A HISTORY OF MACROECONOMETRIC
MODEL-BUILDING

A History of Macroeconometric Model-Building

Ronald G. Bodkin
University of Ottawa

Lawrence R. Klein
Benjamin Franklin Professor of Economics
University of Pennsylvania

Kanta Marwah
Carleton University

Edward Elgar

Published by
Edward Elgar Publishing Limited
Gower House
Croft Road
Aldershot
Hants GU11 3HR
England

Edward Elgar Publishing Company
Old Post Road
Brookfield
Vermont 05036
USA

British Library Cataloguing in Publication Data

A history of macroeconometric model building.
  1. Econometric models
  I. Bodkin, Ronald G. II. Klein, Lawrence R. (Lawrence
Robert) III. Marwah, Kanta
  330.015195

ISBN 1 85278 369 9

Printed in Great Britain by
Billing & Sons Ltd, Worcester

Contents

v

Figures

Tables

Contributors

James Ball, London Business School

Anton P. Barten, Tilburg University (on leave from Catholic University of Louvain)

Abel Beltran-del-Rio, Wharton Economic Forecasting Associates

Roger Bolton, Williams College

Raymond Courbis, Université de Paris-Nanterre

Bert G. Hickman, Stanford University

Sean Holly, Centre for Economic Forecasting, London Business School

Kazuo Sato, Rutgers University

Preface

The background foundations of macroeconometrics had their origin in nineteenth-century investigations dealing with various aspects of quantitative economics. As we note in Chapter 1, the Walrasian system lends itself to numerical analysis, in the form of approximations, of course, but it was not subjected to empirical study by its creators. Rather, at the origins, it was conceptual. Some other nineteenth and early twentieth-century foundations of our subject were based on advances in economic theory, but there are no human survivors today to document a treatise on these aspects of the history of economic thought.

There are, however, pioneers still living, who have contributed directly to the early works in macroeconometrics. Professor Jan Tinbergen and Dr J. J. Polak are prime examples. Trygve Haavelmo began his theoretical researches just before World War II, and Colin Clark, who died late in 1989, was another early contributor (mainly on the empirical side). Of course, there are many students and some colleagues who have had direct contact with Ragnar Frisch, Michal Kalecki and others who were pioneers in the current century.

In our view, the major development of macroeconometric models on the world scene took place just after the Second World War and its origins can be traced to the moving spirit of Jacob Marschak, who organized a team effort at the Cowles Commission (then at the University of Chicago) in 1943–4. That team had essentially three divisions: economic theory (model specification); statistical inference (model estimation, testing, and application); and model construction (including data preparation and numerical calculation). As A. P. Barten notes in Chapter 6, similar developments took place shortly afterwards in the Netherlands at the Central Planning Bureau, under Professor Tinbergen.

A compelling reason for writing the present volume is to capture some first-hand information of the early participants, both from the first empirical phase which dates back to the 1930s, largely in Europe, and from the second phase that started with the Cowles effort beginning in 1943–4. As one of us (Klein) was finishing his doctoral studies at MIT in the summer of 1944, Jacob Marschak told him about the team that Marschak was assembling at the Cowles Commission. Marschak's comment, as he invited the young Klein to join this team, was, 'What this country needs is a new Tinbergen model!' He had in mind, of course, the preparation of a macroeconometric model that would be realistic enough to be used in the formation of postwar macroeconomic policy.

There are many survivors from that team, although Jacob Marschak and Tjalling Koopmans did not live long enough to contribute directly to this tale of *living history*. There are still many active participants from the large model-building efforts that took place in the period from approximately 1950 to the present time. Of course, the developments of the 1980s are not yet embedded in history, and so in general we have treated these only in a sketchy fashion.

We have sought in this volume on macroeconometric history to tap the memories of many participants of the past few decades who created the macroeconometric models of Latin America, the socialist countries, India, Japan, Canada, some Western European countries, and, of course, the United States. (We regret that we were unable to obtain a chapter on the history of model-building in the socialist countries; the interested reader might wish to consult H. T. Shapiro's 'Macroeconometric Models of the Soviet Union and Eastern European Economies: A Tabular Survey', which was published in the November 1977 issue of *Econometrica*.) Apart from J. J. Polak's insightful attempts at international model-building at a very early stage, in the late 1930s, which he resumed after the Second World War, there was not much work in this field until the 1970s, but that is now an explosive activity, to which a full chapter (Chapter 14) is devoted in this book. Regional model-building, within a single country, bears some of the same characteristics as international model-building; and the former subject is also treated in a chapter (Chapter 13, reprinted from the *Journal of Regional Science*). Unfortunately, the treatment in this book of *multi*regional econometric models, for a single country, is somewhat sketchy, but there are a number of references to this challenging development which the interested reader can pursue.

Thus, every aspect of macroeconometric model-building is not covered in this work, but we feel that most of the salient features are. There is some attention paid to the present situation and to the future outlook, even though the principal purpose has been to document the historical record while there was still time to draw upon the memories of some of the actors. We feel confident that in many cases the histories have been checked with some of the important pioneers who have not been directly involved in preparing chapters, and it definitely appears to us that a reasonable account of what did happen has been rendered.

Some attention has also been paid to expected future developments, even though this part has been written by those who participated actively in the history. Thus this discussion lays out the development path through the eyes of practitioners, rather than through those of the critics. There have always been critics, since Tinbergen's first contributions and even earlier, but enormous progress has been achieved even in the face of this criticism and, we feel confident, will continue to be achieved in the face of present criticism.

When all the contributions of the present volume are read as a whole, it becomes evident that macroeconometric modelling activity has been widespread. From the first empirical macroeconometric models of the Netherlands and of the United States, there has been a flowering in many countries, in many types of economic systems, and at many levels, from regions often defined by the jurisdiction of a local government to the world as a whole. This is a very impressive outpouring of work, and it continues to flow at a rapid pace. This seems to be a good time to pause, to digest the material written by some of the actors, and to take a reading on where the activity appears to be going, as well as on where one thinks it ought to go.

Next, it seems appropriate to indicate the institutional affiliations of our eight contributing authors (for seven chapters). As indicated above, all of the eight have had extensive experience in the design, construction and use of macroeconometric models, and all have an interest (as confirmed by their contribution to this volume) in the history of macroeconometric model-building. Sir James Ball is Professor of Economics at the London Business School, where he also served as Principal from 1972 to 1984. Anton Barten is currently Professor of Economics at Tilburg University in the Netherlands, where he is Director of the CentER for Economic Research; he has been Professor of Economics at the Catholic University of Louvain (from which he is on leave and to which he expects to return this fall) since 1966. Abel Beltran-del-Rio has for many years been associated with WEFA [Wharton Econometric Forecasting Associates], an econometric research and forecasting organization founded by Lawrence R. Klein; he is currently Director of the Mexican Econometric Project (CIEMEX–WEFA) of that organization. Roger Bolton is Professor of Economics at Williams College in Williamstown, Massachusetts; he spent the Fall of 1989 as a Visiting Professor at the Robert M. LaFollette Institute of Public Affairs of the University of Wisconsin (Madison). Raymond Courbis, after ten years at INSEE (*Institut National de la Statistique et des Etudes Economiques*), where he built the first French medium-term model, has been Professor of Economics at the Université de Paris–Nanterre since the mid-1970s and also Director of the GAMA (*Groupe d'Analyse Macroéconomique Appliquée*), which specializes in economic modelling, forecasting and quantitative macroeconomics. Bert G. Hickman is Professor of Economics at Stanford University, where he has served since the mid-1960s; he was one of the major initiators of the

LINK Project, about which he is writing in this volume. Sean Holly is affiliated with the Centre for Economic Forecasting of the London Business School, where he has worked with Professor Ball in recent years. And Kazuo Sato, who has served as Professor of Economics at Rutgers University since 1984, has had extensive experience with Japanese macroeconometric models. (We note that the reader can obtain further bibliographical information about Professors Barten, Ball, Courbis, Hickman, and Sato in Mark Blaug, ed., *Who's Who in Economics*, Second Edition, Cambridge, Mass., MIT Press, 1986.)

Finally, in the course of writing this book, we have acquired many debts, intellectual and of other kinds, which it is a pleasure to acknowledge. First, for permission to reprint, we wish to thank Irma Adelman for allowing us to reproduce two important graphs as well as two long quotations. We also wish to thank the North-Holland Publishing Company, a branch of Elsevier Science Publishers B.V., and Economics Editor Joop Dirkmaat in particular, for permission to reprint (with minor changes) Anton P. Barten's paper on the history of Dutch macroeconometric model-building, which has become Chapter 6 of this volume. Finally, we should like to thank the Regional Science Research Institute, publisher of the *Journal of Regional Science*, and its Director, Dr Benjamin Stevens, for permission to reprint (again with minor modifications) an article in the November 1985 issue by Roger Bolton, which has become Chapter 13.

In addition, a number of people have made excellent contributions by reading the whole manuscript or various parts of it, in varying drafts. Chapter 1, a portion of which has been published twice elsewhere, received helpful comments from Eric G. Davis, Robert Dimand, Don Patinkin, Thomas K. Rymes, and Jan Tinbergen. Chapter 2 was read by Jan Tinbergen, who sent helpful comments in a letter dated 31 March 1986; of course this does not imply that he endorses everything that is said in this chapter. Chapter 3 was the subject of helpful comments by Raymond Courbis, Manfred Gilli, and André Keller, during Bodkin's sabbatical in France and Switzerland during the first half of 1984. Chapter 9 (on the history of Canadian macroeconometric modelling) was presented in various drafts on three occasions (at a seminar held at Queen's University in September 1984, at the annual meetings of the Eastern Economic Association in March 1985 and at the annual meetings of the Canadian Economics Association in May 1985); helpful comments on these or other occasions were received from Elbert V. Bowden, Bobbi Cain, Marcel Dagenais, Mervin Daub, Frank T. Denton, Patrick Grady, John F. Helliwell, André Plourde, Ross Preston, John A. Sawyer, and H. E. L. Waslander. (André Plourde deserves our particular thanks, for his helpful comments on the MACE model and his meticulous review of the material of the entire chapter, at a final stage of manuscript preparation.) Michael C. McCracken provided helpful comments on Chapters 16 and 17, as did Jan Kmenta, who also read the whole manuscript at a late stage. The late Jacques Henry also read large portions of the entire manuscript at an early stage of preparation. Two final comments seem in order. First, although we have not followed all of the comments that we received, this book is undoubtedly better for the comments that we did accept. Second, in general the acknowledgements of our eight chapter authors (in seven chapters) appear in the individual chapters below, though we make one exception to this rule in our next paragraph.

As well, the word 'debts' suggests a financial obligation, and we should like to acknowledge generous financial support of our home universities (the University of Ottawa, the University of Pennsylvania, and Carleton University, respectively). Bodkin in particular received a Faculty Leave Fellowship from the Social Science and Humanities Research Council of Canada for the 1983–4 academic year, which enabled good progress to be made on the book; he also received two internal research grants from the University of Ottawa. Moreover, Marwah received an analogous internal grant from Carleton University. In addition, Chapter 7 on macroeconometric modelling in the UK was first written by Sir James Ball alone in 1984, while an updated version was produced in late 1989 by Ball and Sean Holly, under ESRC (Economic and Social Research Council [of the United Kingdom]) grant no. B0250012.

Finally, we should like to thank two other groups of individuals, without whom the preparation of a work like this would be impossible. We have benefited from a series of excellent typists at the University of Ottawa and at Carleton University; while it would be impossible to name them all, we should like to single out Louise Clément, Manon Leclerc and Chi Puong at the University of Ottawa and Patricia Nagy and Gwen McBride at Carleton University. Last and far from least, we should like to thank our publisher, Edward Elgar (who always seemed to know just the right target to set at the final stage) and his associates, Barbara J. Church and Julie Leppard.

Ronald G. Bodkin
Lawrence R. Klein
Kanta Marwah

PART I

INTRODUCTION

1 Antecedents of macroeconometric models

1 Introduction

Econometric models have not sprung forth as entirely new creations, like Athene out of the brain of Zeus. Instead, there have been a number of developments in the history of economics that foreshadowed the arrival of these intellectual constructs. In this chapter, we shall focus on four such antecedents which seem particularly important to us. The first is the set of models of general equilibrium, which were first developed by Léon Walras as an abstract system and later extended by Vilfredo Pareto so that, in principle, these models become capable of empirical estimation. The second was the set of two mathematical models of the business cycle in the early 1930s, constructed by Ragnar Frisch and Michal Kalecki, which anticipated the econometric approach. The third major antecedent has been Keynes's *General Theory* and the subsequent development of this approach, of which the operational heritage has been enormous. Indeed macroeconometric models have largely been designed until very recently to implement the Keynesian system, however much these models may have evolved since their beginnings, just prior to the Second World War. The final major antecedent was the empirical literature on Keynesian macroeconomic concepts, particularly on consumption functions, which flourished between the publication of Keynes's *General Theory* (in 1936) and the outbreak of the Second World War (or the publication of Tinbergen's *Business Cycles in the United States of America, 1919–1932*) late in 1939. Before launching into these four major themes, we may examine briefly five related antecedents.

François Quesnay's *tableau économique* was a major accomplishment for his time, and it is reasonable to regard this construct as the first stylized macroeconomic model. Moreover, the *tableau* was both quantitative and dynamic, designed as it was to indicate cyclical (or perhaps secular) improvements or decay. A second related development could be Karl Marx's discussion in *Capital* of the two schemes of simple commodity reproduction and extended commodity reproduction, which easily lend themselves to representations in terms of abstract models. There was, in addition, Marx's concern to measure statistically his own theoretical concepts, such as the rate of surplus value. However, in our view, modern econometric modelling owes relatively little to Karl Marx's theories and method of inquiry, at least directly. A third subsidiary antecedent is neoclassical theory, particularly the neoclassical theory of the firm, which

3

in several variants has been used to develop theories of the demand for the various factors of production, which have become incorporated into a number of current econometric models. In this regard, it is worth noting that both Jevons and Marshall, two of the founders of the marginalist or neoclassical approach, foresaw an increasing role for measuring the hypothetical concepts of their theories in the evolution of their discipline.[1]

In this connection, we may also cite the work in the 1930s on two-sector models by Griffith C.Evans (1934), which was later extended to an index number interpretation by his student-colleague, F. W. Dresch (1938). Evans, who was primarily a mathematician, developed an interrelated model based on neoclassical theories of production for two sectors, which produced consumption goods and capital goods respectively. With total labour input given exogenously and total capital input constrained by the output of the capital goods sector, the problem was to maximize total consumption output by a suitable allocation of the labour and capital inputs between the two sectors. Dresch then provided the aggregation theory to move from the microeconomic to the macroeconomic plane; this was a development quite apart from Keynes's theory of underemployment equilibrium being developed contemporaneously. Essentially, Dresch showed that Divisia indices of the prices and the quantities for the Evans model satisfied, for the macroeconomy, the same relationships that Evans had postulated for the microeconomy.[2]

A fourth related theme is the thought and work of the German Historical School; here the connection is somewhat indirect, although we shall attempt to make the antecedents more apparent. Although it must be admitted that leading members of this school, such as Wilhelm Roscher and Gustav Schmoller, would probably not have been sympathetic to macroeconometric model-building, it may nevertheless be claimed that the painstaking empirical and statistical work of some of the members of this school, such as the curves of expenditures on various consumption categories of Ernst Engel, would easily fit into a modern econometric model (and indeed they have done so, on a number of occasions). We should not wish to imply that a current model-building is impregnated with *historismus*, requiring a unity of all the social sciences (with due attention paid to the unique characteristics of particular nations) before progress can be made. Nevertheless modern model-building does have a number of characteristics in common with the methods of the German Historical School. In both cases, the subject is the quantitative interpretation of economic history, and so the careful assembling of such data is an essential feature of both approaches. In addition, the typical macroeconometric model uses relationships which are broader than conventional macroeconomic theory. Moreover the relativity of economic laws is well confirmed by practising econometricians; the general experience has been that a typical macroeconometric model cannot be left unmaintained (that is, with unadjusted parameter values) for a period longer than two to four years, or it will go 'sour', becoming an unfit tool for purposes of prediction or of policy simulation. Re-estimation is thus an important part of model maintenance.[3]

The fifth and possibly the most important antecedent of macroeconometric modelling was the work on classical statistics around the turn of the twentieth century, when individuals such as R.A. Fisher, Gosset, Karl Pearson and others built on the foundations of probability theory developed earlier by Gauss, Laplace and others. Mary S. Morgan (1984, 1987) has shown that early econometricians did *not* consistently and clearly conceive of their discipline as resting on probabilistic foundations, until Trygve Haavelmo introduced this approach (by means of a stochastic perturbation whose realizations were turned over to the laws of chance) in the early 1940s. Even given its late appearance, it is fair to state that this approach has revolutionized applied econometrics in general and macroeconometric model-building in particular, as well as serving as the basis for numerous propositions in theoretical econometrics.

2 Léon Walras and the elements of pure economics

Econometric models are, above all, logical systems, in which the behaviour of the whole is not always predictable from the nature of the parts which compose the entire system. One of the earliest and clearest views of the economy as a system is that of Léon Walras, in his *Eléments d'économie politique pure*.[4] Walras glimpsed the functioning of a purely competitive economy in static equilibrium as a coherent system that could be represented by a consistent set of equations for prices and quantities, which the market would solve itself by means of the *tâtonnement* process. In Walras's own words (as translated by William Jaffé),

> And this result is obtained purely and simply by the automatic operation of the mechanism of free competition. The law of supply and demand regulates all these exchanges of commodities just as the law of universal gravitation regulates the movements of all celestial bodies. Thus the system of the economic universe reveals itself, at last, in all its grandeur and complexity, a system at once vast and simple, which, for sheer beauty, resembles the astronomic universe.[5]

In turn, Walras's system has been an inspiration to several generations of econometricians, as they have attempted to find empirical counterparts to his abstract systems of equations. Although we shall argue below that current macroeconometric models are quite different (even in the spirit of the analysis) from Walras's highly abstract models, nevertheless the notion of the economy as a system has been retained and developed.

Accordingly, before presenting some detailed points of Walras's discussion and noting some differences with current econometric models, a review of Walras's development of his view of the economy may be appropriate. After presenting some introductory material (principally definitions), Walras launches into his discussion of the purely competitive economy, which he represents through successively more complicated models. The first model of general equilibrium (in Part II) is one in which stocks of two commodities are exchanged; after this, exchange is generalized (in the second model of general equilibrium, in Part III) to the exchange of fixed stocks of many commodities. In this context, it can be argued that *rareté* (marginal utility, as modified by scarcity or position on the marginal utility schedule)[6] is 'the' fundamental 'cause' of value in exchange; Walras apparently felt a strong need to vindicate the theory of his father, Auguste Walras, as William Jaffé has indicated on a number of occasions. The third model of general equilibrium, which appears in Part IV, is probably the best known of all; here Walras introduces production phenomena and allows land, labour and capital to make their appearance as primary factors of production. Although Walras initially assumed fixed coefficients of production (as in Leontief-style input–output analysis), by the definitive edition he was willing to permit variable coefficients of production, and so the possibility of a marginal productivity theory of output and income distribution was indeed present. Even more interesting are the two final models of general equilibrium. In Part V, the model of general equilibrium is generalized to include individual savings functions, interpreted as the demand for claims to future income, and also capital formation and the price of capital goods (at times interpreted as share prices on the stock exchanges or *bourses*). Equation-counting criteria are met in this context, but Walras takes some pains to show (in his Lesson 28) that the interaction between the savings and investment functions plays a major role in the determination of the rate of interest, despite the caveat that '(t)heoretically, all the unknowns of an economic problem depend on all the equations of economic equilibrium' (p. 307). Despite the neoclassical orientation of this result, the concern with savings functions and the implicit relationships for investment bring us close to a major concern of current-day econometric model-builders. However the underpinning in terms of marginal utility is not lost sight of in the third and fourth models of general equilibrium, as Walras comes back to the maximization of effective utility and the tendency of a purely competitive system to generate at least a relative maximum of the utility functions of its economic agents.

The fifth and final model of general equilibrium may be found in Part VI, 'Theory of Circulation and Money'. Here Walras permits (in principle) inventories of all commodities, particularly cash balances; this leads him directly into monetary theory and discussions of several sorts of financial markets.[7] Walras makes an attempt to preserve his marginal utility theory of value in this context, by imputing *rareté* to the service of money, which has no direct utility of its own. The discussion of this model comes down to a view of the long-run neutrality of money (the level of prices being strictly proportional to the stock of money, after an exogenous increase in the latter) although, interestingly, there appears to be a short-run effect of the stock of money on interest rates. Discussions of bimetallism and of foreign exchange (including our modern concern, the rate of exchange of a given country's money) conclude this discussion.[8] In particular, money has become a flesh-and-blood commodity fulfilling the standard functions, including a store of value, rather than being no more than a disembodied *numéraire*; in addition, absolute prices, rather than mere relative prices, may now be determined.

It is interesting to note that, on occasion, Walras considered the possibility of an empirical implementation of his system. Thus, in discussing price determination under monopoly (Lesson 41), which significantly comes after the statement of the five models of general equilibrium, Walras speaks of 'relat[ing] the rational and rigorously exact equations of exchange and production to the empirical and approximative equation of sales written as a function of price' (p. 440). Earlier, in his discussion of the fifth model of general equilibrium (in the discussion of bimetallism in particular), he states (article 289, p. 348):

> If we were to replace the above arbitrary and indeterminate functions or curves, in whole or in part, by statistically derived functions or curves having concrete coefficients, we could calculate approximately the real effects of a resumption of the coinage of silver on the basis of a given legal ratio between the values of gold and silver moneys.

This sentence indicates not only the anticipation of the possibility of an econometric estimation of the parameters of a behavioural equation, but also a recognition that an estimated model, employed as a complete system, is capable of generating some tentative and approximate answers to policy issues, in what we now call policy simulations. Thus it can legitimately be claimed that, despite his rational bias (to be discussed below), Walras foresaw, at least in part, some of the uses to which the descendants of his systems might be put.

This issue is brought into focus by Walras's treatment of the savings function. In the first three editions of his work, Walras treated the savings functions as an 'empirical datum' in which the utility maximization process was at most implicit; this is something which has at least a family resemblance to the consumption functions of modern econometric models. By the Definitive Edition, there has been a slight but significant change in the formulation. New savings are treated like any other good which is acquired to maximize utility or satisfaction, and the derivation is 'rational' rather than 'empirical'. Admittedly, the savings function (or the sum of individual demands for net income, in the Definitive Edition) always depends on the same arguments, namely the prices of the natural agents, the prices of the various produced capital goods, the prices of the final goods and services, and the rate of interest. Noticeably absent from a modern point of view is an income effect (which is appropriate enough, in a full employment economy). The shift from an empirical relationship to a 'rational' one, based on utility maximization over time (if only implicitly), is probably important as indicating the direction in which Walras thought that the search for insight should go.[9]

This caveat would almost certainly be underlined by the greatest Walras scholar of our century, the late William Jaffé, were he able to read (and criticize) the above interpretation. In reaction to Morishima's treatment of Walras's *Éléments*, Jaffé has argued that:

> The *Éléments* was intended to be and is, in all but the name, a realistic utopia, i.e. a delineation of a state of affairs nowhere to be found in the actual world, independent of time and place, ideally perfect in certain respects, and yet composed of realistic psychological and material ingredients.[10]

Jaffé also argued that Walras had a vehement dislike for 'facts' and the 'observation of facts' [statistics?] and that he denounced their manifestations in a number of areas: art, literature, philosophy, science, and, of course, economics. Jaffé goes on to argue that the *Éléments* were intended to be 'an abstract expression and rational explanation of the phenomena of the real world',[11] rather than a slavish reproduction of these real world data or statistics. In this view, Walras would not have been sympathetic to the interpretation of his system as a mere description of a real-world economy and hence would have been unenthusiastic about econometric estimation of his system.

Indeed the limitations of the Walrasian system as a direct representation of a modern economy should perhaps be given additional emphasis. Upon additional probing, it is clear that the Walrasian model is quite unsuitable for direct econometric estimation, and indeed it is Jaffé's contention that it was never intended to be fitted directly, despite a few passages like the one quoted above, which suggests that Walras himself may have thought of it in this light. Thus the hypothesis of pure competition would appear to be singularly inaccurate as a description of a modern economy, while the amount of detail required for the implementation of any of the last three models described above would appear to be prohibitive. Perhaps the biggest problem is whether the system has any relevance in a context of persistent unemployment; in a seminal article, Robert W. Clower (1966) has argued that Walras's Law will not hold in an underemployment context and that demand (consumption) functions contain quantity variables, such as real income, in such a context.[12] Although Morishima (1980) contends that '... Walras narrowly missed the chance to meet the first Keynesian problem of involuntary unemployment due to overdeterminacy', it seems fair to assert that Walras appears to have been quite neoclassical in his approach to involuntary unemployment.[13] Moreover Clower contends that the acceptance of the Walrasian paradigm negates the essential message of Keynes's *General Theory*. Even if one does not wish to go this far, it is clear that current macroeconometric models cannot be regarded as a direct empirical implementation of the Walrasian system.[14]

To elaborate this point somewhat further, we may note that the Walrasian system is a set of simultaneous equations which is meant to describe the working of the economy; that is, in one interpretation the solution to the system should correspond with observations of the economy. In a similar way, we can think about the set of simultaneous equations that is (arguably) implicit in Keynes's *General Theory* as being a description of the economy. The solution to the Keynesian equation system should also correspond to observations of the economy. There are, however, important differences between the two systems:

1. The Walrasian system generates a set of micro-variables of the economy, while the Keynesian system generates a set of macro-variables.
2. The solution of the Walrasian system as interpreted by K. J. Arrow and G. Debreu (1954), for example, satisfies full economic equilibrium. There is full employment, perfect competition and static equilibrium. The Keynesian system was posed as a simultaneous equation system that did not necessarily have full employment equilibrium, did not necessarily impose the conditions of perfect competition and could generate dynamic as well as static solutions. The Walrasian system in full equilibrium with perfect competition can be shown to satisfy the welfare conditions for a Pareto optimum. The same cannot be said of the solution to the Keynesian system.

As the next paragraph will elaborate, both the Keynesian and Walrasian systems are formulated as a set of simultaneous equations for the whole economy, their principal point of similarity. They are not partial systems.

Does this mean, therefore, that the Walrasian general equilibrium theory has no relevance for current-day macroeconometric modelling? In our view, such an assertion would be far too extreme; Walras's great contribution of the view of the economy as a system (exemplified in the quotation of the beginning of this section) permeates macroeconometric modelling today. This view (akin to the notion of *gestalt* in the school of psychology of that name) is now second nature to econometric model-builders; yet the view was virtually completely absent a century ago and took a long time to become the dominant one in our century. It is in this limited but very important sense that current-day econometric models are descendants of the five models of general equilibrium sketched in the *Éléments*. (Of course, the concept of a system of simultaneous equations should be sharply distinguished from that of equilibrium; examples of one without the other are not difficult to find.) In comparison to this central similarity, the important differences noted above become secondary. Thus detail can be reduced upon suitable aggregation (even though it must be admitted that aggregation itself can be another source of imprecision and error).[15] The hypothesis of pure competition can be regarded as a simple first approximation, to be replaced by more accurate hypotheses as the context under discussion warrants. The price flexibility implied by the *tâtonnements* carried out by the Walrasian *crieur* seems particularly inappropriate in the context of discussions of inflation in the second half of the twentieth century; here one might prefer to substitute the hypotheses of price formation sketched out by the late Arthur M. Okun (1981). And of course the equilibrium described by a current-day econometric model will usually allow for involuntary unemployment, so that consumption (and other expenditure) functions will generally be functions of quantity variables in general and of real income in particular. Another important difference is that the Walrasian models of general equilibrium are generally regarded as static, timeless descriptions of the economy (viewed as purely competitive), while current-day econometric models are dynamic representations for which a static equilibrium position may not even exist.[16] Nevertheless it is our view that these differences are not so important as the essential view of the economy as a global system, one whose behaviour as a whole is not readily explicable in terms of the functioning of the various pieces that separately comprise the system. In this way, current econometric models owe a great deal to the French expatriate who held the chair in economics at the Academy of Lausanne, Switzerland, for over 20 years.[17]

3 Vilfredo Pareto's version of general equilibrium economics

Vilfredo Pareto, Léon Walras's successor at Lausanne, developed and refined the latter's general equilibrium analysis. Because we have discussed Walras's models at some length, we shall be relatively brief with regard to Pareto's representations of price formation in a purely competitive economy.[18] Once again, we feel that it is the basic concept of the economy as an interdependent system which is important, rather than the specific details of the representation. However there are two differences between Walras's and Pareto's versions of the general equilibrium system that are worth noting here: Pareto's system is more abstract and (paradoxically) appears also to be more oriented towards empirical implementation, at least in principle. Let us take up each of these points in turn.

Pareto's general equilibrium analysis can be found in Chapters III to VI of the *Manuale* (1906) (and also in the relevant sections of the mathematical appendix). All commentators agree that the analysis is on a very abstract plane. As interpreted by T. W. Hutchison (1966), the model contrasts the tension between tastes on the one hand and obstacles to the satisfaction of human wants on the other, with the equations of general equilibrium describing the markets' resolution (in realistic terms) of this conflict. Tarascio (1973) would appear not to disagree with this characterization, but he adds the interpretation that there appear to be two models of general equilibrium in these four chapters. In Chapter III, there is a very abstract description of the competitive system purely in terms of transformations of economic quantities, while Chapters IV to VI are concerned with 'a less general study of "tastes" and "obstacles", their interaction, and equilibrium resulting from such interactions'.[19] Accordingly, the Walrasian distinction between exchange, production, capital formation (*'capitalisation'*) and the formation of prices of financial assets disappear; all economic phenomena display an essential unity. This was just as well for Pareto, as he wished to exorcize those elements of Walras's formulation of general equilibrium theory that were overly subjective in his view, such as the importance of *rareté* (marginal utility) in the determination of exchange value. In addition, Pareto sought to correct a small but important (in his view) error in Walras's theory of production, according to which the coefficients of production (as a group) were sometimes regarded as fixed for purposes of the analysis and sometimes regarded (also as a group) as variable. For Pareto, the truth was that some particular coefficients of productions were always variable when factor prices varied and others (for example, the number of cocoa beans required to produce a chocolate bar of a given size) were largely fixed by technology, at least for all practical purposes.

At the same time, it is interesting to observe that Pareto appears to have designed his system so that it might eventually serve for purposes of empirical or even econometric testing. Thus it might be recalled that his discussion of general equilibrium in the *Manuale* is preceded by an exposition of the 'logico-experimental' method in economics and is followed by some interesting discussion in chapters on population, money and applied economics in general. Moreover Pareto himself was not averse to statistically applied work to verify his hypotheses, work that anticipates some of the applied econometric research of the current period. Thus, as T. W. Hutchison (1966) notes, among Pareto's most interesting ideas were his applied econometric investigations, in particular those in the *Cours* (1896) where he developed the form of the highly skewed frequency distribution that was meant to be applied to distributions of income and wealth and which has come to be called the 'Pareto Law', and also his work on business cycles or crises, which was built on the impressive pioneering work of Clément Juglar with monetary statistics. Indeed, as Tarascio (1973) has pointed out, when Pareto came to apply his equilibrium systems to problems of monetary and unemployment theory he was content to work with aggregates, rather than continuing to deal exclusively with the individual elements of an economy. This is an obvious link to modern macroeconometric modelling.

Finally, Pareto's methodological approach, the so-called 'logico-experimental method', appears to have been very much oriented toward empirical testing. Pareto apparently believed in a clear exposition of one's theoretical propositions, eliminating normative content as much as possible, and then confronting the implications of this theoretical framework with the 'facts' of experience to the largest extent possible. Tarascio (1968) has made a detailed study of Pareto's methodology and he concludes that not only did Pareto anticipate much of the current discussion of the philosophical underpinnings of economic knowledge,[20] but also that he would have been quite sympathetic to current-day macroeconometric model-building. Accordingly, even more than Walras, Pareto may be claimed as a direct antecedent of current macroeconometric modelling activity.

4   Ragnar Frisch and Michal Kalecki

In the early 1930s, some important work was done in macroeconomic theory in general and on some abstract models of fluctuations in the aggregate economy in particular. This work, which was effected prior to the publication of Keynes's *General Theory* (but after the publication of his *Treatise on Money*) helped lay the groundwork for the construction of the early macroeconometric models. We have already referred to the papers of G. C. Evans (1934), C. F. Roos (1930), and Edward Theiss

(1933). However, in our view, the two most important papers were those by Ragnar Frisch (1933) and Michal Kalecki (1935). Additional support for this judgement may be adduced from the fact that Jan Tinbergen's contemporaneous survey piece, in *Econometrica* (1935), devotes considerable attention to the work of both Frisch and Kalecki.

Ragnar Frisch's 'Propagation Problems and Impulse Problems in Dynamic Economics' (1933) constructs a simple model of the business cycle which is explicitly dynamic. Investment demand has two components: net investment depends upon the rate of change of the production of consumption goods (the Aftalion or J. M. Clark accelerator), while replacement investment depends upon the current level of output of the consumer goods industries. (Depreciation is viewed as proportional to the initial capital stock; but Frisch assumes a strict proportionality between this capital stock and the related level of output.) A second equation is obtained by taking the desired level of cash balances to be a linear function (with no constant term) of the production of consumer goods and producer goods separately; this might be interpreted as a transactions demand for money. The consumption equation, which is definitely pre-Keynesian, depicts a natural tendency for consumption standards to grow, checked only by the tendency to rein in consumption as the desired level of cash balances increases as well. Finally, Frisch obtains oscillations by making the distinction between investment demand and the production of capital goods. Frisch writes an integral equation which supposes that the production of capital goods lags behind the level of gross investment demand by a constant amount of time. After manipulating his small system of equations, Frisch obtains another small system of mixed difference-differential equations, which he solves by 'the method of trial solutions'. If 'reasonable values' for the structural parameters are substituted, the solution paths are all damped cycles. However Frisch recognizes that the substitution of 'reasonable values' for the structural parameters is no substitute for rigorous econometric work. With one of his prescient insights, he declares, 'I think, indeed, that the statistical determination of such structural parameters will be one of the main objectives of the economic cycle analysis of the future.' His surrounding argument makes it quite clear that he feels that, in order to set forth a full explanation, this kind of work is needed to coordinate and complement the huge mass of empirical or descriptive facts concerning the business cycle already available at the time at which he was writing.[21]

A similar (but distinct) model was presented by Michal Kalecki in the 1933 meetings of the Econometric Society held in Leiden, and published two years later in *Econometrica* (1935). Kalecki's model makes a further distinction: we now have deliveries of capital goods, as well as investment demand and production of capital goods (investment in the national accounts). Kalecki's system is more or less as follows. Investment demand depends positively on realized profits and negatively on the initial stock of capital. Profits (of capitalists) depend only on their own spending (investment goods production and capitalists' consumption), via a sort of multiplier principle which anticipates that of Keynes's *General Theory*. (There is implicitly a capitalists' consumption function in this analysis.) Kalecki has effectively the same equation as Frisch in which capital goods production (investment in a national income accounting concept) is an integral of investment demand experienced for a fixed period between the present and the constant lag in capital goods production. Deliveries of new capital goods lag investment demand (which could be interpreted as new orders) by exactly the length of this fixed lag. Finally, the rate of change of the capital stock is simply the difference between the deliveries of new capital goods and the level of depreciation, assumed constant in Kalecki's model.

This system (in fullest form, of six dynamic equations in six unknowns) can be reduced to a mixed difference-differential equation in each of the variables of the system. This mixed difference-differential equation may or may not have a cyclical solution. Kalecki then uses rudimentary statistical data of the United States for crude estimates of the parameters of his system, which are the amount of depreciation (its rate), the parameters of the capitalists' consumption function, and the constant lag of deliveries of investment goods behind new orders. He was encouraged to find that 'realistic' values of these parameters yielded (maintained) cycles, and also that the period of the cycle was ten years, which he regarded as reasonable. Peripheral discussions in this article consider a multiplier process affecting workers' consumption and incomes, the modification of the model to allow for a growth context, and considerations of financial factors. However, for our purposes, the major significance of Kalecki's pioneering effort is that it appears to represent a step towards an econometric approach to business cycle problems, and hence a step towards the development of macroeconometric models.[22]

5   Keynes, *The General Theory*, and the revolutions in macroeconomic theory and measurement[23]

The most important single antecedent for the construction of macroeconometric models must be John Maynard Keynes's *The General Theory of Employment, Interest and Money* (1936). Moreover this is a point that would command wide agreement. Thus Richard Stone asserted, in his Keynes Lecture in Economics of 1978:

> For there is no doubt that in its day Keynes' book had done probably more

than any other to encourage the systematic estimation of national accounts magnitudes and the construction of econometric models. (Stone, 1980, p. 62)

Similarly, Don Patinkin (1976) argues:

> Furthermore, and most important in the present context, the desire to quantify the *General Theory* provided the major impetus for the exponentially-growing [sic] econometric work that began to be carried out in the late 1930's on the consumption, investment, and liquidity-preference functions individually and, even more notably, on econometric models of the Keynesian system as a whole. (Patinkin, 1976, p. 1092)

Indeed, it may be noted that for many years macroeconometric models have been constructed as essentially empirical counterparts to the Keynesian system; only in recent years have econometric models based on alternative paradigms (monetarist, radical or Post-Keynesian) appeared.[24]

Keynes's *General Theory* itself is worth a cursory review in this context. After six chapters of introductory material, there follow three chapters (grouped together in a section called 'Book III, The Propensity to Consume') which treat the consumption function and an associated concept, the multiplier. The notion of consumption as a relatively stable function of a few explanatory variables, including community income, appears to cry for empirical verification and Keynes himself made some preliminary attempts, using early national income data for the United Kingdom developed by Colin Clark and for the United States developed by Simon Kuznets, to verify his hypotheses.[25] However, it must be admitted that the bulk of the work of the empirical testing of the Keynesian system was left for others, particularly after Keynes's severe heart attack in 1937.

Other parts of *The General Theory* contain concepts that are easily put into a theoretical formulation susceptible to econometric testing and estimation without much difficulty. Thus Book IV, entitled 'The Inducement to Invest', contains an extended discussion (in Chapters 11 and 12) of a concept called 'the marginal efficiency of capital'. Without too much manipulation this discussion can be recast in the form of an investment demand function and so be confronted with statistics on business fixed investment and some of its hypothetical determinants. Book IV also contains an extended discussion of what Keynes called 'liquidity-preference' generally, scattered through five chapters (Chapters 13 to 17 of the work); again, one could attempt to render the liquidity-preference function operational and then to estimate its parameters, which indeed was done by A. J. Brown (1939) and by James Tobin (1947) in the immediate postwar period. Finally, Book V, 'Money-Wages and Prices', contains three chapters (Chapters 19 to 21) and concludes the central theoretical corpus of the work. Depending upon one's preferences, this portion of

The General Theory could be formulated as an aggregate supply function relating real national product to the price level or its rate of change or (corresponding to the breakdown of Book V into three separate chapters) as an employment function (an inverted short-period production function), an equation for the determination of the money wage rate, and an equation for the determination of the aggregative price level.[26] It should be noted that Keynes attempted empirical verification of none of these other relationships, although his theoretical discussion and his example with regard to the consumption function would appear to have pointed the way.

But would Keynes himself have approved of this use of his theoretical apparatus? The answer would appear to be 'no', on the basis of two important pieces of evidence: the strictures in *The General Theory* against the representation of his macroeconomic theory as a set of mathematical relationships ('mathematical economics', as he called it) and his September 1939 review of Part I of Tinbergen's study for the League of Nations.

About Keynes's attitude towards mathematically formulated economic theory (which is so essential for econometric modelling of any type, not just macroeconometric models) little need be said.[27] However his review of Tinbergen warrants some comment. Keynes was quite critical of this approach to macroeconomic research,[28] and the tone of his comments suggested that Tinbergen was largely wasting his and the profession's time, if not practising alchemy. The specific criticisms are, in general, reasonably taken, although Keynes's enthusiasts must be embarrassed by the suggestion that linear difference equations may be incapable of generating cyclical fluctuations in themselves, so that (according to Keynes) Tinbergen may be engaged in the task of explaining cycles (in the endogenous variables) by cycles (in the exogenous variables). The other criticisms seem quite reasonable in themselves and appear to have stood the test of time; thus Keynes's various remarks could be interpreted as pointing to single equation bias, the bias of omitted variables, measurement errors in the explanatory variables,[29] the possible mis-specification entailed in assuming linearity throughout the full range (and beyond) of the dependent variable, and (especially) problems of structural change (that is, the possibility that all the past data utilized for parameter estimation may not be homogeneous or may emanate from different universes). Keynes's remarks may also be taken to be a criticism of crude empiricism that may be entailed in the determination of time lags without a suitable theoretical foundation or in the introduction of time trend variables to capture ill-defined secular forces. Keynes also points to the difficulties of an econometric estimation of the effects of an explanatory variable, in the case in which this particular variable has very little movement during a particular historical episode (the influence of the rate of interest on investment expenditures during the 1930s comes to mind as an example). While nearly all of these points are reasonable and most have been (implicitly) incorporated into econometrics textbooks today,[30] Keynes certainly seems to have had relatively little appreciation of the difficult nature of the problems that Tinbergen was attacking and of the generally unsatisfactory nature of non-econometric solutions to this class of problems. Indeed it can be asserted without too much fear of controversy today that intuitive estimates of concepts such as the multiplier or the effect of a certain fiscal policy on the economy are even more likely to be misleading than the econometric estimates, despite the limitations of the latter.[31]

Beyond the specific issues of econometric technique, there is a more general position regarding methodological approach, as Klant (1985), Lawson (1985) and Pesaran and Smith (1985) have pointed out. One can argue that, owing to instability of structures in the social universe, no econometric test is possible; the best that econometricians can do is to *measure* or estimate, as (in this view) testing is a technical impossibility. Klant, Lawson, and Pesaran and Smith argue (with differing degrees of emphasis) that this indeed was Keynes's position, and that this is why Keynes reacted so vehemently against Tinbergen's League of Nations study, which was attempting to test alternative theories of the business cycle. By contrast, it is claimed (by Pesaran and Smith) that Keynes would have been far more sympathetic to Tinbergen's earlier work (1937), which put the emphasis on estimation, and solution of practical policy problems.[32] A secondary reason why econometric technique can never test critically a received theory (in this view) is that most (or even all) theories are under-identified or at least ambiguous. Accordingly, for econometric testing, supplementary hypotheses must be provided. But if a theory fails a given econometric test, an ardent proponent of that theory can always claim that the fault lies in the supplementary hypothesis furnished for testing purposes, rather than in the central core of the theory. This critique resembles the 'Post-Keynesian' critique of deterministic or econometric models, where it is held that no coherent model, macroeconometric or otherwise, can capture the essential message of Keynes, which in this view is held to be an emphasis on the important role of uncertainty, the uniqueness of particular historical episodes, the underdetermination or the indeterminacy of the macroeconomic system, among other points.[33] Nevertheless it would appear that Klant and also Pesaran and Smith (but not Lawson) agree that building forecasting models and econometric research are useful things to do, in the face of serious policy problems. Pesaran and Smith even argue that Keynes would not have been unsympathetic to this approach and that he did something similar in his approach to the practical problems of the day, for example in 'How to Pay for the War' and 'Can Lloyd George Do It?'

However this should not be regarded as the end of the matter. Richard Stone (1980) argues that, under the pressure of economic policy-making under wartime conditions, Keynes changed his attitudes toward economic statistics ('political arithmetic') and even towards econometric modelling. Moreover Keynes was associated with the 'Cambridge Research Scheme' of the National Institute of Social and Economic Research during the period just before the Second World War (1938 and 1939), and much of this research had a strong quantitative and econometric flavour. Stone feels that, in the light of the timing of these activities, 'the Tinbergen episode seems even more bizarre'. Moreover, both Patinkin (1976) and Stone note that, when Alfred Cowles first proposed to Keynes that he be President of the Econometric Society, he first protested that 'whilst I am interested in econometric work and have done something at it at different times in my life, I have not recently written anything significant or important along these lines, which would make me feel a little bit of an imposter'.[34] Thus, as Patinkin rightly points out, we are entitled to infer that Keynes saw himself as someone who had made important contributions to econometrics at one stage of his life; we are also probably entitled to infer that his critical views on econometric modelling had moderated somewhat by that date (1944). This inference is also indirectly corroborated by the fact that Stone reports that Keynes delighted in his personal reunion with Tinbergen right after the end of the Second World War in Europe (in July 1945), speaking enthusiastically not only of Tinbergen's personal qualities but also of his work.[35]

Ultimately, however, the issue of Keynes's final views on the econometric developments that his macroeconomic theory to a large extent stimulated is a secondary issue.[36] It now seems clear that *The General Theory* was a tremendous stimulus, not only to macroeconomic theory in general, but to macroeconometric model-building in particular. Indeed, as succeeding chapters will detail, for nearly a generation and a half after the publication of *The General Theory*, macroeconometric models constructed in the spirit of Keynesian theory dominated the model-building process; only around the beginning of the 1970s did alternative paradigms of macroeconomic theorizing begin to be incorporated into the macroeconometric models. Moreover, Keynes's theorizing completed the steps that Pareto, Evans, Roos, Frisch and Kalecki had taken away from Walras's microeconomic analysis, allowing researchers to deal with concepts and quantities that were much easier to measure in practice. This in turn permitted a return to the sweeping, aggregative concepts of Quesnay's *tableau économique*, with, however, a much higher degree of precision. This aspect of the 'Keynesian Revolution' opened the field to macroeconometric model-building.

6   Statistical testing of Keynesian concepts between the publication of the *General Theory* and Tinbergen's *Business Cycles in the United States of America, 1919–1932* (1937 to mid-1939)

As noted in the preceding section, a number of the concepts of Keynes's *General Theory* appeared to cry out for empirical verification (or refutation). Most of this discussion centred around the consumption function (or 'propensity to consume', as Keynes had termed it). An exception to this generalization was the 1939 study of the 'Demand Schedule for Idle Money' by A. J. Brown, which attempted to test the Keynesian theory of liquidity-preference, especially against the alternative loanable funds theory. Although Brown was not able to reject the loanable funds theory (particularly its Wicksellian version), he found evidence also in favour of the theory of liquidity-preference. In particular, the demand for idle money was negatively and significantly related to the long-term rate of interest (that on government consols) and to the rate of change of a price index for final demand; it also appeared to be secondarily related to a measure of business transactions and, possibly, to the transactions of financial institutions.[37] Thus an important concept from *The General Theory*, other than the consumption function, was subjected to empirical scrutiny and found reasonably satisfactory.

A number of studies subjected the consumption function to further statistical examination, and much discussion followed these statistical studies.[38] Hans Staehle (1937) fitted a consumption function in which the average propensity to consume for German wage earners (the proportion of labour income spent in retail sales, smoothed by a four-quarter moving average) was fitted to data over the period 1928–34 and was found to be negatively related both to labour income measured in wage units and also to a measure of the inequality in the distribution of *personal* income. As Staehle insisted on the importance of this latter variable and on his view that others had not taken it into account (at least to the extent that its importance warranted), this generated some controversy. (See Dirks, 1938; Staehle, 1938; Keynes, 1939a; and Staehle, 1939.) We need not comment in detail on this debate, other than to remark that none of the participants in the debate presented alternative regressions to support their alternative interpretations (or to defend their original position).[39] Another early study was that of J. J. Polak (1939), but since his consumption functions for the United States over the period 1919–32 are virtually identical (as he notes in this article) with those of Tinbergen (1939), which is discussed in the following chapter, we shall content ourselves by merely mentioning this study. Finally, the Stones (Richard and W. M.) published a study (1938–9) in which aggregative consumption functions (with global consumption as a function of aggregate income and of a time trend) were fitted for Germany (two periods), the United Kingdom, the Netherlands, Sweden (two periods) and the United States. Reasonably good fits were obtained, and the Stones felt that their explanation was quite adequate.[40]

The work of Richard and W. M. Stone was oriented, at least in large part, towards gauging the empirical magnitude of Keynes's concept of the multiplier. (The Stones also checked the results of their time series regressions against family budget studies and 'Kahn's method of leakages', and, as all three approaches gave similar results, they were encouraged.) Among the leakages distinguished were imports, personal savings and (negatively) reductions in induced government transfer payments (such as the dole) with economic recovery; interestingly, the Stones considered induced taxes as an illegitimate leakage. On the basis of some rough calculations, they estimated that these leakages varied from 0.35 to 0.60 as a proportion of GNP, implying a value of the multiplier, for the developed countries surveyed, from 1.67 to 2.86, largely depending on the degree of openness of the economy in question.[41] Colin Clark, in two articles around the same time (1937, 1938), used impressionistic statistical techniques (based on his pioneering work in developing national income statistics for the British economy) to work up estimates of the expenditures multiplier for two subperiods, 1929–33 and 1934–7. He found that the estimated multipliers were 1.5 and 2.1 respectively (or somewhat higher if a correction were made for a possible autonomous shift in the import demand function), thus confirming Keynes's hypothesis that the multiplier would be greater under depressed conditions. Finally, Michal Kalecki (1939), in the Appendix of Chapter 2, presents estimates of his version of the investment multiplier, for the USA for the period 1919–35, based on Simon Kuznets's national income data for that country.[42] Kalecki estimates a multiplier of 2.25, on the basis of his estimation of a reduced form relationship, with a time lag of roughly four months. It may be mentioned that the time diagram of the calculated and the measured values of national income, within the sample period, shows a very tight fit, with turning-points largely reproduced, and Kalecki felt that his theoretical formulation was solidly corroborated.[43]

We may close this section (and this chapter) by reviewing a small macroeconometric model constructed by E. A. Radice (1939) as a dissertation at Oxford University. In his 1939 League of Nations study, Tinbergen not only cites Radice's work but also remarks that, among all the formal macro-theoretical models constructed to represent Keynes's system, only Radice's has all of its parameters estimated. (The parameter estimates come from Colin Clark's national income statistics of the UK economy, and the sample period is, in general, somewhat longer than that indicated in the title of this article, generally from 1924 to 1936.) In point of fact, Radice's was a very simple model, from the point of structure and specification. There were two identities and four behavioural equations, making six in total. One identity relates GNP to net income paid to individuals, business savings and capital consumption allowances. The behavioural relationships include a personal savings function, a business savings function (with profits plus interest received as the only explanatory variable) and a profits-generating mechanism, linking profits (plus interest received) to gross investment. (All four of the behavioural relationships have only unique explanatory variables, so that the explanations seem fairly simplistic, from a modern perspective. Although this is never stated explicitly, one supposes that the economic variables are deflated for changing price (or wage) levels.) The final behavioural equation, the key relationship of the model, is Radice's investment function, a version of the acceleration principle, in which the rate of change of gross investment lags behind a proportional multiple of the second derivative of GNP by a constant time lag, estimated by Radice to be 7 or 8 quarters. More interesting than the simple structure of the model is the associated mathematical analysis. Because of the existence of a mixed differential-difference equation (the function for gross investment), this model can, under some circumstances, produce cycles. In point of fact, this is the case for the fitted values of the parameters obtained. The bulk of the article, indeed, is devoted to a discussion of the character of the cyclical implications of the fitted model. The point estimates suggest a slightly explosive cycle, but Radice feels that neutral or damped cycles would appear to be within the realm of possibility (or, more technically, within the two standard error range of the structural parameter estimates). Sensitivity analysis is carried out in some detail, and the possibility of asymmetrical upswings and downswings is considered. While recognizing the limitations of his statistical base, Radice was encouraged by the close agreement of the estimated periodicity of the cycle generated by his fitted model and the apparent periodicity observed in the British economy. This evaluation seems fair; like Tinbergen's seminal efforts, Radice's attempts should be judged as insightful and pioneering.

Notes

1. Sawyer (1976) has emphasized that Jevons believed strongly in the statistical measurement of his theoretical constructs, particularly at the aggregate level, even though he did not live to have a chance to implement his programme. Alfred Marshall, in his celebrated article (1897), 'The Old Generation of Economists and the New', stated

clearly that one of the tasks of the twentieth-century development of the discipline would be to estimate and to measure, or in other words, to find empirical counterparts to, the theoretical structure that had already been developed by the end of the nineteenth century.

2. The basic Evans model was also used in two contemporaneous contributions dealing with business cycles, C. F. Roos (1930) and Edward Theiss (1933). (See also Roos's fuller development of his theories in his 1934 book; Roos's global views of the various pieces of a functioning economy anticipate, to a certain extent, macroeconometric model-building.) Building on Evans's approach, Roos (1930) developed a model which gave a differential equation in a typical price, which had cyclical solutions. Indeed, the business cycle was conceived as one of fluctuations in prices in general, with fluctuations in production (and hence employment) as an appendage. Theiss (1933) constructed a similar model of cyclical fluctuations of the economy based on Evans's equations of supply and demand. It is interesting to note that Theiss's approach, which consisted of solving linear differential equations of second degree or higher, was intended for empirical application. It is also interesting to note that, for Theiss, the principal source of the business cycle was the long lag in the period of production, which tended to produce over-corrections. (Today we are familiar with this possibility because of the development of cobweb models of agricultural markets.)

3. It is interesting to note as well that the techniques of econometric modelling have invaded economic history itself, where this approach is called 'cliometrics'. However, the view of the subject summarized in this paragraph definitely antedates cliometrics.

4. First published in 1874; *édition définitive*, 1926. All references in this book will be to Jaffé's masterful translation (1954), which furthermore contains a number of collation notes among the several editions of Walras' *Éléments*, as well as some interesting commentaries by the translator of a number of the points under discussion.

5. Walras, p. 374. It is interesting to note that this summary view appears at the end of the discussion of the sequence of theoretical models of general equilibrium, before Walras launches into discussions of 'applied' topics such as structural changes occurring during economic growth, doctrinal points, monopoly, and some theoretical aspects of taxation.

6. This is our interpretation of Walras's special use of this term. It should be noted that Jaffé leaves the French word untranslated in his English text.

7. It is very interesting to note that the discussion in article 273 (especially pp. 317–18) suggests that Walras not only had the transactions and wealth (or speculative) motives for holding cash, but also the finance demand for money that Keynes added after the publication of the *General Theory*.

8. In article 314 (p. 374), Walras states clearly the classical price-specie flow mechanism of David Hume, with reinforcing income effects mentioned in earlier editions but deleted by the time of the Definitive Edition.

9. On these points, see Lesson 23, especially article 242 (pp. 274–6) and also the attached translator's note h, pp. 587–8 of Jaffé's translation of the Definitive Edition. It is interesting to note that Milton Friedman (1955) considers this change to be a definite deterioration of the presentation, as he felt that the older Walras was misled by considerations of pure form and 'the substance which the form was to represent was no longer part of him'.

10. Jaffé (1980) p. 530.

11. Jaffé (1980) p. 530. The reader may observe that our translation is slightly different from the one presented by Jaffé himself on the following page.

12. Fundamentally, Walras's Law need not hold in this context, because the aggregative analogue to the household budget constraint applies only to the notional or full-employment demand functions, while in an underemployment context the realized or effective demand functions need not be globally consistent with virtual (full-employment) equilibrium. (For example, some households may plan to supply more labour and hence demand more goods than their depressed labour markets may permit.)

13. The only place in the book where there is (to the best of our knowledge) a discussion of

involuntary unemployment appears on pp. 432–3, in the context of the lesson on price fixing and monopoly. Here Walras states the neoclassical view that, if the wage rate is set too high (either because of minimum wage laws or other pressures), the results will be unemployment or underemployment.

14. Of course we do not wish to be understood as asserting that the presence of unemployment (whether voluntary or not, whether as an equilibrium phenomenon or not) is essential to a macroeconometric model, as the counter-example of the Sargent model (1976) illustrates in a clear fashion. Rather, the presence of persistent unemployment as explained by the model is characteristic of particular models, especially those constructed in a Keynesian or neokeynesian framework.

15. Thus the demands for the myriad of final products aggregate into the consumption functions for households, the investment functions for business enterprises and (in an open economy) export and import demand functions. Realism would also suggest the introduction of another agent making expenditures, namely the public authorities; however, this is not a fundamental modification.

16. Of course, this position is debatable, as Morishima (1980) claims that Walras's static models can easily be dynamized to encompass a theory of economic growth and possibly also to take cyclical phenomena into account; Jaffé (1980) vigorously challenges Morishima on these points. In any case, the traditional interpretation of the Walrasian system is one of a static model of the competitive process of price formation.

17. Similarly, Henry W. Spiegel appears to share this view in his text on the history of economic thought (1971), as he argues (p. 556) that modern econometric model-builders are, in one sense, the heirs of Léon Walras and his system of equations. Indeed, Professor Spiegel appears to assert that modern econometric models (along with Leontief's input–output system) go some distance to overcoming the criticism that the Walrasian system is purely formal and not really capable of generating substantive conclusions about the economy (a criticism that goes back at least to Friedman's review of Jaffé's translation, 1955).

18. Following Jaffé's review (1972) of Ann S. Schwier's translation of Pareto's *Manuel* (the French, not the Italian, version) and the debate among Jaffé, the Schwiers, and Vincent J. Tarascio, in the March 1974 issue of the *Journal of Economic Literature*, we have decided to rely primarily on secondary sources of the Paretian models of general equilibrium, namely Hutchison (1966) and Tarascio (1973) especially pp. 395–403. However we have examined the original Italian version (1906) of the *Manuale*.

19. Tarascio (1973) p. 397. In this connection, it may be noted that the concept of 'obstacles' is quite general and includes such diverse phenomena as (a) the tastes of other economic agents, (b) barriers of space and time, (c) forms of social organization, and (d) property tenure systems affecting the ownership of complementary factors of production, as well as the more traditional limitations on the stocks of economically produced final goods and services (or, on a slightly longer term perspective, the ease and facility of production).

20. Tarascio (1968, p. 136) states, 'The economics profession has, to a remarkable extent, adopted Pareto's views on the verification problem, although his contribution has always remained implicit in the technical discussions of his contributions to economics'.

21. A related question is whether the business cycle is a real, a monetary, or a mixed phenomenon. It is interesting to note that Frisch argues that his transactions demand for money is only an auxiliary relationship and that his is really not a monetary theory of the cycle. However it is worth noting that, in Frisch's system, without the need for cash as a brake on the dynamic evolution of production, the cycle is eliminated, exactly as it is if the distinction between gross investment and the production of capital goods is obliterated.

22. In this context, it is interesting to note that Frisch, in some prefatory remarks, of which he is the sole author, to Frisch and Holme (1935), a supplementary article, argues that Kalecki should not impose a maintained or neutral (i.e. a non-damped, non-explosive) cycle on the parameter values which he selects for his model but, rather, the parameter values should be 'empirically determined'. This, too, represents a step towards the

construction of a full macroeconometric model. (The bulk of the Frisch–Holme article is devoted to demonstrating a proposition about the existence of a cyclical solution to Kalecki's model which is longer than the fixed lag postulated; this proposition, while true, and its demonstration need not concern us here.)

23. The major part of the argument of this section has already been published in Bodkin, Klein, and Marwah (1986).

24. Suggestions for alternative models have come from other sources such as the school of rational expectations (e.g. R. E. Lucas, 1976 or Thomas J. Sargent, 1976) or the time-series, 'little theory' approach of Christopher A. Sims (1980).

25. Keynes's methods of attempting to corroborate his theoretical constructs (an informal examination of the data, grouping the years in pairs) seem rather casual, and it is no surprise to learn that Patinkin (1976) was unable to reproduce Keynes's estimate (between 2.5 and 3) for the multiplier for the US economy. (This might conceivably be the case because Patinkin not unreasonably considered only contiguous years, while Keynes may have carried out his estimation over two more widely separated years.) In any case, in that Keynes then inferred a parameter value of the marginal propensity to consume from the estimated multiplier, it seems likely that he carried out the first instance of reduced form estimation, as Patinkin notes.

26. Thus Keynes appears (in Chapter 21) to have interpreted the marginal productivity condition of neoclassical economics (the equality of the marginal physical product of labour to the ratio of the nominal wage rate to the price of final output) as a relationship for the determination of final goods prices, rather than as a labour demand relationship, at least under conditions of less than full utilization of the labour force.

27. Stone traces Keynes's views on this subject to his own personality conflicts regarding a lack of success as a research mathematician. Patinkin sees these remarks as a ritualistic continuation of Marshall's attitudes, but also feels that Keynes's comparative advantage did not lie in this field. Presumably Keynes made his peace with mathematically oriented economic theory, as he seems to have acquiesced to Meade's (1936–7) and Hicks's (1937) representations, in fairly tight mathematical terms, of his basic system.

28. We may note that, in his private correspondence, especially with R. F. Harrod and R. F. Kahn, Keynes showed himself to be even more sceptical than in the published review. See Moggridge (1973) pp. 285–306, for a substantiation of this point.

29. This point brings us back immediately to the rudimentary character of national income data in Great Britain during the 1930s, and hence this point would appear to have been particularly pertinent at the time of Keynes's review. (By contrast, the US Department of Commerce was already producing estimates of national income on a regular basis by 1935.) Whether Keynes contributed to the improvement of this situation or whether, *au contraire*, he hindered some useful developments that were taking place in any case is a point of dispute between Stone (1980) and Patinkin (1976), following some correspondence with Colin Clark.

30. Keynes also appears not to have had a full appreciation of the technique of multiple regression as an artificial manner of holding other influences constant, as he asserts in his review that the technique requires the explanatory variables to be 'largely independent' statistically. On the other hand, an apologist for Keynes might interpret his remarks as anticipating the problem of strong multicollinearity, which is so often encountered in applied econometrics.

31. Opinions on Keynes's performance in this episode have certainly varied among commentators, over the years. Thus, almost 40 years ago, one of us (Klein, 1951) characterized Keynes's review of Tinbergen's work as 'one of his sorriest professional performances'; even with the passage of time, Klein sees no reason to revise this evaluation. On the other hand, Patinkin summarizes this same review and concludes that Keynes was more right than incorrect, as well as observing that he (Patinkin) finds it depressing to note how many of Keynes's criticisms are still relevant today. Another evaluation is that of Stone, who, while conceding the validity of some individual points, regards Keynes's review as 'a model of testiness and perverseness'; in particular, he argues that Keynes failed to realize that the new technique might have been exactly what might be

very helpful 'to quantify the multiplier [for example, as in Clark's contemporaneous (1938) article] and other parameters of *The General Theory*'. Moreover, Johannes J. Klant, who is generally sympathetic to what he regards as Keynes's basic methodological position, concedes, 'Keynes displayed much ignorance and misunderstanding of what Tinbergen had done' (Klant, 1985, p. 91). Finally, Tinbergen himself appears not to have commented again, once he wrote a rejoinder (1940) to Keynes's review. In an article that is generally of an expository nature, written shortly after Keynes's death, Tinbergen (1948) did not comment on Keynes's 1939 critique, perhaps out of respect for a recently deceased intellectual opponent (in this matter). Even in 1986, in reviewing a first draft of this chapter, Professor Tinbergen did not comment specifically on this issue.

32. However, Tinbergen in his concluding remarks of *An Econometric Approach to Business Cycle Problems* (1937) clearly mentions testing various received theories as one of the advantages of such an approach. Nor has much changed in this regard. For example, a recent exposition of methodological and philosophical issues in econometric practice (Hendry, 1980) placed great emphasis on econometric techniques as a means of resolving conflicts among rival theories. Hendry, incidentally, reviewed the Keynes–Tinbergen interchanges and expressed great doubt that Keynes could have really meant his apparent position, namely that empirical methods in general and econometric techniques in particular were unsuitable for resolving conflicts among rival economic theories!

33. Taken to its logical extreme, such a philosophical position would appear to imply that no macroeconomic policies (stabilization policies in particular) are possible, because, if the structure of the economy is so unstable, one can never be sure of what one is doing. In this regard, the proponents of this point of view would appear to join Robert Lucas (1976) and the rational expectations school, who argue that the parameters of the system are highly unstable, at least with a shift in the policy regime itself, thus rendering both economic policy and macroeconometric estimation extremely difficult, if not impossible.

34. Quoted by Stone (1980) p. 63, and by Patinkin (1976) p. 1092 (all but the final phrase, 'which would make me feel a little bit of an imposter').

35. Stone (1980) concludes his review of the episode by noting that the renewal of the contact had convinced Keynes that Tinbergen's work should be given 'every scope and opportunity', and he (Stone) asserts, 'Nothing could show better the difference between Keynes' first impersonal impressions and his considered view based on personal experience' (p. 64). At the same time, we may note that Lawson (1985) has argued that Stone's analysis at most explains the *force* of Keynes's critique of Tinbergen, without 'explaining away' his well-founded (according to Lawson) logical objections. Moreover it could be argued (as Don Patinkin did in commenting on an earlier draft of this section) that an emotional reunion right after a cataclysmic war is hardly a set of circumstances under which a detached, rational reappraisal of a previous opinion can be carried out.

36. If Keynes had lived to the ripe old age of his parents, it seems likely that his views would again have evolved further, under the combined influences of additional evidence and the further thinking of himself and others about these problems. What direction his further thoughts would have taken is, at this point, a matter of pure speculation.

37. The significance of the first of these two supplementary explanatory variables suggests that the method of eliminating active balances employed by Brown may not have been completely successful.

38. Elizabeth W. Gilboy (1939), in a running debate with Professor Acheson J. Duncan of Princeton University (and with Keynes himself), remarked that Keynes's propensity to consume was a statistical, rather than a psychological, law or tendency. This turned out to be prophetic, at least as a general tendency.

39. Dirks (1938) did put forward the interesting hypothesis that Staehle's results could be explained more simply by income and income change as explanatory variables, owing to what the late T. M. Brown (1952) was to call 'habit persistence'. In retrospect, it

seems clear that most qualified observers would agree with Richard and W. M. Stone that Staehle exaggerated the practical importance of this additional explanatory variable.

40. Although it was published somewhat later than Tinbergen's League of Nations study, for the sake of completeness we may mention Paul A. Samuelson's 1941 study of 'A Statistical Analysis of the Consumption Function'. Although Samuelson was not to make his career as an applied econometrician, this study is one of the best of the early work on the aggregative consumption function. Samuelson discusses his variables at length, considering a number of alternatives and defending the specification selected. His best formulation has real, per capita consumption as a linear function of real, per capita 'income received' (a sort of disposable income variable) and of real, per capita business savings (which presumably measures increases in household wealth due to increasing claims on the corporate sector); the estimated marginal propensity to consume was 0.81.

41. The Stones considered, on the basis of some fragmentary evidence, that the multiplier appeared to be largely constant over time, within a given country.

42. In this connection, we may raise the question of whether Kalecki did develop independently a macroeconomic model that contained all of the essential elements of the Keynesian system. There are legitimate differences of opinion on this subject, but Kalecki's model of the business cycle, his version of liquidity preference and the equations of his system predate the later formal interpretations by Hicks (1937) and Meade (1936–7) of the Keynesian system as a total model. A literal interpretation of the writings of Keynes and Kalecki might lead some scholars, such as Don Patinkin, to conclude that Kalecki did not independently develop a mainstream Keynesian model. However the spirit and novelty of Kalecki's contributions are such as to lead one to conclude that it was, indeed, a separate discovery of the same basic system. In this regard, mention might be made of Kalecki's version of the consumption function (which put an explicit emphasis on the functional distribution of income), of Kalecki's investment function (which made the sophisticated distinction between orders and shipments or deliveries), and of Kalecki's alternative to liquidity preference theory, in which the income velocity of money is made an increasing function of the rate of interest. We also know that Kalecki treated these three components as a dynamic system whose solution was meant to describe the economy as a whole.

　Apart from the formal question of macroeconometric model-building, it is clear that Kalecki was not able to round out his theory with profound insights into the functioning of financial markets and the formulation of high-level policy, which was the hallmark of Keynes's unusual influence. Kalecki's theory was drafted for a professional audience, while Keynes went far beyond a circle of econometricians and other professional economists. He was talking to major policy- and decision-makers.

43. Although they were published a few years after Tinbergen's study, mention may be made of Mordecai Ezekiel's two studies (1942a, 1942b). Ezekiel attempted to get an empirical counterpart of the savings and investment functions of macroeconomic theory, and so (by appropriate observation or manipulation) he would have been able to calculate the likely location of possible equilibrium positions and hence the implicit multiplier generated by any possible shift in the investment function. More than half a century later, it is interesting to note that Ezekiel explicitly acknowledged in these articles helpful comments from (among others) Alvin H. Hansen, Paul A. Samuelson – and John Maynard Keynes. Ezekiel's work was criticized at the time by one of us (Klein, 1943), largely on the grounds that (in modern language) Ezekiel had not paid sufficient attention to the problem of identification.

References

Arrow, Kenneth J. and Gerard Debreu (1954) 'Existence of an Equilibrium for a Competitive Economy', *Econometrica*, vol. 22, no. 3 (July) pp. 265–90.

Bodkin, Ronald G., Lawrence R. Klein and Kanta Marwah (1986) 'Keynes and the Origins of Macroeconometric Modelling', *Eastern Economic Journal*, volume 12, no. 4 (October–December) pp. 442–50. (This piece was also published in O. F. Hamouda and J. N. Smithin (eds), *Keynes and Public Policy After Fifty Years, Volume 2: Theories and Method* (Gloucester: Edward Elgar Publishing Limited, 1988) pp. 3–11.

Brown, A. J. (1939) 'Interest, Prices and the Demand Schedule for Idle Money', *Oxford Economic Papers*, no. 2 (May) pp. 46–69.

Brown, T. M. (1952) 'Habit Persistence and Lags in Consumer Behavior', *Econometrica*, vol. 20, no. 3 (July) pp. 207–23.

Clark, Colin (1937) 'National Income at its Climax', *Economic Journal*, vol. 47, no. 186 (June) pp. 308–20.

―――― (1938) 'Determination of the Multiplier from National Income Statistics', *Economic Journal*, vol. 48, no. 191 (September) pp. 435–48.

Clower, Robert W. (1966) 'The Keynesian Counter-Revolution: A Theoretical Appraisal', pp. 103–25 in F. H. Hahn and F. P. R. Brechling (eds), *The Theory of Interest Rates* (New York: St Martin's Press, 1966).

Dirks, Frederick C. (1938) 'Retail Sales and Labor Income', *Review of Economic Statistics*, vol. 20, no. 3 (August) pp. 128–34.

Dresch, F. W. (1938) 'Index Numbers and the General Economic Equilibrium', *Bulletin of the American Mathematical Society*, vol. 44 (February) pp. 134–41.

Evans, Griffith C. (1934) 'Maximum Production Studied in a Simplified Economic System', *Econometrica*, vol. 2, no. 1 (January) pp. 37–50.

Ezekiel, Mordecai (1942a) 'Statistical Investigations of Saving, Consumption, and Investment: I, Saving, Consumption, and National Income', *American Economic Review*, vol. 32, no. 1 (March) pp. 22–49.

―――― (1942b) 'Statistical Investigations of Saving, Consumption, and Investment: II, Investment, National Income, and the Saving-Investment Equilibrium', *American Economic Review*, vol. 32, no. 2 (June) pp. 272–307.

Friedman, Milton (1955) 'Léon Walras and His Economic System', *American Economic Review*, vol. 45, no. 5 (December) pp. 1190–1201.

Frisch, Ragnar (1933) 'Propagation Problems and Impulse Problems in Dynamic Economics', pp. 171–205 in *Economic Essays in Honour of Gustav Cassel, October 20th 1933* (London: Frank Cass and Company Limited).

Frisch, Ragnar, and Harald Holme (1935) 'The Characteristic Solutions of a Mixed Difference and Differential Equation Occurring in Economic Dynamics', *Econometrica*, vol. 3, pp. 225–39.

Gilboy, Elizabeth W. (1938) 'The Propensity to Consume', *Quarterly Journal of Economics*, vol. 53, no. 1 (November) pp. 120–40.

―――― (1939) 'Reply' [to comments by Acheson J. Duncan and John Maynard Keynes], *Quarterly Journal of Economics*, vol. 53, no. 4 (August) pp. 633–8.

Hendry, David F. (1980) 'Econometrics – Alchemy or Science', *Economica*, vol. 47, no. 4 (November) pp. 387–406.

Hicks, John R. (1937) 'Mr Keynes and the "Classics"; A Suggested Interpretation', *Econometrica*, vol. 5, no. 2 (April) pp. 147–59.

Hutchinson, T. W. (1966) *A Review of Economic Doctrines 1870–1929* (Oxford: Clarendon Press).

Jaffé, William (1972) 'Pareto Translated: A Review Article', *Journal of Economic Literature*, vol. 10, no. 4 (December) pp. 1190–1201.

―――― (1974) '"Pareto's Three Manuals": Rebuttal', *Journal of Economic Literature*, vol. 12, no. 1 (March) pp. 88–91.

―――― (1980) 'Walras's Economics as Others See It', *Journal of Economic Literature*, vol. 18, no. 2 (June) pp. 528–49.

Kalecki, Michal (1935) 'A Macrodynamic Theory of Business Cycles', *Econometrica*, vol. 3, pp. 327–44.

―――― (1939) 'Investment and Income', Chapter 2 (pp. 42–74) of *Essays in the Theory of Economic Fluctuations* (New York: Farrar & Rinehart, Inc.).

Keynes, John Maynard (1936) *The General Theory of Employment, Interest and Money* (New York: Harcourt, Brace & Company).
_____ (1939a) 'Mr. Keynes on the Distribution of Incomes and the "Propensity to Consume": A Reply', *Review of Economic Statistics*, vol. 21, no. 3 (August) pp. 128–9.
_____ (1939b) 'Professor Tinbergen's Method', *Economic Journal*, vol. 49, no. 195 (September) pp. 558–68.
Klant, Johannes J. (1985) 'The Slippery Transition', pp. 80–98 in Tony Lawson and Hashem Pesaran (eds), *Keynes' Economics: Methodological Issues* (London and Sydney: Croom Helm).
Klein, Lawrence R. (1943) 'Pitfalls in the Statistical Determination of the Investment Schedule', *Econometrica*, vol. 11, nos. 3–4 (July–October) pp. 246–58.
_____ (1951) 'The Life of John Maynard Keynes', *Journal of Political Economy*, vol. 59, no. 5 (October) pp. 443–51.
Lawson, Tony (1985) 'Keynes, Prediction, and Econometrics', pp. 116–133 in T. Lawson and H. Pesaran (eds), *Keynes' Economics: Methodological Issues* (London and Sydney: Croom Helm).
Lawson, Tony and H. Pesaran (eds) (1985) *Keynes' Economics: Methodological Issues* (London and Sydney: Croom Helm).
Lucas, Robert E., Jr (1976) 'Econometric Policy Evaluation: A Critique', pp. 19–46 in Karl Brunner and Allan H. Meltzer (eds), *The Phillips Curve and Labor Markets* (Amsterdam: North-Holland Publishing Company, 1976), Carnegie-Rochester Conference Series on Public Policy, vol. 1, *Supplement* to the *Journal of Monetary Economics*.
Marshall, Alfred (1897) 'The Old Generation of Economists and the New', *Quarterly Journal of Economics*, vol. 11 (January) pp. 115–35.
Marx, Karl (1906) *Capital*, vol. 1, Modern Library Edition (New York: Random House, Inc.).
Meade, J. E. (1936–7) 'A Simplified Model of Mr. Keynes' System', *Review of Economic Studies*, vol. 4, pp. 98–107.
Moggridge, Donald (ed.) (1973) *The Collected Writings of John Maynard Keynes*, vol. XIV, *The General Theory and After, Part II, Defence and Development* (London: Macmillan).
Morgan, Mary S. (1984) 'The History of Econometric Thought: Analysis of the Main Problems of Relating Economic Theory to Data in the First Half of the Twentieth Century', PhD Thesis, London University, 1984. (This work was also published in 1987 by Cambridge University Press under the title, *The History of Econometric Ideas*.)
_____ (1987) 'Statistics without Probability and Haavelmo's Revolution in Econometrics', in L. Krüger, G. Gigerenzer and M. S. Morgan (eds), *The Probabilistic Revolution, vol. 2, Ideas in the Sciences* (Cambridge, Mass., and London: Bradford Books and MIT Press).
Morishima, Michio (1980) 'W. Jaffé on Léon Walras: A Comment', *Journal of Economic Literature*, vol. 18, no. 2 (June) pp. 550–8.
Okun, Arthur M. (1981) *Prices and Quantities: A Macroeconomic Analysis* (Washington, DC: The Brookings Institution).
Pareto, Vilfredo (1896–7) *Cours d'économie politique/Professé à l'Université de Lausanne*, vols 1 and 2 (Lausanne: Rouge). (This work has been republished as Volume 1 of the *Oeuvres complètes de Vilfredo Pareto*, G. H. Bousquet and G. Busino (eds) (Geneva: Droz, 1964).
_____ (1906) *Manuale di economia politica con una introduzione alla scienza sociale*, no. 13 in the Piccola biblioteca scientifica (Milan: Società editrice libraria, 1906). (We have consulted the 1974 reprinting, published in Padova, Italy, by Casa editrice dolt. Antonio Milani.)
Patinkin, Don (1976) 'Keynes and Econometrics: On the Interaction between the Macroeconomic Revolutions of the Interwar Period', *Econometrica*, vol. 44, no. 6 (November) pp. 1091–1123.
Pesaran, Hashem and Ron Smith (1985) 'Keynes on Econometrics', pp. 134–50 in T. Lawson and H. Pesaran (eds), *Keynes' Economics: Methodological Issues* (London and Sydney: Croom Helm).

Polak, J. J. (1939) 'Functions in United States Consumption, 1919–1932', *Review of Economic Statistics*, vol. 21, no. 1 (February) pp. 1–12.

Radice, E. A. (1939) 'A Dynamic Scheme for the British Trade Cycle, 1929–1937', *Econometrica*, vol. 7, no. 1 (January) pp. 47–56.

Roos, C. F. (1930) 'A Mathematical Theory of Price and Production Fluctuations and Economic Crises', *Journal of Political Economy*, vol. 38, no. 5 (October) pp. 501–22.

_____ (1934) *Dynamic Economics: Theoretical and Statistical Studies of Demand, Production and Prices*, Cowles Commission Monograph No. 1 (Bloomington, Indiana: The Principia Press, Inc.).

Samuelson, Paul A. (1941) 'A Statistical Analysis of the Consumption Function', Appendix to Chapter 11 (pp. 250–60) in Alvin H. Hansen, *Fiscal Policy and Business Cycles* (New York: W. W. Norton & Company, Inc.).

Sargent, Thomas J. (1976) 'A Classical Macroeconomic Model for the United States', *Journal of Political Economy*, vol. 84, no. 2 (April) pp. 207–37.

Sawyer, John A. (1976) 'Stanley Jevons and the Development of Scientific Method in Economics', Working Paper No. 7602 of the Institute for Policy Analysis of the University of Toronto, mimeographed, September.

Schwier, J. F. and Ann S. Schwier (1974) 'Pareto's Three Manuals', *Journal of Economic Literature*, vol. 12, no. 1 (March) pp. 78–87.

Sims, Christopher A. (1980) 'Macroeconomics and Reality', *Econometrica*, vol. 48, no. 1 (January) pp. 1–48.

Spiegel, Henry William (1971) *The Growth of Economic Thought* (Englewood Cliffs, New Jersey: Prentice-Hall).

Staehle, Hans (1937) 'Short-Period Variations in the Distribution of Incomes', *Review of Economc Statistics*, vol. 19, no. 3 (August) pp. 133–43.

_____ (1938) 'New Considerations on the Distribution of Incomes and the "Propensity to Consume" (partly in reply to M. Dirks)', *Review of Economic Statistics*, vol. 20, no. 3 (August) pp. 134–41.

_____ (1939) 'A Rejoinder' [to a reply by John Maynard Keynes], *Review of Economic Statistics*, vol. 21, no. 3 (August) p. 129.

Stone, Richard (1980) 'Keynes, Political Arithmetic and Econometrics', Keynes Lecture in Economics 1978, pp. 55–92 of the *Proceedings of the British Academy*, London, vol. 64, 1978 (Oxford: Oxford University Press).

Stone, Richard and W. M. Stone (1938–9) 'The Marginal Propensity to Consume and the Multiplier: A Statistical Investigation', *Review of Economic Studies*, vol. 6, pp. 1–24.

Tarascio, Vincent J. (1968) *Pareto's Methodological Approach to Economics: A Study in the History of Some Scientific Aspects of Economic Thought* (Chapel Hill: The University of North Carolina Press.

_____ (1973) 'Vilfredo Pareto: on the Occasion of the Translation of his *Manuel*', *Canadian Journal of Economics*, vol. 6, no. 3 (August) pp. 394–408.

_____ (1974) 'Vilfred Pareto and the Translation of his *Manuel*', *Journal of Economic Literature*, vol. 12, no. 1 (March) pp. 91–6.

Theiss, Edward (1933) 'A Quantitative Theory of Industrial Fluctuations Caused by the Capitalist Technique of Production', *Journal of Political Economy*, vol. 41, no. 3 (June) pp. 334–49.

Tinbergen, Jan (1935) 'Annual Survey: Suggestions on Quantitative Business Cycle Theory', *Econometrica*, vol. 3, pp. 241–308.

_____ (1937) *An Econometric Approach to Business Cycle Problems* (Paris: Hermann et Compagnie).

_____ (1939a) *A Method and its Application to Investment Activity*, Part I of *Statistical Testing of Business-Cycle Theories* (New York: Agathon Press Inc., 1968). (Originally published in Geneva by the Economic Intelligence Service of the League of Nations in 1939.)

_____ (1939b) *Business Cycles in the United States of America, 1919–1932*, Part II of *Statistical Testing of Business-Cycle Theories* (New York: Agathon Press, Inc., 1968).

(Originally published in Geneva by the Economic Intelligence Service of the League of Nations in 1939.)

_____ (1940) 'On a Method of Business-Cycle Research: A Reply', *Economic Journal*, vol. 50, no. 197 (March) pp. 140–54.

_____ (1948) 'The Significance of Keynes's Theories from the Econometric Point of View', Chapter 18 (pp. 219–31) in Seymour E. Harris (ed.), *The New Economics* (New York: Alfred A. Knopf).

_____ (1986) letter to Ronald G. Bodkin, dated 31 July.

Tobin, James (1947) 'Liquidity Preference and Monetary Policy', *Review of Economics and Statistics*, vol. 29, no. 2 (May) pp. 124–31.

Walras, Léon (1954) *Elements of Pure Economics* (Homewood, Illinois: Richard D. Irwin, Inc.). (A translation, by William Jaffé, of the Edition Définitive of *Eléments d'économie politique pure* (Paris and Lausanne: R. Pichon et R. Durand-Auzias and F. Rouge, 1926).)

2   Econometric model-building at the origins

1   Introduction

In this chapter we shall review three early contributions to macroeconometric modelling. Pride of place has to go to Tinbergen's seminal contribution of 1939, *Business Cycles in the United States of America 1919–1932*, which was published under the auspices of the League of Nations.[1] Accordingly we review this work in the second section of this chapter. Lawrence R. Klein's early efforts in the field of econometric modelling may be found in his 1950 volume, *Economic Fluctuations in the United States, 1921–1941*, and our considered thoughts (including Klein's) on this effort may be found in Section 3 of this chapter. Macroeconometric modelling was first used for purposes of formulating economic policy in Holland, the native country of Tinbergen, where the Dutch Central Planning Bureau took the econometric models originally constructed by Tinbergen and developed them so that they were especially suitable for economic policy. The fourth and final section of this paper reviews this effort, thus overlapping, to a certain extent, Anton P. Barten's work in Chapter 6.

Thus we are looking at some pioneering efforts in this area of scholarship, but we do not claim that we are reviewing the very earliest efforts in this discipline. As both Stone (1980) and Theil (1971) have noted, Tinbergen published (in Dutch) a 24-equation model of the Netherlands economy, around 1935, and indeed a preliminary version of this model was presented to the Fifth European Meeting of the Econometric Society, held in that year.[2] Thus our survey looks at representative pieces rather than attempting to be an exhaustive compilation.

2   Tinbergen's Business Cycles in the United States of America, 1919–1932

Introduction

The edition of this seminal work that we used is the Agathon Press edition of 1968, which contains a contemporary preface by Jan Tinbergen. Nearly 30 years after the publication of his work, Tinbergen regarded his model of the US economy during the interwar period as being primarily of historical interest; he concedes that better working models of the US economy (such as the Klein–Goldberger Model or the Brookings Model) now (1968) exist. He does, however, say that his 1939 model has one feature that has been neither explicitly rejected nor incorporated by later model-builders, namely the role of stock market speculation in the US economy, particularly around 1929.[3] Even here, however, he concedes that this factor may not be as important an element in the postwar US economy as it was in the interwar period. Finally, he notes with pleasure that the idea of using econometric models to simulate alternative paths of the evolution of an economy, particularly for policy purposes, is much better established now (at the end of the decade of the 1960s) than it was just before the outbreak of the Second World War.

We may note that Tinbergen's was an annual model of the US economy, fitted by ordinary least squares to data for the period 1919–32. There were 31 behavioural equations and 17 identities,[4] for a total of 48 equations. If we follow Tinbergen's own classification of the grouping of equations (except for suppressing his definitional equations subsector, which is precisely a collection of 16 identities, and instead associating each identity with a model sector) we may decompose this model into four sectors or related groups of equations. The first sector may be called a final demand sector, and it consists of three consumption functions, three investment demand equations, and eight identities, for a total of 14 equations. The second sector is what we call the price-wage sector (Tinbergen terms it 'Supply or Price Equations for Goods and Services'), and it is composed of five behavioural equations and one identity. A financial sector and an income distribution sector (or, as Tinbergen would call it, an 'Income Formation' sector) complete the model; the former has 10 behavioural equations and five identities for a total of 15 equations, while the latter has 10 behavioural equations with a detailed breakdown of the functional distribution of income (including wages, profits, interest payments, rent payments and salaries) and three identities, for a total of 13 equations. Some slightly greater detail regarding the structure of the model will be given in the following subsection.[5]

In reading Tinbergen's work from a current perspective, a number of differences (some superficial, some more essential) will strike the modern reader. Even the notation is somewhat different from what has become conventional; thus Tinbergen's symbol for the calculated value of the dependent variable is the ordinary symbol with an asterisk, rather than with a circumflex ('hat') accent. Also, in this volume, the symbol C denotes the current value of the capital stock of corporations (not consumption expenditures) and G is the realized value of capital gains, not government expenditures.[6] Regression coefficients are presented in general in stark form, being unadorned with coefficients of determination, standard errors of estimate, Durbin-Watson test statistics (of course), or even standard errors of the individual regression coefficient estimates. (It might be noted, however, that Tinbergen does compute these individual standard errors when their evaluation may be considered essential to the testing of the hypothesis under consideration, while an idea of the tightness of the fit of the overall relationship is given by his time diagrams, which are presented for all of the behavioural relationships and a number of the technical approximations.) At times, even the language is somewhat different from current usage; for example, on p. 171, the term 'stocks' is used to mean inventories, not equities or shares.

Other features of the model which differ from a modern treatment are more subtle. All of the relationships of the model are linear, including linearizations of relationships that would naturally be non-linear. (In view of the primitive nature of computing techniques at the time, this is quite understandable.) Tinbergen uses fractional lags as approximations to distributed lags, again reflecting the state of the art with regard to theoretical econometrics and computing technology at the time.[7] As noted above, the model was estimated by ordinary least squares; it was this aspect of the work that evoked Haavelmo's discussion (1943) of simultaneous equations biases of ordinary least squares estimation a few years later. We note as well that the bulk of Tinbergen's discussion is devoted to model specification, hypothesis testing and description of the final relationships selected. There is a relative absence of full system simulations, either to test specific relationships or to describe the functioning of the economy as a whole. (Again, in the light of the computing technology of the day, this was quite comprehensible.) In place of the full system simulations that are presented in modern studies, we have dynamic multiplier calculations (which, after all, are system-wide, in principle) and the reduction of various subsystems, which Tinbergen studies at some length to draw conclusions concerning the nature of the business cycle, at least for the United States for the interwar period. (More on this below.) Finally, as already noted above, the treatment of the fiscal aspects of government is extremely sketchy, and standard simulations of variations in tax or public expenditures policy could not be performed with the Tinbergen model in any case,[8] although this did not stop him (as we shall see below) from calculating a numerical value of the multiplier in a dynamic context.

The structure of the model
We may begin with the exogenous variables, as these are treated rather summarily by Tinbergen himself. In fact, Tinbergen does not have a portion of his book where he discusses the exogenous variables explicitly; rather, on occasion, when discussing a behavioural equation or identity, he will mention *en passant* that a certain variable entering this relation is 'autonomous', 'external' or 'exogenous'. Indeed we have inferred a final list of exogenous variables from his Appendix A, 'List of Variables

Included in System'; where a variable exists in his final system but does not have an equation or identity that could be interpreted as providing a proximate explanation of that variable, we take the variable in question to be exogenous.[9] (Of course, the text discussion helps in this classification.) We may note that there are few truly exogenous variables in Tinbergen's final model, as he was perhaps still influenced, to a certain degree, by the Walrasian tradition of a largely closed or internally contained model. We have identified five such exogenous variables: P (security holdings of the Federal Reserve system); Au (the US gold stock), which may be a doubtful exogenous variable in a fixed exchange rate system; f, the supply of agricultural output made available to the internal US market; q^B, an index of construction costs,[10] and t, a time trend, which of course is a quintessential exogenous variable, as time will pass regardless of the evolution of economic activity. Note that two of these five exogenous variables could be regarded as policy instruments, both of which refer to monetary policy.

The 'redundant' or non-final exogenous variables are of some interest also. Both exports and imports, in value and in volume terms, are taken as exogenous, which appears to be a doubtful treatment of imports (if it mattered), even in the context of the relatively less open US economy of the interwar period. A parameter for the degree of inequality in the personal distribution of income is also taken as exogenous, but this variable does not enter the final consumption function, for which it had been employed as a tentative explanatory variable.   Turning to the final demand sector, we may note that the principal consumption function explains nominal (current-dollar) consumption expenditures in terms of wage and salary incomes, non-rural property incomes (which includes corporate managers' salaries),[11] capital gains, two price terms (one to allow for possible speculative profits affecting consumption, and one to correct for the use of nominal variables) and a time trend, perhaps to allow for the slow drift upwards over time of consumption standards.[12] Because of multicollinearity between the two income variables, Tinbergen estimates their associated coefficients in an indirect manner. His final estimate is that the marginal propensity to consume wage and salary income is 0.95 (which Polak (1939) claimed was consistent with the results of family budget studies), while the marginal propensity to consume non-agricultural property income is 0.77. Interestingly, the marginal propensity to consume out of capital gains was estimated to be 0.28 (and statistically significant by the usual criteria); this result suggests the possible disruptive influence of stock market fluctuations in the interwar US economy. Tinbergen also spent four pages explaining that he had *not* disaggregated total consumption expenditures into the demand for durables and non-durables separately. Finally, we note from the time diagram on p. 39

of this work that the fit for the principal consumption function appeared to be reasonably tight, with major turning-points effectively reproduced.[13]

The three equations for investment demand form a reasonably articulated subsector, as one might expect from Part I of *Statistical Testing of Business Cycles*. In this subsector, the three dependent variables are in constant dollars, although the explanatory variables, which include price indices and corporate profits, are, of course, in current dollars. Expenditures on plant and equipment investment (which Tinbergen called 'durable producers' goods and non-residential building') depended positively on corporate profits and on the spread or margin between finished goods prices and estimated wage costs and negatively on the price of investment goods and on the interest yield on common stocks or shares; all of these variables are subject to a lag of half a year. There was also a time trend as an additional explanatory variable, 'to account for slow changes in the capital intensity of production'. Investment in residential construction depended positively on corporate profits, a time trend, and an index of rents paid and negatively on an index of construction costs, on the long-term interest rate on bonds, and on the stock of houses already in existence. All of these explanatory variables were entered for the current period, with the exception of the stock of houses, which was supposed to operate with a lag of four years (not quarters). The inventory investment equation (technically, an equation for the stock of inventories) is limited to inventories of finished consumer goods and expresses the tendency of the level of inventories to vary with current and past sales, as modified by the negative influence of the short-term rate of interest and a time trend, representing secular economies in the holding of inventories. As judged by the relevant time diagrams, all three investment demand equations display reasonably close fits, despite some tendency for these equations to miss turning-points (particularly the inventory equation). Nevertheless Tinbergen characterized this latter equation as 'one of the least satisfactory parts of the present study', which he attributed to a 'lack of adequate data'.

We may now turn to the price-wage sector of the model, which Tinbergen interprets as reflecting the supply side of a typical purely competitive industry, solving out (in general) an expression for the market-determined wage or price in terms of variables that could shift either the supply or demand function. However Tinbergen's formulation is robust in the sense that the specification is reasonable with other forms of market structure also. We may now briefly review the five structural equations of this sector. Money wage rates depend positively on the level of production in the private economy (as a proxy for private employment), the consumer price index, and a time trend (as a proxy for improving labour productivity and changing labour market institutions (trade union power, legislation and so forth)); the lag involved is roughly five months and the fit was reasonably tight, reproducing all the major turning-points of the sample period. For the equation explaining the prices of consumer goods and services (excluding rent) the level of this price index varies directly with the wage rate and with farm prices (as elements of cost), while it varies negatively with a time trend (which is interpreted as reflecting the cost-reducing properties of trend increases in labour productivity). The lag here is roughly 2 1/2 months and the fit was reasonably good. Tinbergen tried the level of production of consumer goods as an additional explanatory variable, but it was not statistically significant. The index of rent paid as a dependent variable varied directly with the total wage and salary bill (regarded as a demand-side variable) and negatively with the stock of houses lagged two years (an obvious supply-side variable, which should have depressing effects on price in a competitive market) and also negatively with the level of consumer prices excluding rents (which was viewed as a demand-side variable, reflecting the influence of other commodities competing for consumer income).[14] The fit was reasonably tight, although the estimated equation failed to reproduce two turning-points in the dependent variable in the 1920s.

Looking at the last two behavioural equations of this sector, we note that the index of farm prices depended positively on the total wage and salary bill (presumably a demand-side variable) and negatively on the volume of agricultural supply to the US market (an exogenous variable, as noted above) and on a time trend. In the free fit, only the first explanatory variable was statistically significant (although all three had the theoretically appropriate signs)[15] and so Tinbergen constrained the coefficient of agricultural supply to have a numerical value that he judged more appropriate, on the basis of extraneous information. The fit, even after the constrained estimation, was reasonably good. Finally, the index of investment goods prices was given a straightforward explanation in terms of the positive influence of the money wage rate and of current and past levels of production of plant and equipment, along with the restraining influence of technological progress (represented, of course, by a time trend). This equation is interesting as well because there was some evidence of a change in structure beginning in 1924 (which Tinbergen interpreted as an increase in the degree of 're-monopolisation'); the time diagram indicates a nearly perfect fit for the subperiod 1924–32. The surrounding discussion of this equation is interesting because it anticipates some later conclusions with regard to the problems of identification. Tinbergen pointed out that, in this case, it is possible to derive estimates of the parameters of both the supply and demand relationships as the price-quantity lags are different in the two cases and as the set of third variables entering the demand equation is different from that entering the supply relationship. This is quite consistent with more sophisticated discussions of identification a decade or so later.

The Financial Sector of the model ('Money and Capital Markets', in Tinbergen's terminology) is its largest sector, with 10 behavioural equations and five identities, or 15 equations in total. In general, the sector was based on a model of portfolio balance, which has the following flavour. Three groups of agents were distinguished, namely banks, non-banking firms and households. Anticipating the Brainard–Tobin 'pitfalls' model (1968), Tinbergen required in principle that balance sheets for each group of agents display accounting consistency and that demands for individual asset or liability items should reflect this constraint. A sequential order to optimizing decisions was supposed, for example 'Banks *first* decide how much money they will allow to be in existence, and *then* distribute this amount over short claims and bonds' (p. 74; italics in original), resulting in a fair degree of independence in the various demands for financial assets. (In particular, it was assumed that the real sector does not have direct repercussions on the financial sector, a point of view that has been dominant in mainstream econometric modelling until the 1970s). Theoretical developments were often tempered by the availability of statistical data or by the results of preliminary experimentation.[16] Tinbergen noted that his results suggest that the Federal Reserve authorities could easily control the long-term bond rate by reasonable open market purchases or sales.[17]

We shall not describe all of the behavioural relationships of this sector in detail (and, indeed, as note 16 indicates, some of these behavioural equations are 'uninteresting'), but instead we shall describe three of the key equations of this sector. The demand for bank deposits (demand and time deposits), which is part of the demand for money, varies directly with the sum of nominal consumption and investment expenditures (a standard transactions demand component), with the market value of all shares of capital stock of corporations (which Tinbergen interpreted as reflecting the 'need for means of payment for speculative purposes') and a time trend (reflecting an increasing demand for idle balances as a consequence of increasing wealth and increasing efficiency in the payments system, according to Tinbergen); the demand for bank deposits also varies negatively with the short-term interest rate, regarded as reflecting the cost of holding idle money. This relationship could clearly be regarded as a confirmation of several of the key ideas of Keynes's *General Theory*. A second interesting relationship is the demand for currency to be hoarded, which is negatively related to a sharp fall in corporate profits from its preceding maximum, a sharp fall being estimated to be one above 7 billion dollars. (The other component of the demand for currency is a fairly standard transactions demand component, as modified by secular changes in payments habits.) Finally, we may summarize the fascinating equation for the determination of an index of share (stock market) prices, which has been the subject of wide comment.[18] Share prices vary directly (and significantly) with dividend yields (based on share values at cost), directly (and significantly) with a speculative component reflecting 'boom psychology', which measured the dynamic effect of a change in share prices maintaining its own momentum and which was estimated as the positive values of the change in share prices in excess of 20 index points,[19] and also directly with a time trend (presumably reflecting an upward trend in price–earnings ratios over the entire period). Share prices also varied negatively (but insignificantly) with the long-term rate of interest (the bond yield), which seems in accord with capitalization formulae; in any case, the time diagram suggested that this variable is of minor importance economically. The time diagram also suggested a moderately tight fit with the upper turning-points faithfully reproduced. (In particular, the upper turning-point of 1929 was followed up and down quite closely, as the 'boom psychology' variable comes into play only for the 1929–30 subperiod of the total sample. Parenthetically, we may note that the comparative study of the November 1939 journal article suggested that US experience during the 1927–30 episode was unique.)

We may review the income distribution sector (or 'Income Formation' sector, as Tinbergen calls it) rather quickly, as these equations are reasonably straightforward.[20] There are three identities in this sector (with, as left-hand side variables, urban property income, accumulated corporate saving, and the net income of all enterprises and government).[21] There are also nine behavioural equations to explain dividend payments, entrepreneurial withdrawals (for unincorporated businesses), interest incomes, capital gains, rental income payments, wages, middle-echelon salaries, corporate managers' salaries, and depreciation allowances, and also an empirical relationship linking corporate profits to overall net incomes of enterprises and government; all of these explanations run in nominal terms. Most property income variables are linked to corporate profits, which is treated as a key explanatory variable of the system. For example, dividend payments are tied to current and lagged corporate profits and accumulated corporate savings (lagged one year); all three explanatory variables have a positive influence, and the fit seemed reasonably tight. Capital gains are linked to current and lagged changes in share (stock market) prices, as one might anticipate. The two salary endogenous variables are linked to corporate profits, but the wage bill is linked to constant-dollar expenditures on the sum of consumption plus private capital formation, the money wage rate and (negatively) to a time trend; the fit was quite good and the surrounding discussion makes it clear that Tinbergen was making several statistical and theoretical approximations to the identity that the wage bill is the product of the average rate of wage compensation and the number of units of employment. The empirical relationship linking corporate profits to net incomes of all enterprises and government had a trend term, implying an increasing share of corporate profits in this larger total as time goes on.[22]

Tinbergen's uses of his model

We may now turn to the uses that Tinbergen makes of his econometric model, which may be found in the final two chapters of his book. It seems clear that these uses are what interested Tinbergen most, and his conclusions on these subjects appear like the ends to which the structure of the model is principally a means. From the point of view of a modern observer, there were several conspicuous omissions, as we have already partially noted. First, there is a complete absence of block simulations (or full model simulations) within the sample period, as a means of testing the hypothesized structure of the model. Second, there were no policy simulations as such, either within or beyond the sample period, even though a primitive multiplier calculation is made. Finally, no forecasting uses of the model were made.[23] Of course it should be kept firmly in mind that rapid electronic computers were just not available at this time, and that the computations involved in model simulation would have been simply prohibitive, in terms of effort. (Indeed it is difficult for anyone who now has ready access to good hardware and software to visualize just how much work effort was entailed in solving equation systems of quite modest size in the 1930s and 1940s.) Nevertheless five specific uses of the model are distinguished, to which we now turn.

From an examination of the individual behavioural equations, Tinbergen drew a number of conclusions about the US economy, at least for the period between 1919–1932. He concluded that profit incomes are highly volatile, while some rentier incomes (for example, dividends, interest incomes) are relatively stable. Fluctuations in nominal values of consumption and investment outlays were mainly characterized by quantity variations, rather than by pronounced price movements. Interest rates (and other costs) had a 'very moderate' effect on investment activity, and in general '(t)he monetary sphere seems to be much less narrowly in contact with the physical sphere than one might expect' (p. 128).

The main use that Tinbergen made of his model is to say something about the stability or instability of the economy; this discussion occupies 33 pages of Chapter VI, along with considerable development in his appendices. Basically a reduction was made in order to arrive at a linear difference equation in a key variable of the system (Tinbergen chooses corporate profits);[24] the coefficients of this derived difference equation can then be examined to see whether they generate cycles and, if so, whether the cycles are neutral, divergent (explosive) or convergent (damped). In the event, the derived difference equation in corporate profits was cyclical, with a period of 4.8 years (thus corresponding somewhat to the National Bureau of Economic Research (NBER)'s reference cycle) and with a fairly pronounced damping factor. However the discussion in the two succeeding sections makes it clear that 'boom psychology' in the stock market and hoarding behaviour on the part of asset holders can reduce the degree of stability in the system (as measured by the damping ratio); indeed, if these changes were pronounced, either of these factors (particularly the effects of a stock market boom) could convert a stable system into an unstable one.

A third use of the model made by Tinbergen is to study the empirical counterpart of Keynes's multiplier. This is done in terms of the derivation of an approximate relationship between total private production (the sum of real consumption and real private investment) as a function of current and lagged real housing expenditures, regarded for this purpose as effectively an exogenous variable (Tinbergen uses the term 'external variable').[25] This approximation led to an estimate of the impact multiplier equal to 4.4 and a long-term multiplier of 5.4. Tinbergen also noted that the intermediate-term multipliers tend to cycle somewhat and that his calculations were strictly valid only for truly exogenous variations in this sort of expenditure, such as that which might be induced by a public works programme. Finally, it is at this point that Tinbergen brought in his implicit discussion of the labour market.

Tinbergen concluded his discussion of Chapter VI by carrying out what we should call a sensitivity analysis on the estimated regression coefficients;[26] if some of the estimated coefficients are increased by 10 per cent, what effect will this have on the estimated stability of the system? His conclusions are quite interesting in this regard. Wage and price rigidity have a slight anti-damping effect. Lower marginal propensities to consume reduce instability, as one might expect. 'It will be seen that a decrease in the elasticity of supply of capital goods diminishes the damping of the cycle; in the case of very serious bottlenecks, the cycle may even become anti-damped explosive' (p. 176). In general, the sensitivity analysis indicated that only marginal changes occur from a 10 per cent increase in the values of the estimated regression coefficients. The only exception to this appeared to be the response of stock market prices to the 'boom psychology' variable (or, equivalently, the response of consumption to capital gains); here, as noted above, the system displays considerable potential for instability.

The fifth, final and perhaps most controversial use of his model made by Tinbergen appeared in his Chapter VII, where he attempted to use his econometric model as a basis for the evaluation of theories of the business cycle catalogued by Gottfried von Haberler in his companion study (1939) for the League of Nations. (We recall to the reader our discussion in Chapter 1, where one interpretation of Keynes's major criticism of Tinbergen's earlier work (1939a) in the famous *Economic Journal* review was the assertion that the testing of macroeconomic theories by econometric techniques is methodologically impossible or at least suspect for all practical purposes.) After recognizing some qualifications of his technique as a means of resolving these issues (these qualifications included uniqueness of particular historical episodes, errors in the data, slow-moving explanatory variables, possible breaks in structure, and multicollinearity), Tinbergen noted that he had difficulty in evaluating partial theories precisely because they tend to be underdetermined systems. Nevertheless his conclusions, on the basis of this rudimentary model of the US economy for the interwar period, tended to be mainly negative. He roundly criticizes monetary theories (for example, Hawtrey's) of the business cycle. Similarly he felt that overinvestment theories of a non-monetary variety (such as the acceleration principle) did not receive much support from his work. However he did admit that the gestation or construction period for physical capital may play a definite and important role, particularly with regard to housing. Similarly theories of cost-price squeezes (W.C. Mitchell) and theories of agricultural disturbances were evaluated negatively, the latter on the basis of the secondary effect on the rest of the system of the exogenous variable, agricultural production for the domestic market.[27] Tinbergen concluded this rather critical chapter with the view that the cyclical character of the system has probably been overrated, as well as with some optimistic assertions about the possibility of intelligent stabilization policy to mitigate the worst excesses of the business cycle. Ironically, his model would appear to have limited scope and relevance to stabilization policy, at least in terms of fiscal policy instruments.

3 Economic Fluctuations in the United States, 1921–1941

In the mid-1940s, the Cowles Commission for Research in Economics provided a hospitable environment for macroeconometric model-building. The results of this early work with macroeconometric systems were published in a monograph at the end of that decade (Klein, 1950). In *Economic Fluctuations in the United States*, three models of the US economy (called austerely Model I, Model II, and Model III) are presented, which we shall review in varying detail. It is interesting to note that, at that time, the principal use made of econometric models was for purposes of testing hypotheses and describing the economy; in addition, the models were also used for calculating values of the expenditures multiplier and Model I was analysed to see what light it might shed on the cyclical nature of the economy. (As the previous section indicated, originally macroeconometric models were considered to be 'business cycle models'.) The models were not applied to policy simulations, to tracking exercises within the sample period, or to forecasts, although forecasting and policy analyses were mentioned by Lawrence R. Klein as an eventual goal of this type of tool (Klein, 1950, p. 1).[28]

The first two chapters of this volume are introductory, as econometric concepts are explained to an audience that would be largely unfamiliar with this type of analysis. The theoretical approach is envisaged as one of Walrasian general equilibrium, in which households maximize a utility function and firms maximize anticipated profits (or, with slightly more generality, the entrepreneur's utility function); the interaction of these two principal sets of agents is then brought together in some behavioural relationships describing the functioning of markets, which can be either purely competitive or else subject to imperfections of competition. However it is admitted that identical structural models could be derived from a variety of theoretical underpinnings; for example, Klein mentions that most of Model I is quite compatible with a Marxian perspective on the American economy. The final chapter (Chapter IV) discusses the adequacy of the data for modelling purposes, and of course, near the beginning of our story, this was even more of a problem than it is currently. All of the models of this monograph were constructed with annual data, although some experimental calculations were made with quarterly data.

We may now summarize Model I, which has already made a pedagogical contribution to the education of two generations of econometricians.[29] This model contained three behavioural equations and three identities; the endogenous variables are the levels of consumption, net investment, the private wage and salary bill, real national income, total property (non-wage) income, and the stock of capital. (All endogenous variables are in constant-dollar terms, and all relationships are strictly linear.) In contrast to Tinbergen's model, the exogenous variables were primarily fiscal in nature: real government expenditures (including net exports), the public wage and salary bill (in deflated terms) and real net indirect tax collections; in addition, a time trend played a role. The consumption function related total consumption to real wages and salaries and also to real gross property income (current and lagged) separately, with a higher marginal propensity to consume out of wages and salaries. Net investment expenditures depended on current and lagged property income and (negatively) on the initial stock of capital. The so-called labour demand equation (a generalization of the constant wage share result of the profit maximization condition with a Cobb-Douglas production function) related the private wage and salary bill to private net national product, current and lagged, and a time trend.[30] The system was closed by three identities: net national product is the sum of the three expenditure items, consumption, net investment, and government (with net exports) expenditures; national income is divided into wage and property income components; and the change in the capital stock is equal to net investment.

Next there was a discussion of identification, in which it was concluded that all the behavioural equations are well identified, owing to the essential presence of a large number of predetermined variables, only a few of which appear in each equation. Estimation was then tackled. The parameters of Model I were estimated in three ways: by the method of (full) maximum likelihood, by the limited-information maximum likelihood technique, and by ordinary least squares methods. The results were fairly similar in the three cases, although Klein noted that the implicit marginal propensity to spend non-wage income is well above unity in the case of the ordinary least squares estimates and either below unity (in the case of the limited-information estimates) or just above it (for the full maximum likelihood technique); he regarded these results as suggesting the superiority of simultaneous equations methods of estimation. Model I was used to analyse the stability of the American economy; solution of the system yielded a third-degree difference equation in real national income (or in other variables), which is linear with constant coefficients but non-homogeneous. Solution of the associated reduced (homogeneous) equation produced cycles that were slightly damped;[31] thus the stability of the system was assured, provided that outside shocks (for example, fluctuations of the exogenous variables) were not too severe. Also a long-term (or dynamic equilibrium) multiplier for net national product was calculated and found to be 1.9, which Klein regarded as much more reasonable than the large values of the expenditures multipliers obtained in some early investigations of the Keynesian system.[32] It is interesting to note that, unlike the later textbook presentations, there was no discussion of impact multipliers, although the concept of interim multipliers (a two-year dynamic multiplier, in particular) was discussed in principle, although no numerical estimates were presented.

Model II contained a consumption function and two identities, which related current-dollar gross national product to the sum of expenditure components and also to disposable income. The one behavioural equation was a consumption function, in which real, per capita consumption was related to real, per capita disposable income (current and lagged) and to the real, per capita level of the money stock, thus testing a Pigou effect.[33] This equation turned out to be exactly identified, and so the technique of indirect least squares could be used for parameter estimation. Estimates of the expenditures multiplier easily fell out from this estimation technique: the long-run (dynamic equilibrium) multiplier was calculated to be 3.37, larger than the estimate of Model I and also too large to be realistic, in Klein's judgement. Although the concept of the impact multiplier was not discussed, by inspection it can be estimated to be 2.36, for this historical period. Again, this would seem high by present knowledge and judgement.

Model III, described as a 'large structural model', contained 12 behavioural equations and four identities. We shall not describe this model in great detail, as its principal importance today is as a precursor of the Klein–Goldberger Model, to be described in Chapter 3. There were three behavioural equations to describe the money market and four behavioural equations (plus one identity) to describe the housing market (including two equations describing the demand for residential construction). There was also a simple consumption function, a labour demand equation that was virtually identical to that of Model I, and an investment demand equation for plant and equipment that was similar to the Model I equation for all net private investment. A demand for inventories equation was also distinguished, while perhaps the most interesting equation of Model III is the so-called output adjustment equation, which was discussed at the end of the theoretical chapter (Chapter II), where it is interpreted as a form of market adjustment mechanism in an imperfectly competitive economy in which real output rather than market price tends to do most of the adjusting. The discussion of that chapter was then taken up in the consideration of the individual equations of Model III; here it was postulated that the output variation by entrepreneurs would vary inversely with the level of excess inventories (as measured by the value of the estimated disturbance or residual of the inventory demand equation) and positively with price level changes, which presumably would give entrepreneurs an added incentive to expand output. The results of the parameter estimation (by either method employed) were consistent with these hypotheses.

Next identification was discussed in general terms, despite the non-linearity of Model III. Klein concluded that each behavioural equation of Model III is probably identified, as a result of the large number of predetermined variables in the system, only a few of which appeared in any given structural equation. The parameters of the system were estimated by two methods, limited-information maximum likelihood and ordinary least squares, and the numerical results were quite similar. Although no formal measures of association between the dependent variable and its predicted values were presented, time diagrams (similar to those presented by Tinbergen) appeared in an appendix for each of the behavioural equations, and in general the fits were relatively tight, although dependent variables expressed as first differences had less close fits. Somewhat disconcerting is the fact that the equation for residential construction of rental housing displayed quite different parameter estimates (with the limited-information method) depending upon whether or not the first year (1921) was included in the sample, although this was not true of the other equations. As suggested above, no policy simulations (including multiplier calculations) or sample period simulations were made with this model, and forecasting uses were not indicated there.

Instead, Model III appears as an intermediate product, one that would be developed into the Klein–Goldberger Model. This is also suggested by the discussion on pp. 114–22, where some alternative hypotheses were tested. Here Klein entertained the possibility that the investment demand equation (for plant and equipment) should depend upon a liquidity variable, which hypothesis did not seem extremely fruitful, judged by sample *t* ratios. In the light of future developments, the most important alternative hypothesis was the possibility of dropping the output adjustment equation and replacing it with three new structural equations: a production function, relating gross private (real) output to labour and capital inputs and a time trend; a wage adjustment equation, relating absolute wage changes to current and lagged unemployment and to two auxiliary variables;[34] and (implicitly) an identity stating that the wage bill is the product of the nominal wage rate (per worker) and the number of employees. After such a modification, equation-counting conditions would still be satisfied. The chapter concluded by reminding the reader that still other alternative hypotheses could be envisaged.

4 The 1955 model of the Dutch Central Planning Bureau

From 1945 to 1955, Jan Tinbergen was Director of the Central Planning Bureau of the Government of the Netherlands. In this capacity he encouraged the development of a number of models of the Dutch economy, which were used for forecasting and policy purposes. In this section, we describe one of these early models, that for 1955.[35] Good, succinct descriptions (in English) of this model may be found in Theil (1961), Klein (1962), and in Chapter 6 below. After a very brief review of the model, we consider in general its use in policy formation in the Dutch context of the 1950s. More complete descriptions may be found in Tinbergen (1956), the Netherlands Central Planning Bureau (1956), and Van den Beld (1965); related material appears in Theil (1961), Hessel (1965), and Barten's discussion below.

In general terms, this model is strictly linear, as any pre-existing non-linear relationships have been linearized by standard approximations. The model places a heavy stress (as compared, say, with the models reviewed in the first two sections of this chapter) on exports and imports, which of course is appropriate for the more open Dutch economy. Five sets of agents are distinguished: government, enterprises, wage-earners, property income recipients, and the rest of the world. There are 12 identities, four institutional equations, and 11 behavioural equations (including two so-called 'technical equations') for a total of 27 equations. The behavioural equations were fitted to a sample of interwar and postwar years combined, by a variety of methods.[36]

We may turn to the extensive use of this model in macroeconomic policy formulation in the Netherlands during the decade of the 1950s, according to Tinbergen (1956), the Netherlands Central Planning Bureau (1956), Theil (1961), Hessel (1965), and Van den Beld (1965). We note that stylized representations of this process are characterized by Tinbergen's famous instruments-targets analysis or Theil's seminal suggestion that the policy-makers maximize a social welfare function, subject to the constraints that the functioning of the economy (as measured by the working econometric model) poses.[37] While each of these approaches was an over-simplified description of policy-making in practice in the Netherlands during this period (as the detailed accounts indicate clearly), we nevertheless consider it significant that this theoretical idealization of the process of macroeconomic policy formulation occurred in this particular environment. In particular, the Central Planning Bureau was the advisory body with a professional orientation, which (according to its publication) attempted to make the discussion of economic policy more rational. Other important agents in the process of Dutch macroeconomic planning were the Central Planning Commission (an advisory body composed of governmental and of private representatives), the Social Economic Council (another advisory body, with emphasis on income distribution aspects), and the Council of Economic Affairs (a cabinet committee, which had the final authority with regard to the macroeconomic plan, as we shall see).

In practice, Dutch macroeconomic planning worked something like this. Data were obtained from the Central Bureau of Statistics, government ministries (departments), the business sector, and the internal expertise of the Central Planning Bureau. Statements of objectives were collected from the ministries. At this point, forecasts (based on the macroeconometric model) were made, under the assumption of no change in the policy regime. It may be noted that Dutch forecasts were (particularly in this context) predictions or statements of the most likely outcome, subject to the constellation of exogenous variables hypothesized; they were definitely not directives or targets. Moreover, as Theil documents extensively in his 1961 work, there was a tendency to underestimate changes (in either direction), which appeared to be the major weakness of the forecasting process.

After these preliminary forecasts were made, a first draft plan was constructed and then was sent to the ministries for comment and criticism. Following this exercise, the Central Planning Bureau would construct a second draft plan, which would be sent to the Central Planning Commission, which would formulate its own critique. A third draft plan was then submitted to the Council of Economic Affairs, which would give its own criticisms, after which the definitive annual macroeconomic plan would be constructed, resubmitted to the Council of Economic Affairs and then adopted by this body. The definitive plan would then be submitted to the parliament for information purposes and also to the individual ministries (on the same basis). It might be published to enlighten the public on official thinking on these subjects, and a conference on the subject might be held by the Central Planning Bureau. Again, it is worth noting that it was the Council of Economic Affairs, not the parliament, which gave the final approval of the definitive macroeconomic plan.

Over the years, macroeconomic planning encompassed stabilization policy over the business cycle, wage policy (with additional inputs from the Social Economic Council), and the issue of the revaluation (appreciation) of the Dutch guilder in 1961. From this summary account, it should be clear that the Central Planning Bureau's rudimentary econometric model played an important role in macroeconomic policy formulation in the Netherlands in the 1950s, even though it was less important than the stylized analyses of Tinbergen and Theil might suggest, and even though judgement was important and even critical at most stages of the process of policy formulation. In turn, this experience is important for our story because it was probably the first instance historically of an important role for macroeconometric modelling in such a context.[38]

Notes

1. In Chapter 1, we have already noted and commented on Keynes's critical review of Tinbergen's early econometric work (in the September 1939 issue of the *Economic Journal*); it has also already been noted that this critical review was directed exclusively towards Part I of *Statistical Testing of Business Cycles* (entitled *A Method and its Application to Investment Activity*) rather than Part II (*Business Cycles in the United States of America 1919–1932*,) which contains the basic econometric model and which is reviewed in the following section.

2. In this connection, it might also be noted that in 1937 Tinbergen published a book entitled *An Econometric Approach to Business Cycle Problems*, in which his econometric model of Holland was also presented. A translation of Tinbergen's mid-thirties article into English appears in his *Selected Papers* (1959). This early work is also discussed in Chapter 6 below.

3. In his survey, Marc Nerlove (1966) noted that Tinbergen's model was the first and last model of the US economy to incorporate the stock market explicitly. This is no longer true, as the MPS model (Ando, 1974) used an index of share prices as an exogenous variable and current versions of the DRI Model (Eckstein, Green and Sinai, 1974, summarized in Intriligator, 1978; also, Eckstein, 1983) include purchases and sales of shares as part of the flow-of-funds analysis of the household sector, with an endogenous mechanism for the determination of the average level of stock market prices. Other models of the US economy of the past decade and a half have also included share prices in a variety of ways.

4. Marc Nerlove claimed in his survey (1966) that there were 18 identities in Tinbergen's model, while 17 such identities appeared in Table 1 of Appendix B of Tinbergen (1939b), to make 48 equations in total. Of course, the number of identities is always arbitrary to a certain extent, as one can add and subtract these relationships by algebraic manipulations, at least within certain limits.

5. The sectors of the model distinguished above, which group the equations on the basis of economic function, should not be confused with another grouping that Tinbergen effects, beginning on p. 132 of his text. Here the equations are separated into various groups, such as the 'monetary group', the 'price group' and the 'strategic group'. The purpose of this grouping appears to be principally computational, in an age in which high-speed computing was absent and so considerable ingenuity had to be exercized in order to make useful reductions of the entire system.

6. Consumption expenditures in current terms are denoted by U, and government expenditures are not explicitly included, being in general left out of the model, which effectively is a model of the private economy, with the fiscal role of government only implicit. (Of course government plays a much larger role in the financial sector, as the summary below will indicate.)

7. Another type of dynamic phenomenon is introduced by the use of cumulants for certain stock variables.

8. Dr Hendrikus Johannes Witteveen, a student of Tinbergen's, studied US economic policy under the New Deal, using Tinbergen's US Model (along with tools of the analysis). However, the economic policy that he analyses is not ordinary fiscal policy (variations in taxes and expenditures), but rather an autonomous increase in the wage level.

9. Tinbergen presents in his text a number of intermediate equations or submodels, before he settles on his final model, and some of the variables appearing in these submodels drop out of the final equations, like rejected candidates at a football training camp. We have gone through these non-final variables and tentatively classified them as endogenous or exogenous, based principally on the surrounding text discussion. We might note incidentally that this element of judgement in the categorization of the exogenous variables of the system probably explains why our classification is slightly different from that of Nerlove in his survey article (1966).

10. Tinbergen admits (p. 71) that this variable deserves to be made endogenous; however, he feels that, in view of its secondary influence in the system of equations, it is not worth the effort to construct a structural equation for this variable, which would thus make it endogenous. We note that this is an early instance of a compromise between perfection and practicality.

11. Other variables included in non-rural property income are rent payments, interest payments, dividends and entrepreneurial withdrawals from unincorporated business income.

12. Tinbergen also fitted two supplementary consumption functions for farmers, one for farmers' ordinary consumption expenditures and one for home-produced goods consumed on the farm. Both are supposed to depend on farm prices alone (as an obvious proxy for farmers' incomes). The fits were not especially tight (particularly for farmers' ordinary consumption expenditures), as judged by the time diagrams on p. 45. (Interestingly, Tinbergen shows by some algebraic manipulations that one can interpret

      farmers' demand quantities for home-produced goods as depending negatively on own price, although with an inelastic price elasticity of demand.)

13. More detail on Tinbergen's principal consumption function, along with more preliminary results, may be found in the contemporaneous (1939) article of J. J. Polak. Professor Tinbergen informs us, in a letter dated 31 July 1986, that J. J. Polak, who later went on to a distinguished career at the International Monetary Fund, joined him and Marcus Fleming at the League of Nations Secretariat towards the end of his (Tinbergen's) contract period. Polak was responsible for the completion of the project.

14. There was also the positive influence of a time trend as an explanatory variable, which Tinbergen interpreted as reflecting the secular influence of the growth in the normal demand for housing.

15. It is interesting to observe that estimated standard errors of the fitted regression coefficients were explicitly provided in this case, but not generally elsewhere, in this monograph.

16. Thus the supply of bonds (*B*) and the supply of shares of capital stock issued by corporations (the symbol *C*, as noted above) turn out to be linear trends and hence essentially exogenous variables, after four and two pages of relatively sophisticated theoretical and econometric discussion, respectively. Here the promise seems greater than the delivery.

17. The more interesting question of the ease of control of the real economy by this instrument is not explored at ths point and is touched on only indirectly in the rest of the volume.

18. Again, Tinbergen's ideas were elaborated in a contemporaneous article (published in the *Review of Economic Statistics*, in November 1939) which also made a comparative study of the formation of share prices in pre-First World-War USA (as well as during the interwar period), Germany, the UK, Belgium, the Netherlands, and the Dutch East India company.

19. In other words, this factor played a role only when the current level of share prices exceeded previous year's value by 20 index points; as measured, there would appear to be a definite simultaneity problem. Tinbergen envisaged the theoretical relationship to be a dependence of share prices on its own rate of change, with a lag of roughly half a year. As we will see in the following subsection, this factor could induce considerable instability into the US interwar economy.

20. It is perhaps worth noting that Tinbergen discusses 11 of these 13 equations rather rapidly (11 pages in total) in his Chapter 5, as though he were rather eager to get on with discussions of the system as a whole.

21. For some obscure reason, this identity is placed in Chapter 5 rather than in Chapter 1 (on 'Definitional Relations'); this probably explains why Nerlove in his survey (1966) counts 32 behavioural equations instead of 31.

22. We have not discussed explicitly Tinbergen's discussion of the 'Definitional Relations' (what we would call identities today), as we have allocated these identities to other sectors of the model. The discussion of the first 16 identities is surprisingly long (at 12 pages), as Tinbergen attempted to gauge the degree of error involved in a linear approximation to most of his non-linear identities; this error generally turned out (with one notable exception, namely the expression for share yields) to be surprisingly small. We might note as well an omission that is quite striking to a modern observer, namely the absence of any explicit modelling of the labour market. Employment, unemployment and the labour force simply do not appear as formal variables of the system. To be fair, we should note that data problems in this area were considerable at that time and that employment and unemployment were discussed informally in interpreting the results of a truncated solution of the model, where Tinbergen supposed that employment expands more or less proportionately to total private production (the sum of real consumption and real private investment outputs) and so the employment multiplier should be similar to the output (expenditure) multiplier.

23. Again, to be fair, we should note that discussions of all three of these potential uses, or

at least their possibilities, appeared in Tinbergen's 1937 volume, *An Econometric Approach to Business Cycle Problems.*

24.   For purposes of this reduction, Tinbergen distinguishes four groups of equations: the 'monetary group', the 'price group', the 'strategic' group, and an unnamed fourth group. These groups are chosen because they are concentrated in certain key variables, particularly if one throws away weak secondary effects. (The ingenuity involved in the approximate solution of a large set of linearized equations without the benefit of a modern electronic computer is quite remarkable.) After several stages of approximate reductions, the final dynamic difference equation in the key variable of the system, its own lagged values, and the exogenous variables of the system (and also the stock of housing with a lag of two years or more) may be found. It should be noted that this final result is only an approximation, of course, and also that the presence of another lagged endogenous variable in the final difference equation of the system is an anomaly that prevents a definitive analysis.

25.   It might be thought curious that this quasi-reduced form led to an expression in terms of the current and lagged values of what was basically an endogenous variable. In fact, Tinbergen's discussion made it clear that he was varying the constant term of the residential construction equation by one unit; thus he was effectively varying the autonomous component of the residential construction equation.

26.   Tinbergen acknowledged the possible reservation that a particular coefficient may assume its observed value because another coefficient has taken its own particular value in the recent past; thus a change in the value of one coefficient could be associated with a change in the structure of the system producing an associated change in the second coefficient. This problem is similar to the celebrated problem of hidden relationships among the exogenous variables of a model. Tinbergen does not present a solution to this difficulty (which Lucas and others have raised in our day), merely recognizing it as a qualification upon the results obtained.

27.   It is interesting to note that Tinbergen came back to these issues in his 1942 *Econometrica* article, 'Critical Remarks on Some Business Cycle Theories'. Despite the title of this article, his remarks contain both positive and negative conclusions. Thus, although most of the criticisms of Chapter VII were repeated, Tinbergen remarked there that his consumption and investment relations tended to support Keynes's theories.

28.   There do exist some unpublished forecasts which Klein made as early as 1945-6 at the Cowles Commission. Albert G. Hart (1976), in his correspondence with the editor of *Econometrica*, has drawn attention to one such forecast in which Klein accurately predicted postwar demand activity to be quite buoyant, belying the conventional wisdom at the time. To some extent, even Klein himself was surprised by his forecasts, which were obtained from an early version of Model III without any constant adjustments. However, 'given the unripe state of his model and the fact that the data consisted in good part of shaky preliminary estimates, he evidently felt no urge to push them to publication' (Hart, 1976).

29.   Good textbook summaries of Model I appear in Theil (1971) pp. 432–7, or Intriligator (1978) pp. 432–6. Theil (1971) pp. 463–8, gives a superb discussion of impact, interim and dynamic equilibrium multipliers in Model I; this discussion is much more detailed than either the original or the summary presented here.

30.   Private net national product is merely total net national product less the government wage and salary bill, given the national income accounting conventions of the US Department of Commerce.

31.   In retrospect, it must be admitted that this conclusion was vitiated by a computational error, but the stability condition, associated with significant damping, continues to hold.

32.   In this regard, mention should be made of Colin Clark's (1949) early econometric model of the US economy, fitted to data for the period 1921–41. Clark's model contained behavioural equations for consumption expenditures less imports, for producers' durable equipment, for total construction investment and for inventory investment; in addition, there were two identities linking gross national product to its

components (including exogenous public spending and exports) and defining sales as gross national product less inventory investment; all variables were deflated by the average hourly wage rate (following Keynes's treatment in *The General Theory*). Clark's inventory investment equation was quite volatile, producing considerable short-term instability in his model. Clark stated (p. 16), 'The outstanding – and alarming – feature of all this is the inherent instability which we find in the system whereby trifling causes can, under certain circumstances, become magnified into major movements of the trade cycle.' Indeed, the troughs of US cyclical experience in the 1930s, as simulated in Clark's model, were even worse than those recorded in the statistical series. (See Clark's Figure 1 on p. 95; the computed troughs of deflated national income in 1932 and again in 1938 are below the measured values.)

33. Given that the money supply variable would include inside money (created against private debt by the commercial banks) as well as outside money, it is doubtful that this is a fully appropriate test of the Pigou effect or of the real balance effect. In any case, the indirect least squares estimates suggested an effect with the theoretically predicted sign and a believable magnitude, which was not, however, statistically significant by ordinary criteria. Nevertheless it may be observed that coefficient of the money supply variable was an estimate of especial importance because there was a great need to know how the accumulation of large cash balances during the Second World War would affect postwar spending on consumer goods and services. This statistically insignificant coefficient estimate would, in fact, have provided an excellent guide, within a complete model.

34. We cannot help remarking that this wage adjustment equation appeared eight years before the late A. W. Phillips wrote his celebrated paper on the subject (1958). Of course, questions of priority for the trade-off relationship are somewhat beside the point, as current observers have traced this relationship back to Irving Fisher or even Karl Marx. (On this point, see P. Sylos-Labini, 1971.)

35. In Theil (1964), p. 36, it is reported, 'The first of this series of models was constructed in the early fifties, its main ingredients being intuition, courage, and least squares. Sophistication came later.' It may be noted that, in a sense, these models were a continuation of Tinbergen's pioneering model of the Dutch economy in the 1930s, mentioned in the introduction.

36. By the time of the model of the late 1950s (as described in Theil, 1964) the behavioural equations were generally estimated by the method of two-stage least squares.

37. Good summaries of these two approaches may be found in Intriligator (1978) Chapter 16, Sections 4 and 5 respectively. Stone (1980) also credits Tinbergen and his colleagues for making the first serious applications of econometric models to problems of macroeconomic policy.

38. Macroeconometric modelling has flourished in the Netherlands in recent years also. The more recent developments in Dutch macroeconometric model-building are also reviewed in Chapter 6 below.

References

Ando, Albert (1974) 'Some Aspects of Stabilization Policies, the Monetarist Controversy, and the MPS Model', *International Economic Review*, vol. 15, no. 3 (October) pp. 541–71.

Brainard, William C. and James Tobin (1968) 'Pitfalls in Financial Model Building', *American Economic Review, Papers and Proceedings*, vol. 58, no. 2 (May) pp. 99–122.

Clark, Colin (1949) 'A System of Equations Explaining the United States Trade Cycle, 1921–1941', *Econometrica*, vol. 17, no. 2 (April) pp. 93–124.

Eckstein, Otto (1983) *The DRI Model of the U.S. Economy* (New York: McGraw-Hill).

Eckstein, Otto, Edward W. Green and Allen Sinai (1974) 'The Data Resources Model: Uses, Structure and Analysis of the U.S. Economy', *International Economic Review*, vol. 15, no. 3 (October) pp. 595–615.

Haavelmo, Trygve (1943) 'The Statistical Implications of a System of Simultaneous Equations', *Econometrica*, vol. 11, no. 1 (January) pp. 1–12. Reprinted in John W. Hooper and

Marc Nerlove (eds), *Selected Readings in Econometrics from* Econometrica (Cambridge, Mass.: MIT Press, 1970) pp. 32–43.

Haberler, Gottfried von (1939) *Prosperity and Depression*, revised and enlarged edition (Geneva: Economic Intelligence Service of the League of Nations).

Hart, Albert G. (1976) 'A Lost Work of Lawrence Klein', correspondence with the editor of *Econometrica*, 9 March.

Hessel, Willem (1965) 'Quantitative Planning of Economic Policy in the Netherlands', pp. 163–73 in Bert G. Hickman (ed.), *Quantitative Planning of Economic Policy* (Washington, DC: The Brookings Institution).

Intriligator, Michael, D. (1978) *Econometric Models, Techniques, and Applications* (Englewood Cliffs, New Jersey: Prentice-Hall).

Lucas, Robert E., Jr. (1976) 'Econometric Policy Evaluation: A Critique', pp. 19–46 in Karl Brunner and Allan H. Meltzer (eds), *The Phillips Curve and Labor Markets* (Amsterdam: North-Holland), Carnegie-Rochester Conference Series on Public Policy, vol. 1, *Supplement* to the *Journal of Monetary Economics*.

Klein, Lawrence R. (1950) *Economic Fluctuations in the United States, 1921–1941* (New York: John Wiley).

_____ (1962) *An Introduction to Econometrics* (Englewood Cliffs, New Jersey: Prentice-Hall).

Nerlove, Marc (1966) 'A Tabular Survey of Macro-Econometric Models', *International Economic Review*, vol. 7, no. 2 (May) pp. 127–75.

Netherlands Central Planning Bureau (1956) *Scope and Methods of the Central Planning Bureau* (The Hague: Government of the Netherlands).

Phillips, A. W. (1958) 'The Relation between Unemployment and the Rate of Change of Money Wage Rates in the United Kingdom, 1861–1957', *Economica*, N.S., vol. 25, no. 100 (November) pp. 283–99.

Polak, J. J. (1939) 'Fluctuations in United States Consumption, 1919–1932', *Review of Economic Statistics*, vol. 21, no. 1 (February) pp. 1–12.

Stone, Richard (1980) 'Political Economy, Economics and Beyond', *Economic Journal*, vol. 90, no. 360 (December) pp. 719–36.

Sylos-Labini, P. (1971) 'Oligopoly, Unions and Inflation', pp. 51–79 in N. Swan and D. Wilton (eds), *Inflation and the Canadian Experience: Proceedings of a Conference* (Kingston, Ontario: The Industrial Relations Centre of Queen's University).

Theil, H. (1961) *Economic Forecasts and Policy*, second revised edition (Amsterdam: North-Holland).

_____ (1964) 'Some Developments of Economic Thought in the Netherlands', *American Economic Review*, vol. 54, no. 2 (March) Part 2, Supplement, *Surveys of Foreign Postwar Developments in Economic Thought*, pp. 34–55.

_____ (1971) *Principles of Econometrics* (New York: John Wiley).

Tinbergen, Jan (1937) *An Econometric Approach to Business Cycle Problems* (Paris: Hermann et Compagnie, éditeurs).

_____ (1939a) *A Method and its Application to Investment Activity*, Part I of *Statistical Testing of Business-Cycle Theories* (New York: Agathon Press, Inc., 1968). (Originally published in Geneva by the Economic Intelligence Service of the League of Nations in 1939.)

_____ (1939b) *Business Cycles in the United States of America 1919–1932*, Part II of *Statistical Testing of Business-Cycle Theories* (New York: Agathon Press, Inc., 1968). (Originally published in Geneva by the Economic Intelligence Service of the League of Nations in 1939.)

_____ (1939c) 'The Dynamics of Share-Price Formation', *Review of Economic Statistics* vol. 21, no. 4, (November) pp. 153–60.

_____ (1942) 'Critical Remarks on Some Business Cycle Theories', *Econometrica*, vol. 10, no. 2 (April) pp. 129–46.

_____ (1956) *Economic Policy: Principles and Design* (Amsterdam: North-Holland).

_____ (1959) *Selected Papers* (edited by L. H. Klaassen, L. M. Koyck and J. H. Witteveen) (Amsterdam: North-Holland).

_____ (1986) Letter to Ronald G. Bodkin, dated 31 July.

Van den Beld, C. A. (1965) 'Short-Term Planning Experience in the Netherlands', pp. 134–62 in Bert G. Hickman (ed.), *Quantitative Planning of Economic Policy* (Washington, DC: the Brookings Institution).

Witteveen, J. H. (1947) *Loonshoogate en Werkgelegenheid* [Wage Level and Employment], No. 39 of Nederlandsch Economisch Instituut [Netherlands Economic Institute] (Haarlem: de Erven F. Gohn, N.V.).

PART II

EXPERIENCE IN THE USA

3 American econometric models of the 1950s: the Klein–Goldberger Model

> ... the utility of models goes beyond their 'didactic value'. They are real and essential elements in the preparation of well-coordinated policies.[1]

1 Introduction

Although Lawrence R. Klein's interwar (1921–41) model prepared for the Cowles Commission 'was an attempt to carry on from Tinbergen's great start with newer data and newer theoretical ideas', it was presented with a number of caveats. For example, it contained only tentative and preliminary steps towards econometric model-building and it did not carry over in all respects to the postwar situation, in spite of the fact that it had provided a reasonably good description of the prewar economic process. Klein himself acknowledged (in the Preface), 'If I were to begin today the project of reconstructing an econometric model for the United States, I believe that I would proceed somewhat differently, benefiting from the knowledge of the weaknesses of the models in the volume.'[2] None the less this model proved highly useful as an exploratory model for structural analysis, forecasting and policy evaluations. And it was precisely as a result of such experience that the interwar model (especially Model III) became a progenitor of the Klein–Goldberger Model which made its debut in 1955.[3]

The Klein–Goldberger Model was initiated as a project of the Research Seminar in Quantitative Economics at the University of Michigan. It was a 'medium size' model, and was truly intended (at the time) to be an up-to-date working model, applicable to practical economic problems like those encountered in business cycle forecasting. A distinctive feature of the model was that it was not viewed as a 'once-and-for-all' effort. It was presented as a part of a more continuous programme in which new data, reformulations and extrapolations were constantly being studied.[4] The model consisted of 15 structural equations, five identities and five tax-transfer auxiliary relationships. It was estimated by the limited information maximum likelihood technique and was based on the annual observations from the split sample period 1929–41, 1946–52. In the genealogy of macroeconometric models, no other model has left such a vast legacy of style and flavour as the Klein–Goldberger Model.[5] It served as the paradigm for many model-builders for a long time to come. However, today, more than three decades since its appearance, it is mainly of pedagogical interest.

2   The model

The structure of the Klein–Goldberger Model may be viewed as the first empirical representation of the broad basic Keynesian system. The mathematical formulations of this system developed by J. R. Hicks and O. Lange were extended in the neoclassical direction through a use of the production function and the marginal productivity condition for the employment of labour. Its very rudimentary trade sector was also specified in terms of neoclassical reasoning. The model dealt with both the real and the monetary phenomena; most, but not all, behavioural equations were specified in real terms, and a very specific blending of real and money values was achieved as both the constant-dollar magnitudes and their associated price deflators were estimated as part of the model. The dynamic components were added in terms of cumulated investment, time trends and Koyck distributed lags. It also contained several non-linearities in terms of the variables, which were subsequently linearized in an approximate manner, in order to obtain the solution of the entire system.

The framework of the model consisted basically of 20 equations,[6] which explained the 20 endogenous variables of the model. These variables were the 'traditional economic magnitudes' referring to activities in the private sectors. The exogenous category included the variables from the public

Table 3.1   Variables of the Klein–Goldberger Model

Endogenous variables (20)
Income (5)
   National income (Y)
   Private wage income (W_1)
   Farm income (A)
   Non-wage non-farm income (P)
   Corporate profits (P_c)
Consumption (C)
Gross private investment (I)
Depreciation (D)
Imports of goods and services (F_i)
Private capital stock (K)
Corporate savings (S_p)
Corporate surplus (B)
Number of wage earners (N_W)

Liquid assets (2)
   Held by persons (L_1)
   Held by enterprises (L_2)
Prices (3)
   Price index of GNP (p)
   Index of agricultural prices (p_A)
   Index of hourly wage (w)
Interest rates (2)
   Yield on short-term commercial paper (i_S)
   Yield on corporate bonds (i_L)

Exogenous variables (19)
Policy variables (9)
   Government expenditures (G)
   Government wage bill (W_2)
   Number of government employees (N_G)
   Net tax on wage income (T_W)
   Net tax on farm income (T_A)
   Next tax on non-wage non-farm income (T_p)
   Corporate income tax (T_C)
   Indirect taxes less subsidies (T)
   Excess reserves of banks as a percentage of total reserves (R)
Variables determined by conditions abroad (3)
   Exports of goods and services (F_E)
   Index of agricultural exports (F_A)
   Import prices (P_I)
Demographic variables (5)
   Index of hours worked (h)
   Number of persons in the labour force (N)
   Number of farm operators (N_F)
   Number of non-farm entrepreneurs (N_E)
   Number of persons in the US (N_p)
Time trend (t)
Constant term

Lagged (additional) variables (24)
18 endogenous: $\{Y_{t-1}, (W_1)_{t-1}, A_{t-1}, P_{t-1}, (P_c)_{t-1}, C_{t-1}, D_{t-1},$
$(F_I)_{t-1}, K_{t-1}, (S_p)_{t-1}, B_{t-1}, (L_1)_{t-1}, (L_2)_{t-1}, P_{t-1},$
$P_{t-2}, (i_S)_{t-1}, (i_S)_{t-3}, (i_S)_{t-5}\}$
6 exogenous: $\{(W_2)_{t-1}, (T_W)_{t-1}, (T_A)_{t-1}, (T_p)_{t-1}, (T_c)_{t-1}, T_{-1}\}$

Notes:
(a)   Farm income (a) was split later into two components: A_1 excluded government subsidies to farmers; A_2 consisted entirely of these payments.
(b)   All the value variables were measured in 1939 constant dollars.

sector governed primarily by 'noneconomic political decisions', variables 'determined largely by forces outside the United States', and the variables measuring the characteristics of the labor force which are 'heavily influenced by demographic trends'.[7] The complete listing of the variables together with their classification has been presented in Table 3.1.

Table 3.1 shows that, altogether, the model contained 63 variables; 20 were endogenous and 43 predetermined. Of the 43 predetermined variables, 19 were current exogenous and 24 were lagged.[8] It is also clear from the table that the model went a big step forward from the earlier small models in terms of a greater degree of disaggregation, although it was less disaggregated than Tinbergen's early US model described in the preceding chapter. For example, among the endogenous activity variables there were five categories of income, two liquid assets, two interest rates and three types of prices. The exogenous set contained five demographic and social environmental variables, and nine policy instruments including, among others, two types of government expenditures and five types of taxes.

Finally, the model presented another advance on the computational front, as it was estimated by the limited-information maximum likelihood technique. The model as a whole can be best described by commenting briefly on the structural characteristics of the individual equations.[9]

The consumption function
The prewar linear consumption-income relations of the previous models had seriously underestimated the postwar expenditures and thus had turned out to be inadequate. Modifications in this simplest version of the Keynesian consumption function were suggested in the Klein–Goldberger model to take account of income distribution, taxes and transfer payments, the influence of wealth and a demographic trend. The highly elaborate consumption function contained at least six explanatory variables: consumption expenditure depended on real disposable wage and salary income, real disposable farm income and real disposable non-farm property income separately, as well as on liquid assets (as a proxy for wealth) held by the households,[10] total population and the lagged consumption expenditures. However the three marginal propensities were not freely estimated; instead, some cross-section information was used to constrain the relative values of these parameters in an appropriate manner.[11] Lagged consumption expenditure was used to measure the influence of the past habits on the present consumer behaviour, as T. M. Brown (1952) had suggested somewhat earlier.[12] It constituted an important dynamic component in the model.

The investment function

The investment demand function, which lumped together business fixed investment, residential construction and inventory investment, was specified in gross form (inclusive of depreciation).[13] Gross investment depended on past non-wage property income (after taxes but before depreciation and including farmers' incomes), on the beginning-of-period capital stock and on liquid assets in the hands of enterprises. Initially the lagged property earnings variable was used as a measure of expected earnings jointly with the capital stock and the rate of interest to arrive at a net rate of return on capital, a main motivating force behind investment. However these data failed to assign a reliable non-zero value to the parameter of the interest rate variable, which was finally dropped from the equation. Liquid assets representing a readily available source of funds measured the preference of many businessmen for internal as opposed to external financing.

Corporate profits, corporate earnings and depreciation

The non-wage, non-farm income component (P) of the model included corporate profits, earnings of unincorporated and professional enterprises, and some sluggishly moving components such as interest, rents and royalties. This necessitated the separation of corporate profits from the aggregate component P, as the latter could no longer be appropriately used as an explanatory variable in the corporate savings equation. Thus corporate profits were separated from P by the use of a simple linear relation whose origins are found in empirical association rather than economic theory.

Corporate savings were determined by corporate disposable income (corporate profits net of taxes), lagged dividend payments and the initial level of accumulated corporate surplus. The last two variables were assumed to have a negative impact on the corporate current savings. (In fact, lagged dividend payments turned out in the final estimate to have a positive, if insignificant, impact, although a preliminary estimate showed lagged dividend payments with a negative coefficient that was almost (t ratio equal to 1.5) statistically significant.) These variables were used on the basis of the evidence presented by Dobrovolsky[14] (on Tinbergen's hypothesis), suggesting that corporations attempt to maintain a stable dividend policy, and, in the case of inadequacy of earnings, it is the current savings which bear the burden of adjustment. (If the accumulated surplus is inadequate, corporations will tend to save more in order to reach target levels more rapidly.)

It was indeed recognized that depreciation in constant prices should be a 'moving average of the past values of gross investment measured also in constant prices', the length of the moving average presumably being determined by the average lifespan of the capital goods; depreciation, none the less, was explained in the model as a simple function of the size of the capital stock and the level of aggregate economic activity, because no explicit series of gross investment prior to 1929 was available. (The positive sign on aggregate economic activity represents additional depreciation attributable to more intensive usage or what Keynes called 'the user cost of capital.')

The production function and the labour demand
The output of the private sector was described by a productive process in which, in addition to labour and capital as two inputs, a time trend capturing the effect of increasing efficiency due to technological change was introduced. The labour input was measured by the number of man-hours. In line with the Keynesian view of the economy, the direct role of the estimated production function was to determine the level of private employment, once aggregate demand established the level of output.

The wage and salary bill by the private sector was explained by a variant of the marginal productivity condition of profit maximization. Under an exponential production process of the Cobb–Douglas variety, this condition implies constancy of factor shares. A more general linear version of this condition was used to determine the real value of the private wage bill (W_1); it was determined by the current and the lagged value of the private output and a linear time trend.

The labour market adjustment equation
This was a strategic equation of the model which split real wages into absolute (nominal) wages and prices. With the institutional observation that wage negotiations usually take place in terms of money and not real wages, the change in the nominal wage rate was explained by the level of unemployment (which had a negative effect), the change in the general price level one year earlier, and a linear trend. Thus the model in dynamic solution implied a conflict between the goals of full employment and price stability; this conflict has been described for many years as a trade-off. It is worth noting that this wage adjustment relation, which had its antecedents in a similar equation in *Economic Fluctuations in the United States, 1921–1941* (1950), which we discussed in the preceding chapter, appeared three years before the late A. W. Phillips wrote his seminal paper in 1958.

The import demand function
The import demand was treated in the model in the same way as the demand for other goods and services by domestic consumers and pro-

ducers; domestic disposable income and lagged imports were the principal determinants. The income was deflated by the price of imports in contrast to the general price level used in the other equations. Thus, to some extent, the relative price effect was implicitly taken into account by the income variable. Nerlove, in his 1966 survey,[15] pointed out that it was the first time that an import demand function was treated explicitly in an econometric model of the United States.

The agricultural sector, income and relative prices
A distinction between farm and non-farm income was made in the consumption function, on the grounds that the farmers have a relatively high propensity to save, particularly on the margin. Accordingly, the model included a separate equation for farm income, which was assumed to depend upon the domestic and foreign demand for the US agricultural products. Thus disposable non-farm income deflated by the index of farm prices, current and lagged, and an index of agricultural exports were the primary explanatory variables used in the equation. The variable measuring the terms of trade for agriculture, employed as a multiplier of non-farm income deflated by the general price level, was introduced in a similar manner to the treatment in the import demand function.

The agricultural sector was closed by a simple linear relationship between the agricultural price index and the general price level. The equation was supposed to capture the element of market influence on agricultural prices; however, its inadequacy to include the intricacies of government price support programmes was recognized. An autoregressive factor associated with inventory holding and price speculation was also attempted as an explanatory variable, but it did not appear in the final estimation.

The monetary sector
The monetary sector contained four equations, a liquidity preference function for the household (L_1), a similar function for the business (L_2), an equation for the term structure of short-term interest rates, and a money market adjustment equation. It was assumed that the main choices for households are between holding securities (long-term bonds or stocks) or cash, and so a general trivariate relation among the holding of liquidity by households, disposable income and the rate of interest was introduced. Following work by A. Kisselgoff (1945) and James Tobin (1947), Klein and Goldberger employed an interesting statistical device to separate the liquidity balances of households into two parts, transactions and speculative (idle) balances; the former were assumed to be proportional to disposable income and the latter depended on the long-term interest rate. The

year (1929) of a high level of economic activity when the computed ratio between cash balances and income was at a minimum (0.14) was assumed to be a year when there were no idle balances. The idle balances for other years were computed by using this proportionality factor for transaction balances; that is, by subtracting 0.14 times disposable income from L_1. Finally, a Keynesian specification of the liquidity preference function was used and these idle balances were estimated as a log-linear function of the long-term interest rate in excess of some minimum (floor) value, which was hypothesized to be equal to 2 per cent. Thus the final form of the liquidity demand function by the households was non-linear, which gave infinite elasticity at a low interest rate.

In contrast to the holding of liquid assets by the households, the liquidity demand by the businesses was assumed to emerge from the three-way choices, money, securities and goods and these were subject to the short-term decision: 'whether to hold inventories for a short period or to hold short-term securities (commercial paper); whether to borrow for a short period or to forego the possibility of inventory gains'. Thus the business transactions demand for liquidity was assumed to be proportional to current business cost and the speculative demand was dependent on the short-term interest rate and the rate of change in the general price level. It was a multivariate general linear relationship without any explicit separation of the two components of liquidity demand and without any constraint on the minimum value of the interest rate.

The long-term interest rate was assumed to depend on the expected level of the short-term interest rate;[16] a best expression for the expected short-term interest rate was empirically found in the linear combination of its 3 and 5 period lagged values, a rather long lag considering that the unit of time used was a year.

Finally, the money market adjustment equation was estimated by using a similar version of the fundamental 'law of supply and demand' by which nominal wages or prices were determined in the model. Under the assumption that the level of excess reserves held by the banks as a percentage of their total reserves are a measure of excess supply in the money market, the rate of change in the short-term interest was made a negative function of this ratio.

It may also be observed here (as Klein and Goldberger themselves pointed out) that, from a purely statistical viewpoint in one-period equilibrium, the entire monetary sector could have been treated as exogenous. It is only with lags that money market variables have an influence on the real sector; they have absolutely no instantaneous feedback effect. One is hard pressed to disagree with Theil (1971, p. 479), who asserts, '... the monetary sector of the model gives an inadequate picture of the phenomenon which it serves to describe'. Nevertheless the monetary sector was viewed by the authors as endogenous and hence integrated into a dynamic treatment of the model.

Parenthetically, we may note that these informal remarks are confirmed by a more formal technique of mathematical analysis (topology) known as the analysis of graphs. André Keller (1979, especially Chapter III, pp. 81–120), in his study of the 'static' (one-period) Klein–Goldberger Model, noted that the 'reduced graph' (*graphe réduit*) had a large simultaneous core, with three essentially predetermined variables (the level of investment, the short-term rate of interest and its long-term analogue) and three after-the-fact or epilogue variables that went nowhere in the system, namely the cash holdings of households, those of corporations and the level of accumulated business savings. In dynamic simulation of the economy, the picture changes dramatically, as private investment, the cash holdings of both households and corporations and accumulated business savings become interdependent. The reduced graph of the dynamic version of the Klein–Goldberger Model shows only the two interest rate variables as essentially predetermined. Another result of the study of the Klein–Goldberger Model by the technique of the analysis of graphs is that the central core of the model can be interpreted as reflecting the importance of the pairing of two variables, total output (real GNP)[17] and the level of the GNP deflator. Keller associates this pairing with the supply and demand adjustment mechanism found in purely competitive markets.[18]

Identities

The model was closed by a set of five definitional identities, a definition of GNP by the types of expenditures, definition of national income by the types of distributive shares, an identity connecting the wage rate, hours of work, employment and the wage bill, the definition of investment in terms of change in capital stock, and the definition of corporate savings in terms of change in the stock of business surplus.

The complete statistical model (the version that appears in Chapter VI of the Klein–Goldberger volume) has been presented in the appendix.

3 The applications of the model

Although the model was still considered by its builders to be highly aggregative, it was subjected to a number of applications: the estimated structure provided tests on some partial hypotheses of economic behaviour, its performance was assessed at great length by both *ex post* and *ex ante* forecasting, it was simulated under a number of policy scenarios and, within a few years of its publication, its dynamic (cyclical) properties were examined under a variety of random shocks.

Forecasting performance

By early 1953, the model was ready for its first application; it was solved to prepare the *ex post* forecasts for 1951 and 1952. In preparing these forecasts, deflated or real liquid assets were treated as exogenously known quantities (as was done in the sample period) and the equations for the monetary sector were suppressed. As noted above, the lagged nature of the liquid assets variables through which the real sector was primarily affected by the monetary sector made them virtually predetermined in any exercise of forecasting for less than two periods ahead. The detailed comparison of the *ex post* forecasts with the actual values led to the conclusion that the model gave 'a reasonably good interpretation of the working of the economy'.[19]

To the best of our knowledge, this was one of the first (if not the first) published[20] uses of an econometric model for regular *ex ante* forecasting.[21] These forecasts were presented for 1953 (prepared in February–March 1953), 1954 (prepared in November–December 1953) and 1955 (prepared in December 1954).[22] The 1953 forecast was based on the originally estimated model. And, in spite of the fact that it was the first year of a new political administration in the United States, whose fiscal policies were not yet clearly formulated, it appeared to be an excellent forecast in anticipating growth in real activity and employment, as its main error lay in overestimating price inflation. As a matter of fact, the 1953 forecast went contrary to the pessimistic consensus of the forecasting fraternity of the day, which was expecting a significant downturn after the middle of 1953. No doubt there was a downturn in the second half of 1953, but the economy registered substantial growth for the entire year as a whole.

Next, the model was updated during 1953 by extending the sample period up to 1952 in preparation for making forecasts for 1954. In addition, three refinements were introduced in the model: 'imports were redefined to include only sales to persons and business in the United States';[23] the variable measuring the farm income, A, was split into two components, A_1 and A_2. A_1 excluded government subsidies to farmers while A_2 consisted wholly of these payments; and the depreciation equation, which was previously based on a simple technical relationship with the stock of capital, was modified to include 'the value of private gross national product in constant prices as an additional variable to show the influence of intensity of use on depreciation of capital' (pp. 89–90).

The 1954 forecast was made public around the time when Colin Clark in Great Britain was predicting a major economic slump in America.[24] The calculations from the model clearly refuted the pessimistic contention of Clark that a slump was knocking at the door.[25] To quote the authors, 'We have just completed forecasts of 1954 and conclude that Mr. Colin Clark is wrong. In answer to the presumed question "when will the next depression occur in the United States according to your mathematical model?", ... we say "not yet".' And finally, 'no matter how extreme we make our policy assumptions, as long as we confine our estimates to plausible magnitudes, the mathematical system leads to forecasts of a mild downturn. We must, however, warn non-mathematical readers that forecasts from statistical models are subject to error ... Nonetheless, it is highly improbable that we could be so much in error that we come to Mr. Clark's disheartening conclusions for 1954' (p. 3). Eventually the 1954 forecast did underestimate the recession somewhat but it was able to pick up the turning-point correctly; the predicted values of the main and important variables were quite close to reality. A principal discrepancy once again was in overestimating price increase.[26]

The 1955 forecast did not appear in the Klein–Goldberger book; it was prepared later by Suits and Goldberger. This forecast, like the previous year forecast, correctly picked up the turning-point but somewhat underestimated the boom. Goldberger (1959) systematically compared the *ex ante* forecasts of the Klein–Goldberger model for 1953, 1954 and 1955 with the alternative predictions generated from the then most familiar 'naive models' of Friedman[27] and concluded that the forecasting performance of the Klein–Goldberger model on balance was superior; the model almost every time and for every variable predicted rightly the direction of change.[28] Thus began a development (the use of econometric models for public forecasting) with the Klein–Goldberger Model which in itself would have been difficult to forecast over 30 years ago. (As Chapter 6 indicates, similar developments were occurring in Holland around this time also.)

The policy simulations and multiplier implications
In addition to arriving at a general prognosis of the actual course of economic activity, the forecasting experiment was used to simulate a variety of policy implications; not less than six variants of forecasts for 1953 and five variants for 1954 associated with alternative sets of fiscal policies were generated. Similarly, several alternative forecasts for 1955 activity were derived. These calculations indicated a two-year multiplier of 1.6 (with endogenous tax collections)[29] with respect to real government expenditure; none the less, this multiplier was essentially a short-run multiplier. In another set of policy experiments, Klein and Bodkin (1964) established the presence of a conflict between the goals of full employment

and price stability, at least in the context of this model.

In a subsequent volume, *Impact Multipliers and Dynamic Properties of the Klein–Goldberger Model*, which appeared in 1959, Goldberger studied extensively the impact and dynamic multipliers of this system for both exogenous and endogenous tax collections. In order to conduct this analysis, Goldberger first reduced the structural model into the form which combined both direct and indirect effects of any change in the predetermined variables on the endogenous variables. The reduced form derivation necessitated linearization of some non-linear terms in the system. Similarly, as the model contained lag responses, Goldberger went beyond the immediate initial period effects in tracing out the delayed, long-run results of a policy decision. The immediate, initial period effects were interpreted as impact multipliers and the long-run delayed effects carried over several periods were treated as dynamic (interim) multipliers. The total multipliers, presumably, included both.

In short, Goldberger treated the estimated model essentially as a difference equation system, with each endogenous variable in the reduced form expressed as a function of current exogenous variables, lagged exogenous variables and only lagged values of the endogenous variables. With any set of initial conditions and the time paths of all the exogenous variables specified, the time paths of the dynamic solutions of the endogenous variables were readily obtained. Different exogenous variable inputs or different parameters generated different time paths and this provided a basis for comparing alternative policies. To illustrate, consider a system of G structural difference equations which relate a vector of G exogenous variables Y with a vector of K exogenous variables X; both endogenous and exogenous variables appear in current form and lagged *one* period. In a familiar matrix notation, the system (after we set the random disturbances equal to their expected value of zero) may be written:

$$B_0 Y_t + B_1 Y_{t-1} + \Gamma_1 X_t + \Gamma_0 X_{t-1} = 0, \tag{3.1}$$

where B_0 is a GxG non-singular matrix of the coefficients of the current endogenous variables, B_1 is a GxG matrix of the coefficients of the lagged endogenous variables, Γ_0 is a GxK matrix of the coefficients of the current exogenous variables, and Γ_1 is a GxK matrix of the coefficients of the lagged exogenous variables. The right-hand side is a null vector of order $Gx1$. The dynamic reduced form of the system can be written as

$$Y_t = -B_0^{-1} B_1 Y_{t-1} - B_0^{-1} \Gamma_0 X_t - B_0^{-1} \Gamma_1 X_{t-1}, \tag{3.2}$$

which is simply the first order difference equation system restated. That is,

$$Y_t = \pi_0 Y_{t-1} + \pi_1 X_t + \pi_2 X_{t-1}, \tag{3.3}$$

whose solution may be described as

$$Y_t = \pi_1 X_t + \sum_{i=1}^{\infty} \pi_0^{i-1} (\pi_0 \pi_1 + \pi_2) X_{t-i}.^{30} \tag{3.4}$$

If there are no lagged endogenous variables in the system $(B_1 = 0, \pi_0 = -B_0^{-1}B_1 = 0$, the solution becomes identical with the simple reduced form,

$$Y_t = \pi_1 X_t + \pi_2 X_{t-1} \tag{3.5}$$

where $\pi_1 (= -B_0^{-1}\Gamma_0)$ is a GxK matrix of the reduced form coefficients of the current exogenous variables and $\pi_2 (= -B_0^{-1}\Gamma_1)$ is a GxK matrix of the reduced form coefficients of the lagged exogenous variables.

Equation (3.4) describes a distribution of the effect of any change in exogenous variables on the endogenous variables over periods of time. The successive coefficient matrices are, for example,

$$\pi_1, (\pi_0\pi_1 + \pi_1), \pi_0(\pi_0\pi_1 + \pi_1), \pi_0^2 (\pi_0\pi_1 + \pi_2),$$
$$\pi_0^3(\pi_0\pi_1 + \pi_2),\ldots$$

The elements of the first matrix π_1, which measure the immediate effect of exogenous change, are the *impact multipliers*, while the elements of the other matrices, which describe the effect during a given later period, are known as *interim multipliers*.[31] The total multipliers will correspond to the elements of π obtained by the summation of these successive matrices,

$$\pi = \pi_1 + (\pi_0\pi_1 + \pi_2) + \pi_0(\pi_0\pi_1 + \pi_2) +$$
$$\pi_0^2(\pi_0\pi_1 + \pi_2) + \ldots ;$$

this implies:

$$\pi = (I - \pi_0)^{-1}(\pi_1 + \pi_2),^{32} \tag{3.6}$$

(provided π_0^n approaches a null matrix so that $(I - \pi_0)$ is non-singular).

Among other things, Goldberger measured the response of the economy to a sustained unit increase in government expenditures (G), to a sustained unit increase in corporate taxes (T_c), and to a sustained unit increase in wages taxes (T_W) over time spans ranging from three to nine years.[33] The impact and interim GNP multipliers obtained with respect to a sustained unit increase in government expenditure are presented in

Table 3.2   *Impact and interim multipliers of GNP with respect to a sustained unit increase in government expenditures*

Year	Taxes exogenous		Taxes endogenous	
Lags	GNP change	Level	GNP change	Level
0	1.386	1.386	1.229	1.229
1	1.421	2.807	0.720	1.949
2	1.078	3.884	0.260	2.209
3	0.680	4.565	0.056	2.265
4	0.323	4.887	− 0.009	2.256
5	0.035	4.922	− 0.029	2.227
6	− 0.177	4.745	− 0.036	2.191

Notes:
(a)   'Change' indicates impact multiplier (lag = 0) and interim multiplier (lag = 1,2...6). 'Level' measures cumulative (total) multiplier up to a given period.
(b)   The table is based on Goldberger (1959, pp. 87, 90).

Table 3.2.[34] The numbers show that the impact multiplier alone does not do justice in capturing the effect of government expenditure. This multiplier builds up over five years (from 1.386 to 4.922) when the tax yields are treated exogenously, settling down eventually to its equilibrium value of 2.93 (as shown in Table 3.3), which remains well above its initial impact value. The multiplier in the endogenous tax case has a similar pattern, except that its expansion phase is foreshortened; starting from 1.229, its impact value builds up to 2.265 in the third year and eventually settles down to an equilibrium point 2.34, as shown in Table 3.3.

The multipliers corresponding to the alternative fiscal policies are presented in Table 3.4. The difference in the impact effects of raising wage taxes and raising corporate taxes on GNP persists for several years but is then eliminated. The intermediate-run effect on GNP of a unit increase in taxes is roughly the same whether the change is made in corporate or in wage taxes.

Goldberger concluded from his detailed analysis of multiplier matrices that in the Klein–Goldberger model 'impact effects may deviate substantially from longer-run effects. The real variables appear to be subject to damped oscillations, whereas monetary variables show monotonic behavior' (p. 100).

The dynamic properties
Towards the end of his extensive analysis of impact and interim multiperiod multipliers, Goldberger examined the dynamic cyclical properties of

Table 3.3   *Comparison of dynamic properties of exogenous-tax and endogenous-tax models*

Property	Exogenous tax model	Endogenous tax model
Cyclical component		
Period	13 years	7 years
Amplitude	0.5400	0.3016
Equilibrium multipliers of government expenditure		
GNP	2.9266	2.3364
Consumption (C)	1.2626	0.8792
Investment (I)	0.6640	0.4572
Private wage bill (W_1)	1.3662	1.1310
Gross profits ($P + D$)	1.4100	0.9571
4-year multipliers of government expenditure		
GNP	4.887	2.256
Consumption (C)	2.252	0.833
Investment (I)	1.765	0.484
Private wage bill (W_1)	2.269	1.085
Gross profits ($P + D$)	2.392	0.849

Notes:
(a)   The table is based on Goldberger (1959, p. 129).
(b)   The section on four-year multipliers is based on a slightly larger reduction of the Klein–Goldenberger model than is the section on equilibrium multipliers.

the system. For this purpose, he judiciously simplified its monetary and real sectors and studied them in isolation. The characteristic roots of the difference equation of the monetary sector indicated that the time paths of the absolute wage rate and price level were close to the instability borderline. The main features of the solution of the real sector have been summarized in Table 3.3. The four characteristic roots of the difference equation system of the real sector containing five endogenous variables with four essential lags were:[35]

Exogenous-tax model:

$$\lambda_1 = 0.9527 \qquad\qquad \lambda_3 = 0.4880 + 0.2483\,i$$
$$\lambda_2 = 0.1760 \qquad\qquad \lambda_4 = 0.4880 - 0.2483\,i$$

Table 3.4   Annual change in and the level of GNP in response to a sustained unit increase in: (a) government expenditure, (b) wage tax function, (c) corporation tax function

Year	(A)		(B)		(C)	
Lags	Change	Level	Change	Level	Change	Level
0	1.229	1.229	−0.682	−0.682	−0.089	−0.089
1	0.720	1.949	−0.516	−1.198	−0.940	−1.029
2	0.260	2.209	−0.243	−1.441	−0.441	−1.470
3	0.056	2.265	−0.086	−1.527	−0.103	−1.523
4	−0.009	2.256	−0.016	−1.543	0.043	−1.530
5	−0.029	2.227	0.012	−1.531	0.079	−1.451
6	−0.036	2.191	0.022	−1.509	0.082	−1.369
7	−0.037	2.154	0.026	−1.483	0.080	−1.289

Notes:
(a) 'Change' indicates impact multiplier (lag = 0) and interim multipliers (lag = 1,2...7). 'Level' measures cumulative (total) multiplier up to a given period.
(b) Taxes are endogenous in all solutions.
(c) The table is based on Goldberger (1959, pp. 90, 94, 95).

Endogenous-tax model:

$$\lambda_1 = 0.8468 \qquad\qquad \lambda_3 = 0.1887 + 0.2353\,i$$
$$\lambda_2 = 0.4595 \qquad\qquad \lambda_4 = 0.1887 - 0.2353\,i$$

The system was considered to be technically stable as the absolute value of all roots is less than unity. The time path of the endogenous variables has monotonic components corresponding to two positive real roots, λ_1 and λ_2, and an oscillatory component corresponding to the conjugate pair of complex roots, λ_3 and λ_4. The periodicity of the cycle is 13 years for the exogenous tax case and seven years for the endogenous. The effectiveness of the taxes as built-in stabilizers also becomes apparent in the comparison of the two sets of equilibrium multipliers, which show the *ultimate* response in the level of endogenous variables to a sustained unit increase in the level of government expenditures; from the values presented in Table 3.3, one can easily compute that the tax leakages reduce the ultimate effect of autonomous expenditure by almost 20 per cent,

$$(\frac{2.93 - 2.34}{2.93} = .201).$$

Thus Goldberger concluded, 'While the introduction of postwar tax rates does not convert a technically unstable system into a stable one, it does reduce the magnitude of the equilibrium effect of autonomous changes and also the amplitudes of the largest characteristic root and the cyclical components of the response path' (p. 129).

Irma Adelman and Frank L. Adelman explored the question of how well the Klein–Goldberger Model succeeded in reproducing the business cycle. In their now classic study (1959),[36] the Adelmans particularly investigated the issues as to whether this model 'really offers an endogenous explanation of a persistent cyclical process', 'whether the system is stable when subjected to single exogenous shocks, what oscillations (if any) accompany the return to the equilibrium path, and what is the response of the model to repeated external and internal shocks'. In dealing with these issues, they proceeded as follows. First, the model was simplified by deleting insignificant coefficients,[37] and the equations for import demand and the two interest rates. Second, the least squares trends for most of the exogenous variables were specified. Third, the observed 1952 values for the remaining 22 endogenous variables including taxes were inserted as initial conditions. And finally the time paths of the endogenous variables of the entire non-linear model (with taxes endogenous) were traced, year by year, for the next 100 years to the year 2052.

The first solution corresponded to the deterministic version of the model with no additional external constraints or shocks. The model exhibited unrealistic stability by producing fluctuations that were excessively damped. The issues raised at the beginning of the study were decided unequivocally, and the Adelmans observed, 'After a brief "settling down" period, the system is quite monotonic and essentially linear. There is no hint whatever of any internally generated business cycle, and, indeed, even in the first few years, the shock of start-up is not sufficient to induce more than a single turning-point in any variable' (p. 602). Under ordinary conditions, with great stability of the external environment, the model was clearly non-oscillatory in nature.

In the second simulation, the system was subjected to a severe and sudden shock in terms of reduction in the government expenditures. The resulting time paths of the variables indicate that, after having been thrown into deep depression, the system recovered in four to five years and settled back to its long-run stable path. Once again, the system was stable in a deterministic environment.

In the next two simulations, the system was exposed to distinct types of random impulses: in shocks of type I, random shocks were superimposed on the extrapolated values of the exogenous variables, and in shocks of type II, random errors were introduced into each of the estimated equations making the system stochastic. The magnitude of these shocks or errors was obtained by random drawings from the appropriate probability distributions, namely a normal distribution having zero mean and variance corresponding to the variance of the residuals in the observed sample.

The time paths associated with shocks of type I are shown in Figure 3.1.[38] The model did generate three- to four-year cycles but their average amplitude was unrealistically small. Finally, the simulation with shocks of type II imposed on the estimated equations told a very different story. Not only did it generate three- to four-year cycles but the overall properties of these cycles appeared to be reasonably realistic. The time paths are shown in Figure 3.2.

The Adelmans investigated further the cyclical properties of the time paths generated with shocks of type II by applying the techniques developed at the National Bureau of Economic Research (NBER) for the analysis of business cycles.[39] They found a startling correspondence between the business cycle produced by the Klein–Goldberger Model and the four-year post-Second-World-War cycles in the US economy. The average expansion of Klein–Goldberger cycles covered 2.6 years, its average contraction only 1.5. The observed figures for the United States economy were 2.1 and 1.8 years, respectively. Similarly, in the cycle produced by the Klein–Goldberger Model, 51 per cent of the individual series had maxima coincident with an upper turning-point of the business

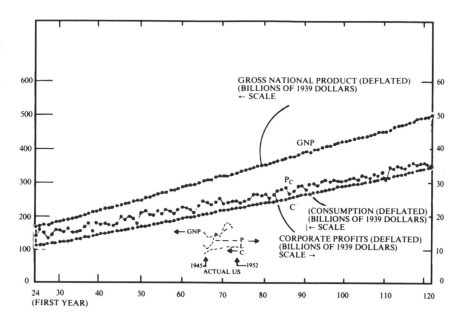

Figure 3.1 Selected time paths under Type I impulses

activity and 52 per cent had minima coincident with a reference trough. The corresponding figures for the US economy were 58 per cent and 52 per cent respectively. This analysis led the Adelmans to the following conclusion about the cyclical properties of the Klein–Goldberger Model:

> All in all, it would appear that there is a remarkable correspondence between the characteristics of fluctuations generated by the superposition of random shocks upon the Klein–Goldberger system and those of the business cycles which actually occur in the United States economy. The resemblance is not restricted to qualitative parallelism, but is, indeed, quantitative, in the sense that the duration of the cycle, the relative length of the expansion and contraction phases, and the degree of clustering of peaks and troughs are all in numerical agreement (within the accuracy of measurement) with empirical evidence. (pp. 614–16)

Finally, their overall observations on the dynamic properties of the model were summarized in part:

> ... our investigation into the dynamic nature of the econometric model of Klein and Goldberger suggests that their equations do not offer an immediate expla-

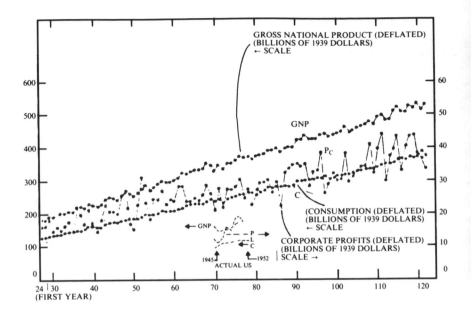

Figure 3.2   Selected time paths under Type II impulses

nation of an internally generated cyclical process. For, in the absence of perturbations, the time paths of the economic variables are monotonic and essentially linear in character. Furthermore, the behavior of the model is remarkably stable, as evidenced by the fact that the solution resumes its unperturbed equilibrium growth trend even after a strong exogenous disturbance ... On the other hand, when random shocks of a realistic order of magnitude are superimposed upon the original form of the Klein–Goldberger equations, the cyclical fluctuations which result are remarkably similar to those described by the NBER as characterizing the United States economy. The average duration of a cycle, the mean length of the expansion and contraction phases, and the degree of clustering of individual peaks and troughs around reference dates all agree with the corresponding data for the United States economy ... All in all, it would appear that the shocked Klein–Goldberger model approximates the behavior of the United States economy rather well. (pp. 619–20)

We may conclude this section by noting that Howrey (1971) has studied the dynamic properties of the Klein–Goldberger Model by an alternative technique, namely spectral analysis in general and a study of the spectrum matrix of the endogenous variables in particular. He finds that the dynamic properties of the model are considerably altered when one passes from the model variant with exogenous taxes to that with endogenous taxes. Finally, we may note that Klein (1969) estimated several variants of an updated version of the Klein–Goldberger, in connection with a study of the properties of several simultaneous equations estimators.

4 The progenies

The legacy of the Klein–Goldberger Model in the history of macroeconometric modelling is indeed vast and all-pervasive. Its impact on the later models can be easily seen from the place it occupies on Michael Intriligator's (1978, p. 452) diagram, 'A "Family Tree" of Macroeconometric Models of the U.S. Economy'. The models of Suits (1962) and Liu (1963) were almost expanded versions of the Klein–Goldberger Model. Its direct descendant was Klein's 'Post-War Quarterly Model', which in turn became a predecessor of the quarterly Wharton models (Wharton, 1967), Wharton Mark III (1972), the model of the Bureau of Economic Analysis (1966) and the Chase Econometrics Model (1971), to name a few. Several other models grew as further offshoots, and the list is long to complete. In addition, the model-builders outside the USA also found their early inspirations in the Klein–Goldberger Model. Klein himself was involved in the construction of a number of them. Econometric model-building spread subsequently not only in the industrialized countries but in the developing countries as well. Among others, models of the United Kingdom, Japan, Canada, France, Italy, India, Israel and Columbia, as well as models of other Latin American countries and the models of Central American economies, were soon constructed. Most of these models owed much to the general style of the Klein–Goldberger Model. Some aspects of this legacy of the Klein–Goldberger Model will be recorded in the following chapters.

5 Other US models of the 1950s

In this section we may briefly review three contemporaneous US econometric models. Valavanis's was built during the first half of the decade, while the Suits and Duesenberry–Eckstein–Fromm models were constructed towards the end of the decade.

Stefan Valavanis (Valavanis-Vail, 1955) constructed an econometric model of US growth experience from 1869 to 1953, based on overlapping decade averages of data assembled by Simon Kuznets and Raymond Goldsmith. The model contained 12 behavioural equations and eight identities. The behavioural equations were: a production function, a relation for capital-labour substitution, a consumption function, an equation for depreciation, an investment demand function, a birth rate equation, an equation for the total size of the labour force, a relation for allocating the labour force between employees and proprietors, a 'wage bargain' equation (which determined the change in the nominal wage rate), equations for both rental and financial incomes, and an equation to determine the income velocity of money or, alternatively, an equation that we might interpret as the demand for real money balances. Valavanis's system was linear in the parameters to be estimated, but not in the variables of the system. His technique of parameter estimation was a version of limited-information maximum likelihood estimation, which was scaled down because of the limited capacity of his computer. We may comment on several of the behavioural equations. The production function was estimated without neutral technical change, but this version showed an unreasonably low marginal productivity of labour and an unreasonably high marginal productivity of capital. Constraining the elasticities of output with respect to the inputs of these two factors to be equal to observed factor shares, Valavanis was able to estimate a rate of neutral technical progress equal to 8 per cent per decade or ¾ per cent per year, which he regarded as reasonable. The consumption function was constructed along the lines of T. M. Brown's 'habit persistence' hypothesis (1952), and real per capita consumption was explained as a function of current real per capita disposable income and the lagged value of the dependent variable. The birth rate equation showed births positively related to the lagged rate of growth of real per capita income (suggesting the consumption aspect of children) as well as containing a negative time trend (to represent the secular forces leading to a decline in the birth rate). The equation for the total labour force, a participation rate equation, suggested a backward-bending supply curve (after correction for population growth, of course). Finally, the 'wage bargain' equation explained the change in nominal wages as a linear function of the percentage of the labour force unionized, the change in the price level, and the percentage of the labour force employed;[40] all three effects were positive. Valavanis then explored some of the dynamic properties of the model; in particular, he examined what he called the 'Domar problem', namely the amount and/or the rate of growth of private domestic investment required to maintain full employment of the labour force. He also looked at the 'inflationary bias' of the US economy. It is interesting to observe that Valavanis concluded his article by predicting an optimistic future for macroeconometric modelling, which in retrospect seems quite justified.

A model of great interest was the Duesenberry, Eckstein, Fromm (1960) model of the US economy. This was a partial model for two reasons: first, it was intended to represent the structure of the US economy only during recession periods and, second, many of the usual components of aggregate demand (business fixed investment, residential construction outlays, and net exports, as well as government expenditures and farm inventory investment) were exogenous.[41] The model was (largely) an example of a quarterly model, which type was coming into vogue in the late fifties.[42] The model contained 10 behavioural equations and 18 identities; among the stochastic equations were an inventory investment equation in which non-farm inventory investment was explained by a loose form of the inventory accelerator and a consumption function in which per capita real consumption as a proportion of lagged per capita real disposable income was explained by a ratchet variable (the ratio of lagged per capita real disposable income to the previous peak of this variable, which of course has a negative influence) and by the lagged value of the dependent variable. The tax-transfer mechanism (including the system of unemployment insurance) was modelled extensively, and also the other aspects of the decomposition of the income side of the national income accounting identity (corporate profits, dividends, inventory valuation adjustment and so forth) were modelled in detail. The model appeared to reproduce well, in simulation, the behaviour of the US economy in the 1957–8 recession, which was not altogether surprising, given the high degree of exogeneity of the system; the primary focus, however, was on the simulation of policies to counteract the hardships of recession. Not surprisingly, the authors concluded that, while the US economy exhibited considerable built-in stability during the typical postwar recession, judiciously selected discretionary policy could improve the response of the economy to exoge-nous shocks. This proposition would appear to be more controversial today than it was at the time that the article was written.

A different sort of focus was represented by Dan Suits's development of the Michigan model during the late fifties and early sixties.[43] As noted above, this model was a lineal descendant of the Klein–Goldberger Model. While policy simulation (in the form of impact and dynamic multipliers) was one of the points of interest of the use of the model, Suits's primary focus was unabashedly economic forecasting. Suits was quite proud of his generally good record for *ex ante* forecasting, and Bodkin's comments on Suits's paper at the First World Congress of the Econometric Society in Rome in 1965 generally agreed that he had not exaggerated the accuracy of his forecasts.[44] The structure of Suits's model was unique and somewhat controversial; in the 1962 version, there were 16 stochastic equations and 17 identities, fitted to annual data in *first difference* form by *ordinary least squares*. (The first difference form was chosen in part to eliminate autocorrelated disturbances (which it will do only if the coefficient of first order autocorrelation is unity or close to it and there is no higher order autocorrelation) but mainly because Suits believed in forecasting first differences rather than levels. The parameters were estimated by ordinary least squares because Suits did not believe that the game of simultaneous equations estimation was worth the candle.) A feature of this model was that aggregate demand was highly disaggregated (especially for that period); consumption expenditures were disaggregated into automobiles and parts,[45] other durables, non-durables, and services; and private investment was disaggregated into business construction, machinery and equipment, durable and non-durable inventory invest- ment, and residential construction. (There was an import demand func- tion, while exports and government expenditures were exogenous.) Also to be noted were a highly developed tax-transfer system, the absence of a monetary sector,[46] and the determination of all variables in real terms. The model was completely linear, as the one non-linear identity was linearized, which again reminds us how much computing technology has developed over the past quarter of a century. Finally, we note that the record of Suits's forecasting illustrates the Theil rule (cited in Chapter 2) that changes tend to be underforecasted. Table 4 of Suits (1967) presents Suits's forecasting record for 1953–65; out of 13 forecasts, the absolute value of the change was underforecasted in ten years, including the three years (1955, 1959 and 1965) when the extent of the boom was missed by a large margin.

Appendix[47]

The estimates are based on the annual split sample 1929–41, 1946–52, and are obtained by the limited-information maximum likelihood technique.

(1)* $C_t = -22.26 + 0.55(W_1 + W_2 - T_W)_t + 0.41(P - T_p - S_p)_t +$
$\qquad\quad$ (9.66) (0.06) $\qquad\qquad\qquad$ (0.05)

$\qquad + 0.34(A_1 + A_2 - T_A)_t + 0.26C_{t-1} + 0.072(L_1)_{t-1} + 0.26(N_p)_t$
$\qquad\quad$ (0.04) $\qquad\qquad\qquad$ (0.075) (0.025) $\qquad$ (0.10)

$\qquad\qquad\qquad\qquad\qquad\qquad \delta^2/S^2 = 1.98$

(2)* $I_t = -16.71 + 0.78(P - T_p + A_1 + A_2 - T_A + D)_{t-1} - 0.073K_{t-1}$
$\qquad\quad$ (4.74) (0.18) $\qquad\qquad\qquad\qquad\qquad\qquad\qquad$ (0.067)

$\qquad\qquad\qquad\qquad\qquad\qquad + 0.14(L_2)_{t-1}$
$\qquad\qquad\qquad\qquad\qquad\qquad$ (0.11)

$\qquad\qquad\qquad\qquad\qquad\qquad \delta^2/S^2 = 2.08$

(3)* $(S_p)_t = -3.53 + 0.72(P_c - T_c)_t + 0.076(P_c - T_c - S_p)_{t-1}$
$\qquad\qquad\quad$ (1.02) (0.06) $\qquad\qquad$ (0.254)

$\qquad\qquad\qquad\qquad\qquad\qquad\qquad\qquad - 0.028B_{t-1}$
$\qquad\qquad\qquad\qquad\qquad\qquad\qquad\qquad$ (0.019)

$\qquad\qquad\qquad\qquad\qquad\qquad \delta^2/S^2 = 0.99$

(4)* $(P_c)_t = -7.60 + 0.69P$
$\qquad\qquad\quad$ (0.54) (0.02)

$\qquad\qquad\qquad\qquad\qquad\qquad \delta^2/S^2 = 1.28$

(5)* $D_t = 7.25 + 0.10\dfrac{K_t + K_{t-1}}{2} + 0.044(Y + T + D - W_2)_t$
$\quad\;\;(0.80)\;\;(0.01)\qquad\qquad\qquad(0.008)$

$$\delta^2/S^2 = 0.94$$

(6)* $(W_1)_t = -1.40 + 0.24(Y + T + D - W_2)_t +$
$\qquad\;\;\;(1.46)\;\;(0.07)$

$$+ 0.24\,(Y + T + D - W_2)_{t-1} + 0.29t$$
$$(0.06)\qquad\qquad\qquad\qquad(0.125)$$

$$\delta^2/S^2 = 2.45$$

(7)* $(Y + T + D - W_2)_t = -26.08 + 2.17[h(N_W - N_G) + N_E + N_F]_t +$
$\qquad\qquad\qquad\qquad\;\;\;(7.27)\;\;\;(0.18)$

$$+ 0.16\dfrac{K_t + K_{t-1}}{2} + 2.05t$$
$$(0.05)\qquad\qquad(0.16)$$

$$\delta^2/S^2 = 1.09$$

(8)* $w_t - w_{t-1} = 4.11 - 0.74(N - N_W - N_E - N_F)_t +$
$\qquad\qquad\quad\;\;(4.85)\;\;(0.61)$

$$+ 0.52(p_{t-1} - p_{t-2}) + 0.54t$$
$$(0.28)\qquad\qquad(0.24)$$

$$\delta_2/S^2 = 2.38$$

(9)* $(F_i)_t = 0.32 +$
$\qquad\quad\;(0.49)$

$+ 0.0060(W_1 + W_2 - T_W + P - T_p + A_1 + A_2 - T_A)_t\dfrac{p_t}{(p_l)_t} + 0.81(F_i)_{t-1}$
$(0.0084)\qquad\qquad\qquad\qquad\qquad\qquad\qquad\qquad\qquad\qquad(0.21)$

$$\delta^2/S^2 = 2.33$$

(10)* $(A_1)_t\dfrac{p_t}{(p_A)_t} = -0.36 + 0.054(W_1 + W_2 - T_W + P - T_p - S_p)_t\dfrac{p_t}{(p_A)}$
$\qquad\qquad\quad\;\;(2.12)\;\;(0.045)$

$-0.007(W_1 + W_2 - T_W + P - T_p - S_p)_{t-1}\dfrac{p_{t-1}}{(p_A)_{t-1}} + 0.012(F_A)_t$
$(0.043)\qquad\qquad\qquad\qquad\qquad\qquad\qquad\qquad\;(0.006)$

$$\delta^2/S^2 = 0.85$$

(11)* $(p_A)_t = -131.17 + 2.32p_t$
$\qquad\qquad\;(15.3)\qquad(0.11)$

$$\delta^2/S^2 = 0.74$$

(12)* $(L_1)_t = 0.14(W_1 + W_2 - T_W + P - T_p - S_p + A_1 + A_2 - T_A)_t +$

$$+ 76.03(i_L - 2.0)_t^{-0.84}{}_{(0.03)}$$
$$(15.31)$$

$$\delta^2/S^2 = 0.73 \text{ (for the logarithmic form of residuals)}$$

(13)* $(L_2)_t = -0.34 + 0.26(W_1)_t - 1.02(i_S)_t - 0.26(p_t - p_{t-1}) +$
$\qquad\quad$ (0.99) (0.03) $\qquad$ (0.19) $\qquad$ (0.06)

$$+ 0.61(L_2)_{t-1}$$
$$(0.06)$$

$$\delta^2/S^2 = 1.72$$

(14)* $i_L = 2.58 + 0.44(i_S)_{t-3} + 0.26(i_S)_{t-5}$
$\qquad\quad$ (0.15) (0.10) $\qquad$ (0.09)

(15)* $100\dfrac{(i_S)_t - (i_S)_{t-1}}{(i_S)_{t-1}} = 11.17 - 0.67R_t$
$\qquad\qquad\qquad\qquad$ (7.81) (0.30)

$$\delta^2/S^2 = 1.59$$

(16) $C_t + I_t + G_t + (F_E)_t - (F_I)_t = Y_t + T_t + D_t$

(17) $(W_1)_t + (W_2)_t + P_t + (A_1)_t + (A_2)_t = Y_t$

(18) $h_t\dfrac{w_t}{p_t}(N_W)_t = (W_1)_t + (W_2)_t$

(19) $K_t - K_{t-1} = I_t - D_t$

(20) $B_t - B_{t-1} = (S_p)_t$

Notes
1. J. Tinbergen (1981).
2. Lawrence R. Klein (1950) Preface, p. viii, dated March 1949.
3. Although the volume *An Econometric Model of the United States, 1929–1952* by L. R. Klein and A. S. Goldberger was published in 1955, some forecasts based on this model were made public as early as November 1953, at a conference on the analysis of economic outlook at the University of Michigan. The same forecasts, in a slightly improved form, were presented later to a wider audience through publication in *The Manchester Guardian Weekly*, 7 January 1954, p. 3.
4. Klein and Goldberger particularly emphasized the need for continuous parameter re-estimation before the model could be used successfully for analysis and forecasting. They acknowledged in the Preface, 'After having spent more than three years at work on the econometric model construction described in this book, we now find ourselves outdated by the basic revisions of the national income accounts made by the U.S. Department of Commerce in mid-summer 1954.' This proved to be prophetic, and many later model-builders have had similar experiences. The only other known case of a continuous econometric project of that time was of the Canadian government. T. M. Brown reported on the 'Canadian Experience in Forecasting from Econometric Models' at the Meetings of the Econometric Society, December 1951. The Canadian experience was described as one of continuous refinement of data, revising and re-estimating equations and testing forecasts. The Klein–Goldberger Model did draw upon this aspect of the Canadian research. (See also Chapter 9 below.)
5. The extent of its legacy is well depicted in a 'family tree' of macroeconometric models of the US economy presented in Intriligator (1978) p. 452.
6. The five auxiliary tax equations were added at the time of making forecasts.

7. However Klein and Goldberger were quick to point out that an assumption that the characteristics of the labour force are exogenous is 'probably the least tenable and should be one of the first to be dropped in future research' (p. 35). This indeed proved to be the case in general in later model-building.

8. The 24 lagged variables contain both exogenous and endogenous variables. This classification is somewhat arbitrary, as the lagged exogenous variables may be counted along with the other exogenous variables.

9. An extended discussion of the model is also available in Henri Theil (1971), pp. 468–83. Also see C. F. Christ (1956) pp. 385–408, and Intriligator (1978) pp. 440–1.

10. The presumption was that, at the individual level, 'liquid assets are highly correlated with overall consumer wealth, and thus serve as a good wealth indicator'. However the authors did point out that, in any future research, the wealth variable should probably be expanded to include the stock of consumer durables.

11. It may be mentioned that the series of disposable income by factor shares were not yet available in the USA; therefore special estimates for the purpose of constructing this model were prepared.

12. And soon afterwards (1954), this formulation was also suggested by Koyck in the context of distributed lags.

13. Lumping inventory investment with other private investments was indeed a shortcoming of the model; it precluded the analysis of the inventory cycle, a major volatile component of the economic activity.

14. S. P. Dobrovolsky (1951).

15. Marc Nerlove (1966) pp. 127–75. It is worth noting that the import demand function is absent in Tinbergen's 1939 model of the US economy (where this variable, though inessential, is taken as exogenous). Also, while there is a theoretical import demand function in Colin Clark's 1949 model of the US economy, in practice this function was merged with the consumption function and so only estimated implicitly.

16. We may here join Benjamin Friedman (1978) in pointing out that, years before the proponents of rational expectations discovered the importance of expectations, they were already being used in Klein's early models.

17. In this connection, the central importance of the real GNP variable is indicated by the result that, if this variable is suppressed (exogenized) from the model, 15 'strongly connected components' (*composantes connexes*) are lost to the model, more than double the number of linkages associated with the second most important (in this sense) endogenous variable of the system, which happens to be the level of the GNP deflator.

18. A similar technique has been developed by Gallo and Gilli (1990), who argue that such qualitative analysis is an essential step in the analysis of the large, complex systems that modern macroeconometric models constitute. Keller also argues that the analysis of graphs, applied to macroeconometric modelling, is an invaluable aid in the construction, solution and estimation of such a model. Of course, in one sense, this analysis has its philosophical foundations in Herbert A. Simon's classical article (1953), in which he attempted to link traditional notions of causality with the modern problem of identification in econometric models. (A more recent discussion of related issues may be found in McElroy's 1978 article.)

19. It may be noted that the value of gross national product was estimated with an error not exceeding 5 per cent.

20. There do exist some unpublished forecasts which Klein made as early as 1945–6 at the Cowles Commission. These were based on Model III of *Fluctuations*. Albert G. Hart (1976) in his communication with the editor of *Econometrica* has drawn attention to one such forecast in which Klein predicted the postwar demand activity to be quite buoyant, contrary to the conventional wisdom of the time.

21. It is important to remember the difference between *ex post* and *ex ante* forecasts while assessing the performance characteristics of any econometric model. In preparing *ex post* forecasts, the actual values of the predetermined variables are used so that the difference between the actual values and the predicted values of the endogenous variables can be purely attributed to the model proper. The *ex ante* forecasts, on the

other hand, are prepared by using the best guesses of the values for the exogenous variables so that the forecasting error represents the combination of both the 'information error' and the model error.

22.   As a matter of fact, annually from 1952 on, the Research Seminar at the University of Michigan started preparing economic forecasts for the forthcoming year. In each case, the forecasts were based on the Klein–Goldberger Model, or some variant of it, supplemented by some extraneous cross-section information. The 1953 and 1954 forecasts mentioned above appeared in the Klein–Goldberger volume and the 1955 forecasts in Suits and Goldberger (1955).

23.   Previously the import variable was computed as 'total purchases in the United States less direct estimates of unilateral transfers overseas by the United States government' (p. 89).

24.   His forecast based on series of equations designed to predict the movements of the business cycle appeared in *The Manchester Guardian Weekly*, 19 and 26 November 1953. Klein and Goldberger published their forecasts for 1954 in the same *Weekly* on 7 January 1954. However a somewhat earlier version of this forecast had been presented to a smaller audience at a conference on the analysis of the economic outlook at the University of Michigan in November 1953.

25.   There is a cartoon printed below the forecast given in *The Manchester Guardian Weekly*, 7 January 1954. A wolf with 'recession' printed at its back is sitting in front of the USA door but looking behind with its head turned towards three rejoicing pigs: Great Britain (Churchill smoking a cigar and making a victory sign), France (playing lute), and one other.

26.   In the Preface of their volume analysing the forecasts, Klein and Goldberger point out that they were quite aware of this tendency in their model. They also emphasize that, although their main assumptions about the fiscal legislation underlying their 1954 forecasts were qualitatively correct, the magnitudes of the government expenditures which they had assumed were at an excessively high level.

27.   See, for example, C. F. Christ (1951) pp. 56–7.

28.   See Table 2.2. on p. 12 of Goldberger (1959).

29.   Endogenous tax collections suppose that the government controls the tax rates rather than the tax yields. An assumption that the government controls the tax yields would be the assumption that tax collections are exogenous.

30.   This reduction, employed, for example, in Theil's (1971, pp. 463–5) statement of dynamic multipliers, is an alternative to the analysis in terms of characteristic equations and characteristic roots.

31.   For example, $(\pi_0\pi_1 + \pi_2)$ for one year later, $(\pi_0(\pi_0\pi_1 + \pi_2)$ for two years later and so on.

32.   Theil (1971, pp. 463–5) has described the detailed derivation of these matrices, in the section that we have previously cited.

33.   In these calculations, the equations for the monetary sector were suppressed with an assumption that the stock of the liquid assets held by the households and the businesses remain unchanged for all time periods. The early calculations had indeed indicated a great deal of dichotomization between the real sector and the monetary sector. In fact, as we have already pointed out, the looseness of the ties between the two could be detected by a qualitative analysis of the model structure. An unpublished study by Bodkin and Davis (1979) also showed that monetary policy, in the Klein–Goldberger Model, exerted a very weak influence on the real economy.

34.   For the complete matrix of multipliers, see Goldberger (1959).

35.   Goldberger (1959) p. 129.

36.   This seminal study of the Adelmans laid the groundwork for a great deal of analysis of the stochastic business cycle; see Hickman (1972).

37.   Whenever the standard error of the regression coefficient was more than twice the size of the coefficient itself, the term was dropped from the equation.

38.   Figures 3.1 and 3.2, which were Figures 3 and 4 in the Adelman's study, have been reproduced from this article.

39.   See A. F. Burns and W. C. Mitchell (1946) and W. C. Mitchell (1951).

40. Again, we note that this relationship anticipates the work of A. W. Phillips (1958) but postdates L. R. Klein's work in *Economic Fluctuations in the United States* (1950).
41. Other key exogenous variables were total population, the price level, unfilled orders for durable goods and the average weekly unemployment insurance benefit. Of course, in a more complete model, a number of these key exogenous variables would have been made endogenous.
42. Perhaps the first quarterly econometric model was Colin Clark's (1949). An early quarterly model was that of Barger and Klein (1954), which made exploratory calculations with a quarterly version of Model I of Klein (1950). These exploratory calculations suggested that quarterly models should ideally be made more than unimaginative variants of corresponding annual models, as the dynamic patterns of response can be captured more precisely with quarterly data.
43. See Suits (1962, 1965, 1967).
44. See, however, Stekler's (1966) more critical evaluation of Suits's forecasts, in which Stekler showed that Suits's *ex ante* forecasts were better than the corresponding *ex post* forecasts of the same events, suggesting that Suits may have been compensating for the deficiences of his model. (Even in the present state of the art, we think that this is quite legitimate.)
45. While one might think that Suits was led to break out this component by the importance of the automobile industry to the regional economy of Michigan, he indicated in the 1962 article that he found it necessary to break it out after missing the extent of the ensuing boom in his *ex ante* forecast for 1955.
46. Thus liquid assets of consumers and corporate bond yields were exogenous variables. Also exogenous (in addition to variables mentioned in the text above) were some miscellaneous tax-transfer variables, the size of the labour force, the numbers of self-employed persons, farm income (in real terms) and construction costs relative to the price level.
47. This is the revised version of the model that appears in Chapter VI of Klein–Goldberger (1955). The tax equations have been omitted.

References

Adelman, Irma and Frank L. Adelman (1959) 'The Dynamic Properties of the Klein–Goldberger Model', *Econometrica*, vol. 27, no. 4 (October). Reprinted in John W. Hooper and Marc Nerlove (1970) *Selected Readings in Econometrics from Econometrica* (Cambridge, Mass.: MIT Press).

Barger, Harold and Lawrence R. Klein (1954) 'A Quarterly Model for the United States Economy', *Journal of the American Statistical Association*, vol. 49, no. 207 (September) pp. 413–37.

Bodkin, R. G. and E. Davis (1979) 'A Simulation by the Klein–Goldberger Model of the 1937–1938 Recession in the U.S.A.', (unpublished) January 1979.

Brown, T. M. (1952) 'Habit Persistence and Lags in Consumer Behavior', *Econometrica*, vol. 20, no. 3 (July).

Burns, A. F. and W. C. Mitchell (1946) *Measuring Business Cycles* (New York: National Bureau of Economic Research).

Christ, C. F. (1951) 'A Test of an Econometric Model for the United States, 1921–1947', *Conference on Business Cycles* (New York: National Bureau of Economic Research).

_____ (1956) 'Aggregate Econometric Models', *American Economic Review*, vol. 46.

Clark, Colin (1949) 'A System of Equations Explaining the United States Trade Cycle, 1921–1941', *Econometrica*, vol. 17, no. 2 (April).

_____ (1953) article in *The Manchester Guardian Weekly*, 19 and 26 November.

Dobrovolsky, S. P. (1951) *Corporate Income Retention, 1915–43* (New York: National Bureau of Economic Research).

Duesenberry, James S., Otto Eckstein and Gary Fromm (1960) 'A Simulation of the United States Economy in Recession', *Econometrica*, vol. 28, no. 4 (October) pp. 749–809.

Evans, M. K. (1974) 'Econometric Models', in W. F. Butler, R. A. Kavesh and R. B. Platt (eds), *Methods and Techniques of Business Forecasting* (Englewood Cliffs, NJ: Prentice-Hall).

Evans, M. K. and L. R. Klein (1967) *The Wharton Econometric Forecasting Model* (Philadelphia: Economics Research Unit, University of Pennsylvania).

Frane, L. and L. R. Klein (1953) 'The Estimation of Disposable Income by Distributive Shares', *The Review of Economics and Statistics*, vol. 35 (November).

Friedman, B. (1978) '"Discussion" on Robert E. Lucas and Thomas J. Sargent's "After Keynesian Macroeconomics"', in *After the Phillips Curve: Persistence of High Inflation and High Unemployment*, Conference Series No. 19 (Federal Reserve Bank of Boston).

Gallo, Giampiero M. and Manfred H. Gilli (1990) 'How to Strip a Model to its Essential Elements', *Computer Science in Economics and Management*, vol. 3, pp. 199–214.

Goldberger, Arthur S. (1959) *Impact Multipliers and Dynamic Properties of the Klein–Goldberger Model* (Amsterdam: North-Holland).

Goldberger, A. S. and L. R. Klein (1954) 'A Mild Down-Turn in American Trade', *The Manchester Guardian Weekly*, 7 January.

Hart, Albert G. (1976) 'A Lost Work of Lawrence Klein', correspondence with the editor of *Econometrica*, 9 March.

Hickman, Bert G. (ed.) (1972) *Econometric Models of the Business Cycle* (New York: Columbia University Press).

Howrey, E. Philip (1971) 'Stochastic Properties of the Klein–Goldberger Model', *Econometrica*, vol. 39, no. 1 (January) pp. 73–87.

Intriligator, M. D. (1978) *Econometric Models, Techniques, and Applications* (Englewood Cliffs, NJ: Prentice-Hall).

Keller, André A. (1979) *Essai sur les structures comparés des modèles macréconomiques de prévision: construction d'une typologie par l'étude des graphes associés et l'analyse factorielle* (Paris: Université de Paris Panthéon-Sorbonne, April).

Kisselgoff, Avram (1945) 'Liquidity Preference of Large Manufacturing Corporations (1921–1939)', *Econometrica*, vol. 13, no. 4 (October) pp. 334–44.

Klein, Lawrence R. (1950) *Economic Fluctuations in the United States, 1921–1941* (New York: John Wiley).

―――― (1964) 'A Postwar Quarterly Model: Description and Applications', *Models of Income Determination*, Volume Twenty-Eight of *Studies in Income and Wealth* (Princeton, NJ: Princeton University Press, for NBER).

―――― (1969) 'Estimation of Interdependent Systems in Macroeconometrics', *Econometrica*, vol. 37, no. 2 (April), pp. 171–92.

Klein, Lawrence R. and Ronald G. Bodkin (assisted by Motoo Abe) (1964) 'Empirical Aspects of the Trade-Offs among Three Goals: High Level Employment, Price Stability, and Economic Growth', Research Study No. 7 (pp. 367–428) of *Inflation, Growth, and Employment*, a Series of Research Studies Prepared for the Commission on Money and Credit (Englewood Cliffs, NJ: Prentice-Hall).

Klein, Lawrence R. and Arthur S. Goldberger (1955) *An Econometric Model of the United States, 1929–1952*, (Amsterdam: North-Holland).

Koyck, L. M. (1954) *Distributed Lags and Investment Analysis* (Amsterdam: North-Holland).

Liebenberg, M., A. A. Hirsch and J. Popkin (1966) 'A Quarterly Econometric Model of the United States: A Progress Report', *Survey of Current Business*, vol. 46.

Liu, T. C. (1963) 'An Exploratory Quarterly Econometric Model of Effective Demand in the Post-War U.S. Economy', *Econometrica*, vol. 31, no. 3 (July).

McCarthy, M. D. (1972) *The Wharton Quarterly Econometric Forecasting Model*, Mark III (Philadelphia: Economics Research Unit, University of Pennsylvania).

McElroy, F. W. (1978) 'A Simple Method of Causal Ordering', *International Economic Review*, vol. 19, no. 1 (February) pp. 1–23.

Mitchell, W. C. (1951) *What Happens During Business Cycles* (New York: National Bureau of Economic Research).

Nerlove, Marc (1966) 'A Tabular Survey of Macro-Econometric Models', *International Economic Review*, vol. 7, no. 2 (May).

Phillips, A. W. (1958) 'The Relationship Between Unemployment and the Rate of Change of Money Wage Rates in the United Kingdom, 1861–1957', *Economica*, vol. 25 (November).

Simon, Herbert A. (1953) 'Causal Ordering and Identifiability', Chapter III (pp. 49–74) of Wm. C. Hood and Tjalling C. Koopmans (eds), *Studies in Econometric Method*, Cowles Commission Monograph No. 14 (New York: John Wiley).

Stekler, H. O. (1966) 'Forecasting and Analysis with an Econometric Model: Comment', *American Economic Review*, vol. 56, no. 5 (December) pp. 1241–8.

Suits, D. B. (1962) 'Forecasting and Analysis With An Econometric Model', *American Economic Review*, vol. 52, no. 2 (March) pp. 104–32.

_____ (1965) 'Forecasting and Analysis with an Econometric Model of the U.S. Economy', unpublished paper presented to the First World Congress of the Econometric Society, Rome, 10 September.

_____ (1967) 'Applied Econometric Forecasting and Policy Analysis', pp. 231–89 in Herman O. Wold, Guy H. Orcutt, Enders A. Robinson, Daniel B. Suits, and Pieter de Wolff, *Forecasting on a Scientific Basis*, Proceedings of an International Summer Institute held at Curia, Portugal, September 1966 (Lisbon: Centro de Economia e financas of the Gulbenkian Foundation).

Suits, D. B. and A. S. Goldberger (1955) 'A Statistical Model for 1955', *Michigan Business Review*, vol. 7.

Tinbergen, Jan (1981) 'The Use of Models: Experience and Prospects', a lecture delivered in Stockholm, Sweden, December 1969, when he received the Nobel Prize in Economic Science. Reprinted in the *American Economic Review*, vol. 71, no. 6 (December) pp. 17–22.

Theil, Henri (1971) *Principles of Econometrics* (New York: John Wiley).

Tobin, James (1947) 'Liquidity Preference and Monetary Policy', *Review of Economic Statistics*, vol. 29, no. 2 (May) pp. 124–31.

Valavanis-Vail, Stefan (1955) 'An Econometric Model of Growth: U.S.A., 1869–1953', *American Economic Review, Papers and Proceedings*, vol. 45, no. 2 (May) pp. 208–21.

4 Expansion and theoretical development during the 1960s: the Brookings Model as a milestone

As our knowledge and understanding of the complex world in which we live increases, so must our tools become more refined and our description more detailed. This is true in economics as in physics where in the span of a few decades the relatively simple Bohr proton, neutron, electron model has given way to the current version with its multitudes of particles and antiparticles.[1]

Introduction

The decade of the 1960s witnessed a quantum leap in macroeconometric model-building. Several models, big and small, emerged on the scene, opening up a whole new vista. At least five major interrelated trends were initiated. Firstly, the models became progressively larger in size, scope and complexity. Klein's Postwar Quarterly Model, which appeared early in the decade, was roughly of medium size, but the Brookings Model, which spanned the second half of the decade (and several years beyond), was considered gigantic at that time. This was truly the first large-scale macroeconometric model, which, in some versions, contained nearly 400 equations. There were other models which, judged by their size and scope, can be placed between the two on the same general spectrum.

Secondly, the degree of theoretical sophistication embedded in these models became increasingly high and, consequently, their operational capability was significantly enhanced. For instance, the conventional macroeconometric models were spliced with input–output models in some cases; intrinsically non-linear relationships no longer needed to be linearized for ease of computation; the dynamic aspects of the models began to be investigated through longer and more complex lag schemes; and, more than ever before, the models were integrated into policy analysis and forecasting applications.

Thirdly, the methodological research in the application of large-scale models succeeded in achieving new and much needed breakthroughs. The timely and contemporaneous advances in the computer technology provided the proper base and scientific environment. The computer routines needed for dynamic and stochastic simulations, among other things, were developed, and the block-recursive structures of the larger models were sought in order to tackle the consistency problem arising from a degrees-of-freedom constraint.

Fourthly, a trend towards an implementation of a team approach was initiated; this became both cause and effect of the growth of larger-scale econometric models as well as of an increase in theoretical sophistication entrenched in them. Of course individual efforts of a highly professional nature also continued and may still be found, but a greater part of the activity in macroeconometric model-building began to take place as a result of team efforts. The team approach, which originated (in a real sense) with the Brookings Model, enabled individual scholars to bring their insight on particular aspects of the economy into play in one overall system. While it also posed problems of coordination of the contributions of specialists, in general, overall project management has been equal to the task.[2] In particular, tools of project management, such as the simulation of one equation (or group of equations) within the context of an overall model, have been extremely helpful.[3] Equally, the use of the computer as a record-keeper (through computerized data banks and with various accounting and computational checks) has also been most helpful.

And finally, there also started the development of an institutional framework that transcends the efforts of the innovator–originator of the model. Just as Henry Ford I no longer manages the Ford Motor Company, Daniel B. Suits no longer operates the Michigan Model. The Wharton Econometric Forecasting Associates was set up as a private organization to run the Wharton Model.[4] This institutional development has the enormous advantage that the model will not die when the interests of the original model-builder move on. Moreover, in the current stage of econometric model-building, this is extremely important, as the lessons of experience, as well as new theoretical developments, must be frequently incorporated if the model itself is to progress.

Leaving these introductory remarks aside, let us review briefly, in their chronological order of appearance, the major models of the 1960s.

A Postwar Quarterly Model (1948–58)

Main features
In a long string of past and present econometric models of the US economy, Lawrence R. Klein's version in the early 1960s was 'A Postwar Quarterly Model'.[5] It was a direct descendant of the Klein–Goldberger (K–G) annual model, and it became a predecessor of the quarterly Wharton models. The National Bureau of Economic Research had for a long time considered annual data inherently inadequate for the study of busi-

ness cycle analysis. Therefore, as soon as the quarterly data for a reasonable span of time became available, a move towards a quarterly model was a natural and pragmatic step. Some prewar quarterly data found in a scanty form had indeed already been exploited by Barger and Klein for methodological purposes,[6] but it was indeed the 'Postwar Quarterly Model' that was developed with the explicit aim of generating accurate short-run forecasts of the course of economic activity, 'to provide an increased empirically supported understanding of the *modus operandi* of our present-day economic system and to develop a tool for testing the effects of alternative economic policies'.[7]

This model, with 29 behavioural equations and eight identities (of which there were tax-transfer auxiliary relationships), was somewhat larger than the Klein–Goldberger Model; as the title implies, it was fitted by quarterly data (for the period 1948–58, thus including the Korean War period) which were seasonally adjusted; and the methods of parameter estimation were limited-information maximum likelihood and two-stage least squares. Distinguishing this model from its annual predecessors and using the K–G Model as a reference point, Klein himself underlined the following main differences that motivated his new research.

First, the Postwar Quarterly Model was less aggregative; some new equations represented an 'obvious decomposition of national product elements', others stemmed 'from more subtle theorizing about patterns of behaviour'. For example, there were three consumption functions (durables, non-durables and services), a similar disaggregation as in the Suits Michigan Model (except of course that automobiles and parts were not separately distinguished), while private investment was broken into plant and equipment (together), residential construction and inventory investment.

Second, in contrast to the K–G Model, in which subjective variables like expectations about consumer purchases and investment outlays were used only in forecasting but were not directly built into the system, in this model, and for the first time, anticipatory data and realization functions were introduced to 'express actual behaviour as a function of expectations'. However, since these expectations were still not explained endogenously, the employment of subjective variables remained quite limited.[8]

Third, because of the nature of the annual data which cannot be used meaningfully to discern inventory-order patterns, the K–G Model (to quote Klein) had 'slurred' the whole issue of inventory investment; at this point, however, explicit relationships among inventories, sales, backlogs and new orders appeared in the model. In short, the inventory investment equation incorporated a form of inventory accelerator, a speculative component, a stock adjustment effect, and an induced effect (from unfilled orders) on the presumed holdings of raw materials. However an endogenous explanation of unfilled orders was still lacking.

Fourth, the concept of capacity output, together with its utilization rate, was introduced in this model. Capacity output was defined as a point on the aggregate production function corresponding to full utilization of the existing labour force and capital stock.[9] The rate of capacity utilization was then simply the ratio of actual output to capacity output, which was in turn available for use elsewhere in the model. Defined in this manner, capacity output and its utilization rate became dependent on the parameters of the ordinary production function for the estimation of which the capital utilization rate itself was needed. This problem of estimating the parameters of the production function was solved by using independently constructed estimates of the capacity utilization rate, which was called the 'Wharton School Index of the Capacity Utilization Rate'.[10]

Fifth, in the K–G Model, some natural non-linearities in the variables were avoided at the cost of introducing some degree of distortion by requiring the national income identities to hold in terms of real or deflated variables. In the Postwar Quarterly Model, such distortions were eliminated by modelling the majority of behavioural equations in real terms but formulating the accounting identities in nominal terms. This led to natural non-linearities in the solution of the system and these were allowed to prevail.

The treatment of the labour force was another distinguishing feature of the model. The labour force was determined endogenously by a stochastic equation which embodied the 'discouraged worker' hypothesis. An element of labour supply consisting of participation by housewives, students and semi-retired persons was shown to move cyclically. They were assumed to enter the labour force when jobs are plentiful and leave the labour force when they are scarce. Therefore a negative association between the labour force and employment rate was sought and found. The wage changes were modelled in the same spirit of the wage adjustment relationship which was used in the K–G Model and popularized by the late A. W. Phillips.

Among the remaining special features of the structure of the model which may be noted are: both imports and exports were endogenous; the reciprocal of velocity was the dependent variable in the demand for cash balances; the monetary authorities were assumed to control or influence directly the bank reserves and the discount rate instead of the stock of cash; and there were at least seven different price levels, which were explained separately; each specific price level was made a function of the general price level or wage level and also of some particular factor affecting that price.

Applications

The model was immediately applied to generate and test *ex ante* forecasts for the first three quarters of 1961. In obtaining these forecasts, the general price level, interest rates and exports were set at predetermined values, and also a certain degree of adjustment of the constant terms was employed. The overall forecasting performance of the model proved quite satisfactory. To quote from comments made by Franco Modigliani,

> I am, therefore, quite pleased to find that the United States economy decided to encourage his [Klein's] activities by producing in the third quarter of 1961 a GNP within a couple of billion dollars of the forecasts made in April 1961, and largely on the basis of information relating only to the last quarter of 1960. The accuracy of the model is even more impressive if stated in terms of change over the last quarter of 1960. (Klein, 1964, p. 42)

And to quote Klein himself,

> On the surface, this appears to have been a good forecast. The prediction of an upturn in the economy after the low point in the first quarter of 1961 was not surprising. Opinion was much divided, however, on the magnitude of the recovery. There is no doubt that many persons were surprised (in government and business) by the magnitude of our increments from first to second quarter and from second to third quarter. This is not to say that we were alone in predicting a substantial improvement in real output, but the model came out in the correct neighborhood when there were great doubts in the minds of many persons that the recovery would be this strong. (Klein, 1964, pp. 28–30)

Another application of this model was to the problem of testing the extent to which the postwar recessions of 1953–4 and 1957–8 might be said to be 'inventory recessions', following Metzler's theory of the inventory cycle. Specifically, the problem posed was 'whether and how much specific dampening of inventory fluctuations in past recessions would have contributed to total output stabilization'. Klein and Popkin (1961) artificially dampened first the fluctuations of inventory investment (around a zero value) and, alternatively, the marginal inventory-sales coefficient by 25 and 75 per cent, respectively, in the two recessions under study and found that fluctuations in output, employment and other key variables were correspondingly reduced. On the basis of these simulation results, they concluded that the characterization of both recessions as 'inventory recessions' was indeed legitimate.[11] And finally, this model also provided an input in the basic calculations of the federal tax reduction bill of 1964.

To sum up, the Postwar Quarterly Model represented another important step forward in the history of macroeconometric model-building. However it had two important structural deficiencies; first, almost the entire component of government sector was treated exogenously, and second, the money market still played a very minor role in the short run. The model was eventually handed over to the Bureau of Economic Analysis (formerly the Office of Business Economics) in the US Department of Commerce, where it has been maintained and operated for several years as the BEA model (Liebenberg *et al.*, 1966, 1971; Hirsch *et al.*, 1974). In this version it contained an expanded and highly-developed government sector, which incorporated several tax rates and monetary policy variables. The model was used for short-term forecasting and policy evaluations by the Department of Commerce and, in one form or the other, by other government agencies, including the (President's) Council of Economic Advisers.

3 The LIU Model

Main features
Contemporaneously with Klein's 'A Postwar Quarterly Model', T. C. Liu, in 1963, presented another quarterly model, which was decribed as an exploratory model of effective demand in the postwar US economy.[12] It was based on a sample of 50 (quarterly) observations from the third quarter of 1947 to the fourth quarter of 1959, and was constructed with a view to analysing certain types of monetary and fiscal policy applications. The model contained 36 endogenous, 16 exogenous and 37 lagged endogenous variables. Of the 36 endogenous variables, 19 were determined by stochastic equations and 17 by definitional identities. Methodologically, the model belonged to the family of non-recursive interdependent systems, and was estimated by ordinary least squares as well as by two-stage least squares.

By comparison with the Klein–Goldberger model, the Liu Model also entailed a somewhat greater degree of disaggregation. There were three consumption functions, as in the Postwar Quarterly Model (consumers' services, durables and non-durable goods), three fixed investment functions (business construction, residential construction and producers' durable equipment), and a submodel of inventory investment (for non-farm business) and price movements. This submodel contained at least three different types of inventory variables: the actual stock, the desired stock and the equilibrium stock. The monetary sector of the model included five liquid assets, five interest rates and the ratio of excess reserves to required reserves. Separate equations were estimated for business liquid assets, personal holdings of currency and demand deposits, and personal holdings of time deposits and savings shares.[13] Nearly all equations contained some lagged variables, which were basically derived from a Koyck–Nerlove distributed lag scheme. Specifically, in the investment and consumption functions, the lagged variables were introduced to recognize the effects of past commitments and future expectations. And also, some 'nonlinearity and asymmetry effects' were captured through the capacity utilization variable.

None the less the structure of the model remained very simple and was deficient at least in two major respects. The entire labour sector was missing, as variables on employment and productivity did not appear explicitly anywhere in the model. Secondly, the entire foreign trade sector representing transactions in goods and services with the rest of the world was treated exogenously.

Applications

Before applying the model under a variety of policy assumptions and shocks, it was tested by generating *ex post* predictions for the second and the third quarters of 1961. With the exception of investment in non-farm business inventories, the extrapolated values were mostly found to be satisfactory.[14] Next, a set of eight simulation scenarios was generated. Each simulation started with the second quarter of 1961 as period 1 and continued for 50 consecutive periods (quarters). These scenarios demonstrated that the economy as described by the model was basically stable.

Simulation I served as a baseline solution for comparison purposes. It was generated by assuming a 'rapid increase in government purchases from the second quarter of 1961 to the end of 1962 (periods 1–7), with balanced budget achieved in the second quarter of 1962 (period 5)'. The results suggested that the model was basically stable and 'the economy was capable of withstanding the shock of a substantial and a fairly rapid reduction in the rate of increase of government purchases, at a price, of course (a mild recession)' (Liu, 1963, p. 327).

Simulations II, III and IV related to the government expenditure and balanced-budget multipliers. Simulation II assumed a one-shot reduction in government expenditure on goods and services in period 2; Simulation III assumed the same reduction in each period; and Simulation IV was based on less rapid increases in government expenditure than those assumed in Simulation I, with a balanced budget achieved in the same period 5.

The results showed that the depressing effect of a one-shot reduction in government expenditure on GNP was transient, and that the effects of a persistent reduction in every quarter were, as expected, more powerful and enduring. In the latter case, the maximum effect was reached only by the eighth quarter. This brought into focus the problem of timing in the use of government expenditure as a counter-cyclical measure. Specifically, it appeared that '(i)f a reduction in expenditure is put into effect only when a boom is already on the horizon and if this lower level of expenditure is maintained for a number of quarters, then the full effect of this policy would be in operation near the trough of the cycle' (ibid., p. 329). The value of the multiplier with respect to government expenditure in the case of a persistent change was found to be in the neighbourhood of 2.25, and in the case of a balanced budget it was substantially less. The pattern of the rate of change in the GNP deflator in these simulations almost corresponded to the path followed by real GNP itself.

Simulations V and VI related to the effects of changes in monetary policy, Simulation V assuming a one-shot increase in the short-term interest rate and Simulation VI a maintained increase. The effects of a one-shot increase in the interest rate on GNP as well as on its deflator were found to be transient, and those of the maintained increase 'fairly substantial in the initial period'. However, interestingly and eventually, in the latter case a kind of real balance effect took over; after 36 periods, the effect on GNP of a maintained increase in the interest rate became positive. Thus it appeared that, 'given a sufficiently long time, the direct and indirect real balance effects become greater than the restrictive effects of higher r_S and r_L interest rates'.

Simulations VII and VIII were rather interesting, as they dealt with the time of the response of fiscal and monetary policies. It was found that '(t)heoretically it is possible, by promptly and repeatedly changing the tax system, to avoid the recession ... and quickly to stabilize the rate of growth of GNP. Such a flexible tax system, however, would be difficult to devise in practice. On the other hand, an immediately responsive interest rate policy deliberately put into effect to counter cyclical movements would destabilize the economy' (ibid. p. 337). The undesirable last result followed from the lag structure of the effects of interest rate changes, thus showing a serious timing problem in the application of monetary policy.

The model results were finally summarized by the caveat that the conditions it portrayed were 'grossly over-simplified' and the limited simulations were 'inadequate' as a reference for making policy suggestions. This model influenced greatly the development of the Liu–Hwa model with monthly data, which appeared almost a decade later, in 1974. (See our discussion in Chapter 5 below.)

4 The Brookings Model

The Brookings Model represented a major milestone in the history of macroeconometric modelling. At the time of its construction in the early 1960s, it was the largest, most highly disaggregated and most ambitious model of the US economy. Moreover it was the first major outcome of team research. Its historic perspective may be underscored in the words of two of the principal participants:

In the continuum of science, time erodes memory, and the fragile achievements of yesteryear soon are forgotten. Today, econometric models of the United States and foreign economies are commonplace. But when we began to construct such a system in the early 1960s, there were few precedents and the viability of large-scale, structural models remained to be demonstrated. The principal achievement of the collaborative, inter-university effort which later became known as the Brookings model was that it blazed a trail followed by many others, leading to a multiplicity of the theoretical developments, models, and economic information systems.[15]

Its inception can be traced to the Social Science Research Council's (SSRC) Conference on Research on the Stability of the American economy held in June 1959, at Ann Arbor, Michigan. At this conference, a general consensus emerged that there was a need for a larger-scale model with many more details than previously used, and such a model should play a central role in the general analysis of business cycle problems and stabilization policies in the short run. Soon afterwards, a Committee of Economic Stability was established, which immediately approved a proposal for the development of a larger-scale econometric model to be sponsored by the SSRC under the co-chairmanship of Professor James S. Duesenberry and Lawrence R. Klein. And the model came to be known as the (SSRC)/Brookings Model.[16]

Structural highlights

The first approximation of the complete model contained over 200 equations (close to 150 were stochastic and the remaining were identities), and later the complete versions of this model permitted determination of more than 400 endogenous variables.[17] The model was estimated by using seasonally adjusted quarterly data for the period 1949–60. To quote from the first volume (Duesenberry *et al.*, 1965), as it was described by its principal investigators,

> In its basic form, our model is similar to its predecessors. Its structure depicts the economy as a set of interrelated dynamic processes involving production, generation and distribution of incomes, price and wage determination and purchases of goods and services by households, businesses and governments. A central role in these processes is played by the mutual feedback between production, income payments and purchases of goods and services ... The dynamic elements in our model, as in others, come from three sources: (1) lagged relationships and rate of change variables; (2) relationships including stock variables, where the stocks are cumulants of flows generated by the model; (3) changing exogenous variables and random shocks. (pp. 5–6)

The model contained a sectoral disaggregation which was much larger than that of any other previous model. Initially, it was fitted with seven producing sectors:

1. Agriculture;
2. Durable manufacturing;
3. Non-durable manufacturing;
4. Regulated industries (transport, communication, utilities);
5. Contract construction;
6. Trade; and a
7. Residual sector.

Indeed there were plans to expand eventually to 32 producing sectors, of which 20 were expected to be two-digit manufacturing industries. Moreover, six aspects of the economy which are either largely influenced by the government policy measures or are affected by the socioeconomic trends were given elaborate treatment. These were (1) agriculture, (2) foreign trade, (3) housing, (4) money and finance, (5) government income and receipts, and (6) demography (marriage rates, household formation, and labour force participation in particular).

A few observations on the various aspects of the model are noteworthy.[18] Consumption expenditures were broken down into five separate categories: new and net used automobiles, other durables, food and beverages, non-durable goods other than food and beverages, and services. The consumption function for each category was assumed to be of a classical type in which income, relative prices, capital stock or lagged consumption, and some additional factors such as credit terms and the availability of instalment financing entered as explanatory variables.

The analysis of investment expenditure included the sectoral models of residential construction, non-farm business plant and equipment, inventories, and orders functions for durable and non-durable manufacturing. Residential construction primarily depended on net household formation, a relative price variable based on a rental price index relative to a construction cost index, some rate of interest and a distributed lag of the past housing starts. As a matter of fact, housing starts were estimated through separate equations and were phased into the residential construction expenditures by a moving average variable. It was this moving average which accounted for the distributed lag effect. The inventories were initially disaggregated by production sectors (durable manufacturing, non-durable manufacturing, trade and others), and the decision process for each was based on the stock adjustment mechanism with some attention paid to the production capacity of the industry and government military orders. However this approach produced large errors in the model solution and the research was later expanded to a greater degree of disaggregation by splitting inventories according to three stages of fabrication (finished goods, semi-finished (in-process) goods and raw materials).

The investment equations generally represented the essential elements of neoclassical theory; they were derived by maximizing an objective function based on the level of discounted profits subject to a (Cobb–Douglas or CES) technological constraint, following theoretical development by Dale Jorgenson (1965). According to his derivation, the user cost or the rental price of capital measured by any of the (humped) distributed lag schemes became the standard explanatory variable in investment equations. This pioneering treatment of investment intentions introduced by Jorgenson was further augmented by realization functions developed by Robert Eisner (1965). The Brookings Model demonstrated for the first time that combining investment anticipation functions with realization functions 'produce[d] superior predictions of investment expenditure than the use of fixed automatic payout mechanisms on the intentions' (Fromm and Taubman, 1968, p. 7).[19]

The production function was normalized on labour requirements and was estimated implicitly following the version developed earlier by Edwin Kuh (1965). The level of employment and the number of hours worked were assumed to depend upon the level and the rate of change in real output, the beginning-of-period capital stock and the lagged values of the dependent variable. Thus the production sector was made dynamic in the framework of an adaptive relationship. The supply of labour primarily depended upon the level of and change in economic activity, as well as on some demographic factors. The Klein–Phillips type of relationship was used to determine wages, and prices were based on mark-ups over unit labour costs. However earlier solutions of the complete model revealed that 'the wages and prices sector was one of the larger contributors of errors in the aggregate results'.

The monetary sector, which was subject to somewhat 'benign neglect' in previous models, was extensively examined in the Brookings Model. Initially, as many as 30 equations were constructed to integrate the financial and the real sectors. There was also a condensed version which consisted of equations explaining households' and business's demands for money and near-money; specifically, there were equations for currency, demand and time deposits, free reserves held by the banks, the rate on time deposits, the term structure of interest rate and the appropriate identities. An extended version covered holdings of financial assets of the nonfinancial corporations, household borrowings, insurance claims, assets and liabilities of the banks, several interest rates and identities. In spite of all that, the interactions between money and real sectors in the Brookings Model remained relatively weak.

Even at its initial stages the Brookings Model had an elaborate public sector. Several specific items in the tax system, government outlays on goods and services, the social security system and welfare payments were separately endogenized. Later on a series of extended simulations with respect to fiscal policy was conducted.

A highly distinguishing feature of the Brookings Model was the methodological splicing of an input–output (inter-industry) system with a macroeconometric model. These two systems were integrated with the explicit aim of achieving the transformation of GNP expenditure components into industry outputs (of the eight producing sectors) and industrial prices into GNP component deflators. Thus the joint model determined both the national income account variables and the input–output variables, once all the parameters were estimated. The splicing technique used may be briefly explained as follows.

Let

$X = (n \times 1)$ output vector
$F = (n \times 1)$ final demand vector
$Y = (k \times 1)$ vector of GNP components
$A = (n \times n)$ square matrix of input–output coefficient a_{ij},
$C = (n \times k)$ matrix of the delivery coefficients c_{ij}, from sector i to the GNP component Y_j.

Then the output flow of the ith sector may be described as:

$$X_i = \sum_j a_{ij} X_j + F_i \tag{4.1}$$

and F_i, by regression analysis, may be expressed as a linear function of the k GNP components,

$$F_i = \sum_j c_{ij} Y_j. \tag{4.2}$$

The accounting restriction specified that the sum of $F_i(i=1,2...n)$ must be equal to GNP. Since the sum of $Y_j(j=1,2...k)$ is also equal to GNP, the c_{ij} coefficients were computed subject to these sums. Thus, for the entire Brookings Model, the transformation of sectoral outputs and GNP components was obtained as follows:

$$X = (I - A)^{-1} F \tag{4.3}$$
$$F = CY, \tag{4.4}$$

which (by substituting (4.4) into (4.3)) was stated as:

$$X = (I - A)^{-1}CY. \tag{4.5}$$

Similarly, in a dual mechanism, the transformation of sectoral industrial prices into GNP deflator components was achieved in an analogous way. Let

V = $(n \times 1)$ value added vector (of GNP originating by sector) corresponding to the gross output vector X
P_v = $(n \times 1)$ vector of sector prices
P_y = $(k \times 1)$ vector of GNP deflator components
B = $(n \times n)$ diagonal matrix of mark-up coefficients transforming value-added into gross output.

The value-added and the gross output of the ith sector can then be described in the production relationship as:

$$X_i = \sum_j a_{ji}X_i + v_i, \tag{4.6}$$

that is,

$$X_i = (1 - \sum_j a_{ji})^{-1}v_i \tag{4.6'}$$

which for n sectors may be expressed as:

$$X = BV \text{ or } B^{-1}X = V, \tag{4.7}$$

where a typical element of the diagonal matrix B is $1/(1 - \sum_j a_{ji})$.

The price transformations can be completed next by using the GNP identities in current prices. For example,

$$P'_v V = GNP = P'_y Y, \tag{4.8}$$

where the ' or transpose symbol in (4.8) indicates the vector dot product and is a form of matrix multiplication.

Substituting (4.5) and (4.7) into (4.8), we have:

$$P'_v B^{-1}(I - A)^{-1}CY = P'_y Y. \tag{4.9}$$

Because (4.9) is an identity which must hold for all conceivable values of Y and of its components, we obtain:

$$P'_v B^{-1}(I - A)^{-1}C = P'_y, \tag{4.10}$$

a row vector of deflators of the k GNP components. Each deflator is simply obtained as a weighted average of the sectoral prices. None the less, the complexity introduced by the feedback of the two systems was enormous, as both had to be solved simultaneously. This brings us to the solution techniques and the simulation aspects of the Brookings Model.

Solution techniques

It is in the area of methodological research that the most lasting contributions of the Brookings Model have been entrenched. The solution techniques and the simulation procedures which have become widely known today emerged from the intensive research undertaken on the Brookings Model during the five-year period 1964–9. There were two principal difficulties, both of which arose from the large size of the model. First, as has been already mentioned above, the model contained over 200 equations (and almost as many predetermined variables), even in the initial stages; however, its estimates were based on a sample of approximately 60 observations for the period 1949–60. Thus there was a fundamental problem of handling the degrees of freedom assumption, which was clearly being violated. Second, the presence of several non-linearities made the solution of the entire model highly complex. The first problem was dealt with by the property of block-recursiveness of the structure of the model and the second was overcome by an appropriate block-linear segmentation of the model.

At the time the Brookings Model was constructed, the simplicity of consistent estimation in recursive systems had become widely known through many publications of Herman Wold (for example, 1954 and 1960).[20] And, although the structure of the Brookings Model was not fully recursive, Franklin Fisher (1965) observed that the system could be divided into several interacting blocks and these blocks could be further ordered in a recursive chain. Thus he called the system approximately block-recursive.[21] A system may be treated as block-recursive if its coefficient matrix formed by the blocks of elements or submatrices can be shown to be triangular, and appropriate conditions on the error terms are met. That is, it may have non-zero submatrices on the principal diagonal and below but only zero submatrices above it. In other words, the elements within each block may be fully interdependent but the ordering of the blocks must be subject to a recursive structure, which may then be interpreted as a causal chain.

On a detailed examination of the Brookings Model, Fisher was able to establish the interconnections among various blocks in a form of a recursive scheme as indicated in Figure 4.1.[22] Blocks of relationships are arranged in such a way that elements within a block (represented, for

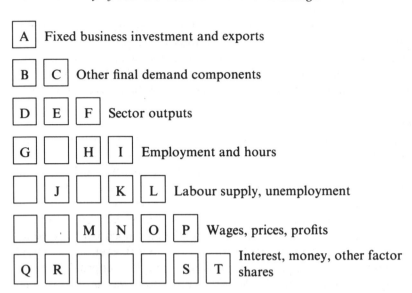

Figure 4.1   Causal block ordering of the Brookings Model

example, by a position of a given row) are mutually interdependent as well as being dependent on the blocks represented by the rows above. However they are independent of the sectoral blocks associated with the rows below. For instance, the initial block, in A, belonging to the top of the array in row one contains fixed investment and export functions and these are basically dependent on the predetermined variables. The second block contains remaining components of final demand; it depends upon itself, in C, as well as on the first block of fixed business investment and exports, in B. Next in the array is a block of sector outputs, which by using input–output methods allocates final aggregate demand among sectors to determine industry outputs. Thus it depends upon itself (through inter-industry structure), in F, and the previous two blocks, in D and E, which determine final demand. The employment and hours block comes next. It depends upon itself, in I, and on fixed business investment and sector outputs, but not on other final demand, as shown by the unlettered block. It is at this stage that production functions are transformed to determine labour requirements. Similarly, labour market conditions are determined next, and these are followed by a block of relationships comprising wages, prices and profits. Labour supply and unemployment can be seen to depend upon other final demand, employment and hours and itself but not on fixed business investment and sector outputs. Finally, the system is completed by a block of equations of the money market, which determine both interest rates and deposits, and also lead to interest income and other factor shares.

This property of block-recursiveness reduced substantially the degree of interdependence in the model, and was thus used ingeniously in obtaining consistent estimates by two-stage least squares and limited-information maximum likelihood techniques. Following the rules devised by Fisher, consistent estimates of the individual equations were first obtained within each block, and then the entire model was re-estimated taking into account the interactions among the blocks.[23] With regard to estimation, it is also important to emphasize that the model structure utilizes a large number of lagged endogenous variables, with some lags as long as eight quarters, and a relatively small number of exogenous variables. The explanation for several variables was thus provided through autoregressive schemes. Key exogenous variables were population and instruments of monetary and fiscal control. Consistent estimates of equations within a particular block were obtained by using the predetermined variables of that block, including the lagged endogenous variables of the preceding blocks, as instruments. The final estimation of the various blocks of the entire model was based on instrumental variables obtained from linear combinations of current and lagged exogenous and lagged endogenous variables from later blocks, together with the predetermined variables associated with a given block.

Alternative policy simulations, with emphasis on cyclical fluctuations and short-run stabilization policies, were the focus of the Brookings Model from the outset. However the non-linearities of the system created an important difficulty in obtaining the solutions required for analysis. After some initial experimentation, an iterative solution of the entire system was finally achieved by making use of block-linear segmentations and the block-recursive structure of the model.[24]

Applications and policy simulations
With the programming problems in obtaining dynamic simulations resolved, the model was tested by *ex post* forecasts for the period from the first quarter of 1961 to the fourth quarter of 1964. It was also subjected to large-scale multiplier calculations and to the analysis of variety of economic policies. The entire 1968 volume prepared by Fromm and Taubman was devoted to these aspects of the model; specifically, the policy issues examined were: the delicate and complex aspects of the balanced budget multiplier, Phillips-type stabilization schemes, the income tax cut of 1964, and the excise tax cut of 1965. The *ex post* forecasts as a whole were fairly accurate, major swings in real magnitudes were captured reasonably well,

and the slowdown in the rate of growth that the economy actually experienced was tracked with a minimal error.

One-quarter *impact* multipliers computed from this highly interdependent system turned out to be somewhat higher than those derived from the existing models, which were generally highly recursive in nature. A high degree of recursion is expected to dampen the initial response of the system to any external shock. A one-quarter impact multiplier of GNP with respect to an increase in consumption expenditure on automobiles was reported by Fromm and Taubman to be 1.59. More interestingly, as a part of the policy analysis, they examined the course of the US economy under a variety of altered conditions while comparing results each time with the baseline solution. In addition to the detailed simulations corresponding to the excise tax cut of 1965, eight of the other experiments reported in *Policy Simulations* (1968) were based on the following different assumptions:

1. an increase in government expenditure on durables;
2. an increase in government expenditure on nondurables;
3. an increase in government employment;
4. an increase in government expenditure on construction;
5. a decrease in personal federal income taxes;
6. a decrease in personal federal income taxes plus monetary policy;
7. a lowering of reserve requirements on demand deposits from 0.149 to 0.139; and
8. an increase in unborrowed reserves of the commercial banks through open market operations.

A close comparison of the results of these policy simulations revealed that the 'largest impacts on real GNP after ten quarters are obtained from the increases in government nondurables and construction expenditures, ... income tax cuts cause the largest spurts in consumption while the monetary variables have the greatest impact on real investment' (p. 28). And, somewhat surprisingly, it was found that 'all stimulative policies cause a fall (in relation to the original solution) in the rate of increase in prices, at least for a period of time' (p. 28).[25] Moreover 'all policies result in the deterioration of the net exports of goods and services account' (p. 29). It was also noted 'that the monetary policy shifts must be substantial if the course of the economy is to be changed, at least in a recessionary situation' (p. 49). Finally, their experiment with respect to the excise tax cut led to the conclusion that, working through the price equations, it 'expands real output by impressive amounts. An increase of up to $2.4 in real GNP is obtained by every dollar given up in tax revenue. In the range of the reductions investigated, the greater the tax cut, the larger the 10-quarter real GNP multiplier. In this experiment, prices fall initially, but, eventually, economic expansion pushes them back towards the original solution' (p. 80).

Finally, Fromm and Taubman evaluated the welfare implications of each policy by applying three different utility functions:

1. Linear: $U_t = \sum_i \beta_i X_i$;
2. Cobb-Douglas: $U_t = \prod_i x_i^{\beta_i}$;
3. CES: $U_t = (\sum_i \beta_i X_i^\delta)$;

where U_t is the utility in period t of the ratio of simulated values to the baseline solution values of the economic objectives (X_i), during the same time period. In the constant elasticity of substitution (CES) function, the value of δ was set successively at 0.5, -0.5, -1.0, and 2.0.

Two separate schemes of weights (β_i) over six arguments $(i = 1,2,....,6)$ were employed to compute the utility indexes. The two schemes of weights were:

1. Equal weights, $\beta_i = 1$ for all i;
2. Proportional weights, β_i average share in real GNP for all expenditure items except one, and 0.5 for all other items.

The six arguments with their proportional weights were as follows:

1. Personal consumption expenditure in constant dollars $(\beta = 0.67)$;
2. Gross private domestic investment other than inventory investment in constant dollars $(\beta = 0.13)$;
3. Government expenditure in constant dollars $(\beta = 0.19)$;
4. The reciprocal of the unemployment rate $(\beta = 0.5)$;
5. Government budget surplus in current dollars $(\beta = 0.10)$;
6. The reciprocal of the GNP implicit price deflator $(\beta = 0.5)$. The utility of outcomes over time was aggregated (to derive the current discounted value) as follows:

$$U_0 = \sum_{t=1}^{m} \frac{U_t}{(1+r)^t},$$

where r denotes a time preference rate (4, 6, 8 and 10 per cent were used) and m is the time horizon limit.

The ranking of the computed utility indexes corresponding to fourteen different types of policies is provided in Tables 5.7–5.9 (pp. 119, 120 and 122) of the volume.

Fromm and Taubman found that, except for one CES function (that with the lowest elasticity of substitution), the shifts in the monetary variables were utility-maximizing policies. After that, still ranking by the utility index, came the government expenditure policies. (If one uses the criterion of the values of the multipliers, the ranking of these two policies would be reversed.) Next came the excise tax cuts (two variants were tried). Finally, using either the utility index or the values of the multipliers, the income tax cuts were at the bottom of the scale.

Fromm and Taubman noted two specific qualifications to this analysis. First, the monetary policies had high ranks on a utility basis because they tended to increase the government surplus, while the fiscal policies decreased it (raised the deficit). But this ignores disruption costs associated with the volatility in money markets and interest rates that discretionary monetary policy may impose, which, it could be argued, are considerable (even if difficult to measure). Secondly, there may be somewhat more *uncertainty* associated with monetary policy than with fiscal policy, particularly if the latter is directed to specific sectors of the economy. (Of course, this does not mean that monetary policy is not powerful, or that it does not have a role to play in stabilization policy, in the view of Fromm and Taubman.)

Finally, the analysis of the welfare implications of the model in terms of the rankings of various policies was closed with a general caveat:

> These orderings of policies are not to be regarded as a prescription for government decisionmakers. Aside from any questions of the validity and accuracy of the model, neither the multipliers nor the utility functions (even if augmented with additional arguments endogenous to the model) reflect the many other considerations which impinge on a policy choice. Such issues as the degree of government intervention, intergroup and interregional inequities, implications for long-run resource allocation and other social costs and benefits which are difficult to quantify must be taken into account. (Fromm and Taubman, p. 123).

They noted as well that, in a practical policy exercise, both the initial conditions and the degree of use of a particular policy instrument must be taken into account.

Stochastic properties

Moving beyond the now classic work of Irma and Frank L. Adelman (1959) with the Klein–Goldberger Model, A. L. Nagar (1969) made an extensive analysis of the dynamic cyclical properties of the Brookings Model. In this task he was particularly aided by a simple method developed by Michael McCarthy to generate random errors with and without serial correlation for perturbing the system. This method was independent of the relationship between the size of the sample (T) and the number of stochastic equations (n).[26] The solution of the system shocked by random errors with specified properties thus generated stochastic simulations.

Altogether, Nagar obtained 20 solutions for each of the 38 quarters for the period 1953: 3 for 1962: 4. The sampling distributions of the stochastic simulations, the relationship between deterministic and stochastic simulations and the time paths of the policy simulations with stochastic shocks provided important insight into the dynamic stochastic structure of the model. The sampling distribution of the stochastic simulations was analysed by its summary statistics, the mean, the standard deviation and the range (minimum and maximum). It was found that, in all cases, the standard deviation and the range of these solutions increased with time. This result was not entirely unexpected because, owing to the presence of lagged endogenous variables, the prediction error builds up rapidly. By and large, the nonstochastic and the mean stochastic solutions were found to be fairly close to each other.

In terms of the accuracy of prediction of the actual course of economic activity as represented by real GNP, it was found

> that the nonstochastic original ('pseudo-realistic') solution tracks the economy reasonably well, especially in early years. The second quarter of 1953, the initial conditions for the solution, was the peak quarter prior to the 1953–54 recession. Whereas the economy's output dropped from that point, the model 'marks time' for two quarters and then begins to drop. After that, the decline in real GNP to the trough of the recession matches that of the economy almost exactly. The same holds true for the rise from the trough to the subpeak at the end of 1955. (Nagar, 1969, p. 442).

Subsequently the model overpredicted the decline in real GNP in early and mid-1956 by a somewhat greater amount than the actual. 'In 1957 the model peaks at the beginning while the economy peaked at mid-year. After the peak, the model shows a mild recession while the economy actually had a more severe decline ... The story for the 1960–61 recession is slightly different' (p. 442).

All in all, it was noted that the model reflected 'cyclical behavior extremely well early in the simulation period and less well as the prediction period is lengthened'. This was not entirely surprising, 'since stochastic shocks in the relationships between endogenous variables are damped in the model but not in the real world. In other words, better predictions of 1957–58 and 1960–61 would have been observed if initial conditions closer to those dates had been selected' (p. 443–4). In terms of the long-term growth path, 'the model passes through the peaks of the post-1953 recessions, a not inconsiderable achievement given that the last peak occurs seven years after the initial simulation quarter'. The model gave a very poor fit on the rate of unemployment. In the policy shocks, the long-run multiplier on real GNP of the income tax reduction appeared to be roughly 1.1.

Epilogue

In due course, the Brookings Model project became the centre for theoretical and methodological research on econometric model-building, and the model played a pivotal role in shaping applied econometric analysis throughout the world. In spite of the fact that the initial aim of the project of a widely accepted operational model for the contemporary short-term economic applications did not fully materialize, and the model was never used as intensively as originally contemplated, the technology generated by the project left a deep impact on the models to come. The project, in the sense of active model maintenance, was terminated in 1972.

For example, soon after, the splicing of a macroeconometric model with an interindustry input–output model became a common feature, among others, of Preston's model (1972, 1975), the Wharton Model (McCarthy 1972; Duggal *et al.*, 1974) and the CANDIDE model (Bodkin, 1976); the detailed financial sector which became a nuclear part of the Fed-MIT-Penn Model grew out of the Brookings project (Section 5 below); an anticipation–realization functional specification developed by Jorgenson and Eisner, which for technical reasons could not be fully implemented in simulations of the Brookings Model, was later fully integrated in the models of Fair (1971), OBE (Liebenberg *et al.*, 1966, 1971) and Wharton; Edwin Kuh's formulation of labour requirements from the aggregate production function was soon extended and incorporated in the revised Wharton Model (McCarthy, 1972); and Albert Ando carried over much of the original work of Paul Taubman and Roger Bolton on the public sector to the Fed-MIT-Penn Model.

As is apparent from the above discussion, it is in the area of methodological developments in the application of large-scale modelling that the most lasting contributions of the whole project have been made, sectoral research apart. On reviewing a decade of research contributions of the Brookings project, Klein (1975) rightly claimed,

> The procedures that are now routine in computer dynamic simulation at virtually every econometric center of the world stem from the research done between 1964 and 1969 at the Brookings model project. This is not to claim that simulation techniques would not have been developed, but they might not have developed in their present form, and it is virtually certain that they would have been seriously delayed but for the technological breakthroughs of the project. (p. 21)

First Charles Holt developed the SIMULATE programme; this was followed by a major further contribution by Edwin Kuh and Lawrence Erdman, who developed a new approach by treating each equation as a separate block. According to Klein, it was the success of the Kuh–Erdman approach with the Brookings Model that finally 'gave rise to the rapid development of Gauss-Seidel programming for dynamic simulation on nonlinear econometric models. Programs with many refinements were written by Michael Hartley and Morris Norman' (Klein, 1975, p. 23).

The Brookings Model was basically a 'modular' composite that continued to evolve over several years. With all its contributions to the art and science of large-scale model-building, it had its critics too. In particular, a critique of Basmann (1972) and an accompanying rejoinder by Fromm and Klein (1972) should not go unnoticed. Basmann's critique was based primarily on that first volume (Duesenberry *et al.*, 1965); it questioned the 'language game of econometric practice' that the model was alleged to have introduced. Addressing mainly the philosophy of statistical inference and its usefulness in ascertaining structural or behavioural relationships, Basmann (to quote Karl Brunner (1972, p. iv)) charged that 'econometric practice has evolved into numerology analogous in some respects to astrology'. After opening his critique with some (presumably)[27] laudatory comments that the Brookings Model 'can safely and justly be regarded as the exemplar of current research into econometrics', and that it 'will set the standard for, and exert a profound influence on, the development of econometrics and its teaching in our graduate schools for decades to come' (pp. 3–4), he assaulted the model on two counts: first, that the structural economic hypothesis represented by the model lacked a sufficient 'sharpness' of formulation to be empirically testably in practice, and second, that 'the quantitative foundations of the hypothesis represented' were seriously defective.

This harsh assessment by Basmann was attributed by Fromm and Klein (1972) to the reading of a non-econometrician, 'an incomplete reading and a misinterpretation and overemphasis of certain statements' in the first volume (Duesenberry *et al.*, 1965). They closed their spirited defence of the model with the remarks:

> ...It is unnecessary here to argue about the nature of science and the discovery of truth. We need merely observe that knowledge is cumulative and that tests of the theories of the present are the stepping stones to the progress of the future. If we pursued Basmann's thesis to its ultimate conclusion, inductive science must perish. Nothing can be quantified absolutely (except by God), for everything is relative. For example, given Einstein's theory of relativity, even a perfect balance could not find two Basmann-equivalent weights.
>
> The economic analysis, stabilization, and growth problems of our day may not be solved by the Brookings model. But neither are they served by Bas-

mann's nihilistic call to return to the fundamentals. We are well acquainted with the principles of quantitative logic, yet thank Basmann for his pedantic restatement. Our only lament is that he did not concentrate his considerable talents on more vital econometric and statistical problems. We need methods of selecting from among alternative specifications, methods for resolving multicollinearity difficulties, complete system nonlinear estimation techniques, better measures of seasonal variation, and many other items to improve the state of economic science. It seems to us that it is Basmann who would be the prophet, not we. If so, then more constructive leadership and contributions are needed than his present critique. (Fromm and Klein, 1972, p. 61)

And so did the task during the 1960s move forward.

5   The MPS Model

We close this chapter with a discussion of the MPS Model (for MIT-Penn-SSRC), which was formerly known as the FMP (or Fed-MIT-Penn) Model. This model, which was begun in the late 1960s, is an ideal link between the present and the following chapter, as the model has flourished throughout the 1970s and was still being maintained in the late 1980s. The model began as a joint project of the Federal Reserve Board and Professors Albert Ando and Franco Modigliani. Later, the Federal Reserve Board dropped out, but the Social Science Research Council (of the United States) joined the project, which thus was given additional viability. The guiding lights of this research have been Professors Albert Ando (of the University of Pennsylvania) and Franco Modigliani (of MIT), particularly the former. The first initials of the institutions of the three principal partners have been permuted to form a charming acronym. The presentation in this section is based on Ando *et al.* (1972), which summarizes the model as it existed in November 1969, despite the fact that the model has evolved (and grown) considerably since then; this is done for ease of access to the secondary sources. Other important sources for this section are Ando (1974), Ando and Modigliani (1969), Helliwell *et al.* (1973), and Intriligator (1978) pp. 448–9.

   The version of the model under study here contains roughly 170 equations, of which 67 are behavioural equations (estimated to a postwar quarterly sample, apparently by versions of the ordinary least squares technique). The technique of block simulations was widely used as a device for selecting the final versions of equations of the model, as Ando and Modigliani (1969) have indicated. In comparison to most of the models of the time, and building on the work of the Brookings Model, the MPS model had an extensive financial sector; in addition, the links with the real sector were developed in some depth. In addition to the Financial Sector, five other model sectors distinguished in Ando *et al.* (1972) are:

Final Demand, Distribution of Income, Taxes and Transfers, the Labour Market and Prices.

We may now rapidly (and abusively) summarize the six sectors of the model. The key equation of the Final Demand sector is the consumption function, in which current consumption per capita is expressed as a 12-term distributed lag of real disposable income per capita (with a long-run MPC of 0.61) and a four-term distributed lag of real wealth per capita (with the long-run effect equal to 0.057, after expressing units in comparable terms).[28] It is interesting to note that the primary effect of restrictive monetary policy is to reduce consumption through a fall in the market value of equities (and hence in the wealth term), via a rise in interest rates. The distinction is also made between consumption expenditures (which include all outlays on durable goods) and the concept of consumption itself, which measures only the value of services rendered by consumer durable goods. Other endogenous categories of expenditure include all outlays on plant and equipment separately, which are based on a version of the rental price of capital and for which equations were developed by Charles Bischoff; equations for the housing market (in which financial factors play a subsidiary role), inventory investment (based on a version of a stock adjustment model), a single equation for imports (recognizing the role of this expenditure category as a safety valve for an overheated economy), and three categories of state and local government expenditures (construction, employee compensation and other), reflecting an econometric version of Wagner's Law. By a count of equations, the Final Demand sector is the largest sector of the MPS model. We note that federal government expenditures and exports are exogenous in the MPS model.

The Distribution of Income sector is a development of ideas in previous econometric models (particularly Brookings), and we may pass over it rapidly. The Taxes and Transfers sector has an interesting submodel of unemployment insurance (payments and contributions) as well as a submodel containing accounting relationships for the deficits of the federal government and all other governments (state and local). The Labour Market sector reflects implicit production function relationships (with lags and short-term productivity effects), in order to obtain requirements for total man-hours employed. There is also an equation for the average number of hours worked per employee, with the number of employees then obtained by identity. The labour force is obtained from a global participation rate equation in which the participation rate has an upward trend during the sample period, together with a predominance of additional worker effects. The amount of unemployment (and, by identity, its rate as a proportion of the labour force) is then obtained residually.

The Prices sector contains two equations that are of particular interest. The wage adjustment relationship (of the Klein–Phillips variety) explains the two-quarter rate of nominal wage change by the corresponding measure for consumer prices (with considerably less than full adjustment for real wages, at a marginal coefficient of 0.42), by the rate of change of corporate cash flow, and finally by changes in the rate of social insurance contributions. The general price level equation explains the evolution of the deflator for non-farm business product in terms of lagged adjustment, the wage rate (with a unitary elasticity in both the long and short run), output per man-hour, material costs and an indicator of current and lagged product market demand pressures; all explanatory variables have the expected signs, and this key price equation can be regarded as incorporating a version of the mark-up hypothesis. Note, however, the unimportance of capital costs (at least explicitly) in this model of price formation. The rest of the sector reflects a general proportionality of all other price deflators to the key deflator, as well as expressing the obvious accounting identities between real and nominal expenditure magnitudes.

The Financial Sector has a detailed submodel of the money markets (the banking sector), with a number of exogenous policy instruments, such as legal reserve ratios and the discount rate of the Fed. There are also equations for the corporate bond rate, the commercial loan rate, the municipal bond rate, and the mortgage rate. In addition, there are equations for time deposits (both passbook deposits and certificates of deposits), as well as for savings and loan associations, mutual savings banks, life insurance reserves, and an identity which measures the flows generated by savings into thrift institutions for purposes of financing new housing. (This latter variable has an obvious application in the Final Demand sector, for the housing starts equations in particular.) However the most interesting equation of this sector (and perhaps the whole model) is the dividend yield equation, in which the ratio of dividends to share prices is explained as a long distributed lag in the corporate bond rate (with a unitary coefficient in total), a long distributed lag in the rate of change of consumer prices (with a negative effect presumably reflecting the attraction of common stocks in inflationary periods), a dummy for the 1962 stock market crash, and a non-linear trend term which has a negative effect over the sample period. While this equation would probably not be very successful for a speculator operating in the New York Stock Exchange, it represents a return to the grand tradition of Tinbergen (summarized in Chapter 2) in attempting to treat the market for shares of equities as endogenous. It also foreshadows some interesting work of Eckstein and associates in the DRI Model (following chapter) in this regard. The entire Financial Sector represents an attempt to capture econometrically the Yale Model of portfolio adjustment (for example, Tobin, 1969) and as such entails a certain number of compromises between theoretical rigour and the exigencies of econometric fitting. It is thus comparable to the RDX2 Model of the Canadian economy, discussed in Chapter 9 below.

The MPS Model has been used extensively for studies of stabilization policy in the context of the US economy, and in particular to attempt to answer the question of the accuracy of the monetarist shorthand view of the US macroeconomy (always assuming that the MPS Model is itself sufficiently accurate to make this judgement!). See, for example, Ando and Modigliani (1969) and Ando (1974). The first study introduced the now familiar concept of dynamic multipliers with a time pattern of an inverted 'U'; additional real income and employment from a maintained stimulus may not only fail to grow forever, but they may even reverse themselves, providing an econometric equivalent to the popular concept of 'crowding out'. Ando and Modigliani also constructed an interesting decomposition of the full multiplier effect from the entire model, adding model sectors successively to yield new insights into the sources of convergence or instability. Ando (1974) argues that the MPS Model suggests that the US macroeconomy is more complicated (and, in particular, less stable) than the monetarist point of view would suggest, a point taken up in Modigliani's presidential address (1977) to the American Economic Association. Helliwell *et al.* (1973) studied linked simulations of the MPS Model with the RDX2 Model of the Canadian economy, which they consider to be a legitimate exercise as the two models are intellectually similar (which in turn is not surprising, as they share a central bank parentage and even some model-builders in common). The results of this study are summarized in Chapter 9 below.

Notes

1. Kermit Gordon in the Foreword to *Policy Simulations with An Econometric Model* by Gary Fromm and Paul Taubman (Brookings Institute and North-Holland, 1968).
2. The reader is warned that the authors write this statement from the perspective of past project managers, so that a possible bias is declared!
3. It is often found, on the basis of such experiments, that the equation (or equation group) which is best on single equation criteria (or an examination of the limited group) is not the best complement to the overall model.
4. Other examples are Data Resources, Inc., and the CANDIDE project of the Government of Canada.
5. Lawrence R. Klein, 'A Postwar Quarterly Model: Description and Applications', in *Models of Income Determination*, Studies in Income and Wealth, Vol. 28, NBER, 1964.
6. Harold Barger and Lawrence R. Klein, 'A Quarterly Model for the United States Economy', *Journal of the American Statistical Association*, Vol. 49, September 1954.
7. 'A Postwar Quarterly Model', p. 42.
8. Specifically, an index of consumer buying plans for new cars and other household

appliances was used in the equation for consumer durables; the data from the Office of Business Economics – Securities and Exchange Commission on investment intentions were used in the equation for plant and equipment; the data on housing starts appeared in the equation for residential construction; and the backlog of orders was used as an anticipatory variable in the inventory investment equation.

9. In the formulation of the aggregate production function, the two inputs, in addition to a time trend, were labour and capital.

10. The Wharton School Index of the Capacity Utilization Rate was constructed as follows. Using seasonally adjusted monthly series, averaged to quarters, time charts for each of the 30 major components of the Federal Reserve Index of Industrial Production were plotted, major peaks were established by inspection, and pairs of successive peaks were joined by linear segments of trend lines. The ratios of actual production to trends drawn through peaks gave the percentage of capacity utilization in each industry. The weighted average of the capacity utilization rates of these industries was used as an index to derive the amount of utilized capital to enter as an input in the production function.

11. There were a number of simplifications made to facilitate the calculation of the simulated time paths, which were then calculated with a desk calculator. The extent to which it is legitimate to break into an economic system and operate on endogenous variables or structural parameters (as distinct from exogenous variables, particularly policy variables) is controversial. Indeed it is possible that the treatment of some other endogenous variable would have produced similar results. Nevertheless the results are at least consistent with the view that these two downturns were 'inventory recessions'.

12. Ta-Chung Liu, 'An Exploratory Quarterly Econometric Model of Effective Demand in the Postwar U.S. Economy', *Econometrica*, vol. 31, no. 3, July 1963, pp. 301–48.

13. Another component of liquid assets, US savings bonds held by consumers and non-profit organizations, was exogenous. Time deposits and savings shares were treated more in the nature of savings rather than liquid assets, as they were 'assumed to be an increasing function of income and the rates of interest they earn' (p. 31).

14. Even in the case of investment in inventories, the 1960–1 turning-point was captured correctly although the magnitudes were inaccurately predicted.

15. The editors in the preface of *The Brookings Model: Perspective and Recent Developments*, eds Gary Fromm and Lawrence R. Klein (North-Holland, 1975).

16. The model was first known as the SSRC model, then was called the SSRC-Brookings model, and finally the Brookings model. More than 30 economists with expertise in particular sectors collaborated in the construction of this model. Various aspects of its construction spanned the decade of the 1960s and beyond. The research has appeared in series of volumes which may be listed chronologically: *The Brookings Quarterly Econometric Model of the United States*, eds J. S. Duesenberry, G. Fromm, L. R. Klein and E. Kuh (Rand McNally and North Holland, 1965); *Policy Simulations with An Econometric Model*, Gary Fromm and Paul Taubman (1968); *The Brookings Model: Some Further Results*, eds J. S. Duesenberry, G. Fromm, L. R. Klein and E. Kuh (Rand McNally and North Holland, 1969); *Tax Incentives and Capital Spending*, ed. G. Fromm (Brookings Institution, 1971); *The Brookings Model: Perspective and Recent Developments*, eds Gary Fromm and Lawrence R. Klein (North-Holland and American Elsevier, 1975). There were also other contributions of the project. For a critique of the model and some ensuing spirited debate, see Basmann and a reply by Gary Fromm and Lawrence R. Klein in *Problems and Issues in Current Econometric Practice*, ed. Karl Brunner (Ohio State University, 1972).

17. Fromm and Klein reported in the first volume (Duesenberry *et al.*, 1965, p. 722), 'The exact number is not easy to state because there are many trivial and definitional equations that we refrain from eliminating by substitution, for matters of convenience.' Of course, it is generally true that the number of identities (and hence endogenous variables) is somewhat arbitrary in a large-scale model.

18. These observations are based on one of the earlier versions, specifically the one presented in the second volume (Fromm and Taubman, 1968).

19. See Chapter 2 by Jorgenson and Chapter 3 by Eisner in Duesenberry *et al.* (1965). This approach was implemented in later macroeconomic models of Fair (1971), OBE (Liebenberg, Hirsch and Popkin, 1966; Liebenberg, Green and Hirsch, 1971) and Wharton (Adams and Klein, 1972).

20. A system is defined as fully recursive if its matrix of linear coefficients of the endogenous variables is triangular and the variance–covariance matrix of the error terms is diagonal. Such a system can be consistently estimated by a series of single equation least squares regressions.

21. The system was approximately block-recursive as 'triangularity' was achieved by ignoring some relatively minor effects and also some lag relationships.

22. Reproduced from Duesenberry *et al.* (1965) p. 28. As we saw in the preceding chapter, this type of analysis is now done more systematically through the applications of graph theory. Some recent examples include Gallo and Gilli (1990), Garbel and Gilli (1984) and Keller (1979).

23. Fisher devised the rules based on the technique of structurally ordered instrumental variables; it consisted of choosing instrumental variables in accordance with the causal ordering of the system. See Fisher, in Duesenberry *et al.* (1965).

24. The breakthrough in this area came around 1965 when Charles Holt developed the SIMULATE programme to solve the Brookings Model. However, the progress in this area has been particularly rapid and Charles Holt's solution programme became obsolescent after a short period. It was displaced by programmes developed by Ross Preston; further contributions were made by Edwin Kuh and Lawrence Erdman, who suggested the use of a single equation block. See the discussion by Fromm and Klein (1969), Chapter II of Duesenberry *et al.*, *The Brookings Model: Some Further Results.*

25. This may well be an artifact due to the use of actual unit labour costs as a key explanatory variable in the price equations together with the phenomenon of short-term productivity gains as a result of increased demand stimulation. Most later models use normalized unit labour costs as an important explanatory variable for the price equations, to mitigate this apparent anomaly.

26. It was valid regardless of whether *n* was larger or smaller than *T*; although Nagar did find some difficulties for the case $n \geq T$. None the less the method was found to be so simple and attractive that it became the basis for stochastic simulations for many more macroeconometric models to come, and thus it opened up an entire new dimension for the analysis.

27. In his further criticism, Basmann even denied that he had meant these remarks to be complimentary. 'I regret that Fromm and Klein inferred from my prediction that I was praising their work' (Basmann in Karl Brunner, 1972, p. 66).

28. As Ando himself (1974) notes, ideally the consumption function should contain disposable *labour* income as the key explanatory variable, following upon the Modigliani Ando–Brumberg life-cycle hypothesis of consumption behaviour. However the data are very difficult to obtain for this concept, and so we have a compromise between theoretical rigour and the exigencies of data gathering, as sometimes happens in macroeconometric modelling.

References

Adams, F. G. and L. R. Klein (1972) 'Anticipations Variables in Macroeconometric Models', in B. Strumpel (ed.), *Human Behavior in Economic Affairs* (Amsterdam: North-Holland).

Adelman, Irma and Frank L. Adelman (1959) 'The Dynamic Properties of the Klein–Goldberger Model', *Econometrica*, vol. 27, no. 4 (October). Reprinted in John W. Hooper and Marc Nerlove, *Selected Readings in Econometrics From* Econometrica (Cambridge, Mass.: MIT Press).

Ando, Albert (1974) 'Some Aspects of Stabilization Policies, the Monetarist Controversy, and the MPS Model', *International Economic Review*, vol. 15, no. 3 (October) pp. 541–71.

Ando, Albert and Franco Modigliani (1969) 'Econometric Analysis of Stabilization Policies', *American Economic Review, Papers and Proceedings*, vol. 59, no. 2 (May) pp. 296–314.

Ando, Albert, Franco Modigliani and Robert Rasche (1972) 'Appendix to Part One: Equations and Definitions of Variables for the FRB-MIT-PENN Econometric Model, November, 1969', pp. 543–98 in Bert G. Hickman (ed.), *Econometric Models of Cyclical Behavior*, vol. 1, no. 36, by the Conference on Research in Income and Wealth (New York and London: Columbia University Press).

Barger, Harold and Lawrence R. Klein (1954) 'A Quarterly Model for the United States Economy', *Journal of the American Statistical Association*, vol. 49, no. 207 (September).

Basmann, R. L. (1972) 'The Brookings Quarterly Econometric Model: Science or Number Mysticism?' and 'Argument and Evidence in the Brookings–S.S.R.C. Philosophy of Econometrics', respectively, Chapters 1 and 3 in K. Brunner (ed.), *Problems and Issues in Current Econometric Practice* (College of Administrative Science, Ohio State University, Columbus, Ohio).

Bodkin, Ronald G. (1976) 'A Large-Scale Input–Output Econometric Model of the Canadian Economy (CANDIDE)', Chapter Two (pp. 27–44) in Karen R. Polenske and Jiri V. Skolka (eds), *Advances in Input–Output Analysis* (Cambridge, Mass.: Ballinger Publishing Company).

Bolton, R. E. (1969) 'Predictive Models for State and Local Government Purchases', in Duesenberry *et al.* (eds) *The Brookings Model*, pp. 223–67.

Brunner, Karl (ed.) (1972) *Problems and Issues in Current Econometric Practice* (College of Administrative Science, Ohio State University, Columbus, Ohio).

Duesenberry, James S., Gary Fromm, Lawrence R. Klein, and Edwin Kuh (eds) (1965) *The Brookings Quarterly Econometric Model of the United States* (Chicago and Amsterdam: Rand McNally & Company and North-Holland).

_____ (1969) *The Brookings Model: Some Further Results* (Chicago and Amsterdam: Rand McNally & Company and North-Holland).

Duggal, Vijaya G., Lawrence R. Klein and Michael D. McCarthy (1974) 'The Wharton Model Mark III: A Modern IS-LM Construct', *International Economic Review*, vol. 15, no. 3 (October) pp. 572–94.

Eisner, R. (1965) 'Realization of Investment Anticipations', Duesenberry *et al.*, (eds), *The Brookings Quarterly Econometric Model*, pp. 95–128.

Evans, M. K. and L. R. Klein (1967) *The Wharton Econometric Forecasting Model* (Philadelphia: Economics Research Unit, University of Pennsylvania).

Fair, R. C. (1971) *A Short-Run Forecasting Model of the United States Economy* (Lexington: D. C. Heath).

Fisher, F. M. (1965) 'Dynamic Structure and Estimation in Economy-Wide Econometric Models', in Duesenberry *et al.* (eds), *The Brookings Quarterly Econometric Model*, pp. 589–625.

Fromm, G. (ed.) (1971) *Tax Incentives and Capital Spending* (Brookings Institution).

Fromm, G. and L. R. Klein (1972) 'The Brookings Econometric Model: A Rational Perspective', in K. Brunner (ed.), *Problems and Issues in Current Econometric Practice* (Columbus College of Administrative Science, Ohio State University).

_____ (eds) (1975) *The Brookings Model: Perspective and Recent Developments* (North-Holland).

Fromm, G. and P. Taubman (1968) *Policy Simulations with an Econometric Model* (Brookings Institute and North-Holland).

Gallo, Giampiero and Manfred H. Gilli (1990) 'How to Strip a Model to its Essential Elements', *Computer Science in Economics and Management*, vol. 3, pp. 199–214.

Garbely, M. and M. Gilli (1984) 'Two Approaches in Reading Model Interdependencies', Chapter 2 (pp. 15–33) in J. P. Ancot (ed.), *Analysing the Structure of Econometric Models* (The Hague : Martinus Nijhoff).

Gordon, Kermit (1968) 'Foreword', to *Policy Simulations With an Econometric Model*, by Gary Fromm and Paul Taubman (Brookings Institute and North-Holland).

Helliwell, J. F., F. W. Gorbet, G. R. Sparks and I. A. Stewart (1973) 'Comprehensive

Linkage of Large Models: Canada and the United States', pp. 395–426 in R. J. Ball (ed.), *The International Linkage of National Economic Models* (Amsterdam and London/New York: North Holland/American Elsevier Publishing Company Inc.).

Hirsch, A. A., B. T. Grimm and G. L. V. Narasimham (1974) 'Some Multiplier and Error Characteristics of the BEA Quarterly Model', *International Economic Review*, vol. 16.

Holt, Charles C. (1965) 'Validation and Application of Macroeconomic Models Using Computer Simulation', in Duesenberry *et al.* (eds) pp. 637–50.

Intriligator, Michael D. (1978) *Econometric Models, Techniques, and Applications* (Englewood Cliffs, New Jersey: Prentice-Hall).

Jorgenson, D. W. (1965) 'Anticipation and Investment Behaviour', in Duesenberry *et al.* (eds) *The Brookings Quarterly Econometric Model*, pp. 35–92.

Keller, André A. (1979) *Essai sur les structures comparées des modèles macroéconomiques de prévision: Construction d'une typologie par l'étude des graphes associés et l'analyse factorielle* (Paris: Université de Paris I Panthéon-Sorbonne).

Klein, L. R. (1964) 'A Postwar Quarterly Model: Description and Applications', *Models of Income Determination*, vol. 28 of *Studies in Income and Wealth* (Princeton, NJ: Princeton University Press, for NBER).

_____ (1975) 'Research Contributions of the SSRC–Brookings Econometric Model Project – A Decade in Review', in Fromm and Klein (eds) *The Brookings Model*.

Klein, Lawrence R. and Arthur S. Goldberger (1955) *An Econometric Model of the United States, 1929–1952* (Amsterdam: North-Holland).

Klein, Lawrence R. and Joel Popkin (1961) 'An Econometric Analysis of the Postwar Relationship between Inventory Fluctuations and Changes in Aggregate Economic Activity', pp. 69–89 in *Inventory Fluctuations and Economic Stabilization*, Part III of Study of Inventory Fluctuations and Economic Instability, Joint Economic Committee of the 87th US Congress, First Session (Washington, DC: US Government Printing Office).

Kuh, Edwin (1965) 'Income Distribution and Employment Over the Business Cycle', in Duesenberry *et al.* (eds) *The Brookings Quarterly Econometric Model*, pp. 227–78.

Liebenberg, M., A. A. Hirsch and J. Popkin (1966) 'A Quarterly Econometric Model of the United States: A Progress Report', *Survey of Current Business*, vol. 46.

Liebenberg, M., G. Green and A. Hirsch (1971) *The Office of Business Economics 70 Quarterly Econometric Model* (Washington, DC: US Department of Commerce, Econometrics Branch).

Liu, T. C. (1963) 'An Exploratory Quarterly Econometric Model of Effective Demand in the Postwar U.S. Economy', *Econometrica*, vol. 31, no. 3 (July) pp. 301–48.

Liu, T. C. and E. C. Hwa (1974) 'Structure and Applications of a Monthly Econometric Model of the U.S. Economy', *International Economic Review*, vol. 15, no. 2 (June) pp. 328–65.

McCarthy, M. D. (1972) *The Wharton Quarterly Econometric Forecasting Model*, Mark III (Philadelphia: Economics Research Unit, University of Pennsylvania).

Modigliani, Franco (1964) 'Comment' [on 'A Postwar Quarterly Model: Description and Applications', by L. R. Klein] in *Models of Income Determination*, vol. 28 of Studies in Income and Wealth (Princeton, NJ: Princeton University Press for NBER) pp. 41–53.

_____ (1977) 'The Monetarist Controversy, or Should We Forsake Stabilization Policies?', *American Economic Review*, vol. 67, no. 2 (March) pp. 1–19.

Nagar, A. L. (1969) 'Stochastic Simulation of the Brookings Econometric Model', in Duesenberry *et al.* (eds) *The Brookings Model*.

Preston, Ross S. (1972) *The Wharton Annual and Industry Forecasting Model* (Philadelphia: Economics Research Unit of the Department of Economics of the University of Pennsylvania).

_____ (1975) 'The Wharton Long-Term Model: Input–Output Within the Context of a Macro Forecasting Model', *International Economic Review*, vol. 16, no. 1 (February) pp. 3–19.

Suits, D. B. (1962) 'Forecasting and Analysis with an Econometric Model', *American Economic Review*, vol. 52, no. 2 (March) pp. 104–32.

Taubman, P. (1969) 'Econometric Functions for Government Receipts', in Duesenberry *et al.* (eds) *The Brookings Model.*

Tobin, James (1969) 'A General Equilibrium Approach to Monetary Theory', *Journal of Money, Credit, and Banking*, vol. 1, no. 1 (February) pp. 15–29.

Wold, H. (1954) 'Causality and Econometrics', *Econometrica*, vol. 22, no 2 (April) pp. 162–77.

_____ (1960) 'A Generalization of Causal Chain Models', *Econometrica*, vol. 28, no. 2 (April) pp. 443–63.

5 American econometric models of the 1970s

1 Introduction

In the preceding chapter, we noted that, in the 1960s, there began five broad, interrelated trends: improvements in computer technology, the implementation of a team approach to econometric modelling, the development of an institutional framework largely independent of the orginator(s) of the models, detailed and large-scale modelling, and increasing theoretical sophistication. Although its critics might dispute this, the Brookings Model appeared to embody all of these new developments. In the 1970s, these trends continued with unabated and even accelerated vigour. One development that should be noted explicitly, however, was the rise of the econometrics consulting house as a commercial entity, as exemplified by DRI (Data Resources, Incorporated) or WEFA (Wharton Econometric Forecasting Associates), as examples of entrepreneurship where (as in many other instances) the founders of the enterprise perceived a demand in the market place and then filled the demand in a less costly and/or better-quality manner than potential competitors. The rise of the commercial econometrics house placed a slightly greater emphasis on the (unconditional) forecasting use of the model,[1] as this application was (and remains) the prime interest of the non-economist consumers of the econometrics enterprise. It is also a key factor in establishing a 'track record,' by which credibility is established. Nevertheless the underlying models remained vehicles for the scholarly study of the characteristics of the American economy, and (as our review of the DRI and Wharton Models in Sections 3 and 4 below will indicate) a number of contributions to applied macroeconomic theory were developed in the context of these models.

The model teams were at times assembled in government organizations, as our review of the BEA (Bureau of Economic Analysis) and St Louis Federal Reserve Models, in Sections 2 and 7 respectively, will indicate. Finally, a number of models (of which the Fair Model reviewed in Section 6, the Hickman–Coen Model reviewed in Section 5, and the Liu–Hwa Model reviewed in Section 8 are typical) were built in the context of a university department of economics. Here individual scholars (either singly or in combination) were able to develop their vision of the macroeconomy, and some of these ideas also contributed to the development of the mainstream econometric model.

We note that, in the mid-1970s, there was an important symposium (based on a continuous seminar of model-builders), on comparative simulation studies of leading US macroeconometric models, in the June 1974, October 1974, and January 1975 issues of the *International Economic Review*.[2] As will be obvious in what follows, we have freely drawn on these articles, which also present a good summary of the state of the art in this area, at that point.[3] Another good summary of the development of US macroeconometric modelling in the mid-1970s appears in Chapter 12 ('Applications to Macroeconometric Modelling') of Intriligator (1978). In general, we summarize the state of the art to the middle of the 1970s, though at times we permit ourselves a forward look to the end of the decade and even into the 1980s. We end this chapter in Section 9 with some concluding remarks.

2   The BEA Model

Lawrence R. Klein's 'Postwar Quarterly Model' had two direct descendants. One, the series of Wharton Models, will be discussed in Section 4 below. The other was first known as the OBE Model of the US Economy (for the Office of Business Economics, US Department of Commerce). When this division changed its name (around 1970) to the Bureau of Economic Analysis, the model naturally became known as the BEA Model. As emphasized in a number of descriptions, the BEA Model had econometric forecasting as its primary focus, with structural analysis an important secondary objective. (In this regard, it resembled its parent, the Postwar Quarterly Model.) It may be noted that the model itself evolved over the years. The original model (Liebenberg *et al.*, 1966) had 36 behavioural equations and 13 identities, for a total of 49 endogenous variables (and roughly 40 exogenous variables). The 1974 version (Hirsch *et al.*, 1974) had 117 endogenous variables (and slightly fewer exogenous variables), of which 67 were directly determined by stochastic equations. By the end of the 1970s, the model had grown much larger.

The structure of the BEA Model, which was in the mainstream, neo-Keynesian tradition, may be summarized rapidly. The seven model sectors were: GNP Component Equations, Price and Wage Rate Equations, the Labour Sector (Employment, Weekly Hours and Labour Force), Non-wage Income Components, Monetary Equations, Miscellaneous Equations,[4] and Identities. We may briefly summarize some interesting features of the model. The price-wage sector is heavily cost-oriented, with only a secondary role for demand pressures (a partial exception to this generalization being the importance of the unemployment rate variable or variables in the equation for the rate of change of wage rates). Total employee hours adjust more rapidly than actual numbers of employees, thus implying a buffer role cyclically for the average work week; in turn, this reflects the quasi-fixed nature of employment over the business cycle, due to non-trivial costs of hiring, training and firing (Oi, 1962). Thirdly, we note that there are behavioural equations for all income components and that the statistical discrepancy is defined residually. However this discrepancy is limited with regard to level and magnitude of change; if these constraints are violated, all of the income components (not just corporate profits, the usual residual category) are revised to enforce the constraint, a somewhat different treatment from most econometric models. Finally, as described in Hirsch (1972) and Hirsch *et al.* (1974), in some versions supply-side constraints were added, limiting both the level of capacity utilization and its absolute change.[5] As one might expect, the presence of such capacity constraints implies that aggregate demand stimulation near full capacity utilization leads to higher price level changes and smaller increases in real output, even allowing for some non-price rationing in these circumstances.

In this review, we shall summarize only the multiplier properties outlined in Hirsch *et al.* (1974); for a discussion of the forecasting properties, the reader is referred to the original article. This article indicates the presence of dynamic multiplier patterns which are inverted Us, as the dynamic multiplier (with regard to real output) starts low (at a less than unitary value), builds to a peak of roughly 2 (starting from a 6 per cent unemployment path) or $1\frac{2}{3}$ (starting from a 4 per cent unemployment path), after 4 or 5 quarters. After this peak, the intermediate-term multiplier declines dramatically, becoming small (roughly $\frac{1}{2}$) or even negative, depending upon the initial state of the economy. As these simulations indicate, in a model with important non-linearities, such as the BEA Model, the initial position can make a great deal of difference with regard to the magnitude of the multiplier.[6] We note that another set of multiplier calculations (accelerated defence expenditures, beginning in the fourth quarter of 1965, with the capacity constraints operative) actually implied negative real multipliers, as more than 100 per cent of these additional expenditures then spilled over into price level increases. This is 'crowding out' with a vengeance. We further note that an examination of the tax receipts multipliers suggests that the balanced budget theorem of intermediate macroeconomic theory is something of an oversimplification.

We observe that Hirsch's simulations (Hirsch, 1972) suggest that the wage-price block, when simulated in isolation, is reasonably satisfactory; as such, this was an improvement over the original 1966 model. Full model simulations over the entire sample period were somewhat less satisfactory, particularly if one looks at the absolute levels of wages and prices rather than their rates of change. The 1972 paper also contains estimates of a long-run trade-off curve, which is fairly steep: zero inflation in the GNP deflator is associated with a 6 per cent rate of unemployment, a 4 per cent rate of unemployment was associated with a 4 per cent rate of inflation,[7] and a 3 per cent rate of unemployment was associated with a rate of inflation of nearly 8 per cent per annum. As indicated in note 3 below, this long-run trade-off curve is fairly similar to two others analysed by Hymans (1972) at the same conference. Finally, we note an interesting asymmetry that Hirsch claimed to discover from his analysis of the BEA Model: starting from a high-inflation initial position, a rapid approach to a target rate of inflation was claimed to entail considerable excess unemployment in the interim, while it was asserted that moving rapidly to a target rate of unemployment in a slack economy would involve only a slight amount of excess inflation.[8]

3   The DRI Model[9]

Perhaps the most successful econometric model ever built, from the point of view of the market test of the product, was the DRI Model of the US economy. (See Eckstein, 1983; Eckstein, Green and Sinai, 1974; and Intriligator, 1978, pp. 449–51.) The DRI Model is regarded as the centre-piece of the DRI information system, but the information system is much broader than the basic model. (For instance, fewer than 1000 time series are required to maintain the basic model, while the information system contains over 20 000 time series.) In another sense, the US model is also a centre-piece, namely in its role as the leading member of the DRI system of econometric models. Thus Data Resources, Inc. has been an example, in the field of economic consulting, of the internationalization of American enterprise. Because of the importance of the paying client to the development of the model, there has been an important emphasis on (*ex ante*) forecasting,[10] but other aspects (such as the development of satellite or peripheral models by users of the basic model) have also received some attention. We note that the DRI Model, which is a quarterly model whose parameters are re-estimated each year, was started in 1969 and has continued to the time of writing, surviving the death of its pioneer–founder.

The DRI Model has been constructed in the mainstream of macroeconomic thinking; although there are heavy elements of neo-Keynesian thinking, supply-side elements have been important since at least the first energy crisis of the mid-1970s. Antecedents of the DRI Model include the Brookings Model and, earlier, the Duesenberry–Eckstein–Fromm Model (both discussed in previous chapters). As Robert Solow (1985) remarked at a memorial session honouring Otto Eckstein, the DRI Model is a nice blend of theoretical rigour and compromise with intractable statistical realities. In addition, it is interesting to note the number of areas in which the DRI Model makes some contribution to the received theory that is pertinent. Some examples will be furnished in outlining the structure of the model.

As summarized in Eckstein, Green and Sinai (1974) or Intriligator (1978), the DRI Model consisted of roughly 700 equations, of which approximately 400 were behavioural equations. In addition, there were roughly 180 exogenous variables. (Later versions have approximately 800 endogenous variables.) The model may be subdivided into seven model sectors: Final GNP Demands; Incomes; Financial; Supply, Capacity and Operating Rates; (Aggregate) Employment, Unemployment and the Labour Force; Prices, Wages and Productivity; and the Industry Sector. The three major sectors of the model, according to the equation counts, are the Industry Sector (at over half the model, with roughly 375 equations), Final GNP Demands (with roughly 130 equations), and the Financial Sector (with more than 100 equations). We may summarize some salient features of each of these sectors. Turning to the Final GNP Demands sector, we note that the theory of consumer behaviour underlying the DRI Model modifies the mainstream theory in this area by highlighting the effects of risk and an uncertain macroeconomic environment, resulting in more volatile behaviour on the part of consumers, particularly with regard to the purchase of automobiles and other consumer durables. The submodel of residential construction gives considerable role to the flow of mortgage funds and other financial factors. Business fixed investment is largely explained according to a Jorgensonian model emphasizing the 'user cost' (rental price) of capital goods, while state and local government expenditures are explained endogenously, in an econometric version of Wagner's Law. The largely standard model of foreign trade is applied in isolation to explain both exports and imports, although in practice there tend to be informal linkages among the national economic models of the DRI international system, so that export equation results tend to be overridden in favour of the results of the import equations of the exporting nation's principal customers. As this entails (at least in principle) some repercussions among the trading partners, an informal simultaneity (in contrast to the formal simultaneous relationships of a linked system of models, like project LINK) is built into the relationships.

The Financial Sector is one of the more critical pieces of the model, and financial constraints and possibilities are very important in conditioning developments in the real economy. There is a complete flow-of-funds submodel which includes the commercial banks, the mortgage market, non-bank financial intermediaries, non-financial businesses, and households. In addition, not only are certain key interest rates modelled, but also the level of stock market prices (as in the MPS Model), recalling the early efforts of Tinbergen in this regard. Variations in the level of equity or share prices influence the real economy through their effect on household financial assets, which in turn is one of the determinants of consumer spending and residential construction. Finally, it may be noted, '... the model confirms recent observations that housing and automobiles are the main interest-sensitive sectors' (Eckstein, 1983, p. 90).

Embedded within the DRI Model is an aggregate production function, which is used to generate estimates of potential output. This aggregate production function takes the form of a Cobb–Douglas production function, with capital, labour, energy, and research and development as the primary factors of production. Interestingly, the productivity slow-down of the US economy in the 1970s is explained implicitly in the DRI framework by energy shortages and by reduced R & D expenditures rather than by a fundamental change in structure; also, at a slightly more disaggregated level, materials shortages (which would have had their principal effect through higher prices) can slow down the growth of aggregate output. With regard to the major sector, Employment, Unemployment and Labour Force, we note that the DRI Model contains a disaggregation of the composition of unemployment by age, race and sex. This social indicator aspect of the model enables one to chart social tensions arising (say) from continuing high unemployment of black teenagers.

Turning to the final two sectors of the model, we may begin with the wage-price sector, which in turn can be decomposed into four subsectors. There is an aggregate wage change equation in which the demand pressures variable is either the unemployment rate or a form of the ratio of real GNP to potential real GNP. In later versions of this equation, the total effect of the rate of change of prices is close to unity, taking both long-run and short-run price expectations into account. The remaining price subsectors may be identified as a wholesale prices block, a block of implicit deflators for categories of final demand (which generally correspond to retail prices), and aggregations of various overall price deflators or indices. Unifying this entire approach is a stages-of-processing approach to price information, which goes back to the work of Popkin (1974) and which traces the cost of effects of wages and raw materials prices through semi-finished goods, wholesale finished goods and the retail levels, with energy prices playing a role at several stages. We note that, in later versions of the DRI Model, a sensitive measure of demand pressures (which is one among several, including capacity utilization rates) is the state of 'vendor performance' (which is an expectational variable measuring the percentage of purchasing executives reporting slower deliveries, in a monthly survey, on the part of suppliers). The wage–price–productivity sector leads to a neat decomposition of the total inflation rate into Core, Shock and Demand components, a decomposition which appeared to fit the facts of the decade of the 1970s (and also the early 1980s) reasonably well. This approach suggests appreciable (but not enormous) costs of disinflating an economy in which inflation has taken root. Also it suggests the classic shape for the short- and medium-term trade-off curves of the American economy, which Eckstein sketches (1983, p. 21) early in his summary of the characteristics of the DRI Model.

Finally, the Industry sector of the model determines the output of roughly 50 industries (in the mid-1970s version, or 75 in the later versions), and also employment and industry investment functions for roughly 30 industrial groupings. Industrial output determination is done on the basis of a regular (square) input–output table, with the first estimates of the industrial outputs so obtained modified by the use of a 'bridge' model. (As noted in the preceding chapter, the use of such a technique in a complete econometric model goes back to the Brookings Model of the US economy and also to a sequence of models constructed more or less contemporaneously by the Economic Planning Agency of Japan.) Industrial employment functions represent an inverted production function, with lagged adjustment to 'desired' or target levels of employment. And industrial investment functions have a twofold purpose: to generate measures of industrial capital stock, which in turn are an input into four sectoral capacity utilization rates, as well as serving as a check on the results of the aggregate investment function.

We may now summarize rapidly some of the salient uses of the DRI Model. Over the years, the most important use, from the viewpoint of the paying clients, has been that of quarterly forecasts of the economy, produced at least four times a year. In discussing this aspect of his organization's work, Eckstein (1983, pp. 24–8) argues that the quality of the forecasts has improved with the third generation DRI Model and is now quite acceptable, as judged by comparisons with forecasts generated by a statistically sophisticated but economically naive alternative, the ARIMA Models.[11] A second use has been that of multiplier analysis (as with other econometric models in the symposium on comparative simulation studies). Several generations of the DRI Model show the familiar 'inverted-U' pattern for the dynamic multiplier (Eckstein, Green and Sinai, 1974, pp. 611–12; Eckstein, 1983, p. 19), although the numerical values of the dynamic multiplier tend to be lower (well less than unity) with the later version of the DRI Model.[12] Eckstein interprets this latter result as validating to a large extent the arguments of the critics of fiscal policy, who claimed that 'crowding out' would inevitably take place. Another interesting application of the DRI Model was Eckstein's study (1978) of the 'Great Recession' (that of 1973–5, which incidentally may have been deprived of its title by American cyclical experience less than a decade later, in 1981–2). In this work, Eckstein analyses perceptively (using the DRI Model to provide counterfactual patterns for the evolution of the economy) the effects of six major shocks to the economy on both the rate of unemployment in 1975 and the rate of inflation in 1974. These six major perturbing events were: the Energy Crisis (the major contributor, according to Eckstein's analysis, to both observed inflation and unemployment and hence highly stagflationary), the Agricultural Price Explosion, monetary policies (1964 to 1974 or 1975), the devaluation of the dollar, price decontrol (for inflation) or price controls (for unemployment), and fiscal policies, 1969–74 (the least important for inflation and, in a sense, for unemployment). Finally, Eckstein's work, towards the end of his life, was devoted in part to testing the rational expectations critique of econometric modelling in general. His conclusion (1983, pp. xi–xii) is quite categorical: '... [C]hanges in policy regime seem to have been among the minor sources of structural change of the economy and of forecasting error in the actual historical record'. He also asserts (p. 41) that businesses and households learn their lessons only gradually and form expectations adaptively from past experience, which a 'tough-minded rationalist' would not consider to fall legitimately within the sphere of 'rationality'.[13]

4   The Wharton Models

The final large-scale team model (or models) that we shall review in this chapter is the series of Wharton Models, originated, maintained, and operated by WEFA (Wharton Econometric Forecasting Associates) under the leadership of Lawrence R. Klein. In this review, we shall limit ourselves mainly to the models in use around 1975, as this set is comparable to the others in the symposium on comparative simulation studies. However some references will be made to earlier and later developments. A representative of the Wharton Model has been in existence continuously since 1963;[14] antecedents for the Wharton Model include Klein's Postwar Quarterly Model, the Brookings Model and Michael Evans's unpublished work. Like the DRI Model, the principal Wharton Model is used heavily and extensively for short-term forecasting, as will be discussed below. The size of the basic Wharton Model has been growing, at a fairly rapid rate: the Evans–Klein version (1968) had roughly 80 equations and approximately 40 exogenous variables; McCarthy's version (Mark III, 1972) had approximately 200 equations and 100 exogenous variables, while some versions for the early 1980s had roughly 1000 endogenous variables.

Turning to a description of the three models discussed in the comparative models simulation studies, we may note that Wharton Mark III has been described (Duggal, Klein and McCarthy, 1974) as a 'modern IS–LM construct'. This seems fair enough, except that we may note that, even with a considerable development of the monetary sector (patterned, according to McCarthy, 1976, upon the then current version of the MPS Model), the IS portion of the model is considerably larger, as much attention has been lavished on the traditional consumption and investment expenditure categories; accordingly, the model is centred in the neo-Keynesian tradition. The investment theory employed is a version of Jorgenson's so-called 'neoclassical' theory of investment. The inventory equations estimate the balance between production and disappearance (for example, via consumption expenditures) of goods. The model makes extensive use of the Wharton capacity utilization index, and indeed capacity output is modelled endogenously (via a Cobb–Douglas production function). Other elements of supply-side forces playing a role in the outcome of economy-wide variables include elements of mark-up pricing, various versions of the Klein–Phillips wage adjustment equation, and a labour requirements function that reflects an inverted production function, with lagged adjustment.[15] A modest breakdown of the total output of the economy into six production sectors (mining, manufacturing, commercial (services), regulated, household and government) is effectuated, but the breakdown is informal, and no use (in Mark III) was made of input–output techniques to carry out this disaggregation on a more rigorous basis.[16] We also note the many long lag distributions in Wharton Mark III, generally on the basis of the Almon polynomial distribution.

The Anticipations Version of the Wharton Model (Adams and Duggal, 1974), which was discussed in the same symposium, is essentially the same model as Mark III, except that three anticipations-style variables (the Michigan Index of Consumer Sentiment, the BEA survey of investment intentions, and housing starts) have been included in the structure of the model, both as explanatory variables and with enough additional equations to explain their formation. Adams and Duggal note that the main changes with regard to the structure of the model come in the areas of personal consumption of automobiles, business fixed investment, and (obviously) residential construction. Adams and Duggal claim a marginal improvement in the forecasting accuracy of the Anticipations Version of the Wharton Model, particularly when anticipations-type variables can be taken as given.[17] In particular, it is claimed that this version is particularly useful for capturing turning-points, always a critical test for econometric model validation. Finally, the relevant multipliers are somewhat smaller with the Anticipations Versions (though the dynamic multipliers still display the well-known 'inverted-U' shape), as the consumer sentiment index replaces the unemployment rate as an explanatory variable in the automobile expenditure equation, which in turn imparts a sizeable effect to exogenous stimulation of the economy, as depicted in the model. (This is true because the unemployment rate appears to be a particularly sensitive indicator of cyclical conditions.)

The Wharton Annual and Industry Forecasting Model (Preston, 1972; Preston, 1975) has been described as a 'younger sibling to the Wharton Econometric Forecasting Model'. The model, with less than 400 equations in 1972, had grown to a scale of over 3000 equations in the early 1980s. In Preston (1972, 1975), eight model sectors are distinguished: Final Demand, Input–Output, Labour Requirements, Sector Wage Rates, Sector Prices, Final Demand Prices, Income Payments and the Financial Sector. Central to the Annual and Industry Forecasting Model, which has been used to make medium-term projections up to 10 years in the future,[18] are two input–output submodels, one on the side of industry output determination for 50 or 63 producing sectors of the economy,[19] and one on the prices side. The problem of variable coefficients in the input–output submodels of the economy is handled by two groups of bridge models, analogously to what was done in the Brookings and DRI Models, although Preston (1975) also introduced variable input–output coefficients by making them functions of relative prices of inputs. In effect, he substituted a restricted CES production function for the original fixed-coefficients model. Finally, we note that the wage adjustment equations (for seven major producing sectors) suggested that labour market pressures operate primarily in leading sectors, which are generally characterized by strong unions. Follower sectors appear to be insensitive to labour market conditions, relying generally on results obtained in the leading sectors.

We may now turn to some of the various uses of the Wharton Models: here we shall discuss forecasting, multiplier studies, policy simulations, and the use of the current Wharton quarterly model in project LINK. Turning to the forecasting application, we note that this has been a principal (if not primary) use of the Wharton Model, since its inception around 1963. Forecasting with an econometric model is not a mechanical process, at least if done in an efficient manner; judgement enters not only in the choice of exogenous variables, but also in the choice of the 'add factors' or constant adjustments.[20] In the case of the Wharton Model, the forecasts have in the past been greatly influenced by the comments of the users at the periodic conferences reviewing the first pass at a forecast of the economy in the short run; some of these users will possess a specialized expertise in particular sectors of the economy and hence will have a feel for the likely short-term evaluation of the economy in their area of expertise. In turn, the short-term forecasts of the economy are often the most important benefit that particular subscribers to the model draw from this service. On the substance of the forecasts, we note that the Wharton Model picked out recessions beginning in 1969 and 1974, thus demonstrating its mettle in that regard. Duggal, Klein and McCarthy (1974) argue that the forecasting record of the Wharton Model was rather good over the difficult period 1972–II to 1974–IV, given all the objective perturbations in the economy (New Economic Policy, dollar devaluation and drastic fluctuations in agricultural and petroleum prices), except for the errors in the GNP deflator. A detailed study of the problem of forecasting with the Wharton Model during this turbulent period appears in McCarthy (1972, Chapter V, pp. 157–89).[21]

We note also that, more recently, an outside observer (McLaughlin, 1980) pointed to the success of the Wharton forecasts for calendar 1979; in particular, it was noted that not only were the Wharton Model forecasts very close to average real GNP growth for the entire year, but also the quarterly patterns of change of this important variable were predicted highly accurately. We also note that Adams and Duggal (1974) noted a marginal improvement in the forecasting ability of the Anticipations Version of the Wharton Mark III Model, particularly with regard to turning-points (and particularly for the phenomena of residential construction and business fixed investment). On the other hand, the exercise with the Wharton Annual and Industry Forecasting Model (Preston, 1972) implied (on the basis of the conditional projections over the 1970–80 decade) an annual growth rate of real GNP equal to 4.4 per cent, an average level of the unemployment rate of 4.7 per cent of the labour force, and an inflation rate of 3.5 per cent per annum. (These numbers are relatively close to the hypothetical 4/4/4 economy referred to above.) In retrospect, these medium-term projections were hopelessly optimistic, but the failure was not principally one of econometric modelling.

Turning to the other uses of the Wharton Models, we have already noted that both the short-term Wharton Model and the Wharton Annual Model show 'inverted-U' patterns for the real government expenditures multiplier, although the level at which the dynamic multiplier peaks is lower (1.64 or 2.0) for the Wharton Annual Model than it is (2.5 or 3.3) for the quarterly Wharton Model. Nevertheless, in both cases, there is evidence of eventual 'crowding out', as the relevant dynamic multiplier drops below 1.0 or even 0.[22] The use of Wharton Mark III for policy analysis is well illustrated in McCarthy's (1972) chapter on the problems of forecasting in the context of massive policy changes; implicitly, the model provides an evaluation of the various components of the policy package, as one evaluates the likely evolution of the economy, with and without each of the components of the total package of policy changes under consideration. In the case under discussion, the various components of the policy change included a 90-day freeze on prices (including rents) and wages, four fiscal policy measures reducing tax receipts, postponement of federal government revenue-sharing with state and local governments, a 5 per cent cut in federal government civilian employment and a six-month delay in the pay increases for these employees, closing the gold window of the Federal Reserve system and a *de facto* devaluation of the US dollar, and a 10 per cent reduction in US foreign aid and the imposition of special import surcharges. These policy changes were analysed, with the use of the Wharton Mark III Model and with some assumptions as to their probable impact on the constant terms of the structural equations (and some other specialized assumptions). At the time, this analysis suggested that the New Economic Policy would have favourable effects on real output, employment and inflation; moreover, in retrospect, these favourable effects appear largely to have been realized, at least for late 1971 and 1972. Finally, we note that the Wharton Model has been the representative model of the US economy in Project LINK since the beginning; for instance, a summary description of the Wharton Mark III Model (McCarthy, 1976) appears in Waelbroeck's volume, *The Models of Project LINK.*

5   The Hickman–Coen Model

We now turn to four models (Hickman–Coen, Ray Fair's, the Liu–Hwa, and the St Louis Federal Reserve) that are more individualistic in nature, in the sense that the model reflected the vision of the principal model-builder or model-builders. The first such model to be reviewed, the Hickman–Coen Model, is perhaps a good transitional case, for, while the model (a medium-term one) reflected Hickman and Coen's emphasis on the supply side (on interrelated factor demands, in particular), the model documentation makes it clear that there was an entire project team that put the model together and maintained it, for a time.[23] Hence this model makes a good transitional case, from the team models reviewed above to the more strictly individualistic models discussed in this half of the chapter.

The Hickman–Coen Model, which is documented in Hickman, Coen and Hurd (1975) and Hickman and Coen (1976), was designed to be a medium-term model, useful for projections 10 years or more into the future.[24] The model contains a blend of Keynesian-style aggregate demand factors and more traditional macroeconometric modelling, along with an emphasis on supply factors, generally with a neoclassical orientation.

Indeed the theorizing is at a relatively sophisticated level, and the model-builders attempted to break new ground in a number of areas. (We shall attempt to cover most of these, in broad outline, in our summary of the model's structure in the next several paragraphs.) The model was fitted to a split sample period of annual data, 1926–40 and 1949–66, and in fact considerable data development work was entailed, as is made clear in Hickman and Coen (1976). The method of parameter estimation was either ordinary least squares or two-stage least squares, depending on the individual equation under estimation. The scale of the model is indicated by the fact that the model had 50 behavioural equations, 120 identities and over 100 exogenous variables.[25] Hickman and Coen started largely afresh in building a medium-term macroeconometric model, drawing as well upon the neoclassical theory of the household, firm and market. Jorgenson's work on investment functions and results from the Brookings Model, the MPS Model, and some of the Wharton Models also appear to have played some suggestive role.

Turning to the structure of the Hickman–Coen Model, we note that there are five aggregate demand sectors ('blocs'): consumption, business investment, housing and residential construction, government purchases of goods and services, and foreign trade. Here we may simply note that business fixed investment is based on a version of Jorgenson's 'user cost' (rental price) of capital, a subject to which Robert Coen has made original contributions, with the underlying demands for the labour and capital factors of production being interrelated through common parameters of the production function.[26] Expenditures on residential construction are the result of a submodel stressing household formation, income flows and, in the short run, market disequilibrium. We note that exports are exogenous in nominal terms, which implies (as noted by Hickman and Coen) an export demand function that has a unitary price elasticity in real terms.[27] Output in the model is implicitly the result of a production function of Cobb–Douglas form; one of the interesting research issues is whether the representation of constant returns to scale or of increasing returns yields a better description of the US economy. The same production function is used to describe potential output, and indeed Hickman and Coen distinguish among potential output, full-employment output and full-capacity output.[28] The basic labour demand function, which explains total employee hours, is based on the same fundamental production function with cost minimization (subject to a lag); the relevant explanatory variables are total output, a time trend (to measure neutral technological change), the ratio of the rental price of capital to the wage rate, and the lagged value of the dependent variable, total employee hours. Thus this equation reflects more than an inverted production function, as optimization (cost minimization) enters the picture. As there is a behavioural equation for average hours worked per employee (reflecting cyclical conditions and secular factors), the total number of employees is obtained by identity. The labour supply equation, which is formulated in terms of employees, has an interesting combination of discouraged worker effects (from the employment ratio) and additional worker effects (when average hours drop, presumably below target levels).[29] Unemployment is then obtained residually.

We note that the model also contains sectors ('blocs') for money stock and interest rates, for money wages, and product price levels. The monetary sector, which contains an elaborate sub-bloc for determining the term structure of interest rates, is based on a Yale-style portfolio balance model of the financial sector in which 'adding-up' properties are respected.[30] The money-wage rate for the private sector was not initially determined by a version of the Klein–Phillips wage adjustment relationship; rather, it reflected the assumption that, in a stable price environment, 'firms set wages in order to achieve the manpower level which minimizes costs of production'.[31] The principal price level (which is the implicit deflator of private non-residential national product net of indirect business taxes) is determined by a variant of the mark-up pricing hypothesis, one in which the mark-up is sensitive to demand pressures, as proxied by the rate of capacity utilization.[32]

Turning to applications of the model, we note that the Hickman–Coen model was particularly useful for studying longer-term policy scenarios as deviations from an established base line solution. This base case need not strictly be a forecast projection. Moreover the model was useful for describing the structure of the US economy during 40 years in the middle of the twentieth century. Thus there is an appendix in Hickman and Coen (1976) which describes alternative measures of resource utilization (capacity utilization, full-employment output utilization, potential output utilization) for a period running from 1924 to 1972 (with a break during the Second World War and immediate postwar years), all based on calculations drawing on the model. The results show the horrendous underutilization of resources during the 1930s, as well as the heavy demand pressures on the system during the Korean War and Vietnam War periods. Interestingly, as noted above, a later study (Coen and Hickman, 1980b) attempted to correct the 1970s model for the defect of ignoring the energy input to gross output, after which they attempted to gauge the likely evolution of potential output for the rest of the twentieth century. (They found a definite suggestion of retardation in the growth rate of potential output for the final 15 years of the current century.)

Turning to the standard multiplier simulations, we note that the Hickman–Coen Model does not appear to have the standard 'inverted-U' pattern for the dynamic expenditures multiplier; rather, the response of real output to a sustained increase in expenditures is just to keep on increasing, at least for 14 years. [33] While it is true that these expenditure multipliers finally peak in year 14, Hickman and Coen (1976) indicate quite clearly that this is probably an artifact, due principally to the introduction of the Canadian–American Automobile Agreement in 1965. On the side of the impact of exogenous changes in a monetary policy variable (a unit change in unborrowed reserves), this policy change had only a transient effect on real output (and also on the level of unemployment and, for 1970s version, on price levels). (This is not terribly surprising, given the tenuousness of the links in the model of the monetary sector to real phenomena as outlined earlier.) For the 1980s version of the Model, price levels now respond more or less proportionately to an increase in the money stock (M_1) in the medium term.

Finally, we note rapidly three other applications of the Hickman–Coen Model, which are developed more fully in the 1976 book. There is a chapter devoted to the issue of 'Constant or Increasing Returns to Scale?'; after weighing the evidence of prediction errors, Hickman and Coen generally feel that the model suggests that constant returns to scale is the more accurate hypothesis. An analysis of the components of aggregate demand (particularly in staged multiplier calculations) suggests the presence of a short-term inventory cycle, even in the context of an annual model. Finally, a comparison of some prewar and postwar characteristics of the economy (particularly in the multiplier calculations) suggests a much greater intrinsic stability of the postwar economy.

6 Fair's Forecasting Model

Another model we wish to consider in this chapter is the 'Short-Run Forecasting Model' of Ray C. Fair (Fair, 1971 and 1974), which incorporated (at that time) Fair's particular vision of the economic process, as well as his philosophy with regard to good practice in econometric forecasting. At 19 endogenous variables (derived from 14 behavioural equations and five identities) and roughly the same number of exogenous variables, Fair's was certainly one of the smallest working models of this stage of the history of macroeconometric model-building. Certainly he situated himself at the 'small model' extreme of the debate between the partisans of big models and small models; as such, he would appear to go against the traditions of the Brookings Model builders and to line up with the approach of Irwin Friend and his associates. (See, in particular, Friend and Jones, 1964, and Friend and Taubman, 1964.) Fair's Model put particular emphasis on the forecasting application, and his results and particular philosophy will be discussed below. In line with this emphasis on short-term forecasting, he placed major emphasis on expectational variables (considered exogenous in the short run), such as the Michigan Survey Research Center index of consumer sentiment and investment anticipations of the OBE–SEC. However theoretical considerations were not neglected, and Fair incorporated some interesting theoretical innovations of his own construction (in whole or in part) in the structure of his system (as the next paragraph indicates). Finally, we note that his model was estimated by techniques that were innovative at the time, incorporating the possibility of correcting simultaneously for both autocorrelated disturbances and simultaneous equations biases. (Fair's default assumption regarding the random disturbance terms of his structural relationships was to assume that they are autocorrelated.) The original model had been fitted to a variable sample period running in general from the first quarter of 1956 to the fourth quarter of 1969, although Fair also generally updated the sample period just prior to each individual forecast.

Turning to the structure of the system, we note that the 19 equations of the system may be decomposed into four blocs or sectors: a monthly housing starts sector, a money GNP (or expenditures) sector, a price sector, and a labour force and employment sector. The housing starts sector, which was estimated from monthly data and then averaged on a quarterly basis before being factored into the expenditures sector, is interesting, as it is assumed that the housing sector of the economy is generally *not* in equilibrium.[34] Separate demand and supply equations for housing starts are estimated by a special technique, which assumes that the short side of the market always prevails. Exogenous variables for this sector included financial variables, such as the interest rate on a special class of mortgages, and some technical variables, such as the number of working days in the particular month under consideration. The expenditures sector was constructed in nominal terms, which Fair believed was justified in the short run. The index of consumer sentiment played an important if supplementary role for the three consumption functions, while investment anticipations were a major part of the explanation of business fixed capital formation. Once housing starts had been determined (on a quarterly basis for the current and the preceding two quarters), the explanation of investment in residential construction was easy. Inventory investment was explained by a flexible accelerator in which sales expectations were taken into account. A simple import demand function completed the sector, as export demand and government expenditures were taken as exogenous (in nominal terms), along with the expectations variables (as already mentioned). The price sector used a GNP gap variable (defined as the difference between an exogenous real potential GNP and last quarter's actual real GNP, less the current change in nominal GNP) to explain the change in the price deflator of private output, in a sort of semi-reduced form that can also be interpreted as a trade-off relationship. With the private output deflator determined, nominal GNP could then be split between price and real components.[35] In the final sector, total man-hours were determined by means of the requirements calculated from a short-run production function (Fair distinguished between total man-hours worked and total man-hours paid for), while requirements for employees represented a related but slightly different process. (Accordingly, average hours worked would implicitly be obtained by identity, were this variable required.) The participation rate of 'primary' workers (males 25 to 54 years of age) followed a time trend, while that for the remaining workers displayed a discouraged worker effect. (Source populations were exogenous variables, in both cases.) Fair tested his model, both with dynamic simulations within the sample period and with evidence beyond it, in order to gauge (among other things) the stability of the fitted behavioural relationships. Evidence from the journal article (1974a) confirmed that five of the 14 behavioural equations from the 1971 book (the two housing starts equations, that for inventory investment, the price change equation, and the participation rate relationship for secondary workers) were relatively unstable.

Turning to the forecasting use,[36] we note that Fair argued that the comparative strength of his model is in the area of forecasting. Indeed, in the book, he claimed that his model had a better *ex ante* or unconditional forecasting performance than either the Wharton or OBE (BEA) Models, although this claim was somewhat attenuated by the time of the journal article.[37] Fair's philosophy of forecasting was somewhat different from the standard type characteristic of most model-builders; he claimed that one should be able to forecast unconditionally without the use of constant adjustments (although he puts a lot of emphasis on the re-estimation of the parameters of the model before each specific forecast, which could be interpreted as a sort of parameter adjustment procedure). Thus Fair claimed to eliminate the subjective element in econometric forecasting (except for the thorny problems of data revisions and also of 'random' phenomena like strikes, which are virtually impossible to incorporate into standard macroeconometric models). In other words, for Fair, forecasting (*ex ante* as well as *ex post*) was considered to be (at least ideally) largely a mechanical process. As an indication of the scientific character of the forecasting process, Fair noted that his forecasts of particular historical episodes improve when the estimated values of the predetermined variables (used, of course, for the *ex ante* forecasts) were replaced, after the fact, by the measured values; this result was not generally obtained with the larger macroeconometric models, such as the Wharton or BEA Models. Finally, Fair subjected his *ex ante* forecasts retrospectively to a considerable amount of analysis, concluding (for instance) that the unemployment rate was slightly underpredicted in the late 1960s and also that inventory investment was difficult to forecast (at least in the context of his model).

Fair's contribution is interesting for at least two reasons. First, it shows that an independent researcher, using inspiration and hard work, can still produce a respectable macroeconometric model; it is not absolutely necessary to have a team effort to do this. Second, Fair's views on forecasting, model size, and related questions were interesting (even though we remain generally unconvinced) and merit consideration in this continuing debate. Fair has continued to evolve his thoughts on model-building, but his contributions after 1975 will not be reviewed in detail here.[38]

7   The St Louis Model

In the late 1960s and early 1970s, an interesting challenge to mainstream, neo-Keynesian orthodoxy in the field of macroeconometric modelling came from several scholars at the Federal Reserve Bank of St Louis. (See Andersen and Carlson (1970a and 1974). A history of the St Louis Model, in which the author reviews its development over time and attempts to situate this model in the larger debate about macroeconomic theory that was taking place at the time, has been written by Donald A. Elliott (1985).) This challenge, which assumed that markets generally clear and that the private economy is stable, was of course part of a wider monetarist challenge in the entire field of macroeconomics. (Interestingly, in the second article, Andersen and Carlson largely reinterpret their results in terms of search theory and the theory of information costs, which they admit were not foremost in their minds at the time of the construction of this model.) The model of Andersen and Carlson and their associates, which has come to be known as the St Louis Model, was small, with only five behavioural equations and four identities. In general, one could regard these behavioural equations as reflecting a collapsing of more fundamental structural relationships and so constituting 'semi-reduced forms'. The behavioural relationships were originally fitted by ordinary least squares to US data running from the first quarter of 1955 to the fourth quarter of 1968. (In the second article, the sample period was extended to the second quarter of 1973.) Andersen and Carlson state that their model was oriented towards policy analysis, rather than towards unconditional macroeconomic forecasting. (The question of the forecasting capacities of the St Louis Model is raised below.)

We may now turn to the structure of the St Louis Model. The key behavioural equation appears to be that for total spending, in which the change in total spending (current nominal GNP) is expressed as a four-quarter distributed lag of the nominal change in the stock of money and also a four-quarter distributed lag of changes in high-employment federal expenditures (also in nominal terms). While both distributed lags contain individual terms which are statistically significant, the coefficients for high-employment federal expenditures are significantly positive for the current and one-quarter lag term and significantly negative for lags of three and four quarters, producing a sum that is barely positive and quite insignificant (in the original version of the model). By contrast, the sum of the coefficients of the money stock changes, current and lagged, is large and highly significant, thus confirming the monetarist point of view. Price level changes in the model (more accurately, the dollar change in total spending due to changes in the GNP deflator) are explained as a function of a five-quarter distributed lag in the excess demand variable and the anticipated change in the price level variable; both of these explanatory variables are the results of identities that will be discussed in the following paragraph, and both the sum of the excess demand variables and also the anticipated price level change variable are highly significant, by standard criteria. Real output changes can then be obtained residually, via an identity that decomposes the change in nominal spending into price and real output components.

Turning to the remaining three identities, we note that the demand pressure variable is defined as the change in nominal spending less the difference between potential GNP (in constant prices) and last quarter's actual level of real GNP, a definition that is quite close to Fair's measure discussed in the preceding section. The anticipated change in prices is a weighted average of past rates of change of the price level (the GNP deflator), going back 17 quarters. (Although the basic weights come from the long-term interest rate equation, they are modified by the inverse of the unemployment rate (scaled to a 'full-employment' base of 4.0) in the quarter contemporaneous with the price level change.) Accordingly, the key expectations equation of the model reflects a theory of adaptive, rather than rational, expectations. The remaining identity defines the real GNP gap as the difference between potential GNP (in constant dollars) and current real GNP, relative to potential GNP. The exogenous variables of the model are simply three in number: the change in the money stock (M_1), the change in high-employment federal government expenditures, and potential or full-employment GNP.

The final three behavioural equations give epilogue 'outputs' (endogenous variables), in the sense that these variables do not affect the solution for the rest of the model, either in the current period or in dynamic simulation.[39] The unemployment rate equation explains unemployment (as a percentage of the labour force) by the current and lagged value of the GNP gap. (As Andersen and Carlson note, this is a version of Okun's Law.) The two interest rate equations (one for a long-term rate and one for a short-term rate) relate the levels of these respective interest rates to the annual rate of change of the money stock (with the expected negative effect) and long distributed lags in both the rate of change of real output and in the rate of change of the price level.[40] As noted above, it is the pattern of the weights of the price level change variable in the long-term interest rate equation (whose sum was insignificantly different from unity in both the original paper and also in the re-estimated version of 1974) that is used to define the anticipated price change variable.

Turning to the applications, we note that the multiplier properties of the St Louis Model are quite different from those of the other models of the US economy reviewed in this chapter. (This comes out quite clearly in Christ (1975, Figure 4 on p. 70), where the change in real GNP per unit change in real government purchases peaks at unity after roughly two or three quarters, and then falls to a slight negative value, after seven or eight quarters. The real multiplier remains negative for the remaining 12 or 13 quarters of the simulation.) Thus, although the St Louis Models has the familiar 'inverted-U' pattern for the real multiplier of government expenditures, it peaks much earlier and at a much lower maximum than the other models represented in this diagram (Wharton, DRI, MPS, BEA, Hickman–Coen, Michigan, Brookings and Fair). Interestingly, in the following diagram, where Christ examines the response of real GNP to a monetary stimulus (M_1 for the St Louis Model, unborrowed reserves for the others), the St Louis Model behaves in a much more similar fashion to several of the mainstream models examined. As with Wharton and DRI, the effect of the monetary stimulus on real GNP is shown by an inverted-U pattern for this policy multiplier; in the case of the St Louis Model, the peak comes after roughly six quarters of the policy stimulus, and the effect turns negative after roughly 16 quarters. In the case of the St Louis Model, of course, the direct effect of monetary stimulation is to raise nominal GNP; while in the short run a fair proportion of this will stimulate real national product, eventually all (or the effect may even be slightly more powerful) of this monetary stimulation will work its way through the system to an effect on prices.

The long-run neutrality properties of the model are also apparent in a particular set of simulations that Andersen and Carlson (1970b) made with St Louis Model. Starting with the year 1970, they simulated the effects of possible growth rates of the money supply at a constant rate of 6,

4 or 2 per cent per year alternatively, for a period of 100 years. (High-employment government expenditures and potential output were simply assumed to grow at the rate of 4 per cent per year.) The results are most interesting. In the 'short run' (that is, for the first 20 and especially the first 10 years), unemployment rates are higher and real growth rates are lower, with lower growth rates of the money supply.[41] Nominal income growth is lower with lower rates of growth of the money supply, and also the rate of change of the price level is lower. But in the long run the neoclassical neutrality properties rule. After 20 (or in some cases, 30) years, the unemployment rate settles down to its assumed full-employment value of 4 per cent, the growth rate of real GNP is at its potential value of 4 per cent per annum, and nominal income expands at the rate of growth of the money supply (6, 4 or 2 per cent respectively). Thus, after 20 years or so, we either get an inflation rate of 2 per cent per year and completely stable price levels or *deflation* at the rate of 2 per cent per year,[42] according to the St Louis Model. (Admittedly, this final effect takes somewhat longer, nearly 40 years in the model simulations, but in this world the long-run neutrality principle remains valid.) These simulations are a remarkable *tour de force*, even if one would never expect to see anything like them in practice, particularly in a representative democracy.

As suggested by the initial results of these long-run simulations, there is built into the St Louis Model a short-run trade-off between inflation and unemployment rates in the following sense: a faster rate of growth of the money supply will produce faster real output growth and hence less unemployment temporarily, but the cost is then a higher future rate of inflation, which will become incorporated into price expectations. Andersen and Carlson made these implicit results explicit in a paper (1972) written for the Conference on the Econometrics of Price Determination. Here, in the context of a critique of the trade-off (Klein–Phillips) curve, they show that their own model does in fact generate a number of short-run trade-off curves, with the familiar negative slope![43]

On the forecasting side, Andersen and Carlson state explicitly (1974, p. 305) that the St Louis Model 'was not designed for exact quarter-to-quarter forecasting'. Such modesty seems quite in order, given the mediocre forecasting performance of the St Louis Model over the 1970s. Thus Stephen K. McNees (1973), in a supplementary comment which was part of a larger study, notes that, by several criteria and either within or outside the sample period, the St Louis Model was less accurate in fore-casting nominal GNP for the USA during the first few years of the 1970s than was the Fair Model. Even for *ex post* dynamic simulations, a disturb-ing feature of the St Louis Model was that it predicted declining price levels during the entire 1961–3 period, when actual price levels were still rising very gently (between 0 and 2 per cent per annum), which of course suggests some model inaccuracy. Indeed the key total spending equation of the St Louis Model has been shown to be subject to considerable instability; two observers (F. De Leeuw and T. Kalchbrenner, 1969) have suggested that a slight adjustment of both the monetary and the fiscal variables produces dramatically different parameter estimates.[44] Moreover, in the re-estimation of the total spending equation reported in Andersen and Carlson (1974), we note that the sum of the distributed lag coefficients on changes in high-employment government expenditures went from 0.05 to 0.54, with the addition of 18 further quarters of observations, which suggests a qualitatively different effect of government expenditures in the long run, even if the estimated difference may not be statistically significant. In addition, as Andersen and Carlson evaluated the St Louis Model in their 1974 paper, two of the shortcomings of this model are that it cannot predict price level developments during a period of worldwide inflation, and also that it failed to capture short-run movements in income velocity.

How, then, may we evaluate the St Louis Model? At the least, it was an interesting challenge to mainstream macroeconometric modelling, and in this regard could be thought of as anticipating the Lucas critique. Moreover it was undoubtedly a useful exercise for the monetarists to attempt to formulate their hypotheses in econometric terms. It also shed some interesting light in the continuing debate among the partisans of large and small models. However, it would appear that a more formidable challenge to the advocates and practitioners of mainstream macroeconometric models comes from the rational expectations school, which is discussed in Chapter 17 below.

8   The Liu–Hwa Model

The final model to be reviewed in this chapter is the Liu–Hwa Model, described in Ta-Chung Liu and Erh-Cheng Hwa (1974). (A preliminary version of the model is described in Liu's earlier article (1969).) The principal innovation of this model is that it was a monthly model, and so it was better able (in principle) to take account of the detailed lag structure of the behavioural relationships. (A lot of the discussion of the two articles centres around this point.) Furthermore, most of the relationships are recursive, rather than simultaneous; if one believes, with Herman Wold and Robert Strotz, that economic behaviour in the 'real world' is virtually never simultaneous and that apparent simultaneity is largely an artifact of the manner in which economic data are collected (generally annually or quarterly), then monthly relationships could be formulated so as to represent more closely the 'true' patterns of behaviour.

As presented in Liu and Hwa (1974), the model contains 51 behavioural equations and 80 identities, for a total of 131 endogenous variables. (The earlier version (Liu, 1969) was much smaller, with only 16 behavioural equations and 17 identities.) The behavioural equations were estimated by ordinary least squares, using monthly data over the period 1954–71 (216 observations in total). Space does not permit a detailed description of the model, but we note that Liu and Hwa subdivided their model into eleven sectors: GNP Components (the traditional aggregate demand relationships); Manufacturers' New Orders, Sales and Unfilled Orders; Employment, Hours and Labour Force; a Financial Sector; Personal Property Incomes; Links between GNP and Disposable Personal Income; Prices, Wages and Unit Labour Cost; a Foreign Trade Sector; GNP Identities; Identities Relating to Capital Stocks; and Miscellaneous Identities. The parentage of the Liu 'Exploratory' Model of aggregate demand (Liu, 1963) is evident, although the gaps and lacunae mentioned in our review of the preceding chapter have now been filled. Thus, as the list of sectors above makes clear, there are now relationships for international trade and for employment, the labour force and unemployment. (Labour productivity measures for the private sector could be calculated from the model's outputs.) Liu and Hwa themselves compare the structure of their model (in broad outline) to the Wharton Mark III and BEA Models, both of which are summarized above. Three behavioural equations seem particularly interesting: that explaining the change in non-farm inventories, the equation for the implicit price deflator of gross private product, and the wage rate change equation. In the equation for the change in non-farm inventories, an inventory–sales accelerator is present to explain planned inventory investment, while the current change in sales (with a coefficient of -0.6) accounts for unintended inventory investment or disinvestment.[45] Other explanatory variables include the real short-term rate of interest (with a negative but statistically insignificant coefficient), which is lagged and the subject of a three-month average; the change in unfilled orders, lagged one period (which may capture growth in inventories of raw materials and goods-in-process); a strike dummy; the beginning-of-period stock of inventories (which would capture stock adjustment effects); and the lagged value of inventory investment (the dependent variable), which further alters the dynamic pattern of adjustment. The implicit deflator for gross private product is explained in level form; the structural explanatory variables are a controls dummy, unit labour costs, and the ratio of real gross private product to the stock of capital,[46] while the lagged dependent variable also appears, with a coefficient of 0.94.[47]

The wage rate adjustment equation explains the annual percentage change in money wage rates as a function of the reciprocal of a weighted average of unemployment rates over the past 12 months, the annual percentage change in consumer prices (with a one-month lag), the annual percentage change in corporate profits (gross of depreciation allowances), a controls dummy (with a negative but statistically insignificant coefficient), and the lagged dependent variable. These three equations, in addition to being important in themselves, serve to give a reasonable idea about the structure of the behavioural equations in this model.

Turning to the multiplier effects of increases in government expenditures (or exports), we note that the Liu–Hwa Model displays the familiar pattern of an inverted 'U' for the dynamic multipliers. Thus, in the case of both government expenditures and exports during the early 1960s, the dynamic multiplier for real GNP peaks after roughly 24 months (2 years) at peak values of 1.7 and 1.8 respectively. For the more prosperous period between the first month of 1968 and December 1971, the dynamic pattern is similar, although the numerical values of the multipliers are lower (exactly as Keynes predicted in the *General Theory*). Thus the government expenditures multiplier peaks after 15 months at a value of 1.13, while the exports multiplier also has a peak after 15 months, with a value of 1.25. Other multiplier calculations show that the effect on real GNP of an increase in non-borrowed reserves is quite powerful, particularly when starting from a position of considerable slack of resource utilization in the system.

Liu and Hwa (1974) examine the sources of prediction error, both within the sample period and beyond it (but with known values of the exogenous variables). They compare their model's full-model simulation errors with those of the Wharton Mark III and the BEA Model, and in general they feel that their model does not suffer in the comparison. (Christ's graphs (1975, p. 63) tend to confirm this view; as long as the monthly Liu–Hwa Model predictions last, the associated forecasting errors tend to be on the low side.) Thus there is some basis for Liu and Hwa's optimistic conclusion, '[t]here is some evidence, therefore, that a monthly model may have advantages in short-term forecasting' (p. 336).

The Liu–Hwa Model, although it was regarded as experimental and a tentative effort in a new direction, was quite stimulating and showed considerable promise. It seems unfortunate that, since the death of Ta-Chung Liu, this direction of research appears not to have been developed further. Perhaps the very difficult problems of generating monthly data in a form suitable for model estimation are a considerable part of the story (or lack of a story).

9 Some concluding remarks

As we intended to suggest in reviewing the seven models highlighted in this chapter, American macroeconometric modelling continued to make much progress during the decade of the 1970s. The models became increasingly sophisticated from a theoretical viewpoint, at times contributing importantly to the debates on central issues of macroeconometric theory. While the contribution of the model-builders was not exempt from criticism (see Chapters 16 and 17 below), the macroeconometric models were in the centre of this debate. It might also be noted that, of the five trends distinguished above (in the introductory section), the team approach to macroeconometric modelling was perhaps the central one, as this trend became the dominant pattern during this decade, despite some notable exceptions (some of which have been discussed in the text of this chapter). Moreover the team approach was also critical for two of the other trends distinguished above, namely detailed and large-scale modelling and also that of increasing theoretical sophistication. The revolution in computer technology also facilitated a team approach and probably gave a comparative advantage to this approach to macroeconometric modelling.

In Chapter 14, we wish to look at an exciting development, the interaction of national econometric models in a sort of world model, with links through international trade and other international economic relationships. We shall conclude this book with some of our best guesses as to the future evolution of macroeconometric model-building. Before launching into these tasks, a survey of some international experience would appear to be relevant. The following seven chapters discuss some of the experience of macroeconometric modelling outside its adopted homeland in the United States. In this context, it should not be forgotten that the first macroeconometric models of the pioneer Tinbergen were constructed for the Dutch, not the American, economy.[48]

Notes

1. Of course, given that all models contain exogenous variables and that in practice adjustments to constant terms (and others, on occasion) are made in virtually all *ex ante* forecasting exercises, no set of predictions can be described in the absolute as 'unconditional'. Moreover, this was often recognized in practice by the preparation of alternative forecasts (that is, forecasts that would be pertinent if some contingencies, deemed somewhat less likely than the evolution of exogenous variables underlying the principal forecast, materialized). Nevertheless, in practice, clients did undoubtedly treat the principal forecasts as the model-builders' best guesses of what was likely to happen to exogenous variables underlying the principal forecast, and it is difficult to see how a reasonable agent could behave otherwise.

2. The formal numerotation was vol. 15, no. 2; vol. 15, no. 3; and vol. 16, no. 1. These articles have been bound together and published as a book (Klein and Burmeister, eds, 1976).

3. We have not summarized the MPS Model (despite its appearance in the comparative

simulation symposium) in this chapter because we have done so at the end of the preceding chapter. The section summarizing the MPS Model makes in our view a good transition for American macroeconometric modelling experience during the 1960s to that of the 1970s, because the MPS evolved importantly during the two decades.

Nor have we summarized the Michigan Quarterly Econometric Model (Hymans and Shapiro, 1974) despite the fact that it, too, appears in this symposium. We have not done so because this smallish model (35 stochastic equations and 24 identities in 1974) was successor to the Suits Model, summarized in Chapter 3 above. (It is interesting to note, however, that, according to Intriligator (1978), another important antecedent of the Michigan Quarterly Econometric Model was a small forecasting model constructed at the Council of Economic Advisers in the late 1960s.) We may note, however, that the Michigan Model suggested (Hymans and Shapiro, 1974) that the American economy is inherently stable in the sense that it exhibits highly damped cyclical fluctuations in response to exogenous shocks; in addition, like many other econometric models, the Michigan Model has a tendency to smooth out unusual stimuli, thus under-reproducing extreme historical change. Hymans's survey article for the Econometrics of Price Determination Conference suggested that the long-run trade-off curve for the Michigan Model was very similar to that for two other current, mainstream models of the US economy that he was able to survey (the OBE (BEA) and the FMP (MPS) Models in particular); moreover this long-run trade-off curve corresponded rather closely to US macroeconomic experience during the individual years of the decade of the 1960s.

4. Half of the equations in this model sector in the 1966 version were concerned with the tax-transfer mechanism; others were technical relationships which concerned the orders-shipments mechanism, the definition of capacity output, and so forth.

5. There was also a constraint in the Monetary Sector, in which a limit was imposed on net borrowed reserves of member banks of the Federal Reserve System.

6. As pointed out in Hirsch *et al.* (1974), a key non-linearity is the hyperbolic relationship of money wage rate changes to the level of the unemployment rate. Another important non-linearity is the multiplicative interaction of prices and quantities in the identity for nominal GNP.

7. This was the period when one of us (Lawrence R. Klein) used to say that the American Economy was a 4 per cent economy – 4 per cent unemployment, 4 per cent inflation, and 4 per cent real annual growth.

8. US experience during the second half of the 1970s would appear to have refuted this assertion, which in any case appears doubtful to us (perhaps with the wisdom of hindsight), even in the context of the simulations reported in this paper.

9. This section is based, in part, on Bodkin's review (1985) of Eckstein (1983).

10. Not surprisingly, Eckstein (1983) stresses *ex ante* forecasting as a test for validating the model, for this is the usual context in which the (paying) client is interested in the results.

11. Interestingly, in the earlier paper, Eckstein, Green and Sinai (1974) point to the poor performance in forecasting price levels and hence nominal GNP; this defect had largely been corrected in the third-generation models, it is asserted. Of course, this is not to imply that economic forecasting with the DRI Model has become perfect; Eckstein (1983) makes the qualification that it is still largely impossible to forecast the exact timing (or magnitude) of minor inventory corrections; also, the forecasts of exogenous variables or phenomena (such as the behaviour of the Federal Reserve system, at the time of writing of his book) represent a limitation on the accuracy of *ex ante* forecasts (which practical users will consider the most important kind).

12. Interestingly, Eckstein, Green and Sinai (1974) assert that dynamic tax receipts multipliers are generally symmetric (but opposite-signed) to the expenditure multipliers, with a numerical value that is generally lower by one unit. Accordingly, in contrast to the BEA Model (and most of the working econometric models of this generation), the DRI multiplier results tend to confirm the balanced-budget theorem of intermediate macroeconomic theory.

13. A more sophisticated critique of the hypothesis of rational expectations is that it allows

economic agents to react only to first moments of expectations. This Eckstein explicitly rejects, arguing that risk and uncertainty may play a role, as businesses and consumers are both generally risk-averse. For instance, the variance of income and other measures of macro and financial risk affect spending decisions adversely, with a considerable impact in some historical episodes.

14. On this point, see McCarthy (1976).

15. In particular, the average work week varies as a by-product of the theoretical (and empirical) result that total employee hours are adjusted more rapidly than the number of employees.

16. In later versions of the Wharton Model during the late 1970s, price equations for final demand did employ input–output weights to obtain a partial mark-up over the prices of intermediate inputs. Also, the manufacturing sector of the model was subdivided into durable and non-durable manufacturing sectors.

17. For short-term forecasting in which the horizon is short enough for the anticipations-type variables to be known, these variables would typically be taken as given (exogenous). By contrast, longer-term forecasting (or counterfactual simulation, as in some multiplier analyses) would require some explanation of these variables, which must then be explained within the model.

18. Medium-term projections are much more 'conditional' than short-term *ex ante* predictions, as there often appears to be a wider range of possibilities for the exogenous variables, particularly the policy instruments. Some observers have gone so far as to argue that, in the long run, the future can be what we choose to make it. In any case, leaving aside this philosophical issue, we note that these medium-term projections are often 'tuned' to the companion model's forecast of the immediate economic future.

19. In Preston (1972), there were 50 producing industries in the square input–output matrix employed in the model. By 1975, pressures for disaggregation had increased this breakdown to 63 industries, which especially included energy detail in response to the oil embargo, the influence of changes in OPEC pricing policies, and other similar disturbances in the economy.

20. A nice description of the techniques of econometric forecasting in general appears in Intriligator (1978) Chapter 15.

21. In particular, a strikingly impressive accomplishment was the preparation of a revised forecast that was completed just two days after former President Nixon's announcement of the New Economic Policy, just in time for a previously scheduled meeting of the users' group.

22. Although the 'inverted-U' pattern is not evident in Table 12 of Duggal, Klein and McCarthy (1974), the discussion in the text makes it clear that this was the case. In addition, the summarizing article by Christ (1975) confirms this and also indicates that dynamic multipliers drop below unity (or zero) if given sufficient time to play themselves out.

23. In particular, the work of Michael Hurd (one of the co-authors of the 1975 journal article) and John Scadding on the monetary sector should be mentioned explicitly.

24. The Hickman–Coen Model has continued to be developed during the 1970s and 1980s; a good summary description of recent modifications to the model may be found in Coen and Hickman (1983), especially pp. 3–14. (Summary descriptions may also be found in Coen and Hickman (1984) and Coen and Hickman (1985), while the modifications of labour supply and demand and potential output sectors may be found in the two 1980 Coen and Hickman papers.) In general, the text discussion will focus on the model in the middle of the 1970s (in order to maintain consistency with our discussion of other American models of the time) but we shall note occasional recent developments. In particular, these modifications have rendered the Hickman–Coen Model far more useful for projection exercises during the final years of the twentieth century (and into the twenty-first). Interestingly, Hickman and Coen (1976) mention that the version of the model surveyed in the text would not be particularly useful for projections after 1973, owing to a failure to include energy constraints on production and to the rise of inflationary expectations, which would have had an impact (in all likelihood) on the

wage-formation process. These defects were remedied to the satisfaction of the model-builders, with the result that the final paper cited above contains projections into the first decade of the twenty-first century. (The remodelled energy sector of the Hickman –Coen Model is discussed in Coen and Hickman (1983) pp. 11–14; we note in particular that final consumer demands for energy are now modelled explicitly, and that energy costs are now part of the process of price formation, both for relative prices and for the general price level.)

25. In Hickman, Coen and Hurd (1975), it is stated that the model contains 50 behavioural equations and 70 endogenous variables. This was apparently a misprint, and the correct number of endogenous variables was evidently 170.

26. We note that several variants for the discount factor were tried in the expression for the rental price of capital services, and ultimately a constant 10 per cent value (independently of current monetary conditions) was preferred to both the nominal and real rates of interest, after tax, on private bonds. (Hickman and Coen have tested this hypothesis again with more recent data and more recent formulations of the model, again arriving at similar conclusions.) Thus monetary policy has only weak effects on private aggregate demand, as there were no real balance effects and the only interest rate effects that exist in the model work through consumer durables and residential construction.

27. The treatment of exports appears to mark an intermediate step between taking this category of final demand as purely exogenous and the fitting of export demand functions, which is now common (and indeed mandatory in linked systems).

28. Potential output is what the economy can produce if the full employment supply of labour (employee hours) is combined with the existing stock of capital. Capacity output, similarly a point on the aggregate production function, is a cost-minimization concept and refers to the output that would be produced if the existing capital stock were combined with that level of the labour input which is optimal (in the sense given above) with existing factor prices and technology. (In later versions of the model, potential output is defined as the level of real national product consistent with full employment at the 'natural' rate of unemployment, which is also given an endogenous representation in the model.)

  Full-employment output, on the other hand, is defined by Hickman and Coen to be that level of output which would have to be demanded if entrepreneurs were to hire, at existing wages and the rental price of capital services, enough employee hours to employ 96 per cent of the (full-employment) labour force.

29. In addition, we note that the real wage affects the participation rate negatively, which can be interpreted as indicating the predominance of an income effect over a substitution effect in the representative individual's theoretical choice of the quantity of leisure to enjoy. Of course, this choice should be understood to take place over a lifetime, the principal issue being the age of entry (or re-entry) into and retirement from the labour force. Later versions of the model disaggregate labour supply considerably; in Coen and Hickman (1980a) there are labour force participation rate equations for 16 age–sex groups.)

30. By contrast, the term structure of interest rates is considerably simplified in later versions of the model, and the monetary aggregate M_1 is simply taken to be an exogenous variable.

31. Hickman, Coen and Hurd (1975) p. 26. Similarly, in Hickman and Coen (1976), it is asserted that their approach to wage determination is one 'utilizing elements of the search theory of unemployment rather than the Phillips curve approach commonly found in macroeconomic models' (p. 2). Nevertheless, in practice, the distinction is not too pronounced, as the fitted wage rate equation does depend on the ratio of the amount of unemployment to the level of employment (this ratio is a transformation of an unemployment rate) and, via the role of expectations, the lagged level of wage rates. In later versions of the model, an expectations-augmented version of the Klein–Phillips relationship was added, in which the rate of wage change depends (among other things) on the ratio of the actual to the natural rate of unemployment.

32. There is a different mark-up equation depending upon whether the aggregate economy

operates according to a regime of constant or increasing returns to scale, because this maintained hypothesis will affect the formulation of the average cost function.

33.   This is clearly shown in Figure 4 (p. 70) of Christ's summary article (1975), where the dynamic multipliers for government expenditures in the Hickman–Coen Model continue to rise more or less monotonically for at least 40 quarters (10 years), although there is a slight cycle imposed on the major trend. By contrast, the pattern of the dynamic multipliers for the other nine econometric models for which this pattern was calculated for at least eight quarters all show the 'inverted-U' shape, although the details may differ to a large extent. However the 1980s Hickman–Coen Model now displays the familiar inverted-U pattern for the dynamic expenditures multiplier (Coen and Hickman, 1985).

34.   Fair's later work (such as Fair, 1984) also stresses the disequilibrium approach to macroeconometric modelling.

35.   It may be noted that output and employment were exogenous in the government and agricultural sectors.

36.   It should be noted, however, that Fair's 1970s model permitted calculation of an impact multiplier, if not dynamic multipliers (as the expectations variables were taken as exogenous); in his case, the impact multiplier is estimated to be relatively low, at 1.23.

37.   Thus, in Fair (1974a), he admits that the *ex ante* forecasts on the basis of the model were not quite as good as those of the ASA/NBER sample of expert (non-econometric) forecasts, while the performance of the Wharton and BEA models were roughly equivalent to this standard. Moreover a decade later (Fair, 1984) he is still less assertive, adopting what he terms a 'wait-and-see' methodology. At this time, he says that all models are mis-specified to a certain extent, in any case, and so rhetorical assertions of superiority may well be out of place.

38.   As a footnote, however, we may note that a more recent version of the Fair Model (Fair, 1984) appears to obey the tendency of macroeconometric models to grow larger. Thus the 1984 version of Fair's model had 30 behavioural equations and 98 identities; these 30 behavioural equations could be partitioned into nine equations representing household behaviour, 12 equations representing firm behaviour, five equations for the financial sector, one import demand equation, and three equations for the government (federal and state and local) sector. Fair's more recent model has been used to investigate the hypothesis that economic expectations are 'rational' (or at least 'model-consistent'), especially for the financial sector of the model. Being of manageable size, the Fair Model has also been adapated to the personal computer, for purposes of teaching and of individual model simulation. (See Blackburn and Case, 1985.)

39.   In fact, the solution of the St Louis Model is exceedingly simple, as it is virtually recursive. The total spending variable depends only on exogenous variables, so that it can be solved immediately. Furthermore the anticipated change in the price level depends only on lagged endogenous variables, so that it is effectively predetermined. Moreover the demand pressure variable depends on total spending changes and an exogenous and a lagged endogenous variable, so that it too can now be readily calculated. At this point, the price component of the change in total spending can be calculated via the appropriate behavioural equation, leaving the change in real GNP to be obtained from the relevant identity. At the end of this process we can calculate the GNP gap variable, the rate of unemployment and the two interest rate variables. Thus there is complete recursivity for a one-period solution of the model. Although there would be considerably more feedback in a dynamic solution (one over several periods), we observe that interest rates never enter the central core of the model and hence are virtually an 'afterthought'.

40.   We note that the lags are somewhat longer (16 quarters rather than 10) for the long-term interest rate equation. Also the constant weights for the current and past rate of change of the price level are modified by the reciprocal of the contemporaneous rate of unemployment (relative to a base of 4.0 per cent), exactly as was done in defining the anticipated price level change variable. Finally, both interest rate equations have a shift dummy taking effect during and after the first quarter of 1961, indicating that interest

rates were roughly a percentage point higher after 1960, at given values of the other explanatory variables.

41. This result emerges even more clearly in the context of some alternative 20-year simulations of the model, where the alternative growth rates of the money stock were 6, 3 and 0 per cent per year.

42. Interest rates follow a familiar pattern: the real interest rate settles roughly down to a constant value (3¼ per cent per year in the case of the long-term bond rate), while nominal interest rates equal approximately the sum of this real interest rate and the experienced rate of inflation, which of course is equal to the anticipated rate, in this context.

43. Andersen and Carlson work with one-year trade-off curves in this paper, but they indicate that this is a matter of pure convenience, as there are a number of other short-run trade-off curves (for example, a trade-off curve for one quarter, another for two years, and so forth) that could be calculated.

44. More recent studies have considerably weakened the view (even employing the St Louis Model as the framework of analysis) that monetary policy alone has an impact on nominal or real national product. See Silber (1971), Benjamin M. Friedman (1977) and (for a methodological criticism) Schmidt and Waud (1973). The titles of the Silber and Friedman articles are quite suggestive: Silber argues that there are 'Republican' and 'Democratic' versions of the key St Louis spending equation, and that the 'Democratic' version indicates that total nominal expenditures are quite sensitive to the fiscal policy variable. Friedman is even more unequivocal, asserting (after some standard qualifications), 'Even the St Louis Model now believes in Fiscal Policy.'

45. This would appear to be a reasonable value for this coefficient, even with monthly data. However, if even 40 per cent of unforeseen demand is met out of production (which of course is not the only interpretation of this result), then this suggests a non-trivial simultaneity, even within the monthly period of observation.

46. While this variable should have a negative coefficient if it represents capital costs factors, its positive coefficient (which is highly significant by conventional criteria) could be interpreted as reflecting the direct influence of demand pressures on price formation.

47. While the size of this coefficient suggests that the price equation might better be formulated in the form of a first difference or of a percentage rate of change, the difference from unity is highly significant, on the basis of a conventional test of statistical significance.

48. For more details, see the following chapter.

References

Adams, F. Gerard and Vijaya G. Duggal (1974) 'Anticipation Variables in an Econometric Model: Performance of the Anticipations Version of Wharton Mark III', *International Economic Review*, vol. 15, no. 2 (June) pp. 267–84.

Andersen, Leonall C. and Keith M. Carlson (1970a) 'A Monetarist Model for Economic Stabilization', *Review of the Federal Reserve Bank of St. Louis*, vol. 52 (April) pp. 7–25.

_____ (1970b) 'Supplementary Materials accompanying "A Monetarist Model for Economic Stabilization"', mimeographed, April.

_____ (1972) 'An Econometric Analysis of the Relation of Monetary Variables to the Behavior of Prices and Unemployment', pp. 166–83 in Otto Eckstein (ed.), *The Econometrics of Price Determination Conference* (Washington, DC: Board of Governors of the US Federal Reserve System).

_____ (1974) 'St. Louis Model Revisited', *International Economic Review*, vol. 15, no. 2 (June) pp. 305–27.

Blackburn, Anthony J. and Karl E. Case (1985) *FAIRMODEL Student Manual: An Economic Laboratory in Theory, Policy, and Forecasting* (Englewood Cliffs, New Jersey: Prentice-Hall).

Bodkin, Ronald G. (1985) Book Review of Otto Eckstein, *The DRI Model of the U.S. Economy, Southern Economic Journal*, vol. 51, no. 4 (April) pp. 1253–5.

Christ, Carl F. (1975) 'Judging the Performance of Econometric Models of the U.S. Economy', *International Economic Review*, vol. 16, no. 1 (February) pp. 54–74.

Coen, Robert M. and Bert G. Hickman (1980a) 'A Disaggregated Annual Model of Labor Supply and Unemployment, 1951–2000', Working Paper WP-80-15, International Institute for Applied Systems Analysis, Laxenburg, Austria, January.

_____ (1980b) 'The Natural Growth Path of Potential Output', Working Paper WP-80-132, International Institute for Applied Systems Analysis, Laxenburg, Austria, August.

_____ (1983) 'Energy Shocks and Macroeconomic Activity: Simulation Results from the Hickman–Coen Model', EMF 7.11, Energy Modeling Forum Working Paper, Stanford University, November.

_____ (1984) 'Tax Policy, Federal Deficits, and U.S. Growth in the 1980s', *National Tax Journal*, vol. 37, no. 1 (March) pp. 89–104. (Also published under the same title in *Prévision et analyse économique*, vol. 5, no. 1 (mars 1984) pp. 7–28).

_____ (1985) 'Social Security and Macroeconomic Activity in 1985–2010: A Forecast with the Hickman–Coen Model', Center for Economic Policy Research Publication No. 70, Stanford University, December.

de Leeuw, Frank and John Kalchbrenner (1969) 'Monetary and Fiscal Actions: A Test of their Relative Importance in Economic Stabilization – Comment', *Federal Reserve Bank of St. Louis Review*, vol. 51, no. 4 (April) pp. 6–11.

Duggal, Vijaya G., Lawrence R. Klein and Michael D. McCarthy (1974) 'The Wharton Model Mark III: A Modern IS–LM Construct', *International Economic Review*, vol. 15, no. 3 (October) pp. 572–94.

Eckstein, Otto (1978) *The Great Recession, with a Postscript on Stagflation* (Amsterdam/New York/Oxford: North-Holland).

_____ (1983) *The DRI Model of the U.S. Economy* (New York: McGraw-Hill).

Eckstein, Otto, Edward W. Green and Allen Sinai (1974) 'The Data Resources Model: Uses, Structure and Analysis of the U.S. Economy', *International Economic Review*, vol. 15, no. 3 (October) pp. 595–615.

Elliott, Donald A. (1985) *The St. Louis Fed's Monetary Model: Whence It Came; How It Thrived, 1970–1983* (New York & London: Garland Publishing).

Evans, Michael K. and Lawrence R. Klein (1968) *The Wharton Econometric Forecasting Model*, second, enlarged edn (Philadelphia: Economics Research Unit of the University of Pennsylvania).

Fair, Ray C. (1971) *A Short-Run Forecasting Model of the United States Economy* (Lexington, Mass.: D.C. Heath and Company).

_____ (1974a) 'An Evaluation of a Short-Run Forecasting Model', *International Economic Review*, vol. 15, no. 2 (June) pp. 285–304.

_____ (1974b) *A Model of Macroeconomic Activity, Volume I: The Theoretical Model* (Cambridge, Mass.: Ballinger).

_____ (1976) *A Model of Macroeconomic Activity, Volume II: The Empirical Model* (Cambridge, Mass.: Ballinger).

_____ (1984) *Specification, Estimation, and Analysis of Macroeconometric Models* (Cambridge, Mass.: Harvard University Press).

Friedman, Benjamin M. (1977) 'Even the St. Louis Model Now Believes in Fiscal Policy', *Journal of Money, Credit, and Banking*, vol. 9, no. 2 (May) pp. 365–7.

Friend, Irwin and Robert C. Jones (1964) 'Short-Run Forecasting Models Incorporating Anticipatory Data', pp. 279–307 in *Models of Income Determination*, Studies in Income and Wealth, vol. 28 (Princeton, NJ: Princeton University Press).

Friend, Irwin and Paul Taubman (1964) 'A Short-Run Forecasting Model', *Review of Economics and Statistics*, vol. 46, no. 3 (August) pp. 229–36.

Hickman, Bert G. and Robert M. Coen (1976) *An Annual Growth Model of the U.S. Economy* (Amsterdam/New York/Oxford: North-Holland).

Hickman, Bert G., Robert M. Coen and Michael D. Hurd (1975) 'The Hickman–Coen Annual Growth Model: Structural Characteristics and Policy Responses', *International Economic Review*, vol. 16, no. 1 (February) pp. 20–38.

Hirsch, Albert A. (1972) 'Price Simulations with the OBE Econometric Model', pp. 237–76 in Otto Eckstein (ed.), *The Econometrics of Price Determination Conference* (Washington, DC: Board of Governors of the US Federal Reserve System).

Hirsch, Albert A., Bruce T. Grimm and Gorti V. Narasimhan (1974) 'Some Multiplier and Error Characteristics of the BEA Quarterly Model', *International Economic Review*, vol. 15, no. 3 (October) pp. 616–31.

Hymans, Saul H. (1972) 'Prices and Price Behavior in Three U.S. Econometric Models', pp. 309–24 in Otto Eckstein (ed.), *The Econometrics of Price Determination Conference* (Washington, DC: Board of Governors of the US Federal Reserve System).

Hymans, Saul H. and Harold T. Shapiro (1974) 'The Structure and Properties of the Michigan Quarterly Econometric Model of the U.S. Economy', *International Economic Review*, vol. 15, no. 3 (October) pp. 632–53.

Intriligator, Michael D. (1978) *Econometric Models, Techniques, and Applications* (Englewood Cliffs, NJ: Prentice-Hall).

Klein, Lawrence R. and Edwin Burmeister (eds) (1976) *Econometric Model Performance: Comparative Simulations of the U.S. Economy* (Philadelphia: University of Pennsylvania Press).

Liebenberg, Maurice, Albert A. Hirsch and Joel Popkin (1966) 'A Quarterly Econometric Model of the United States: A Progress Report', *Survey of Current Business*, vol. 46, no. 5 (May) pp. 13–39.

Liu, Ta-Chung (1963) 'An Exploratory Quarterly Econometric Model of Effective Demand in the Post-War U.S. Economy', *Econometrica*, vol. 31, no. 3 (July) pp. 301–48.

_____ (1969) 'A Monthly Recursive Econometric Model of United States: A Test of Feasibility', *The Review of Economics and Statistics*, vol. 51, no. 2 (February) pp. 1–13.

Liu, Ta-Chung and Erh-Cheng Hwa (1974) 'Structure and Applications of a Monthly Econometric Model of the U.S.', *International Economic Review*, vol. 15, no. 2 (June) pp. 328–65.

McCarthy, Michael D. (1972) *The Wharton Quarterly Econometric Forecasting Model Mark III* (Philadelphia: Economics Research Unit of the University of Pennsylvania).

_____ (1976) 'Quarterly Model of the U.S.A.: Wharton Mark III', pp. 349–96 of Waelbroeck (ed.), *The Models of Project LINK*.

McLaughlin, Robert L. (1980) 'Never, Never – Repeat – NEVER Forecast Recession', *Business Economics*, vol. 15, no. 3 (May) pp. 5–15.

McNees, Stephen K. (1973) 'A Comparison of the GNP Forecasting Accuracy of the Fair and St. Louis Econometric Models', *New England Economic Review*, September/October, pp. 29–34.

Oi, Walter (1962) 'Labor as a Quasi-Fixed Factor', *Journal of Political Economy*, vol. 70, no. 6 (December) pp. 538–55.

Popkin, Joel (1974) 'Consumer and Wholesale Prices in a Model of Price Behavior by Stage of Processing', *Review of Economics and Statistics*, vol. 56, no. 4 (November) pp. 486–501.

Preston, Ross S. (1972) *The Wharton Annual and Industry Forecasting Model* (Philadelphia: Economics Research Unit of the University of Pennsylvania).

_____ (1975) 'The Wharton Long-Term Model: Input–Output within the Context of a Macro Forecasting Model', *International Economic Review*, vol. 16, no. 1 (February) pp. 3–19.

Schmidt, Peter and Roger N. Waud (1973) 'The Almon Lag Technique and the Monetary Versus Fiscal Policy Debate', *Journal of the American Statistical Association*, vol. 68, no. 341 (March) pp. 11–19.

Silber, William L. (1971) 'The St. Louis Equation: "Democratic" and "Republican" Versions and Other Experiments', *Review of Economics and Statistics*, vol. 53, no. 4 (November) pp. 362–7.

Solow, Robert M. (1985) 'Reflections on Macroeconomic Modelling: Confessions of a DRI Addict', *Eastern Economic Journal*, vol. 11, no. 1 (January–March) pp. 79–83.

Waelbroeck, Jean (ed.) (1976) *The Models of Project LINK* (Amsterdam/New York/Oxford: North-Holland).

PART III

COMPARATIVE EXPERIENCE

6 The history of Dutch macroeconometric modelling 1936–86

*Anton P Barten**

1 Introduction

'A dynamic theory of the business cycle, if fully elaborated in precise terms, so as to do some justice to the enormous complexity of the real world, requires a highly complicated mathematical technique and presents formidable problems from the purely logical point of view.' In this way Haberler concludes Part I of his famous *Prosperity and Depression*, of which the first edition appeared in 1937. In a footnote he refers to the work of Frisch and Tinbergen as an example of this approach.

This statement by Haberler well expresses the intellectual challenge of constructing a framework which would bridge the gap between the business cycle theory of those days and the reality of economic fluctuations. The approach taken by Frisch and Tinbergen, but also by others (for example, Kalecki), consisted in applying the mathematics of solving (linear) differential and difference equations to sets of economic relations. By assigning sufficiently realistic values to the constants in such a system, one might be able to simulate a dominant wave-like movement of the economy with a periodicity of about 8–11 years: the business cycle.

In this sense two of the many contributions of Frisch and Tinbergen to the development of a mathematical theory of the business cycle are of special interest, because they specifically aim at matching theory and facts.[1] Seen against the backdrop of later developments, these attempts are rather crude, but at their time they were quite novel. A brief review of them might help recreate the intellectual landscape in which the first full-fledged macroeconometric 1936 model of Tinbergen appeared.

The contribution of Frisch (1933), presented orally at the Leyden meeting of the Econometric Society in 1933, addresses itself to the issue of the endogenous nature of the business cycle. As he patiently explains, cycles can be generated by non-periodic impulses depending on the intrinsic characteristics of the economic system. To generate cycles the system should relate the present to the more or less distant past. In the simple case of a linear economy, the cyclical nature follows from the value of the parameters of the underlying relations. By selecting for these some more or less realistic values (a marginal capital–output ratio of 10, a depreciation rate of 20 per cent, and so forth) Frisch is able to let his model generate cycles of 8.6, 3.5 and 2.2 years, superimposed upon a monotone damped component.

In the Frisch model the basic imbalance giving rise to cyclical movements is the one between the production of producer or investment goods on the one hand, and that of consumer goods on the other. Prices do not play any role. In the model of Tinbergen (1935), however, the price level is playing the leading part. One may summarize his model as a hog-cycle or cobweb model for macroeconomic consumption. With quarterly data for the United States (1920–33) and for Germany (1925–33), the supply of consumer goods (volume) and the demand for these (value) are explained as a function of the retail price level, its change and a trend. The two equations are fitted by the method of least squares, with the coefficients divided by the correlation coefficient. One may consider this three-equation model (the third equation being the identity linking price, volume and value) as the first published estimated macroeconomic model.

In many respects this first model is very primitive when compared with the model which Tinbergen employed for his paper which was read at the 1936 annual meeting of the Dutch Association of Economics and Statistics. This latter model truly marks the beginning of a long tradition of model-building and for that reason alone deserves a detailed discussion, which follows in the next section.

The 1936 Tinbergen model gave the construction of models, of the Netherlands and in the Netherlands, a head start. Over the years, many models have been constructed, for the Netherlands as well as for other countries, regions, blocks of nations and the world. It is not the purpose of the present contribution to review them all. A quick glance at the survey of Uebe *et al.* (1986) would show such an endeavour to be self-defeating. The emphasis will instead be on how Dutch modelling activity responded to the needs of macroeconomic policy, how it incorporated new theoretical insights concerning the working of the economy and how it absorbed technical innovations in estimation and model simulation. To limit further the scope, models that have not lived beyond a doctoral dissertation are not discussed; nor are other models that have hardly been put to use. This historical review also concentrates on the Dutch tradition. Many models of the Netherlands have been built as part of multinational modelling projects. One of the first of these is to be found in Von Hohenbalken and Tintner (1962). These will also be left out. Still it is possible that models have been omitted that in the view of some should have been included. This may have happened because the author was not aware of their existence, or as the result of a conscious decision to keep the review within reasonable bounds.

The paper is organized as follows: The 1936 Tinbergen model, together with a later variant of it, is discussed in some detail in the next section. One had to wait until 1953 before the Central Planning Bureau (CPB) installed its first model. Since then, however, it has been *the* centre of model-building in the Netherlands. The string of models developed and used by the CPB in the late 1950s and in the 1960s is reviewed in Section 3. The following section is then devoted to the newer generations of models produced at the CPB since then. The virtual monopoly of the CPB in modelling came to an end in the mid-1970s. Section 5 summarizes some of the models that have been constructed at other institutions. Section 6 will, from a distance, look back at this half-century of model-building.

The pioneering role of Dutch model-building in the earlier years stands out clearly. This justifies the telescopic structure of this paper with its focus on the more distant past at the cost of less detail on more recent developments.

2 The 1936 Tinbergen model

The title of the English translation – Tinbergen (1959) – of the 1936 paper is 'An Economic Policy for 1936'. It nicely summarizes the slightly long-winded question which serves as the title of the original paper: 'Is a recovery in the domestic economic situation of this country possible, with or without action on the part of the Government, even without an improvement in our export position? What can be learned about this problem from the experience of other countries?' This was the question the Board of the Association put before Tinbergen, then associated with the Central Bureau of Statistics (CBS) and part-time professor at the Netherlands School of Economics in Rotterdam. Tinbergen limited himself mainly to the first part of the question. He specifically built his model to answer it.

Economic conditions in the Netherlands had become worse and worse between 1929 and 1936. World trade, on which the country depended so much, had dropped by 30 per cent. Net national income per capita at constant (market) prices had decreased by 18 per cent. Registered unemployment had gone up from 2.8 per cent in 1929 to 17.4 per cent in 1936 (see CBS, 1979). Quantitative import restrictions and higher tariffs aimed at keeping foreign competition on the domestic market at bay. Minimum prices for farm produce were introduced to maintain farmers' income at subsistence levels. Nominal wages of those that had a job, however, had gone down less than the cost of living index. Moreover consumption per capita had not changed much since 1929 but its distribution was more unequal. The surpluses of central government of the late 1920s had turned into a series of deficits. The government headed by Colijn tried hard to curtail its expenditures. The trade balance was less negative than in more prosperous years because imports had decreased more than exports. Colijn defended the position that without a sound currency there was no way back to prosperity. He kept the guilder at its (overvalued) gold parity in a world where the major currencies had already left the gold standard years earlier.

What, then, could be done to reduce unemployment and to restore prosperity, while respecting some balance of the current account? Would matters improve by themselves if left alone? A public works programme, perhaps, as proposed by the socialist movement in their Labour Plan? More import restrictions? Rationalization? Reduction of profit margins? Or of wages? Or perhaps a devaluation, risking foreign reprisals?

Tinbergen's model tried to supply the means to formulate an answer to these questions. It is worthwhile to have a close look at it. It is a system of 24 linear equations, of which 15 are reaction equations with estimated coefficients, in most cases. Six equations contain lagged endogenous variables on the right-hand side, making it a dynamic model. We will take up various aspects in turn.

Variables
The variables are mostly quantities, prices and values of labour, consumption, exports of goods, imports of finished consumer goods and those of production equipment, imports of raw materials for the production of consumer goods or for that of producer goods. The distinction between consumer goods and producer goods is typical for a school of business cycle theory of that time. A strategic role is played by non-wage or other income, also called 'profits' by Tinbergen. One misses concepts like inventory changes, government consumption, gross national or domestic product, indirect and direct taxes, which are familiar components of most models since the system of national accounts was fully developed. Investment or gross fixed capital formation is implicitly defined. Absent from the model are monetary and financial variables, like the interest rate, money supply and various forms of credit. The exogenous variables are the world price level, the price levels of the various imports, the volume of world trade, the income from investment abroad, that is, the international environment. The time trend is, of course, also an exogenous variable. Note that exports of goods and their prices are endogenous in the 1936 Tinbergen model.

Data
The observations on the variables are taken from various sources. The paper gives the annual values for 1923 to 1933 for all variables. For 1934 most values are given; for 1935 the information is less complete. All equations but one are estimated for an 11-year sample period, 1923–33. In

the case of equations with lagged variables, the relevant 1921 and 1922 values are absent, but they can be reconstructed from the graphs of the equations. The prices are scaled so that the average for 1923–33 equals 100. The values are expressed in units of 17.54 million guilders, being the 1923–33 average of the wage bill, after division by 100. The quantities are defined accordingly.

Specification
The model is conceived as a business cycle model. The equations describe variations around a linear trend. This is reflected in the fact that the variables in the equations are expressed as deviations from the 1923–33 mean, while many equations contain a trend term. This term is omitted from the presentation of the equations but can be retrieved from the graphs.

Estimation
Most of the equations have been estimated by least squares, or rather by a variant of least squares also known as diagonal least squares. The least squares regression coefficients are divided by the correlation coefficient to correct for the asymmetry in the treatment of left-hand side and right-hand side variables in ordinary least squares. Since most of the correlation coefficients are close to one, this correction is (fortunately) of minor importance.

In a few equations, multicollinearity prevented the obtaining of plausible values for some of the coefficients. These were then assigned a reasonable value. Next to the intercepts, at most three regression coefficients per equation were estimated. Tinbergen, helped by B. Buys, performed the calculations with paper, pencil and slide-rule. Redoing these calculations using a computer showed differences in the outcomes, but none of those were consequential – see Dhaene and Barten (1989). Inconsistency due to simultaneity is an academic question if the sample covers only 11 observations. Moreover, the coefficients of multiple determination (R^2) are generally rather high. To silence all doubts on this score, the residuals of the Tinbergen equations have been regressed on the explanatory variables using as instrumental variables the exogenous ones of the system. The resulting chi-square values are so small that the hypothesis of no inconsistency cannot be rejected. It appears, however, that the estimates are very sensitive to the data. Using one more observation may make a considerable difference for the point estimates. This corresponds with the finding of Denton and Kuiper (1965) that in very small samples the point estimates tend to be more sensitive to the data than to the method.

Identities
The model contains two additive definitions. One describes total consumption as the sum of consumption by wage-earners, identical to the wage bill, and that of other income earners. The other one defines total output as the sum of consumption and commodity exports. The data do not obey this latter identity. The other seven identities are linearizations of the relations in which value equals quantity times price. As an example, take the case of commodity exports.

$$U_A(t) = u_A(t) + 0.88p_A(t) - 88. \tag{6.1}$$

Here U_A, u_A and p_A are the value, volume and price of commodity exports, respectively; t represents a year. The value of 88 is the 1923–33 average of both U_A and u_A. As a measure of the precision of the approximization one may use the R^2. It is 0.984.

Reaction Equations
We will present some examples and start with the consumption function. The model explains consumption as a function of income but in a differential way. A first component is consumption by wage-earners. The members of this group are supposed to consume all of their primary income (L) without delay. Other income (Z) is only partially (68 per cent) paid out to its earners and with an average delay of 0.27 years. Of this amount (E) 26 per cent is consumed now and next year. Tinbergen's function is written as:

$$E'(t) + E'(t+1) = 0.26 \, E(t) - 1.8 \, t + 224.07, \tag{6.2}$$

where E' is consumption by 'other income' earners. The constant has been added to make it simple to work with the level values of the variable. The R^2 of this equation for the 1923–32 sample period is 0.94. The marginal propensity to consume out of paid-out other income is only 13 per cent. This seems somewhat low, considering that farmers, retailers and artisans are among these income earners. For comparison, we add here the least-squares re-estimation results of this equation:

$$E'(t) + E'(t+1) = 0.229 \, E(t) - 1.793 \, t + 229.9 \tag{6.3}$$
$$ (0.054) (0.274) (10.27)$$
$R^2 : 0.942 \quad SER : 2.18 \quad DW : 2.07$
Sample period 1923–32,

where the standard errors are given in parentheses below the coefficients,

SER denotes the standard error of regression and *DW* the Durbin-Watson statistic. Clearly, the differences are minor. Note that relative prices do not influence consumption levels.

Investment equation

The model does not contain an investment variable as such. No doubt data were lacking for this concept. Tinbergen assumed that investment activity is proportional to imports of means of production. The factor of proportionality is three times larger when these means are raw materials rather than finished products, reflecting the assumption that $\frac{2}{3}$ of the value of the finished product is value added. The dependent variable of his investment equation is thus $v_A' + 3y_A'$, where v_A' is imports of finished means of production and y_A' is imports of raw materials (inputs) for the production of investment goods. The explanatory variable is 'other income' (Z) and a trend:

$$v_A' + 3y_A' = 0.51\ Z(t-1) + 2.93\ t - 48.10, \tag{6.4}$$

with $R^2 = 0.887$. Athough perhaps profit expectations is the appropriate explanatory variable, no information about that is available and past profits are the best proxy for it. The rate of interest does not appear in this equation. It is a relatively unimportant part of total investment costs in the first place and its role does not show up in empirical investigations. Prices of shares are roughly parallel to profits so there is no room for them in this equation. Tinbergen (1935) found little unambiguous evidence of the acceleration principle, which was so popular with the business cycle analysts of that era. This explains the absence of production changes in (6.4). Explaining investment by profits will turn out to be characteristic for Dutch modelling. In the model, the y_A' part of investment determines the amount of labour in the producer goods industry (b). Moreover the degree in which investment goods are locally produced rather than completely imported, as measured by $y_A' - v_A'$, is made dependent on the difference between the price of imported investment goods and that of locally produced ones $(q_A' - q)$.

Labour demand

The portion of total labour (a) working in the consumer goods industry $(a - b)$ is considered to be engaged in processing imported raw materials for consumption (x_A') and to a much lesser degree in processing finished consumer goods (u_A'). The equation reads:

$$a(t) = b(t) + 0.2\ u_A'\ (t) + 1.0\ x_A'(t) - 0.28\ t + 23.05. \tag{6.5}$$

The coefficients of u_A' and of x_A' have not been estimated. The importance of the effects can be gauged from the respective elasticities: 0.12 for a with respect to u_A' and 0.41 for a with respect to x_A'. The R^2 of this equation is 0.905. In the model u_A' and x_A' depend on total production (u), while the extent to which consumer goods are home-produced rather than fully imported depends on the differential of consumer prices (p) and the price of imported inputs into the production of consumer goods.

Consumer prices
Tinbergen's price equations represent supply behaviour. In this model demand determines the quantities, sometimes independently of prices, as in the case of consumption, while supply sets the prices, mostly independently of the quantities. The basic ingredient is a cost component consisting of import price of the raw materials, the wage rate (l) and a productivity trend. The profit margin depends on the corresponding foreign price level and, in the case of consumption, on the total quantity produced (u). The consumer price equation, for example, takes the following form:

$$p(t) = 0.15 \, (r_A' + 2l - 6t) + 0.04 \, p_A' + 0.08 \, u(t) + 24.20 \qquad (6.6)$$

The coefficients in the cost term have not been estimated. Still, the equation has a very close fit: $R^2 = 0.980$. The effect of the price level of imports of finished consumer goods (p_A') is weak and statistically sensitive. When the equation was re-estimated it turned negative, although not significantly different from zero. In a later version of the model (see Tinbergen, 1937), it was omitted. As is evident from (6.6), long-run price homogeneity is not respected.

Wage rate
In the 1936 Tinbergen model, the equation for the wage rate (l) is specified as follows:

$$\Delta l(t) = 0.27 \, \Delta p(t-1) + 0.16 \, a(t) - 16.28, \qquad (6.7)$$

which shows that the change in the wage rate is made dependent on the change in the cost of living in the preceding year and on the level of employment (a). In a sense, this specification anticipates a Klein–Phillips type of wage determination. Its R^2 equals 0.897, which is not too high, but the standard deviation of the residuals is less than 1 per cent of the sample mean. There is a problem with this equation, however. In the stationary state Δl and Δp are zero and a equals 101.75, regardless of the exogenous conditions. This implies that all measures of economic policy that do not change the intercept in (6.7) cannot affect the employment level in the long run. The same is true for external conditions like world trade. This is an unfortunate property for a model oriented towards the design of an employment policy. At the time of its presentation, this aspect seems to have escaped the attention of its author. However, in a revision (Tinbergen 1937), this question was replaced by:

$$l(t) = 0.36 \, a(t-1) - 0.9 \, t, \tag{6.7a}$$

which avoids the problem just mentioned.

Export equation
Commodity exports u_A are proportional to world trade and depend positively on the world price level lagged one quarter and negatively on the price of exports. The elasticity of exports with respect to its own price is -1.43, when evaluated for the sample mean, while that with respect to the world price level is 2.38. These values centre around -2, the value of the substitution price elasticity of exports implicit in an earlier study by Tinbergen (1936b) and incorporated in so many of the later Dutch models.

Other income
The 'other income' or profit variable (Z) plays a major role in the model. Its structural equation is a mixture of a definition and of a reaction function. The variable itself was calculated as the estimated national income of persons plus the non-distributed income of enterprises minus the wage bill. Only the latter appears as such in the model. The other two components are implicitly approximated by the equation. A first part is made up of the value-added (the term was not yet in use) of the production of consumer goods, production equipment and commodity exports, from which the wage bill is subtracted and to which income from investments abroad (the colonies overseas) is added. Profits are not only the rewards of production. They can result from speculation or from appreciation of inventories, which are considered to be related to the increases in import prices of raw materials and of finished consumer goods. The value of financial investments is taken to be reflected in profit levels. As the change in this value can be considered as part of profits, the equation contains a term in $\Delta Z(t)$, introducing a further element of dynamics into this equation. The coefficients of the second part of the equation have not been estimated by regression methods but resulted from an educated guess. The equation displays a considerably high fit. It is of interest to note that Z peaked in 1928. It dropped as early as 1929 because exports remained

constant (at a high level) while income from abroad continued its decrease since 1926. In the model, only lagged Z appears as explanatory variable. It determines investment and the consumption of non-wage earners. Because it absorbs virtually all other variables in the model, the Z equation plays a pivotal role in the dynamic interactions of the model.

Simultaneous interdependence

Qualitative structural analysis shows that the model consists of a central simultaneous block of 14 equations, preceded by two recursive equations and followed by a string of eight post-simultaneous recursive equations. The degree of simultaneity is considerably reduced when the wage rate (l) is made independent of employment (a).

Solution procedures

The model does not contain policy instruments as variables. Policy changes were introduced as exogenous shifts in the relevant equations. Replacing the other exogenous variables by assumed values and the lagged variables by observed values, Tinbergen solved the model in two steps. First, by way of substitution and elimination, all endogenous variables, except the wage rate, are expressed in terms of the wage rate, the lagged wage rate, the lagged increase in consumption prices, lagged profits (Z) and a constant. Next, a small recursive system in the five endogenous variables that also appear in lagged form is set up, which is then solved simultaneously and consecutively, resulting in a time path for these variables, one for each policy alternative. These time paths were then used to calculate the values of the other endogenous variables. One of the time paths corresponds to no specific policy. It served as the reference solution. As such it could serve as a pure prediction. Still as Driehuis (1986) remarks, Tinbergen did not pay much attention to it. He was more interested in the differential policy effects that can be read off from the differences between the time paths for the various policy and the reference solution. His approach is the one model-users employ too to evaluate their simulations. However the Tinbergen model is linear and has constant multipliers. There are, then, simpler ways to calculate the differential effects.

Multipliers

The linearity of the model has been used to derive the reduced form, the impact, interim and total multipliers of an incidental autonomous increase in investment in year $t = 0$ by one unit on gross domestic product ($GDPQ$), on employment (a), on consumer prices (p), the trade balance (TBV) and on other income (Z) for the years $t = 0, ..., 10$. The last row represents the sum of all the multipliers over $t = 0, ..., \infty$. The first column resembles most closely the Keynesian investment multiplier concept. (*GDPQ* is defined here as $u + 2y'_A - u'_A - x'_A$.) As may be observed, it is less than one. This low value can be explained as follows. Derived investment increases only the following year because it depends on $Z(t-1)$. There is a small derived increase in consumption of about 0.36. The gross effect of a 1.36 production increase entails imports of 0.65, resulting in a net effect of 0.71. Observe that this is the total effect of an autonomous increase in investment on *GDPQ*, that is, national value added, which combines the *direct* and *derived* effect. In the model the structural share of value-added to investment is 0.5. Thus the total effect is 1.4 times the direct effect as far as value-added is concerned. As further appears from Table 6.1, the trade balance (*TBV*) is reduced, as a result of the increase in imports. Employment and prices go up. The second year effect is still attractive but already substantially less than the impact effect. In later years the effects become small. Pump-priming does not work here. Note the fluctuating sign of *Z*, indicating a two-year cycle. Table 6.2 gives the effects of a permanent unit increase in autonomous investment. The bottom line gives the change in the stationary state; it appears to be small. The zero for employment is due to the nature of wage rate equation (6.7). Table 6.3 displays the effects of a permanent increase of all foreign prices by one unit (about 2 per cent). The impact in year 0 is rather small but that in year 1 is substantial. Note the perverse *J*-effect on the trade balance.

The increase in foreign prices relative to domestic prices causes in this model a shift from imports of finished goods to imports of raw materials and hence only a rather limited decrease in imports, which is more than compensated by the increase of imports due to the induced domestic expansion. The volume of exports is rather insensitive. It depends on the difference between the world price level and the export price level, which is never allowed to be large because the export price level depends positively on the world price level. The effects on GDP and employment are initially strong but taper off. Domestic prices adjust to the international ones. As the last line of Table 6.3 shows, there is even an over-adjustment, owing to the absence of price homogeneity in the model. This last line also shows that employment returns to its old level, as is implied by equation (6.7). Still, real wages as well as other income are higher.

Dynamic characteristics
The interim multipliers show a gradual decrease. The endogenous fluctuations of the model are definitely damped. When the eigenvalues that characterize these fluctuations are calculated, they turn out to be all real and less than one in absolute value. The non-zero ones are 0.9723, −0.9421, 0.1148 and 0.1075, respectively. The first two are close to one in

Table 6.1 Multipliers of autonomous investment (single one-unit impulse in $t = 0$)

Year	GDPQ	a	p	TBV	Z
0	0.710	0.420	0.049	-0.650	0.994
1	0.422	0.226	0.059	-0.396	0.177
2	0.010	0.015	0.035	-0.069	-0.050
3	-0.006	-0.015	0.038	-0.031	0.025
4	-0.043	-0.017	0.030	-0.016	-0.063
5	-0.014	-0.018	0.035	-0.023	0.019
6	-0.042	-0.017	0.028	-0.015	-0.058
7	-0.014	-0.017	0.033	-0.021	0.016
8	-0.039	-0.016	0.027	-0.014	-0.052
9	-0.015	-0.016	0.031	-0.020	0.013
10	-0.036	-0.015	0.025	-0.014	-0.048
$\sum_{0,\infty}$	0.050	0.000	1.360	-1.845	0.353

Table 6.2 Multipliers of autonomous investment (permanent increase by one unit from t = 0 on)

Year	GDPQ	a	p	TBV	Z
0	0.710	0.420	0.049	−0.650	0.994
1	1.132	0.646	0.108	−1.046	1.171
2	1.142	0.661	0.143	−1.115	1.121
3	1.136	0.646	0.181	−1.146	1.146
4	1.093	0.629	0.211	−1.162	1.083
5	1.079	0.611	0.246	−1.185	1.102
6	1.037	0.594	0.274	−1.200	1.044
7	1.023	0.577	0.307	−1.221	1.060
8	0.984	0.561	0.334	−1.235	1.008
9	0.969	0.545	0.365	−1.255	1.021
10	0.933	0.530	0.390	−1.269	0.973
∞	0.050	0.000	1.360	−1.845	0.353

Table 6.3 Multipliers of foreign price increase (devaluation) (permanent increase by one unit from t = 0 on)

Year	GDPQ	a	p	TBV	Z
0	−0.021	0.017	0.161	0.272	3.086
1	1.665	0.840	0.334	−0.559	2.611
2	1.286	0.667	0.351	−0.339	2.290
3	1.253	0.624	0.395	−0.342	2.444
4	1.186	0.606	0.413	−0.339	2.244
5	1.217	0.587	0.456	−0.372	2.391
6	1.134	0.568	0.474	−0.375	2.214
7	1.160	0.554	0.514	−0.406	2.344
8	0.085	0.540	0.532	−0.409	2.185
9	0.107	0.523	0.569	−0.438	2.299
10	0.039	0.510	0.587	−0.442	2.157
∞	0.207	0.000	1.426	−0.999	1.607

absolute value. This corresponds with the rather slow convergence of the multipliers. The negative one corresponds with the two-year cycle, mostly owing to the way that the consumption function (6.2) is formulated and to the determination of other income (Z). For a business cycle model, the absence of conjugate pairs of complex eigenvalues is somewhat disappointing, because these would have caused more interesting cyclical patterns. The two-year cycle is more an artifact of the model than a reflection of the real state of affairs.

Implementation
Tinbergen investigated seven different policy scenarios. Two of these involved a devaluation of the guilder by 30 per cent. He found this option the most attractive alternative. He addressed the meeting of the Dutch Economics Association on 24 October 1936, but his paper was already available in September. On 27 September the minister–president Colijn abandoned the gold parity of the guilder, reluctantly following the example of the People's Front government of France and that of Switzerland. The guilder was effectively devalued by 17–20 per cent.

Evaluation
One cannot help but be deeply impressed by the enormous step forward that the Tinbergen 1936 model constituted. With virtually no antecedents, Tinbergen produced a model of no less than 24 equations, justified on the basis of economic reasoning and empirical experience, fitting well the scarcely available data. It made it possible to answer questions of great practical importance with an exceptional degree of consistency. Artus *et al.* (1986) consider the model's linear structure, the weakness of its theoretical basis and the non-empirical nature of some of the coefficients as its basic weaknesses, as seen from the present point of view. One need not entirely agree with this judgement. Surely from the 1936 point of view, the linear structure was a strong point of the model. The theory behind it was much more articulate than contemporaneous contributions, even including that of Keynes (1936), while reliance on non-estimated coefficients is even today a common feature. Perhaps, with a collective experience of over 50 years, one would do certain things differently now. Perhaps the limitations of the approach are somewhat better realized, because of that experience. Still, this does not detract from the unique qualities of the original contribution. Going over the old text, trying to derive again the published results, one finds out over and over again that every detail is justified, that little or nothing is left to luck, but almost all is consciously selected.

Sequel

Tinbergen (1937) was somewhat more than a version in English of his 1936 paper. It not only contained a more elaborate discussion of the dynamics involved, but also the model was changed in a number of ways. As already mentioned, the wage equation (6.7) was replaced by (6.7a), making the model more suitable. The consumption function (6.2) with the slightly awkward left-hand side was changed into:

$$E' = 0.065 \,(E(t) + E(t-1)), \tag{6.2a}$$

reducing the somewhat spurious two-year cycle which was in part caused by the original equation. The savings equation was changed in a similar way. Commodity exports and export prices were made exogenous. The model then comprised 22 equations. Minor adjustments were made to the equation of the consumption price and that of other income. The total of long-run multiplier effects on employment are now non-zero. The impact multiplier of autonomous investment on GDP is 0.73, close to the value of Table 6.1, but the long-run multiplier is now 0.88, still below one but substantially higher than the 0.05 of Table 6.2. All eigenvalues characterizing endogenous dynamics are real. The dominant one is -0.44, negative, but rather small. The other non-zero ones are 0.17, 0.03 and -0.02, respectively. There is a dominating two-year cycle, which soon dies out. Tinbergen (1938) developed still another model for a report by the Dutch Labour Council on employment policy. Although it differed from its predecessors, the differences are rather minor. One of Tinbergen's co-workers, J. J. Polak (1939), used the 1936 model to derive for the Netherlands a reduced form equation for domestic activity as a function of world trade and the exchange rate. Such kinds of equations were estimated for seven other countries. It was the first attempt at setting up an internationally linked, multi-country model, as Hickman also notes (Chapter 14 below).

In the meantime, Tinbergen had temporarily moved from the Central Bureau of Statistics to Geneva as an expert with the Economic Intelligence Service of the League of Nations. There he refined the methodology, in Tinbergen (1939a) and, assisted by Polak, he constructed a 50-equation model for the United States (Tinbergen, 1939b).[2] This project was sharply criticized by Keynes (1939) and Tinbergen (1940) replied.[3] As Keynes feared, Tinbergen's reaction to this critique was not so much to give up model-building but 'to drown his sorrows in arithmetic'. More specifically, a 39-equation model for the United Kingdom was constructed. It was published much later, in Tinbergen (1951). Around the same time, as noted in Chapter 1, Radice (1939) published a pocket-size forecasting model for the United Kingdom. It is not our purpose to go further into these developments. In any case, the Second World War effectively stopped activities in this area. When later on they were resumed on both sides of the Atlantic, as in Klein (1950) and Klein and Goldberger (1955), one could start with the knowledge that model-building was indeed feasible, because Tinbergen had amply demonstrated this proposition by constructing relatively large econometric models for three countries in slightly more than three years.

3   Modelling at the Central Planning Bureau: the early years
In 1945, the Centraal Planbureau (in English, the Central Planning Bureau, here abbreviated as CPB) was established with Tinbergen as its director. Its 1947 charter states as its main duty the formulation of a 'balanced system of forecasts and directives for the Netherlands economy'. A macroeconometric model of the type Tinbergen had been pioneering would have been the perfect tool for this task. However the Second World War had left the Dutch economy in ruins. An extensive system of rationing of imports, consumption and investment was put in force to make the most out of what was available. Coffee, for example, was rationed until 1951. Housing was rationed much longer. A more or less refined model implicitly assuming free interaction among the major economic variables was of little use in this situation. As recovery proceeded, a gradual relaxation of the physical controls became possible. At the same time the need for a model, able to make consistent predictions for the uncontrolled variables, made itself felt.

The problems of the early 1950s centred around the balance of payments, employment, the wage level (centrally fixed) and the level of investment. Unemployment was increasing in spite of an active emigration policy. The model that was eventually adopted was directed at policy formulation for these issues. It was published in an Appendix to the Central Economic Plan 1955 and is therefore known as the '1955 Model'. It had been constructed earlier and was already in use in 1953. It was adjusted marginally in later years. Here we will base ourselves on CPB (1956), which gives the structural form of the 1955 model without commentary. It served as a basis for the prediction and policy advice of the CPB for most of the 1950s.[4]

The 1955 model consists of 27 equations describing the major macroeconomic aggregates as defined by the system of national accounts. The equations are expressed as the first differences of the variables. The model is hardly dynamic. Preceding year levels enter in linearizations. Only the investment equation, based on the flexible accelerator mechanism, is truly dynamic. At the time of the construction of the model, postwar time series of sufficient length for estimation were not available. Its coefficients, therefore, were based on input–output information, on regressions on prewar data, including cross-sectional data and on information about the tax and social security systems. In some cases simply a plausible value was used. Taxes and unemployment allowances are endogenous. A number of other income transfers are exogenous. Monetary variables are absent. To appraise the model better, we shall look at some of the structural equations in detail.

1955 consumption function

It is in the same spirit as the one for the 1936 Tinbergen model. Combining the equations for consumption out of wages and out of other income, we have:

$$\Delta C(t) = 0.85 \, \Delta L_B(t) + 0.40 \, \Delta Z_B(t) \tag{6.8}$$

where C is private consumption expenditure, L_B disposable wage income and Z_B disposable other income. As compared with the 1936 Tinbergen model, wage-earners have a lower propensity to consume, while other income earners have a higher one.

1955 investment equation

Investment is explained by the flexible accelerator principle in first differences:

$$\Delta i(t) = 0.10[2.5(\Delta v(t) - \Delta n(t)) - i(t-1)] + \Delta i_v(t) - \Delta d(t) \tag{6.9}$$

with i being net investment, i_v replacement investment, d depreciation, v gross output of enterprises and n changes in inventories, all measured in constant prices. The coefficient 0.10 is the speed of adjustment and 2.5 is the marginal capital–output ratio, adjusted for the optimal degree of utilization of capacity. This equation has been revised in later versions of the model. Among other things, dwellings have been excluded from the capital stock. Correspondingly, rents have been subtracted from v and the coefficient of 2.5 was lowered to 1.8. The model treats n, i_v and d as exogenous. Note that the choice of the accelerator explanation is very much at variance with the Tinbergen approach to investment, which uses (expected) profits as the explanatory variable. In practice, equation (6.9) was not fully utilized for prediction. Predictions were in part based on an investment survey with the largest firms.

1955 labour demand

This equation is based on Verdoorn's Law – See Verdoorn (1949, 1951) – which states that the rate of growth of labour productivity is 0.6 of the rate of growth of production. Consequently, the rate of growth of labour demand is 0.4 times that of production. No allowance is made for substitution of labour by capital or vice versa.

1955 imports equation

Imports are related to the categories of final demand, using measures of import content obtained from an input–output table. In this way, it is possible to differentiate between the low import-intensive outputs like consumption, exports of services and government expenditures on the one hand, and the high import-intensive other outputs, namely investments and exports. Here also, there are no price effects.

1955 exports equation

Exports are made dependent on the difference between the export price and the competing world market price level with an elasticity of − 2, based on prewar studies by Tinbergen. Since the model explained the export price level as the average of a cost component and the competing international price level, the price difference would be small and the price-dependent component relatively unimportant. The portion of exports that does not depend on prices is fixed exogenously.

1955 price equations

The role of prices in the 1955 model was modestly limited to converting quantities into values. Their equations are based on cost components: wages, import prices and autonomous shifts in indirect taxes. As in the 1936 model, price homogeneity is not respected.

The 1955 *multipliers* of GNP with respect to autonomous investment and government expenditure are about 0.5 and 0.9, respectively, reflecting the high import content of domestic expenditure.

With respect to the 1936 Tinbergen model, the 1955 model takes a step forward in its compatibility with the system of national accounts and in the explicit presence of variables related to government action. It scores lower because of the virtual absence of dynamics, the very limited price–quantity interaction and the somewhat weaker empirical basis. While in the 1936 Tinbergen model only foreign price and world trade are exogenous, the 1955 model treats as exogenous many other, domestic, variables, such as depreciation and inventory changes, which are really endogenous. Also the wage rate is exogenous. This was justified by the wage policy at that time, which fixed a uniform wage increase. The wage rate was a kind of policy instrument.

Forecasting at the CPB was – and remains – an almost continuous activity. The 1955 model was used for that purpose only twice, perhaps three times, a year. Several *ad hoc* adjustments then had to be made to render these forecasts plausible. In the meantime the forecasts were updated informally.

The model played a much more important role in the design of economic policy. It could be used to draft a table indicating the consequences of particular measures of economic policy, like those of an indirect tax increase, for employment, investment, consumer prices, and the current account of the balance of payments. The lack of dynamics helped here, because only current effects were relevant. Such a compact table – see for example the *Centraal Economisch Plan 1957* – enabled decision-makers to choose their favourite policy menu. Locally, these tables acquired a certain fame under the name *'spoorboekje'*, the railway timetables.

The model was also important internally at the CPB. Because of its relative transparency, people could easily grasp the underlying reasoning. The staff became model-minded. It also homogenized their vision of the working of the economy. Until proved wrong, the model was taken to be right. With a more complicated model, such a change of attitude would have been more difficult and slower.

As was also noted in Chapter 2, the fact that an official institution was using a macroeconometric model was internationally unique. At the time models were being built elsewhere, for example by Klein, as academic exploits. Official institutions remained sceptical about the possibilities of such models for their work. The CPB was clearly doing path-breaking work.

The 1955 model is basically a short-run model. For the formulation of *long-range projections*, a different type of model is needed. It was designed by Verdoorn (1956). It is a model of 17 equations, many of them non-linear in the variables and coefficients. The latter have been obtained in various ways. There is some correspondence with the 1955 short-run model. Demand for labour and capital are simple functions of GNP only. The price elasticity of exports is -2. The model is a growth model for an open economy. Long-run equilibrium of the balance of payments basically determines the rate of growth of output. Given this, equilibrium on the labour market implies the rate of growth of income. Exports are determined via accounting identities. Exports and income determine savings available for investment, which then have to correspond with the capital needed. The over-determination of the model can be used to turn assumptions into endogenous variables. The most optimistic forecast for a

20-year period ending in 1970 implied an annual growth rate of per capita GNP of 1.7 per cent. In reality it turned out to be 3.6 per cent, more than twice as large. This underestimation is, however, mostly due to the under-estimation of the exogenous component of exports (world trade). Rather than the assumed 4.8 per cent growth rate, its actual value was more than double, at 10.3 per cent annually.

The need for a better *short-run* model was clear. Its construction was conceived as a large-scale project ('An Econometric Analysis of the Neth-erlands Economy') with wide support. The initiative was taken by Tinber-gen and Idenburg, the Director-General of the Central Bureau of Statis-tics (CBS). In addition to the CPB and the CBS, the Netherlands Economic Institute in Rotterdam and the Mathematical Center in Amsterdam participated. Some support was obtained from the Nether-lands Science Foundation. Koyck, of the Netherlands School of Econ-omics, and Verdoorn were the principal investigators. As it turned out, the centre of gravity of the project was the CPB, where Verdoorn was in charge of it.

A first stage of the project was the construction of an adequate data base. For the postwar years, most of the data needed were normally published by the CBS. However the first usable year was 1948. When working with changes and lags, few postwar observations were available. A joint effort of CBS and CPB resulted in a data base for the period 1922–39. For the first versions of the new model, roughly 22 annual obser-vations were now available, of which 16 dated from before the Second World War. These latter data points were of interest because they showed more fluctuations than the postwar ones, which were mainly trends. To avoid arriving at a model which would be better geared to the remote past than the more recent and relevant one, the postwar observations were weighted twice as heavily as those of the 1923–38 period. The data set for the prewar period was not published as such. Only recently the CBS released more or less detailed national accounts for the years 1921–39 – see Van Bochove and Huitker (1987).

The combination of the two data bases entailed another problem. The levels of the variables were perhaps not comparable across the two per-iods. Under the assumption that relative changes, however, were compar-able, the equations of the new model were formulated in terms of percent-age changes of the variables. An additional advantage was that the coefficients become elasticities. The accounting identities have to be 'linearized' as expressions in percentage changes. The price–quantity-value identities are almost naturally linear in those transformations.

The initial versions of the model (see the 1958 paper of Verdoorn and van Eyk) were estimated by ordinary least squares. Calculations were performed by hand, using desk calculators. One was, of course, very much aware of the development of simultaneous equation estimation techniques by the Cowles Commission in the late 1940s and early 1950s. In fact Theil (1954) developed the method of two-stage least squares (2SLS) at the CPB as part of the modelling project. This method assumes that the list of exogenous and lagged endogenous variables is known and smaller in number than the number of observations. For the initial stage of model-building, where various alternatives for structural equations are being 'screened', the first condition is not satisfied. The second condition is even more precarious for models of more than a few equations and with a variety of lag patterns. In any case, given the small sample size, any worry about inconsistent estimation seems to be excessively scrupulous.

Still, the 1961 version of the new model was estimated by a version of 2SLS, in particular the one developed by Kloek and Mennes (1960). It is the model used for the drafting of the Central Economic Plan 1961 and published as its Annex 1. It is a system of 36 equations, linear in the percentage changes of the current variables, with one notable exception: the rate of unemployment, used as a proxy for capacity utilization, appears in some equations in a non-linear transformation. As compared with the 1955 model, the 1961 model is fully dynamic. It also has more of the economy described as endogenous. The wage rate is still exogenous, even though the central wage policy had been relaxed some years before. Monetary variables appear: time and demand deposits at the end of the year, as an indicator of liquidity, and the discount rate of the Central Bank. The quantities respond to price variations. The model is much more geared to the Dutch economy of the late 1950s and early 1960s than the 1955 model, which still reflected so much the extreme scarcities of the years immediately after the Second World War. It is also less demand-driven (or Keynesian) than its predecessor. Investment is explained mainly by profits rather than by output, returning in this manner to the Tinbergen approach. To highlight some of the model's features, we shall discuss some of its structural equations.

1961 consumption function
Using the symbol ∇ to indicate percentage changes, the equation for private consumption reads:

$$\nabla C(t) = 0.64 \ \nabla \ L_B(t - \tfrac{1}{2}) + 0.17 \ \nabla \ Z_B(t - 2/3) \qquad (6.10)$$
$$+ \ 0.46 \ \triangle \nabla \ P_c(t) - 0.16 \ \triangle \nabla \ C(t-1) + 0.05 \ \nabla \ C'(t-1) - 0.63$$

with P_C being the price index of private consumption and $\nabla \ C'(t-1)$ the percentage change in demand and time deposits at the end of the preceding year.

One may note the relatively complicated dynamics: lags and changes of percentage changes. The use of lagged consumption $C(t-1)$ as explanatory variable in the consumption function goes back to Brown (1952), who interpreted it as habit persistence. It can also be justified by the type of reasoning which nowadays is associated with the Error Correction Mechanism (ECM), originally proposed by Sargan (1964) and more recently reintroduced by Davidson *et al.* (1978). The short-run income elasticities of 0.64 and 0.17 are rather low, while their long-run counterparts are even smaller in contrast with the hypothesis of long-run proportionality of consumption and (permanent) income postulated by Friedman (1957). The deposits variable (C^r) is a proxy for available liquid assets. We note that price inflation appears to stimulate real consumption, in contrast to the results obtained in the DRI Model of the US economy during the 1970s and early 1980s (preceding chapter).

1961 investment equation
The dependent variable of the investment equation is the percentage change in non-residential private investment in fixed assets. Its explanation is almost perfectly that of an ECM. The long-run equilibrium value depends on other income after taxes, the price of investment goods, liquidity (C^r) and the degree of utilization of capacity. The current first difference in this variable explains the short-run fluctuations around this level. The dependence on other income or profits is a typical supply-side feature of the model. (Under)utilization of capacity is proxied by the rate of unemployment, which enters this equation in a non-linear way. For low employment values the effect on investment is very strong, reflecting the need for investment when the economy is operating at a high level of capacity utilization. This indeed was the case for the Dutch economy in most of the 1950s and 1960s.

1961 labour demand
The equation of labour demand reflects on the one hand Verdoorn's Law, with an elasticity of 0.39 (rather than 0.4!), and on the other hand a profit effect. This is another supply-side feature. The differential between import and domestic production prices also plays a role, albeit minor.

1961 imports equation
This equation links imports to the categories of final demand in roughly the same way as the 1955 version does, except that it is more refined dynamically. Also differential price effects appear.

1961 exports equation
The long-run price elasticity of exports is now close to -3. Furthermore Dutch exports are depicted as growing 1.5 times faster than competing exports. A non-linear capacity effect represents the preference of producers for the domestic market. One can also say that it captures the 'Zijlstra effect': the increase of interest of the producers in exports when domestic demand stalls.

1961 price equations
These are basically refinements of the 1955 equations, with cost per unit of output as the major explanation. The export price depends in part also on the competing price level. The consumer price equation also contains an ECM. None of the prices react explicitly to variations in demand.

As already remarked, the 1961 model is in many respects superior to the 1955 model. Specifically, its dynamics were much more refined. The use of ECMs predates their popularity in British econometrics by 15–20 years. Still, the basic economic reasoning was rather similar to that of the 1955 model, except for the explanation of investment.

The 1961 model was soon followed by updates like the Model 62.10 – see Verdoorn and Post (1964) – and the Model 63D. One of the new features was the introduction of an equation for the wage rate, reflecting, with considerable delay, the fact that central wage policy, or incomes policy in general, was virtually abandoned. The wage rate was made dependent on a Koyck lag pattern in prices, productivity and unemployment. The role of unemployment in this equation was twofold. First, it represents the idea launched by Klein (1950) and Phillips (1958). Secondly, it reflects the decision to make the model more sensitive to capacity utilization in general. One finds non-linear capacity effects in other structural equations (those for investment, exports, imports, labour demand and export price) as well. The effect of capacity (under)utilization as measured by the rate of unemployment (w) is specified as:

$$10 \log (w+2) - 0.2\, w,$$

with the coefficients selected on the basis of some experimentation. The importance of the role of this variable in the model can be explained by the conditions of over-full employment under which the Dutch economy was operating at the time. At the same time, the newer models were stripped of the ECMs of the 1961 model. A first monetary equation was introduced, namely the one for deposits (C'), needed to make predictions more than one year ahead. Deposits also appeared in the investment equation, where they played a major role.

Verdoorn and Post (1964) paid considerable attention to the solution of a model with a non-linear capacity utilization variable, which, given the general preoccupation with linear models and their solution techniques, posed a problem at that time. Computers still had to become somewhat faster in order to handle large-scale iterative procedures.

Model 63D was left basically unchanged until 1969 when it was re-estimated; see Verdoorn *et al.* (1970, 1971). The extension of the sample period to 1966 made it possible to include additional variables in the various reaction equations. Although these additional variables and the revised point estimates of the coefficients made a difference to the multipliers and the predictions, the line of reasoning of the 69-C model is not drastically different from that of its predecessor. Of interest is the introduction of a (negative) effect of investment on employment. It is a first move away from the implicit assumption of mutual independence of labour and capital in production.

During the 1960s the need for medium-term analysis and forecasting made itself felt. As Smithies (1957) pointed out, the distinction between (on the one hand) business cycle models like the Tinbergen ones, which explain short-run fluctuations around a given trend, and (on the other hand) growth models of the Harrod-Domar type, which explain the long run but are silent about the short run, is unsatisfactory. There is a need for integration of both approaches. One can also say that typical short-run models concentrate on the adjustment of demand to existing capacity, and that long-run models explain the development of production capacity, taking appropriate effective demand for granted.

Medium-term models, then, should aim at the mutual adjustment of supply and demand. This is the central theme of the CS Model of Van den Beld (1967, 1968),[5] in which available capacity follows from a linear production function. Production is determined by the various categories of expenditures. In the structural form, the relative overcapacity acts negatively on investment, positively on exports (Zijlstra effect) and negatively on some of the prices and on the creation of liquidities by the banking sector. The consequence is an increase in demand quantities and a reduction in supply, eliminating after a few years the over-capacity. Many of the 24 reaction equations of the CS Model are simplified versions of the corresponding equations of the Verdoorn class of models. Employment, for example, follows Verdoorn's Law with an elasticity of 0.462 and is not related to investment activity. The investment equation of the CS Model, however, differs drastically from that of the annual models. Here, next to over-capacity, production and to some extent relative liquidity are the determinants, while profits do not play a role. Supply conditions are represented by over-capacity. In general, the CS Model allows little room for price effects. From a computational point of view, it is of interest to note that the model contains six linear equations, with breaks, and that it is otherwise contemporaneously linear but consecutively non-linear. These complications could be handled without problems.

The CS Model shares with the short-term model the role of capacity utilization as an explanatory variable in some of the structural equations. While in the short-term model tendencies to restore capacity to a normal level are very weak, they constitute the essence of the CS model. This mode, however, was very much an experimental one. Still, it was innovative in several respects: it explicitly aimed at a prediction of the full-time path several years ahead; it was non-linear; it incorporated explicitly a production function; and it treated the interrelations between the real and the monetary sector endogenously. It clearly meant another approach to modelling than that with which the CPB had become identified. It has served as a source of inspiration for the newer generations of models at the CPB.

4   Modelling at the Central Planning Bureau: the later years

The appetite grows with the eating. Once year-to-year prediction and policy analysis are under control, one wants to monitor the economy with a greater frequency. At the end of the 1960s a quarterly model was developed; see Driehuis (1972). The Central Bureau of Statistics did not until recently (1986) publish a full-fledged system of quarterly national accounts. The missing time series has to be constructed by the CPB itself using various methods, one being the interpolation method of Boot *et al.* (1967). The series used (1951: 1–1965: 4) were either without season by the nature of their derivation or were seasonally adjusted. The reaction equations were specified in terms of logarithms of the variables. This is not really a break with the tradition of the Verdoorn class of models with variables expressed in percentage changes, as those are virtually proportional to changes in logarithms. Koyck lag patterns and finite lag structures were used to represent the various types of inertia in adjustment and expectations formation.

The Driehuis model consists of 68 equations, of which 21 are estimated reaction equations. In many respects, these reaction equations were similar to their counterparts in the annual model, but there are some important differences. For example, several specifications are explicitly based on a neoclassical optimization scheme. Employment and investment, for example, are both influenced by the user cost of capital in relation to the wage rate, introducing at last some degree of substitution between labour and capital. They also depend on production on the one hand and on profits after taxes on the other.

Also relative liquidity and the utilization rate of labour are assigned a role. This eclectic approach is somewhat balanced by the symmetric treatment of the demand for labour and that for capital. In virtually all reaction equations, capacity utilization plays a role. It is a step back from the CS model in that only labour is used in the definition of capacity. It is also inconsistent with the use of a Cobb–Douglas production function with full substitutability. Still, its presence in so many equations supplies a unifying element to the model and in this way acknowledges the CS model. It also shares with the latter the presence of the liquidity rate as an endogenous explanatory variable in several structural equations. It is of interest to note that the long-run price elasticity of commodity exports is -2.045, again in line with the tradition.

The innovative aspect of the Driehuis model is, of course, its quarterly nature. In other aspects it is obviously the offspring of both the Verdoorn and the Van den Beld type of models, but its specifications are justified in a theoretically more appealing way. Its analytical content is more substantial. The Driehuis quarterly model was used for short-run predictions for most of the 1970s, until succeeded by KOMPAS. This latter model also integrated components of the VINTAF approach, which we will therefore discuss first.

The annual models usually formulated a relatively simple relation between employment on the one hand and production by enterprises on the other. Demand for labour was in these models basically independent of capital. Through most of the 1960s there was a strong empirical correlation between output and employment. In the late 1960s and early 1970s, the Netherlands witnessed a further growth in output but stagnating employment. As the labour force was still increasing, this led to increasing unemployment. The CPB predictions consistently missed this development. They overestimated employment.

At the CPB, Den Hartog and Tjan (1974) approached this problem by formulating a vintage production model, the core of the later VINTAF models. In this model production capacity is determined by installed equipment, with a constant capital–output ratio. Each unit of equipment requires a certain amount of labour, depending on the vintage of the equipment. The labour requirement per unit of equipment decreases by about 5 per cent from one vintage to the next. Capacity increases because of new investment, while it decreases because old equipment is scrapped. Scrapping occurs for two reasons. The old equipment becomes either technically obsolete or economically unprofitable, because the labour required for its operation is too expensive. The scrapping rule makes labour demand sensitive to real wages. Installation of equipment, investment, is undertaken to replace scrapped capacity or in response to gross profits after taxes. Stagnating employment in manufacturing with growing output and capacity can then be seen to follow from a replacement of old vintages with high labour requirements by new ones with low labour requirements.

The idea of a vintage production function goes back some time in the literature (see Johansen (1959) and Solow (1960) for example), but was not given an operational implementation. It is the great merit of Den Hartog and Tjan to have surmounted the rather formidable empirical complications of the approach, although this sometimes meant cutting the Gordian knot. Their work justly drew international attention.

The vintage production bloc is embedded in a full model. The equations in this model are partly linear in the levels of the variables, partly in the logarithms of the variables, and partly in terms of percentage changes. VINTAF II, the second version of the model, contains 112 equations; see Den Hartog (1980). Apart from the production block VINTAF II is not essentially different from its predecessors. The long-run substitution elasticity of export demand in VINTAF II is − 1.7!

A new phenomenon occurred. The presentation of VINTAF II and its use for policy analysis caused considerable discussion. A special double issue of *De Economist* (vol. 124, 1976, issue 1/2) was published with both a translation of Den Hartog and Tjan (1974) and critical comments and a discussion of related topics. A lively debate developed in *Economisch-Statistische Berichten* in the period August 1977–August 1978, triggered by a provocative contribution by Driehuis and van der Zwan (1978). The debate led to further research on the specification and estimation of vintage models as summarized by Den Hartog (1984).

The discussion around VINTAF II was novel. Never before had a CPB model been so closely analysed in public. The critique directed itself primarily at the model assumptions and no so much, as had sometimes happened before, at the model outcomes. The CPB models were no longer sacrosanct.

The VINTAF model, surely not perfect, was clearly a step forward over the earlier annual models. Its data base was completely postwar. It was not confined by linearity of its relations. Its major innovation, though, was to explain potential demand for labour in conjunction with investment activity.

In the early 1980s VINTAF was succeeded by FREIA. This model, documented by Hasselman *et al.* (1983), integrates a model of the real sector largely based on VINTAF with a monetary model developed at the CPB. Its empirical basis is formed by annual time series for the period 1954–1975. (The sample period ran to 1978, in some cases.) Its real part consists of 257 equations. The monetary submodel contains 75 equations.

The real submodel has a more refined explanation of investment in equipment, for which expected sales play a role, in addition to replacement needs and profitability. Actual employment is described as a weighted mean of the demand and supply of labour with the weights depending on the tension on the labour market. In this way 'disequilibrium modelling' has found a foothold in the CPB modelling tradition. The growth in relative size of the public sector with the ensuing need to try to keep it under control led to a large set of equations for general government and social security.

The addition of a monetary submodel is the important new element of FREIA. It reflected the increased interest in the functioning of the money and financial markets and their interdependence with the real sectors of the economy. For the private and banking sector, an optimal portfolio explanation is used. Such an approach was employed earlier outside the CPB by Knoester (1974, 1980). FREIA takes the adjustment costs of changing the portfolio into account. Also a rationing mechanism is introduced in case the desired amounts of assets may not be available.

The financial surpluses (deficits) of the non-banking sector result from the real part of FREIA. The interest rate and some asset holdings are fed back from the monetary model to the model of the real sector. Here also, 'disequilibrium modelling' has been practised in cases where interest rates were not supposed to clear markets and strict rationing was not applied. The exchange rate is treated as an exogenous variable. However the discrepancy between export prices and competing export prices is used as a proxy for expected exchange rate modifications.

It is perhaps not entirely fair to its authors (van den Berg *et al.*, 1983) to state that the KOMPAS model is a quarterly version of FREIA. In any case, the construction of the two models was coordinated. Like FREIA, KOMPAS has a vintage production block. It also has a similar monetary submodel. KOMPAS too has a large number of equations describing the government and social security sector. The need to specify at the same time the quarterly time structure of the interactions made it more than a simple copy applied to quarterly data: the fact that the computer listing of the model contains 851 equations clearly reflects this.

The enormous degree of detail for many variables contrasts with a consumption function which is hardly different from the old Tinbergen formulation, apart from a minute interest rate effect. Not only is its specification primitive, but also no distinction between durables and non-durables has been made.

It is of interest to note that Koyck lag patterns have not been used to specify delayed effects. In the case of a Koyck lag pattern, the use of the Koyck transformation leads to the presence of the lagged dependent variable on the right-hand side of the equation, as is well known. This can cause problems if this variable is not well determined. The errors are propagated into the future when simulating several periods ahead. Some 24 different lag patterns were used instead for the specification of the KOMPAS equations. In general, KOMPAS relies less on estimation to determine coefficients than earlier models. The long-run price elasticity of exports, for example, is simply set at -2.

To maintain two models of similar inspiration is a waste of means. It is also confusing. It was only natural to merge FREIA and KOMPAS into a single model, FK 85, presented as 'a quarterly macro economic model for the short and medium term' – see Van den Berg *et al.* (1987). It is a quarterly model. Its monetary block is taken from KOMPAS. The real submodel is a refined version of the earlier one. Disembodied technological progress is made endogenous by allowing for a slower rate of obsolescence in times of slack and low wage increases. It introduces an element of substitutability after the instalment of equipment. The exogenous reduction in labour requirements per unit of equipment from vintage to vintage, which was originally 5 per cent in VINTAF, was further reduced from 3.8 per cent in FREIA and KOMPAS to 1.9 per cent. Private consumption was given a more sophisticated specification. Next to current disposable income, wealth effects and the rate of interest were allowed to play a role. Other adjustments were made in the real submodel to take into account recent experience with the earlier specifications.

Given the open nature of the Dutch economy, the ability to analyse the international environment is of the greatest importance. The BUMO model of the CPB, as developed in Okker and Suyker (1985) and Suyker (1986), describes the world by way of five interlinked submodels: one each for West Germany, the United States, the Rest of the OECD, the OPEC countries and the Rest of the World.

The special model for West Germany reflects the fact that that country is the main trading partner of the Netherlands and that the Dutch guilder is tightly linked to the Deutschmark. Economic conditions in the United States affect the Dutch economy less directly, but still rather strongly. The growing importance of international monetary and financial relations expresses itself in the presence of monetary submodels and linkages in BUMO. Recently, the monetary submodel has been revised too. The exchange rate as well as the monetary policy of the central bank were made endogenous, as explained in Hasselman *et al.* (1987).

Finally, the development of sectoral models may be mentioned. Draper *et al.* (1987) present VINSEC, a six-sector model. It applies the VINTAF approach to sectors. In this way it meets the criticism as stated in Driehuis *et al.* (1983a), that the macroeconomic models were too integrated. The

BETA model distinguishes fourteen sectors. We shall not go into a detailed discussion of these models, in part to limit ourselves to macroeconomic models and in part because they fall outside the period of review, which ends with 1986.

Looking back at 35 years of modelling at the CPB, the first impression is that of continuity with gradual change. The 1955 and 1961 models borrowed from the 1936 Tinbergen model. The 1961 consumption, investment and export equations are very much like those of Tinbergen. The VINTAF investment equation comes close to that of the 1961 model. Change occurred in response to recent experience or to the need for information. The introduction of labour market pressure in the 63D model reflected the experience of an over-full employment economy with strongly reduced multipliers. This idea was further elaborated in the CS model, with a more general definition of tension, involving both labour and capital. The Driehuis quarterly model clearly builds on this tradition with an increasing attention to the analytical justification of the specified equations. Both the CS and the Driehuis models were meeting a need for information: the first about medium-term development, the other concerning very short-run prediction and analysis. The stagnation and decline of employment in the manufacturing industry and the inability to explain it with the available models led to VINTAF, which, apart from its use of a vintage production function, is similar to its forerunners. The earlier models already contained some endogenous monetary variables. The increasing interest in monetary feedbacks in the 1970s naturally led to the development of a full-fledged monetary model linked to a traditional real sector, yielding FREIA and KOMPAS. These models have at the same time extensive sets of equations for social security and general government, meeting a need for detailed information about the variables in question. The merger of FREIA and KOMPAS does not constitute a break with tradition.

At first sight, it seems that modelling at the CPB was very much inward-looking. Deviations from the tradition were based on own experience and not on developments in the literature or on the experience of other model-builders. Of course, initially there were few competitors to learn from, but partial econometric studies were readily available. Since the mid-1960s modelling has been widespread internationally, but one finds few references to other modelling projects in the CPB publications and progress reports. One has the impression that, on the contrary, model design and usage at the CPB have had a considerable impact on similar work outside the Netherlands, although it is not a simple matter to trace such effects.

The relative insulation of the intellectual environment of CPB modelling has had the advantage that there was no obvious pressure to jump on the bandwagons of Scandinavian dualism, monetarism, rational expectations, supply-side economics, disequilibrium modelling and so on as these came and went. In fact the CPB models are not easy to classify according to the fashionable nomenclature of modern macroeconomics. The consumption function is usually purely Keynesian, but the investment equation is generally characteristic of a supply-side approach. In fact most of the more recent models nicely balance supply and demand explanations.

Our review has not been overly critical. Criticism from the point of view of present knowledge is rather easy but irrelevant. More important is the question as to what extent the models reflected the state of the art at the time they were constructed. The first models simply were the state of the art. Later on, however, discrepancies could show up. My personal feeling is that the treatment of employment is the truly weak element in the models. The early CPB models explained employment in a very simple and crude way, independently of investment activity. Then all of a sudden VINTAF supplied a rather elaborate framework, rigidly tying employment to investment vintages. A more flexible approach, taking into account the heterogeneity of the labour force and of the supply of jobs as to age, sex, schooling and location might have been indicated. What about the effect of social security and the wage structure on supply and demand? In view of the seriousness of the unemployment problem, one would have expected a much more refined analysis than the models offered.

Until some 10 years ago (that is, until the mid-1970s), the CPB dominated model-building in the Netherlands. Its experience, type of staff, data base and contacts with the centres of decision-making gave it a natural comparative advantage over, say, university teams. In one domain, that of monetary model construction, the CPB has not exploited that advantage. The first models of the monetary and financial sector, such as Knoester (1974), were academic exercises. The monetary models of the CPB, and of the central bank, have, to a certain extent, taken their cue from these efforts.

The virtual monopoly of the CPB in model-building in the Netherlands in the early years effectively gave the CPB model the status of unassailable truth, of the only possible description of reality. Its predictions and simulations were taken too much as certainty and not enough as possibilities with a limited degree of probability. Ignoring the tentative and random nature of models leads to problems when the realizations fall short of the predictions. Fortunately, in more recent years, the CPB has had competitors presenting alternatives which may, if they differ from the CPB analysis, create some reasonable doubt or, if they agree with it, corroborate it. Modelling activities outside the CPB are the subject of the next section.

5 Modelling at other institutions

Until the mid-1970s, no other Dutch institution or research group under-took the construction of a macroeconometric model of the Netherlands. In other countries, and specifically the United States, model-building was mainly an activity of academic research teams; see Nerlove (1966). In part, the absence of university-based models can be explained by lack of pub-lished data. The data constructed by the CPB/CBS team for the prewar period and the quarterly data underlying the Driehuis quarterly model were not published. This in a way reinforced the monopoly position of the CPB. There is some evidence that the material would have been made available on request, but it was not until 1976 that a team at the Econo-metrics Institute of the *University of Groningen* developed its GRECON model as an alternative to the current CPB model: the 69C. By that time the postwar time series published by the CBS were long enough for reliable estimation without the prewar data. The GRECON model was used for the first time to produce forecasts for 1977. These were published in a March issue of *Economisch-Statistische Berichten*. This exercise was repeated annually, with a re-estimated and slightly changed version of the model – see Voorhoeve (1986).

The GRECON project aimed at a relatively concise model. The 1977 model contains 18 equations, of which nine are reaction functions. The 1986 version has only 10 reaction functions supported by 23 definitional equations. The models are linear in annual percentage changes. The linearity made it possible to apply the method of two-stage least squares in its unadulterated form.

The specification of the equations is somewhat *ad hoc*. In the 1978 model, for example, private gross investment (excluding houses) is made dependent on output and on the unemployment rate, without any refer-ence to production functions, relative prices and the like. The 1986 version of the investment equation also contains output but the unemployment percentage is replaced by gross profit per unit of production, returning to the long-established Tinbergen–Verdoorn tradition in this respect. Private employment depends positively on domestic production and negatively on the wage rate. In the 1977 to 1982 version, the coefficient of domestic production is close to the Verdoorn 0.4 value. It increases for later versions, to reach the value of 0.64 in the 1986 version. In general, the equations of the early GRECON models look very much like simplified versions of the 69C model of the CPB. GRECON distinguishes itself from that model not so much in the specification of the equations as in the careful econometric estimation and complete documentation.

In the latter part of the 1970s, Driehuis of the *University of Amsterdam* started the SECMON project. It aimed at filling the need for a sectoral analysis of the Dutch economy. SECMON-A, constructed under commission by the WRR, the Wetenschappelijke Raad voor het Regeringsbeleid (Scientific Council for Government Policy), is a static model covering four sectors: agriculture, manufacturing, construction and services. It also contains a small monetary sector. The SEO, Stichting voor Economisch Onderzoek (Foundation for Economic Research), in Amsterdam adopted the project in 1980. SECMON-B extended its predecessor, being dynamic and covering 10 rather than four sectors, but it had no monetary component. It was succeeded by SECMON-C, in which wages and prices were also modelled. SECMON-D is a further revision. The model is used for research and analysis under contract with various official agencies, non-profit organizations and private firms. SECMON-D consists of 700 equations. It is an annual model. The category of firms consists of 18 sectors, of which nine are in manufacturing and six are various types of services.

Driehuis *et al.* (1983b) supplied in some detail information about SEC-MON-C, which serves as the basis for our discussion. Basically, SEC-MON is an input–output-type model, generating gross output per sector as the sum of intermediate deliveries to other sectors and of final demand. An input–output framework is also used to link sectoral prices to those of primary inputs. Among the categories of final demand, total private consumption is explained in roughly the same way as the 1955 CPB model, namely as a simple function of disposable wage and disposable other income. It is next allocated over commodity groups as a function of total consumption and a relative price term. Group X (others) is determined as the difference between total consumption and that of the other groups. Private investment is directly determined by sector, either exogenously or as a function of disposable other income, in line with the Tinbergen–Verdoorn tradition. Scandinavian dualism enters the model when the exports for the exposed sectors are made dependent on the price differential between domestic prices and the world price level. Of course this dualism is also present in the price formation per sector, where the prices of the exposed sectors follow international prices.

SECMON-C uses for the capital-intensive industries a linearized clay–clay vintage production model – see Driehuis *et al.* (1979). It differs from the CPB model in the sense that scrapping does not occur when the oldest vintage in use is not profitable any longer but when the cost of operating the old equipment exceeds the total costs of installing and using the newest vintage. The labour requirements of the vintage in use determine the employment in the capital–intensive industries. Since scrapping depends on wage costs, employment is sensitive to wages. Employment in the labour-intensive sectors depends mainly on value-added per sector.

SECMON-C distinguishes itself from CPB models by its sectoral dimension. However the economic mechanism underlying the determination of the endogenous variables is not basically different from that which is incorporated in the CPB models.

After more than a decade of preliminary detailed studies, the Econometrics Research and Special Studies Department of *De Nederlandsche Bank* (DNB), the Dutch central bank, developed an integrated monetary/real model, named MORKMON, for quarterly data; see Fase (1985). It is the natural desire of a policy-maker like the central bank to have a macroeconometric model of its own. Close cooperation between model-builder and model-user is of crucial importance to arrive at a model that meets, even anticipates, the needs of the policy-maker. It also contributes to the confidence the latter has in the model, while at the same time making the policy-making aware of its limitations.

MORKMON was preceded by two versions of MOKMON, the monetary block; see Fase (1981). The development of the submodel for the real sector had to wait until the quarterly series needed were constructed. The data used for estimating MORKMON are mostly time series, starting with the first quarter of 1970 and ending with the fourth quarter of 1979.

Before entering on a discussion of MORKMON, the question may be asked why both DNB and CPB were so late in developing interlinked real/monetary models, late not only in comparison to what was done abroad, but also in comparison to the 1967 CS model of Van den Beld as a forerunner of such a model and to the relatively detailed monetary model of Knoester (1974) and its integration with a model of the real sector; see, in particular, Knoester and Buitelaar (1975). As far as DNB is concerned, a possible explanation is that its econometrics unit needed time, after being set up in 1971, to build up staff and experience. The CPB had been engaged in monetary analysis since its beginning. It is not clear why it did not try much earlier than FREIA to integrate that analysis with the model for the real sector.

We return again to the DNB model MORKMON. Its monetary submodel consists of over 50 equations. The unifying principle is an optimal portfolio model for the private sector. Such a model explains the composition of the portfolio by the total amount to be invested and all relevant interest rates. The interest rates are in their turn explained by reaction equations. The monetary block also contains a description of the foreign exchange market. The guilder/dollar exchange rate depends on the volume of interventions by the central bank, changes in interest rates in the

Netherlands, Germany and the United States, the difference in the US and German inflation rates and the balance of payments surplus, combining the three alternative explanations of exchange rates in one equation. The major determinant, however, is the Deutschmark/dollar exchange rate, which is exogenous in the model. Consequently, the endogenous component of the guilder exchange rate is minor.

The real part of MORKMON comprises 90 equations. Seventeen of these are reaction functions. Their specification follows in certain respects the CPB tradition. Private consumption depends separately on disposable labour income and disposable other income, gross investment is determined by disposable other income (or profits), and prices are explained as a function of costs and a constant mark-up. Still, there are differences. Private consumption and gross investment also depend on the long-term rate of interest. The long-run price elasticity of exports is −1.2, rather lower than the value used by the CPB. Employment is not based on a vintage production model, although it is made dependent on the stock of capital goods. The latter are decreased by scrapping without identifying the vintage. Since scrapping increases with labour costs, the wage rate affects the capital stock and thus employment negatively. A further feature is the distinction made between output and sales of the private sector. Actual output is determined as a function of expected sales and the desired level of inventories, relative to current levels. In this way output is made to depend negatively on inventory levels. The two submodels are linked by interest rates and liquidity positions coming from the monetary block and by the private sector's savings surplus, the government deficit and the balance on current account coming from the real block.

MORKMON is in many respects similar to the comparable CPB models, although its monetary block was developed at the same time and quite independently of that of the CPB models. Such similarity does not mean that MORKMON is redundant. An institution like the central bank should be able to express its views in the form of a model, which is, or can be, optimally geared to its needs.

The Macroeconomic Policy Unit of the *Erasmus University Rotterdam* started its RASMUS project in 1982. It aims at studying the international ramifications of macroeconomic policy by constructing sets of interrelated national models. It started with a model for the United States and one for a block of six members of the European Community. As the project developed, a model for the Dutch economy was introduced separately. The interesting aspect of this project is its complementarity to the other Dutch models, which usually treat the international environment in a rather global way and offer few opportunities to study the consequences of international policy coordination.

Recently, the Centre for Cyclical and Structural Research (CCSO) of the *University of Groningen* produced the first version of the CCSO annual model of the Dutch economy; see Kuipers *et al.* (1987). In spirit, it is rather close to the VINTAF line of models. However its vintage model is of the putty–clay variety, allowing for substitution between labour and capital for the newest vintage. A detailed discussion of this model would carry us from the past into the present and thus outside the time interval of this survey.

Other models of the Dutch economy have been constructed in the time period of this survey. No doubt a number of doctoral dissertations contain such models. Some models have been published as articles or books, for example Knoester (1980). We shall not discuss them here. The attention has been centred on models that are part of a continuing operation, that are being renewed and are being used. As the models that were discussed show, the CPB tradition appears to have had a strong demonstration effect. Even though other models attempt to be different from those of the CPB, in order to offer an alternative, they still have very much in common with them.

6   Concluding remarks

The modelling activities reviewed here have not been undertaken for their own sake, out of intellectual curiosity. They were set up to help provide answers to the economic policy problems of their time. Up to a point, such policy concerns are reflected in the models. For example, the finely detailed description of the government and social security sector corresponds to the increasingly detailed nature of economic policy. New insights into the working of the economy have been gradually incorporated. Most of these were internally generated in response to shortcomings of previous models. The upheaval in macroeconomics in the 1970s has left some traces in the models.

Modelling activity has increased over time. Several conditions have been favourable to this development. First of all, there has been the development of the system of national accounts after the Second World War. These accounts supply in a consistent way the lion's share of the data needed for model-building. Incidentally, the fact that the CPB and the DNB had to construct independently their quarterly series indicates that the Central Bureau of Statistics had not been playing the role which, given its fine tradition, one would have expected.

Secondly, econometric techniques have been developed specifically to estimate dynamic simultaneous systems. The work of the Cowles Commission,[6] directed by Tjalling Koopmans, at the University of Chicago and of Henri Theil, first at the CPB and later at the Netherlands School of

Economics, deserves mention in this connection. Although most of the techniques apply ideally to linear models, they can be easily adapted to estimate non-linear models as well.

Thirdly, calculation has become easier. From the slide-rule, via the manually operated and electric desk calculator, the first-generation electronic ARMAC in Amsterdam, various other generations of computers to the super-computers, a long way has been travelled. With the increased memory size and speed of computers, there are now virtually no limits on the size of models and non-linearities can be handled with relative ease.

Fourthly, the number of people able to specify and estimate the structural relations, to simulate the full models and to interpret the results has increased. Initially, it was a matter of on-the-job training. After econometrics became a special field in Dutch universities, the supply of potentially competent modellers was built up gradually.

Fifthly, models and model outcomes were initially treated with great scepticism by professional economists, both inside and outside government. As the number of people able to understand the possibilities and limitations of models increased, criticism based on ignorance was replaced by a more constructive attitude. This did not mean that the models were simply swallowed hook, line and sinker, but that the criticism was directed at specific properties of the models, which could then be amended.

Sixthly, models became theoretically more consistent. The individual structural equations are increasingly specified on the basis of some theory involving several of them. In other words, the specifications tend to be more analytical and less *ad hoc*. This increases the claim to plausibility of the model, perhaps at the empirical cost of some of the goodness of the fit.

The increasing internal consistency of models is no luxury. As models become larger and larger, they become less and less easy to control; that is, they can produce predictions which are hard to understand in an intuitive way. One has to base a model on relatively few principles, elaborated perhaps in many directions, but rigorously applied in each case. In this way one may avoid the models becoming a big black box. To remain in control over models that are continuously increasing in size and complexity constitutes in my opinion the intellectual challenge for the current generation of model-builders.

This generation will no doubt continue to build on the work of its predecessors. Working in a Dutch environment, one would almost naturally be absorbed into the strong Dutch modelling tradition, which started with the 1936 model of Tinbergen. In retrospect, that model seems to be a true act of creation. Out of virtually nothing, there appeared a medium-sized macroeconometric dynamic policy model for an open economy. It is difficult to appreciate fully the methodological innovation that it represented. The fact that macroeconometric modelling is now commonplace the world over is perhaps its best testimonial.[7]

Notes

* The author of this chapter wishes to thank Professor J. Tinbergen for his readiness to answer questions concerning his 1936 model, forcing him to go back in memory more than 50 years, Professor H. den Hartog for the information supplied about modelling at the Central Planning Bureau, and Professor M. M. G. Fase for his help in obtaining copies of older publications and for his constructive comments on an earlier draft of this paper. Also Professor V. Ginsburgh and Dr Peter Solar are thanked for their useful comments. Geert Dhaene faithfully undertook the work of running the 1936 Tinbergen model on the computer of Louvain University. The involvement of all these people in this paper does not reduce in the least the responsibility of the author for its shortcomings. Professors Bodkin, Klein and Marwah wish to thank the North-Holland Publishing Company, and the Economics Editor, Joop Kirkmaat, in particular, for the permission to reprint in the present volume, with minor changes, Professor Barten's paper, which originally appeared in Driehuis, Fase and Hartog (eds), *Challenges for Macroeconomic Modelling* (Amsterdam, 1988) pp. 39–88.

1. See also the related discussion in Chapters 1 and 2 above.
2. See the more detailed discussion in Chapter 2 above, and also De Wolff (1983).
3. This debate is reviewed in Chapter 1 above.
4. This model has also been summarized in Chapter 2 above. Because that discussion is largely complementary to the present account, the two descriptions have been allowed to coexist in this volume.
5. The CS in the name 'CS Model' refers to Conjincturer-Structurer or Cyclical/Structural, expressing the intermediate nature of the model as a synthesis of a short-run (cyclical) and a long-run (structural) model.
6. For more details on this subject, see Clifford Hildreth (1986) especially pp. 14–52.
7. The reader may wish to compare the chapter author's conclusions with the volume authors' general lessons from the macroeconometric model-building experience and with prospective future development, presented in Chapters 16 and 17 below.

References
Artus, P., M. Deleau and P. Malgrange (1986) *Modélisation macroéconomique* [Macroeconomie Model-Building] (Paris: Economica).

Boot, J. C. C., W. Feibes and J. H. C. Lisman (1967) 'Further Comments on the Derivations of Quarterly Figures from Annual Data', *Applied Statistics*, vol. 16, pp. 65–75.

Brown, T. M. (1952) 'Habit Persistence and Lags in Consumer Behavior', *Econometrica*, vol. 29, pp. 355–71.

Centraal Bureau voor de Statistiek [Central Bureau of Statistics] (1979): *Tachtig jaren statistiek in tijdreeksen* [Historical Series of the Netherlands 1899–1979] (Staatsuitgeverij, 's-Gravenhage).

Central Planning Bureau (1956) *Scope and Methods of the Central Planning Bureau* (The Hague: Centraal Planbureau).

Davidson, J. E. H., D. F. Hendry, F. Srba and S. Yeo (1978) 'Econometric Modelling of Aggregate Time Series Relationships between Consumers' Expenditure and Income in the United Kingdom', *Economic Journal*, vol. 88, pp. 661–92.

Den Hartog, H. (1980): 'Employment in the Netherlands: The Analysis by the Central Bureau on the Macro Level', in *Unemployment: the Dutch perspective* (A. Maddison and B. Wilpstra, eds) (The Hague: Ministerie van Sociale Zaken en Werkgelegenheid).

—— (1984) 'Empirical Vintage Models for the Netherlands: A Review in Outline', *De Economist*, vol. 132, pp. 326–49.

Den Hartog, H. and H. S. Tjan (1974) 'Investeringen, lonen, prijzen en arbeidsplaatsen', Central Planning Bureau, Occasional Paper, 1974/2, The Hague. The English translation of a revised and extended version appeared as: 'Investments, Wages, Prices and Demand for Labour (a Clay–Clay Vintage Model for The Netherlands)', *De Economist*, vol. 124 (1976) pp. 32–82.

Denton, F. T. and J. Kuiper (1965) 'The Effect of Measurement Errors on Parameter Estimates and Forecasts: A Case Study Based on the Canadian Preliminary National Accounts', *The Review of Economics and Statistics*, vol. 47, pp. 198–206.

De Wolff, P. (1983) 'Jan Tinbergen als modellenbouwer' [Jan Tinbergen Model-Builder], *Economisch-Statistische Berichten*, vol. 68, pp. 308–11.

Dhaene, G. and A. P. Barten (1989) 'When It All Began: The 1936 Tinbergen Model Revisited', *Economic Modelling*, vol. 6, no. 2, pp. 203–19.

Draper, D. A. G., A. Nieuwenhuis and H. S. Tjan (1987) 'Vinsec, een model met zes produktiesectoren van de Nederlandse economie voor de middellange termijn'; [Vinsec, a Model with Six Production Sectors of the Dutch Economy for the Medium Term], Occasional Paper 40 (Centraal PlanBureau, 's-Gravenhage).

Driehuis, W. (1972) *Fluctuations and Growth in a Near Full Employment Economy: A Quarterly Econometric Analysis of The Netherlands* (Rotterdam: Universitaire Pers [University Press]).

——— (1986) 'De methodologie van de macro-economische modellenbouw in Nederland in de jaren dertig [The Methodology of Macroeconomic Model-Building in The Netherlands in the 1930s], in *Economie als Spel* [Economics as a Game] (W. Driehuis and R. A. de Klerk, eds) (Leiden: Stenfert Kroese) pp. 115–22.

Driehuis, W. and A. van der Zwan (1978) *De voorbereiding van het economisch beleid, critisch bezien* [The Preparation of Economic Policy, a Critique] (Leiden: Stenfert Kroese).

Driehuis, W., K. A. Heineken and A. F. de Savornin Lohman (1979) 'De werkgelegenheid in kapitaalgebruikende bedrijfstakken' [Employment in Capital–Using Industries], in *Samenleving en Onderzoek* [Sociology and Research] (J. J. Klant, W. Driehuis, H. J. Bierens and A. J. Butter, eds) (Leiden: Stenfert Kroese) pp. 147–82.

Driehuis, W., E. C. van Ierland and P. J. van den Noord (1983a) 'Toekomstscenario's in discussie' [Scenarios for the Future under Discussion], *Economisch-Statistische Berichten*, vol. 68, pp. 696–704.

Driehuis, W., E. C. van Ierland and P. J. van den Noord (1983b) 'A Sectoral Model for the Netherlands Economy, SECMON-C', mimeo, Foundation for Economic Research of the University of Amsterdam.

Fase, M. M. G. (1981) 'Financiële activa, rentevorming en monetaire beheers-baarheid. Proeve van een monetair kwartaalmodel voor Nederland' [Financial Assets, Interest Rates and Monetary Control. A Tentative Quarterly Monetary Model for the Netherlands] in *Zoeklicht op Beleid* [Focus on Policy] (E. den Dunnen, M. M. G. Fase and A. Szasz, eds) (Leiden: Stenfert Kroese).

——— (1985) *MORKMON, A Quarterly Model of The Netherlands Economy for Macro-Economic Policy Analysis*, Monetary Monographs, no. 2 (Dordrecht: Nijhoff).

Friedman, M. (1957) *A Theory of the Consumption Function* (Princeton: Princeton University Press).

Frisch, R. (1933) 'Propagation Problems and Impulse Problems in Dynamic Economics', *Economic Essays in Honour of Gustav Cassel* (London: George Allen & Unwin) pp. 171–205.

Haberler, G. (1937) *Prosperity and Depression*, 3rd edn 1946 (Lake Success: United Nations).

Hasselman, B. H., V. R. Okker and R. J. A. den Haan (1983) *FREIA, Een macroeconomisch model voor de middellange termijn* [FREIA, A Macroeconomic Model for the Medium-Term] (Centraal Planbureau, 's-Gravenhage).

Hasselman, B. H., F. A. M. van Erp and H. R. Timmer (1987) 'The Central Planning Bureau Monetary Model of the Dutch Economy', paper presented at the A. E. A. [Association des économistes appliqués] (Geneva: Conference on Financial Modelling, January).

Hildreth, C. (1986) *The Cowles Commission in Chicago, 1939–1955* (Berlin, Heidelberg, New York: Springer-Verlag).

Johansen, L. (1959) 'Substitution versus Fixed Production Coefficients in the Theory of Economic Growth: A Synthesis', *Econometrica*, vol. 27, pp. 157–76.

Keynes, J. M. (1936) *The General Theory of Employment, Interest and Money* (London: Macmillan).

_____ (1939) 'Professor Tinbergen's Method', *The Economic Journal*, vol. 49, pp. 558–68.

Klein, L. R. (1950) *Economic Fluctuations in the United States, 1921–1941* (New York: Wiley).

Klein, L. R. and A. S. Goldberger (1955) *An Econometric Model of the United States, 1929–1952* (Amsterdam: North-Holland).

Kloek, T. and L. B. M. Mennes (1960) 'Simultaneous Equations Estimation Based on Principal Components of Predetermined Variables', *Econometrica*, vol. 28, pp. 45–61.

Knoester, A. (1974) 'Een stelsel monetaire vergelijkingen ten behoeve van een empirisch macro-model voor Nederland' [A System of Monetary Equations for an Empirical Macro Model of The Netherlands], *Maandschrift Economie*, vol. 38, pp. 473–530.

_____ (1980) *Over geld en economische politiek* [On Money and Economic Policy] (Leiden: Stenfert Kroese).

Knoester, A. and P. Buitelaar (1975) 'De interacties tussen de monetaire en de reële sector in een empirisch macro-model voor Nederland' [The Interactions between the Monetary and Real Sector in an Empirical Macro Model of The Netherlands], *Maandschrift Economie*, vol. 39, pp. 493–548.

Kuipers, S. H., G. H. Kuper and E. Sterken (1987) 'The CCSO Annual Model of the Dutch Economy, Specification, Estimation and Forecasting', mimeo (Faculty of Economics, University of Groningen).

Nerlove, M. (1966) 'A Tabular Survey of Macro-Econometric Models', *International Economic Review*, vol. 7, pp. 127–75.

Okker, V. R. and W. B. C. Suyker (1985) *Assessing Foreign Influences on the Dutch Economy, BUMO, an Experimental Modelling Approach* (Centraal Planbureau, 's-Gravenhage).

Phillips, A. W. (1958) 'The Relation between Unemployment and the Rate of Change of Money Wage Rates in the United Kingdom, 1861–1957', *Economica*, new series, 25, pp. 283–99.

Polak, J. J. (1939) 'International Propagation of Business Cycles', *The Review of Economic Studies*, vol. 6, pp. 79–99.

Radice, E. A. (1939) 'A Dynamic Scheme for the British Trade Cycle, 1929–1937', *Econometrica*, vol. 7, pp. 47–56.

Sargan, J. D. (1964) 'Wages and Prices in the United Kingdom: a Study in Econometric Methodology', in *Econometric Analysis for National Economic Planning* (P. E. Hart, G. Mills and J. K. Whitaker, eds) (London: Butterworths), pp. 22–54.

Smithies, A. (1957) 'Economic Fluctuations and Growth', *Econometrica*, vol. 25, pp. 1–52.

Solow, R. M. (1960) 'Investment and Technical Progress', in *Mathematical Methods in the Social Sciences, 1959* (K. J. Arrow, S. Karlin and P. Suppes, eds) (Stanford: Stanford University Press), pp. 89–104.

Suyker, W. B. C. (1986) *Het reële deel van BUMO: de vergelijkingen en een historische simulatie* [The Real Part of BUMO: Equations and Historical Simulation] (Centraal Planbureau, 's-Gravenhage).

Theil, H. (1954) 'Estimation of Parameters of Econometric Models', *Bulletin de l'Institut International de Statistique*, vol. 34, pp. 122–9.

Tinbergen, J. (1935) 'Annual Survey: Suggestions on Quantitative Business Cycle Theory', *Econometrica*, vol. 3, pp. 241–308.

_____ (1936a) 'Kan hier te lande, al dan niet na Overheidsingrijpen, een verbetering van de binnenlandse conjunctuur intreden, ook zonder verbetering van onze exportpositie? Welke leerng kan ten aanzien van dil vraaptuk worden getrokken uit de ewaringen van andere lander?' [Is a Recovery in the Domestic Economic Situation of this Country Possible, with or without Action on the Part of the Government, even without an Improvement in our Export Position? What Can Be Learned about this Problem from the Experience of other Countries?], *Prae-adviezen voor de Vereeniging voor de Staathuishoudkunde en de Statistiek* ('s-Gravenhage), pp. 62–108.

_____ (1936b) 'La disparité des prix et le commerce extérieur' [The Imbalance of Prices and Foreign Trade], *De Nederlandsche Conjunctuur*, vol. 20.

_____ (1937) *An Econometric Approach to Business Cycle Problems* (Paris: Hermann).

_____ (1938) 'Arbeidsproduktiviteit en werkgelegenheid' [Labour Productivity and Employment], Bijlage III van *Onderzoek naar de blijvende werkloosheid en haar bestrijding* [Inquiry into Lasting Unemployment and its Abatement], Rapport van de Commissie – van der Waerden, Hoge Raad van Arbeid, pp. 181–230.

_____ (1939a) *Statistical Testing of Business-Cycle Theories, Vol. I: A Method and its Application to Investment Activity* (Geneva: League of Nations).

_____ (1939b) *Statistical Testing of Business-Cycle Theories, Vol. II: Business Cycles in the United States of America, 1919–1932* (Geneva: League of Nations).

_____ (1940) 'On a Method of Statistical Business-Cycle Research. A Reply', *Economic Journal*, vol. 50, pp. 141–54.

_____ (1951) *Business Cycles in the United Kingdom, 1870–1914* (Amsterdam: North-Holland).

_____ (1959) 'An Economic Policy for 1936', *Jan Tinbergen Selected Papers*, L. H. Klaassen, L. M. Koyck and H. J. Witteveen, eds (Amsterdam: North-Holland), pp. 37–84.

Uebe, G., G. Huber and J. Fischer (1986) *Macro-Econometric Models – an International Bibliography* (Aldershot: Gower).

Van Bochove, C. A. and T. A. Huitker (1987) 'Main National Accounting Series, 1900–1986', National Accounts Occasional Paper NA-017, Central Bureau of Statistics.

Van den Beld, C. A. (1967) *Dynamiek der ontwikkeling op middellange termijn* [The Dynamics of Medium-Term Development], Inaugural lecture, Netherlands School of Economics.

_____ (1968) 'An Experimental Medium-Term Macro Model for the Dutch Economy', in *Mathematical Model Building in Economics and Industry* (London: Griffin), pp. 31–48.

Van den Berg, P. J. C. M., F. J. H. Don and J. Sandee (1983) *KOMPAS, Kwartaal-Model voor prognose, analyse en simulatie* [Quarterly Model for Forecasting, Analysis and Simulation] (Centraal Planbureau, 's-Gravenhage).

Van den Berg, P. J. C. M., G. M. M. Gelauff and V. R. Okker (1987) 'The FREIA–KOMPAS Model for the Netherlands: A Quarterly Macro-Economic Model for the Short and Medium Term', Occasional Paper 39, Centraal Planbureau, 's-Gravenhage.

Verdoorn, P. J. (1949) 'Fattori che regolano lo sviluppo della produttività lavoro' [Determinants of the Development of Labour Productivity], *L'industria*, pp. 3–11.

_____ (1951) 'On an Empirical Law Governing the Productivity of Labour', *Econometrica*, vol. 19, pp. 209–10.

_____ (1956) 'Complementarity and Long-Range Projections', *Econometrica*, vol. 24, pp. 429–50.

Verdoorn, P. J. and J. J. Post (1964) 'Capacity and Short-Term Multipliers', in *Econometric Analysis for National Economic Planning*, P. E. Hart, G. Mills and J. K. Whitaker, eds, (London: Butterworths) pp. 179–98.

Verdoorn, P. J. and C. J. van Eyk (1958) 'Experimental Short-Term Forecasting Models', paper read at the European meeting of the Econometric Society, Bilbao, Spain.

Verdoorn, P. J., J. J. Post and S. S. Goslinga (1970) 'The 1969 Re-estimation of the Annual Model: Model 69-C', mimeo, Central Planning Bureau.

Verdoorn, P. J., J. J. Post and S. S. Goslinga (1971) 'Het Jaarmodel 1969' [The Annual Model 1969], Bijlage A *Centraal Economisch Plan 1971* [Central Economic Plan 1971] (Centraal Planbureau 's-Gravenhage) pp. 181–201.

Von Hohenbalken, B. and G. Tintner (1962) 'Models of the OEC Member Countries, the United States and Canada, and their Application to Economic Policy', *Weltwirtschaftliches Archiv*, vol. 89, pp. 29–85.

Voorhoeve, W. (1986) *Short-Term Economic Forecasting in Practice: The Grecon Case. Econometric Fundamentals and Empirical Results Using Data of the Dutch Economy*, doctoral dissertation, University of Groningen.

7 Macroeconometric model-building in the United Kingdom*

James Ball and Sean Holly

The purpose of this chapter is to provide an historical background to macroeconometric model-building in the United Kingdom over the last 35 years. There is no doubt some dispute as to where the line should be drawn between macro and micro model-building, and clearly the two are linked in a number of significant ways. As a rough guide, macroeconometric model-building is interpreted here as the activity of constructing complete equation systems of the economy for such purposes as economic forecasting, the simulation of dynamic behaviour of the macroeconomy and the evaluation of the consequences and feasibility of macroeconomic strategies. That interpretation and the way in which it is applied is in itself somewhat arbitrary, but it is of practical importance to draw a line between the development of econometric relationships. This is not intended to be a history of applied econometrics, and this rules out reference to much interesting material which has affected the construction of complete economic systems themselves.

One should in addition, by way of introduction, make the point that, while the references to important work are clearly intended to be as full as possible in the space available, it is in our view neither practical nor interesting to attempt a complete enumeration of all the macroeconometric models of the United Kingdom that have been built and used over this period. (In any case, this has been done by others; see G. Ucbe *et al.*, 1988.) At the time of writing there are many. Some exist within the official government machine, such as the models used by HM Treasury and the Bank of England. Some exist within semi-public institutions such as the National Institute of Social and Economic Research. Others, such as the models of Liverpool University and of the London Business School, have been built and used within a university framework. Still others have been developed by consultants and stockbrokers, and the results provided to clients and customers. Model-building has been a mushrooming activity, and one could spend the entire chapter simply describing and evaluating

*We are grateful to Alan Budd, David Currie and Peter Smith for comments and assistance in the prepration of this chapter, a first draft of which was written by Professor Ball in 1984. This research was carried out under ESRC grant No. B01250012.

existing models. Apologies must be given in advance to those whose models and work are not referred to.

The approach of this chapter therefore is to eschew cataloguing and detailed description, and to focus instead on historical events and ideas that underlie existing econometric models in the United Kingdom at the present time. It begins with an historical overview of what we see as the main 'events' which have influenced model-building, and thoughts about model-building in the United Kingdom. This is followed by the consideration of some theoretical, philosophical and technical issues which affect current activities and attitudes. Finally, we attempt a brief summary of what we see currently as the 'state of the art'.

1   Econometric models since the 1950s

While a considerable amount of econometric work had been carried out by Richard Stone and others prior to the 1950s, the only complete and somewhat rudimentary model of the United Kingdom constructed within the United Kingdom was put together by Radice (1939). (This model is described in some detail in Chapter 1 above.) Tinbergen constructed a model of the business cycle in the United Kingdom published in 1951 (Tinbergen, 1951) and, in the late 1940s, Colin Clark built a model of the US rather than the UK economy (Clark, 1949). However, in the late 1950s, between 1957 and 1960, three developments took place which reflect the beginning of serious and sustained work on large-scale model-building for the UK economy, although only two were in effect completed and only one survived for further and continuous development.

These three developments owed little or nothing to each other. The first two began at about the same time in 1957–58, one at the London School of Economics (LSE) and one at the (then) Oxford University Institute of Statistics. At the LSE, the late Sir Maurice Kendall sought to develop a dynamic model of the economic system, drawing heavily on the general approach to the specification of dynamic models that had been reflected in the writings of A. W. Phillips (for example, Phillips, 1954). The essential point about models of this kind is that they were set out as differential equations rather than in difference equation form, which had been the custom in the setting up of earlier models of the Dutch and the US economies. This created some difficulty in estimating parameters when the gap had to be bridged between the theoretical system and the available data. This work was not in fact completed, but is of interest, given that it reflected a growing interest in the behaviour of economic systems. Indeed problems of securing adequate funding for the extension of the project were material in influencing Sir Maurice's decision to resign his chair at the LSE and to move to the world of consulting. (See *The Times*, 8 August 1961.)

At the Oxford Institute of Statistics, work began on a full-fledged model of the United Kingdom economy under the supervision and leadership of Lawrence R. Klein. There were two significant characteristics of the Oxford model. The first was that it was the first major model of its size to be estimated on the basis of quarterly data. With the notable exception of the US model of Clark (already referred to) and a further small model built by Barger and Klein (1954), other US and Dutch models had been constructed using annual data. This raised in a more acute fashion than hitherto the problems of seasonal adjustment and the specification of lag structures within the model.

Secondly, owing to the absence of national income data on a quarterly basis, the central output variable around which the model was constructed was the index of industrial production. In general, as reported in Klein *et al.* (1961), a large amount of the time had to be spent constructing and manipulating the available data to provide the data base that the specification of the model required. The methods of estimating and using the model itself were primitive indeed. All preliminary estimation was carried out using desk calculators, although at a later stage computer programs were developed to provide simultaneous estimates. The solution of the final model also had in effect to be worked out by hand with a desk calculator. One major forecast was in fact attempted and published (Klein *et al.*, 1959). In the event, with the departure of Klein to the United States in 1958, the model was not maintained, remaining until some years later an isolated and heroic effort in the face of many difficulties.

The third and major sustained research activity was the establishment of the Cambridge Growth Project in 1960. In many respects this represented a larger and more ambitious project with somewhat different objectives, at least in its early stages, from the Oxford model and the early work of Kendall. The Oxford model was predicated on the assumption that one was interested in making forecasts and studying the behaviour of the economy under different types of policy regime. The Kendall work reflected more of a profound interest in the dynamic properties of the economic system *per se*. The Cambridge Project at that time (although it became different at a later date) was not concerned with either of these things. It was concerned with trying to understand the probable consequences of various sets of assumptions – rather specifically the requirements that a particular set of growth rates of consumers' expenditure would place on the rest of the economic system. 'Requirements' in this context were to be thought of in terms of the investments in different areas of the economy and the individual outputs that would be necessary if the target levels of consumption were to be achieved. With this kind of model, it could be seen, for example, that certain final configurations of consumption were *prima facie*, implausible; for example, a given industry might have to invest and increase its output to a degree that was clearly unlikely.

Early papers of importance which contain overviews of the Project at this time were Cambridge Department of Applied Economics (1962) and (1964). Illustrative of the purpose towards which the model was to be put is Stone (1964). The important feature of this project in its early development was its focus on detailed inter-industry analysis. (See, for example, Cambridge Department of Applied Economics, 1963.) Moreover the early model, as already implied, was inherently static, although the problem of examining the transient path of the model from the initial point to the target year was discussed in Cambridge Department of Applied Economics (1964). In more recent years the Growth Project focused on the development of a multi-sectoral dynamic model of the economy. The Growth Project has been the major activity and leader of attempts to build more disaggregated models of the British economy which reflect detailed industrial analysis. A more up-to-date version of the 'static' model was provided in Barker (1976). Given this version of the model, much effort was made to develop a more sophisticated approach to policy analysis using the targets and instruments approach.

During the 1970s, Cambridge Econometrics, a consulting firm based on the work of this project, was formed to encourage industrial participation. Cambridge Econometrics has joined other groups in the United Kingdom which have published regular assessments and forecasts of economic prospects.

From the Oxford Model until the middle of the 1960s, little happened in the field of what might be described as conventional aggregate economic model-building. With the availability at last of quarterly national income data, if on a limited sample, a first attempt was made by Ball and Burns to put together a small model of the economy and to produce some simple multiplier simulations, reported in Ball (1966). In the same year, Ball and Burns began the publication of the first regular series of economic forecasts produced from a very similar model, which appeared under their names in the *Sunday Times* three times a year for the next ten years. The kind of model that existed and was in use at the London Business School (LBS), together with its multiplier properties, is set out in Ball and Burns (1968). A later version was described by Ball *et al.*, in Renton (1975). From this point on, the development of this kind of model accelerated substantially and it is worth pausing to consider, from an historical point of view, why this was the case.

As was evidenced by the history of the Oxford model, to which reference has been made, there were considerable data problems over a long period for anyone who wanted to build a model of the United Kingdom based on quarterly data. Nevertheless annual models might have been built, and they were not. Systematic and regular forecasting of the economy had of course been carried out by the Treasury for its own purposes for many years while, in the public domain, the foundation of the *National Institute Review* in 1959 heralded regular forecasts provided for public consumption. There were also forecasts provided by certain consultants who retailed these to their clients. However, while these forecasting exercises took place within the discipline of the national accounting framework, no attempt was made to integrate the various pieces of analysis that went into the forecast into a complete and computable model of the economy as a whole. At the official level such as the Treasury there was, in principle at least, no reason to lack resources for such a development. However, at the official level, there was undeniably a strong and profound scepticism as to the value of such an undertaking. It must at the same time be remembered that, in those days, there was also a close and very personal relationship between the National Institute and the Treasury, with personnel and ideas moving freely between the two.

The attitude to econometric model-building that appeared at official level merely reflected a rather general scepticism in the economics profession at large in the United Kingdom about the application of mathematical and statistical techniques to economic problems. The generation which headed the profession had no doubt been affected in some measure by Keynes's views on the subject, particularly as exemplified in his famous review of Tinbergen (Keynes, 1939). Some have suggested that Keynes's attitude was merely an extension of an attitude also made manifest in part by Marshall, although in an insightful analysis of Keynes's views on this subject Sir Richard Stone has suggested that this is all too simple an interpretation (Stone, 1978); see also the discussion in Chapter 2 above. Nevertheless casual empiricism at least suggests some negative inclination among British economists with a serious mathematical background to apply it to the analysis of economic relationships. Or, to the extent to which this was done, these individuals had a tendency to hide the formal structure. In so far as the activity was regarded as legitimate, it assisted at least in the formulation of pure theory, but stopped short of a full-blooded application to statistical data.

If we leave on one side the Cambridge Growth Project already referred to, the desire to link together forecasting and policy analysis systems on the part of the model-builders was a prime motivation for much of the work that took place in the late 1960s and early 1970s. But, to give some idea of the not unrepresentative attitude of much of the economics profession of the time, one can best quote the address of the distinguished former Chief Economic Adviser to the Treasury, Sir Alec Cairncross, to the Royal Economic Society in 1969. Referring to the process of economic forecasting, he said: 'I cannot discover any occasion on which the Royal Economic Society has ever discussed this new activity, in which an increasing number of economists are now engaged' (Cairncross, 1969, p. 797). At a later stage in his address, he expressed much scepticism with regard to more formal modelling as applied to the forecasting process:

> Just as some people feel in no need of recent data, others feel in no need of elaborate models. They find it sufficient to establish a trend and extrapolate. Or they conduct surveys of business expectations and build a forecast round the results ... My own sympathies lie more with the unsophisticated second group who at least have an ear to the ground, than with the often oversophisticated first group, who take a bird's eye view of the situation. (Cairncross, 1969, p. 799)

Later opinion would probably suggest that, in practice, the contrast is too starkly drawn, but it is fair to say that the majority of economists in the United Kingdom at that time would have agreed firmly with Sir Alec, who went on to say further that: 'Forecasts based on economic models convey an illusion of continuity that can be highly dangerous' (Cairncross, 1969, p. 800). The implicit suggestion seemed to be that random events dominated systematic behaviour to a degree that rendered the development of more formal models of the economy a dangerous game.

The second major constraint on the development of econometric models was simply finance. As the Cambridge Growth Project originally supported by the Ford Foundation had already demonstrated, the formation and maintenance of the teams required to sustain serious model-building exercises was expensive in relation to the meagre resources available, if not expensive in absolute terms. The advances that took place outside the official world in the late 1960s and the early 1970s owed nearly all to the foundation and the use of funds made available by the Social Science Research Council (of the United Kingdom), which took over part of the funding of the Cambridge Growth Project, as well as the funding of the work carried out at the London Business School, at the University of Southampton and at the National Institute. The Institute also received substantial support from Her Majesty's Treasury. In addition, the Social Science Research Council supported related work in the 1970s on estimation and control problems at Queen Mary College (and subsequently at Imperial College). As late as 1974, the then Chairman of the Social Science Research Council (SSRC), Professor Alan Peacock, observed that 'The crusade against quantification in Economics [in the UK] has never reached the dimensions of a religious persecution, but at times there has been formidable opposition to overcome ...' (Renton, 1975, p. v). He went on to say that the SSRC had now become a major supporter of work in the field, and would continue to support this work, believing in encouraging different approaches to model-building and forecasting methods.

The initial SSRC funding enabled the model-building work started at the London Business School to be continued and developed. Much of the development consisted in expanding the size of the system by disaggregating parts of the model and endogenizing more variables. At the same time, funds were made available to the University of Southampton for the development of a new model which was described originally at an initial SSRC conference on model-building and forecasting held in Southampton, reported in Hilton and Heathfield (1970) and further described in Heathfield and Pearce (1975).

The Southampton model project was a much more ambitious and complicated affair than the London Business School's. While the LBS continued with the development of a rather traditional Keynesian-type model in the tradition of Klein and Goldberger (1955) and the early version of Wharton Model (see Evans and Klein, 1968), the Southampton approach attempted to move directly to a multisectoral dynamic model of the economy based on a disaggregation of total output into 14 industries:

> To translate a conceptual framework based on economic theory into a system of equations with each variable designated so as to correspond with some identified data series is no small task, particularly when the number of series called for is something in excess of 1500. (Heathfield and Pearce, 1975, p. 83)

In essence, the Southampton model at the outset reflected an even more ambitious attempt to model the economy than the Cambridge Growth Project to which we have referred. The Cambridge Growth Project remained essentially static in nature through much of its early and middle years. While the number of sectors it purported to deal with were many more than those proposed for the Southampton model, the direct introduction of dynamic behaviour based on quarterly data brought major complexities of both a theoretical and practical nature. In many respects the model may have been ahead of its time. In the event, research on the model terminated in the 1970s, and it was never completed in the way in which its progenitors had originally intended.

The production of the first econometric forecasts by the London Business School in 1966, and the establishment of the research projects at London and Southampton, supported by the SSRC, preceded stirrings both at the National Institute and the Treasury. The National Institute history over this period has been clearly set out in Worswick (1975) and more recently in Jones (1988).

As already recorded, the Institute had been publishing forecasts since 1959, although these were not derived from any formal model. During the 1960s, increasing attention was paid to the use of certain econometric relationships as part of the forecasting process, particularly under the influence of Wynne Godley (for example, Godley and Shepherd, 1964); Godley and Gillion, 1965). As described by Worswick, the approach in the mid-1960s was to ensure that, for a given set of forecasts of exogenous variables, the forecasts of the endogenous variables satisfied the appropriate accounting identities, satisfied what statistical equations existed and were thought to be reliable and, finally, made good sense in areas where no such equations existed.

The strategy the Institute subsequently followed in extending its activities in the field was to build two models of the economy. The first and larger one was built by Byron and reported in Byron (1970). This model consisted of 22 behavioural equations and 51 identities. The parameters of the model were estimated, and some experimentation carried out with it. Worswick commented on it (Worswick, 1975, p. 68): 'The results however were quite unsatisfactory, and it seemed clear to me that there would be a very long way to go indeed before we could envisage bringing that particular model into regular use.'

Instead, the Institute gathered its existing relationships into an 11-equation model, together with some nine identities, and this model was ready for trial in the summer of 1969, and used in the August forecast of that year. The model in use at the time had been set out in Surrey (1971), and it is interesting to note Worswick's subsequent comment on its use (Worswick, 1975, p. 74):

> Let us then try to sum up experience so far of the use of an economic or econometric model in regular forecasting. *None of us would now envisage trying to do without it*, but our reasons for saying this are rather different from those which we might have expected when we first set out along this path. The advantages of the model are a) it ensures that the forecasts satisfy the accounting identities, b) it enables us to distinguish that part of our knowledge of the system which can reasonably be incorporated into equations and that part which cannot or not yet, c) it permits us to make adjustments in any part of the model and to compute the consequences with great speed. In short, it is a very handy tool. [Italics added]

It is interesting to compare this comment with the fears of Sir Alec Cairncross quoted above.

Meanwhile, back in the Treasury, despite no doubt considerable reservations, cautious progress was undertaken towards model-building. The then Treasury approach to economic forecasting has been well described by Roy (1970) and the subsequent history of this period summarized in

Shepherd, Evans and Riley (1975). The forecasting process could be described as being interdepartmental, with the Treasury coordinating the process and assembling the final forecast. To oversimplify the process, individual departments were given certain assumptions about the possible growth of GDP, on which they based their own forecasts of their particular concerns. For example, those responsible for housing forecast investment in residential construction, and so on. Elsewhere the balance of payments group prepared forecasts of world trade and exports. Finally, these forecasts were integrated with behavioural equations reflecting consumption and import behaviour to produce a second round estimate of GDP, an iterative process modified with judgements made at the relevant interdepartmental meetings that the Treasury organized and chaired.

The way the Treasury chose to move cautiously forward was to commission Ball and Eaton of the London Business School to undertake the task of describing in formal terms (that is, in terms of quantifiable equations) what in effect the Treasury were implicitly assuming about economic relationships. Some of these relationships were of course explicit. Some had to be inferred and, as recounted in Roy (1970, p. 473), certain other relationships were left for them to specify and estimate, including a function for non-housing investment in order to close the system.

The object of the exercise at this stage was not to provide a model that would be directly used for forecasting or for the consideration of policy alternatives. It was simply to provide a framework for updating the existing official forecast as new information, either new data or new views about certain exogenous variables, came into view. The computer program subsequently written by Eaton permitted the insertion and manipulation of the residuals of the model so that the equations, when suitably modified by the residuals, reflected exactly the official forecast which was initially obtained in the same way as before. Of course, in technical and model terms, the Treasury rapidly advanced from this position, and their own version of a full-scale model was first used fully operationally in the forecasting exercise of June–July 1970 (Shepherd, Evans and Riley, 1975, p. 30).

There is little doubt that, from the mid-1960s, the work carried out and reflected in the forecasts produced by the London Business School had a considerable multiplier effect both on interest in econometric modelling for policy analysis and for forecasting. The most significant fact about it was not that it was particularly original, which it was not at the time. The point was really rather more like that of Dr Samuel Johnson about the dog dancing, namely not that it was necessarily done particularly well; rather it was simply that it was done at all. On balance, what the work established was also not so much that econometric models might lead to some major improvements in forecasting but that, if sensibly handled, they were not obviously going to do it any worse. Moreover, as the quotation from Worswick (1975) indicates, it was now seen that these models were tools rather than mechanical devices. At the official level, the contribution made by the London Business School to the initiation of work in the Treasury has already been recorded. At a later stage in the 1970s, the London Business School model also provided the basis from which the Bank of England began developing its own capability in the econometric model-building and forecasting field, by supplying the model at that time with appropriate software and a member of staff transferred from the School to the Bank to run it. By the early 1970s, econometric models provided the basis for what were at that time seen as the three major forecasts provided on a non-commercial basis for the United Kingdom economy, namely the London Business School, the National Institute and the Treasury.

During the 1970s, the models of these three institutions expanded and changed, in ways that are broadly described in the next section. However the inventory of models expanded. While the Cambridge Growth Project continued to develop and flourish, a new Cambridge model was developed under the leadership of Wynne Godley, and under the banner of the Cambridge Economic Policy Group (CEPG).

From a visible point of view, the starting-point of the CEPG was what came to be known for a period as the New Cambridge Economics. The initial view put forward in a number of newspaper articles in 1973 and later was that government fiscal intervention had by and large been destabilizing because it had misunderstood the impact of the government deficit on the economy. Fluctuations in the current account of the balance of payments, it was argued, were primarily the result of changes in the public sector financial deficit. As a matter of accounting identity, of course, the current account of the balance of payments is equal to the sum of the financial deficits of the public and the private sectors. It was initially claimed that the private sector surplus was 'small' and stable although, following further model-building work, this was amended to the claim that the private sector deficit was predictable.

The conclusion that the CEPG drew from this in the early stages was that what were described as conventional models of the economy, a description which at the time could equally be applied to the models of the London Business School, the National Institute or the Treasury, were bound to give the wrong answers in projecting the effects of changes in economic policy because insufficient attention was given to the effect of financial flows on the current account of the balance of payments. Early versions of the New Cambridge Economics laid some stress on the forecasting issue. Forecasting the balance of payments on current account, long ago regarded as one of the more difficult variables to forecast, was in effect claimed to be easy. All that had to be done was to determine the government's prospective deficit or surplus. The analysis implied that this very simple theory provided insights that were vastly superior to anything that could be provided by the more conventional and elaborate model of the economy being used by the Treasury at that time. This striking conclusion attracted the attention of the politicians, always on the lookout for simplicity on the one hand and a stick with which to beat the Treasury on the other. (See Ninth Report of the Expenditure Committee, 1974.)

From these beginnings the CEPG went on to produce its own complete model of the economy and began projections on an annual basis, which were published in the *Cambridge Economic Policy Review* starting in February 1975. A particular version of the model is set out in Cripps and Godley (1976). Further discussion of the model and the general influence of the CEPG is left over until the next section.

In the late 1970s and early 1980s, all the models so far discussed more or less underwent further extension and revision. Most of them grew rapidly, the Treasury model being an outstanding example. By the end of the decade, it was represented by some 600 equations and identities; the London Business School model had grown to 280, and the National Institute to 150. As will be seen in the next section, however, these models had not necessarily developed in the same way. There were differences emerging in the approach to model-building, and the beliefs as to how the underlying economy operated. The growth in the size and complexity of these systems produced new challenges, and the models that were associated with them are conveniently discussed more in connection with the development of these ideas in the following sections, than simply as part of the historical view that we have just taken.

By the early 1980s there were many other models, associated with consultants and stockbrokers, which provided information both for clients and publicly for the world at large. In so far as the published forecasts emanated from a formal econometric model, they were (with the exceptions explicitly considered below) derived from the general model-building approaches of the major groups which had sponsored the research and progress in this field in the United Kingdom.

2   Alternative methodological approaches to model-building

In the previous section, some attempt was made to provide a chronology of macroeconometric model-building in the United Kingdom in the 1960s and 1970s. In so doing, we have touched on some of the reasons why such model-building was undertaken and hinted at some of the differences which have existed between the model-builders. Differences of viewpoint have more clearly emerged over these years among model-builders as to their underlying beliefs of how the economy functions and how it should therefore be modelled. At the same time, there have been differences of viewpoint, of what one might describe as a technical nature rather than simply an economic one, as to the precise research strategy and methodology that should be followed.

In the 1960s and early 1970s, the predominant economic orthodoxy in the United Kingdom was Keynesian. The specific character of the Cambridge Growth Model, with its emphasis on inter-industrial analysis and its use of a linear expenditure system to explain consumer demand, could hardly be said to have reflected any particular general view about economic behaviour (see Cambridge Department of Applied Economics, 1962). In the absence of any serious dynamics, it was not confronted with some of the short-term adjustment issues which, in part, came to divide model-builders at a later stage. On the other hand, the conceptual framework which, from an economic point of view, basically guided the early model-building developments of the London Business School, the National Institute and the Treasury was unashamedly Keynesian, building up multiplier/accelerator models of a kind, although the early models differed in some details and in scope. In so far as these modelling developments were intended to result in forecasting as well as policy analysis, the early model-builders in the United Kingdom would have undoubtedly subscribed to the view expressed by Sir Alec Cairncross (Cairncross, 1969, p. 805) that: 'On the whole, I doubt whether bad theory has played a major part in forecasting errors in this country over the past decade or two.'

We were all Keynesians then, brought up in a world of pegged exchange rates, in which the total supply of money was taken simply to respond to the demand for it, in which the behaviour of the economy was fully discussed in terms of flows, and virtually the sole channel through which monetary policy was assumed to affect the economy was through interest rates. Whatever the catholicity of views about monetary effects on the economy among monetarists and Keynesians alike across the water in North America, fiscality was king in the United Kingdom, and those few of a monetarist persuasion at the time were merely figures in the curiosity shop. The models built and developed were essentially expenditure models with fixed exchange rates, a limited treatment of the government sector and financial flows, and little or no monetary influences on economic behaviour, either through interest rates or otherwise. The competition between the London Business School, the National Institute and the

Treasury as the three main producers of public forecasts (and, in the case of the first two, quantified policy analysis in the public domain) was to develop more effective and efficient models of the economy within what might be called the general Keynesian paradigm. As time went on, this took the form in part of more detailed analysis, endogenizing variables that had hitherto been treated as exogenous, and disaggregating certain significant variables in the models. The principal debates of the late 1960s were not so much among the model-builders themselves as to the content and economic framework of their models. The major debate was between those who, for one reason or another, were opposed in general to the model-building activity, and those who believed that there were distinct advantages in further development.

However, in the early 1970s, attacks were made on the 'conventional' model-builders (excluding under this definition the Cambridge Growth Project) from two quite distinct points of view. The first was of a technical nature, relating to the strategy of model-building. The second was a concern with the economic specification of the conventional models, which has already been discussed as the New Cambridge Economics. Finally, at a later stage in the 1970s, model-building began to be affected by the growing influence of work on rational expectations.

The first had, in practice, three distinct but related elements. To begin with, largely owing to the influence and interest of Jeremy Bray, control theorists began to take an interest in the application of optimal control methods to the analysis of economic policy. (See, for example, Bray, 1970.) Bray was not alone in this, as witness a significant early British contribution from Livesy (1971). Livesy went on to participate in the application of control methods to the analysis of policy options with the use of the static Cambridge Growth Model.

It was, however, on Bray's initiative that a project financed by the Social Science Research Council was put together at Queen Mary College London, and subsequently transferred to Imperial College, under the leadership of John Westcott. The point at issue was not simply the importance and value of applying control theory to economic models. Indeed, the initial Queen Mary project was actually described as a Programme of Research into Econometric Methods, which clearly implied something of wider scope than simply the application of control theory to economic models.

Thus, while the first point was that economists ought to be paying more attention to the control literature than they were, there were two other interrelated items on the agenda. The first was the trend, even in the early 1970s, towards substantially larger and larger econometric models in terms of the number of equations and variables involved. Moreover the models were also highly non-linear. This posed considerable problems for the advocates of optimal control, since typically real applications of optimal control theory had, for the most part, involved models that were small relative to the econometric models that were being produced, and which were also linear. This raised the whole question of how necessary it was to build such large models if the object of the exercise was simply to forecast certain key variables in the economy, such as the rate of economic growth, the rate of inflation, the rate of unemployment and the current account of the balance of payments.

On top of this, questions were raised about the way in which the equations of the so-called conventional econometric models were actually estimated. Much of the econometric statistical literature of the 1950s and 1960s had dealt with the familiar problems of the estimation of simultaneous systems of equations, in which the lag structures of the models appeared to be somewhat arbitrary and primitive, and it was suggested that superior results to those conventionally obtained in the economics field could be obtained by the application of time series methods proposed by Box and Jenkins (1970) and by Astrom and Bohlin (1965).

Given the difficulties of scale and linearity, and the belief that better methods existed for estimating the specification and dynamic structures of economic relationships than econometricians were characteristically using, the Queen Mary group proceeded to specify and estimate their own small model of the United Kingdom economy of some 12 equations, which was known as PREM 1. The estimates of this model were given in Wall *et al.* (1975). Subsequent attempts to improve the model (Holly *et al.*, 1979), while still keeping it small, ran up against the difficulty that few economists were convinced by the specification. Moreover the explosion of inflation in the mid-1970s made the assumption of linearity more and more untenable. To overcome some of these difficulties, attention was switched to working with one of the main macroeconomic models. In 1975, the London Business School made its model available to PREM and this was used as a test case for a number of new approaches. A linearization of the large model was tried with linear optimal control techniques applied to the linear version. Non-linear optimization techniques were also explored. In a comparison of the two approaches (Zarrop *et al.*, 1979), non-linear optimization proved to be better, and this has been the approach which has been pursued since then by the Imperial College group. As we shall see later, others were to develop the linearization approach further.

The application of optimal control techniques was taken seriously enough to establish a Treasury committee of outside economists and statisticians to make recommendations on the value and feasibility of applying such methods to economic policy-making in the United Kingdom, which reported in 1978 (Committee on Policy Optimisation, 1978). The Committee concluded, among other things, that:

> ... optimal control applications (to existing models) are 'feasible', in the literal sense of the word, although there are still problems and questions with regard to the treatment of uncertainty and the choice of algorithms. Our central conclusion however is that optimal control techniques are at present best looked at as part of the total procedure of model building, testing and use. Within the context there were few who gave evidence to us who would rate optimal control techniques as the first priority over other problems of estimation and data improvement ... (Committee on Policy Optimisation, 1978, p. 12)

Work in the area of optimal control continued to receive support and, in 1979, a joint project was begun between the London Business School and John Westcott's group to further the application of optimal control to large models.

As far as methodology and estimation problems are concerned, a proper account of developments that have contributed in the United Kingdom requires a separate paper. However, following on from the viewpoint of some of the control theorists who have suggested that more powerful methods of estimation have been open to model-builders than those they have used, it is worth commenting on one debate that has distinguished the approaches of different groups.

This relates to the extent to which it is believed that the underlying properties of the behaviour of the economy can be ascertained largely by statistical estimation from available data sets. The point is to what extent the behaviour of the models is determined by the *a priori* constraints that are imposed by the model-builder before estimation of relationships, and which have significant effects on the dynamic properties of such models, particularly in the longer term. A good example of the problem is whether the slope of the Klein–Phillips curve can be left to empirical determination rather than prior specification. As pointed out in the United Kingdom context by Ball, Burns and Laury (1977), the behaviour of the wage determination equations has significant effects on the longer-term properties of aggregate econometric models with regard to the effects of exchange rate changes under both pegged and floating regimes. The approach of the National Institute, as described by Ormerod (1979a), suggests that the model should consist of the 'best' set of relationships that can be estimated from the available data set. At the London Business School, however, much of the work of the mid-1970s and after was affected by the prior beliefs that, in the longer run, the overall model should exhibit approximately the characteristics of a system which was homogeneous of degree zero in absolute wages and prices (see Ball, Burns and Warburton, 1979). The Cambridge Economic Policy Group has also claimed that its view of the economy and the relationships that have been developed for their model are strictly rooted in the available empirical evidence as reflected in detail by the available data sets, suggesting that the model specification is relatively free of significant prior hypotheses about the way in which the economic system functions (Cripps and Fetherston, 1979). In practice, no doubt, matters are not black and white on this issue. Nevertheless there have been clear differences of emphasis as to the information content of available data and the methods of determining it.

Some help with building (testable) long-run theoretical restrictions into macro-models was to come from developments in applied econometrics. The challenge to conventional econometric methods from control theorists and time series advocates, which we discussed earlier, stimulated a reappraisal at the LSE. The starting-point for this reappraisal was the seminal paper by Denis Sargan (Sargan, 1964). Sargan showed how the wage and price equations in Klein *et al.* (1961) could be made homogeneous by introducing long-run proportionality between wages and prices via an 'error-correction' term. Inspiration for this was drawn in part by the earlier work of Phillips, who showed how feedback mechanisms could be used in economic systems. These methods allowed modellers to combine long-run *a priori* theoretical properties, with short-term dynamic adjustments, which were consistent with the data. More recent theoretical developments associated with 'cointegration' techniques have provided an even firmer basis for error-correction models. Almost going full circle, statistical conditions have now been established by which static regressions can reveal the long-run properties of trended, non-stationary time series independent of the process of dynamic adjustment. The use of this class of modelling techniques is now commonplace among the majority of macroeconometric modellers in the United Kingdom.

3   Alternative conceptual frameworks

As recorded at the beginning of the last section, the basic conceptual framework that underlay the development of the earlier United Kingdom aggregate econometric models was Keynesian. The initial challenge to the so-called conventional approach came from the New Cambridge economics, which has already been briefly described. The earlier models recorded in Renton (1975) failed to incorporate flow-of-funds behaviour and to provide appropriate links between the behaviour of the government sector and, in particular, the government sector and the real economy.

While the Cambridge Economic Policy Group developed their ideas into a new full-scale model of the economy possessing the properties to which they had drawn attention, a significant step change away from the Keynesian paradigm was taken by the London Business School model of the economy. (See, for example, Ball, Burns and Laury, 1977; Ball, Burns and Warburton, 1979.) These developments were influenced from two directions. The first was the international monetary literature, as exemplified by Johnson (1972) and Dornbusch (1976), which provided the theoretical basis for linking together monetary and exchange rate changes. The second was the failure to make any kind of adequate prediction of the behaviour of the economy in the recession of 1975; in particular there was a widespread failure to account for the drastic fall in real consumption in the United Kingdom in that year.

The developments that took place rested on three propositions. The first was that relative monetary movements could be a key element in determining exchange rate behaviour, thus opening up a new linkage between monetary change and the inflation rate. When combined with the view that, in practice, fiscal changes had important monetary effects, another important route for 'crowding-out' in the economy was established other than simply through the behaviour of nominal interest rates. The second important element was the view that emerged as a result of the experience of 1975 and the behaviour of the personal savings ratio, namely that saving and consumption behaviour had to be accounted for in terms of stock adjustment phenomena. Thus accelerating inflation would, at the outset, cause a rise in the personal savings ratio as savers sought to restore the real value of their monetary assets. This explanation was much disputed, particularly by those who argued that the rise in the savings ratio was simply a response to uncertainty resulting from higher unemployment. (See, for example, the summary of Otto Eckstein's discussion of this point in the context of the DRI Model of the US economy, as reported in Chapter 5 above.) An important question was therefore what would happen as the inflation rate fell. In fact, subsequently, as inflation fell sharply, so did the savings ratio, while the general level of unemployment continued to rise. Finally, it came to be believed that it was unreasonable to accept estimates of the pass-on of price inflation into wage determination with a coefficient that was materially less than unity. The net result of building these propositions into the models was that, while they remained apparently Keynesian in the shorter term, fiscal expansion tended, under a flexible exchange rate regime, to be ultimately dissipated in inflation rather than having lasting effects on real output and employment. (We have something of a similar trend in the evolution of American models, surveyed in Chapters 3 to 5 above.) Because of the significance of the role of the money supply in such models, and its effect via the exchange rate, they were described as reflecting international monetarism, to be distinguished from so-called conventional monetarism by the fact that the neutrality of such models in the longer run did not depend essentially on a neoclassical specification of the labour market.

The London Business School was the first to move away from the Keynesian paradigm of the 1960s, while retaining the basic income–expenditure framework. But a much more far-reaching challenge to the whole concept of macroeconometric modelling and policy analysis was mustering in the United States. (See also the discussion in Chapter 17 below.) The challenge came on a number of fronts. Friedman had long questioned the efficacy of Keynesian fine-tuning, and the early neglect of monetary influences in macro-models. Lucas (1976) went much further than this, and from the perspective of rational expectations with competitive equilibrium models – in which all markets cleared immediately, by assumption – questioned the basis of models, the parameters of which were supposedly invariant to shifts in policy regimes. Lucas and Sargent (1981) sharpened this attack, and concluded that: '... modern macroeconomic models are of *no* value in guiding policy and that this condition will not be remedied by modifications along any line which is currently being pursued' (Lucas and Sargent, 1981, p. 296; italics in original).

Sargent and Wallace (1975) had earlier established, in a model with perfectly flexible prices and rational expectations, that there was no role for systematic macroeconomic policy, indeed that there was no *need* for a stabilization policy. These attacks from the New Classical school were to bear fruit in the United Kingdom in a number of developments in macroeconometric modelling during the 1980s.

4 Developments in the 1980s

Before we turn to a discussion of some basic themes running through model developments in the 1980s, it is worthwhile describing a number of events that have affected United Kingdom macroeconometric modelling as a whole.

In the early 1980s there was a re-examination of the basis for public support through the SSRC (renamed the Economic and Social Research Council (ESRC) in 1984). After the publication of the SSRC Subcommittee Report on 'Macro-Economic Research in the United Kingdom', it was decided to fund this activity through a consortium comprising the Bank of England, the Treasury and the SSRC. It was also decided to establish a Macroeconomic Modelling Bureau with the remit to improve accessibility to macroeconomic models, to promote general understanding of the properties of the United Kingdom models, and to allow comparisons between models to be made. The Bureau began operation in September 1983 at the University of Warwick under the direction of Kenneth Wallis.

There was also a number of new entrants to and exits from the group of publicly funded modellers. The City University Business School (CUBS) began to receive funding in 1983 for a model oriented towards the supply side, under the direction of Mike Beenstock. At the same time, the CEPG had its funds withdrawn. At the time, various (political) interpretations were placed upon these events. But it is more likely that the CEPG fell foul of the coming orthodoxy in econometric methodology that has had such an impact upon the standards of econometric practice in United Kingdom macro-modelling during the 1980s.

In fact ESRC funding of the CUBS model lasted only four years. With the departure of Mike Beenstock to Israel, funding was withdrawn in 1987. At the same time, support for the Cambridge Growth Project was withdrawn. Support was then diverted to a patchwork of small projects on vector autoregressive modelling, computable general equilibrium modelling, econometric testing, and housing, as well as a new initiative on micro- to macro-modelling. It is far too early at this stage to judge what impact these projects will have on the mainstream models at London Business School, Liverpool and the National Institute.

At the beginning of the 1980s, macroeconometric modellers in the United Kingdom – as elsewhere – found themselves assailed on a number of fronts. There was the intellectual assault from the New Classical school, in the United States, alluded to above. In 1979 a new Conservative government was elected with a programme of radical, market-oriented reform, and a purported abandonment of the use of demand management. The abandonment of exchange controls in 1979, financial deregulation, trade union reform and cuts in marginal (though not average) tax rates threw up countless problems for modellers as they attempted to capture the empirical effects of these measures on incentives to produce, save, invest and work.

In the economy, the rise in unemployment in 1980/1, the appreciation of the real exchange rate in 1979/80, the onset of North Sea oil, and the adoption of monetary and fiscal targets within the framework of a Medium-Term Financial Strategy – adopted by the Conservative government in 1980 from a proposal by Budd and Burns – placed enormous strains on the descriptive power of the mainstream macroeconometric models.

The responses took a variety of forms. As before, we shall eschew cataloguing and detailed description and concentrate on underlying ideas. We shall attempt to describe developments under three headings – the role of expectations, the modelling of the supply side, and developments in policy formulation, bearing in mind that there is considerable overlap.

5   The role of expectations

The challenge mounted by the New Classical school went to the heart of conventional macroeconometric modelling. But an important distinction needed to be drawn between expectations which were forward-looking and prices which were perfectly flexible. Both of these conditions are necessary for the neutrality propositions of Sargent and Wallace to hold. Once we allow prices to be sticky, whether because of overlapping contracts in labour markets, or because of the costs of processing information and changing prices, quantity adjustments become important. But there is also another important distinction between the markets in which prices are sticky and markets in which there is immediate clearing. In asset markets, low transactions costs and potentially large returns to arbitrage, even with risk premia, make it unlikely that known events or expected outcomes are not immediately discounted into asset prices. However prices in product and labour markets can be sticky.

In the United Kingdom the first model which incorporated forward-looking, or what should really be called 'consistent' expectations (Walters, 1971), was the Liverpool model. This was the first econometric model to incorporate both market-clearing and consistent expectations. The first published version of the Liverpool model was described in Minford (1980), though work on the model began in 1976. The first version effectively exogenized natural rates of unemployment and output. A 'supply' side was added subsequently and described in Minford (1983). A full description of the latest version of the model is contained in Minford *et al.* (1984). The model is regarded by its proprietors as belonging to the class of equilibrium or 'New Classical' rational expectations models.

Movements in output – around its natural rate – are dominated by price surprises, while inflation depends directly on monetary growth (using a narrow measure). The natural rate of unemployment is determined within the labour market, and depends – as does the real wage and equilibrium output – upon unemployment benefits, taxes on both employees and employers and on the trade unionization rate, as well as the real exchange rate. Because of the presence of this open economy effect, the aggregate supply curve is upward-sloping, rather than vertical as in the closed economy case.

At the London Business School, the distinction between perfectly flexible asset markets and slowly adjusting product and labour markets was adopted. The first attempt to incorporate rational expectations into a quarterly macroeconometric model in the United Kingdom was Holly and

Corker (1984), though Fair (1979) achieved it earlier for the United States. The United Kingdom attempt involved only expectations of the exchange rate. However a much more ambitious approach to modelling asset markets was adopted by Keating (Budd *et al.*, 1984; Keating, 1985). This did not mean that the monetary approach to the determination of the exchange rate introduced by Ball and Burns was abandoned. Rather, the model was extended to allow for more general portfolio considerations. The result was that three asset prices – the price of foreign exchange, bond prices and the price of shares – were determined in a forward-looking market-clearing framework.

At about the same time, some significant developments in the application of consistent expectations were occurring at the National Institute. There the emphasis was on expectations of quantity adjustments. Terms in expected output began to appear in a number of expenditure equations for inventories and investment, as well as in employment equations. Expected prices appeared in the wage equations, and the expected exchange rate in the exchange rate equation (Hall and Henry, 1988). Work was also proceeding at HM Treasury, though there exploration of the role of 'consistent' expectations was confined largely to the exchange rate.

From the beginning of 1985, the London Business School began publishing forecasts with consistent expectations; the National Institute quickly followed, later that year. Thus by the mid-1980s there were three United Kingdom macroeconometric groups – London Business School, Liverpool and the National Institute – publishing regular forecasts with 'consistent' expectations.

6 Modelling the supply side

The modelling of the supply side came onto the agenda of macroeconometrics after the first oil shock in 1973, as it became clear, especially in the United States, that the existing framework could not cope with the effects of a large change in relative price.

Of course, it has rarely been true that Keynesian-type, demand-oriented models have lacked a supply side. As is clear from Lucas, the expectations-augmented Klein–Phillips relationship can be reinterpreted as a supply curve, with deviations of output from trend driven by price surprises. Lawrence Klein (as in Klein, 1979), commenting on the need to take more account of the supply side, argued that: 'In a subtle way, supply factors are implicitly taken into account in the macroeconomic Keynesian model if the IS-LM construct is extended to include price determination, a production function, labour supply and labour demand' (Klein, 1979, p. 266). But he also argued that a full treatment of the supply side required an input–output system.

Developments in the United Kingdom broadly followed Klein's recommendations, though with less attention to the input–output side than he might like. But there were also a number of extra influences shaping the modelling of the supply side. The first was the very sharp rise in unemployment in 1980–1. The second was the emphasis which the new Conservative government placed on the importance of incentives.

One of the most marked features of the way in which unemployment was discussed and modelled in the 1980s was the attention given to the role of a labour market. Steve Nickell has expressed it as follows:

> [Sargan] ... was one of the first to try to make some theoretical sense of the Phillips correlation by pointing out that, at least in the long run, the Phillips curve must be about real and not nominal wages. This fundamental insight has, of course, been extended in a multitude of ways although not until the theoretical work of Friedman ... Phelps ... Mortensen ... and the empirical work of Lucas and Rapping ... was the *market* for labour returned to the centre of the stage. However ... subsequent empirical work on wages has still been dominated by the Phillips curve paradigm with the labour *market* firmly in the background. By this I mean that wage equations are not typically treated in conjunction with their natural market partner, namely employment. Indeed the usual partner of a wage equation is a price equation – thus we have the 'wage-price sector' whose sector here refers to a part of a model rather than a sector of the economy. (Nickell, 1984, p. 14; italics in original)

The debate about employment focused upon the relative contributions made by demand and supply factors. The earliest work from this perspective among macro-modellers in the United Kingdom was that of Beenstock (1979) and Minford (1983). However the econometric modelling of the labour market in the United Kingdom quickly came to be dominated by the ESRC-supported Centre for Labour Economics (CLE) at the LSE, under the direction of Richard Layard. The CLE has never regarded itself as part of the macroeconometric fraternity. It did put together a complete annual model of the United Kingdom, but this model has never been used for forecasting or kept up to date. Nevertheless the CLE's approach to modelling the labour market has had a profound effect on the majority of macroeconometric models. Essentially their approach has involved a model of imperfectly competitive product markets. Firms determine employment, given the real wage, which is the outcome of a bargain between firms and trade unions. Any factors which affect the bargaining strengths of the two parties will in principle alter the real wage. Thus a number of both supply and demand factors can be at work influencing the real wage, and through the mechanism of the labour market fixing the 'natural' rate of unemployment. The NAIRU (non-accelerating inflation rate of unemployment) then depends upon a number of structural factors such as a mismatch between available workers and available jobs, upon taxes on both employees and employers, on trade union power and upon unemployment benefits (Layard and Nickell, 1985). It can also depend upon the existence of unemployment itself; being unemployed makes it more likely that someone will be unemployed in the future, as *unemployed* human capital deteriorates, and so the intensity of job search diminishes (Budd *et al.*, 1988).

A clear picture of the treatment of the labour market in each of the models can be seen from the 1986 *Review of the Macroeconomic Modelling Bureau* (Wallis *et al.*, 1986, ch. 5), which provides an econometric evaluation of the labour market in all the publicly supported models (CUBS, London Business School, Liverpool, National Institute) as well as in those of the Bank of England and HM Treasury. A number of features stick out. First, all of the models are expressed in terms of real (expected) wages. The controversy of the 1970s concerning the pass-on of price rises into nominal wages has been replaced by complete unanimity.

Secondly, with the exception of the Cambridge Growth Project (CGP), which uses the change in unemployment, the *level* of unemployment appears in all wage equations. In principle, therefore, each of the models (excepting CGP) has a 'natural' rate of unemployment. The final issue concerns what supply-side influences affect the real wage in each of the models. In the Liverpool model, both unemployment benefits and the extent of trade unionism (measured by its density) have a powerful impact on real wages. Unemployment benefits also appear in the CUBS and London Business School wage equations. In the case of the London Business School, this effect was much weaker, and less well determined. In the case of the Bank of England model, the income tax rate appears, while the indirect tax rate features in the London Business School model, and both the income tax rate and taxes on employment appear in the Treasury's model. No supply-side variables of this type appear in the models of either the CGP or the National Institute.

We do not wish to overemphasize the similarities between the models, since substantial differences still exist. The effects of taxes and benefits and trade unions on real wages and on unemployment remain contentious both among the macro-modellers and the academic community at large. The strength of the effect of unemployment on real wages also remains in dispute. One line of argument suggests that the long-term unemployed have a substantially weaker (if not negligible) effect on real wages compared with the short-term unemployed, and more recently this kind of distinction has been incorporated into some of the macro-models (Budd *et al.*, 1988).

One other feature of the mid-1980s was the increasing role which was being given to factor prices and to interest rates in the macroeconometric models (Kelly and Owen, 1985). This is important for two reasons. First, stronger interest rate effects increase the potency of monetary policy. Interest rate effects work through two channels: there is a direct expenditure effect on consumption, investment and inventory investment, and an indirect effect via the exchange rate, which, if expectations are forward-looking, jumps immediately in response to an increase in interest rates. Secondly, the incorporation of factor prices and interest rates also opens up channels by which taxes on profits, interest payments, employment and wages affect decisions to save, invest and to work.

The new emphasis on the labour market made it more natural to group the treatment of wages with employment (to explain unemployment), so it is reasonable that prices should be grouped with output to explain supply. It is along these lines that the incorporation of a complete supply side into the London Business School model has moved. This model is still organized around the income–expenditure accounts but GDP is no longer directly demand-determined. Instead output is set at the sectoral level by both supply and demand factors. A distinction is also drawn between goods which are exported and those which are supplied to the domestic market. Output, or aggregate supply, is then made consistent with decisions on the expenditure side by adjustments to inventories and by making imports the difference between domestic absorption and domestic output (Dinenis *et al.*, 1989). (The similarity with several of the French models, reviewed in the next chapter, may be noted.)

Again, this represents a development of the earlier monetary approach to the determination of the exchange rate and the current account. The monetary approach was in part a reaction against the elasticities approach to the current account, and, in order to sharpen the distinction, those advancing the monetary approach suppressed the role of relative prices in achieving adjustment between traded and non-traded goods, and focused on the way in which the domestic price level was set under fixed and floating exchange rates. However if we wish, in a complete model of the open economy, to understand how adjustment takes place after an internal or external disturbance, we need to capture the role relative prices play in sectoral adjustments, and to explain what determines the real exchange rate. Nothing is lost by allowing key supply and demand elasticities to affect sectoral adjustments within the open economy.

In summary, then, the expansion of a 'supply side' in the United Kingdom macroeconometric models involved a number of uneven developments in the modelling of labour and product markets. In so far as it is fair to generalize, this has involved a much greater role for relative prices, a widespread acceptance of the importance of long run homogeneity of degree zero in absolute wages and prices, and a greater – though highly disputed – role for taxes and benefits to alter incentives to save, invest and work.

7   Policy formulation

The Conservative government's conscious abandonment of demand management and its adoption of a medium-term financial strategy to guide fiscal and monetary policy would appear to have undermined the usefulness of the work which had begun in the 1970s into the application of control methods to macroeconometric models. Nevertheless work continued.

The Imperial College group continued with its application of non-linear optimization techniques to large models, taking in the National Institute model along the way. A copy of the Treasury model was also obtained. Subsequently the Imperial College group wrote computer programs for economists in HM Treasury to use (Melliss, 1984). Thus, by the mid-1980s, the technical equipment to carry out optimal control exercises had spread to the London Business School, to the National Institute and to the Treasury, and more recently it has reached the Bank of England.

However the rational expectations revolution also had serious implications for the use of optimal control techniques, and this prompted a rethink of the whole technical approach to policy formulation. To quote Kydland and Prescott:

> Even if there is an agreed-upon, fixed social objective function ... discretionary policy ... does not result in the social objective function being maximized. The reason for this apparent paradox is that economic planning is not a game against nature but, rather, a game against rational economic agents. We conclude that there is *no* way control theory can be made applicable to economic planning when expectations are rational. (Kydland and Prescott, 1977, p. 127; italics in original)

On the face of it, this largely technical dispute has little to do with the nature of macroeconometric model-building in the United Kingdom. In a narrow sense this is true, since the criticisms of Lucas and Sargent had provided sufficient reasons for re-examining the way in which expectations were being treated in macro-models. However the importance of the Kydland and Prescott paper was that it changed the way in which the use of models for policy simulations was perceived, and it threw an illuminating light on the nature of economic policy-making when there is a deliberate change in regime. Previously unfamiliar notions, such as the 'credibility' of an economic strategy, became commonplace in discussions of economic policy. Suppose, for example, a new government announces the adoption of a counter-inflationary strategy based upon a restrictive fiscal and monetary strategy. If it is widely believed that the government will stick to its guns, then it is possible that the economy will adjust quickly to a lower path for inflation, with little loss of output. However, if there is the widespread expectation that, on the basis of past experience, a government will reverse its anti-inflationary policy in the face of rising unemployment, then the policy will not be believed, and possibly significant output losses will be experienced if the government continues with its strategy, until the government is believed. However there is a further twist to this story.

Once the government has built up a reputation for being tough, it then may have an incentive to cheat by reneging on its previous policy. There are a number of ramifications of this line of argument discussed more fully in Currie (1985) and Holly and Hughes Hallett (1989). Overall, the effect that this kind of analysis has had on the uses to which macro-models are put is to show that the role of macro-models in the conduct of economic policy cannot be divorced from larger aspects of political economy. If we wish to understand how a set of policy proposals might impinge on the economy and we use a macroeconometric model which incorporates consistent expectations, proper regard must be given to the way agents in the economy might look at the proposals, with regard both to their credibility and to their sustainability.

There were also a number of subsidiary issues in the area of policy formulation that were evident in the 1980s. We have already described how the Imperial College group moved over to the use of non-linear optimization techniques and applied them successively to each of the main quarterly macro-models. However, more or less at the same time, as Imperial dropped the use of linear techniques, the linear approach was being picked up by others and developed, especially in the direction of rational expectations. In 1982, the Programme of Research into Small Models (PRISM) began work at Queen Mary College under the direction of David Currie. This research had two key features. It developed the linear framework of optimal control theory to allow for forward-looking expectations, and ultimately extended the framework to handle dynamic games and international policy coordination. Secondly, the first models to which these techniques were applied were very small, though theoretically coherent.

The parameters were not estimated directly but were culled from a variety of plausible empirical estimates. The PRISM models were largely convincing at the theoretical level, in contrast to the early Imperial College model discussed earlier, but they still did not carry sufficient conviction because of the lack of a firmer empirical basis. Thus work began again in the United Kingdom on deriving linearized versions of the large macro-models. The techniques used drew upon previous work which had been under way at Cambridge University that in turn drew on classical techniques for the control of engineering processes (Macie, Jouskey and Vines, 1982). The work on linearization of large models and the application of the PRISM techniques to linear models came together to allow the examination of a variety of policy rules.

8   The current state of the art

While, as recorded earlier, the basic conceptual framework in the 1970s that underlay the construction of aggregate mainstream econometric models was of an inherently Keynesian nature, developments in the 1980s have continued to move in other directions, as discussed in the last section. In 1979 Alan Budd, in reviewing the main models, took the following view:

> As far as the structure of the models is concerned, three issues deserve particular emphasis, either because they illustrate the greatest difference between the models or because they represent the sharpest break with previous conventional views. The general issues are: what is the importance of money? what are the short- and long-run effects of changes in fiscal policy? and what are the short- and long-run effects of changes in the exchange rate?

At the time of writing (late 1989), some tentative agreement has emerged on some of these issues, but there still remains considerable disagreement. In the case of the United Kingdom, the dispute about the role of money in the economy has historically been of an entirely different nature from the disputes between the so-called Keynesians and monetarists of the United States. In the latter case, there has been no serious disagreement as to whether money 'matters', or whether changes in interest rates and monetary aggregates do or do not have material economic effects. The argument has not been about whether money matters, but about the limits to discretionary monetary and fiscal policy, as well exemplified in Franco Modigliani's presidential address to the American Economic Association (Modigliani, 1977). The key question in the United States has been whether it is both possible and desirable to iron out fluctuations in economic activity by discretionary monetary and fiscal intervention.

In the United Kingdom, for much of the 1960s and 1970s, the issue has been a much cruder one, starting from the point of view that money and monetary variables play little role in affecting either real output or the behaviour of prices. To believe that monetary policy is as important an element of macroeconomic policy as fiscal policy was to court the epithet of 'monetarist'. The belief in the unimportance of money and, in some sense, the primacy of fiscal policy had been a key feature of United Kingdom thinking with regard to macroeconomic policy until recently. It is hardly surprising, therefore, that this attitude was reflected in the work of the earlier econometric model-builders.

There were, we believe, three reasons for this. The first is the hangover from the late 1930s, which suggested that monetary policy had a very limited role to play in the process of recovery from slump conditions. The well-known enquiries into the effects of interest rates on investment decisions, carried out both in the United Kingdom and in the United States, suggested that changes in nominal rates had little effect. Sometimes this was presented in the form that you could lead the horses to water (by providing funds), but you could not persuade them to drink – or you can pull on the string of interest rates but not push. All this added up to a considerable scepticism as to the significance of monetary policy (however defined) and to the elevation of fiscal policy, whose effects on economic activity were believed to be more direct and effective. All this was no doubt at the back of people's minds during the earlier postwar period.

Secondly, it is of major importance to take into account the significance of the open character of the British economy. In the United States, debates about the importance of monetary policy have historically taken place under the broad umbrella assumption of a closed economy, although this is less so in the post-OPEC world. In the United Kingdom, it is impossible to do that. Unfortunately much of the postwar discussion of these issues in the United Kingdom also failed to take into account the significance of the Bretton Woods agreement and the pegged exchange rate system for the conduct of British economic policy. The maintenance of parity with the dollar restricted the ability of the monetary authorities to control the total supply of money. Overall monetary adjustments took place through the balance of payments. The quantity of money accommodated itself by and large to the demand for it, and became essentially a dependent rather than an independent variable. World inflation was dominated by the financial conservatism exercised for many years by the United States. Thus, to a significant degree of approximation, the United Kingdom controlled neither its money supply nor its inflation rate, despite the rhetoric with which successive Chancellors of the Exchequer presented their budgets. Thus the myth arose that, during the 1950s and 1960s, successive governments pursued Keynesian policies and money did not matter. The error was of course to jump to that conclusion from the more or less correct presumption that, under the operation of the system, benign neglect of changes in the money supply did not in fact matter that much, as far as influencing domestic economic activity was concerned. However, once the exchange rate was floated in 1972, the whole situation changed, since in principle it meant that control over the money supply was regained, and monetary adjustments now took place through changes in the exchange rate and, subsequently, prices.

Lastly, considerable difficulties had been experienced in the United Kingdom over a long period of time in relating financial variables in general to developments in the real economy. As has been alluded to in previous sections, there has been greater success during the 1980s in identifying significant interest rate effects on most categories of investment and consumption expenditure, though the strength of these effects remains in dispute. Wealth effects have also become important. The role of monetary policy has also been reinforced by the much closer relationship in the United Kingdom macroeconometric models between changes in interest rates and changes in the exchange rate. The precise specification of the relationship varies from model to model, depending upon the use of 'consistent' expectations and the role given to proximate determinants such as North Sea oil. But it is clear that convergence is occurring towards an uncovered interest parity condition with some adjustment for risk premia. This convergence reflects as much the difficulties of estimating reduced forms of exchange rate equations as the theoretical attractions of using an arbitrage relationship in an efficient, forward-looking exchange rate market. It also reflects the greater interest in the exchange rate as a channel for the transmission of monetary policy and as an intermediate target. This interest resulted from the severe difficulties which were experienced with the use of targets for the monetary aggregates during the 1980s.

The commitment of British governments to monetary targets began in the mid-1970s. In the 1980s monetary targeting was enshrined in the Medium-Term Financial Strategy, which laid down targets for a number of years ahead. The particular form that these targets took reflected the previous tendency for the velocity of circulation to rise slowly over time. As it was, the velocity of circulation, as in many other industrialized countries, fell steadily during the 1980s. This made the use of monetary targets particularly difficult for economic policy, so there was an increasing interest in using the exchange rate as an intermediate target. Thus, while there is now greater agreement about the effects of monetary policy on the economy, there is less agreement about precisely how that policy is to be operated.

It is clear that the issues posed by Alan Budd (1979) cannot be dealt with simply in terms of econometric investigations. The questions of the importance of money and the degrees of homogeneity in the available models, which affect the longer-term responses to fiscal and monetary changes, all pivot on the critical question of the aggregate supply response of the economy to a change in the level of nominal demand. The overall elasticity of supply of the system is a critical element in the neutrality debate in general, as are such particular questions as whether changes in the nominal rate of exchange can cause permanent shifts in the real rate of exchange. (See, for example, Ball, 1977.) As we have pointed out above, there is now much more agreement among macro-modellers in the United Kingdom that money illusion cannot be a long-run feature of any economy. Modelling the supply side of the United Kingdom economy is still at a relatively early stage, and no broad consensus on how it should be approached has yet emerged. It should be clear that the problem is not so much one of determining capacity in any *physical* sense, but lies in determining and measuring the degree of *economic* capacity that exists. Weakness in modelling the supply response imposes considerable limitations on the use of existing models, particularly if policies aimed at inducing supply shifts (such as increasing competition or incentives, or promoting trade union reform) lie at the heart of policies being pursued by a particular government. One of the problems may reside in the nature of the time series data that we use. Many of the tax rates, the effects of which we are interested in determining, have varied comparatively little over time compared with most macroeconomic series. This makes it difficult to capture whatever effects there might be on savings, investment and work. One way around this difficulty is to make more use of the recent growth in microeconometric work, which uses very large pooled data sets of households and firms. These data sets may help us to get a better idea of the supply-side effects of various policies. Currently, some effort is being put into seeing how this information could be used in macroeconometric models.

Despite the differences that exist in the structures of the individual models, they have not differed greatly in terms of short-term forecast performance. Some crude forecast comparisons between the London Business School, the National Institute and the Treasury for much of the 1970s are given in Ball (1978) and the figures for the London Business School have been updated by Robinson (1983). Table 1 of Ball (1978) sets out 18-month predictions and realizations for much of the 1970s for gross domestic product, consumer expenditure, and the rate of inflation where possible. The observed absolute errors over these periods are easily within the average range of adjustments in the data themselves five years after the rate of initial publication. The update given in Robinson (1983) for the London Business School continues to support that idea that, since the 1960s, there has been some improvement in the capacity to forecast both real output and prices in the short term, but it is impossible to say to what extent this has been due to the development of the models or to the increased skills of the forecasters themselves. Given the standard errors of the data themselves, it is hardly likely that we shall see much, if any, improvement in the recorded forecast errors, so that the worth of such models and forecasting exercises must probably be judged on the basis of what we can now do. Burns (1986) provides an analysis of Treasury forecasts and notes that, while there has not been an obvious improvement in short-term forecasting, there are signs that two-year forecasts have improved over time, though Wallis (1989) found that forecasts made two years ahead by the London Business School and the National Institute did not exhibit a similar improvement. One of the undoubted benefits flowing from the Macroeconomic Bureau at Warwick University is that it has replaced irregular analysis of forecasts with systematic annual studies. By the end of 1989 it will have a repository of seven annual forecasts made by the publicly supported groups. This will provide a rich source for the systematic study of forecast performance. Furthermore the Bureau can also decompose forecast errors into those due to incorrect assumptions about exogenous variables, those coming from model errors, and those which reflect the forecaster's judgement.

It turns out that, for the purposes of determining policy, the precise differences in models' structures and coefficient estimates are probably much less than one would suppose. When placed in a policy context, none of the models of which we are aware suggest that important permanent gains in real output and employment can be obtained by major fiscal expansion without an unacceptable cost either in terms of inflation or in terms of the effect on the current account of the balance of payments. Policy packages to take care of these side effects tend to take one of two forms – a flexible exchange rate combined with direct controls over incomes and prices (the National Institute type of solution) or a general tariff on imports (the CEPG type of solution). The protagonists then divide into three groups: those who argue that the balance of payments is a constraint to fiscal expansion, which can best be dealt with by combining incomes policy with devaluation; those who espouse protectionism and reject the devaluation option; and finally those who do not believe that the balance of payments is a constraint, that the basic constraint is underlying supply behaviour, for which devaluation as such and protectionism are quite irrelevant. The precise models employed by the protagonists differ, even if they fall into the same camp. The important point to make here is that none of these models are in any sense adequately specified to test the policy packages that are put forward. The political implications of wage restraint and the price that would have to be paid for it lie completely outside the formal models, for which the incomes policy in practice means the exogeneity of the money wage rate. As far as protectionism is concerned, leaving on one side the political question of retaliation, the supply-side specifications of the models are quite inadequate to trace through the consequences of a general tariff on inflation, profits and aggregate supply. The impact of a tariff would appear as a restriction on imports in the model, which begs the material questions to which the models, as such, provide no answers.

These problems are illustrated in the papers contributed to Posner (1978). Each of the main model-builders was asked to make use of their existing models to re-examine the economic history of the first Wilson government, starting in 1964, and the Heath government, starting in 1970. The results given and the subsequent discussion suggest that the range of policy options, for example the use of incomes policies and protection introduced into the models in the way described above, had produced more significant differences in the results than the differences in the model structures themselves.

It is now widely recognized that aggregate models of the economy are significant tools in the hands of analysts as part of the process of scanning and interpreting the economic environment. Despite the scepticism of many about economic forecasts and the acknowledged limitations of such models, there will continue to be a need for forecasts and for writing alternative scenarios, and this cannot be achieved in any more efficient way. Modern technology in the form of computer capability and software has now made it possible to handle very large systems with ease.

The 1980s have been a particularly unsettling time for macroeconometric modelling in the United Kingdom and elsewhere. The models appear to have weathered the serious intellectual challenges that have emanated from the New Classical school, though much work still needs to be done. The role of models in both forecasting and policy analysis has increased, though not necessarily in ways we anticipated ten years ago. To quote the views of a Treasury economist:

> ... it might seem at first sight that modelling has a less important role in policymaking in the Treasury than it used to have. It is certainly true that we serve up fewer numbers from policy simulations straight to Ministers. That in itself does not, of course, mean that such work is less influential. Economists in the Treasury still comment on the whole range of macroeconomic policy issues, and provide quantification where necessary. The Treasury model is vital in this process because, first, it is essential when numbers are needed; and second, it is an invaluable aid to clear thinking, especially since the interactions are usually too complex to work through in one's head or in a simple analytical model. We could not operate at all effectively in policy analysis without the model, even if we never show ministers a single number. (Odling-Smee, 1989, p. 34)

Further developments in models in the United Kingdom are likely to be dominated by a period of consolidation. It may be premature to claim that a degree of broad consensus is emerging. Nevertheless it is striking how much the United Kingdom models have developed over the last decade. The widespread use of consistent expectations in forecasting and policy analysis, the acceptance of the need for wage and price homogeneity, the modelling of the labour market and approaches to explaining the exchange rate all suggest that the models are moving together. However there is still disagreement about the extent to which all markets need to clear immediately, though we suppose that everyone agrees that markets do clear eventually. The Liverpool model is commonly regarded as the most extreme on this issue. However, since the Liverpool model is annual, the clearing of all markets in the space of one year may not be such a long way from what the quarterly models are starting to suggest.

The main area of significant disagreement, as we have already remarked, remains the empirical role of incentive effects on the supply side. The new microeconometrics may in time help to resolve this issue also.

References

Astrom, K. J. and T. Bohlin (1965) 'Numerical identification of linear dynamic systems from operating records', *Proceedings of the IFAC Conference on Self-Adaptive Control Systems*, Teddington.

Ball, R. J. (1966) 'Economic model building for control', *The Advancement of Science*, March.

―――― (1977) 'The theory of employment revisited', in H. Allach, R. Helmstadter and R. Henn (eds), *Quantitative Wirtschaftsforschung: Wilhem Krelle zum 60 Geburtstag* (Tübingen: Mohr) pp. 25–42.

―――― (1978) 'Assessment of short-term economic forecasts', *Economic Outlook* (Aldershot: Gower).

―――― (1983) 'Economic Management and Aggregate Supply', in F. G. Adams and B. G. Hickman (eds), *Global Econometrics. Essays in Honor of L. R. Klein* (Cambridge MA: MIT Press) pp. 239–61.

Ball, R. J. and T. Burns (1968) 'An econometric approach to short-run analysis of the United Kingdom economy, 1955–66', *Operational Research Quarterly*, 19, pp. 225–56.

Ball, R. J., B. D. Boatwright, T. Burns, P. W. M. Lobban and G. W. Miller (1975) 'The London Business School Quarterly Econometric Model of the United Kingdom Economy', in G. A. Renton (op. cit.) pp. 3–38.

Ball, R. J., T. Burns and J. S. E. Laury (1977) 'The role of exchange rate changes in balance of payments adjustment – the United Kingdom case', *Economic Journal*, 87, pp. 1–29.

Ball, R. J., T. Burns and P. J. Warburton (1979) 'The London Business School Model of the United Kingdom economy: an exercise in international monetarism', in Ormerod (op. cit.) pp. 86–114.

Barger, H. and L. R. Klein (1954) 'A quarterly model of the United States economy', *Journal of the American Statistical Association*, 49.

Barker, T. S. (ed.) (1976) *Economic Structure and Policy: Cambridge Studies in Applied Econometrics No. 2* (London: Chapman and Hall).

Beenstock, M (1979) 'Do United Kingdom Labour Markets Work?' *Economic Outlook*, 3, June/July, pp. 21–31 (Aldershot: Gower).

Box, G. E. P. and G. M. Jenkins (1970) *Time Series Analysis, Forecasting and Control* (San Francisco: Holden-Day).

Bray, J. (1970) *Decision in Government* (London: Victor Gollancz).

——— (1979) 'Current model testing procedures of United Kingdom modellers', in Ormerod (op. cit.), pp. 330–42.

Budd, A. P. (1979) 'The present state of the art', in Ormerod (op. cit) pp. 1–22.

Budd, A. P., G. Dicks, S. Holly, G. Keating and B. Robinson (1984) 'The London Business School econometric model of the United Kingdom', *Economic Modelling*, vol. 1, no. 4.

Budd, A. P., P. Levine and P. Smith (1988) 'Unemployment, vacancies and the long-term unemployed', *Economic Journal*, vol. 98, no. 393.

Burns, T. (1986) 'The interpretation and use of economic predictions', *Proceedings of the Royal Society of London*, series A., no. 407, pp. 103–25, reprinted in *Predictability in Science and Society* (eds) J. Mason, P. Mathias and J. H. Westcott (London: Royal Society and British Academy).

Byron, R. (1970) 'Initial attempts in model building at NIESR', in K. Hilton and D. F. Heathfield (op. cit.)

Cairncross, A. (1969) 'Economic Forecasting', *Economic Journal*, 79, December, pp. 797–812.

Cambridge Department of Applied Economics (1962) *A Computable Model of Economic Growth*, no. 1 in *A Programme for Growth* (London: Chapman and Hall).

Cambridge Department of Applied Economics (1963) *Input–Output Relationships 1945–1966*, no. 3 in *A Programme for Growth* (London: Chapman and Hall).

Cambridge Department of Applied Economics (1964) *The Model in its Environment: A Progress Report*, no. 5 in *A Programme for Growth*, (London: Chapman and Hall).

Clark, C. (1949) 'A system of equations explaining the United States trade cycle 1921–1941', *Econometrica*, 17, April.

Committee on Expenditure (1974) *Ninth Report* (London: HMSO).

Committee on Policy Optimisation (1978) Report CmND, 7448 (London: HMSO).

Cripps, T. F. and W. A. H. Godley (1976) 'A formal analysis of the Cambridge Economic Policy Group model', *Economica*, 43, November, pp. 335–48.

Cripps, T. F. and M. J. Fetherston (1979) 'Cambridge Economic Policy Group Methodology', in Ormerod (op. cit.)

Cripps, T. F., M. J. Fetherston and T. S. Ward (1978) 'The effects of different strategies for the United Kingdom economy', *Economic Policy Review*, no. 4, March.

Currie, D. A. (1985) 'Macroeconomic policy design and control theory – a failed partnership?', *Economic Journal*, vol. 95, pp. 285–306.

Dinenis, E., S. Holly, P. Levine and P. Smith (1989) 'The London Business School econometric model: some recent developments', *Economic Modelling*, vol. 6, no. 3 (July).

Dornbusch, R. (1976) 'The Theory of Flexible Exchange Rate Regimes and Macroeconomic Policy', *Scandinavian Journal of Economics*, vol. 78, no. 2.

Evans, M. K. and L. R. Klein (1968) *The Wharton Econometric Forecasting Model, Studies in Quantitative Economics No. 2* (University of Pennsylvania).

Fair, R. C. (1979) 'An Analysis of a Macro-Econometric Model with Rational Expectations in the Bond and Stock Markets', *American Economic Review*, vol. 69, no. 4 (September).

Godley, W. A. H. and J. R. Shepherd (1964) 'Long-term growth and short-term policy', *National Institute Economic Review*, 29, August, pp. 26–38.

Godley, W. A. H. and G. Gillion (1965) 'Pricing behaviour in manufacturing industry', *National Institute Economic Review*, 33, August, pp. 43–7.

Godley, W. A. H. and T. F. Cripps (1973) 'Why the government's economic strategy is dangerous', *The Times*, 5 September.

Hall, S. G. and S. G. B. Henry (1988) 'Rational expectations in an econometric model: NIESR Model 8', *National Institute Economic Review*, 114, November, pp. 58–68.

Heathfield, D. F. and I. F. Pearce (1975) 'A view of the Southampton econometric model of the United Kingdom and its trading partners', in G. A. Renton (op. cit.) pp. 83–124.

Hilton, K. and D. F. Heathfield (1970) *Econometric Study of the United Kingdom* (London: Macmillan).

Holly, S. and B. Corker (1984) 'Optimal Feedback and Feedforward Stabilisation of Exchange Rates, Money, Prices and Output Under Rational Expectations', in *Applied Decision Analysis*, A. J. Hughes Hallett (ed.) (Dordrecht: Klywer and Nijohoff).

Holly, S. and A. J. Hughes Hallett (1989) *Optimal Control, Expectations and Uncertainty* (Cambridge: Cambridge University Press).

Holly, S., B. Rustem, J. H. Westcott, M. B. Zarrop and R. Becker (1979) 'Control Exercise with a Small Linear Model of the United Kingdom Economy', in *Optimal Control for Econometric Models: An Approach to Economic Policy Formulation*, S. Holly, B. Rustem, and M. B. Zarrop (eds) (London: Macmillan).

Johnson, H. G. (1972) 'The monetary approach to the balance of payments theory', in *Further Readings in Monetary Economics* (London: George Allen & Unwin) pp. 229–49.

Jones, K. (1988) 'Fifty years of economic research: A brief history of the National Institute of Economic and Social Research 1933–88', *National Institute Economic Review*, 124, May, pp. 36–62.

Keating, G. (1985) 'The financial sector of the London Business School Model', in *Advances in Monetary Economics*, D. Currie (ed.) (Croom Helm, London) pp. 86–126.

Kelly, C. and D. Owen (1985) 'Factor Prices in the Treasury Model', Government Economics Service Working Paper, no. 83.

Keynes, J. M. (1939) 'Professor Tinbergen's method', *Economic Journal*, 49, September, pp. 558–68.

Klein, L. R. (1979) 'Managing the Modern Economy: Econometric specification', in *Optimal Control for Econometric Models: An Approach to Economic Policy Formulation*, S. Holly, B. Rustem and M. B. Zarrop (eds) (London: Macmillan).

Klein, L. R. and A. S. Goldberger (1955) *An Econometric Model of the United States 1929–52* (Amsterdam: North-Holland).

Klein, L. R., R. J. Ball and A. Hazelwood (1959) 'Econometric forecasts for 1959', *Bulletin of the Oxford University Institute of Statistics*, vol. 21, no. 1 (February).

Klein, L. R., R. J. Ball, A. Hazelwood and P. Vandome (1961) *An Econometric Model of the United Kingdom* (Oxford: Basil Blackwell).

Kydland, F. E. and E. C. Prescott (1977) 'Rules Rather than Discretion: the Inconsistency of Optimal Plans', *Journal of Political Economy*, pp. 473–9.

Layard, R. and S. J. Nickell (1985) 'The causes of British unemployment', *National Institute Economic Review*.

Livesy, D. G. (1971) 'Optimising short-term economic policy', *Economic Journal*, 81, September, pp. 525–46.

Lucas, R. E. (1976) 'Econometric policy evaluation: a critique', in K. Brunner and A. H. Meltzer (eds), *The Phillips Curve and Labor Markets* (Amsterdam: North-Holland).

Lucas, R. E. and T. J. Sargent (1981) 'After Keynesian macroeconomics', reprinted in *Rational Expectations and Econometric Practice*, R. E. Lucas and T. H. Sargent (eds) (Boston: George Allen & Unwin) pp. 295–320.

Macie, J., M. Jouskey and D. Vines (1982) 'The Design and Performance of a Multivariant Macroeconomic Regulator' in *Proceedings of the I.E.E.E. Conference on Applications and Multivariant Control*, July (Hull, U.K.)

Melliss, C. (1984) 'Some experiments with optimal control on the Treasury Model', Government Economic Service Working Paper no. 67.

Minford, A. P. L. (1980) 'A rational expectations model of the United Kingdom under fixed and floating exchange rates', in Carnegie-Rochester Conference Series on Public Policy, vol. 21, Amsterdam, North-Holland.

Minford. A. P. L. (1983), 'Labour market equilibrium in an open economy', *Oxford Economic Papers*, November.

Minford, A. P. L., S. Marwaha, K. Matthews and A. Sprague (1984) 'The Liverpool macroeconomic model of the United Kingdom', *Economic Modelling*, vol. 1, no. 1 (January) pp. 24–62.

Modigliani, F. (1977) 'The monetarist controversy or, should we forsake stabilization policy?', *American Economic Review*, 67, March, pp. 1–19.

Nickell, S. J. (1984) 'The modelling of wages and employment', in *Econometrics and Quantitative Economics*, D. F. Hendry and K. F. Wallis (eds) (Oxford: Blackwell).

Odling-Smee, J. (1989) 'The exchange rate and external trade: A comment', in *Policymaking with Macroeconomic Models*, A. Britton (ed.) (Aldershot: Gower).

Ormerod, P. (1979a) *Economic Modelling* (London: Heinemann).

Ormerod, P. (1979b) 'The National Institute Model of the United Kingdom economy: Some current problems', in Ormerod (op. cit.) pp. 115–40.

Phillips, A. W. (1954) 'Stabilisation policy in a closed economy', *Economic Journal*, 64, June, pp. 290–323.

Posner, M. V. (ed.) (1978) *Demand Management* (London: Heinemann).

Radice, E. A. (1939) 'A dynamic scheme for the British trade cycle, 1929–37', *Econometrica*, vol. 7, no. 1 (January).

Renton, G. A. (ed.) (1975) *Modelling the Economy* (London: Heinemann).

Robinson, P. W. (1983) 'Forecasting errors: the track record', *Economic Outlook* (Aldershot: Gower) July, pp. 24–33.

Roy, A. D. (1970) 'Short-term forecasting for central economic management of the United Kingdom economy', in K. Hilton and D. F. Heathfield (op. cit.)

Sargan, J. D. (1964) 'Wages and prices in the United Kingdom: a study in econometric methodology', in *Econometric Analysis for National Economic Planning*, P. E. Hart, G. Mills and J. K. Whitaker (eds) (London: Butterworths) pp. 22–54.

Sargent, T. J. and N. Wallace (1975) 'Rational expectations, the optimal monetary instrument and the optimal money supply rule', *Journal of Political Economy*, vol. 83, no. 2.

Shepherd, J. F., H. P. Evans and C. J. Riley (1975) 'The Treasury short-term forecasting model', in G. A. Renton (op. cit.) pp. 38–65.

Stone, R. (1964) 'British economic balance in 1970: a trial run on Rocket', in *Econometric Analysis for National Economic Planning*, P. E. Hart, G. Mills and J. K. Whitaker (eds) (London: Butterworths).

_____ (1978) 'Keynes, Political Arthmetic and Econometrics', *British Academy Seventh Keynes Lecture in Economics*, May.

Surrey, M. (1971) 'The analysis and forecasting of the British economy', *NIESR Occasional Paper* **XXV**.

Tinbergen, J. (1951) *Business Cycles in the United Kingdom 1870–1914* (Amsterdam: North-Holland).

Uebe, G., G. Huber and J. Fischer (1988) *Macro-Econometric Models – An International Bibliography* (Aldershot: Gower).

Wall, K. D., A. J. Preston, J. W. Bray and M. M. Preston (1975) 'Estimates of a simple control method of the United Kingdom economy', in G. A. Renton (op. cit.) pp. 398–446.

Wallis, K. F. (1989) 'Macroeconomic forecasting: A survey', *Economic Journal*, 99, March, pp. 28–61.

Wallis, K. F., P. G. Fisher, J. A. Longbottom, D. S. Turner and J. D. Whitley (1986) *Models of the U.K. Economy: A Third Review by the ESRC Macroeconomic Modelling Bureau* (Oxford: Oxford University Press).

Walters, A. A. (1971) 'Consistent expectations, distributed lags and the Quantity Theory', *Economic Journal*, 88, pp. 273–81.

Worswick, G. D. N. (1975) 'National Institute experience with econometric models', in G. A. Renton (op. cit.) pp. 66–82.

Zarrop, M. B., S. Holly, B. Rustem and J. Westcott (1979) 'The design of stabilisation policies with large non-linear econometric models: two possible approaches', in Ormerod (op. cit.) pp. 171–92.

8 Macroeconomic modelling in France[1]
Raymond Courbis

1 An overview: a late start but an old concern in France

Forecasting economic development was shortly after the Second World War a preoccupation of the French government, for both the medium term (for preparation of the 'Plan') and the short term (for the 'economic budgets'). However, it was only in the middle of the 1960s, with FIFI for the Plan and ZOGOL for government budgets, that operational macroeconomic models were effectively used for forecasts and simulations. Until then, planners and short-term forecasters used only informal methods.

The building of the FIFI and ZOGOL models was a drastic change. Since then, macroeconomic modelling has developed rapidly, especially since the second half of the 1970s. Historically, there were three major periods. From 1940 to 1965–7, economic projections, medium-term as well as short-term, rested on an informal approach. The forecasting system was developed during that period and its development went hand with hand with that of the national accounts and the statistical system. It was thus asserted in 1950 (Gruson, 1950, p. 517) that 'the annual Government budget must be presented within the framework of a national economic budget, and that this latter can only be prepared if one considers the national accounts, describing after the facts the main factors of economic activity during the past year'. At the origin of the French national accounts, there was a desire to apply these tools for both 'economic budgets' and the 'Plan'.[2] Conversely, some French models constructed at a later date were influenced by this interrelated development of both the national accounts and projection methods.

The second period, from 1966 to the middle of the 1970s, saw the birth of the first formal operational models: FIFI for the medium term, built in 1966–8 and used from 1968 until 1978 for the preparation of the Sixth and Seventh Plans, and ZOGOL for the short term, built in 1966, for the preparation of the 'economic budgets' and used in 1967–9, followed by DECA and STAR for the economic budgets of 1970–3 and 1974–7. These models introduced important changes, especially FIFI. Constructed for informing the government's economic decisions, both FIFI and ZOGOL were built within the *public service*, at the Institute of Statistics (INSEE) and the Direction de la Prévision (Forecasting Branch), both of which were divisions of the Ministry of Finance. At this time, the Government of France had a definite monopoly of macroeconomic model-building.

Finally, the period from the middle of the 1970s witnessed the birth of 'second-generation' models which emphasized the dynamics of the economy. While previously the distinction had been between short-term and medium-term models, the major distinction became that between annual and quarterly models. New modelling institutions appeared outside the government,[3] with the creation of GAMA (1972), OFCE (1981) and IPECODE (1982). Five large-scale annual models were built: DMS (INSEE), MOGLI (GAMA), COPAIN (Direction de la Prévision), the OFCE annual model and HERMES-France (Ecole Centrale de Paris). Four quarterly models were also built in the second part of the 1970s, and the 1980s, after a first experiment at the Banque de France, namely METRIC (INSEE), ICARE (IPECODE), PROTEE (GAMA) and the OFCE quarterly model.[4] In all, there were nine major macroeconomic models of the French economy. Modelling became pluralistic and a recent change has been, for the projections of the Tenth Plan, to use the results of four institutions (INSEE, Ecole Centrale de Paris, GAMA, IPECODE), instead of only using the INSEE model.[5]

Accelerated development of modelling since the 1970s
The acceleration since the 1970s of French model-building has several explanations. First, there were technical factors, both for computer programming and for econometric estimation. Difficulties in programming and equation estimation were very important for the first models. Several months of programming work were needed for a large-scale model such as FIFI (the programme, written in Fortran by the authors of the model, had more than 5000 lines). In the middle of the 1970s, important progress in productivity was effected, thanks to computer programs made available for solving a model. The use of SIMSYS (built at the Economic Council of Canada, for the solution of the Canadian CANDIDE Model) helped INSEE in the building of DMS and METRIC and helped GAMA in the building of MOGLI and PROTEE; SIMSYS was also used later by the Ecole Centrale de Paris for HERMES. New computer packages have now been used for a few years, such as TROLL, G, and MODULECO, but the use of SIMSYS was very important in building dynamic models in the 1970s.[6]

Secondly, statistical progress in the 1970s played an important part. The lengthening of series (for FIFI, for instance, only annual series for the period 1959–66 were available at a sectoral level), has permitted a better treatment of lags.[7] The building by INSEE in the 1970s of series for the capital stock has made estimation of production functions easy. The same applies to the detailed quarterly models in the 1970s, as a result of the quarterly accounts by INSEE, which have become available only since 1973.

Thirdly, there are human reasons. The creation of CEPE (Centre d'Etudes des Programmes Economiques (Centre for the Study of Economic Policies)) in 1959 inside the Ministry of Finance, greater attention given progressively to econometrics and modelling at ENSAE (the school of INSEE) in the middle of 1960s, and a more developed teaching of econometrics and modelling in the universities since the 1970s have all played an important role in the development of 'human resources' for macroeconometric modelling. (INSEE, the Forecasting Branch, and GAMA have also contributed.)

Institutional reasons also played their part. The creation of GAMA in 1972, and of OFCE and IPECODE in 1981–82,[8] directly stimulated the 'supply' of models. Finally, there was the development of economic studies and comparisons of existing models.[9]

All of the above are part of the explanation for the accelerated development of model-building in France.

Specific factors in the French experience
American model-building was primarily academic until the 1950s, whereas French modelling efforts were both instrumental and governmental. The purpose of the French models was to enlighten government choices for short- and medium-term economic policy; this explains some specific factors of the French models:

1. They employed integrated and detailed national accounts, which describe in an interrelated way the accounts of the different economic agents. Using the model in this way allows a projection of national accounts. Accounts identities were described both in terms of agents and of operations, but an implication was the introduction of a great number of variables (even if some were not too important from an economic point of view).
2. They were generally large-scale models, owing to the use of a national accounts framework and the willingness to describe economic policy instruments in detail (as well as the introduction of a sectoral disaggregation).
3. They emphasize, for the medium term, the role of supply. In a model like FIFI, built in 1966–8 for the Plan, supply directly determines production in manufacturing (production depends on demand only for the 'sheltered' sectors). Therefore medium-term growth depends much more on investment financial possibilities than on demand.

At the same time, the theoretical background of French models was also pluralist, with a Keynesian or neo-Keynesian approach for ZOGOL, DECA, METRIC, DMS, HERMES or OFCE; a 'competitioned economy' approach for FIFI, MOGLI or PROTEE, in which 'exposed' sectors' profitability plays an important part in the determination of growth; a new-Cantabrigian logic for STAR, which emphasizes the link between growth and the wages-profits share; a monetarist approach for SIMPLET, a quarterly model built at the beginning of 1970s at the Banque de France; and a disequilibrium models approach for recent but still experimental work. Pluralism is found with a large diversity in France; this too contrasts with the dominance of the Keynesian paradigm in the United States.

2   From the beginning to the 1960s

In France, operational macroeconomic models were born in the middle 1960s, whereas forecasting and the interest in a modelling approach were much older. The 1907 crisis obliged the government to find a means of forecasting 'periodic crises' with the construction of leading indicators, but it was only after the First World War that the 'Service de la Statistique Générale' (General Statistical Office) built economic indicators. The initiative concerning the analysis of the (short-term) economic situation remained in private hands (with, in particular, the works of J. Dessirier and C. Rist).

The creation in November 1938 of the 'Institut de Conjoncture' (Business Cycle Institute) at the ministry of National Economic Affairs (A. Sauvy headed it until March 1945) gave evidence of an interest by government in forecasting economic developments, but it was not funded until September 1941. In 1946 the Institut de Conjoncture merged with other public agencies to become the Institut National de la Statistique et des Etudes Economiques (INSEE), the current French Statistical Office.

Due to the Institut de Conjoncture, an interest appeared in the modelling approach. André Vincent, a researcher of the Institut de Conjoncture, recognized the importance of model-building techniques. As early as 1943, Vincent wrote a book on business fluctuations, while in an appendix (Vincent, 1943, pp. 75–7) he gave an example of a model and stated the method and its possibilities and limitations. This model had 15 equations and introduced a distinction between consumption and equipment goods; its major importance was that it was a numerical one (even if mainly illustrative). Indeed a solution over a seven-year period was presented.

Thus the notion of a 'model' appeared in 1943, but it was only in May 1944 that, in a report of the Institut de Conjoncture, one finds an attempt (due to Vincent) to build and use a model for analysing the evolution of the French economy in the immediate postwar period (to 1948).[10] However rudimentary the model was (containing *a priori* assumptions and no econometric estimation, because of gaps in the statistical data available at that time), it remained interesting both for its approach and for its objectives. Based on a determination of production from the side of labour supply, it allowed the analysis of the evolution of real wages and purchasing power. This approach emphasized quite well the economic problems of that time, as well as displaying the possibilities of the modelling approach.

With the 1946 integration of the Institut de Conjoncture into INSEE, these first model-building attempts did not continue, but in 1950 C. Gruson (the 'father' of the French national accounts) argued also for a modelling approach in his famous 'Note on the Conditions of Building National Accounts and a National Economic Budget' (Gruson, 1950). For Gruson, the link between the various economic variables could be 'fully presented only in mathematical terms'. He proposed a theoretical model of 88 equations, with 11 identities. Production in real terms was determined by supply (this generalized Vincent's scheme), and equilibrium between demand (calculated in value terms) and real supply was achieved by prices. (This mechanism was the logic of a 'gap model'.)

In addition to its theoretical interest, Gruson's model provided a general framework for the building of national accounts and the development of the statistical system. It was also used in 1951 and 1952 as the theoretical background for the preparation of 'economic budgets'. Such an approach corresponded, however, with a full-employment economy in which production was related to supply and available labour, but economic conditions changed with the return to a market-oriented economy. The theoretical 'model' underlying the preparation of 'economic budgets' changed consequently in 1953 and a quite Keynesian approach (SEEF, 1953) was adopted.

If the SEEF logic was considered as a 'model', this would have constituted a poor model, because of gaps in the statistical data and also a certain mistrust of econometrics.[11] Nevertheless it provided a general framework for the short-term projections, even if this was done on an informal basis. For about 15 years, the elaboration of 'economic budgets' (that is, the projection of annual national accounts one year ahead)[12] rested on an informal approach. In 1958–60 a new modelling attempt was made, but this effort failed to become operational as a result of various problems (SEEF, 1960).

Until the preparation of the Fifth Plan, in 1963–6, French planning was also based on an informal and normative approach (the purpose of projections was to determine suitable development paths and not really to forecast actual outcomes). The detail of the projections kept increasing;[13] a projection of an input–output table was introduced with the Third Plan; a projection of a flow of funds table appeared with the Fourth Plan; and finally, with the Fifth Plan, an analysis of the nominal values and prices, instead of only an analysis in volume terms, was presented.

However, at the beginning of 1960, an interest in modelling price level movements appeared with the works of Nataf and Thionet (1962) and Thionet (1961). These works were based on a cost approach and on the projection of business accounts by industry. But they remained experimental.

The work on the Fifth Plan initially corresponded to a very simple and aggregated input–output model with employment equations (INSEE, 1966), which were used for determining the rate of growth needed for a full utilization of the labour force, but rapidly a less formal (but more detailed) approach was, as before, adopted. Experimentally, however, an optimization model was developed by CERMAP[14] on behalf of the Planning Office (Nataf, 1965; Moustacchi, 1965) to illuminate the consequences of shorter working time. But as it was too simple (a two-period model in only physical terms) this model had no practical interest (Fourquet, 1980, p. 285). The introduction of an informal approach to programming in value (that is, an analysis of income distribution in view of an incomes policy) for the Fifth Plan led, however, to a dramatic change that was introduced for the Sixth Plan, with the use of the FIFI Model.

For the purpose of the Fifth Plan a price projection was needed, but the studies in 1964–6 (Courbis, 1965, 1968a) questioned the logic of these projections for the Plan. A determination of prices by costs was first considered (as in the Nataf and Thionet model) but it led, for several manufacturing sectors, to an increase in production prices that were not compatible with the increases in foreign prices. Thus it was necessary for these sectors (the 'exposed' sectors) to determine domestic price levels by foreign prices. However, if this was done, profits and self-financing became incompatible with the investment and production targets of the Fifth Plan. The lesson learned was that it was necessary to determine production from investment possibilities that were feasible financially.

These sectoral projections could only partly be taken into account in the Fifth Plan, but they prepared the ground for the Sixth Plan's 'modelling revolution', with the construction of the FIFI model.

3　The FIFI Model, a tool for the preparation of the Sixth and Seventh Plans

For the preparation of Sixth Plan, it was decided to build a model to explain the channels of influence of the Plan. After the failure of CER-

MAP, INSEE was asked to do this by the Planning Office. An optimization model was wanted by the Planning Office, but in fact a *simulation* model was built, as only such a model could be sufficiently representative of the economic realities. This was the FIFI Model (FIFI means 'physical–financial').

Built in 1967–8 at the 'Service des Programmes' of INSEE, by R. Courbis, M. Aglietta, C. Seibel and A. Saglio (on FIFI, see Aglietta and Courbis, 1969; Courbis, 1972a; Aglietta, Courbis and Seibel, 1973; and Bussery, Courbis and Seibel, 1975), FIFI was used until 1978 for the preparation of the Sixth Plan (1971–5) and the Seventh Plan (1976–80).

FIFI was based on observed economic evolution, as interpreted by the experience of previous studies: for the Fifth Plan a disaggregation of the productive system and an introduction of an analysis in value terms and also a detailed national accounts framework for the synthesis of a disaggregated economy and R. Courbis' sectoral studies (for the Fifth Plan). FIFI emphasized the importance of pricing behaviour with regard to foreign competition; the need to take into account the 'self-financing' requirements of firms, namely a consistency between self-financing and investments; the necessity to take supply into account when determining production (the limitation of self-financing and investment possibilities leading to a limitation of supply); and finally the view that a normative approach was not suitable if one wanted to determine what was actually possible.

FIFI is a multisector simulation model which divided the productive system into seven industries (the Fifth Plan studies considered 68 branches at the level of the input–output table and 29 sectors for the projections of prices and firms' accounts, but this was considered too detailed). FIFI combined an input–output table (the 'Tableau d'Echanges Interindustriels', or TEI), and an income distribution analysis (the 'Tableau Economique d'Ensemble', or TEE), with a projection of firms' accounts and prices by industry. The analysis of income distribution and economic policy instruments was considered in a detailed way. Consequently, FIFI was a large-scale model, with about 1300 equations for its Sixth Plan version and about 2000 for its Seventh Plan version.

From an economic point of view, FIFI emphasized *supply* (and more particularly the supply of the manufacturing sector and the firms' 'self-financing' behaviour (Courbis, 1968b, 1973a, 1975a). This theory stipulates that firms – for protection against financial risks – search for an optimal self-financing ratio.

The theoretical background of FIFI is the theory of 'competitioned economies' (*économies concurrencées*) (see Courbis, 1969, 1971a, 1973c, 1975a). This theory emphasizes the distinction between 'sheltered' and 'exposed' sectors, in an economy open to foreign competition. For the 'sheltered' sectors, domestic production is determined by demand. A Keynesian schema (Figure 8.1) can be applied and prices can move in such

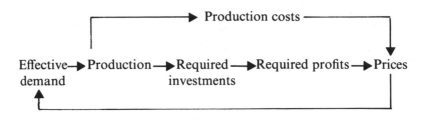

Figure 8.1   Economic links in the sheltered sectors

a way that they are consistent with increases in unit costs and the sectors' self-financing needs.

For the 'exposed' sectors, the evolution of domestic prices is constrained by foreign prices. If cost pressures exist, self-financing resources are low and this reduces investment and capital growth. Supply will be limited and so will production, but foreign trade (in particular imports, which are considered as perfectly substitutable) allows the gap between demand and supply quantities to be filled.[15] (See Figure 8.2.)

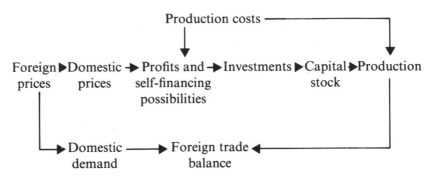

Figure 8.2   Relationships in the exposed sectors

According to the sector under consideration, production is determined either by supply ('exposed' sectors) or demand ('sheltered' sectors), and prices are determined either by foreign prices or by unit costs and self-financing considerations, respectively. The coexistence of those two categories led to some original properties described by the theory of 'competitioned economies'. Linkages are *asymmetric*: 'exposed' sectors have a leading effect on 'sheltered' sectors, but the reverse is not true. An increase in demand and production in 'sheltered' sectors leads to higher employment and lower unemployment in the short term. This in turn involves (the Klein–Phillips mechanism) a higher rate of growth of nominal wages. In turn, the profitability and self-financing of the 'exposed' sectors would be reduced, as would production and employment in these sectors.

A growth in employment in 'sheltered' sectors leads to a reduction in production and employment in the medium term in 'exposed' sectors, so a growth in real demand from domestic sources does not much influence total employment (Courbis, 1971a, 1975a). The focus is on supply, which explains the choices of a supply policy in the Sixth Plan (Courbis and Pagé, 1973). Institutionally, using FIFI involved a change in the behaviour of planners, who now emphasized a macroeconomic approach, instead of focusing on a detailed study of production in terms of demand (the 'generalized market study' as it was termed by P. Massé). Financial factors played a major role in FIFI (through the self-financing behaviour of firms), but the projections of the flow-of-funds table (the 'Tableau des Opérations Financières' or TOF) continued to remain excluded from the model.

No financial feedback was explicitly introduced in FIFI, but it was possible to take this into account by modifying the parameters of the model on the basis of results of the TOF projection. This was made during the preparation of the Sixth Plan, but there was a desire to introduce financial factors explicitly into the FIFI model. In summer 1969 a proposal was made by R. Courbis (see Courbis, 1971b, 1971c) with the idea that, for an 'indebted economy' such as the French, the supply of external long-term funds for firms should be rationed. This limitation had, for reasons of solvency, an impact on the self-financing ratio which firms had to obtain, and consequently it affected investments or prices. Simulations in 1970–1 with FIFI (Courbis, 1970, 1972b) revealed the importance of such a feedback. This was also studied on a 'small version' of FIFI by Rossignol and Roux-Vaillard (1973), (mini-FIFI-TOF).[16] Consequently, a projection of the TOF was integrated to FIFI (FIFI-TOF) (INSEE-DP-CGP, 1973). Certainly overburdened with too much detail, the project FIFI-TOF was never finished, and it met with official opposition.[17]

Nevertheless FIFI influenced the authors of the STAR Model, with a 'financial feedback' on investment, and a similar mechanism of 'integration' was later employed in the DEFI model (Villa, 1982a). (This introduced a financial and monetary block into mini-DMS, the reduced version of the DMS model, which followed FIFI in 1978.)

The FIFI version used for the Seventh Plan (Bussery, Courbis and Seibel, 1975) was similar to the one used for the Sixth Plan, with mainly technical improvements, but also there was a less rigid relation between domestic and foreign prices (Bussery, Courbis and Seibel, 1975, pp. 391–419; Rossignol (1975).

4   The 'economic budgets' models: from ZOGOL to COPAIN

When FIFI was adapted to the planners' problems, it was not a short-term model. Thus a specific model was needed for 'economic budgets'. The ZOGOL model was built in 1965–6, followed by several models: DECA, STAR and COPAIN, all of which were intended to solve these problems.[18]

ZOGOL and DECA

Built jointly in 1965–6 by INSEE and the Direction de la Prévision, ZOGOL (named after the model-builders P. Herzog and G. Olive) was the first short-term model used in France (Herzog and Olive, 1966).[19] It was used in 1966–8 for studies related to 'economic budgets'. To a large extent, ZOGOL formalizes the previous informal approach. It is a global model (one product). In its first version of 1965–6 (ZOGOL I), it had 107 equations, but only 10 were true behavioural equations.

Like the 1953 SEEF model, ZOGOL was a Keynesian model, but prices were also endogenous (with a feedback on exports). Wages, however, were exogenous because of the problems with a simultaneous determination of prices and wages. The structure of ZOGOL was simple and (in contrast to FIFI) emphasized effective demand, but it had the distinction of having been the first short-term model to be actually used for 'economic budgets'.

Because of its static form, ZOGOL could not be used for projections of more than a year. The purpose of DECA (model of *DE*mande et *C*omportement d'*A*utofinancement (literally, demand and the behaviour of self-financing)) was to improve upon ZOGOL in this regard. Built in 1967–8 at the Direction de la Prévision (Billaudot, 1971), this annual model (like FIFI and ZOGOL) was used from January 1969 until 1972 for the preparation of economic budgets.

DECA succeeded ZOGOL, and was influenced by FIFI in several respects, in particular its approach to 'firms' self-financing behaviour'. The most important improvements were:

1. The endogenization of wage rates: in the manner of FIFI, the wage rate depended on the increase in consumption prices and on the unemployment level (Klein–Phillips–Lipsey relation). Prices had an impact directly on foreign trade and household consumption.
2. A revision of some specifications, in particular those for imports and exports.
3. The introduction of firms' 'self-financing behaviour'. The general

scheme of FIFI was used in DECA while constructing a short-term model. The general view was that firms seek a 'normal' rate of self-financing, depending on the rhythm of investment growth. In the short term, the actual self-financing rate may be different from the normal rate, which leads to imbalance: if the actual rate is down (up), the rise in prices is accelerated (slowed down), and firms' investments are stimulated (reduced). At the same time, investment depends also on a capacity indicator; so the investment equation is like a 'profits accelerator' equation.

In DECA production remained determined by demand, as in ZOGOL. The 'price-wages' block was more satisfactory and the feedback of prices on foreign trade more complete. Finally, the determination of investment and the impact of unemployment on wages gave dynamic properties to the model (with a key role for self-financing behaviour in short-term dynamics) and so this model can be used for projections several years ahead.

The model remained, however, quite Keynesian, as demonstrated by the Malgrange (1972) study on a simplified small-scale version of DECA (with only 23 equations instead of 200 for the detailed model).

STAR

Being a dynamic model, DECA could be used for projections several years ahead but, in contrast to FIFI, its validity in the medium term was limited, owing to its emphasis on demand. However it was necessary to make a connection to indicative planning in order to take into account the increasing uncertainties of the 1970s. In other words, it was necessary to consider as well medium-term problems in the models used in the preparation of the 'economic budgets'. The STAR model was a first answer to this problem and constitutes 'the start of a short-medium term model' (GRM, 1972, p. 24).

Built in 1971–3 by the 'Groupe de Recherche Macroéconomique' (GRM) (Macroeconomic Research Group) at the Direction de la Prévision, STAR was used from 1973 to 1976 for the preparation of economic budgets for 1974–7. From a theoretical point of view, STAR ('*Schéma Théorique d'Accumulation et de Répartition*') (Theoretical Framework for Investment and Income Distribution) (GRM, 1972; Boullé *et al.*, 1974; Boyer *et al.*, 1973, 1974; Mazier, 1974, 1975) took as antecedents models built previously for France: ZOGOL, DECA and FIFI. Therefore it was influenced by theoretical views from the Cantabrigian school (N. Kaldor and J. Robinson) on income distribution, and also the analysis of K. Boulding and F. Modigliani on the role of the financial system.

From FIFI it kept both the idea of self-financing dominating capital accumulation (investment) and potential growth. From DECA it retained the idea that annual balance between the actual and normal rates of self-financing influenced income distribution and so the possibilities for self-financing. Finally, like ZOGOL and DECA, STAR was considered a model for 'economic budgets' and so it was restricted to a 'global' analysis (one product), whereas the Plan implies a sectoral disaggregation.

From N. Kaldor and J. Robinson's theoretical works, the main idea was the interaction between profits and accumulation: on one side the rhythm of investment influences effective growth and profits, while on the other investment depends on anticipated profit rates.

Finally, from Modigliani and Boulding, STAR retained the main role of the financial system in the necessary macroeconomic balance between income distribution and the distribution of sectoral outputs. Financial flows affect income distribution and have an impact on the rate of profit. In turn, the rate of profit depends on the structure of firms' financing (private agents are rationed on the financial market, an idea developed in the 'FIFI-TOF project').

The structure of the STAR model was organized around three groups of relationships:

1. The relationship of capital accumulation influencing profits: for a given level of capital accumulation and growth in real terms, demand in current prices could be calculated in terms of income components (contrary to other models, there was no equation for the wage rate and the wage bill–profits share was directly determined).
2. The relationship of profits influencing capital accumulation: firms' investments in current prices depended both on self-financing (as in FIFI and DECA) and on external financing possibilities (these in turn depended on households' savings).
3. The relationship of growth influencing profits: the level of profits depended on real output and on the capital stock, as well as the financial structure inherited from previous years.

The first two groups fully determined an equilibrium in current prices (in value terms) and in particular nominal production levels and effective profits, but they had to be consistent with the rate of growth. Thus the price level was determined to achieve consistency between production in value and in volume terms. There was no explicit price equation (as in ZOGOL or DECA) but only an 'implicit' determination in such a way as to equalize the required and the realized rates of profit (Mazier, 1975); for a discussion of this point, see also Courbis (1977) pp. 89–97.

The structure of the STAR appears quite original; if Keynesian in value terms, it introduced an impact of supply factors on realized production (as did FIFI). The volume–value share determination was a central piece of the model and permitted an understanding of the stagflation that prevailed at this time. However it appeared from historical simulations that the determination of inflation was biased (Boyer *et al.*, 1973), calling into question the validity of the profits–growth relationship for determining the price level. Firms' realized profitability also played an important role in the dynamic properties of the model (which presented some similarities with the theoretical model of R. M. Goodwin, 1951).

As with FIFI and DECA, the properties of the STAR model have been studied on a small simplified version. Those studies (Deleau and Malgrange, 1975; Oudet, 1975, 1976; Andrighetto *et al.*, 1975) helped the understanding of STAR as well as showed the value of such studies.

COPAIN

Built at the end of the 1970s, COPAIN (*CO*mportements *PA*trimoniaux *IN*tégrés) (Integrated Financial Behaviour) aimed at giving the Direction de la Prévision a new instrument to prepare 'economic budgets', with the objective of analysing the medium-term impact of short-term policy measures (Dehove *et al.*, 1981). It was constructed to replace STAR (which became non-operational because of a new system of national accounts); and also to coordinate the use of several specific models built at the Direction de La Prévision.

COPAIN resembles the second-generation dynamic annual models that we shall study further on, but its links with previous models are also obvious: a global analysis, an implicit price level determination, and the same computer package.

From an economic point of view, the focus was on *financial conditions of capital accumulation*: the 1973 oil shock had accelerated the movement to lower rates of profit margins for firms and an increasing level of indebtedness, so there was a need for an 'integrated analysis of financial behaviour'. (There is a similarity with the 'self-financing' approach of the FIFI model but in FIFI this was in terms of annual flows and not in terms of 'balance sheets', as in COPAIN.) The assumption was made in COPAIN of a 'borrowing norm' at which the firms aim, and this norm depends on inflation, which depreciates debt. Inflation is consequently determined in such a way as to produce realized self-financing that is consistent with the 'borrowing norm'.

The COPAIN authors criticized traditional explanations in econometric models based on the interaction of wages and prices. They explained inflation by the role of the 'borrowing norm'. Realized borrowing adapts to desired borrowing. The price level is such that it induces the required self-financing margins. The other part of the model was much more traditional, with a neo-Keynesian scheme: production is determined by effective demand but with a feedback effect of productive capacity utilization on foreign trade.

In COPAIN three points must be emphasized: the introduction of wealth effects for household consumption; a formulation of import demand in which the elasticity of demand is variable and tends to unity when demand increases; 'integration' of a 'financial sector' and the endogenous determination of interest rates,[20] with a feedback on real variables and on prices (in particular by the channel of the 'borrowing norm').

COPAIN was a global model (as were the previous 'economic budgets' models), but it introduced a distinction between manufactured and non-manufactured products for the determination of production and foreign trade. The size of COPAIN was consequently limited, with 350 equations, of which 100 were behavioural.

It is questionable to analyse indebtedness to deduce the level of prices. An analysis of COPAIN multipliers by Schubert and Zagamé (1983) showed a zig-zag pattern of variation, whose explanation is to be found in the COPAIN price mechanism and the determination of direct indebtedness in level form and not as a rate. It seems that it would have been better to have had an explicit price equation (in which one determinant could have been the gap between the realized borrowing rate and its norm).

5   Dynamic multisectoral annual models of the second generation: DMS, MOGLI, OFCE and HERMES

The short-term medium-term consistency problem
Because of two institutionalized requirements for economic projections (the preparation of the 'Plan' and the preparation of 'economic budgets'), the choice in the 1960s was to build two models: a medium-term (FIFI) and a short-term model (ZOGOL, then DECA). The former emphasized structural problems but assumed a regular path (such an assumption was relatively legitimate in the 1960s and early 1970s); the latter analysed fluctuations but could only be used a few years into the future.

Thus a sort of dichotomy prevailed, but as early as 1965 the necessity to introduce consistency between the short-term and medium-term projections was felt. During the execution of the Fifth Plan, a tentative reconciliation was made between the Plan's projections and the 'economic budgets', but for the Sixth Plan this was attempted during the process of preparation. On this occasion, an attempt was made to use FIFI and DECA at the same time, but difficulties appeared because of the two-year limitation of the DECA model and because of differences in the macroeconomic background of the two models.

The purpose of the STAR model was to solve such problems but, being a global model, it could only be used for preparation of the 'economic budgets'. For the Plan, a sectoral disaggregation was necessary; consequently the choice was made to continue using FIFI for preparing (in 1973–6) the Seventh Plan, but to begin work in 1974 for the construction of a new model: DMS, which became operational in 1978. At the same time, GAMA built (in 1974–8) the MOGLI model with the same objective. Later, in the early 1980s, two other 'dynamic' annual models were also built: the OFCE model and (at the Ecole Centrale de Paris) the HERMES-France model.

DMS

The DMS model (abbreviated from its name, *D*ynamic *M*ulti-*S*ectoral Model) was built at INSEE. A first version became operational in 1977 (Fouquet *et al.*, 1976, 1978) and was used in 1978 for re-examination of the Seventh Plan. A second version (INSEE, 1980a, 1980b; Charpin and Fouquet, 1982) followed in spring 1979 for the preparation of the Eighth Plan; a third version in 1982 for preparing the 1982–3 Plan and the Ninth Plan; finally a fourth version (DMS 4) was published in 1987 (INSEE, 1987).

Designed as a successor to FIFI, the DMS model has similarities to this model on several points:

1. the introduction of a sectoral disaggregation (11 industries for non-financial activities);
2. a detailed national accounts framework;
3. the role of profits in the determination of investment (by a 'profits accelerator' equation) and in the formation of prices;
4. the impact of supply and productive capacities in manufacturing on foreign trade (a supply limitation or an increase in domestic demand leads, as in FIFI, to a decrease of exports and an increase in imports).

To some extent DMS was also inspired by STAR with an explicit determination of the path to equilibrium and the role of prices in this equilibrium for balancing demand and supply. Unlike FIFI, DMS is a neo-Keynesian model not only in the short term but also in the long run. In the short run, production is determined by effective demand, with, however, a consideration of supply feedbacks (by the channel of the capital utilization rate in manufacturing) on external trade, prices and investment. In the medium and long term, the dynamic of DMS is managed by the evolution of the 'capital utilization rate' (a function of investment in previous years) and the 'rate of profits' (which depends on the current value of the capital stock). There is a *double dynamic of accumulation*: capital in real terms determines productive capacities and capital in value terms requires a certain level of profits. Investment accumulation fixes capital growth in both volume and value terms but is itself dependent on short-term disequilibrating movements in terms of capital utilization and effective profits.

Nevertheless DMS appears quite neo-Keynesian: effective demand determines production and prices are determined in such a way that there is sufficient investment and the needed profits (with, however, a prices feedback on external trade and net effective demand). The neo-Keynesian properties of DMS are well demonstrated by analysing its multipliers. (See Guillaume and Muet, 1979, and Guillaume, 1978, for DMS 1; and INSEE, 1987, for DMS 4. See also Artus and Muet, 1980, and Schubert and Zagamé, 1983, for a comparison with other models.) A sustained increase in demand induces, as with any Keynesian model, a durable increase in production. For DMS 1, the multiplier increases steadily towards its asymptotic value. For DMS 4, the multiplier develops more rapidly but has a lower asymptotic value.

Owing to its sectoral disaggregation and its detailed national accounts framework, DMS is a large-scale model: about 1000 equations for DMS 1, 1900 for DMS 2 and 2900 for DMS 4. It is easy to understand that, as for FIFI, DECA or STAR, a simplified version was built for a better understanding of this large model or for some specific experiments. Two simplified versions were built: Mini-DMS (Brillet, 1981a, 1981b, and INSEE, 1986) with two sectors (manufacturing and other sectors), having roughly 200 equations; and Micro-DMS with one sector and only 30 equations in its final version (Brillet, 1988).

Mini-DMS has three objectives:

1. To allow a better understanding of DMS [Bianchi, Brillet and Calzolari (1984); Bianchi, Brillet and Panattoni (1987)].
2. To determine optimal economic policy by using gradient methods [Anglard and Brillet (1982)].
3. To be the starting-point of three specific models. The three models come from Mini-DMS: Mini-DMS-Energy (Brillet *et al.*, 1982; Mouttet *et al.*, 1983); and Mini-DMS-Transport (Bureau, 1985), which have each isolated a specific sector from the non-manufacturing sector: energy or transportation. DEFI (Villa, 1982a, 1982b) was intended to introduce a 'financial block' (see also Cohen and Rocca,

1983, for a development of 'financial integration', which is a problem in DMS[21]).

Micro-DMS, which is a theoretical, small version of DMS, was designed for analysing its properties in the long-term (Brillet, 1988; Brillet, Le Van and Malgrange, 1986; Deleau, Le Van and Malgrange, 1988). It was used also for analysis of efficient stabilization policies, in the face of stochastic perturbations (Deleau, Le Van and Malgrange, 1984a, 1984b).

MOGLI
Built at GAMA in 1974–8 and used regularly since 1979 for forecasts and economic policy simulations, MOGLI (*MO*dèle *GLI*ssant (Sliding Model), to designate its dynamic character) is a multisectoral dynamic model (see Courbis, Fonteneau, Le Van and Voisin, 1980, 1982; to study multipliers, see also Fonteneau and Le Van, 1982; and see Schubert and Zagamé, 1983, for a comparison with DMS and COPAIN). The purpose of MOGLI is the same as that of DMS but its theoretical background differs; not a neo-Keynesian model, MOGLI is based on a dynamic version of the 'competitioned economies' theory proposed by R. Courbis (see Courbis, 1980 and 1982).

The interest of the underlying theory of the MOGLI model is to reconcile a neo-Keynesian approach for the short term and a 'competitioned economies' approach for the long term. While effective demand determines production in the short run, it is supply-oriented in the long run. While DMS takes into account the impact of disequilibrium for only the labour market (unemployment), the goods market (capital utilization) and for profitability, MOGLI introduces also the impact of a gap between foreign prices and domestic prices for the 'exposed' sector. In the short term, substitutability between imports and production is limited, so domestic prices may differ from foreign prices (expressed in national currency) but such a gap cannot persist: if domestic prices are higher (lower) than import prices, imports increase (decrease) progressively until production levels, unit costs and domestic prices become consistent with foreign prices.

In the long term (see Courbis, 1980, 1984, and Courbis and Le Van, 1982, for empirical simulations on a simplified version of MOGLI), there is a constant growth rate path, with the same rate of increase for domestic and import prices, and also a constant rate of capacity utilization and a perfect substitutability between imports and production.[22] Production is determined by supply (and investment possibilities) and not by demand as in the short term, and production prices by foreign prices and not by unit costs as in the short term. In the long term, the results of the static version of the 'competitioned economies' theory (as developed in FIFI) hold asymptotically.

The interest of MOGLI is to reconcile the Keynesian demand-oriented approach and a supply approach. Two other characteristics should also be emphasized: an attempt to endogenize government behaviour and also that of the Banque de France for interest rates; and a strong non-linearity (due to the role of supply and disequilibrium mechanisms) so that the MOGLI multipliers strongly depend on the size of the shocks and the historical conditions during which the shocks occur.

Like DMS and FIFI, MOGLI is a large-scale model (around 1300 equations) because of its sectoral disaggregation, its national accounts framework and the (partly) endogenized behaviour of government.

OFCE annual model

Built in 1982–3 at OFCE, the OFCE annual model (Fonteneau, 1983; Boutillier and Durand, 1986) comes from Mini-DMS. In addition to revisions of the main equations, an adaptation of Mini-DMS was made for a better analysis of the foreign sector, a disaggregation into three industries instead of two, and the addition of a financial and monetary sector (Boutillier and Villa, 1985); some specifications are also taken from other models (METRIC, DEFI and MOGLI).

The most interesting is the financial and monetary sector: the supply of long-term credits is rationed by the Government of France (as was previously assumed in FIFI-TOF and STAR), but no constraint exists for short-term credits; commercial banks (as assumed in METRIC, DEFI or COPAIN) provide all the needed financing and consequently the interest rate depends on commercial banks' refinancing conditions, as proposed by Courbis (1971d).

HERMES-France

Built from 1980 to 1984 at the Ecole Centrale de Paris (Faubry, Moncomble, Vidal de la Blache and Zagamé, 1984), HERMES-France is the most recent (at the time of writing) of the French annual macroeconomic models. It constitutes the French part of the HERMES multicountry model built for the EEC Commission.

Designed at the end of the 1970s (that is, after the two oil shocks), HERMES emphasizes *energy problems*. Like labour and capital, energy is a factor of production (this allows a better analysis of the impact of energy prices on productive structures). Energy is considered a composite good with a disaggregation into eight products, for a better analysis of demand and of the substitution relationships between imports and domestic production.

Except for energy analysis, HERMES' structure is comparable to DMS,[23] but it also takes specifications from other models. Like DMS, HERMES-France is a large-scale model (around 1500 equations), owing to its disaggregation into nine industries and the disaggregation of energy into eight products.

6 Quarterly models

Short-term forecasting and quarterly model-building
If in France annual model-building dates from the middle of 1960s, quarterly modelling began to be developed in the middle 1970s, for statistical reasons (INSEE had developed quarterly national accounts only at the beginning of the 1970s), but also as a result of French practice itself.

In the United States, the focus is often on cyclical regularities and aims at constructing 'leading indicators', whereas the French school (Fayolle, 1987) aims at eliciting causalities and sequences that explain the current situation. First of all, methodological efforts have been made for producing business and households surveys, which give information on the intentions and expectations of economic agents. Until the middle of the 1970s, very short-term forecasts and analyses were consequently made by INSEE on the basis of surveys and short-term economic indicators.

However, as long ago as the 1940s, Vincent – one of the fathers of the French short-term forecasting school – was emphasizing the interest of the 'models method' (Vincent, 1947). Despite this, for almost thirty years, short-term cyclical analysis was studied by informal methods, but the realization of such surveys permitted the introduction of 'opinion variables' in models.

It was only at the beginning of the 1970s that a quarterly model was first built in France – the SIMPLET model at the Banque de France – but this was rapidly followed by the construction of the much more ambitious METRIC model at INSEE in the 1970s, and then, in the 1980s, by ICARE (at IPECODE), PROTEE (at GAMA) and the OFCE model.[24]

SIMPLET
Built in the early 1970s at the Banque de France by J. H. David (1972, 1975), the SIMPLET model is a very small model with only seven equations. It uses directly available quarterly data.

Like the well-known St Louis model, SIMPLET is a *monetarist* model. Activity in manufacturing is directly analysed in value terms (it depends on the stock of money, the government budget surplus, exports and the rate of capacity utilization). By calculating directly the price level increase, a function of nominal wage rates and labour productivity, activity in real terms can be deduced, but, contrary to the St Louis model, prices do not depend on the gap between realized and potential production. This is not a consistent assumption.

METRIC

The SIMPLET model was a seminal work, but it was constrained by the availability of data. The situation changed on that point in 1973 when quarterly national accounts became operational at INSEE. This enabled the construction of a more ambitious model, METRIC (*Modèle* *Econo-métrique* *TRI*mestriel de la *Conjoncture*) (Quarterly Econometric Business Cycle Model), built at INSEE with the help of the Direction de la Prévision.

METRIC is a large-scale model owing both to its sectoral disaggregation and to its integrated national accounts framework: about 400 equations for the first version (INSEE, 1977), about 900 for the second version (Artus *et al.*, 1981); and 950 for a recent version (Bloch *et al.*, 1988), which aims at taking better account of supply effects (METRICX).

METRIC's structure is neo-Keynesian (as it is of the 'accelerator-multiplier' type with a determination of inflation by the Klein–Phillips curve and the 'price-wages' loop). However three extensions in METRIC should be emphasized:

1. It takes into account the impact of disequilibria at four levels: first (like annual models) at the level of production (the gap between potential and actual production); secondly, in the labour market (unemployment); thirdly, at the level of the firms' financing requirements, namely the gap between available and needed financial resources, which is a contribution of METRIC, and finally credit (when the demand for credit is rationed).
2. It introduces a financial and monetary sector. In the French context of an 'indebtedness economy', the general interest rate is determined by the Banque de France interest rate and the commercial banks' refinancing conditions.[25] For securities, funds are on the contrary rationed by government demand; this was previously a central assumption of the FIFI-TOF project. Contrary to other models, exchange rates are determined in the second version of METRIC (from the 'portfolio' behaviour of the Banque de France, following a 'reaction function').[26]
3. In also introduces opinion variables and indicators of expectations (data are available with the INSEE household and business surveys). Four survey indicators are modelled: the available production capacities, opinions on inventories, opinions concerning financial difficulties, and short-term expectations of prices. The introduction and

endogenization of such variables is interesting because this formalizes the practice of French forecasters of the very short-term period.

In the very short term, a Keynesian scheme is also adapted: total supply, and therefore production, are determined by expected demand (and inventory requirements) and not by effective demand. In the very short term, inventories equilibrate aggregate demand and supply, but the gap between actual and desired inventories influences supply, in such a way that production is, after a few quarters, determined by effective demand (the point where aggregate supply is equal to aggregate demand).

Because of the great number of equations, a simplified version (Mini-METRIC), as well as a very small version (Micro-METRIC), have been developed, as was the case for other models. Studies have been made which enabled a better understanding of the short-term and long-term properties of METRIC (Malgrange, 1983; Kuh, Le Van and Malgrange, 1984; Malgrange, 1988; Le Van and Malgrange, 1988; see also Brillet, Le Van and Malgrange, 1986, for a comparison with Micro-DMS). In the short term, METRIC looks like a Keynesian model with flexible prices and the long-term solution dominated by the 'wage-prices' loop (however the impact of prices on real variables is weak until four or five years have elapsed). If the model is stable, it appears that this stability has its limits, owing to the quite complete indexation of wages.

While the first two versions of METRIC focused mainly on the short term, more attention to long-term problems is given in the new version (METRICX). In this new version, supply has a more important role, with, in particular, the adoption of specifications stressing the correction of 'errors'.

ICARE, OFCE and PROTEE
The construction of METRIC demonstrated both the feasibility of, and the interest in, building large quarterly models, in particular to take into better account the impact of disequilibria and lags.[27] It stimulated research and, following METRIC, three operational quarterly models were built in the 1980s:[28] the OFCE quarterly model, the IPECODE's ICARE model, and the GAMA's PROTEE model.

The OFCE quarterly model, built from January 1983 to April 1984 (Sterdyniak *et al.*, 1984), comes from the Mini-METRIC simplified version. However there is more attention paid to medium-term properties. A financial block is introduced, with the interest rate determined by refinancing costs, as in METRIC, but exchange rates are exogenous.

ICARE (*I*pecode *C*adre pour l'*A*nalyse et la *R*éflexion *E*conomique) (Ipecode Framework for Economic Analysis and Reflection) was built in

1982–3 at IPECODE (IPECODE, 1983). A new version was recently built; see Dumazet and Khong (1989). This is a large-scale model with a disaggregation into six industries and a detailed national accounts framework. The main interesting points are: a detailed treatment of taxation; a detailed projection of firms' accounts; an analysis of business investment by industry and product (and not only by product as in other models). No monetary and financial sector is introduced, and interest and exchange rates are exogenous. The variation in inventory level is directly determined (and is not the result of a confrontation between aggregate demand and supply). Opinion variables are not introduced.

PROTEE (*PRO*jection *T*rimestrielle de l'*E*volution *E*conomique) (Quarterly Projection of Economic Evolution) (Courbis and Salmon, 1986), the final quarterly model surveyed here, was developed in GAMA from 1982 to 1986. This model was designed to be used frequently (each month since January 1985 for updating short-term forecasts), and so it has only roughly 200 equations. From an economic point of view, the structure of the PROTEE model follows the specification of MOGLI but with an adaptation for the very short term. Like METRIC, supply in the very short term is determined by expected demand (and inventory requirements); in the short term (a few quarters), production is demand-determined, but in the long term the model becomes supply-oriented. Consequently, as simulations demonstrated, PROTEE can be used not only for very short-term and for short-term forecasts but also for forecasts 10–15 years into the future. The indexation of wages is endogenized, which extends its validity to both low and high inflation regimes.

7   Recent trends in research

Initiated in the middle of the 1960s, macroeconomic model-building in France has developed rapidly since the middle of the 1970s and especially since the early 1980s. The environment has been stimulating. Besides the construction of the models, recent trends have been characterized by:

1. A development of methodological studies on models with both comparisons (Artus and Muet, 1980; Schubert and Zagamé, 1983; Bureau and Norotte, 1984) and studies of 'simplified versions'. A theoretical simple version was also built by CEPREMAP (Deleau, Malgrange and Muet, 1981, 1984); see also for studies of this small model, Malgrange (1985); Kuh, Le Van and Malgrange (1984); and Brillet, Le Van and Malgrange (1986).[29]
2. An increasing interest in long-term analysis. As early as the 1970s, a central point of the theoretical background of the MOGLI model

(and afterwards of the PROTEE model) was to guarantee the existence of a long-term steady-rate solution, which permitted the projection of the model for a number of years. Conversely, studies made in the 1980s on the simplified versions of the DMS and METRIC models analysed in particular the long-term properties of these models (see above). Clearly, the objective is to have a short-term model that one can still use in the long term,[30] but progress still has to be achieved (Boyer and Malgrange, 1989) in this area. In particular, it would be necessary to endogenize technical progress.[31]

3. A widening of the field covered by models, with in particular attempts at taking into account politico-economic interrelationships (Aubin *et al.*, 1985).[32]

4. An interest in the study of an optimal policy. As macroeconometric models were simulation models, one question that was raised very early was how to use these models for determining an optimal policy. A first attempt was made in 1967–70 with a simplified version of DECA (Deleau, Guesnerie and Malgrange, 1972, 1973) but other studies were to be made only much later, for the preparation of the Eighth Plan (Gauron and Maurice, 1980) and of the Ninth Plan (Catinat and Maurice, 1984). By assuming that the model (here DMS) was a linear one, the impact of a mixed policy can be calculated as a linear combination of the impacts of simple policies. Optimizing the total impact for a given preference function and allowing for the constraints enable a calculation of the weight of each simple policy (see also Brillet *et al.*, 1987). Such an optimization was made only in static terms for the Eighth Plan, but in dynamic terms for the Ninth Plan. However, for both Plans, a critical assumption was the linearity of the model. In an experimental way, attempts have recently made for optimization with a non-linear model (with Mini-DMS or Micro-DMS; see Anglard and Brillet, 1982, 1984; Deleau, Le Van and Malgrange, 1984a, 1984b; Brillet, Le Van and Malgrange, 1986).

5. A tendency to use, in a complementary way, time-series methods, either for the updating of exogenous variables or for the projection of the constant adjustment factors. Chassin (1985), with a simplified version of PROTEE, has compared four approaches: the use of only an econometric model; the use of this model with a forecast of constant adjustment factors following a Box-Jenkins method; a simple univariate Box-Jenkins model; and a Box-Jenkins model with transfer functions. The second solution, which is quite simple, appears efficient.

6. The use of micro computers: HERMES-France can now be used on micro computer (Vielle, 1988) and a version of PROTEE on micro

computer is being tested.[33] Such a trend should accelerate and contribute to progress in macroeconometric model-building.

Since the beginning of the 1980s, another structure has also begun to be explored: a disequilibrium models approach. In line with the 'fix-price' model of Barro and Grossman, the idea is that economic agents can be rationed if there is a disequilibrium between demand and supply quantities. A first attempt with annual data was made by Vilares in 1980–1, later published in Vilares (1987), in which only firms can be rationed. A few years later, a first attempt with quarterly data was developed by Artus, Laroque and Michel (1984), subsequently improved in Artus, Avouyi-Dovi and Laroque (1985). The model permits the calculation of the probabilities of 'Keynesian unemployment' and 'classical unemployment' regimes. The 'Keynesian' regime seems more likely for the period under consideration (1963–83), a conclusion which results also from the work of Lambert, Lubrano and Sneessens (1984). The previous attempts considered only global models (only one product) but more recently a model has been proposed by Artus, Avouyi-Dovi and Laffargue (1987, 1989), with two sectors: manufacturing and non-manufacturing.[34] However a problem appears for all these models, as the passage from one regime to another is discontinuous. Consequently it is more convenient to consider the possibility that the different regimes can coexist, and to introduce (and endogenize) the proportion of firms in each regime. Data are available with the surveys of enterprises. Such an approach was recently applied by Gagey, Lambert and Ottenwalter (1987), and by Bleuze, Leroux and Muet (1988).

As argued above, progress in the methodological, theoretical, and practical domains is being made. This augurs well for further development of French macroeconomic model-building.[35]

Notes

1. We will only consider here models built in France, but models of the French economy have also been developed (since the 1970s) abroad as elements of multicountry models. Nor do we consider (a) multicountry models which have been built in France (let us, however, note the very early building of the MOISE models in the 1960s; see Le Go and Lafay, 1967 and Courcier and Lafay, 1972); (b) regional or multiregional models for France or French regions (for a survey of which, see Courbis, 1983a); (c) input–output models: two large I/O models of the French economy were built, one by INSEE (INSEE, 1982) and the other by Courbis and Sok (1983) in GAMA; (d) cliometric models, like the one built by Bourguignon and Lévy-Leboyer (1984) for France in the nineteenth century (see also Lévy-Leboyer and Bourguignon, 1986). For more detail on the French macroeconomic modelling experience, see also Courbis (1989).
2. For this period, see Fourquet (1980) and Boyer (1981).
3. Attempts were also made at the end of the 1960s in CEPREMAP, and in the 1970s by the 'Laboratoire de Conjoncture et de Prospective' and at University of Paris IX-Dauphine, but these brief efforts did not lead to operational models.

4. A quarterly model, the MUSCAT model, was also recently built at the University of Paris I but its purpose is academic. On this model, see Vergnaud (1986), and Jacquinot and Loufir (1987) for a simplified version.
5. For ten years, a comparison of the official short-term forecast has been regularly made (twice a year) with non-official forecasts by a technical group of the 'Commission des Comptes de la Nation'. (This group was established in 1979 by the Minister of the Economy and Finance with the participation of non-official forecasting institutions such as BIPE, COE, GAMA, IPECODE and OFCE.)
6. The availability of good modelling packages is quite important; this is why INRIA began at the end of the 1970s to build the MODULECO programme (which, however, is not much used now).
7. The use of increasingly elaborate econometric packages also contributed greatly.
8. GAMA (Groupe d'Analyse Macroéconomique Appliquée) (Group for Applied Macroeconomic Analysis) is a research centre of the University of Paris-Nanterre; OFCE (Observatoire Français des Conjonctures Economiques) (French Observatory of Business Cycle Studies) belongs to the 'Fondation des Sciences Politiques' (Political Science Foundation); IPECODE (Institut pour la Prévision Economique et le Développement des Entreprises) (Institute for Economic Forecasting and Business Development) is an institution with business financing.
9. For a general survey of econometric work, see Zagamé (1987) and INSEE-DP (1986, 1988). For a comparison of French models, see in particular Artus and Muet (1980), Schubert and Zagamé (1983), and Bureau and Norotte (1984).
10. This projection, given in the May 1944 report of the Institut de Conjoncture, is reproduced (with a few changes) in Vincent (1947, pp. 386–402), with a comparison with actual data.
11. Founded at the beginning of the 1950s, SEEF (Service d'Etudes Economiques et Financières) (Financial and Economic Studies Centre) was a division of the Ministry of Finance. It was in charge of building and using French national accounts. In 1965, SEEF was transformed into the 'Direction de la Prévision' (which is in charge of the short-term forecasts and the preparation of economic policy for the Minister of the Economy and Finance).
12. 'Economic budgets' ordinarily correspond to a forecast (or projection) one year ahead but 'exploratory budgets' consider a forecast two or three years into the future.
13. On the methods used for preparation of the first Plans, see Courbis (1973b) and Boyer (1976).
14. CERMAP (Centre d'Etudes et de Recherches Mathématique Appliquées à la Planification) was a research centre which was founded by the Planning Office in the beginning of the 1960s. It merged with CEPREL in 1968 to become CEPREMAP.
15. However foreign supply is not perfectly substitutable in FIFI; consequently, import prices are partly flexible, varying with the level of imports. This means that domestic demand has an impact (but a limited one) on the production of the 'exposed' sectors.
16. On the simplified version of FIFI, namely Mini-FIFI, see Deleau (1973).
17. On the FIFI-TOF-project, see also Courbis (1971c) and Courbis and Vajda (1971).
18. With four models in 15 years, the lifetime of an 'economic budgets' model was short, while the FIFI model has been used for the preparation of the Plan over 10 years.
19. The ZOGOL model was originally presented only in a working paper (Herzog and Vajda, 1966) and was not published. A presentation can, however, be found in Bénard (1972, pp. 439–56), Guillaume (1971, pp. 202–6) and Stoléru (1970, pp. 518–21). See also Herzog (1968).
20. Such a determination by the refinancing conditions of commercial banks was previously introduced in METRIC and was also used later in other models. See below in the text and note 25.
21. The basic idea of the 'financial integration' in the possible submodel DEFI is that, owing to solvency constraints, firms aim at having an optimal borrowing ratio (a function of the real interest rate and the average duration of external debts). For adjusting the realized ratio to the optimal one, firms can act either on investments (a

function of demand and/or of profits and borrowing possibilities) and/or prices. (An increase in prices reduces the realized borrowing ratio, but econometrically this appears to be possible only for the non-manufacturing industries, that is the 'sheltered' sectors.) This is (except that it is expressed in terms of the balance sheet and not of annual flows) the same idea as that of the 'self-financing' behaviour mechanism introduced in the 1960s by R. Courbis in the FIFI model.

In DEFI, exchange rates can be endogenous (as in the later DMS 4 model) and wealth effects were also introduced.

22.   As with FIFI, in the static version of the 'competitioned economies' theory, there is no problem with regard to consistency between production growth and that of the labour force: the long-term, steady-rate solution is such that we have a constant rate of unemployment (which leads to an increase in wage rates and unit costs that are consistent with the increase in import prices).

23.   The first project manager of the HERMES-France model was H. Guillaume, formerly one of the authors of the DMS model.

24.   A quarterly macroeconomic model was also built recently in the University of Paris I (see note 4 above) but with an academic purpose.

Another quarterly model, PITI (Coutière, Pacaud and Teyssier, 1980) was also built at the Direction de la Prévision during the second part of the 1970s. Its purpose was to adapt the STAR approach to a quarterly model and to describe better the transfers of wealth resulting from inflation. Although a quarterly model, PITI did not focus on very short-term disequilibria and was only an experimental model. However, the general approach of PITI was to be followed by the authors of the annual COPAIN model.

25.   As previously proposed by Courbis (1971d), a similar approach was later introduced in the COPAIN model and the two (annual and quarterly) OFCE models.

26.   DMS was later, however, to introduce the possibility of flexible exchange rates, which would be determined by the establishment of an equilibrium in the balance of payments.

27.   The availability of better econometric packages contributed greatly to a better analysis of lags in METRIC and also in the other French quarterly models.

28.   The PITI model built at the end of the 1970s at the Direction de la Prévision was only an experimental model and the MUSCAT model of the University of Paris I is an academic model.

29.   The pedagogic model MIC-MAC (a mini-model solved on micro-computer) is derived from the mini CEPREMAP model. (On MIC-MAC, see Muet, Bleuze and Giraud, 1987a, 1987b.)

30.   Such an interest in a 'long-term' analysis is not completely new. A long-term multisectoral model was previously built at the end of the 1960s for the preparation of the Sixth Plan (the model ANTOINE, a Johansen-type model; on this model see Stoléru (1968). However difficulties appeared in solving this model and only a linear version was used practically (for determining only the social rate of discount for the Sixth Plan) (Bernard, 1968; Bernard and Mairesse, 1970).

31.   An attempt at endogenizing the impact of research and development on technical progress was made in GAMA, but it has still to be introduced in a model.

32.   An attempt at a detailed analysis of non-marketed' activities was also made at the end of the 1970s in the AGORA model (Peaucelle *et al.*, 1981, 1983). The construction of a multiregional model (REGINA) by GAMA in the 1970s (Courbis, 1975b, 1979, 1982) also constituted an attempt at enlarging the field of the national macroeconometric models.

33.   A simplified version (MUSCADET) of the MUSCAT model was also developed at the University of Paris I and is workable on micro computer (Jacquinot, Loufir and Mihoubi, 1988). A micro computer program has also been developed by the Direction de la Prévision for a rapid calculation of analytical effects (Bureau and Laury, 1988).

34.   An interesting conclusion of these studies is that production of the non-manufacturing sector is not rationed by supply but by effective demand. For manufactured goods,

domestic demand is not rationed by supply and it is by means of external trade that one has an equilibrium between production (determined by supply) and domestic demand. This looks quite similar to the results of the 'competitioned economies' theory.

35. It may be remarked that, after a decline at the beginning of the 1980s, more interest is being paid (at the time of writing) to the use of macroeconometric models.

References*

Aglietta, M. and R. Courbis (1969) 'Outil pour le Plan: le modèle FIFI' [A Tool for the Preparation of the Plan: the FIFI Model], *Economie et Statistique*, no. 1, May, pp. 45–65.

Aglietta, M., R. Courbis and C. Seibel (1973) *Le modèle FIFI, tome 1: Présentation générale et utilisation* [The FIFI Model, Part 1: General Presentation and Use] (Paris: INSEE) Insee Collections, séries C, no. 22.

Andrighetto, B., B. -A. Oudet and J.-P. Guerin (1975) 'Décompositon spectrale et effets d'une perturbation à court terme: application à STAR' [Spectral Decomposition and the Effects of Short-Term Disturbances: Application to STAR], *Annales de l'INSEE*, no. 20 September–December, pp. 129–40.

Anglard, P. and J.-L. Brillet (1982) 'Utilisation d'une méthode de gradient pour la recherche d'une politique économique optimale: application au modèle MINI-DMS' [Using the Gradient Method for the Study of an Optimal Policy: Application to the MINI-DMS Model], INSEE, Service des Programmes, March (Paper presented at the *Ninth International Conference of Applied Econometrics*, Budapest, 28 March–1 April).

Anglard, P. and J.-L. Brillet (1984) 'Using an Optimization Algorithm to Solve Simple Policy Problems. Application to the MINI-DMS Model', paper presented at the *Sixth Conference of the Society for Economic Dynamics and Control*, Nice, June.

Artus, P. and P.-A. Muet (1980) 'Une étude comparative des propriétés dynamiques de dix modèles américains et cinq modèles français' [A Comparative Study of the Dynamic Properties of Ten US Models and Five French Models], *Revue économique*, vol. 31, no. 1, January, pp. 88–120.

Artus, P. and M. Volle (1982) 'The METRIC Model: Presentation, Simulation and Multipliers', *Econometric Modelling in Theory and Practice*, J. Plasmans (ed.) (The Hague: Martinus Nijhoff) pp. 123–58.

Artus, P., G. Laroque, and G. Michel (1984) 'Estimation of a Quarterly Macroeconomic Model with Quarterly Rationing', *Econometrica*, vol. 52, no. 6, November, pp. 1387–1414.

Artus, P., S. Avouyi-Dovi and G. Laroque (1985) 'Estimation d'une maquette macroéconomique trimestrielle avec rationnements quantitatifs; [Estimation of a Small Quarterly Macroeconomic Model with Quantity Rationing], *Annales de l'INSEE*, no. 57, January–March, pp. 3–25.

Artus, P., M. Deleau and P. Malgrange (1986) *Modélisation macroéconomique* [Macroeconomic Model-Building] (Paris: Economica) (especially Chapter 2).

Artus, P., S. Avouyi-Dovi and J. P. Laffargue (1987) 'Un modèle économétrique de deséquilibre à deux secteurs et son apport à l'analyse des politiques économiques' [An Econometric Model of Disequilibrium with Two Sectors and its Contribution to the Analysis of Economic Policy], *Observations et diagnostics économiques (Revue de l'OFCE)*, no. 21, October, pp. 211–36.

Artus, P., S. Avouyi-Dovi and J. -P. Laffargue (1989) 'A Disequilibrium Econometric Model of the French Economy with Two Sectors and Endogenous Prices and Investment', paper presented to *Project LINK Meeting*, Paris, 28 August–1 September.

Artus, P., J. Bournay, P. Morin, A. Pacaud, C. Peyroux, H. Sterdyniak and R. Teyssier (1981) *METRIC, Une modélisation de l'économie française* [METRIC, A model of the French Economy] (Paris: INSEE).

Aubin, Ch., J. -P. Berdot, D. Goyeau and J. -D. Lafay (1985) *Un modèle politico-économique de la France (1966-1982)* [A Politico-Economic Model of France (1966–1982)], Final

*For a more complete bibliography, see Courbis (1989).

Report for the DGRST, University of Poitiers, IRAPE (Institut de Recherche et d'Analyse Politico-Economique) May.

Bénard, J. (1972) *Comptabilité nationale et modèles de politique économique* [National Income Accounting and Models for Economic Policy] (Paris: Presses Universitaires de France).

Bernard, A. (1968) 'Modèle de croissance à long terme linéarisé pour l'economie française' [A Linearised Long-Term Growth Model for the French Economy], *Bulletin du CEPREMAP*, no. 2, July.

Bernard, A. and J. Mairesse (1970) 'Un modèle de croissance à long terme linéarisé pour l'économie française' [A Linearised Long-Term Growth Model for the French Economy], *Cahiers du Séminaire d'Econométrie* (Paris: CNRS) no. 12, pp. 23–65.

Bernard, Y. and P. -Y. Cossé (1974) *L'Etat et la prévision macroéconomique* [Government and Macroeconomic Forecasting] (Paris: Berger-Levrault).

Bianchi, C., J. -L. Brillet and G. Calzolari (1984) 'Analyse et mesure de l'incertitude en prévision d'un modèle économétrique. Application au modèle mini-DMS' [Analysis of Forecasts and Measurement of Uncertainty from an Econometric Model Application to the Mini-DMS Model], *Annales de l'INSEE*, no. 54, April–June, pp. 31–62.

Bianchi, C., J. -L. Brillet and L. Panattoni (1987) 'Uncertainty and Stability in a Macro-Econometric Model', *Annales d'Economie et de Statistique*, no. 6–7, April–September, pp. 347–68.

Billaudot, B. (1971) 'Le modèle Deca' [The Deca Model], *Statistiques et etudes financières, Séries Orange*, no. 1, pp. 5–46.

Bleuze, E., V. Leroux and P. -A. Muet (1988) 'Offre, demande et compétitivité industrielle: les apports d'un modèle économétrique de déséquilibre intégrant des données d'enquêtes' [Supply, Demand and Manufacturing Competitiveness: Result from an Econometric Model of Disequilibrium with Business Survey Data], *Observations et diagnostics économiques (Revue de l'OFCE)* no. 23, April, pp. 175–91.

Bloch, L., A. Kadjar, R. Rabemananjara, P. Ralle, D. Allard, P. Boeuf, J. -P. Fraichot and J. -F. Loue (1988) 'Présentation du modèle METRICX' [Introduction to the METRICX Model], *Economie et Prévision*, no. 85, pp. 5–26.

Boullé, J., R. Boyer, J. Mazier and G. Olive (1974) 'Le modèle STAR' [The STAR Model], *Statistiques et Etudes financières, Series Orange*, no. 15, pp. 1–68.

Bourguignon, F. and M. Lévy-Leboyer (1984) 'An Econometric Model of France During the 19th Century', *European Economic Review*, vol. 25, pp. 107–41.

Boutillier, M. and P. Villa (1985) 'Politique monétaire en économie d'endettement vue à travers le modèle OFCE-annuel' [Monetary Policy in an Indebtedness Economy: A View with the Annual OFCE Model], *Observations et diagnostics économiques (Revue de l'OFCE)*, no 13, October, pp. 119–47.

Boutillier, M. and B. Durand (1986) 'Investigations in the Causal Structure of the Yearly OFCE Model', *Journal of Economic Dynamics and Control*, vol. 10, no. 1–2, pp. 131–7.

Boyer, R. (1976) 'La croissance française de l'après-guerre et les modèles macroéconomiques' [Postwar Growth of the French Economy and Macroeconomic Models], *Revue économique*, vol. 27, no. 5, September, pp. 882–939.

――― (1981) 'Les modèles macroéconomiques globaux et la comptabilité nationale: un bref historique' [Global Macroeconomic Models and National Income Accounting: A Brief History], *CEPREMAP Working Paper*, no. 8108, May.

Boyer, R. and P. Malgrange (1989) 'Formalisation du long terme: une revue de littérature' [Formalization of the Long Term: A Survey of the Literature], *CEPREMAP Working Paper*, no. 8906.

Boyer, R., J. Boullé and J. Mazier (1973) 'Présentation et étude d'un modèle d'accumulation et de répartition de l'économie française (STAR)' [Presentation and Analysis of a Model of Accumulation and Distribution for the French Economy (STAR)], paper presented at the *European Meeting of the Econometric Society*, Oslo, 28–31 August.

Boyer, R., J. Mazier and G. Olive (1974) 'Un nouveau modèle de prévision macroéconomique: STAR' [A New Forecasting Macroeconomic Model: STAR], *Economie et Statistique*, no. 77, April, pp. 29–48.

Brillet, J. -L. (1981a) *MINI-DMS, modèle macroéconomique de simulation* [MINI-DMS, a

Simulation Macroeconomic Model] (Paris: INSEE) (Collection Archives et Documents) no. 35.

―――― (1981b) 'La dynamique de mini-DMS' [The Dynamics of Mini-DMS], INSEE, Service des Programmes, INSEE Working Paper, no. 320/113.

―――― (1988) 'Propriétés de long terme de la maquette MICRO-DMS' [Long-Term Properties of Micro-DMS], *Modélisation en biologie et en économie* [Model-Building in Biology and Economics] (J. Demongeot and P. Malgrange (eds) (Dijon: Librairie de l'Université) pp. 171–201.

Brillet, J. -L., C. Le Van and P. Malgrange (1986) 'Stabilité structurelle des modèles macroéconométriques; optimisation dynamique et incertitude' [Structural Stability of Macroeconometric Models: Dynamic Optimization and Uncertainty], *CEPREMAP Report*, October.

Brillet, J. -L., C. d'Hose, F. Mouttet and J. -P. Morand (1982) 'Energie et économie: le modèle Mini-DMS-Energie' [Energy and the Economy: the Mini-DMS-Energy Model], *Economie et Statistique*, no. 146, July–August, pp. 73–85.

Brillet, J. -L., P. Malgrange, J. Maurice and J. -P. Puig (1987) 'Planning and Optimisation: the French Experience', *Keynesian Theory, Planning Models and Quantitative Economics*, G. Gandolfo and F. Marzano (eds), vol. II, (Milan: Dott. A. Giuffrè Editore) pp. 525–38.

Bureau, D. (1985) 'Présentation générale de MINI-DMS Transport' [General Presentation of the MINI-DMS Transport Model], Direction de la Prévision, Ministère de l'Economie et des Finances, Working Paper, no. 13/C35, 24 January.

Bureau, D. and M. Norotte (1984) 'Simulations de mesures de politique économique: une classification typologie' [Simulations of Economic Policies: A Classification], *Economie et Prévision*, no. 63, pp. 3–37.

Bureau, D. and B. Laury (1988) 'IMVS: un outil pour l'analyse macro-économique des politiques sectorielles' [IMVS: A Tool for Macroeconomic Analysis of Sectoral Policies], *Economie et Prévision*, no. 86, pp. 3–15.

Bussery, H. R. Courbis and C. Seibel (1975) *Le modèle FIFI, tome II: les équations* [The FIFI Model, Part II: Equations] (Paris: INSEE), INSEE Collections, séries C, no. 37–8.

Catinat, M. and J. Maurice (1984) 'Analyse quantitative de la stratégie macro-économique du IXe Plan' [Quantitative Analysis of the Macroeconomic Strategy of the Ninth Plan], *Revue économique*, vol. 35, no. 6, November, pp. 1007–80.

CGP (1976) *Modèles monétaires de l'économie française* [Monetary Models of the French Economy] (Paris: Documentation française) Collection of the Planning Office, 'Economie et Planification'.

Charpin, J.-M. and D. Fouquet (1982) 'The DMS Model, Version 2', *Econometric Modelling in Theory and Practice*, J. Plasmans (ed). (The Hague: Martinus Nijhoff) pp. 53–81.

Chassin, J.-B. (1985) *Apport des techniques Box-Jenkins à la construction d'une maquette trimestrielle de l'économie française* [Contribution of Box-Jenkins Methods to the Construction of a Small Quarterly Model of French Economy], doctoral dissertation, University of Paris-Nanterre and GAMA, June.

Cohen, D. and M. Rocca (1983) 'Une étude intégrée de l'économie française en deux secteurs' [An Integrated Study of a Two-Sector Model of the French Economy], *Economie et Prévision*, no. 59, pp. 23–45.

Courbis, R. (1965) La prévision des prix à moyen terme et les problèmes de financement des entreprises pendant le Ve Plan [Medium-Term Price Forecasting and Business Financial Problems During the Fifth Plan], report of INSEE for the preparation of the Fifth Plan, November.

―――― (1968a) *Prévision des prix et étude sectorielle des entreprises pendant la préparation du Ve Plan* [Price Forecasting and Sectoral Analysis of Firms during the Preparation of the Fifth Plan] (Paris: Imprimerie nationale) and *Etudes et Conjoncture*, vol. 23, no. 11, November, pp. 3–280).

―――― (1968b) 'Le comportement d'autofinancement des entreprises' [The Self-Financing Behaviour of Firms], *Economie appliquée*, vol. 21, no. 3–4, pp. 749–821.

―――― (1969) 'Developpement économique et concurrence étrangère' [Economic Development and Foreign Competition], *Revue économique*, vol. 20, no. 1, January, pp. 37–83.

_____ (1970) 'Comportements financiers et développement économique' [Financial Behaviour and Economic Development], *Economie et Statistique*, no. 12, May, pp. 27–44.

_____ (1971a) *La détermination de l'équilibre général en économie concurrencée* [Determination of General Equilibrium in a Competitioned Economy] (Paris: Editions du CNRS) 2nd edn, 1980.

_____ (1971b) 'Monnaie, financement et croissance en économie de concurrence' [Money, Financing and Growth in a Competitioned Economy], *Etudes de calcul économique*, R. Courbis, G. Fourcade and H. Guillaume (eds) (Paris: Presses Universitaires de France) pp. 9–141.

_____ (1971c) 'L'intégration des opérations financières dans le modèle à moyen terme FIFI utilisé pour la préparation du Plan français' [Integration of Financial Variables in the Medium-Term FIFI Model Used for the Preparation of the French Plan], paper presented at the *Fifth International Conference on Input–Output Techniques*, Geneva, 11–15 January 1971, INSEE Collections, no. 320/1077, November 1970.

_____ (1971d) 'Marché international des capitaux et politiques monétaires nationales' [International Capital Markets and National Monetary Policy], *Economie appliquée*, vol. 24, no. 3, pp. 379–411.

_____ (1972a) 'The FIFI Model Used in the Preparation of the French Plan', *Economics of Planning*, vol. 12, no. 1–2, pp. 37–78.

_____ (1972b) 'Tarifs publics et équilibre économique' [Public Prices and Economic Equilibrium], *Economie et Statistique*, no. 30, January, pp. 19–27.

_____ (1973a) 'Le comportement d'autofinancement des entreprises et le modèle FIFI' [Firms' Self-Financing Behaviour and the FIFI Model], *Annales de l'INSEE*, no. 12–13, January–August, pp. 3–28.

_____ (1973b) 'Les méthodes de planification française: évolution et perspectives' [Method of French Planning: Evolution and Prospect], *Revue Suisse d'Economie politique et de Statistique*, vol. 109, no. 3, September, pp. 317–40.

_____ (1973c) 'La théorie des "economies concurrencées", fondement du modèle FIFI' [The Theory of 'Competitioned Economies': Theoretical Background of the FIFI Model], *Revue économique*, vol. 24, no. 6, November, pp. 905–22 (with erratum in the issue of September 1974, p. 898).

_____ (1975a) *Compétitivité et croissance en économie concurrencée* [Competitiveness and Growth in a Competitioned Economy] (Paris: Dunod) 2 volumes, doctoral dissertation, University of Paris, 1971.

_____ (1975b) 'Le modèle REGINA, un modèle du développement national, régional et urbain de l'économie française' [The REGINA Model, A Model of National, Regional and Urban Development of the French Economy], *Economie appliquée*, vol. 28, no. 2–3, pp. 569–600.

_____ (1977) *Les modèles de prix pour la prévision et la planification* [Price Level Models for Forecasting and Planning] (Paris: Dunod).

_____ (1979) 'The REGINA Model, A Regional–National Model for French Planning', *Regional Science and Urban Economics*, vol. 9, no. 2–3, May–August, pp. 117–39.

_____ (1980) 'Une reformulation dynamique de la théorie des économies concurrencées' [A Dynamic Reformulation of the Theory of Competitioned Economies], *Economie appliquée*, vol. 33, no. 1, pp. 5–43.

_____ (1982) 'La théorie des économies concurrencées et ses applications: de FIFI à MOGLI' [The Theory of Competitioned Economics and its Applications: From FIFI to MOGLI], *Economie et Finances Internationales*, J. L. Reiffers (ed.) (Paris: Dunod) pp. 395–424.

_____ (1983a) 'L'expérience française de comptabilité et modélisation régionales' [The French Experience in Regional Accounting and Modelling]. *Espace et Localisation* [Space and Location], J. H. P. Paelinck and A. Sallez (eds) (Paris: Economica), pp. 157–72.

_____ (1983b) 'La prévision économique en France' [Economic Forecasting in France], *Futuribles*, no. 71, November, pp. 75–91 (partly reproduced in *Problèmes économiques*, no. 1868, 4 April 1984, pp. 27–32).

——— (1984) 'Compétitivité, importations et chômage' [Competitiveness, Imports and Unemployment], paper presented at the *Annual Meeting of the French Economic Association*, Paris, 24–5 September, GAMA Paper no. 486.

——— (1989) 'La modélisation macroéconomique en France: des origines à nos jours' [French Macroeconomic Model-Building: From the Beginning to the Present], *GAMA Study*, no. 587.

Courbis, R. and P. Vadja (1971) 'Financement et planification' [Financing and Planning], *Economie et Statistique*, no. 24, June, pp. 13–29 (with erratum in no. 26).

Courbis, R. and J. P. Pagé (1973) 'Techniques de projection macroéconomique et choix du Plan français' [Methods for Macroeconomic Projection and the Choices of the French Plan], *Revue économique*, vol. 24, no. 6, November, pp. 951–87.

Courbis, R. and C. Le Van (1982) 'Fondement et simulation sur maquette de la dynamique à long terme du modèle MOGLI' [Background and Simulation with A Simplified Model of the Long-Term Dynamics of the MOGLI Model], *Second CNRS-NSF Seminar on Macroeconomic Modeling in France and the US*, Gif-sur-Yvette, 7–9 December.

Courbis, R. and H. Sok (1983) 'Le modèle ANAIS, un modèle inter-sectoriel détaillé de l'economie française' [The ANAIS Model, A Detailed Input–Output Model of the French Economy], *Prévision et Analyse économique (Cahiers du GAMA)* vol. 4, no. 2, June, pp. 73–101.

Courbis, R. and P. Salmon (1986) 'Le modèle PROTEE, un modèle trimestriel de l'économie française. Présentation générale et utilisation' [The PROTEE Model, A Quarterly Model of the French Economy: General Presentation and Use], *Second French–Polish Seminar on Modelling*, Nanterre, 29–30 May, GAMA Paper no. 544.

Courbis, R., A. Fonteneau, C. Le Van and P. Voisin (1980) 'Le modèle MOGLI' [The MOGLI Model], *Prévision et Analyse économique, (Cahiers du GAMA)* vol. 1, no. 2–3, July–December, pp. 1–318.

Courbis, R., A. Fonteneau, C. Le Van and P. Voisin (1982) 'The MOGLI Model: A Pluri-Sectoral Econometric Dynamic Model of the French Economy', *Econometric Modelling in Theory and Practice*, J. Plasmans (ed.) (The Hague: Martinus Nijhoff) pp. 27–52.

Courcier, M. and G. Lafay (1972) 'Simulation économique multinationale' [Multicountry Economic Simulation], *Statistiques et Etudes financières, Séries Orange*, no. 8, pp. 27–58.

Coutière, A., A. Pacaud and R. Teyssier (1980) 'Piti: éléments pour un modèle à prix implicites trimestriels intégré' [Piti: Elements for an Integrated Quarterly Model with Implicit Determination of Prices], *Statistiques et Etudes financières, Séries Orange*, no. 41, pp. 39–87.

David, J. -H. (1972) 'Un modèle de l'économie française inspiré des thèses monétaristes' [A Monetarist Model of the French Economy], *Bulletin trimestriel de la Banque de France*, no. 5, November, pp. 23–56.

——— (1975) 'A Monetarist Model of the French Economy', *Econometric Research in European Central Banks*, F. Masera, A. Fazio and T. Padoa-Schioppa (eds) (Rome: Banca d'Italia) pp. 45–95.

Dehove, M., A. Fauqueur, J. -P. Gaudemet, M. Husson, J. Mathis, G. de Monchy and D. Vallet (1981) 'Le modèle COPAIN: comportements patrimoniaux et intégration financière' [The COPAIN Model: Behaviour of Wealth and Financial Integration], *Economie et Prévision*, no. 48, pp. 1–70.

Deleau, M. (1973) 'Une étude des mécanismes du modèle MINIFIFI' [A Study of Mechanisms of the MINIFIFI Model], *Annales de l'INSEE*, no. 12–13, January–August, pp. 159–215.

Deleau, M. and P. Malgrange (1975) 'Etude des mécanismes du modèle STAR' [Study of the Mechanisms of the STAR Model], *Annales de l'INSEE*, no. 20, September–December, pp. 35–93.

Deleau, M. and P. Malgrange (1978) *L'analyse des modèles macroéconomiques quantitatifs* [Analysis of Quantitative Macroeconomic Models] (Paris: Economica), in particular Chapter 9 on the STAR model.

Deleau, M., R. Guesnerie and P. Malgrange (1972) 'Planning, Uncertainty and Economic Policy: the OPTIMIX Study', *Economics of Planning*, vol. 12, no. 1–2, pp. 79–114.

Deleau, M., R. Guesnerie and P. Malgrange (1973) 'Planification, incertitude et politique économique. L'operation OPTIMIX' [Planning, Uncertainty and Economic Policy: The OPTIMIX Study], *Revue économique*, vol. 24, no. 5, September, pp. 801–36, 'Une procédure formalisée d'adaptation du Plan à l'aléa' [A Formalized Procedure for Adapting the Plan to Random Occurrences] and no. 6, November, pp. 1072–1103, 'Résultats numériques' [Numerical Results].

Deleau, M., P. Malgrange and P. -A. Muet (1981) 'Une maquette représentative des modèles macroéconomiques' [A Simplified Representation of Macroeconomic Models], *Annales de l'INSEE*, no. 42, April–June, pp. 53–92.

Deleau, M., C. Le Van and P. Malgrange (1984a) 'Stabilisation efficace des systèmes économiques en présence d'incertitude: expérimentation avec une maquette du modèle DMS' [Efficient Stabilisation of Economic Systems with Uncertainty: Experiments with a Simplified Version of the DMS Model], *Revue économique*, vol. 35, no. 3, May, pp. 507–36.

Deleau, M., C. Le Van and P. Malgrange (1984b) 'The Uncertainty Frontier as a Global Approach to the Efficient Stabilisation of Economic Systems: Experiments with the MICRO-DMS Model', *Applied Decision Analysis and Economic Behaviour*, A. J. Hugues Hallett (ed.) (Dordrecht: Martinus Nijhoff) pp. 97–117.

Deleau, M., P. Malgrange and P. -A. Muet (1984c) 'A Study of Short-run and Long-run Properties of Macroeconometric Models by Means of an Aggregative Core Model', *Contemporary Macroeconomic Modelling*, P. Malgrange and P. -A. Muet (eds) (Oxford: Basil Blackwell) pp. 215–46.

Deleau, M., C. Le Van and P. Malgrange (1988) 'Le long terme des modèles macroéconométriques' [The Long Term in Macroeconometric Models], *Essais en l'honneur d'Edmond Malinvaud* [Essays in Honour of Edmond Malinvaud] (Paris: Economica and E.H.E.S.S.).

Dumazet, D. and V. Khong (1989) 'ICARE 1980. Le modèle ICARE en nouvelle base de comptabilité nationale' [The ICARE Model Based on the New National Accounts], *Revue de l'IPECODE*, no. 22, pp. 11–43.

Faubry, E., J. -E. Moncomble, O. Vidal de la Blache and P. Zagamé (1984) 'Le modèle Hermès-France' [The Hermes-France Model], *Economie et Prévision*, no. 66, pp. 3–29.

Fayolle, J. (1987) *Pratique contemporaine de l'Analyse conjoncturelle* [Contemporary Practice of Business Cycle Analysis] (Paris: Economica).

Fonteneau, A. (1983) 'Le modèle OFCE-annuel' [The OFCE Annual Model], *Prévisions et Analyse économique (Cahiers de GAMA)*, vol. 4, no. 1 (March).

Fonteneau, A. and C. Le Van (1982) 'Les multiplicateurs du modèle MOGLI' [The Multipliers of the MOGLI Model], *Prévision et Analyse économique (Cahiers du GAMA)*, vol. 3, no. 1, March, pp. 7–75.

Fouquet, D, J. -M. Charpin, H. Guillaume, P. -A. Muet and D. Vallet (1976) 'DMS, modèle de prévision à moyen terme' [DMS, A Medium-Term Forecasting Model], *Economie et Statistique*, no. 79, June, pp. 33–48.

Fouquet, D., J. -M. Charpin, H. Guillaume, P. -A. Muet and D. Vallett (1978) *DMS, modèle dynamique multi-sectoriel* [DMS, A Dynamic Multisectoral Model] (Paris: INSEE), INSEE Collections, séries C, no. 64–5.

Fourquet, F. (1980) *Les comptes de la Puissance, Histoire de la compatabilité nationale et du Plan* [The Accounts of Power: History of the National Accounts and the Plan] (Paris: Editions Encres).

Gagey, F. J. -P. Lambert and B. Ottenwalter (1987) 'Déséquilibres sur le marché du travail: une estimation à partir d'enquêtes de conjoncture' [Disequilibrium in the Labour Market: Estimation with Survey Data], working paper.

Gauron, A. and J. Maurice (1980) 'Des politiques économiques pour le VIIIe Plan: une exploration de l'ensemble des possibles' [Economic Policies for the Eighth Plan: An Exploration of Possibilities], *Revue économique*, vol. 31, no. 5, September, pp. 894–929.

Goodwin, R. M. (1951) 'The Nonlinear Accelerator and the Persistence of Business Cycles', *Econometrica*, vol. 19, no. 1 (January), pp. 11–17.

GRM (1972) 'Présentation de STAR (Schéma théorique d'accumulation et de répartition).

Note de synthèse' [Presentation of STAR (The Theory of Accumulation and Income Distribution): A Synthesis], *Working Paper DP*, Direction de la Prévision du Ministère de l'Economie et des Finances, Groupe de Recherche Macroéconomique (GRM), September.

Gruson, C. (1950) 'Note sur les conditions d'établissement d'une comptabilité nationale et d'un budget économique national' [Note on Conditions for Building National Accounts and A National Economic Budget], *Statistiques et Etudes financières*, no. 19, July, pp. 517–38. (See also complementary tables in the issue 20–21, August–September 1950, pp. 633–76.

Guillaume, H. (1971) *Modèles économiques* [Economic Models] (Paris: Presses Universitaires de France).

———— (1978) 'Les multiplicateurs de politique économique de DMS: Analyse menée sur une maquette simplifiée du modèle' [The Economic Policy Multipliers of DMS: An Analysis with a Simplified Version], *Annales de l'INSEE*, no. 32, October–December, pp. 57–108.

Guillaume, H. and P. -A. Muet (1979) 'Simulations et multiplicateurs dynamiques du modèle DMS' [Simulations and Dynamic Multipliers for the DMS Model], *Revue économique*, vol. 30, no. 2, March, pp. 207–43.

Herzog, P. (1968) *Prévisions économiques et comptabilité national: Etudes des méthodes de projection à court terme* [Economic Forecasting and National Accounting: A Methodological Study for Short-Term Projections] (Paris: Presses Universitaires de France).

Herzog, P. and G. Olive (1966) 'Le modèle de projection à court terme ZOGOL I' [The Short-Term ZOGOL I Model], INSEE–DP Working Paper, Division des Budgets économiques de la Direction de la Prévision et Division des Comptes et Projections économiques à court terme de l'INSEE, 20 May.

INSEE (1966) 'Méthodes de programmation dans le Ve Plan' [Programming Methods of the Fifth Plan], *Etudes et Conjoncture*, vol. 21, no. 12, December, pp. 1–173.

INSEE (1977) 'METRIC, Modèle économétrique trimestriel de la conjoncture' [METRIC, A Quarterly Econometric Model for Business Cycle Study], *Annales de l'INSEE*, P. Nasse, G. de Menil, P. Artus, J. Bournay, P. Morin, R. Porcher, F. Yohn and C. Zaidman, no. 26–27, April–September, pp. 1–364.

INSEE (1980a) 'Le modèle DMS: principales différences entre la version base 62 et la version base 71' [The DMS Model: Principal Differences Between the 1962 Base Year Version and the 1971 Base Year Version], INSEE, Services des Programmes, Working Paper no. 320/168, April.

INSEE (1980b) 'Une représentation de l'économie française: le modèle DMS' [A Representation of the French Economy: The DMS Model], *Revue économique*, vol. 31, no. 5, September, pp. 930 81.

INSEE (1981) 'Document de présentation au Plan de la version provisoire DMS3' [A Presentation Paper to the Office of the Plan of the Provisional DMS3 Version], *Note INSEE*, Services des Programmes.

INSEE (1982) *PROPAGE, Modèle détaillé de l'appareil productif français* [PROPAGE, A Detailed Model of the Production Process in France], P. Rossignol, C. Bismut, J. Colmant, M. Demotes-Maynard, C. Dupuy, J. Ho Ta Khahn, F. Koepp, C. Zaidman and P. Zagamé) (INSEE Collections, séries C, no. 103).

INSEE (1986) *Modèle Mini-DMS en 1985* [The Mini-DMS Model in 1985] INSEE, Service des Programmes, Working Paper no. 320/16, 31 January (2 vols).

INSEE (1987) *DMS-4, modèle dynamique multisectoriel* [DMS-4: A Dynamic Multisectoral Model] (Paris: INSEE) INSEE Collections, séries C, no. 139.

INSEE–DP (1986) *Reports des Groupes d'Etudes Macroéconométriques Concertées* [Reports of the Macroeconometric Studies Groups] INSEE – Direction de la Prévision (5 reports).

INSEE-DP (1988) *Groupes d'Etudes Macroéconométriques Concertées. Document complémentaire de synthèse* [General Report of the Work of the Macroeconometric Studies Groups], Report of INSEE – Direction de la Prévision, August.

INSEE–DP–CGP (1973) 'Modèle FIFI-TOF (version non intégrée)' [The FIFI-TOF Model (Non-Integrated Version)], Report of INSEE – Direction de la Prévision – Commissariat Général de Plan, March.

IPECODE (1983) 'ICARE, modèle conjoncturel de l'économie française' [ICARE, A Business Cycle Model of the French Economy], *Revue de l'IPECODE*, G. Maarek, H. Delessy, P. Guevalot, F. Le Peltier, J. -P. Morand, no. 1, March, pp. 1–296.

Jacquinot, P. and A. Loufir (1987) 'MUSCADET, une maquette du modèle MUSCAT' [MUSCADET, A Simplified Version of the MUSCAT Model] (University of Paris I, Centre de Mathématiques et d'Informatique) Working Paper, October.

Jacquinot, P., A. Loufir and F. Mihoubi (1988) 'Muscadine: logiciel de résolution de Muscadet. Manuel d'utilisation' [Muscadine: A Computer Program for the Muscadet Model. Handbook] (University of Paris I, Centre de Mathématiques Economiques et d'Informatique and Centre de Macroéconomie et d'Analyse des Déséquilibres) Working Paper, January.

Kuh, E., C. Le Van and P. Malgrange (1984) 'Une étude de la dynamique structurelle des modèles macroéconomiques' [A Study of Structural Dynamics of Macroeconomic Models], *CEPREMAP Working Paper*, July.

Lambert, J. -P., M. Lubrano and H. -R. Sneessens (1984) 'Emploi et chômage en France de 1955 à 1982: Un modèle macroéconomique annuel avec rationnement' [Employment and Unemployment in France from 1955 to 1982: An Annual Macroeconomic Model with Rationing], *Annales de l'INSEE*, no. 55–56, July–December pp. 39–76.

Le Go, Y. and G. Lafay (1967) 'Présentation d'un modèle de projection à moyen terme des échanges internationaux' [Presentation of a Medium-Term Projection Model of International Trade Flows], *Economies et sociétés*, vol. 1, no. 5, May, pp. 93–128.

Le Van, C. and P. Malgrange (1988) 'Hiérarchie temporelle dans un modèle macroéconomique. Application à une maquette du modèle METRIC' [The Hierarchy of Time in a Macroeconomic Model. Application to a Simplified Version of the METRIC Model], *Modélisation en biologie et en économie* [Model-Building in Biology and Economics], J. Demongeot and P. Malgrange (eds) (Dijon: Librairie de l'Université) pp. 51–64.

Lévy-Leboyer, M. and F. Bourguignon (1986) *L'économie française au XIXe Siècle* [The French Economy in the 19th Century] (Paris: Economica).

Lévy-Leboyer, M. and F. Bourguignon (1986) *L'économie française au XXe Siècle* [The French Economy in the Twentieth Century] (Paris: Economica).

Malgrange, P. (1972) 'Etude analytique du modèle DECA' [Analytic Study of the DECA Model], *Annales de l'INSEE*, no. 11, September–December, pp. 85–139.

_____ (1983) 'Steady Growth Paths in a Short Run Dynamic Model: The Case of the French Quarterly Model METRIC', *CEPREMAP Working Paper*, no. 8321, October.

_____ (1985) 'Sentiers stationnaires des modèles macroéconomiques: leçons de la maquette du CEPREMAP' [Steady State Growth Paths of Macroeconomic Models: Lessons from the Simplified CEPREMAP Model], *Optimalité et Structures* [Optimality and Economic Structure], G. Ritschard and D. Royer (eds) (Paris: Economica) pp. 173–94.

_____ (1988) 'The Structure of Dynamic Macroeconometric Models', *CEPREMAP Working Paper*, no. 8802.

Mazier, J. (1974) *Modèles de court-moyen terme: un schéma théorique d'accumulation et de répartition* [Short-Term–Medium-Term Models: A Theoretical Framework for Savings and Income Distribution], doctoral dissertation, University of Paris I, September.

_____ (1975) 'Les prix dans les modèles macroéconomiques appliqués: détermination implicite ou explicite' [Prices in Applied Macroeconomic Models: Implicit or Explicit Determination], *Revue économique*, vol. 26, no. 3, May, pp. 447–77.

_____ (1978) *La macroéconomie appliquée* [Applied Macroeconomics] (Paris: Presses Universitaires de France), in particular Chapter VI on STAR.

Moustacchi, A. (1965) 'Application d'un modèle d'allocation des ressources à la planification française. Ses enseignements' [Application of a Model of Resource Allocation to French Planning. Its Contributions], World Congress of The Econometric Society, Rome (CERMAP Report).

Mouttet, F., C. Plateau, J. -L. Brillet and J. -P. Morand (1983) *Mini-DMS-Energie, Modèle des interactions économie-énergie* [Mini-DMS-Energy: A Model of Interactions Between the Economy and Energy] (Paris: INSEE) Collection 'Archives et Documents', no. 74.

Muet, P. A. (1979) 'La modélisation macroéconomique: une étude de la structure et de la dynamique des modèles macroéconométriques' [Macroeconomic Modelling: A Study of the Structure and Dynamics of Macroeconometric Models], *Statistiques et Etudes financières, Séries Orange*, special issue, pp. 1–62.

Muet, P. -A., E. Bleuze and Ch. Giraud (1987a) *MICMAC. La macroéconomie par la microinformatique* [MICMAC: Macroeconomics with a Microcomputer] (Paris: Economica).

Muet, P. -A., E. Bleuze and Ch. Giraud (1987b) 'MICMAC: un logiciel micro-informatique pour l'analyse macroéconomique' [MICMAC: A Microcomputer Program for Macroeconomic Analysis], *Observations et Diagnostics économiques (Revue de l'OFCE)*, no. 21, October, pp. 237–61.

Nataf, A. (1965) 'Variante marginale d'un Plan. Problèmes d'ajustment' [Marginal Variants of the Plan. Adjustment Problems] in *Modelli econometrici per la programmazione* [Econometric Models and Programming Techniques] G. Parenti (ed.) (Florence: Scuola di Statistica) pp. 197–218 and 400–2.

Nataf, A. and P. Thionet (1962) 'Le modèle à moyen terme à prix variables SEEF' [The SEEF Medium-Term Model with Variable Prices], *Etudes de Comptabilité National* (Paris: Imprimerie nationale) no. 3, pp. 35–86.

Oudet, B. (1975) 'La dynamique à court terme des modèles macroéconomiques: application à STAR' [The Short-Term Dynamics of Macroeconomic Models: Application to STAR], *Annales de l'INSEE*, no. 20, September–December, pp. 95–128.

—————— (1976) *Etude de la dynamique déterministe à court terme des modèles macroéconomiques: application au modèle STAR* [Study of Determinist Short-Term Dynamics of Macroeconomic Models: Application to the STAR Model], doctoral dissertation, University of Paris IX–Dauphine, January.

Peaucelle, I., P. Petit and Y. Saillard (1981) 'Le modèle AGORA: Présentation succincte et analyse de quelques multiplicateurs' [The AGORA Model: A Brief Presentation and Analysis of Some Multipliers], *CEPREMAP Working Paper*, no. 8122.

Peaucelle, I., P. Petit and Y. Saillard (1983) 'Dépenses publiques: structure et évolution par rapport au PIB. Les enseignements d'un modèle macroéconomique' [Public Expenditure: Structure and Evolution with Respect to GNP: The Lessons of a Macroeconomic Model], *Revue d'Economie politique*, vol. 93, no. 1, pp. 62–85.

Rossignol, P. (1975) 'La nouvelle donnée économique et le modèle FIFI' [The New Economic Conditions and the FIFI Model], *Economie et Statistique*, no. 64, February, pp. 5–17.

Rossignol, P. and P. Roux-Vaillard (1973) 'MINIFIFITOF: maquette du modèle français de planification. Etude de l'intégration des opérations financières' [MINIFIFITOF: A Simplified Version of the French Planning Model: Analysis of the Integration of Financial Variables], *Annales de l'INSEE*, no. 12–13, January–August, pp. 59–158.

Schubert, K. and P. Zagamé (1983) 'Comparaison de trois modèles français: DMS, MOGLI et COPAIN' [Comparison of Three French Models: DMS, MOGLI and COPAIN], *Prévision et Analyse économique (Cahiers du GAMA)*, vol. 4, no. 2, June, pp. 7–35.

SEEF (1953) 'Méthodes d'établissement des comptes provisoires de la Nation et des budgets économiques; [Methods for Building Provisional National Accounts, and Economic Budgets] (Services des Etudes Economiques et Financières), *Statistiques et Etudes financières*, no. 53, May, pp. 396–420.

SEEF (1960): 'Modèle Nachtigal' [The Nachtigal Model] (Services des Etudes Economiques et Financières), Ministère des Finances, SEEF, Division des Comptes et Budgets économiques, *SEEF Paper*, no. 89, October.

Sterdyniak, H., M. -A. Boudier, M. Boutillier, F. Charpin and B. Durand (1984) 'Le modèle trimestriel de l'OFCE' [The Quarterly OFCE Model], *Observations et Diagnostics économiques (Revue de l'OFCE)*, no. 9, October, pp. 137–78.

Stoléru, L. (1968) 'Etude d'un modèle global d'évolution à long terme de l'économie française' [Study of a Global Long-Term Model of the French Economy], *Cahiers du Séminaire d'Econométrie* (Paris: CNRS) no. 10, pp. 64–92.

—————— (1970) *L'équilibre et la croissance économiques* [Economic Equilibrium and Growth] (Paris: Dunod) 3rd edn.

Thionet, P. (1961) 'Indices prévisionnels de prix des agrégats de production des secteurs par la méthode des budgets économiques' [Forecasting Prices of Production by Industry with the Economic Budgets Method], *Bulletin de l'Institut International de Statistique*, vol. 38, second issue, pp. 141–8.

Vergnaud, E. (1986) *Structure et exploitation d'un modèle macroéconomique trimestriel* [Structure and Use of a Quarterly Macroeconomic Model], doctoral dissertation, University of Paris I (modèle MUSCAT).

Vielle, M. (1988) 'Le modèle HERMES-France sur Microtroll' [The HERMES-France Model with Microtroll], University of Paris 5 and Ecole Centrale of Paris, Working Paper, (paper presented at the Planning Office Meeting on French Models on Microcomputers, 29 January, 1988).

Vilares, M. -J. (1987) 'Un modèle macroéconomique pour l'étude des changements structurels. Théorie et application à l'économie française' [A Macroeconomic Model for the Study of Structural Changes. Theory and An Application to the French Economy], *Macrodynamique et déséquilibre*, J. -P. Fitoussi and P. -A. Muet (eds), Paris, pp. 185–206 (with a comment by P. Villa, pp. 207–10). (A first version of this paper was presented in 1981 at the Amsterdam European Meeting of the Econometric Society.)

Villa, P. (1982a) *Modélisation macroéconomique des structures financières. Le modèle DEFI* [Macroeconomic Model-Building of Financial Structures. The DEFI Model] (Paris: INSEE), Collection 'Archives et documents', no. 53.

———— (1982b) 'Politique économique et objectif de change (Une analyse à l'aide du modèle DEFI)' [Economic Policy and Exchange Rate Targets (An analysis with the DEFI Model)], *Internationalisation et autonomie de décision, Repères pour le choix français* [Internationalisation and Decision Autonomy: Guidelines for French Policy Decisions], H. Bourguinat (ed.) (Paris: Economica) pp. 343–66.

Vincent, A. (1943) *La conjoncture, science nouvelle* [Business Cycle Analysis, A New Science] (Paris: Editions de 'La vie Industrielle').

———— (1947) *Initiation à la conjoncture économique* [Introduction to the Economic Analysis of Business Cycles] (Paris: Presses Universitaires de France).

Zagamé, P. (1987) 'L'expérience française de modélisation macroéconométrique: bilan et perspectives' [The French Experience of Macroeconometric Model-Building: Evaluation and Prospects], *Revue d'Economie politique*, vol. 97, no. 5, September–October, pp. 485–528.

9 Canadian macroeconometric modelling, 1947–79 and selectively beyond

1 Introduction

Macroeconometric modelling came to Canada at a fairly early stage of the development of this discipline. As described by T. M. Brown (1970a), the first econometric model project took place in the Department of Reconstruction and Supply and was begun in the Summer of 1947, when Lawrence R. Klein came to Canada to serve as a consultant for the project. Moreover, when Nerlove wrote his survey article (1966), it is interesting to note that four out of the 25 models surveyed were Canadian; the only country for which more models were reviewed was the United States. We may also note that an important landmark in the evolution of Canadian macroeconometric modelling was the symposium in the May 1979 issue of the *Canadian Journal of Economics* (with papers by Waslander, Jump, de Bever and Maxwell, Foot and Sawyer, and Helliwell *et al.*), in which the dynamic properties of the TRACE Model, RDX2, the University of Toronto's Quarterly Forecasting Model, and CANDIDE Model 1.2M were compared.[1] We observe that, although macroeconometric modelling had a slow and steady development during the rest of the 1940s, the 1950s, and most of the 1960s, the impetus to rapid and pronounced development of this discipline came only at the end of the 1960s and then continued strongly into the decade of the 1970s. This trend has continued unabated into the decade of the 1980s, and we survey in a very selective fashion some developments beyond the symposium just mentioned. In recent years, the use of macroeconometric models by business forecasting services, such as Informetrica Limited, the Conference Board of Canada, Data Resources of Canada, Chase Econometrics Canada (now the Canadian arm of Wharton Econometric Forecasting Associates) and Woods Gordon, has given an additional fillip to model development and application.[2]

Before launching into the specifics, we may note that macroeconometric modelling in Canada has been subject to many of the same trends as occurred elsewhere in the developed, market economies. The growth of the modelling activity was partially demand-led (owing to an emphasis on Keynesian-style aggregate demand policy early in the period, and later to a regulatory environment in which quantitative estimation could be, at a minimum, a valuable supplement). Of course, supply forces (for example, the growth of computing capacity, the increased training of specialists in this particular area and possibly the development of macroeconomic theory) played a non-trivial role as well in this process. At this point, we are not prepared to identify the exact contribution of trends in government and the underlying economy, or the new developments in macroeconomic theory or in improved estimation techniques and computing facilities. All that we wish to say is that all of these played an important role on occasion, and we shall attempt to highlight some of them in the summary to follow. As Daub makes clear in his discussions (1985, 1987), the econometric modelling industry may well have a quite cyclical character, periods of expansion and rapid growth being followed by periods of consolidation and maintaining previously won gains. In the late 1980s, we appear to be in a period of consolidation, perhaps induced by uncertainties in the aggregate economy. However other explanations are possible: the Lucas critique of macroeconometric modelling has gained a number of converts (see our discussion in Chapter 17), and the advent of the powerful microcomputers capable of handling medium-sized econometric models may be another force for downscaling.

The plan of this chapter is as follows. After these brief introductory remarks, Section 2 describes some of the models of the government of Canada, beginning with those associated with T. M. Brown (1952, 1964, and 1970a), continuing with the work of Brown's associate, Sydney May (1966), and culminating with John Kuiper's Department of Finance Model (1970). In Section 3, we look at a model that stresses the openness of the Canadian economy, Rhomberg (1964). The strong and sustained efforts of the Research Department of the Bank of Canada, which have produced the series of Models RDX1, RDX2 and RDXF, are reviewed in Section 4. Section 5 looks at the models of the University of Toronto's Institute for Policy Analysis, and, in particular, at the TRACE Model, the Quarterly Forecasting Model, and (most recently) the FOCUS Model. In Section 6, we review the CANDIDE project, which ran for over a decade and a half (from the summer of 1970) and produced a number of models, including CANDIDE Models 1.0, 1.1, 1.2, 2.0 and 3.0; TIM (The Informetrica Model) is an obvious offshoot of this development. In Section 7, attention is paid to two individual models of the Canadian economy with interesting properties (neither of which is maintained at present), namely the models constructed by Tsurumi (1972) and Marwah (1978). Developments in the 1980s are briefly surveyed in Section 8; we use the report of the July 1982 seminar in Ottawa (O'Reilly *et al.*, 1983) as a point of departure for this survey. Our discussion here can be quite brief and even arbitrarily selective, as the period 1980–5 has been very well described in a recent paper by Patrick Grady (Grady Economics and Associates, 1985). Finally, some concluding remarks appear in the last section.

We may note that, although this survey has attempted to be comprehensive, we by no means claim that it is exhaustive. In particular, we have not covered a number of econometric models of the Canadian economy that have been constructed either in government departments or privately but have not been published; this is particularly true for models of the Canadian economy constructed outside Canada.[3] In particular, we focus only on comprehensive macroeconometric models, leaving to one side models of individual sectors of the economy, industry models, and models of economic regions of Canada. Finally, because we take the year 1979 as a dividing point, our treatment of the post-1980 period is quite brief and selective. We note that, as an indication of the burgeoning of macroeconometric modelling activity, we survey over 25 macroeconometric models of Canada in this chapter, which is exactly the number of models that Nerlove summarized in 1966 in his review of world macroeconometric modelling.

2 T. M. Brown and the models of the Government of Canada up to the end of the 1960s

In Chapter 17 of his book, *Specification and Uses of Econometric Models* (1970a), the late T. Merritt Brown describes in some detail the first Canadian macroeconometric model, which was put together during the Summer of 1947 by himself and two other professionals, with Lawrence R. Klein retained for the summer on a consulting basis. The contrast with modern methods is striking: in place of mechanized data banks, data were assembled by hand, and all calculations were done on desk calculators, rather than by computers. Towards the end of the summer, the team began to train data clerks to take over the tasks of routine computation. Thus the Government of Canada (under the leadership of the late C. D. Howe and O. J. Firestone) began a venture in the use of econometric models as an aid to policy formulation and (especially) for purposes of short-term forecasting. This section will describe several members of the series of models built for these purposes. The first model was built in the Department of Reconstruction and Supply; with the disappearance of this department, the model project was transferred to the Economics Branch of the Department of Trade and Commerce, where it remained until 1964. The final two members of this series of models were constructed in the Department of Finance.

Model I, with six behavioural equations, three equations for net taxes (taxes less transfers or subsidies) and four identities, is already a rather sophisticated model. This model is somewhat more advanced than Klein's interwar model (Model III of *Economic Fluctuations in the U.S.*) and anticipates some of the developments of the Klein–Goldberger Model. The model was non-linear, and so its solution was far from trivial; nevertheless this problem was overcome, and the model was honed on predicting immediate developments in 1947 and 1948. Brown describes in detail some of the processes of generating these forecasts. Suffice it to say the model tended to under-predict consumption demand (and hence real national product) in the immediate postwar period, but the subsequent inflationary pressures were reasonably well captured, once full-employment constraints were introduced in the model.

The project continued, and Brown indicates the thinness of the resources devoted to it (1970a, Chapter 18). The normal complement was one or two professional economists and one or two data or computing clerks. Sydney J. May joined the project in 1949, and May was to carry on after Brown's departure in 1959. By 1957, electronic computers were employed for some of the more tedious calculations. Brown makes it clear that data reconstruction, even more than model development on an abstract plane, was an essential activity of the project.

Model IIIE, constructed in 1950, was based on a sample of data from the two subperiods 1927–41 and 1946–9. This model contained seven behavioural equations (thus one more than Model I), all estimated by ordinary least squares except for the consumption function, which was estimated by the technique of limited information maximum likelihood estimation, three net taxation equations, and five identities. The consumption function maintained the distinction between labour and property disposable income (with a higher marginal propensity to consume the former), but there is now the lagged dependent variable to measure the role of 'habit persistence', as explained by Brown in his celebrated 1952 *Econometrica* article.[4] In addition, this consumption function has a prewar–postwar dummy variable, to allow for the apparent upward shift in the immediate postwar period. (Brown interprets this upward shift as reflecting the increased liquidity of the typical postwar household, which unfortunately could not be measured from the data which the project had at its disposal at that particular time.) The six other behavioural equations are an investment demand equation (on a gross rather than a net basis), an import demand equation, an equation for wage determination in the private sector, a production function, an equation for average hours worked per year per employee in the private sector, and an equation for the determination of the total private wage and salary bill. Most of these behavioural equations show a close relationship to the Klein Model III or Klein–Goldberger Model analogues; hence we shall not comment in detail about them. However we may note that the import demand equation, while containing a standard relative prices variable (the ratio of import prices, tariff-adjusted, to domestic prices), whose coefficient has the expected sign but is not statistically significant, contains two unusual income variables, namely lagged property income after taxes and exports. This import demand equation is one of the first to be estimated for a macroeconometric model. The hours equation relates this variable negatively to the level of unemployment, while the wage rate determination equation is a variant of the Klein–Phillips relationship. We note that, in three out of the seven behavioural relationships, there is a dummy variable to allow for an upward shift in the constant term between the prewar and postwar subperiods.[5] The three net tax equations explain direct taxes on labour income, direct taxes on property income, and (implicitly) indirect taxes less subsidies. The usefulness of the model for purposes of policy simulations is limited by the fact that no parameters of the tax system are included explicitly in these three relationships. Identities for national income (from the income side), gross national product (from the expenditure side), the total tax receipts of government, the level of unemployment and the stock of producers' capital complete the system. The exogenous variables include government expenditures, exports, capital consumption allowance, inventory investment and the labour force. Model IIIE was used for short-term forecasts and also for multiplier studies, resulting in an impact multiplier for government expenditures equal to 1.15. Although Brown suspects that dynamic (or intermediate) multipliers would build up, he points out that an unexpected use of multiplier tables is to illuminate structural defects in the model.

By the end of the 1950s, the scale of the current model of this series had grown considerably. Model VIII, dated January 1958 and described in Brown (1964), had six sectors of the model (40 equations in total); Model IX (built in the autumn of 1959) had eight sectors and 49 equations in total. (The increase in the number of behavioural equations was somewhat more modest, as this magnitude went from seven in Model IIIE to nine in Model VIII and 12 in Model IX). Because Model IX was the last model that Brown built directly and also because he appears to have preferred this model to Model VIII,[6] we shall concentrate our description of this stage in the project on the later model.

Model IX is fitted to a prewar–postwar sample, and the behavioural equations are estimated by the method of two-stage least squares. The eight model sectors were as follows: a household sector (three behavioural equations and one identity); a business sector with six behavioural equations; a labour market sector with one new behavioural equation; an international sector with no new relationships, as three key variables are exogenous and the demand for imports already appears in the business sector; a money market sector with two behavioural equations and three identities; a government sector with five tax and transfer equations; three identities for the 'Global Market for Final Goods' and finally a miscellaneous sector of some 24 identities and definitions.

We may highlight a few of the salient details of the Model IX. The exogenous variables remain largely as they were in Models I and IIIE, except that population source magnitudes (for the labour equation) and high-powered money (the monetary base) and the associated reserve ratio now enter as exogenous variables. (The latter two variables serve, in principle, as instruments in monetary policy simulations.) The model distinguishes three production sectors: government, agriculture and the private non-farm sectors. The consumption function now has labour disposable income, property disposable income and lagged consumption as the explanatory variables (even though the property disposable income variable has a small and statistically insignificant coefficient); the prewar-postwar dummy was replaced by a liquid assets variable in immediately preceding versions, but this explanatory variable no longer played a role in Model IX. (Liquid assets play a role – negatively – in the labour force participation rate equation and in the supply equation for hours of work.) The participation rate equation also has the real wage in the non-agricultural private sector as an explanatory variable with a negative influence, suggesting a backward-bending supply curve. A separate inventory investment demand equation, which implicitly distinguishes unintended from desired or 'equilibrium' inventory changes, is now broken out. The aggregate production function shows increasing returns to labour and capital as variable factors of production, as it did in Models I and IIIE. The import demand function continues to have a relative price effect (which Brown feels is too weak quantitatively as well as being statistically insignificant); the income effects are broken down by category of aggregate demand, with inventory investment and machinery and equipment purchases giving rise to strong import demand components. The import demand function also has a 'trigger' explanatory variable, namely the discrepancy between a standardized 3 per cent rate of unemployment and the actual rate when this discrepancy is positive; thus imports are one of the safety valves of an overheated economy. This trigger variable also plays a role in the wage equation, which also has the amount of unemployed hours as an explanatory variable (with a negative influence). Finally, there are two alternative equations for the determination of the key price level in the system, the implicit deflator of the gross domestic flows of new final goods and services. In the short run, this variable is determined by an adjustment of the lagged value of this deflator to the percentage discrepancy between gross domestic flows of new final goods and services demanded and those supplied; in the medium term, with inventory investment set equal to the desired change, the price level can be obtained by equating real gross domestic flows of new final commodities demanded and supplied.

According to May (1966), this sometimes resulted in an 'exaggerated price sensitivity' of this aspect of the model. We note that Model IX, like its predecessors, appears to have been used principally for short-term forecasting,[7] despite the fact that there were a number of policy instruments available for purposes of policy simulation or multiplier analyses.

These somewhat natural applications were made by Sydney May (1966) with a successor model, Model XIV, constructed in the autumn of 1963 on the sample period 1927–41 and 1946–61, using ordinary least squares and two-stage least squares as estimation techniques.[8] The model contains 11 behavioural equations and 58 identities or technical relationships, for a total of 69 endogenous variables. The 11 behavioural equations are three consumption functions (broken down among consumer durables, non-durable goods and consumer services), three investment functions (inventory change, plant investment and investment in machinery, with residential construction exogenous); the Klein Model I labour share equation (intepreted as a labour demand equation); equations for imports, hours worked, and the money wage rate; and, finally, an equation for the direct determination of the price level, which May interprets as closing the real system in lieu of the production function, which indeed is absent from Model XIV. Some key filiation of ideas may be indicated quickly. Two of the three consumer demand equations (non-durables and services) have a lagged dependent variable, to represent the formation and persistence of habits (as explained above). The wage rate equation still has a trigger variable, although the critical rate of unemployment is now 4 per cent of the labour force. The trigger variable was by contrast absent from the import demand function, in which the explanatory variables were a measure of the relative price of imports, four categories of final expenditures (gross investment in machinery, expenditure on consumer durables and, less importantly, non-durable consumption expenditures and inventory investment) and a time trend. It is also interesting to note that, picking up a theme developed by Tinbergen in his 1939 US model, the lagged change in an index of the prices of industrial common stocks appears as an explanatory variable in the equation explaining business fixed investment in machinery and equipment, which May indicates was a difficult relationship to fit satisfactorily. May applies his model to study optimal policy formulation in the Tinbergen–Theil context, which occasioned much comment at the conference in August 1965, held at the University of Western Ontario and convened by the Economic Council of Canada, where he originally presented his paper. May also studied the government expenditures multiplier (the dependent variable being real non-farm output) for both the original non-linear model and a linearized variant of his model: in both versions, the impact multiplier was small (1.29) and in both cases the interim multiplier built up over time, reaching a value of 1.71 (original model) or 2.00 (linearized variant) in the fifth year.

The final member of this series that we shall discuss was that produced by John Kuiper, then of the Econometrics Section of the Department of Finance, in early 1970. According to Kuiper's unpublished manuscript (1970), the Department of Finance took over the maintenance and development of this series of models in the autumn of 1964. Model XVI, of which an earlier version was summarized in Tsurumi's survey article on Canadian macroeconometric models (1973), was produced early in 1970.

Model XVI has 90 equations, of which 20 are behavioural equations and were fitted (in general) to the split sample period 1927–41, 1946–68 by the technique of ordinary least squares. The model represents an evolutionary development from previous members of this group of models and so will only be described in grand outline. We note that there are now four categories of consumption expenditures, as consumer durables spending has now been broken down into automobiles and other consumer durables. (The lagged dependent variable plays a role in all four consumption category regressions, and financial variables, household debt in particular, play a role in the two consumer durable regressions.) The exogenous categories of final demand are residential construction, government spending and exports. The trigger variables have disappeared, but the supply side is represented by a short-run productivity relationship for the private non-farm sector, showing increased productivity gains with increasing output; wage formation and price determination (particularly the former) appear also to be somewhat sensitive to demand pressures. As one might expect, the government budget identities are developed in some detail, and there are a number of variables for policy instruments on both the public expenditure and taxation sides, although the principal use of the model appears to have been in the domain of economic forecasting. (Records of the actual use for economic forecasting are extremely scanty, probably for reasons outlined in note 7.)

With the appearance of Model XVI and the departure of John Kuiper in the summer of 1970, macroeconometric modelling at the Department of Finance entered a new stage. In particular, for a time, the Department used versions of other models surveyed in this chapter (such as QFM of the University of Toronto and RDX2 of the Bank of Canada). Eventually these proved unsatisfactory, and the Department of Finance developed its own macroeconometric model, QFS (Quarterly Forecasting System). As described in Grady Associates (1985), QFS is a large quarterly model (668 equations, of which 196 are behavioural) used for internal forecasting purposes within the Department of Finance. As one might expect, this model has considerable detail with regard to the government sector (particularly government revenues). It is also claimed that the model was constructed following a 'bottom-up' (use of sectoral specialists) rather than a 'top-down' (application of general principles) approach. However it would take us too far afield to describe QFS in detail, particularly in view of the good summary available in Grady Economics Associates (1985).[9]

3 A model reflecting the openness of the Canadian economy: the Rhomberg Model

Before passing on to our discussion of the Rhomberg Model, we may note the macroeconometric model of the Canadian economy built by Richard E. Caves and Richard H. Holton as a relatively small part of their comprehensive study of Canadian economic growth, both past and perspective. (See Caves and Holton, 1959, especially pp. 129–40.) Their long-term econometric model of the Canadian economy was fitted by ordinary least squares to semi-decade averages; in this respect (as in others), it resembles the Valavanis Model of the US economy, discussed in Chapter 3 above. The model contained three identities and nine behavioural equations fitted over the period 1901–55 (11 observations of 5-year averages in all). For our interest, the key behavioural equations were those for imports, exports, gross immigration and gross emigration, thus recognizing the great openness of the Canadian economy to external influences. From our perspective, this model should be described as 'experimental', and apparently that would appear to be the self-evaluation of Professors Caves and Holton, as they seemed discouraged by the quality of the fits of the behavioural equations and did not use the model to forecast future Canadian economic growth. In any case, the absence of policy instruments among the exogenous variables would have precluded policy simulations, as the only explicit exogenous variables were a weighted average of the GNPs of the United States and the United Kingdom (Canada's principal trading partners during the first half of this century), the death rate of the Canadian population (births were endogenous), and a time trend.

Perhaps the most significant early econometric model of the Canadian economy was that constructed by Rudolf Rhomberg (1964), which broke new ground on the subject of the determination of the rate of foreign exchange in a floating regime and also had an interesting discussion of the comparative efficiency of both monetary and fiscal policy under a floating rate, as contrasted with a fixed rate, regime. Rhomberg even introduced his discussion with a small, non-econometric prototype model, in which the essential points from his principal model (econometric in nature) were highlighted.

Some of the details of Rhomberg's (principal) model may now be described. The model was fitted to data from the first quarter of 1952 to the fourth quarter of 1959, generally by the technique of limited-information maximum likelihood estimation. The model, which clearly depicts the dependence of the Canadian economy on that of the United States, contains 17 behavioural equations and two identities (one for the balance of payments and also the standard national income accounting identity for real gross national product). Among the behavioural equations are seven that might be characterized as aggregate demand relationships: a consumption function, four investment functions (private investment is split into residential construction, non-residential construction, machinery and equipment, and non-farm inventory investment), an export demand function and an import demand function. With regard to the functions, we might note that the three fixed investment functions appeared to be quite interest-sensitive, while the inventory investment equation had an interesting interpretation in terms of voluntary and involuntary components of inventory investment. The import and export demand functions can be given standard interpretations in terms of price and income effects, with significant price terms in both cases (and a price and/or exchange rate elasticity of -2 for exports and -1 for imports). There are three price level equations (one each for the implicit price deflators of gross national product excluding farm inventory investment, of exports and of machinery and equipment expenditures, respectively); the principal price level equation depicts the GNP implicit deflator as dependent on the implicit deflator for imports (after correction for variations in the exchange rate) and on the level of real gross national product (seasonally adjusted), in what might be interpreted as an approximation to a trade-off curve. As the fiscal sector is not modelled directly and as seasonal adjustment is generally carried out in the regression equations, there are two technical relationships: one linking disposable income to gross national product (both in real terms) and one linking seasonally-adjusted real gross national product to its non-seasonally-adjusted analogue. The monetary sector is represented by two equations, for short-term and long-term interest rates respectively; the former can be interpreted as a simple liquidity preference relationship and the latter as a simple term structure relationship with a positive premium for illiquidity in dynamic equilibrium.

The remaining three behavioural equations, which explain US direct investment in Canada, net US long-term portfolio investment in Canada, and the exchange rate, were the most novel (at the time) and hence may be described in greater detail.[10] US direct investment in Canada depends principally on US economic activity, as measured by the deviations from a linear trend of real US GNP. Secondary explanatory variables, which, however, are not statistically significant, are real investment in plant and the differential between the Canadian and US long-term rates of interest. By contrast this latter variable has a very large and statistically significant coefficient in the equation for net US portfolio investment in Canada,[11] for which the other explanatory variable (other than the seasonal dummies) is the cumulated total of US foreign investment. (The regression coefficient indicates that Canada received, on the margin during the sample period, roughly 8 per cent of total US net foreign investment in the form of this particular long-term capital flow.) The exchange rate, defined as the US dollar price of a Canadian dollar so that an upward movement represents an appreciation, depends positively and significantly on two explanatory variables – the short-term interest rate differential between Canada and the United States and also the lagged value of the exchange rate – and negatively (and significantly) on short-term capital inflows (credits to non-residents). The three effects can be interpreted as an interest differential effect, an inertia effect, and an 'overhang' effect; notice, as Nerlove (1966) points out, that movements in official reserves have no (direct) effect in the determination of the exchange rate.[12] Another interpretation of exchange rate determination in the Rhomberg model is that the exchange rate is the price of international speculative flows or short-term capital movements, and indeed Rhomberg inverts this equation to make short-term capital inflows the left-hand side variable, when the system is converted to a model of the Canadian economy under a fixed exchange rate regime.

Before discussing the principal use that Rhomberg made of his model, the exogenous variables may be briefly indicated. The policy instruments are government expenditures (which represent fiscal policy), the money supply (which represents monetary policy) and (under a floating rate regime) the change in international reserves that the government wishes to achieve. (If the float is 'clean', this target will presumably be close to zero.) Under a fixed rate, the exchange rate itself becomes an exogenous policy instrument and the change in reserves becomes an endogenous variable, determined in the first instance by the balance of payments identity. The other (non-policy) exogenous variables include the import price deflator, all other types of long-term capital flows (other than the two determined in the model), world export prices, world industrial production, US real gross national product, US net foreign investment (in nominal terms), US interest rates, a time trend, and the three seasonal dummies. There are also a number of lagged endogenous variables, so that the system displays a number of dynamic effects.

As noted above, Rhomberg's principal focus was a comparison of the efficacy of both monetary and fiscal policy under the two different regimes of fixed and floating exchange rates. Like all of the studies of this vintage, there are no full model simulations during the sample period as a means of validating the model. Instead, the use made by Rhomberg of his model was multiplier analysis, after a linearization of the system. This allowed him to calculate impact and dynamic (medium-term or intermediary) multiplers; some additional (somewhat heroic) assumptions enabled Rhomberg to calculate equilibrium multipliers as well. As indicated above, the conversion of the model of Canada under a floating rate to one under a fixed rate regime was done by the reinterpretation of the exchange rate equation as a short-term capital flow equation, with the indicated change in the endogeneity and exogeneity of both the rate of exchange and of the change in reserves. In addition, some assumption (for example, at the extremes, full linkage or complete sterilization) must be made concerning the relationship between the movements of official reserves (under a fixed rate system) and the change in the money supply. Rhomberg makes an extensive number of multiplier calculations, which all show that the numerical value of the fiscal policy multiplier is higher under a fixed rate system (particularly with fully endogenous money) than it is under a floating rate regime. (This is so because the exchange rate must remain unchanged under a fixed regime, rather than appreciate, thus dampening the fiscal stimulus, as it would have, under a floating rate system.) For example, the impact multiplier of an increase in government expenditures was 1.5 under a floating rate regime but 1.8 under a fixed rate system (with either sterilized or fully endogenous money), and the relative difference in the efficacy of fiscal policy is heightened when one studies the dynamic multipliers, particularly with fully endogenous money. By contrast, monetary policy appears (from a study of the money supply multipliers) to have a 'comparative advantage' under a floating rate system, as the depreciating exchange rate (due to both a passive current account balance and the capital account's also becoming passive, the result in turn of reduced interest rates) reinforces the directly stimulative effects of lower interest rates.[13]

Another early model that recognizes the openness of the Canadian economy is that of Officer (1968), which he claims is built around the determination of the (spot) exchange rate rather than the standard national income accounting identity. The sample period was the first quarter of 1951 to the first quarter of 1962 (45 observations in total), a period of a floating exchange rate, at least officially. There were 50 behavioural equations, which were generally fitted by some variant of two-stage least squares, and also some 58 identities. In general, seasonal adjustment was performed directly in the regression equations themselves.

We note that the exogenous variables of the Officer model include import prices, other developments in other economies, Canadian direct foreign investment outside Canada, a time trend and seasonal dummies. The exogenous policy instruments include several types of government expenditure, direct tax receipts, monetary and debt management policy instruments (such as reserve ratios) and the change in official reserves. Officer calculates impact multipliers with respect to roughly 40 of the most important exogenous variables. We may simply note that he found the impact multiplier of government expenditures on real national income to be small, between 1.1 and 1.4, depending on the type of government expenditures and the concept of national income under consideration. There were, however, no dynamic simulations or even calculations of dynamic multipliers. At this point, the Officer model appears to be primarily of interest for historical reasons and because it was a useful training ground for one of the principal authors of the RDX1 and RDX2 models, to which we now turn.[14]

4   Models of the Bank of Canada: RDX1 and RDX2

At this point in the narrative, we describe the models of one of the continuing projects for econometric models of the Canadian economy, those of the Research Department of the Bank of Canada. It seems appropriate to begin with the RDX series of models, as this group of models (particularly the RDX2 Model) has been the industry standard for a number of years. Moreover RDX2 has had a strong influence on a number of subsequent Canadian macroeconometric models, in part because the 'alumni' of this project have gone on to develop such models with new organizations. It may be observed that, since the late 1960s, team projects have tended to be the predominant force in Canadian econometric modelling, even though individual efforts (such as those summarized in Section 7 below) have not been totally absent. Also it may be noted that we shall not enter into the detail of individual equations, owing to a desire to give a concise account. Readers interested in the details of the specifications are referred to the individual publications cited below and listed in the references at the end of this chapter. It is interesting to note that interpretations of the motivations of the senior management of the Bank of Canada in permitting, and indeed encouraging, these developments have varied among commentators.[15]

RDX1 (for '*R*esearch *D*epartment e*X*perimental – Version 1') was a quarterly model of the Canadian economy with 101 equations, of which

50 equations were behavioural equations and the remainder were identities. (See Helliwell *et al.*, 1969a, 1969b.) The behavioural equations were generally fitted to data running from the first quarter of 1952 or 1953 to the fourth quarter of 1965, by either the technique of ordinary least squares or a version of instrumental variables estimation (in the context of simultaneous equations); the estimation technique did not, in general, make an appreciable difference in parameter estimation. As one might expect of a model built in the research department of a central bank, financial links affecting the real economy were stressed (although, for RDX1, these links were principally interest rate effects rather than quantity influences from the financial flows and stocks). The model was also quite open to foreign (particularly US) influences, reflecting structural characteristics of the Canadian economy. It is interesting to note that the final specifications were in many cases selected by comparing results under full system dynamic simulations, and the authors of RDX1 claim that they were among the first groups of model-builders to use this procedure.[16]

As described in Helliwell *et al.* (1969a), the structure of RDX1 may be decomposed into five model sectors: (1) private aggregate demand (decomposed in turn into consumption expenditures, a submodel of residential construction, business investment, and export and import demands); (2) income distribution, employment, and prices; (3) the government sector; (4) a (domestic) financial sector; and (5) international capital flows. We may note that RDX1 was built in the context of a fixed rate of foreign exchange, and so this important variable is exogenous.[17] We may briefly note the following aspects of the structure of RDX1: the consumption equations reflect a weak version of the permanent income hypothesis; residential construction is quite sensitive to financial influences (both interest rates and financial flows); and labour inputs adjust (with a time lag) to the real demand (namely the appropriate production magnitudes) for these factor services. Wages and prices are rather cost-oriented, with the wage rate change being determined by a wage adjustment equation of the Klein–Phillips variety. The government sector has submodels for personal income tax collections and for unemployment insurance payments. In the financial sector, the key interest rate is the average yield on federal government securities with three years or less to maturity, and this variable is highly sensitive to US influences. With international capital flows explained, one can keep track, via the balance of payments identity, of changes in the level of official reserves.

The dynamic experiments with RDX1 (as summarized in Helliwell *et al.*, 1969b) showed some interesting results. Although the impact multipliers were small (between 1.08 and 1.36), they had a tendency to build, with only a faint suggestion of a tendency to decline after hitting a peak.[18]

There was also a very interesting analysis of a trade-off curve in the full model context, in which variations in the rate of inflation were plotted against variations in the rate of unemployment, using policy instruments which maintained the level of foreign exchange reserves constant. The well-known inverse relationship appeared, although it was also interesting to note that the inflationary cost of a reduction in unemployment was higher when the process was started from a rate of unemployment that was already low (and also that the non-linearity of this inverse relationship was more pronounced when this initial unemployment rate was low).

With continued development work at the Research Department of the Bank of Canada, RDX1 soon became obsolete. By contrast, its successor, the RDX2 model, was fruitfully used during most of the 1970s and well into the 1980s. Moreover, as we noted above, no other Canadian macroeconometric model has had as large an influence on the development of later models. We may distinguish two versions of RDX2. The version of the first half of the decade, described in Helliwell *et al.* (1971), contained 258 equations (of which 141 or 142 were behavioural equations fitted to data beginning some time in the 1950s and generally ending in the fourth quarter of 1968);[19] accordingly, RDX2 was considerably larger than its predecessor. The version of the second half of the 1970s, which was the version employed in the models symposium of the May 1979 issue of the *Canadian Journal of Economics* mentioned above, was larger still, with 516 equations in total.[20] (See Bank of Canada, 1976a, 1976b; as the title of the first reference indicates, the sample period was updated to end in the fourth quarter of 1972, which was useful to capture some contemporary experience with a floating rate.) The behavioural equations were in general fitted by ordinary least squares, and it is interesting to note that RDX2 contained behavioural equations for two phenomena that were exogenous in RDX1, namely the rate of foreign exchange and the level of international migration (both immigration and emigration).[21]

We may briefly summarize the structure of RDX2; this rapid summary follows closely the presentation of Maxwell (1978). In Helliwell *et al.* (1971), the five model sectors of RDX1 are disaggregated further into 21 model sectors for RDX2. Disaggregation proceeds on two other planes as well: foreign trade (and foreign financial) linkages are disaggregated between the United States and the rest of the world (in part to facilitate the linked simulations with the MPS Model of the US economy, briefly discussed below), and government budget items are disaggregated between federal and provincial–municipal levels. It seems fair to describe the RDX2 model as depicting the Canadian economy as being in disequilibrium almost continuously, although always moving toward equilibrium in the absence of further (stochastic or systematic) disturbance. Thus the strong distinction is made between intended inventory investment (reflecting the traditional sales accelerator) and unintended inventory investment, which acts as a buffer to sudden changes in aggregate demand.[22] Other features of the RDX2 model worthy of comment include the use of a production function as a technological constraint on the amount of output ultimately obtainable from the available set of productive inputs, with, however, considerable variation in the levels of short-run productivity (which varies directly with the pressure of aggregate demand). Labour input varies, of course, with the state of aggregate demand, but average weekly hours adjust more rapidly than employees. The labour force is endogenous, with discouraged worker effects predominating in the short (and medium) run, so that the labour force expands in periods of high demand. As in RDX1, wage and price formation is cost-oriented, with an emphasis on normal unit labour costs and the costs of imported materials, although demand pressures play a supplementary role. In RDX2 (unlike its predecessor), wage formation is regarded as emanating from a long-term target of labour negotiators of maintaining labour's share, so that real wage rates rise in the long run at the same rate as normal labour productivity.

The financial sector is constructed around a model of portfolio adjustment of the major financial institutions, which reflects the public's changing preferences (due to changing wealth, interest rates and other determinants) for the various financial holdings possible. Short-term interest rates are determined in RDX2 by a reaction function of the monetary authorities,[23] while long-term rates reflect a term structure relationship in which US rates play a critical role also. A key output of the financial sector is a critical rate of return called the 'supply price of capital' (from the Yale approach to financial theory), which affects investment and consumption decisions in these sectors of the model. International capital flows also reflect portfolio decisions (on the part of both borrowers and lenders) and equations to explain this category of the balance of payments are developed. Finally, there are behavioural equations for both private and the official demand for spot foreign exchange and also (in a floating rate regime) for the forward rate of foreign exchange; in a floating rate system, the spot rate is viewed as the Canadian dollar price of one US dollar which will equilibrate the balance on current account with that of 'normal' capital flows (long-term capital flows and any non-speculative short-term flows); in other words, it is a market-clearing price once all speculative capital flows have stabilized.

Two uses of RDX2 (which was also used for a large number of policy simulations during its long life) may be indicated briefly here. The multiplier calculations of de Bever *et al.* (1978), as summarized in de Bever and

Maxwell (1979), displayed the now standard 'inverted-U' shape for multiplier calculations, with the regular multipliers beginning at a low value (roughly 1.0 in the case of RDX2), climbing slightly (to a peak of approximately 1.4 after three years for RDX2), and then trailing off towards zero (the RDX2 real multiplier was 0.5 after 10 years). This pattern, which also characterized the other Canadian models in the model symposium, is modified if the exchange rate and immigration links are allowed to influence the model calculations. With the exchange rate links, de Bever and Maxwell's article (1979) suggested that the effects of a sustained increase in government expenditures would be cyclic, while permitting international migration to be endogenous suggested that a sustained increase in government spending can be a source of additional growth in this context.[24] RDX2 was also the subject of some very interesting linkage experiments with the MPS model of the US economy. (See, in particular, Helliwell *et al.*, 1973 and Helliwell, 1976.) A principal conclusion of this group of experiments was (as the title of Helliwell's 1976 article suggested) that the important linkages between the US and Canadian economies are not only the traditional trade linkages, but that financial effects and factor (labour) flows may be even more important responses to stimulative policy in one of the two North American economies.

Finally, we may observe that recent work in the modelling area at the Research Department of the Bank of Canada has centred on the development of a successor to RDX2, a model called RDXF. Here the emphasis has been on the development of a model with forecasting capabilities (and hence the 'F' in the model mnemonic).[25] RDXF is somewhat smaller than the second version of RDX2, at 403 equations, of which 208 are behavioural equations; it is nevertheless broadly similar to its predecessor. RDXF was used as the Bank's entry in the comparative models seminar of July 1982, held in Ottawa under the auspices of the Bank of Canada and the Department of Finance. (As noted in the introduction, the results of this seminar later appeared in O'Reilly *et al.*, 1983.)

5 Models of the Institute for Policy Analysis of the University of Toronto

The Institute for Policy Analysis (which has a longer formal name, 'The Institute for the Quantitative Analysis of Social and Economic Policy') has been involved in an econometric modelling project (with first an annual model and later quarterly models) since 1966. In the early days of the project, regular forecasts were produced for commercial and government subscribers, who thus helped to finance the model-building projects. After the first quarter of 1977, according to Jump (1979), the production of regular quarterly forecasts was left to Data Resources of Canada (see

Section 8 below), and the researchers of the Institute for Policy Analysis concentrated exclusively on scholarly work.[26] We may briefly describe two of these models and mention the development of a third.

The TRACE (for *To Ronto Annual Canadian Econometric*) Model dates from 1968 and went through many versions until 1979, when active maintenance of this model was no longer carried out. (Mark I is described in Choudhry *et al.*, 1972, while the paper in the 1979 models symposium is based on Mark IVE.) Because of easy accessibility, we summarize the Model IIIR version (in Sawyer *et al.*, 1976), on which the experiments for fixed contrasted to floating rates of foreign exchange (Carr, Jump and Sawyer, 1976) were performed. The TRACE Model is an annual model of the Canadian economy, estimated (for Mark IIIR) by ordinary least squares to data for 1947–71 (in general).[27] As used in practice, TRACE tends to be medium-term in outlook, with (conditional) projections made some five to 10 years into the future on the basis of this model. As described in Choudhry *et al.* (1972), TRACE can be thought of as a statistical, dynamic application to an open economy of a neo-Keynesian aggregate supply and demand apparatus. (In turn, the neo-Keynesian aggregate supply and demand apparatus can be regarded as a generalization of the IS–LM framework to allow varying price levels.) The set of roughly 145 exogenous variables of Mark IIIR, which contains 44 behavioural equations and 139 identities, or 183 equations in total, includes tax rates, some government expenditure variables, world prices, US economy variables (real incomes, interest rates etc.), variables from other foreign economies, dummies, a time trend, housing starts,[28] Canada–US Auto Pact variables, the average labour force participation rate of males 25 to 54 years of age, the supply of money (M1), and a number of statistical residuals or discrepancies. As described in the following paragraph, the rate of foreign exchange can be exogenous or endogenous, depending on the regime in force. The scope of the model is indicated by the 14 model sectors: there are groups of equations for consumption expenditures, government expenditures on goods and services, business gross capital formation, international trade, national income accounting identities, production (and potential output), wages and price levels, employment and hours, factor incomes, taxes, government revenue and expenditure account, interest rates, investment and savings accounts, and international capital flows and the exchange rate. We note that the lags in TRACE are often quite long; business fixed investment is determined by a variant of the Jorgensonian investment theory; and the key production sector is business non-agricultural output, as the disaggregation with respect to production is quite rudimentary with only government, personal sector, and basic primary (agriculture, fishing, and trapping) production distinguished separately. Other disaggregation is also fairly minimal in TRACE; for instance, the consumption sector distinguishes only two categories of expenditure, durables and other (services and semi-durable and non-durable goods), although foreign trade is broken down between the United States and all other trading partners and the government sector is disaggregated among all levels of government. The basic production concept is that of a Cobb-Douglas two-factor (labour and capital) production function for business non-agricultural output, and this concept underlies the theory of the investment demand function, the concept of potential output, and some of the labour demand relationships.

Turning to the applications of TRACE, we note that, from 1969 to 1979 (when it was replaced by the FOCUS Model), TRACE served honourably as the representative Canadian model in Project LINK. (See Chapter 14.) In a very interesting simulation study, Carr, Jump and Sawyer (1976) applied version Mark IIIR of TRACE to study various differential responses of the Canadian economy, depending upon whether the Canadian economy was functioning under a fixed or floating exchange rate regime. As noted above, Mark IIIR contains an international capital sector (based on a theory of portfolio adjustment for either stocks or flows, depending upon the case at hand); in a floating rate regime, the exchange rate calculated by the model is an equilibrium one (one that neither accumulates nor discharges international reserves) and is computed by iterative simulations of the model. Carr *et al.* (1976) simulated expansionary fiscal policy (and two other experiments); interestingly, they found (contrary to Rhomberg, 1964) that the dynamic fiscal multiplier was larger in a flexible rate regime, at least for the first three years.[29] Finally, we note that, according to the Foot and Sawyer article in the 1979 models symposium, the TRACE Model has a number of sources of dampening of expansionary impulses, such as increased imports, higher interest rates and higher induced price levels. Taking the standard multiplier simulation (fixed exchange rate, and fixed stock of money), Foot and Sawyer report a monotonic decline of the dynamic multiplier, with an impact multiplier of 1.9, which then decreases to 1.2, 1.0, and 0.5, after three, five, and 10 years respectively. Another interesting finding for the TRACE Model from the models symposium was that, under static conditions, the long-run marginal propensity to consume implied by the model exceeds 1.0 (after more than six years of constant stimulus have passed); this obviously pointed up a weakness in the TRACE Model which subsequent revisions were able to correct.

The workhorse of the Institute for Policy Analysis's forecasting effort was QFM (the *Q*uarterly *F*orecasting *M*odel), which was a reduced neo-Keynesian model of roughly 75 equations and 30 exogenous variables in its real sector (see Jump, 1972), at times supplemented by a moderately detailed financial sector. QFM as a forecasting instrument was supplemented by frequent meetings of the project subscribers, at which the projections were discussed in some detail. QFM had a moderately detailed aggregate demand sector (with, however, exogenous residential construction expenditures, export demands and government expenditures in nominal terms) and a rather sensitive wage-price sector. In comparison to TRACE, QFM had a rudimentary production sector and an absence of international capital flow relationships. In the models symposium, it was found that QFM was reasonably conformable to the general pattern of real dynamic multipliers; indeed, the QFM dynamic multipliers had the classical shape of an inverted 'U', beginning with an impact multiplier of 1.4, rising to a maximum dynamic multiplier of 2.7 after roughly 12 quarters, and then falling off to a value of -0.3 after 10 years.[30] However the dynamic volatility of the wage-price sector implies that the nominal multipliers (ratio of the variation in nominal GNP to the original stimulus, also evaluated in current dollars) simply soar over time and are quite inconsistent with the other dynamic nominal multipliers studied in this symposium. Indeed Jump expresses on a number of occasions in this article (1979) the inconsistency of asking a short-term forecasting model to run for 40 quarters, when the model has been typically used in a forecasting mode only for eight quarters into the future. But in turn this argument could be disputed, as QFM has also been described as a policy-simulation model. While it is true that the fault could have been with the three other models compared in this symposium, the circumstantial evidence is against this interpretation, and in fact QFM was abandoned (in favour of FOCUS) in part as a result of this comparative models study. Finally, mention should be made of Jump's unpublished 1976 study, presented at the annual meeting of the Canadian Economics Association in Quebec City, of the 'expected' evolution of the price level (on the basis of QFM) in which he compared this predicted evolution with the measured path of the price level, in the presence of a new disturbance, the federal government's new anti-inflation programme, announced on Thanksgiving Day, 1975. On the basis of this comparison, Jump concluded that the effects of the Anti-Inflation Board and associated measures were minimal (up to the time of his study) and that the observed deceleration in inflation during the first half of 1976 would have occurred in any case.

The FOCUS (*FO*re*C*asting and *U*ser *S*imulation) Model is a lineal descendant of QFM and so it has been constructed in much the same spirit; however, it incorporates some elements of a monetarist approach, judiciously blended with the basic neo-Keynesian concepts. The FOCUS

Model is much larger than QFM, with roughly 250 equations (of which approximately 180 are behavioural) and with some 350 exogenous variables. In addition, the FOCUS Model has been constructed with a view to correcting the weaknesses of QFM; for example, there are equations for both single-family and multiple-unit housing starts in the FOCUS Model, variables which were implicitly exogenous in QFM. Another innovation is that the FOCUS Model offers the choice of two price level regimes: one based on a mark-up over labour, energy, import and tax costs and a second based on neoclassical market-clearing of aggregate supply (real private domestic production) and demand. (See Grady Economics and Associates, 1985, pp. 89–90.) The FOCUS Model was represented in the Department of Finance's July 1982 Models Symposium (Peter Dungan and Joan Head, 1982; O'Reilly *et al.*, 1983), and it appeared that the responses of the FOCUS Model to outside stimuli were reasonable in general, even in the context of a cross-models comparison.

6 The CANDIDE project and associated models

The CANDIDE (*CA*Nadian *D*isaggregated *I*nter-*D*epartmental *E*conometric) Project began in mid-1970, under the leadership of the Economic Council of Canada (ECC), following consultants' reports by Bodkin and Denton (1970) and Matuszewski (1970). The project terminated in 1987 when the Economic Council of Canada decided to cease active maintenance of a version of the CANDIDE Model, although a lineal descendant of CANDIDE still exists (at the time of writing) at Informetrica Limited. Initially an inter-departmental project (as the acronym asserts), management of the model then currently in use and development of new versions came to be increasingly concentrated in the project group at the ECC. In total, there were four permanent project managers: Michael C. McCracken (1970–2, under whose leadership Model 1.0 was developed);[31] Ronald G. Bodkin (1972–4, whose team developed Model 1.1); H. E. L. ('Bert') Waslander (1974–6, who was responsible for versions 1.2 and 1.2M, which is described in Waslander, 1979); and Ross S. Preston (1976–87), who led his team in the development of Models 2.0 and 3.0 (see Preston *et al.*, 1979). The role of Michael McCracken in implementing the consultants' reports and in coordinating the efforts of a number of junior econometricians, often on temporary loan from a cooperating federal department, cannot be overstated. At the beginning, it was far from clear that this model would actually function; success, when it finally came, was all the more welcome in that it was by no means assured.[32]

In this historical summary, we shall concentrate (perhaps inevitably) on Model 1.1, as this was the version of the CANDIDE Model which has the most readily accessible documentation. We shall, however, refer to other versions and present brief commentaries on Models 2.0 and 3.0 and on an associated model. In any case, there is a fair resemblance among all of the variants of the CANDIDE Model, though inevitable progression and development have occurred.

The CANDIDE Model was a large, medium-term model of the Canadian economy; as the acronym implies, there was a fairly extensive industrial breakdown or disaggregation, and indeed there were two input–output submodels (one on the side of real output determination and one on the side of industrial price formation) embedded in the overall model. (In turn, the input–output submodels of the CANDIDE Models rested on some fundamental development work on rectangular input–output systems, carried out at Statistics Canada during the 1960s by such scholars as Terry Gigantes, Tadek Matuszewski, the late Paul Pitts, and J. A. Sawyer.) In Model 1.1, there were some 2049 equations, of which 616 were behavioural equations (estimated by ordinary least squares over a 1955–71 sample period, in general), 427 were input–output identities associated with the two input–output submodels of the system, and the remaining 1006 equations were other identities. The 453 exogenous variables reflect price and real output developments outside Canada, particularly in the United States,[33] some categories of imports and exports, most basic demographic phenomena (such as the average fertility rate of females of child-bearing ages), some international financial transactions, capital stock scrappage levels, a number of policy instruments (particularly fiscal policy instruments, such as tax rate parameters, but also three monetary policy variables and the exchange rate),[34] dummies and time trends (which are intended to capture unique historical circumstances) and miscellaneous exogenous variables (which include a number of adjustment items). According to the overview in the first chapter of Bodkin and Tanny (1975), Model 1.1 could be decomposed functionally into eight 'supersectors': final demands by ultimate use, derivation of real domestic product by industry, labour supply and requirements, wage and prices, private and government revenues, national income accounting relationships, financial flows, and anterior (recursive) sectors. We note that, in the first supersector, aggregate consumption is determined initially by an analysis of savings (contractual and discretionary); disaggregated consumption categories (43 in number), required (among other detailed expenditure categories) to work the industrial output determination submodel, are obtained from a variant of the Houthakker–Taylor model of consumption outlays (Houthakker and Taylor, 1970); there is a developed submodel of residential construction expenditures; most categories of government expenditures on goods and services (disaggregated, in addition, by the various levels of government) are endogenous; and the standard model of the demand for goods and services traded internationally is applied to most of the categories of exports and imports. Other aspects of the structure of CANDIDE Model 1.1 worth commenting on include the existence of an endogenous labour force (due to participation rate equations reflecting a preponderance of discouraged worker effects for four out of the five age–sex population groups),[35] the largely cost-oriented nature of wage and price determination in Supersector IV (with, however, a subsidiary role for demand pressures), and the submodel of personal income taxation reflecting the introduction in 1974 of indexation into the system of Canadian income taxation. The key domestic rate of interest (the three-month Treasury Bill rate) was determined by internal liquidity and transactions factors, as modified by conditions in US financial markets. There were also a number of equations for capital flows in the balance of payments, which could have formed the basis of a theory of the exchange rate in a floating rate regime. Finally, the recursive supersector (Supersector VIII) contains a complete demographic submodel which generates total population and its decomposition by families, households, and age–sex groups (for determination of the labour force) endogenously.[36] (Although most of the basic determinants, such as specific death rates and a general fertility rate are exogenous, net immigration is endogenous and tied (with a lag) to conditions in Canada; because of this lag, this sector can be solved initially, before the solution of the large simultaneous core of the model.) It may also be noted that CANDIDE is a general purpose model in which the industrial detail is an essential element; as Waslander (1979) points out, 'it is not possible to simulate only the aggregates in CANDIDE, since they are related to each other through their components' (Waslander, 1979, p. 141).

The usages of the CANDIDE Model have been many and varied; in this summary, only a few can be indicated. In the 1979 models symposium (for which the research was done three years earlier, as noted in the introduction), Waslander (1979) studied the dynamic multiplier for CANDIDE Model 1.2M (similar to 1.1, with a small but important difference described in the article cited) for the standard simulation (a sustained $400 million increase in 1961 dollars in federal non-wage expenditures, with the stock of money held constant). In Model 1.2M, the impact multiplier was 1.7, while the dynamic multiplier shows a general downward trend, so that the fourth year value was 1.4 and the tenth year dynamic multiplier was 0.5. The Waslander study also showed the uneven effects of aggregate expansion on the various production sectors of the economy, as in general sectors exposed to foreign competition suffered from the deterioration in the terms of trade (rise in domestic relative to foreign prices), while most 'sheltered' sectors (such as services) expanded more than the economy-wide average in general. The results of these multiplier analyses were much more reasonable than in CANDIDE Model 1.0, where the dynamic multipliers tended to explode (rise indefinitely) or even in Model 1.1, where the dynamic multiplier showed no apparent tendency to decline after the passage of a certain amount of time. By contrast with earlier versions of CANDIDE, the general pattern of the dynamic multiplier of CANDIDE Model 1.2M was much more conformable to those of the other econometric models studied in the 1979 symposium.

The CANDIDE Model has been used extensively to make conditional projections into the medium-term future (say five to 10 years beyond the present). Thus the first use of the CANDIDE Model, summarized in the Economic Council of Canada's Ninth Annual Review (1972), *The Years to 1980*, stressed the growth prospects which seemed to be unfolding at that time, following a severe recession at the beginning of the 1960s and a somewhat milder one (in attempting to squeeze the inflation out of the system) at the beginning of the 1970s. (In retrospect, the projections of the Ninth Annual Review were hopelessly optimistic, as they did not take into account worldwide inflationary pressures, energy shocks and productivity slow-downs.) Seven years later, CANDIDE Model 2.0 was used (in the Sixteenth Annual Review, 1979, *Two Cheers for the Eighties*) to trace out much more sombre medium-term prospects in view of some fairly hefty energy price increases in prospect for the immediate future. It was interesting to observe that, the worse the supply shock that was assumed, the worse was the deterioration of economic performance in terms of standard objectives: low inflation rates, low rates of unemployment and low deficits in government budgets and in the balance of payments. However it was still true that, in the context of various policy instruments operated in the medium term (three to five years here) with given prospective energy price increases, there was still a trade-off between the objectives of reduced inflation and lower unemployment (at a rather pronounced level of each). In the years intervening between these two dates, especially under the chairmanship of André Raynauld, the CANDIDE Model was used as a technical base to generate 'performance indicators', which were intended to show intermediate (three to four years) proximate objectives for macroeconomic policy.

There were a myriad of other uses of the CANDIDE Model, also. Thus, Siedule, Skoulas and Newton (1976) modified the basic version of CANDIDE Model 1.1 (by adding more age–sex groups in considering labour force participation and by testing for the presence of specific effects induced by the 1971 reform of the system of unemployment insurance). They then attempted to gauge the extent to which the modifications in the system of unemployment insurance increased the measured rate of unemployment, as a result of increased labour force participation (but without additional employment) under the more generous arrangements of the reformed system. Based on Siedule, Skoulas and Newton's simulations, Bodkin and Cournoyer (1978) estimated that these measures may have added an additional 1.3 percentage points to the rate of unemployment, for a given setting of aggregate demand pressure. CANDIDE has also been used to project requirements for occupational categories (in the medium term); in addition, the now defunct federal Department of Regional Economic Expansion experimented with a regional version of the CANDIDE Model. This version was not a success, owing in part to weak linkages among spending, production, labour markets and incomes.

In the 1982 Models Symposium held at the Department of Finance, two off-shoots of the CANDIDE Project were represented: CANDIDE Model 2.0 and TIM (*The Informetrica Model*). CANDIDE Model 2.0 (whose structure is described in some detail in Preston *et al.*, 1979) is similar to earlier versions of the CANDIDE Model, yet there are some important differences: the industrial structure of the model is more balanced (so that there are the same number of industries for output determination, wage and price formation, employment and hours, and capital stocks and investment) and also expectational phenomena play a larger role. (Thus the expected rate of change of the price level depends in part on observed rates of change of the money stock, so that this version is less purely neo-Keynesian than its predecessors. Also in this vein, federal government deficits require financing decisions, which in turn have an impact on present and future developments in the economy.) As noted above, the rate of foreign exchange is determined endogenously (in a reasonably satisfactory fashion) in Model 2.0. TIM, at roughly 3900 equations (1984 version), was still larger; it has been used by Informetrica Limited (a private consulting firm headed by Michael C. McCracken) for medium-term projections (and also for short-term forecasting, to a certain extent); the large size of TIM reflects in part the desire to design a variant of the CANDIDE Model that would be useful in the construction of satellite or peripheral submodels, which could then be appended to the main structural model to produce estimates of industrial detail, regional disaggregation or some other phenomenon of interest. (This sort of modification can be particularly useful in consulting work.) Finally, we note that the CANDIDE project also produced a final version of the CANDIDE Model, Model 3.0, in 1984–5. Model 3.0 incorporated still more monetarist theoretical constructs, and so continued the trend away from the purely mainstream Keynesian approach of the early CANDIDE Models.[37]

7 Other individual econometric models of the Canadian economy: Tsurumi and Marwah

In this section, we look at two individual efforts in modelling the Canadian economy econometrically. Some interesting ideas, which form part of the larger history of economic thinking in Canada, have resulted in consequence. In turn, these models illustrate once again that there is a role for the individual modeller–innovator who wishes to construct a representation of his/her particular vision of the economy.

A very interesting individual effort was Hiroki Tsurumi's four-sector model of the Canadian economy (Tsurumi, 1970, 1972, 1973). The version of Tsurumi's model published in 1972 had 52 behavoural equations and 34 independent identities, for a total of 86 equations. The model was estimated from annual data of the Canadian economy, by a variety of estimation techniques, such as non-linear least squares, two-stage least squares, and a variant of the two-stage least squares technique developed by J. D. Sargan to handle simultaneously the problems of autocorrelated residuals and simultaneous equations biases.[38] One distinguishing feature of Tsurumi's model was the disaggregation of the economy into four productive sectors: primary industries (agriculture, forestry and fishing); mining and manufacturing; construction; and the services sector (which includes public utilities, transport, wholesale and retail trade, finance, public administration and other services). A second distinguishing feature of Tsurumi's model was the presence of wage and price links with the US economy; hence, in addition to trade and financial influences, US wage and price variables appeared in the Canadian wage and price equations, which could be interpreted as direct wage-price links in a world of multinational corporations and international unions (beyond those reflecting a common environment with regard to demand or cost pressures).

The 52 stochastic equations of the Tsurumi model may be decomposed into four consumption functions, seven investment functions, five foreign trade functions (two export equations and three import equations), four wage equations, 11 price equations, eight ordinary production functions and capacity production functions (one of each for each of the productive sectors), one equation to explain the labour force participation rate, two interest rate equations and three other financial sector equations, three tax and transfer equations, and finally four sectoral product equations. We may briefly discuss some of these behavioural equations. The four consumption functions had as dependent variables real, per capita consumption of durables, semi-durables, non-durables, and services, respectively; the explanatory variables were real, per capita disposable income (with a distributed lag in the case of durables) and relative prices (which term was absent for consumer services and statistically insignificant in the durables equation). Turning next to the four sectoral wage functions, we note that the dependent variable was the sum of wages, salaries and supplementary labour income divided by the number of employees; the explanatory variables were the rate of unemployment (which was significant only in construction and absent in services), real output per employee, and either the consumer price index (agriculture and services) or the corresponding US wage rate. All explanatory variables had the expected signs (even when not statistically significant), and the coefficient on the corresponding US wage rate was roughly 0.75 in both the construction and the mining and manufacturing sectors, which could be interpreted (as indicated in the preceding paragraph) as reflecting independent pressures toward price synchronization. The four sectoral production functions were of the Cobb-Douglas variety, and the capacity production functions were of exactly the same kind (with the same estimated coefficients), except that the inputs were the available capital stock (rather than that utilized) and the sector's share of the available labour force (rather than the portion actually employed). Finally, we note that the equations for industry output determination were an informal translation of categories of final demand into expected sectoral real national product originating, without the benefit of an explicit input–output table. (For instance, mining and manufacturing output was explained by the sum of the three goods categories of consumption expenditures plus business fixed investment and services output was explained by disposable income (a somewhat surprising choice) and also by government services.)

The identities of Tsurumi's model were relatively straightforward and require no additional comment. The exogenous variables of the system were generally what one would expect: the level of the Canadian population and the rate of frictional unemployment, world prices (including US sectoral wages and prices), US, UK and Japanese real national incomes, the Bank of Canada discount rate and two US interest rates (one short-term and one long-term), three types of government expenditures, a time trend and two dummies, and several other minor Canadian variables, such as the inventory valuation adjustment, interest and miscellaneous investment income, income of unincorporated non-farm business, income of farm operators, and farm inventory investment. In some respects, the model gave the impression of being quite simplistic, particularly in the areas which were not its principal focus of study. Thus, for example, the consumption functions were quite rudimentary (even by the standards of the time), the industry output determination mechanism appeared quite *ad hoc* and even non-theoretical, and the direct personal taxes equation was overly simple. In addition, the rate of frictional unemployment was set at 2 per cent of the labour force, its minimum value over the entire sample period, which certainly did not allow for the possibility of over-full employment during the sample period, to say nothing of possible structural shifts of this parameter. Tsurumi's 1972 article was an ingenious application of his model to simulate the possible effects of wage parity with the United States, a burning question at that time. Finally, it should be remembered that Tusurmi built this model largely on his own, with only a $5000 research grant from the old Canada Council; judged in this light, his product was indeed impressive.

The other model surveyed in this section is Kanta Marwah's MOP-CAP Model, fitted (by two-stage least squares) to Canadian data from 1954:2 to 1971:4. MOP-CAP refers to *M*oney, *O*utput, and *P*rices, as studied (in part) through *CAP*acity equivalent ratios; as the name implies, Marwah's model had six other ratios which were analogues to the capacity utilization rate (the ratio of real GNP to capacity GNP, as measured by peak-to-peak trends) and which were drawn from each of the product, the factor and the money markets and from the government sector.[39] The model presented an innovative and provocative approach to the study of inflation. Its central core was based on the notion that, in our present market system, a series of rapidly changing short-term *demand choices* are constantly imposed on long-term *supply decisions*. The demand choices regulate the actual state of the economy, whereas the supply decisions generate its potential capabilities. By measuring the degree to which the potential capabilities are utilized at a given point of time, the capacity-equivalent ratios measured the divergence (or deviations) between the demand choices and the supply decisions. These were treated as activity variables that indicate market pressures and thereby determine the state of economic expectations and drive the entire system.

The model was definitely small-scale in nature, with only 10 behavioural equations and 12 identities. There was a heavy emphasis on the monetary sector, which was treated in five of the behavioural equations and six identities. (In this expanded analogue of the LM curve of macroeconomic theory were determined directly the components and the total of the stock of money as well as a short-term interest rate, the yield on three-month treasury bills, and the long-term government bond rate.) However the model was not strictly monetarist in nature,[40] but rather was an eclectic blend of monetarist, neo-Keynesian and long-term supply-side effects. Marwah herself regarded the model as a generalization of the textbook IS–LM schema to include factor markets so that wages (the average hourly wage in the manufacturing sector) and prices (the implicit deflator of gross national expenditure) became endogenous variables. Without entering into the details of the individual equations, we may note two interesting results which follow from the estimation of the parameters of this model. First, there appeared to be some evidence (a highly significant *t* ratio) for the existence of 'crowding out', in the sense of a perverse negative partial effect on real GNP of an increase in the realized government deficit. Secondly, there appeared to be a fair tendency of the banking system to supply more money (out of a given total of reserves) when profitability (as measured by the differential between the short-term rate of interest and the rate of change of the price level) increased. Finally, we note that Marwah simulated the model within a subperiod of the sample observations, and in general she was satisfied with its capability to reproduce the broad patterns observed in the data for several key endogenous variables. It should be noted that Marwah did not further develop this model, in part because of a structural shift in central bank policy following Governor Bouey's Saskatoon speech in September 1975.

8 Some developments in the early 1980s: Data Resources of Canada, MACE and the Conference Board of Canada

As noted in the introduction, econometric modelling has burgeoned in Canada since the beginning of the 1980s. At the July 1982 seminar at the Department of Finance, macroeconometric models represented (in addition to those already described in preceding sections) were QFS (the Quarterly Forecasting System of the Department of Finance itself), the model of Chase Econometrics of Canada, the Data Resources of Canada Model, SAM (*S*mall *A*nalytical *M*odel) of the Bank of Canada, and the MACE Model of Professor John F. Helliwell and associates from the University of British Columbia. In this section, we are going to describe a non-random sample of these additional models, namely the Data Resources Model and MACE; in addition, we shall briefly describe the two models underlying the frequent forecasts of the Conference Board of Canada.

The Data Resources of Canada Model (Hyndman, 1977) was also represented at the July 1982 symposium at the Department of Finance. Two direct antecedents of this model are the QFM of the University of Toronto (Section 5 above) and also the DRI Model of the US economy (see Chapter 5). In the 1977 version, this model has 515 equations, of which 180 are behavioural equations generally estimated from recent Canadian data by ordinary least squares (OLS). The model may be decomposed into 10 sectors (Consumption; Investment and Housing; Government; Foreign; Prices; Labour and Potential Output; Profits; GNP, Income and Savings; Financial; and Industry Output Determination). We may briefly note that foreign trade is decomposed into 10 export and 10 import categories, in order to be consistent with DRI's broader international economic information system, of which econometric models are the centre-piece. Other aspects of model structure which bear comment are the following: (1) the use, in the Prices Sector, of a detailed stages-of-processing submodel (based ultimately on work by Popkin, 1974), which accounts explicitly for the level of indirect taxation (with 148 equations, this sector is easily the largest of the entire model); (2) the use of a Cobb-Douglas production function to measure potential output of the Canadian economy, using work by J. A. Sawyer of the University of Toronto to measure the upward drift in the 'full-employment rate of unemployment' (from 3.4 per cent of the labour force in 1964 to 5.2 per cent in 1974, reflecting principally changes in the system of unemployment insurance); (3) use of an input–output submodel (similar to that of the DRI Model of the US economy or the CANDIDE Model) to explain output determination for 29 Canadian industries; and (4) an endogenous exchange rate. In the explanation of the exchange rate (the Canadian dollar price of a US dollar), significant explanatory variables include the change in the stock of international reserves (with positive changes strengthening the Canadian dollar), the sum of the current and long-term capital account balances, the differential between short-term Canadian and US interest rates, a measure of the ratio of US portfolio wealth to Canadian portfolio wealth, a polynominal distributed lag in the exchange rate itself, and two dummy variables (one for the oil embargo in the first and second quarters of 1974, and one for the election of a *Péquiste* government in Quebec during the fourth quarter of 1976 and the first quarter of 1977). All of the explanatory variables of this OLS regression (fitted to data from 1971:1 to 1977:1) have theoretically expected signs, recognizing that a positive sign denotes a weakening of the Canadian dollar (as a rise in the price of a US dollar corresponds to a decrease in the value of the Canadian dollar). This equation has its antecedents in the work of Rhomberg and the RDX2 Model, reviewed earlier in this chapter.

In applying this submodel of exchange rate determination, David McClain (1977) notes that the election of a *Péquiste* government was directly responsible for a deterioration of the value of the Canadian dollar equal roughly to two cents US. In other words, this equation suggested that the prolonged fall in the value of the Canadian dollar which began with the election of the *Parti Québécois* in Quebec was merely a correction that would have occurred in any case. McClain also projected (in October 1977) a continuing deterioration (with a cycle) of the Canadian dollar over the coming three years (up to the end of 1980), although in retrospect he underestimated the extent of this deterioration.

Next, we turn our attention to the MACE (for *MAC*ro and *E*nergy) Model of the Canadian Economy, built by John F. Helliwell and associates at the University of British Columbia's Programme in Natural Resource Economics. (See Helliwell *et al.*, 1985. A more recent version may be found in Helliwell *et al.*, 1987.) Broadly speaking, MACE is a supply-oriented model of the Canadian economy with two principal industries, one of which produces, transports, refines and distributes energy (the energy-producing sector), while the other (the energy-using sector) does everything else. An important intellectual antecedent of the MACE Model is the RDX2 Model (a natural enough linkage, in view of Helliwell's previous work), particularly with regard to the modelling of production processes and financial links. The MACE Model may be decomposed into seven sectors, of which the first five are more or less traditional in macroeconometric modelling: (1) supply and factor demands (23 equations); (2) personal and foreign expenditure on goods and services (six equations); (3) prices, wages, and national income (10 equations); balance of payments and capital movements (six equations in the portfolio model version); (5) government and private finance (15 equations); (6) an energy sector, with six sub-blocks; and (7) two blocks of linkages between the energy sector and the rest of the model (one in either direction). An indication of the scale of the model is given by the fact that (in our count) the first five model sectors contain 60 equations, of which 26 are behavioural equations. MACE is an annual model with most of the behavioural equations fitted to data over the period 1955 to 1980, usually by two-stage least squares.

We may comment in slightly more detail on the first five sectors of the model. The supply sector distinguishes three principal factors of production: labour, capital and energy, in a vintage production function in which capital and energy are first bundled in a CES (constant elasticity of substitution) representation. Then this bundle is nested within a Cobb-Douglas production function for gross output (also a CES production function, in the 1987 version of the model) in which labour in efficiency units is the other productive input. We note that the aggregate production function suggests a minuscule slow-down in productivity beginning at the end of 1976; in practical terms, the separation of the economy into energy and non-energy sectors and the inclusion of energy in the production function of the non-energy sector eliminates any appreciable reduction of total factor productivity during the 1970s, as Helliwell (1984) showed explicitly elsewhere. The key equation in the personal and foreign expenditure sector is the consumption function, in which real, per capita consumption is explained by the real, per capita level of the wage and salary bill plus government transfers to persons after an estimated correction for direct personal taxation (with a regression coefficient of 0.82), and by the real, per capita wealth of the private sector (with a marginal coefficient equal to 0.02). The key equation in the sector of prices, wages and national income would appear to be the wage equation, which explains the percentage change in the annual wage per employee of the energy-using sector as a function of lagged wage rate changes and the rate of change of prices (constrained so that the long-run effect of price changes is unity), a terms-of-trade effect (which is sizeable but apparently not statistically significant), two indicators of demand pressure, and two dummy variables which suggested downward pressure of roughly three percentage points annually for the years 1977 and 1978, reflecting former Prime Minister Trudeau's Anti-Inflation Board. In the fourth sector (balance of payments and capital movements), four alternative mechanisms are envisaged for the determination of the exchange rate: a portfolio model, parity of the nominal interest rate, purchasing power parity, and a fixed exchange rate. In the first mechanism, which is the preferred explanation, the change in the exchange rate (the Canadian dollar price of a US dollar) is negatively related to the net balance on current and long-term capital account (with credits measured with a positive sign), thus producing a depreciation of the Canadian dollar if this measure of the balance of payments turns passive. The sector of government and private finance has behavioural equations for corporate income tax-receipts (in the energy-using sector of the economy), for direct personal taxes, and for government transfers to persons; indirect taxes are the subject of an identity. Finally, we may note that the set of exogenous variables of the system includes the following policy instruments: real government expenditures on goods and services, various tax rates and receipts (such as the direct personal tax rate, the rate of indirect taxation in the energy-using sector, indirect taxes net of subsidies in the oil and gas industry and the constant term of the corporation income tax equation) and the exchange rate (in one regime).[41] Other key exogenous variables of the model include incomes abroad and prices of foreign producers, US interest rates, population variables, the natural rate of unemployment, the real supply price of capital (somewhat questionable), parameters of the production function, adjustment items, a time trend and dummy variables.

The MACE Model has had a number of fruitful applications in the area of the interaction of energy development with the rest of the economy, with potential for even more. Among the problems studied have been the results of a rise in world oil prices at the beginning of the 1980s, the effects on the Canadian economy of a restoration of an oil sands investment project, and the consequences of increased exports of natural gas. It may be noted that the MACE Model suggested that the effects of a rise in the world price of oil might not have been so deleterious to the Canadian economy (with regard to increased inflation and unemployment and reduced real growth) as those implied by the CANDIDE simulations reviewed in Section 6 above.

Finally, we may briefly summarize two models of the Conference Board of Canada, which have a common strand in their orientation towards econometric forecasting. The AERIC (for *A*pplied *E*conomic *R*esearch and *I*nformation *C*entre) Model of the Canadian economy, a quarterly model estimated by ordinary least squares to a sample period generally including the 1960s and 1970s, was of medium size, with 151 endogenous and 182 exogenous variables. Because the emphasis was on short-term forecasting (the typical forecast produced ran eight quarters into the future), there was a great emphasis placed on the precise estimation of lag structures and other dynamic aspects of the relationships. Also this orientation explains the separation of inventory investment for detailed study and the substitution, in many forecasts, of survey data on business fixed investment (after suitable adjustment) for the corresponding equations of the model.[42] The AERIC Model was largely neo-Keynesian in orientation, and so the key block of the model was that of Final Demand. The four other blocks of model equations were Inventories, Output and Employment, Income Distribution and the Financial Sector. The exogenous variables were generally what might be expected but we note that the exchange rate was exogenous in the AERIC Model, despite a managed float during most of the 1970s. (For more details on the AERIC Model, see the Conference Board in Canada, 1976.) Bodkin *et al.* (1979) found that the forecasting performance of the AERIC Model was quite satisfactory, both absolutely and in comparison to available alternatives.

Since 1982, the AERIC Model has been replaced by the Medium-Term Forecasting Model (MTFM) at the Conference Board of Canada. (See London and Stokes, 1982.)[43] The MTFM is also a quarterly model of the Canadian economy, but, with slightly more than 800 equations (of which roughly 300 are behavioural equations, fitted in general to a sample period from 1961 through 1979), it is considerably larger than the AERIC Model. The greater scope of MTFM may also be indicated by listing the 14 sectors of the model: Consumer Expenditures; Housing and Residential Construction Expenditures; Non-Residential Fixed Investment and Inventories; Government Current Expenditures; Imports; Exports; Output; Employment, Hours and Labour Force; Prices; Income Distribution; Taxes and Transfers; Financial Markets; International Capital Flows and Exchange Rates; and Energy. As this listing indicates, MTFM is more supply-oriented than was the AERIC Model; also sectoral production functions (and sectoral output constraints) play a non-trivial role in the functioning of the model. The output sector is based on an input–output submodel of industry output determination, like that of CANDIDE or the

Table 9.1 Tabular presentation of principal models surveyed

Principal model surveyed	Other versions	Scale	Method(s) of parameter estimation	Comment on exogenous variables	Important summary characteristics
1. Model IX of T.M. Brown	Models I, IIIE, VIII	Small (48 equations)	Two-stage least squares	Monetary and fiscal policy instruments available	'Habit persistence' hypothesis for the consumption function; 'trigger variable' when unemployment rate falls below 3 per cent.
2. Model XVI (Dept. of Finance)	Model XIV (Sydney May)	Small (69 equations)	OLS	Number of policy instruments on both the expenditure and taxation side	Disaggregation of consumptions; model used internally for economic forecasting.
3. Rhomberg Model		Small (19 equations)	Limited information maximum likelihood; OLS	Exogeneity of exchange rate, change in international reserves switches, depending upon exchange rate regime	Floating exchange rate modelled, so that efficacy of fiscal (and monetary) policy can be compared between fixed and floating rate regimes.
4. Bank of Canada, RDX2 (2nd half of 1970s)	RDX1 RDX2 (1st half of 1970s) RDXF	Large (516 equations)	OLS (in general)	Exogeneity limited, e.g. money supply explained by a reaction function of the monetary authorities	Additively consistent portfolio holdings model of the financial sector; openness to the US economy in a number of respects. Attention to theoretical niceties, such as the distinction between planned and unplanned inventory investment.
5. TRACE, Model IIIR (Institute for Policy Analysis of the University of Toronto)	Other variants of TRACE (more distantly, QFM and its successor, FOCUS)	Medium (183 equations)	OLS	Housing starts exogenous; rate of foreign exchange can be either exogenous or endogenous, depending on regime in force	Medium-term in outlook; Canadian 'representative' to project LINK for many years; many specific studies.

Table 9.1 Tabular presentation of principal models surveyed continued

Principal model surveyed	Other versions	Scale	Method(s) of parameter estimation	Comment on exogenous variables	Important summary characteristics
6. CANDIDE Model 1.1	CANDIDE 1.0, 1.2M, 2.0, 3.0, TIM	Very large (over 2000 equations)	OLS and variants	Owing to anterior population submodel, only basic aspects of population (e.g. crude fertility rate) are exogenous	Integration of two rectangular input–output submodels into main model. Industrial output detail. Medium-term outlook. Originally, inter-organizational cooperation.
7. Tsurumi's 4-Sector Model	(Several variants)	Small (less than 100 equations)	Gamma distributed lags; two-stage least squares and variants; non-linear least squares OLS, with Almon lags	Many US variables included here	Four producing sectors of the economy: primary industries, manufacturing and mining, construction, services; used to simulate effects of wage parity with the USA.
8. Data Resources of Canada Model, 1977 version	(Has as antecedents QFM and DRI Model of US economy); several versions	Large (515 equations)		Foreign variables formally exogenous, but model is designed to be operated in tandem with DRI's broader international economics information system	Stage-of-processing submodel of final demand prices; use of I/O submodel to explain industrial output determination. Model oriented towards usefulness to clients.
9. MACE (*MAC*ro and *E*nergy), John Helliwell and Associates at the University of British Columbia		Medium (when all seven model sectors are included)	Two-stage least squares, and other techniques	Include a number of policy instruments and (more questionably) real supply price of capital	Basic distinction of the economy between energy-producing and energy-using sectors; neat explanation of apparent downtrend in productivity growth after 1975.
10. Medium-Term Forecasting Model (MTFM) of the Conference Board of Canada	AERIC Model (antecedent)	Large (over 800 equations)	OLS	Dummy variable on the election of a *Péquiste* government in Quebec suggested a modest effect of this event in depreciating the external value of the Canadian dollar	Medium-term outlook (as the acronym suggests); model oriented towards forecasting, both in short run and in medium term (standard horizon is 20 quarters).

Data Resources of Canada Model; the real gross domestic product originating in 21 industries (and also public administration and defence) is so determined. Industrial price formation is essentially determined in a stage-of-processing prices submodel. As indicated above, in MTFM the exchange rate is endogenous (in contrast to the treatment in the AERIC Model), and it is interesting to note that the Conference Board's estimate of the depressing effect on the Canadian dollar of the election of a *Péquiste* government in Quebec is very close to that of the Data Resources of Canada Model; the coefficient of this dummy variable suggested that the direct effect of this event was to raise the Canadian dollar price of a US dollar by rough 1 ¾ cents. Finally, we note that MTFM is certainly more medium-term in orientation (as the acronym implies), especially with regard to forecasting and conditional simulations; in particular, the standard forecast horizon with MTFM is 20 quarters or five years.

9   Conclusions

Macroeconometric model-building has flourished in Canada, aided by a judicious balance of governmental and private support. Private support has by no means been limited to university research; in the past decade, consulting firms, sparked by the traditional profit motive, have made very useful contributions to the development of this discipline. The authors are aware of the difficulties of recording the romance of econometric model-building, as distinct from the dry bones of external events, yet romance there has been, and the excitement and *esprit de corps* in some of the workplaces turning out pioneering efforts has at least been mentioned.

As noted in the introduction, macroeconometric modelling in Canada was already well developed in the mid-1960s, when Marc Nerlove wrote his well-known survey article (1966). After more than two decades, Canada appears to have, at a minimum, kept up with developments in this fast-moving field. Canadians can be justly proud of a number of innovations that have been made in macroeconometric models of the Canadian economy, such as work on the determinants of a floating exchange rate (beginning with Rhomberg in 1964) or the use of full model simulations as a validation device, which was employed by the builders of the RDX1 Model in the late 1960s. More generally, Canada appears to have been almost an ideal environment for the construction of important model-building efforts: while the intellectual environment has benefited from the important stock of intellectual capital of American society (which has been readily available to Canadian model-builders), the objective conditions of the Canadian economy are and have been quite different, in a number of important respects, from those of the US economy. This unique combination of a similar intellectual milieu and different objective circumstances has been quite favourable to progress in econometric model-building. Moreover, to the extent that Canadian conditions are more similar to those in other developed economies (and also to those in some of the developing countries), results obtained in econometric modelling in Canada can be (and have been) readily generalized on the international scene. Table 9.1 shows the principal models we have considered.

As this chapter is already quite long, we shall save the reader a detailed prognosis (forecast?) of future developments in this field. (See, however, Chapter 17 below; we anticipate that Canada will continue to benefit from innovations available generally to the scholarly community.) At this point, all indications suggest that this will be one of the leading sectors of economic research for many years to come; we expect the macroeconometric models of 20 years from now to be as much an improvement over present efforts as these have been with regard to the pioneering efforts of T. M. Brown, May, and Rhomberg.

Notes

1. As Waslander pointed out in a letter, the model comparison work was done principally in 1975, the delayed publication resulting from the usual lags of the publication process in scholarly journals.
2. A related subject is the history of macroeconomic forecasting in Canada, which is the subject of a stimulating study by Mervin Daub (1985), which was later incorporated in his book (Daub, 1987). As Sawyer has remarked in a comment on Daub's work, one might well wish to make the distinction between the macroeconometric model (even as a generator of forecasts) and the forecasts themselves (which of course need not be econometric in origin). Some forecasters have even been known to make the bases of their forecasts obscure, even when these are econometric in origin, in an attempt to render their services more appealing and hence more profitable, at least in the short run. Of course, this can be at the expense of scholarship and the contribution to our knowledge in this area.
3. Uebe *et al.* (1988) indicate that there are indeed a number of macroeconometric models of Canada that have been built outside Canada, such as the one built by the Economic Planning Agency of Japan. (See also Chapter 10 below.)
4. The argument is developed more fully in Brown (1952). It is interesting to note that the consumption function of Model IIIE is identical to that of the *Econometrica* article, which itself is embedded in a small scale econometric model of two behavioural equations and two identities.
5. For the import demand function, the postwar shift is actually negative, while a smooth time trend is used in the equation for wage rate adjustment.
6. In a note written to Ronald G. Bodkin on 6 May 1970, T. Merritt Brown stated that he regarded the three models described in his *Specification and Uses* book (Brown, 1970a) as more 'straightforward' than Model VIII (described in Brown, 1964), particularly the third one (Model IX), for which he felt that the specification and theoretical formulations were better respected. (He also indicated that he preferred the model constructed for the Royal Commission on Health Services (Brown, 1965) to Model VIII.)
7. According to Daub (1985), a marked change in the willingness of Federal government departments to make their aggregative economic forecasts available occurred after the late 1950s, as a result of the 'Diefenbaker Affair'. This refers to the incident in which the new Conservative government (first elected in 1957) claimed to have found a confiden-

tial forecast of a forthcoming recession, which they accused the predecessor Liberal government of doing nothing to counteract. To this day, according to Daub, some Canadian federal government departments appear to be wary of macroeconomic forecasts, possibly as a result of this experience.

8. May's model and study are summarized in Bert G. Hickman's (1969) international survey of the macroeconometric models of 10 countries. Hickman presents a nice summary of the 12 econometric models represented (the United States and Australia were represented by two models), before proceeding to the comparative multiplier properties of these models. Hickman found enough of a convergence of the several multipliers (both impact and medium-term multipliers) to conclude that 'modern mixed enterprise systems are characterized by stable response mechanisms and small dynamic multipliers'. It seems unlikely that a current study would find as much convergence in an analogous international sample, as even multiplier estimates from different econometric models of the same country may show points of divergence, as indicated by the symposium on Canadian models in the May 1979 issue of the *Canadian Journal Models of Economics*, mentioned in the introduction to this chapter.

9. In closing this section, it is worth mentioning Leo Bakony's 1959 econometric model of Canada, which was an offshoot of his doctoral dissertation at the University of Washington. As summarized in Nerlove (1966), Bakony's model had 10 behavioural equations, fitted by ordinary least squares to the period 1947:2 to 1958:2, along with two identities. This model incorporated much of the Klein–Goldberger specifications, along with T. M. Brown's habit persistence hypothesis for the consumption function. Nevertheless, as Nerlove notes, the model gives the impression of an intermediate or even incomplete product. (For example, the capital stock is exogenous, even though both gross investment and depreciation are determined within the model.) Still, Bakony continued his work on econometric modelling of the Canadian economy, particularly at the Economic Council of Canada during the mid-1960s. Later versions of this model stressed the determination of potential output (see Bakony, 1967), which was a focal point of policy analysis at the Economic Council during its first years.

10. According to the self-criticism that Rhomberg performed in a later publication (1966) these three equations were apparently the most subject to structural change, a result that has been corroborated by unpublished student papers written in 1982 for a course taught by Bodkin on 'Models for Economic Policy'.

11. It is this equation which gives a tremendous sensitivity of the capital account of the balance of payments to upward movements in Canadian interest rates, which in turn means that, during the sample period at least, fiscal stimulation would imply an upward movement of the exchange rate (appreciation of the Canadian dollar), as the credits on the capital account more than offset the deterioration of the current account, rather than a depreciation; this in turn would deaden the effects of fiscal stimulation. This is a result which emerges both in the theoretical prototype model and in the Rhomberg model itself.

12. Of course, there will be indirect effects through all the other equations of the simultaneous system, particularly the balance of payments identity.

13. Mention might also be made of Rhomberg's subsequent study (1966), in which an annualized, updated and corrected version of his 1964 model was used to study the evolution of Canada's balance of payments and its national product during the 1960–4 period. Rhomberg found substantial (favourable) effects of the policy-induced depreciation of the Canadian dollar on both the current account balance and on Canadian real national income.

14. This is not to imply that Lawrence H. Officer played the leading role in the development of the RDX1 and RDX2 sequence of models. This honour, it appears, must go to John F. Helliwell, according to a number of reactions to an earlier draft of this chapter, on the part of knowledgeable individuals. Moreover Professor Helliwell was one of the authors of the 1979 *CJE* comparative models symposium, and, as we shall see in Section 8 below, has continued to do innovative work in the 1980s. Interestingly, the remaining two principal authors of the RDX1 Model, Harold T. Shapiro and Ian A.

Stewart, both developed econometric models of Canada as their doctoral dissertations, but in their two cases (as contrasted to that of Lawrence H. Officer) the dissertations were not subsequently published. Nevertheless it may be presumed that their work also found a subsequent input, at least in part, in the RDX sequence of models.

15. Thus Courchene (1981) remarks:

> Moreover, it is possible to view the development in the mid-1960s of the Bank of Canada's econometric model and the accompanying input of consultants from the academic world as an attempt to smooth over the rift that had developed between the economists and the Bank.

By contrast, Daub (1985) views the Bank models as an important integrating device in the research strategy of this organization. Of course, these two explanations are not mutually exclusive.

16. See Helliwell *et al.* (1969b) pp. 383–4. Certainly, we have not found any *published* reference to this technique of model construction prior to 1969.

17. Other important exogenous variables included US interest rates, world economic activity, world trade prices, demographic variables, tax rates (and some tax receipts), a number of financial variables, dummy variables (including seasonal dummies), and time trends.

18. After 16 quarters, the interim (dynamic) multipliers remained as high as 2.13 (for the 16-period simulation starting in the first quarter of 1958) or 2.72 (for the 1964 simulation).

19. In our classification, we should prefer to call equation 16.4 of Helliwell *et al.* (1971) an identity rather than a behavioural equation, as no fitted parameters are involved in determining the required cash reserve ratio of the chartered banks.

20. These can be broken down into 161 behavioural equations, 164 ordinary identities, and 191 tax structure equations.

21. In other respects, the broad nature of the exogenous variables is similar to that of the RDX1 model.

22. Consumption is explained by a variant of the permanent income hypothesis, with private sector wealth and income distribution playing additional roles. Residential construction is (as in RDX1) quite sensitive to financial factors and to mortgage approvals (generated by the financial sector) in particular. Business fixed capital formation is explained by the production function model alluded to in the text, with additional hypotheses to generate desired stocks of plant capital and equipment capital, which are then translated into actual investment in business plant and in machinery and equipment (separately), via a stock adjustment mechanism. Exports, imports and (most) government expenditures are determined endogenously also.

23. Thus we have the interesting phenomenon of one section (the Research Department) of a large organization modelling the behaviour of another section (the decison-making authorities), an approach that raises a number of philosophical issues (such as those concerned with determinism and free will) that we shall not attempt to resolve here.

24. The graph on p. 167 of de Bever and Maxwell (1979) yields another interpretation, namely that the sustained increase in government expenditures might induce explosive fluctuations in the economy in this context. De Bever and Maxwell argue that this interpretation is not appropriate, and we are inclined to agree.

25. In contrast to the forecasts of private forecasting services (or those of the Conference Board of Canada), the forecasts on the basis of RDXF have not been published or even circulated privately, to the best of our knowledge. Indeed, although most of the equations of RDXF have been published in Technical Report 25, three critical equations have been omitted, namely that for demand deposits and currency (M1), that for the spot rate of foreign exchange in a floating rate regime, and that for the official excess demand for foreign exchange.

26. This is of course not to imply that the production of a defensible *ex ante* forecast of the economy is not a scholarly activity, as a great amount of systematic (and even ingeni-

ous) thinking must go into the preparation of such a forecast. In addition, much can be learned from this sort of periodic exercise, as the experience of Wharton EFA in the United States and the London Graduate School of Business Model Group in the United Kingdom demonstrates, along with the experience of the Institute for Policy Analysis itself. However the relatively large amount of sheer legwork probably implies that a strictly academic institution does not have a comparative advantage in this area, at least in the Canadian context.

27.   For Mark I, two-stage least squares estimation with principal components was employed; the experiments of Nelawi (1977) suggest that this does not make a major difference.

28.   Interestingly, this variable was endogenous in Mark I, as it is in a number of other Canadian econometric models.

29.   The reason for this is that the capital inflow effect is not nearly so large in TRACE as it was in Rhomberg's model, with the consequence that the exchange rate depreciates (rather than appreciates) under fiscal stimulus in a flexible rate regime, with an additional fillip to the multiplier. With Mark IVE, this effect takes four years to show up, as reported in Foot and Sawyer (1979).

30.   Even in the context of the dynamic 'real' multiplier, QFM appeared to display extreme behaviour as its peak was higher and its descent more rapid than those of the other three models represented in this cross-models symposium. (See Helliwell *et al.*, 1979.) Accordingly, QFM had the lowest terminal (10-year) dynamic multiplier and was, in fact, the only one of the four models examined to have had a negative tenth year multiplier. (This is not patently ridiculous, as the 'correct' structure of the economy might conceivably be cyclical.)

31.   See McCracken (1973) for a fairly detailed description of the first model of the CANDIDE Project, Model 1.0. Further details of Model 1.0 may be found in CANDIDE Project Papers nos 2 to 17.

32.   The *esprit de corps* that existed in those early days appears to have been virtually unbelievable; teams worked well into the night to ensure that model sectors would be available by the deadlines set. Some of this story is also retold in Daub (1985).

33.   In practice, with medium-term (five to 10 years) projections into the future, the values of most of the US exogenous variables were obtained from similar projections of the Wharton Annual and Industry Forecasting Model, an econometric model of the US economy fairly similar in spirit and structure to the CANDIDE Model. See Preston (1972).

34.   In principle, the exchange rate was an endogenous variable in Model 1.1, at least when the country was operating in a floating rate regime. In practice, this mechanism functioned rather poorly (that is, failed to track at all well the experienced exchange rate during the historical sample period) and so the model was always operated in a fixed exchange rate mode for non-experimental simulations. It is our understanding that some progress with regard to modelling the exchange rate was made in Model 2.0 (see Preston *et al.*, 1979) following some developments in the literature.

35.   For prime-age (25 to 54 years) males, the rate of labour force participation is exogenous in Model 1.1.

36.   In practice, this sector was used only for projections into the future, as known population values were substituted for the results of this sector in simulations of historical periods.

37.   According to one of our commentators, the increasingly monetarist nature of Model 3.0 was due in part to cross-fertilization from the SAM (Small *A*nalytical *M*odel) of the Bank of Canada. (For a summary description of SAM, see Grady Economics and Associates, 1985.)

38.   A technical point is that Tsurumi favours the Gamma distributed lag, and uses this form of distributed lag (in preference to the Koyck or Almon) wherever a distributed lag is appropriate. It should be noted that, almost two decades later, Tsurumi's Gamma distributed lag does not appear to have passed into widespread use.

39.   Other capacity-like ratios studied in the model included the ratio of employment to the

labour force (the complement of the actual unemployment rate), the ratio of the actual budget surplus (excluding transfer payments) to its high employment value, the traditional income velocity of money (the ratio of nominal GNP to the stock of money), and the 'density of money' (the ratio of the 'potential' supply of money to the actual level). (The 'potential' supply of money is the maximum amount that can be created, given existing currency holdings, total reserves in the system, and legal reserve ratios.) The remaining two ratios were the peak price relative and the peak wage relative; these are respectively the ratios of actual levels of the price index and the wage rate to their corresponding peak-to-peak trends.

40. In this regard, it is comparable to the early efforts of Thomas J. Courchene and Alex K. Kelly (1971) in modelling the Canadian macroeconomy econometrically, which, however, is monetarist in inspiration but incorporates a number of mainstream Keynesian ideas.

41. As estimated, the MACE Model offers no apparent 'handles' for monetary policy because, following the RDX2 treatment, a key instrument of monetary policy (high-powered money) has been made endogenous through the use of a reaction function. In simulation, however, the supply of high-powered money can be treated as an exogenous variable, in which case the equation for the demand for money should be inverted to determine (proximately) the short-term rate of interest.

42. This is a forecasting technique that is already more than two decades old; Suits (1962) mentions this method in discussing his forecasts with his own model, a successor to the Klein–Goldberger Model, discussed in Chapter 3 above.

43. A good description of the MTFM Model may also be found in Grady Economics and Associates (1985) especially pp. 22–4.

References

Bakony, L. I. (1959) 'A Quarterly Econometric Model of the Canadian Economy', abstract of a paper given at the Chicago Meeting of the Econometric Society, 27–29 December 1958, *Econometrica*, vol. 27, no. 2 (April) pp. 296–7.

_____ (1967) 'A Medium-Term Model of Canada: A Prospectus', Economic Council of Canada, mimeographed paper, April 1966, revised June 1967.

Bank of Canada (1976a) *The Equations of RDX2 Revised and Estimated to 4Q72*, Bank of Canada Technical Report No. 6 (Ottawa).

_____ (1976b) *A Sectoral Analysis of RDX2 Estimated to 4Q72*, Bank of Canada Technical Report No. 6 (Ottawa).

_____ (1981a) *The Equations of RDXF, September 1980 Version*, Bank of Canada Technical Report No. 25 (Ottawa).

_____ (1981b) *The Structure and Dynamics of RDXF, September 1980 Version*, Bank of Canada Technical Report No. 26 (Ottawa).

Bodkin, Ronald G. and Frank T. Denton (1970) 'Report on Medium-Term Economic Models', mimeographed, January.

Bodkin, Ronald G. and Stephen M. Tanny (eds) (1975) *CANDIDE Model 1.1*, CANDIDE Project Paper No. 18, Vol. 1 (Ottawa: Information Canada).

Bodkin, Ronald G., and André Cournoyer (1978) 'Legislation and the Labour Market: A Selective Review of Canadian Studies', pp. 62–89 in Herbert G. Grubel and Michael A. Walker (eds), *Unemployment Insurance: Global Evidence of its Effects on Unemployment* (Vancouver: The Fraser Institute).

Bodkin, Ronald G., Victoria Cano-Lamy, Edward Chow, Jean Fortin, Leslie Gunaratne, John Kuiper and Christine Serrurier (1979) '*Ex Ante* Forecasting of the Canadian Economy', *Journal of Post Keynesian Economics*, vol. 1, no. 3 (Spring) pp. 16–40.

Brown, T. M. (1952) 'Habit Persistence and Lags in Consumer Behaviour', *Econometrica*, vol. 20, no. 3 (July) pp. 355–71.

_____ (1964) 'A Forecast Determination of National Product, Employment, and Price Level in Canada, from an Econometric Model', pp. 59–96 in *Models of Income Determi-*

nation, vol. 28 of Studies in Income and Wealth (Princeton, NJ: Princeton University Press) for the National Bureau of Economic Research.

_____ (1965) *Canadian Economic Growth*, Study for the Royal Commission on Health Services (Ottawa: Queen's Printer).

_____ (1970a) *Specification and Uses of Econometric Models* (Toronto: The Macmillan Company of Canada Limited).

_____ (1970b) Note to Ronald G. Bodkin, dated 6 May 1970.

Carr, J. L., G. V. Jump and J. A. Sawyer (1976) 'The Operation of the Canadian Economy under Fixed and Flexible Exchange Rates: Simulation Results from the TRACE Model', *Canadian Journal of Economics*, vol. 9, no. 1 (February) pp. 102–20.

Caves, Richard E. and Richard H. Holton (1959) *The Canadian Economy: Prospect and Retrospect* (Cambridge, Mass.: Harvard University Press) especially pp. 129–40.

Choudhry, Nanda K., Yehuda Kotowitz, John A. Sawyer and John W. L. Winder (1972) *The TRACE Econometric Model of the Canadian Economy* (Toronto and Buffalo: University of Toronto Press).

Conference Board in Canada (1976) *The AERIC Short-Term Quarterly Forecasting Model of the Canadian Economy*, revised edn (Ottawa: The Conference Board in Canada).

Courchene, Thomas J. (1981) 'The Interaction Between Economic Theory and Bank of Canada Policy', pp. 147–89 in David C. Smith (ed.), *Economic Policy Advising in Canada* (Montreal: C. D. Howe Institute).

Courchene, Thomas J. and Alex K. Kelly (1971) 'Money Supply and Money Demand: An Econometric Analysis for Canada', *Journal of Money, Credit, and Banking*, vol. 3, no. 2, part 1 (May) pp. 219–44.

Daub, M. (1985) 'A History of Canadian Aggregate Economic Forecasting', *Journal of Business Administration*, vol. 15, no. 1/2 (Autumn) pp. 377–83.

Daub, Mervin (1987) *Canadian Economic Forecasting in a World Where All's Unsure* (Kingston, Ontario: McGill-Queen's University Press).

de Bever, Leo and Tom Maxwell (1979) 'An Analysis of Some of the Dynamic Properties of RDX2', *Canadian Journal of Economics*, vol. 12, no. 2 (May) pp. 162–70.

de Bever, L., U. Kohli and T. Maxwell (1978) *An Analysis of the Major Dynamic Properties of RDX2*, Bank of Canada Technical Report No. 13 (Ottawa, June).

de Bever, L., D. K. Foot, J. F. Helliwell, G. V. Jump, T. Maxwell, J. A. Sawyer and H. E. L. Waslander (1979) 'Dynamic Properties of Four Canadian Macroeconomic Models: A Collaborative Research Project', *Canadian Journal of Economics*, vol. 12, no. 2 (May) pp. 133–9.

Dungan, Peter and Joan Head (1982) 'The Response of FOCUS to Various Monetary Policy, Fiscal Policy and Exchange Rate Shocks', paper presented to a seminar at the Department of Finance, July.

Economic Council of Canada (1972) *The Years to 1980*, Ninth Annual Review (Ottawa: Information Canada).

_____ (1979) *Two Cheers for the Eighties*, Sixteenth Annual Review (Hull, Quebec: Supply and Services Canada).

Foot, David K. and John A. Sawyer (1979) 'Some Dynamic Properties of the TRACE Model', *Canadian Journal of Economics*, vol. 12, no. 2 (May) pp. 170–81.

Grady Economics and Associates Ltd. (1985) *The State of the Art in Canadian Macroeconomic Modelling*. report prepared for the Economic Forecasting Division, Department of Finance, Government of Canada, Ottawa, March.

Helliwell, John F. (1976) 'Trade, Capital Flows and Migration as Channels for the International Transmission of Stabilization Policies', pp. 241–78 in Ando, Herring and Marston (eds), *International Aspects of Stabilization Policies*, Conference Series No. 12 (Boston: Federal Reserve Bank of Boston).

_____ (1984) 'Stagflation and Productivity Decline in Canada, 1974–82', *Canadian Journal of Economics*, vol. 17, no. 2 (May) pp. 191–216.

Helliwell, John F., T. Maxwell and H. E. L. Waslander (1979) 'Comparing the Dynamics of Canadian Macromodels', *Canadian Journal of Economics*, vol. 12, no. 2 (May) pp. 181–94.

Helliwell, John F., Lawrence H. Officer, Harold T. Shapiro and Ian. A. Stewart (1969a) *The Structure of RDX1*, Staff Research Study No. 3 of the Bank of Canada (Ottawa: Bank of Canada).

_____ (1969b) 'Econometric Analysis of Policy Choices for an Open Economy', *Review of Economics and Statistics*, vol. 51, no. 4 (November) pp. 383–98.

_____ (1969c) *The Dynamics of RDX1*, Staff Research Study No. 5 of the Bank of Canada (Ottawa: Bank of Canada).

Helliwell, J. F., F. W. Gorbet, G. R. Sparks and I. A. Stewart (1973) 'Comprehensive Linkage of Large Models: Canada and the United States', pp. 395–426 in R. J. Ball (ed.), *The International Linkage of National Economic Models* (Amsterdam and London/New York: North-Holland/American Elsevier Publishing Company).

Helliwell, John F., Mary E. MacGregor, Robert N. McRae, André Plourde and Alan Chung (1987) 'Supply-Oriented Macroeconomics: The MACE Model of Canada', *Economic Modelling*, vol. 4, no. 3 (July) pp. 318–40.

Helliwell, John F., Harold T. Shapiro, Gordon R. Sparks, Ian A. Stewart, Frederick W. Gorbet and Donald R. Stephenson (1971) *The Structure of RDX2*, Parts 1 and 2, Staff Research Study No. 7 of the Bank of Canada (Ottawa: Bank of Canada).

Helliwell, John F., Robert N. McRae, Paul Boothe, Ardo Hansson, Michael Margolick, Tim Padmore, André Plourde and Reg Plummer (1985) 'Energy and the National Economy: An Overview of the MACE Model', pp. 17–85 in Anthony Scott (ed.), *Progress in Natural Resource Economics* (Oxford: Clarendon Press).

Hickman, Bert G. (1969) 'Dynamic Properties of Macroeconometric Models: An International Comparison', Chapter Thirteen (pp. 393–435) of Martin Bronfenbrenner (ed.), *Is the Business Cycle Obsolete?*, volume based on a conference of the Social Science Research Council Committee on Economic Stability (New York: John Wiley).

Houthakker, H. S. and Lester D. Taylor (1970) *Consumer Demand in the United States: Analyses and Projections*, 2nd edn (Cambridge, Mass.: Harvard University Press).

Hyndman, R. M. (1977) *The Data Resources Model of the Canadian Economy* (Toronto: Data Resources of Canada, November).

Institute for Policy Analysis [of the University of Toronto] (1977) *FOCUS: Quarterly Forecasting and User Simulation Model of the Canadian Economy* (Toronto: Institute for Policy Analysis, November).

Jump, Gregory V. (1972) *The University of Toronto Quarterly Econometric Forecasting Model: A Description of its Real Sector* (Toronto: Institute for Policy Analysis of the University of Toronto, April).

_____ (1979) 'The Quarterly Forecasting Model', *Canadian Journal of Economics*, vol. 12, no. 2 (May) pp. 150–61.

Kuiper, J. (1970) 'Model XVI – An Econometric Model of the Canadian Economy', mimeographed, Department of Finance of the Government of Canada, February.

London, A. and E. Stokes (1982) *The Medium-Term Forecasting Model (MTFM): An Overview* (Ottawa: The Conference Board of Canada, June).

Marwah, K. (1978) 'Towards Money, Output and Prices: A Capacity View of Inflation (MOP-CAP)', *Empirical Economics*, vol. 3, no. 1, pp. 1–29.

Matuszewski, T. (1970) 'Rapport au Comité provisoire sur les modèles économiques à moyen terme', mimeographed, Laboratoire d'économétrie, Université Laval, 19 January.

Maxwell, T. (1978) 'A Primer on RDX2', *Bank of Canada Review*, January, pp. 3–10.

May, Sydney (1966) 'Dynamic Multipliers and their Use for Fiscal Decision-Making', pp. 155–87 of *Conference on Stabilization Policies*, convened by the Economic Council of Canada (Ottawa: Queen's Printer).

McClain, David (1977) 'Quebec, Energy and the Outlook for the Canadian Dollar to 1980', *Canadian Review* [of Data Resources of Canada] vol. 1, no. 6 (October) pp. 41–8.

McClain, David and Kathryn Riepe (1977) 'The Data Resources Model [of the Exchange Rate] of the Canadian Economy', *Canadian Review*, vol. 1, no. 6 (October) pp. 49–50.

McCracken, M. C. (1973) *An Overview of CANDIDE Model 1.0*, CANDIDE Project Paper No. 1 (Ottawa: Information Canada).

Nelawi, Joseph E. (1977) 'Consistent Estimation of Real Econometric Models with Undersized Samples: A Study of the TRACE (Mk IIIR) Econometric Model of the Canadian Economy', *International Economic Review*, vol. 18, no. 1 (February) pp. 163–79.

Nerlove, Marc (1966) 'A Tabular Survey of Macro-Econometric Models', *International Economic Review*, vol. 7, no. 2 (May) pp. 127–75.

Officer, Lawrence H. (1968) *An Econometric Model of Canada Under the Fluctuating Exchange Rate* (Cambridge, Mass.: Harvard University Press).

O'Reilly, Brian, Graydon Paulin and Philip Smith (1983) *Responses of Various Econometric Models to Selected Policy Shocks*, Bank of Canada Technical Report No. 38 (Ottawa, July).

Popkin, Joel (1974) 'Consumer and Wholesale Prices in a Model of Price Behavior by Stage of Processing', *Review of Economics and Statistics*, vol. 56, no. 4 (November) pp. 486–501.

Preston, Ross S. (1972) *The Wharton Annual and Industry Forecasting Model* (Philadelphia: Economics Research Unit of the University of Pennsylvania).

Preston, R. S., C. Braithwaite, B. Cain, D. Desaulniers, B. L. Eyford, S. Gilby, B. K. Lodh, P. Nevin, J. E. Ramin, P. S. Rao, H. M. Saiyed, C. St. Jean, T. T. Schweitzer, J. D. Whillans and M. Willis, *CANDIDE Model 2.0: Model Description*, Volumes One and Two (Ottawa: Economic Council of Canada, October).

Rhomberg, Rudolf R. (1964) 'A Model of the Canadian Economy under Fixed and Fluctuating Exchange Rates', *Journal of Political Economy*, vol. 72, no. 1 (February) pp. 1–31.

_____ (1966) 'Effects of Exchange Depreciation in Canada, 1960–64', pp. 99–125 in *Conference on Stabilization Policies*, convened by the Economic Council of Canada (Ottawa: Queen's Printer).

Sawyer, John A. (1984) letter dated 4 December to Ronald G. Bodkin.

Sawyer, J. A., J. L. Carr, N. K. Choudhry, G. V. Jump, Y. Kotowitz and J. W. L. Winder (1976) 'The TRACE Mark IIIR Annual Model of the Canadian Economy', Chapter 7 (pp. 115–60) in Jean Waelbroeck (ed.) *The Models of Project LINK* (Amsterdam, New York and Oxford: North-Holland).

Siedule, Tom, Nicholas Skoulas and Keith Newton (1976) *The Impact of Economy-Wide Changes on the Labour Force: An Econometric Analysis* (Ottawa: Supply and Services Canada).

Suits, Daniel B. (1962) 'Forecasting and Analysis with an Econometric Model', *American Economic Review*, vol. 52, no. 2 (March) pp. 104–32.

Tsurumi, Hiroki (1970) 'A Four-Sector Econometric Model of The Canadian Economy', Discussion Paper No. 8 of the Institute for Economic Research of Queen's University, mimeographed.

_____ (1972) 'Effects of Wage-Parity and Prices Synchronization between Canada and the United States on Canadian Economic Growth: Simulation Experiments with a Macro-Model', *International Economic Review*, vol. 13, no. 3 (October) pp. 644–78.

_____ (1973) 'A Survey of Recent Canadian Macro-Econometric Models', *Canadian Journal of Economics*, vol. 6, no. 3 (August) pp. 409–28.

Uebe, Goetz, Georg Huber and Joachim Fischer (1988) *Macro-Econometric Models: An International Bibliography* (Aldershot: Gower).

Waslander, H. E. L. (1979) 'The Dynamic Properties of CANDIDE Model 1.2', *Canadian Journal of Economics*, vol. 12, no. 2 (May) pp. 139–50.

10 Econometric models of the Japanese economy
Kazuo Sato*

1 Introduction

Since the pioneering work of Jan Tinbergen (1939; see also Chapter 6 above), macroeconometric model-building has gone through a history of half a century. Like the career of a professional, its evolution exhibited three successive stages of growth, namely, learning, practice and maturity.

This pattern of evolution is very clear in the case of the United States, the forerunner in this field. Stage 1 was from the late 1940s to the 1950s, the era of small annual models, the most celebrated of which was Klein and Goldberger (1955). With the accumulation of more time-series data and the rapid improvement of computer capability, stage 2 began and continued through the 1960s, the era of large-scale quarterly models, the most prominent of which was the Brookings model (Duesenberry *et al.*, 1965). In stage 3, the 1970s and onward, these models were put to practical use. A few commercial forecasting services were set up. Also, national models were linked together in order to analyse and predict the international transmission mechanism of economic activity (see Chapter 14 below).

Serious pursuits of macroeconometric model-building were introduced into Japan in the late 1950s, some 10 years later than in the United States. This initial time lag, however, was very quickly eliminated as Japan's econometric profession moved forward through the next quarter century. Thus, in Japan, stage 1 ran from the late 1950s to the early 1960s, stage 2 was concentrated in the late 1960s, and stage 3 has continued thereafter. By now, it may be that, outside of the United States, model-building as an activity flourishes most in Japan.

This paper documents Japan's history of model-building in a chronological order. The three stages are reviewed successively in Sections 2, 3 and 4. The current state of model-building and economic forecasting is examined in Section 5. A tabular survey of the leading contemporary macroeconometric models is given in the appendix.

*The period up to 1979 was covered in my earlier survey (Sato, 1981); the present survey brings it up to 1988. In preparing this updated version, I owe special thanks to Professor A. Amano, C. Moriguchi, M. Saito and S. Shishido for helping me to fill many missing gaps in my literature search. There are many model-builders in Japan who supplied materials for both surveys – too numerous to be named here individually. I wish to thank them collectively.

2   The first stage: learning

In model-building efforts, Japan was initially about 10 years behind the United States. Some reasons for this lag were that, owing to disruptions in academic life through the Second World War, Keynesian macroeconomics did not reach the mainstream of the economics profession until later, that econometrics was an unknown subdiscipline of economics, and that not enough statistical data were available.

As regards macroeconomic theory, it took time for Keynesian theory to take root in Japan. Though the policy of aggregate demand management was put into practice by Finance Minister Korekiyo Takahashi in 1932, prior to the appearance of Keynes's *General Theory* (1936), the general public was not sufficiently exposed to Keynes's new ideas. Though Keynes's preface to the Japanese edition of his book was dated 4 December 1936, a year after his original preface, the Japanese edition appeared on 15 December 1941, a week after Pearl Harbor! The second printing was released in August 1942, but then the book remained out of print until the third printing appeared in May 1949. Keynesian macroeconomics had to wait until the 1950s before being popularized.[1]

As for econometric theory, the quantitative approach was unfamiliar before the Second World War. The discipline of economic statistics was under the heavy influence of the German Historical School, which emphasized a complete enumeration of the population. While sampling theory was known in mathematical statistics, it was anathema to economic statisticians in Japan. As for applied econometrics, there were some early attempts at estimation of demand functions, but this activity belonged to a very small minority.

With regard to statistical data, it goes without saying that national income statistics are indispensable to macroeconometric model-building. Though there were earlier attempts at national income estimation before the Second World War, it was in the early 1950s that the national income and product accounts came to be officially prepared on a continuing basis by the Economic Planning Agency (EPA).[2] The first official report for the year 1951 was published in 1953. The official annual data cover the period of 1930–44 and 1946 onwards. Quarterly data first became available in the second quarter of 1951. The data base was initially meagre, and econometricians had to wait about 10 years before they could embark on any full-scale model-building exercises for the postwar period.

With the country cut off from international cultural exchanges through the Second World War, Japanese economists of the older generation found themselves quite behind the times. There was a great deal of catching up to do. The quickest way to fill the gap was to study abroad, so many economics students went to the United States for graduate study from the early 1950s on when such opportunities opened up. The 1950s were thus a period of importing and digestion of economic theory and econometrics.[3]

The acquired knowledge had to be applied to practice. It is no coincidence that model-building began to be practised in earnest in Japan in the late 1950s. As a matter of fact, the inception of model-building can be dated a few years earlier. The very first model-building attempt was due to Isamu Yamada (1948) of the Institute of Economic Research of Hitotsubashi University. A little later, Shozaburo Fujino and Yoshimasa Kurabayashi (1952) of the same institute produced a model. However these were very small, primitive models, little better than learners' products. After this early foray, Hitotsubashi economists were to shun macroeconometric model-building.[4] The major stimuli in model-building came from universities in Tokyo and Osaka.[5]

TCER models

The very first attempt at building an economy-wide model was made by Tadao Uchida and Tsunehiko Watanabe, both in their early thirties, at the Tokyo Center for Economic Research (TCER), a private group of young economists in Tokyo which held regular seminars to stimulate members' academic interest (the group is still active). The first Uchida–Watanabe model, called TCER Model I, was made public in 1957. It was very primitive by present standards; it consisted of five behavioural and two definitional equations based on annual national income data for the period 1951–6.

Better known is TCER Model II, which was published in Uchida and Watanabe (1959). In preparing this model, the authors imitated Colin Clark's model of the American economy (1949) in order to see whether an American model could also apply to Japan. The data were now quarterly values covering 19 quarters (1952:3–1957:1). The model consisted of five behavioural and two definitional equations. The dependent variables of the former were consumption (private plus public), imports, private fixed investment, private residential construction, and private inventory investment. The first four variables were functions of real GNP, while the fifth was a function of total sales, namely GNP minus inventory investment. Hence two identities were added to define GNP and sales. Note that the model was strictly demand-determined and neither prices nor financial variables appeared.

After this humble beginning, the TCER econometricians continued their efforts and the TCER models went through successive versions. Thus TCER Model III adapted the Klein–Goldberger Model of the US economy, consisting of 16 equations (11 behavioural and five definitional) for the period of 28 quarters (1951:3–1957:4) (Uchida and Mori, 1960). TCER Model IV took a different tack by constructing two annual models, one for the prewar years (1926–40) and the other for the postwar period (1951–9). TCER Model V was an elaboration and extension of Model III, developed by introduction of more details on fiscal policy. Several versions were prepared and used for comparing simulation results. The model size expanded considerably. For instance, Model V-8-2 had two versions – I without and II with details on public finance. Version I consisted of 30 equations (18 behavioural and 12 definitional). These versions were constructed by Tadao Uchida and Kei Mori and several papers were published (for example, Mori, 1963a, 1963b).

Thus, by 1963, considerable expertise had been accumulated by the TCER econometricians. Tadao Uchida and Tsunehiko Watanabe emerged as two prominent leading macroeconometricians.

Osaka University models
Osaka University was a relatively young national university with specialization in science, technology, and medicine. After the Second World War, it added the faculties of humanities and social sciences. In creating its economics department, it was decided that it should be non-Marxian, unlike other established economics departments, which were (and still are) dominated by Marxians. In this orientation, the contribution of Yasuma Takata (1883–1972), one of the most prolific writers on economics in Japan, was great. Takata conceived of the establishment of a research institute attached to the department and gave his junior colleague Michio Morishima, who was in his very early thirties, an academic leadership in running the institute. The institute came into being in the mid-1950s with the faculty including Hukukane Nikaido, Shin'ichi Ichimura, and Masahiro Tatemoto, among others. This was the beginning of the Osaka University Institute of Social and Economic Research.[6] As one project which was intended to distinguish the new institute, the institute thought of starting a team of young econometricians on the construction of a large-scale model of the Japanese economy. Thus the ISER organized late in 1959 an econometric team (including the present author as a member). Lawrence R. Klein was called in as an adviser to the project. In addition to the authors of the 1964 paper – Shin'ichi Ichimura, Lawrence R. Klein, Susumu Koizumi, Kazuo Sato and Yoichi Shinkai – the team included at one time or another Masahiro Tatemoto, Mitsuo Saito and Hiroshi Atsumi.

The project was ambitious. The model was to describe all parts of the economy – production, consumption, foreign trade, wages and prices, financial sector and so on. It was expected to take account of salient features of the economy, such as the dual structure in industry, migration of labour from agriculture to industry and indirect financing. Thus industry was divided into heavy industry, textiles and other manufacturing with large and small firms separately identified. A special financial sub-sector model was constructed with considerable details (Ichimura, 1962). The final version of the model contained 211 equations (102 behavioural and 109 definitional) – roughly comparable in size with the Brookings Model of the US economy, which started its preparation in 1961.

The initial intention of the team was to publish details of the model, including its mathematical properties and simulation results. Unfortunately the team was broken up before the work was fully completed, as some key members left the university. Ichimura *et al.* (1964) gave the skeleton structure of the model and the data base, but no adequate explanation was published until the whole model structure was fully documented in Ichimura *et al.* (1977). Two factors made this project difficult. One was the massive data requirements of this highly disaggregated model; a major part of the research effort had to be spent on preparing time-series data from primary statistical sources. Another was the poor level of computer facilities. The model was too large to be manageable by the computer facilities which were at the team's disposal in the early 1960s.[7]

However this team exercise served its historical mission, since it demonstrated the feasibility of a large-scale model from the data base available in the 1950s that could reflect special features of the Japanese economy. It also promoted academic interchange between Kanto and Kansai econometricians.[8]

In addition to this gigantic ISER model, the Osaka University project was instrumental in producing three famous models, one by Klein and Shinkai, another by Klein, and a final one by Ueno.

Klein–Shinkai Model   To supplement the main model, a small annual model was built by Klein and Shinkai (1963) to describe economic changes of Japan covering the prewar (1930–6) and postwar (1951–8) years and consisting of 22 equations (15 behavioural and seven definitional). Characteristics of the model are the inclusion of both prewar and postwar periods distinguished by a shift variable in the form of a dummy, the inclusion of demographic variables, and the emphasis on the price-wage formation. (For a retesting of the model, see Blumenthal, 1965.)

Klein's long-term model   Klein (1961) wanted to describe in bold relief Japan's long-term economic growth in the spirit of Valavanis-Vail (1955) and Klein and Kosobud (1961), which referred to American economic growth. In this exercise, Klein connected 12 quinquennial observations

from 1878–82 to 1933–7. Productivity ratios and the labour force participation ratio were explained as trends. The birth and death rates were
quadratic functions of per capita output. Non-primary production was
made to respond to the expansion of the country's capacity to import.
While the model was crude, it inspired another econometrician to
continue with larger, more detailed long-term growth models of Japan.

Ueno's long-term model   Hiroya Ueno is another econometrician who
has been active in model-building. He served as a consultant to the Osaka
University project while he was on the faculty of Nagoya University. His
interest in long-term model-building was stimulated by the Klein–Shinkai
efforts. Thus he produced a long-term model of the Japanese economy
going further back in time than the Klein–Shinkai model. His period
covered 1920–36 and 1952–8 (Ueno, 1961, 1963) with a dummy variable
distinguishing the two subperiods. As the national income data did not go
beyond 1930 at that time, Ueno relied on industrial production series. His
model therefore highlights long-term changes in the industrial structure
over the period of Japan's modern industrial development. The model
consisted of 38 equations (22 behavioural and 16 definitional).

After this exercise he was placed in charge of a long-term model for the
government's Medium-Term Economic Plan (to be discussed in Section
3). The result of his related work was published in Ueno and Kinoshita
(1965, 1968). Later on, he continued his research at the Economic
Research Institute of the Economic Planning Agency, extending the time
period to 1906–37 and 1954–68 and switching to the national income
series prepared by Kazushi Ohkawa and associates for their Long-Term
Economic Statistics project (Ueno *et al.*, 1971).

Other models
There were a few other model-building exercises apart from the two major
groups noted above.[9] Prominent among these were (1) the Ministry of
International Trade and Industry (MITI) model in three versions with a
special emphasis on industrial production; (2) the short-term prediction
model in successive versions by the Economic Research Institute of the
Economic Planning Agency (see Section 3); (3) Ueno's short-term model;
and (4) the initial efforts of Takao Fukuchi of the International Christian
University (Tokyo) in model-building, particularly regional models.

The late 1950s to the early 1960s were the period of learning by doing.
Econometricians had to master the art of model-building by themselves.
Moreover the data period was still short and electronic computer facilities
were just becoming available to them. None the less the econometricians
had a good time, like children with new toys. They were still playing with

econometric models, not fully sure of their practical capability, which remained unknown and untested.

3 The second stage: practice

The Japanese government has been engaged in preparing and publishing medium-term national economic plans since 1948. In the period of our first stage, there were six such national plans: I (the first provisional plan for economic recovery, May 1948, for 1949–52); II (the plan of economic recovery, May 1949, for 1949–53); III (the plan of economic autonomy, January 1951, for 1951–3); IV (the five-year plan of economic autonomy, December 1955, for 1955–9); V (the new long-term economic plan, December 1958, for 1957–61); and VI (the income-doubling plan, November 1960, for 1960–9). These plans set up various plan targets, globally for real GNP growth and sectorally by industry. Except probably for the last plan, they were not grounded on any macroeconomic model.[10] Hence there was little consistency between the global target and the sectoral targets. In addition, the national government started the practice of announcing its macroeconomic predictions late in December for the next fiscal year (April to March) as essential background materials for national budget-making. The 1955 fiscal year was the first instance of this practice. These short-term predictions suffered from the same shortcomings as the medium-term plans, because of the lack of internal consistency.[11]

This unsatisfactory state of affairs was inevitable as the economics profession itself was still struggling with macroeconomics and macroeconometrics in the 1950s. With the progress of knowledge in these fields, it was a matter of time before the bureaucracy came for advice to econometricians in order to improve its plan-making and predictions. Thus our stage 2 begins in 1964, when the government decided to pull econometricians out of their playground and to put them to hard work building its seventh postwar plan, called the Medium-Term Economic Plan (January 1965 for 1964–8). Before proceeding to this important phase of our stage 2, let us take note of two important developments on the research front.

Two new research institutions began to operate in the late 1950s and early 1960s. The first is the Economic Research Institute of the Economic Planning Agency, which was set up in 1958. Apart from the National Income Division, which was installed as a part of the Institute, it was established as a link between the national government and the academic profession so that applied economic research could be promoted. Its director-general (who was given the official rank of a ministerial bureau director-general) received a tenure of three years, to be chosen (in principle) alternately from inside the Economic Planning Agency and from the universities (again, alternating between Kanto and Kansai). The first director-general was Kazushi Ohkawa of the Institute of Economic Research of Hitotsubashi University. The research division consists of several senior research officers, the majority of whom are appointed from the university faculties. Each senior officer heads a research team of junior officers (partly from the Institute staff and partly from universities), who would work on a certain research topic to be completed within the tenure of the team leader. When the assignment is completed, the preliminary research results are to be published in *Keizai Bunseki*, a journal (irregularly published) of the Institute, and the final full-length results in a monograph of the Institute. So far, 41 such monographs have been published. One continuing assignment was the short-term econometric forecasting model.

Another new institution that came into being a little later is the Japan Economic Research Center (JERC), which was created in association with the *Nihon Keizai Shimbun* (Japan Economic Journal), a major business daily. The centre was set up in December 1963 under the directorship of Saburo Okita, who had resigned from the Economic Planning Agency (he served as a foreign minister in the late 1970s). The centre is a private institution supported by contributions from member firms. Its primary objective is to disseminate economic information through public lectures, round-table panel discussions, workshops, seminars and the like and also to train junior officers of member firms in economic and business research through its training programme. One important project in which trainees participate is the quarterly forecasting exercise. The centre maintains a small research staff of its own with library facilities, physically located on the premises of the newspaper.

These two new institutions considerably increased academic economists' involvement with the government and the private sector.

Medium-term economic plan models
Econometric models were definitely introduced into plan-making for the first time in the seventh plan, namely the Medium-Term Economic Plan, which was announced in January 1965 for the plan period of 1964–8. The sixth plan, that is, the celebrated Income Doubling Plan, had to be revised soon after it was announced because the economy performed much better in the first half of the 1960s than that ambitious plan had anticipated. This was the onset of the rapid-growth era, which was to last into the early 1970s. Thus a revision was requested for the remainder of the plan period. The request was formally accepted by the government in January 1964. The final draft was to be produced by October of the same year.

In this rush job, econometric models came onto centre stage. A group of econometricians was appointed to the Econometric Subcommittee to give the quantitative framework to the seventh plan. The overall model consisted of four submodels. The first was a long-term model based on Ueno's earlier work and was intended to show long-term directions that Japan's economic development and growth would take. In this version, the submodel covered the period of 1906–39 and 1951–60, consisting of 21 equations (11 behavioural and 10 definitional). The second was a 'medium-term' model covering the period 1954–63 with semi-annual observations. It consisted of 60 equations, equally divided between stochastic and definitional equations. The model was a direct descendant of TCER models, since its builders were Tadao Uchida, Tsunehiko Watanabe and Masahiro Tatemoto. The model was designed to predict short-term changes.[12] Since the plan was to provide more disaggregated targets at the industry level, the medium-term model was to be linked to an input-output model,[13] which was supervised by Ken'ichi Miyazawa. The linkage was provided by specifying highly disaggregated consumer demand functions (including consumer price formation equations). This final part was the responsibility of Kotaro Tsujimura.[14]

The 1965 plan clearly established the reputation of the econometric approach. Thus the Committee for Econometric Model Analysis (Keiryo Iinkai) was permanently installed in the Economic Deliberation Council, an advisory body to the Economic Planning Agency. A dozen or so members are appointed from among academic econometricians and its secretariat is the Division for Econometric Model Analysis, Planning Bureau, Economic Planning Agency.[15] The committee has been in charge of providing the quantitative framework for all subsequent plans. Since its installation, the committee has dealt with eight plans.[16] Over time, the model structure did not basically change for nearly 10 years. A change was made in the 1977 plan exercise by introducing multi-sector models in the medium term (five years), the long term, and the very long term.[17,18]

Interactions were reciprocal between plan-makers and econometricians. While the latter's models provided the basic framework for the economic planners to follow, the former's requirements gave new orientations to further model developments.

The pilot model for short-term prediction of the economic planning agency
The Economic Planning Agency's Economic Research Institute had been experimenting with short-term prediction models (SP) since 1960.[19] After the Medium-Term Economic Plan was prepared, the Institute mobilized its seven units to produce a new 'pilot' model. The work began in 1965.

There were roughly 20 versions to this model.[20] An expanded version of the pilot model was prepared in 1967 under the name of the Short-Term Economic Prediction Master Model, consisting of 125 equations (60 behavioural and 65 definitional (Shishido *et al.*, 1970). In the late 1960s, the pilot model contained 53 equations (23 behavioural and 30 definitional).

The JERC short-term forecasting model
After the completion of the government's medium-term plan model, Uchida and Watanabe were asked by the JERC to carry on their model for the purpose of short-term economic predictions. The project was also funded by the Central Research Institute of Electric Power Industry (Denken). The first full-length report of this model is found in Uchida *et al.* (1966). The model in this report consisted of 35 equations (23 behavioural and 12 definitional). The behavioural equations could be classified as follows: eight on expenditure components, three on income distribution, three on taxes, five on price changes, one on wage change, one on employment,one on labour's share, and one on industrial production. Subsequent versions of the model are larger.[21]

The econometricians' participation in the plan-making of the Medium-Term Economic Plan demonstrated the practical utility of macroeconometric model analysis. Continued efforts to elaborate short-term prediction models and to try economic forecasting based on these models gave enough confidence to practising model-builders. Also the historical circumstances were kind to them, since rapid economic growth, which was running at full steam into the early 1970s, virtually guaranteed success to any econometric forecasting effort at that time.

4   The third stage: maturity
Macroeconometric models had proved their worth. Those macroeconometricians who mastered the techniques went on their own ways and began to construct their individual models. Thus a tremendous proliferation of models followed. As early as 1972, knowledgeable model-builders commented that Japan was probably the world leader as regards the number of macro-models developed so far (Tatemoto and Uchida, 1972, p. 1). Subsequent developments should place Japan, if not at the top, at least abreast of the United States in this field. Needless to say, such an exuberance of model-building activity makes any survey of the field a very difficult task; therefore our survey of stage 3 models has, by necessity, to be selective. First of all, finding the location of existing models is by itself a major enterprise.[22] Only a few of them publish specifications in a

readily accessible form. A number of model-builders failed to respond to the present writer's request for information. This lack of communication has made the coverage of this survey far from being truly comprehensive. Even so, as will be seen below, there are already too many models to allow us to give each model a full review in the limited space.

It is useful here to outline relevant events that took place in the decade and a half of stage 3 from the early 1970s to the mid-1980s. During this period there were ups and downs in model-building activity. Japan's rapid growth, which lasted through the decade of the 1960s, faced a transition period in the early 1970s. Its demise came with the first oil shock of 1973–4. The inflation rate went above 20 per cent in 1974 and the economy was confronted by a severe recession. Needless to say, macroeconometric forecasting failed miserably. The honeymoon came to an end for the model-builders, who had to reassess their own work in the light of these failures. At the same time, Japan's national accounts shifted from the old to the new versions of the UN System of National Accounts. It took some time before the new edition became available, in early 1979. The revision was substantial (available from 1965 onwards for broad aggregates and from 1970 on for disaggregated accounts), and the scope of statistical coverage was expanded considerably. This necessitated extensive respecification and re-estimation of all active models. In the meantime, Japan's decelerated economic growth became a permanent feature. Investment fell sharply, but saving did not in the private sector. The resulting excess private saving was absorbed into government deficits. Also Japan became more open to international trade and capital transactions, thereby making its economy more susceptible to external shocks. These new developments have greatly increased the demand for macroeconomic forecasting and revised models have had to take them into account adequately. Thus the early 1980s have witnessed renewed interest in model-building activities.

In the meantime, the Japanese computer industry came into maturity. Computer facilities made rapid strides in the private and public sectors. Large-scale computer systems of domestic make were installed in universities (especially the national universities) and became liberally accessible to their faculties.[23]

A related noteworthy development is the growth of electronic data bank services. The *Nihon Keizai Shimbun* (Japan Economic Journal) set up a data bank bureau, which maintains the Nikkei Economic Electronic Data Service (NEEDS), allowing subscribers access to its data bank through time-sharing computer terminals. Similar services are provided by other institutions, for example, the Nomura Research Institute, which markets its data bank of a few thousand economic time-series throughout the world via its international computer network. Other ancillary data, such as input–output tables and corporate income statements and balance sheets, are computerized and commercially available.

To academic researchers, however, these data services are limited in coverage and very expensive. Accordingly, in 1983, an ambitious inter-university consortium was organized with the objective of creating a comprehensive data bank on all aspects of social sciences, albeit with dominant emphasis on economics. The project was funded by the Ministry of Education for three years, 1983–5, and directed by Shuntaro Shishido of the University of Tsukuba, with the participation of more than a hundred social scientists from various universities.[24]

Reflecting these new changes, model-building has also been transformed. Models have tended to be larger and more differentiated. Combining a macro-model with an input–output table has been a popular line of model-building, especially suited to simulating the effect of an external shock to a particular segment of the economy. As external transactions have become a significant influence on Japan's domestic economy while Japan's presence has grown in the world economy, international linkage models have been developed. Also other economic sectors, which used to be treated as largely exogenous, have come to be endogenized. Two examples are the monetary-financial sector and the government sector.

In the late 1970s and early 1980s, public interest in short-term forecasting recovered, and a large number of private and public institutions have joined the forecasting community. They make extensive use of macro-models.

On another front, following academic dissension abroad, a counter-attack was staged by monetarists against Keynesian macro-models. Monetarists have been vocal, especially from their stronghold at Japan's central bank, Bank of Japan (BOJ), though the mainstream of macroeconomics still remains Keynesian in Japan. A few monetarist macro-models have been tried using Japanese data.

In view of these recent developments, we classify major macro-models of stage 3 into five groups, according to their functions and objectives. The classification is somewhat arbitrary as these criteria are not necessarily mutually exclusive: I general equilibrium and projection models; II special-purpose models; III international linkage models; IV short-term forecasting models; V monetarist models. Each group is further divided into subgroups. A brief description is given of each individual model. In what follows, a model is identified by a three-digit code, for example, 1A1. References are limited to either the most representative, the latest, or relatively accessible (preferably in English). The reader is reminded that there are many other models (less important, it is to be hoped) which are not touched upon.

I   General equilibrium and projection models
General equilibrium models   Academic econometricians are more interested in studying the working of a macro economy than in forecasting.
For this purpose, general equilibrium theory provides a challenging test-
ground. There have been at least two such models. As their principal
objective is theory testing, they are not maintained on a continuing basis.

> 1A1: Keio multi-sector model (Tsujimura and Kuroda, 1974; Tsujimura, Kur-
> oda and Shimada, 1981). Keio University's Economic Observatory elaborated
> the annual multi-sector model, which Kotaro Tsujimura, its leader, developed
> for the government's 1965 Medium-Term Economic Plan. This medium-sized
> model was intended to analyse the general equilibrium structure of the Japa-
> nese economy by connecting behavioural equations to successive versions of
> the input–output table. The demand–supply equilibrium of money, goods and
> services is emphasized.
> 1A2: Interindustry general equilibrium model (Saito, 1974). Mitsuo Saito of
> Kobe University expanded the input–output model by endogenizing consump-
> tion functions, making production coefficients variable according to the Cobb–
> Douglas technology, and determining outputs and prices by equating demand
> and supply quantities in each industry. While this model has not been main-
> tained, the idea of inter-industry price formation is carried into Saito's later
> modelling, such as 2C1 (described below).

Projection models   There are macro models specifically designed for
medium- to long-term projections. Some of them are described below[25]

> 1B1: EPA medium-term macro model (Economic Planning Agency, 1965,
> 1966), Committee for Econometric Model Analysis, 1967, 1968, 1970, 1973,
> 1977.) The Committee for Econometric Model Analysis of the Economic
> Deliberation Council, with the assistance of econometric staff of the Planning
> Bureau of the Economic Planning Agency, kept up a small semi-annual model
> inherited from the 1965 Medium-Term Economic Plan. The model was used as
> a policy model for providing medium-term plan targets. It was discontinued
> and replaced by Model 1B2.
> 1B2: EPA medium-term multi-sector model (Committee for Econometric
> Model Analysis 1977, 1980, 1984 and Ueno, 1980). The model was prepared in
> 1977 by the Committee for Econometric Model Analysis to provide highly
> disaggregated projections for the government's medium-term planning. Semi-
> annual behavioural equations cover all aspects of economic activity (both
> supply and demand) with imperfect quantity and price adjustments embedded
> in them. These equations are connected with an input–output table (14 indus-
> tries/15 commodities).
> Attached to this model is a long-term turnpike multi-sector model (with 10
> sectors in the 1980 version and the maximum of 33 sectors in the 1984 version)
> in order to trace the optimum turnpike trajectory for economic growth
> (through maximizing cumulative consumption) subject to various external

constraints. The model was utilized to provide long-term projections for a 1982 Economic Deliberation Council study, *Japan in Year 2000* (1982).

1B3: EPA–Kinoshita multi-sector model (Kinoshita *et al.*, 1982; Kinoshita, 1983, 1984). This is the Japan Model of a World Trade and Industry Model (3A3) constructed at the Economic Research Institute of the Economic Planning Agency under the direction of Soshichi Kinoshita of Nagoya University. It is an annual model (1963–78) with 22 sectors separately identified. Its heavy emphasis is on the production side (estimating equations by industry for domestic demand, imports, production, capacity, capacity utilization, employment, wages, prices, value added, and capital consumption). The financial side, however, is represented by one equation (the bank rate). Linked with other national/regional models and trade linkage models (by commodity), the model is used to assess the impacts of changes in comparative advantages and protectionism on Japan's industrial structure.

1B4: JERC medium-term projection model (JERC, 1986). The Japan Economic Research Center, with Hiromichi Muto in charge, has been issuing medium-term projections (five years ahead) every year (the twelfth in 1986). Projections are based on a successive approximation technique (see 4D1). A macroeconometric model of medium size is employed as one of the inputs into the projections. Simulations are reported based on the model.

II   Special-purpose models

Embedded in an economy-wide model, a special-purpose model highlights a certain specific sector or aspect of an economy in order to provide structural analysis and/or projections and simulations. These models are divided by topic.[26]

Public finance

2A1: Medium-term public finance model (Kansai Keizai Kenkyu Center [Kansai Economic Research Centre], 1980). The KERC organized in 1978 a study group directed by Chikashi Moriguchi of Kyoto University to study the country's public finance position. A large-size annual model detailing the public sector was constructed. It was linked to the Kyoto University Model (4B1) to produce medium-term (1979–85) policy simulations.

Financial sector

2B1: *Bank of Japan econometric model* (Bank of Japan, 1972). The Bank of Japan's Statistics Department built a medium-sized quarterly macro-model in 1972 and revised it in 1978. It details the financial sector, paying particular attention to special features of Japan's financial structure, in particular to the fact that the interest rate was not a market-clearing variable. (See 4A4 for the BOJ's official forecasting model.)

2B2: KERC financial model (Kansai Keizai Kenkyu Center, 1984). As a sequel to its public finance model (2A1), the KERC reconvened its study group headed by Chikashi Moriguchi with an assignment of endogenizing the financial sector within an overall macro-model. The work was undertaken in 1982 and 1983, and the final report was published in 1984. This medium-size quarterly model was employed for investigating multiplier properties in response to a change in the discount rate, a change in nominal public fixed investment, and the introduction of a sales tax.

Natural resources/energy

2C1: KIC econometric model (Kansai Joho Center [Kansai Information Center], 1978). The KIC organized a study group in 1976–8 directed by Mitsuo Saito of Kobe University to construct a macroeconometric model with the specific objective of predicting the macroeconomic effects of resource constraints (imported food and petroleum). This small macro-model was linked to an inter-industry price model (1A2) in order to estimate the price effect of scarce resources. A computer program system was developed for future development of the model.

2C2: Kobe University energy model (Saito and Oono, 1985). Mitsuo Saito continued his work on the energy problem of Japan in association with Takayuki Oono of Kagawa University. This medium-sized annual model (1961–79) is a Keynesian-type model covering all aspects of the economy but with special focus on the external sector (19 equations) and the price sector (35 equations). Final demands are disaggregated in order to give a prominent place to energy demands. Price equations incorporate input–output information. Production functions are specified as two-level CES (constant elasticity of substitution) functions. The model is used to evaluate the impact of an oil price change on the entire economy.

2C3: Computable general equilibrium (CGE) model (Ezaki, 1986). Mitsuo Ezaki of Kyoto University constructed a CGE model (as developed by the World Bank), with special emphasis on the energy industry. The economy is divided into 12 industries with four institutional sectors (business, households, government and external). Each industry is given a Cobb-Douglas production function. There are 12 product markets, one labour market, and one foreign exchange market, in which product prices, the wage rate, and the exchange rate are to be determined via demand–supply equilibrium. The exchange rate is taken as the numeraire since the financial side is yet to be developed. As a bona fide CGE model, some 500 parameters in the model are either predetermined from the 1980 Input–Output Table or borrowed from other studies. The model is used to evaluate the macroeconomic effects of changes (a doubling and a halving) in imported oil prices.

2C4: Saitama University energy model (Murota, 1985; Ito and Murota, 1984). Yasuhiro Murota of Saitama University has built an energy model for projections of energy demand and supply. The model includes a Japanese macro-model and a US model, in addition to the detailed modelling of energy demand and supply at the global level. The model is used for projecting energy demand and supply in 1995. The Japanese model is a very small one, consisting of real expenditures, production (cost shares of capital, labour, and energy in translog forms), implicit deflators and income distribution measures.

The external sector

2D1: Kobe University FLEX model (Amano, 1982). Out of his long-standing interest in Japan's external transactions, Akihiro Amano of Kobe University went heavily into econometric studies of Japan's external sector. His earlier work is Amano *et al.* (1973), which built a balance-of-payments model. From 1978 he turned his attention to the endogenous determination of the yen exchange rate. For this purpose he built a medium-sized model with heavy emphasis on the external sector (FLEX 4, 1982) which contains 94 equations for the domestic sector and 87 equations for the external sector. The model went through a few revisions until FLEX 4B (1982). Further work has been temporarily suspended as Amano has been busy advising the builders of the EPA World Economy Model (4A2).

Socioeconomic indicators

2E1: JERC social indicator model (Uno, 1978). Kimio Uno of the University of Tsukuba, with the assistance of the JERC's Econometric Unit, prepared a social indicator model, which explains changes in demographic and environmental indicators within a macroeconometric model.

III   International linkage models

With the globalization of economic activities and resource constraints at the worldwide level, a number of supranational macro-models have come into being since 1968 when Project LINK started its activity. Some of these models are discussed in Chapter 14 below. However, as six of them have been constructed or organized in Japan, we briefly touch on them now (see Amano, 1985, for a detailed comparison of the performances of these six models).

World economy models

3A1: EPA world economy model (Economic Planning Agency, 1982, 1984, 1987). As Japan is no longer a small country, it is necessary in macroeconomic forecasting to take a full account of international repercussions of Japan's actions. With this objective in mind, the Economic Research Institute of the Economic Planning Agency began in April 1979 to construct a giant quarterly world macro-model connecting nine major countries (United States, United Kingdom, France, Germany, Italy, Canada, Japan, Australia, and Korea). Each country has its own model, ranging from large (247 equations for the United States) to small (92 equations for Korea). In addition, the rest of the world is divided into six regions. A trade linkage model connects those countries and regions. One express objective of this exercise is to determine exchange rates as endogenous variables. The first version of the model was published in

February 1982, the second in February 1984 and the third in September 1987. It is very actively employed for international policy simulations.[27] Its submodel of Japan (4A3) is used for domestic short-term predictions.

3A2: Tsukuba–FAIS world model (Shishido *et al.*, 1980). Shuntaro Shishido of the Institute of Socio-Economic Planning, University of Tsukuba, in association with the International Economic Forecast Project of the Foundation for Advancement of International Science (FAIS), which is located at the University of Tsukuba, developed a worldwide annual econometric model. The work started in 1974 and, since 1978, annual economic predictions have been announced every spring. The model covers 19 countries and four regions including developed, developing and centrally planned economies. Its model of Japan (4B2) is employed for domestic annual economic predictions.

3A3: EPA–Kinoshita world trade and industry model (see 1B3). At the Economic Research Institute of the Economic Planning Agency, a team headed by Soshichi Kinoshita of Nagoya University started in 1979 constructing a multi-country, multi-sector annual model of international trade and industry. With the initial focus on Japan, the United States and Korea (later expanded to France, Germany, Italy, the United Kingdom, Asian NICs [Newly Industrialized Countries], ASEAN [Association of South-East Asian Nations], other developed, and the rest of the world), the model links national multi-sector models through trade linkage models (with 21 industries separately identified). The principal objective is to evaluate the impacts of shifting comparative advantages and rising protectionism upon the industrial structures of Japan and of other countries.

3A4: FUGI model (Onishi, 1983). Akira Onishi, of the Center for Global Modelling, Soka University, and some associates started in 1976 working on an ambitious annual world economy model, called the Future of Global Interdependence (FUGI) Model, with the objective of preparing medium- to long-term projections for the world economy, especially with respect to North–South economic relations. The model consists of a Global Macroeconomic Model (GMEM), Global Input–Output Model (GIOM), and Global Metal Resources Model (GMRM). The GMEM covers 54 countries and eight regions, with the total number of equations at about 12 000. Models for developed countries are effective-demand-type models covering not only the real but also the financial side, with additional emphasis on government finance, balance of payments, official development aid payments and private direct investment in developing countries.

Asian link models

The economic interdependence between Japan and East Asian and Southeast Asian countries is large. Yet the latter countries are often lumped together into one region in international linkage models. Therefore two attempts have recently been made to connect Japan and the United States to East Asian and Southeast Asian countries individually.

3B1: ELSA (Institute of Developing Economies, 1985). The Institute of Developing Economies (Tokyo) organized in 1981 a four-year project, with international cooperation, for the construction of an econometric link system for ASEAN (ELSA). Country models were built for five ASEAN countries (Indonesia, Malaysia, Philippines, Singapore and Thailand), Hong Kong, South Korea, Taiwan, the United States and Japan. Country models are linked together via an international trade matrix. The Japanese model (as well as those of the United States and Hong Kong) was a simple monetarist model with seven equations (see 5A2).

3B2: Asian Link System (Ezaki, 1979, Ezaki *et al.*, 1984, Ichimura and Ezaki, 1985). The Center for Southeast Asian Studies, Kyoto University, organized in 1978, with international cooperation, an Asian Link System project, which covers the same 10 countries as the ELSA (3B1). The 10 country models plus the rest-of-the-world model (divided into three regions) are linked by an international trade model. Country models, which are not standardized, vary in size from 73 equations (Indonesia) to 20 equations (the Philippines). The objective of the system is to analyse the structure of economic interdependence via dynamic and policy simulations within the sample period. The model of Japan in this system was developed by Ezaki and Moriguchi of Kyoto University. It is a small annual model of effective-demand-type with no financial sector, no industry breakdown, and no disaggregation for traded commodities.

IV   Short-term forecasting models

In model-building exercises, short-term forecasting attracts the greatest attention as it is the most readily understandable output of those exercises. Short-term forecasting has a considerable history behind it. The Japanese government has been issuing its annual economic outlook every December for the following fiscal year (beginning 1 April) since 1954. The number of forecasts has risen over time. For the year 1967, Muto (1980) cites 18 forecasts. By 1985, the number exceeded 40 (Sato, 1986). These forecasts are conveniently put together in a January or February issue of the Japan Economic Research Center's bi-monthly bulletin and in Toyo Keizai's *Economic Statistics Yearbook*. Most of them, it is understood, are based on various macro-models.[28]

Models in this category are basically of the demand-determined Keynesian type. The expenditure and distribution sides of the economy are usually well described, though they differ in the degree of disaggregation (for example, how far consumption is divided among different types of goods and services). The production and employment sides are more aggregative. The price and wage sector is generally based on the Klein–Phillips curve and the mark-up relation; the tightness of the market is (sometimes) an additional explanatory variable. Depending on the primary objective, models also differ in the details of the foreign sector. Some models are highly detailed on this score, while others may merely take total merchandise trade. Probably the greatest difference appears in the financial sector. Some models are virtually non-financial while others emphasize real–financial interactions. Needless to say, those models look very much alike in their basic characteristics since they are all of the same genus. Many of them trace their ancestry back to the 1965 Medium-Term Plan.

Who are those forecasters and who among them carry more weight than others? In these respects, Japan and the United States differ in an important manner. For one thing, the government's annual forecasts carry a very heavy weight in Japan, as is natural in a country in which the national government is looked upon for more direct intervention in the private sector. For another, there is only one commercially-run forecasting service in Japan, whose commercial success is reportedly far from being satisfactory. There seems to be a public perception in Japan that economic forecasts are public goods. In fact, when there are so many public and private forecasters around who supply their forecasts free of charge, customers are unwilling to pay for forecasts unless they are specifically tailored to meet their special needs. On this point, Japan's big firms pride themselves in possessing an excellent research staff of their own which can develop in-house models and forecasts.

In any event, there is a large variety of economic forecasters in Japan. They are classified below by status.

Government agencies

4A1: EPA's annual economic outlook. In order to facilitate national budget-making for the next fiscal year (beginning on 1 April), the national government, with the Economic Planning Agency in charge, announces its Annual Economic Outlook in late December. The Outlook contains annual forecasts on real GNP growth, inflation rates, gross national expenditure components in current and constant prices, industrial production, balance of payments items and so on. Coming from the government, these forecasts are taken seriously by the private sector. While macro-model forecasts must provide the basic data, there are many arbitrary adjustments in these forecasts in order to reconcile various ministries' demands.

4A2: EPA's short-term prediction (SP) econometric model (EPA, 1978). The model had an early start, as noted in Section 3. It was kept up with successive revisions by the EPA's Economic Research Institute through the 1970s. The model, eventually a compact forecasting model of a standard type, was used actively for short-term predictions for policy-making and policy simulations as requested by the government. The final version was SP-19, built in 1979. It was replaced by 4A3 in 1982.

4A3: EPA world economy model (see 3A1, Yoshitomi *et al.*, 1981; Sadahiro *et al.*, 1987). This gigantic model, constructed originally in 1979–81 and having been revised twice already, contains a Japanese model, which replaced SP-19 (4A2) as the official model of the Japanese government. The Japanese model remains large, with more than 200 equations. The model is an all-round one.

4A4: BOJ short-term forecasting econometric model. As distinct from its Macro-Econometric Model (2B1), the Bank of Japan's Research and Statistics Department has maintained for quite some time another medium-sized model (about 170 endogenous and 50 exogenous variables in it). The model is a Keynesian type with a comprehensive coverage of the economy (expenditure components, production, employment, prices, balance of payments and financial variables). The bank employs this model for quarterly predictions and policy simulations for monetary policy decision-making. Strictly for internal use, the model is confidential to outsiders.[29]

4A5: Ministry of Finance model (Sawa *et al.*, 1987, 1988). As a relative newcomer to model-building,[30] the Ministry of Finance (MOF) economists also pursued this activity in their research office (which was upgraded to the Institute of Fiscal and Monetary Policy in 1985). Under the supervision of Takamitsu Sawa of Kyoto University, the group built two models, one very small-scale (16 equations) and the other somewhat larger (56 equations). The models are basically Keynesian but price changes are affected by the GNP gap. The primary objective of constructing these models is to conduct structural analysis, namely, identifying behavioural changes before and after 1975. A comparison of alternative methods of estimation concludes that 3SLS and FIML perform better than OLS and TSLS.

4A6: Other ministries. The Ministry of International Trade and Industry (MITI), which prepares *inter alia* medium-term projections of energy demand and supply, reportedly maintains its own macro-model. If so, the model is not in the public domain. Other ministries likewise engage in short- and medium-term predictions of variables of their respective interests. They may also have macro-models.

University econometricians

4B1: Kyoto University macro-model (KYO). This quarterly macro-model is a relative newcomer to the field of short-term forecasting. It was constructed for the first time in 1975 (Amano, Ban and Moriguchi, 1976) to serve as a national model for Project LINK (to replace 4D8). Since then, the model has been revised annually and short-term forecasts have been conducted regularly in association with the Kansai Economic Research Center. Chikashi Moriguchi of Kyoto University has remained its principal supervisor.[31] The model seems to have achieved a high status. In its earlier versions, the model was heavy on the real side, especially in the external sector, but very light on the financial sector. Since then, the financial and government sector models have been attached (see 2A1, 2B2).

4B2: Tsukuba–FAIS annual model (see 3A2). This compact annual model is the Japan Model in the Tsukuba FAIS World Model. Its principal architect has been Shuntaro Shishido of the University of Tsukuba, who had been in charge of the 1960s of the Economic Planning Agency's short-term prediction pilot and master models when he was a senior officer of the EPA. The model is small and of a standard type. Annual forecasts have been made every spring since 1978 for the forthcoming fiscal year.

4B3: Keio University macroeconometric model (KOMN2) (Hamada, 1978,

1984). Fumimasa Hamada of Keio University (Economics) has long been interested in analysing the short-term macroeconomic behaviour of the Japanese economy, especially the interdependence between financial and real variables and the effects of fiscal and monetary policies. He has continued his model-building efforts. Having developed an efficient computer program, he maintains his compact model on his personal computer.

4B4: Kei Mori's quarterly macroeconomic model (KS53). Having engaged in model-building since the very early 1960s, Kei Mori of Keio University (Science and Technology Faculty) has maintained a medium-sized macro-model. The model endogenizes the financial sector, the exchange rate, and new issues of national bonds. The model is revised every year. Reportedly the model is employed for the purpose of graduate training.

Commercial forecasting

4C1: NEEDS Model (NEEDS, 1984). The NEEDS (Nikkei Economic Electronic Data Service) Model is the only commercially operated macro-forecasting model in Japan. The Nihon Keizai Shimbun's Data Bank Bureau has been running this model since 1973. (Its initial adviser was Tadao Uchida.) The quarterly model has frequently been revised and its size varies from one version to the next. The model is fairly standard and covers all macro aspects more or less evenly. It is a correspondent with the DRI Model in the United States (Eckstein, 1983).

Think tanks

4D1: JERC quarterly forecasts by successive approximations (Katsumura, 1977). Since 1967 the JERC's Short-Term Forecasting Unit has been issuing quarterly forecasts. Its hallmark is the technique of successive approximations. The econometric approach provides basic inputs for forecasts; then these forecasts go through several steps of 'successive approximation', adding many other pieces of extraneous information, including subjective judgements of experts and the forecasters themselves. There is a faith that this approach ensures better internal consistency and injects more flexibility than the purely econometric techniques. Hence this is not based purely on a macro-model. However the JERC forecasts have attained professional respectability in Japan.

4D2: JERC short-term forecasting model (JERC, 1976). Starting with the short-term forecasting model prepared by Uchida, Watanabe *et al.* at the JERC's Econometric Unit in the late 1960s, this relatively compact quarterly model was kept up there with periodical quarterly forecasts (as distinct from 4D1). The model was more detailed on production and prices but was very light on the financial side (only two equations). Because of the mounting cost of maintaining the model and the duplication with 4D1, the model was discontinued in 1979.

4D3: JERC simultaneous inter-industry model (Ueno and Muto, 1975; Ueno,

1980). The model consists of six institutional sectors (households, non-financial corporations, banks, general government, central bank and external) and 12 industries. Activities in these industries are connected with those at the macroeconomic level, namely expenditure, income distribution and price formation. The model contained another large submodel on industrial financing, along with two submodels on pollution and household portfolio choices. Behavioural equations were estimated with semi-annual observations. The model was discontinued because of the heavy cost of maintenance.

4D4: RINE model. The Research Institute of National Economy is a non-profit research outfit, originally created in 1945, which is engaged in disseminating economic information to the business sector, which supports the institute through its membership subscriptions. One of its ongoing projects is its quarterly and annual economic predictions. The model is reportedly very small.

4D5: NRI model (Nomura Research Institute, 1982). Originally a research unit of the Nomura Securities Co., the NRI became a separate entity in April 1965. One of its continuing projects is short-term forecasting undertaken by its Economic Research Unit. Its medium-sized quarterly model covers the entire economy comprehensively.

4D6: MRI model. As a research arm of the Mitsubishi zaibatsu, the Mitsubishi Institute of Economic Research was long active in economic research before the Second World War. More recently, it was renamed the Mitsubishi Research Institute, and its new work included macroeconomic forecasting on an annual basis. Its macro-model is reportedly of a medium size (specifications not available to the present reviewer).

4D7: Daiwa macro-model (Daiwa Securities Co., 1978). Daiwa Securities Co. has been active in quarterly forecasting. Its quarterly macro-model was originally developed from the Economic Planning Agency's SP Model (4A2) in 1967 by the company's research staff. Periodical forecasting began in March 1970. Later, the activity was transferred to the company's newly-founded Economic Research Institute. The model is a standard type, covering all macro aspects more or less evenly, though its coverage of the financial sector is relatively strong. The model is constantly re-estimated. It links up with the Wharton Econometric Forecasting Associates in the United States.

4D8: Denken macro-model (Denken, 1983). The Denken or the Economic Research Institute of the Central Research Institute of Electric Power Industry has long been active in macro-model-building. Originally, the model was developed from the Tatemoto–Uchida–Watanabe Model of the 1965 Medium-Term Economic Plan as it was transferred to the JERC. The first 1970 version was built by Uchida and Tatemoto on behalf of the Institute and served as the Japanese model in Project LINK. The model went through several revisions, sometimes drastic. However it has always been kept small. Because of the nature of its sponsor, the model includes equations for electricity and energy.

4D9: Other think tanks. There are a few other think-tank forecasters, especially those related to securities companies such as Nikko and Yamaichi. Their annual and semi-annual forecasts are based on macro models, which are not examined here.

Private enterprises Those who have swelled the roster of short-term forecasters in recent years are banks, life insurance companies and general trading firms. They generally have their own macro-models. In addition, it is reported that there are many other firms, especially in manufacturing industries, such as automobiles, steel and electronics, which employ their in-house models for specific economic predictions. These models are restricted to internal use.

V Monetarist models

The models reviewed so far are by and large Keynesian. In particular, aggregate demand is the sum of expenditure items and aggregate supply is moderately upward-sloping in the short run. Autonomous injections thus have multiplier effects. Monetarism and later New Classical Macroeconomics (NCM) view these phenomena in a different light. Aggregate demand is very strongly (if not entirely) governed by the quantity of money; aggregate supply is positively related to the excess of the actual over expected price levels. When expectations are rational, this excess reduces to zero, except for a random error. Thus the position of the aggregate supply curve is determined by the natural rate of unemployment subject to random shocks. The money supply is a crucial determinant of macroeconomic activities. Autonomous injections have little power. To monetarists, then, Keynesian macro-models are incorrect. A simple model which relates nominal national income to money supply can perform as well as a large structural model as far as very aggregative variables are concerned. The very first such model for the US economy was the St Louis Model developed by Andersen and Carlson (1970) at the Federal Reserve Bank of St Louis.

Just as Keynesianism came late to Japan, monetarism also took some time before developing roots there. Yoshio Suzuki (1982), a prominent Bank of Japan economist, reports Milton Friedman's visit to Japan in the summer of 1963, when Friedman speculated that the money supply must be leading price changes by two quarters in Japan just as in the United States. The BOJ Research Department carried out a small study in 1963 which verified Friedman's conjecture. The finding was incorporated into Suzuki's book (1964). However Suzuki remained basically a Keynesian, and his well-received book (1974, English edition 1980) on Japan's monetary system was based on the Tobin approach. In the meantime, Friedman in 1968 introduced the concept of the natural rate of unemployment, which was to emphasize the role of inflationary expectations. The Japanese economy had already been inflationary before the great inflation took place in the wake of the 1973–4 oil shock. Inflationary expectations, which were engendered by rapid monetary expansion, seemed to be the root cause. In this regard, Suzuki was inspired by Keran (1970), a study by another St Louis Fed economist on Japan's business cycles, which were allegedly induced by fluctuations in the money supply. This is the very first self-contained monetarist model of the Japanese economy.[32] However monetarists needed more rigorous theorizing to convince even themselves of the persuasiveness of their own approach, and such a theory was provided by New Classical Macroeconomics, which rediscovered the rational expectations hypothesis that enabled inflationary expectations to be endogenous; empirical tests for this hypothesis came in quick succession from the mid-1970s in the United States. As Suzuki (1982) acknowledges, it was in 1979 that Suzuki and his fellow BOJ economists were made fully aware of the importance of this new approach through the interest of junior economists in the Special Studies Division of the Bank (which was elevated in October 1982 to the Institute for Monetary and Economic Studies).

Work has flourished along monetarist and New Classical Macroeconomic lines in the BOJ Institute (whose current director-general is Suzuki).[33] This, however, is not the place to review the monetarist literature in Japan.[34] It suffices to note here that monetarists have been more interested in hypothesis-testing than in model-building. Hypothesis-testing is concerned with the proposition that 'money causes income' and with the neutrality of money (Okina, 1985, 1986).

When it comes to model-building, monetarist models are very aggregative and small-scale, as they are not really interested in producing detailed forecasts. In fact, there are only a very few full-fledged monetarist macromodels, to the best of my knowledge.

5A1: EPA–Shimpo monetarist model (Shimpo *et al.*, 1978; Shimpo, 1980, 1985). The model is a typical monetarist model. Of 12 equations, five are behavioural. The change in nominal GNP is dependent on (current and lagged) changes in money supply, government spending and export earnings. Price level changes are influenced by a demand pressure variable, anticipated inflation (based on business intention surveys), and import price changes. Anticipated inflation rates are explained by changes in the wholesale price index (WPI) and the trend deviation of the velocity of money. The unemployment rate is a function of the GNP gap. Changes in the wholesale price index are due to the demand pressure variable, (lagged) inflation anticipations and import price changes.

5A2: ELSA Japan model (See 3B1; chap. 8 of the Institute of Developing Economies (IDE) 1985). Mitsuru Toida and Hiroshi Osada of the IDE (Tokyo) present a seven-equation monetarist model of Japan. Five equations are behavioural: (1) changes in nominal GNP due to changes in money supply, government spending and exports; (2) price-level changes based on its lagged values, changes in the ratio of nominal GNP to potential output and import price changes; (3) the production function of potential output; (4) investment as a function of real output, the capital stock and the relative price of oil; (5) real imports as a function of real output and relative import prices. Two identities are real output (as the ratio of nominal output to the price level) and the growth rate of the capital stock.

5 Issues in macro-model-building

Model structures[35]
Japan's macro-models, with strong emphasis on the demand side, are almost exclusively Keynesian, and, as such, they are quite similar as far as the core portion is concerned, that is, with regard to expenditure functions, production functions (usually Cobb-Douglas), employment functions, wage-price functions (Klein–Phillips curve) and so on.[36] In degrees of coverage, they differ notably with regards to the government, financial and external sectors. Attempts have been made by a few model-builders to endogenize some variables which are usually treated as exogenous, such as government expenditure, money supply, labour supply and the exchange rate.

One way to compare model properties is via simulation analysis, such as comparing the time profiles of dynamic multipliers. As Saito and Moriguchi (1985) report,[37] the models that they compare yield fairly similar results among themselves, which are not dissimilar from those observed for American models. For instance, the dynamic multiplier values showing the effects of a permanent increase of government investment expenditure (nominal) upon GNP (nominal) are, when averaged for models under comparison, 1.37, 2.00, 2.38, 2.76 and 3.04 over the successive five quarters. While variances tend to widen over time, there is little dispersion in the impact multiplier (between 1.24 and 1.44).[38]

An important issue is the stability of coefficients. When an economy goes through structural changes, behavioural equations are likely to be subject to considerable change. The Japanese economy experienced structural changes several times. A significant one occurred between the prewar and postwar periods. Within the postwar period, excluding the late 1940s with their postwar dislocation, there have been three distinct subperiods, namely, a period of normalization in the 1950s, the rapid-growth era of the 1960s to the early 1970s, and the 'stable' growth period since the mid-1970s. Did the economic structure remain unchanged so that equations can be estimated for the entire period? For the first two subperiods, Moriguchi (1979, 1983) conducted a Chow test to see if coefficient estimates could be judged unchanged between them (1956:1 to 1965:4 and 1966:1 to 1976:1). His finding was that the null hypothesis is rejected with respect to, for example, the consumption function and the fixed investment function. Among others, Moriguchi takes note that personal consumption responds, in the later period, more to expected inflation, fixed investment has a longer gestation period and responds more to firms' internal funds position, the Klein–Phillips curve has shown a wage drift, and the demand for labour has a higher adjustment speed. I have seen no similar test for the most recent years, namely between the rapid-growth and slow-growth periods. There is, in the view of the writer, no doubt that the structural change that took place between these two subperiods was great.[39] Practising econometricians have faced a dilemma here. If they limit their sample period to the last subperiod, the sample size is too small and some coefficient estimates have large standard deviations because economic relationships seem to have become less stable after the first oil shock. So far, a compromise has been accepted by extending the sample period to the years before 1975.

Estimation methods
Econometric theory has taught us that a simultaneous equation system ought to be estimated by sophisticated econometric techniques which minimize simultaneity bias. In Stage 2, econometricians took this advice seriously. For example, Tatemoto, Uchida and Watanabe (1967) opted for the two-stage least squares (TSLS) and the limited-information maximum likelihood (LIML) methods. In Stage 3, however, Japanese econometricians have reverted to the ordinary least squares (OLS) method. Thus, with rare exceptions, Japanese models are currently estimated by OLS. This is because econometricians have learned that the OLS is the simplest, cheapest and most robust – free from the rather arbitrary choice of instrumental variables involved in the TSLS and LIML. Serial correlation difficulties have been taken care of by the application of the Cochrane-Orcutt iterative procedure.

One study which compared performances of these three alternative estimation techniques is Ban (1979), which examined within-sample and post-sample prediction errors for the Kyoto University Model (4B1, 1977 version). He concluded that the OLS estimator gave, 'on the average, the best performances ... in the one-period prediction over the within-sample periods' and the LIML estimator gave, 'on the average, the best performances ... in the one-period prediction over the post-sample periods'. In other words, there was 'sufficient evidence to contend that the LIML class is superior' (Ban, 1979, p. 21).[40]

Cost of model maintenance
To develop a new model is extremely expensive. Even maintaining an already established model in a routine manner is expensive because it requires the full-time presence of professional econometricians and some support staff. (Updating time-series data is no longer a problem, as the

data bank offers such data on a regular basis at a fixed fee. In the case of Japan, the organization NEEDS has become a popular data source.) The Daiwa Securities Institute retains five professionals to run its macro-model (4D7) and sends a junior member for a year's apprenticeship at the organization, Wharton Econometric Forecasting Associates. The Institute (or rather its parent company) bears this heavy cost because, on the one hand, it believes that trained staff will prove useful for other research functions and, on the other, it has a sense of public mission (such as helping the government to produce economic projections).[41] NEEDS, the only commercial forecasting establishment in Japan, maintains three professionals on a rotating basis (assigned from the parent newspaper's research department). As the subsidiary's financial fortune rises and falls, it often leads to a headache for the parent company.

Performance checks
To check how well a macro-model performs, one has to evaluate the success of its predictions. There are a number of ways to do this. One of them is post-mortem analysis. It shows where the errors of prediction come from, such as misspecifications of the model adopted, structural changes not reflected in the model, errors in the assigned values of exogenous variables, and so on. What makes this analysis difficult to undertake is the fact that macroeconometric forecasters in Japan (as elsewhere) often engage in small modifications to their models (fine-tuning, constant-term adjustments, or 'licking the pencil' as the Japanese expression goes). So full details of the predictions, particularly the basic assumptions about the assigned values of exogenous variables, are not usually published (with a few exceptions).[42]

If a simulation analysis is undertaken to compare predictive powers of competing models by standardizing them with common data and sample periods, it should provide us with valuable insights. The only study which came close to this exercise is Hatanaka and Saito (1974). They took five major (but anonymous) models in order to compare short-term predictive powers by examining errors of predictions four quarters ahead with respect to some 30 endogenous variables. The forecast year was 1971, which covered a recession. The authors found that econometric predictions were very unsatisfactory, even in comparison with the naive model (extrapolations of past trends). If these models all performed poorly in the high-growth period, one could not expect them to perform well after 1973.

Macroeconomic forecasting
Predictions and projections have long been familiar in Japan. National economic plans, which started in the late 1940s, set up medium-term

targets for macroeconomic variables, though they are apt to be mainly exercises of lip service, as Japan is not a planned economy. Since the end of 1954, the national government has been engaged in announcing its annual 'economic outlook' for the next fiscal year.

As the model-building exercise became popularized in the late 1960s, there appeared a number of private-sector forecasting institutions which provided macroeconomic forecasts – more often annual or semi-annual than quarterly. Annual forecasts are for the next fiscal year (starting on 1 April) and are usually announced towards the end of the calendar year.

Some Japanese newspapers carry these annual forecasts as a special feature in their New Year edition. The most convenient source of those alternative forecasts is the Japan Economic Research Center's semi-monthly bulletin. One of its early-year issues (which is now the 1–15 January issue) assembles a large number of annual forecasts with the forecasters' explanatory notes. The number of forecasters reported in this source was 18 in 1967 and rose to 23 in 1969–71. Then the number fell sharply to six, in 1974. This decline must have been largely due to the loss of confidence on the part of forecasters as well as of the general public in face of rising uncertainties on the macroeconomic scene. As the economy moved into the phase of decelerated growth and macroeconomic stability was regained, the number of reporting forecasters increased. In 1980, it was 20. In the early 1980s, this number rose sharply. For the year 1988, there were 39 forecasters.[43]

Another source, equally convenient and with larger coverage (with semi-annual forecasts when available), is Toyo Keizai's *Keizai Tokei Nenkan* (Economic Statistics Yearbook). Its 1988 edition reports 52 forecasters. They are broken down by type as follows: 22 research institutions (think-tanks and the like), 20 commercial banks, six life insurance companies, and four trading companies. Many of the 22 research institutions have been reviewed in Section 4.

A number of these forecasters are engaged in quarterly forecasting on a continuing basis. For quarterly forecasts, one must go to forecasters' respective periodicals, though newspapers carry feature articles when forecasts have been greatly revised owing to the occurrence of some unforeseen major event, such as the large appreciation of the yen in early 1986. A convenient source has become available as far as some aggregative variables are concerned. Since January 1984, an international monthly journal, *Economic Forecasts* (Amsterdam: North Holland), has been publishing short-term macroeconomic forecasts of major countries of the world. The Japanese correspondent is Professor Shuntaro Shishido, formerly of the University of Tsukuba and, since 1987, President of the International University of Japan. As of now, nine forecasters are covered. They are, for quarterly forecasts, Kyoto University (4B1), JERC (4D1), RINE (4D4), Nomura (4D5), Daiwa (4D7), and NEEDS (4C1) and, for annual forecasts, EPA (4A1), Tsukuba-FAIS (4B2) and Mitsubishi (4D6).[44]

Annual forecasts can be graded for predictive power after the year is passed. Kanamori (1977) mentions that he did such grading for 1967–9 when he was a staff member of the JERC, but had to suspend the exercise since the JERC's own forecasts (4D1) did not perform particularly well, and responsible researchers at some banks became despondent over the poor rating they had received. None the less, Kanamori provides an interesting comparative study of some of these forecasts of 1974–6.

A more systematic, quantitative approach was taken by Muto (1980), who compared a few major private annual forecasts for the period 1967–78 (JERC (4D1), JERC (4D2), RINE (4D4), NRI (4D5) and Daiwa (4D7)) against the naive forecast (applying the growth rates of the year just passed) with respect to rates of change of GNP (real, nominal), private consumption (nominal), housing investment (nominal), business fixed investment (nominal), and private inventory investment (nominal). Among other interesting findings, Muto found that the private forecasts did not do much better than the naive forecasts if judged by the size of the root-mean-squared errors.

The period covered by Muto (1980) was not favourable to macroeconometric forecasts. Sato (1986) did a follow-up study by shifting the period to 1976–84, in which the Japanese economy moved onto a 'stable' path of low growth. A comparison of government forecasts and consensus private forecasts (average of all private forecasts covered in the Toyo Keizai source) was made with the naive forecasts with respect to rates of change of real GNP, industrial production, the implicit GNP deflator, the consumer price index, and the wholesale price index. This time, for all the variables except the GNP deflator, the naive forecasts gave the poorest results. Going one step further, the study set up a forecast-generating function in which the current forecast is a linear combination of the expected value of the current growth rate and the growth rate observed for the year which has just passed. As the expected value is equal to the actual value plus a random error, the forecast growth rate is regressed on the two successive growth rates. Regression results should show how well forecasters forecast and whether they are backward-looking or forward-looking (including a test of the rational expectations hypothesis). It is seen that the national government has been much more backward-looking than the consensus private forecast. Both, however, significantly overforecast the inflation rate (the GNP deflator). The exercises are replicated on a dozen private forecasts for which the time series data are (nearly) continuously available with respect to the real growth rate and the inflation rate. As for the former, the coefficient of determination ($\bar{R}^2$) ranges from 0.09 to 0.80, indicating wide diversity in forecasting ability among those forecasters.[45] As for the latter, $\bar{R}^2$ is in a much narrower range, from 0.60 to 0.84, and all forecasts overestimate by 1 to 2 percentage points.

While not all forecasts have performed equally well, informed opinion holds that the good ones among them have demonstrated satisfactory performance by international standards.[46] More in-depth analysis of forecasting performances seems to be difficult because of the constant-term adjustments, which are extensively employed by Japanese forecasters. According to one knowledgeable forecaster, 'clean' forecasts, in the sense that they are relatively free of fine-turning, are few.[47]

Critical views

Large-scale macroeconomic model-building exercises have been criticized on various accounts. Mainstream economists of the Keynesian persuasion ought to be sympathetic with this sort of work, but some of them have expressed concern and scepticism. For instance, Shozaburo Fujino of the Hitotsubashi University Institute of Economic Research, who is a leading quantitative economist himself, commented as follows: 'As Japanese macroeconomic models have become larger and larger, theoretical reflections and reconsiderations which should accompany them constantly have become less and less visible and the state of "measurement without theory" has set in' (Fujino, 1980, p. 204).[48]

Others, especially in the monetarist camp, believe that 'small is beautiful'. So long as our interest is in highly aggregated variables, such as the growth rate and the inflation rate, why should we bother with a gigantic model? A small model may perform as well as a large model.[49] Thus monetarist models have the virtue of being small and straightforward. The monetarist approach has led to the time-series or multivariate autoregressive approach. In Japan, the time-series approach has not been popular, except among the monetarists.[50]

Summary

Without trying really to be comprehensive, we have already counted more than 40 full-fledged macro-models in Stage 3, many of which are still in active operation. If we had tried to be really exhaustive by looking into every nook and corner and adding a number of special-purpose models, we could easily have expanded our list beyond one hundred. This is the best indicator of macroeconomic model-building currently going on in Japan. The Japanese macroeconometric profession ought to be commended for this thriving business. If there is anything which should be criticized, it is the seeming lack of communication within the model-building profession[51] and the absence of a market test which weeds out the weak and incompetent.[52] However the author of this chapter has faith that time will solve these problems.

Notes

1. It is not that the *General Theory* was unknown. In fact, a few leading economic theorists of Japan picked up the book soon after its publication and even introduced it in the classroom. But they were a minority. The book was really seriously studied in the late 1940s after the end of the Second World War, when a number of expository books appeared in Japan.
2. The Economic Stabilization Board was created in August 1946 as a government ministry in charge of enforcement of economic policy measures for the reconstruction of the Japanese economy. The first annual White Paper on the economy was published in February 1947. The Economic Stabilization Board was later reorganized into the Economic Planning Agency, which had less direct involvement in policy enforcement.
3. Before the Second World War, Japanese economics had been under the strong influence of German institutionalism. Marxism then came in and was growing until it was suppressed in the late 1930s. Anglo-Saxon economics was relatively less popular.
4. Staff members of Hitotsubashi University, especially its Institute of Economic Research, expended their intellectual energy on constructing their massive and monumental *Long-Term Economic Statistics of Japan since 1868*, a project which started in the early 1950s. Its first volume was published in 1965; two volumes are still to be published out of the 14-volume set. For an English summary, see Ohkawa and Shinohara (1979).
5. Most prominent in academic economic research are Hitotsubashi University, Tokyo University, Kyoto University, and Osaka University among the national universities and Keio University among the private universities.
6. The original intention of covering sociological research (Takata was initially a sociologist) was never realized but the term 'Social' remains in the institute's official title.
7. In following historical developments of model-building in Japan, one cannot miss considering how poor computer facilities were in our Stage 1. Before the mid-1950s, practising econometricians had to depend on pencils, abacuses (at which the Japanese were very adept), and at best manual hand calculators. In the late 1950s, electric digital calculators (made in America and Western Europe) became available, but they broke down very easily. Computing was a highly labour-intensive exercise, made feasible only because of the then prevailing cheap labour of research assistance. In the very early 1960s, high-speed electronic computers were introduced, but a few years were to pass before universities could instal them for academic research.
8. Two major academic centres of Japan are the Kanto or Tokyo metropolitan area and the Kansai or Kyoto-Osaka-Kobe metropolitan area.
9. The early survey of Nerlove (1966) covers the Osaka ISER, Klein-Shinkai, and Ueno models only. For other models, see MITI (1964) and Koizumi (1963).
10. For such a model, see Osamu Shimomura (1961), who was an economic adviser in a private capacity to Prime Minister Hayato Ikeda, who was responsible for the Income Doubling Plan. See also Bronfenbrenner (1965).
11. This evaluation is due to Watanabe (1969, 1970).
12. For the characteristics of this model, see Tatemoto, Uchida, and Watanabe (1967). Watanabe and Tatemoto resigned from the committee before the completion of the assignment, because of a disagreement with the government about the final plan target figures (Watanabe, 1969, p. 116, and 1970). Both Watanabe (1926–76) and Uchida (1923–86) are now deceased. The sole survivor, Tatemoto, in his presidential address to the Japan Association of Economics and Econometrics in 1987, reported the re-estimated version of the 1967 model based on recent data (1966–84) (Tatemoto, 1988).

This model consists of 26 behavioural equations (including three new ones) and eleven identities.

13. An input–output table was officially prepared for the first time for the year 1951. From 1955 on, an analogous table has been prepared every five years.

14. For the details of the overall model, see Economic Planning Agency (1965, 1966). Other members of the Econometric Subcommittee were Kazushi Ohkawa (chairman), Masao Baba, Akira Yajima, and Yasuhiko Yuize. Shuntaro Shishido was the principal liaison officer of the Economic Planning Agency.

15. The committee remains active. Over the last 10 years it has produced three reports – fifth (1977), sixth (1980) and seventh (1984). In 1984, the committee consisted of 21 members.

16. For details, see its seven successive reports from 1966 to 1984.

17. For the long-term optimization model, see Tsukui and Murakami (1973, 1979).

18. The model size has been expanding rapidly. The number of endogenous variables in the medium-term multi-sector model was 691 in the 1977 version and 1156 in the 1984 version.

19. For SP–1 (1960) and SP–2 (1963), see MITI (1964).

20. For an early sample, see Shishido *et al.* (1968).

21. The 1969 version consisted of 71 equations (32 behavioural and 39 definitional). See Watanabe and Uchida (1969).

22. In my first literature search for Stage 3 (Sato, 1981) I benefited much from the advice of Chikashi Moriguchi, who made available to me the list of participants in the Kyoto Econometric Models Project, which he organized. This project holds semi-annual conferences of leading model-builders. The first meeting was held in November 1977 and they are still running.

   My second literature search for the early 1980s was facilitated by two survey papers of Japan's econometric models, which were presented to the autumn 1985 Convention of the Japan Association of Economics and Econometrics, namely, Saito and Moriguchi (1985) on domestic models and Amano (1985) on international linkage models.

23. The Japanese government maintained the 'Buy Japanese' policy for national university computers, with the market shared by three major computer firms (Hitachi, Fuji and Nippon Electric). For the development of Japan's computer industry, see Shinjo (1988).

24. On progress reports of this project, see its newsletter, *Statistical Data Bank*. The project is fully explained in its first issue (October 1983).

25. Besides those discussed in the text, some recent projections have been as follows:

Author of projection	Date	Projection year
Research Institute of National Economy (*a*)	Sept. 1987	1990
Nomura Research Institute (*b*)	Apr. 1984	1993
Mitsui and Co. (*b*)	Jan. 1985	1990
Japan Industrial Bank (*b*)	Jan. 1984	1990
Japan Economic Research Center (*c*)	Feb. 1988	1993, 2000
Japan Economic Research Center (*a*)	Dec. 1987	1992

   (*a*)   As quoted in Toyo Keizai, *Keizai Tokei Nenkan* (Economic Statistics Yearbook), (Tokyo: Toyo Keizai, 1988).
   (*b*)   As quoted in Toyo Keizai, op. cit., 1985.
   (*c*)   Japan Economic Research Center (1985).

26. Among those topics not reviewed here, honourable mention may be made of regional models, which were popular at one time (the 1960s), and of models of social security and medical care, which are getting popular.

27. See the discussion paper series of the Institute, which reports the proceedings of international symposia on the World Economic Model with the participation of foreign and Japanese economists.

28. Forecasters announce their own short-term forecasts in their special bulletins and/or regular periodicals. Newspapers report some of them.

29. Therefore 'neither the specific structure of the model nor predictions therefrom are released to the public' (a private communication from Mr Shoichi Ogawa, Associate Advisor, Research and Statistics Department, Bank of Japan).

30. MOF prepares medium-term projections on public finance (for example, its January 1985 report on the fiscal balance up to 1988). These projections seem to have been obtained from a relatively crude non-econometric model.

31. The name of the model is expected to be changed as Professor Moriguchi moved to the Institute of Social and Economic Research of Osaka University in April 1986.

32. Keran's recursive system is as follows (variables in growth rates):

> imports→foreign reserves→money supply→nominal GNP
> 2Q lag   1Q lag   2Q lag
>
> no lag

33. Note, however, that the two BOJ models (2B1, 4A4) are of the Keynesian type. They are maintained by the Bank's Research Department, not by the Institute.

34. Most of this literature can be found in the Bank of Japan Institute's periodicals, *Kin'yu Keykyu Shiryo* (14 issues from January 1979 to September 1982), *Kin'yu Kenkyu* (quarterly from October 1982) and *Monetary and Economic Studies* (quarterly from June 1983) as well as its discussion papers (available in English).

35. A more detailed tabular survey (as of the end of the 1970s) is available in Sato (1981) for the following models: 1A1, 1B1, 2A1, 2C1, 2D1, 2E1, 4A2, 4A3, 4B1, 4B2, 4C1, 4D1, 4D2, 4D7, 4D8. Saito and Moriguchi (1985) review the following models: 1B2, 1B3, 2C2, 2C3, 2D1, 4A3, 4A5, 4B1, 4B2, 4B3, 4B4, 4C1, 4D3, 4D8. Amano (1985) reviews 3A1, 3A2, 3A3, 3A4, 3B1, 3B2.

36. Saito and Moriguchi (1985) give an equation-by-equation comparison of structural parameter estimates for consumption, business fixed investment, housing investment, inventory investment, merchandise exports and imports, production functions, and demands for financial assets.

37. Reported are the effects of fiscal policy (an increase in government spending and a cut in the corporation income tax), oil shocks, wage increases and exchange rate changes. These have been computed by the model-builders themselves.

38. See Saito and Moriguchi (1985), table 3–1.

39. After this was first written, an attempt was made to test for structural change during the mid-1970s, with the use of the two MOF models (4A5), as reported in Sawa *et al.* (1987, 1988).

40. Ito, Ban, *et al.* (1984) repeat this exercise with respect to the Japanese model of 4A3 by comparing performances of OLS, TSLS, and FIML. See also Sawa *et al.* (1987, 1988).

41. I owe these points to Dr T. Taya of the Daiwa Securities Institute.

42. Analysis of prediction errors was often reported for the EPA–SP model (4A2) in *Keizai Bunseki*. The EPA medium-term models (1B1, 1B2) do likewise. For the Kyoto University model (4B1) and the FLEX model (2D1), see Moriguchi (1983) and Amano (1983), respectively.

43. For changes in the number of forecasters covered in the *JERC Bulletin*, see Muto (1980). For 1988, see *JERC Bulletin*, No. 551–2 (1–15 January 1988).

44. See Shishido (1984).

45. The GNP growth rate is the weighted average of growth rates of GNP components. Thus one should be able to pinpoint principal sources of prediction errors of the GNP growth rate. Takeuchi *et al.* (1985) did this exercise by applying the principal component analysis to the 1983 and 1984 forecasts.

46. This remark is based on private communication with Professor Lawrence R. Klein, who looked at performance comparisons of project LINK models.

47. The exceptions which he cites include the Kyoto University model (4B1), the Daiwa model (4D7) and the NEEDS model (4C1). Of course, it hardly needs to be emphasized that this vice (if it be one) is not unique to Japanese forecasters.

48. The same point was made by Takamitsu Sawa (1980), who is one of Japan's leading

econometric theorists. Sawa not only criticizes macroeconometric models but also is even more critical of the time-series approach.

For an interesting dialogue on macroeconometric models, see Uzawa and Uchida (1980). A critical position is taken by Hirofumi Uzawa, who has long foresaken the neoclassical camp, and a supportive position by Tadao Uchida, the initiator of macro-model-building in Japan.

49. See the foreword of S. Kobayashi, Executive Director of the Institute of Developing Economies, to ELSA (Institute of Developing Economies, 1984).
50. The Special Studies Department of the Bank of Japan (1981) sponsored a panel discussion of leading Japanese econometricians to review the possibility of reconciling the two approaches, but there were few constructive suggestions.
51. This is based, first, on my personal impression derived from my talks with Japanese model-builders and, second, on the list of participants in Professor Chikashi Moriguchi's semi-annual meetings of the Kyoto Econometric Models Project – participants are mostly academic model-builders, with very few business forecasters.
52. As noted earlier, forecasts are provided free of charge except for the commercially operated NEEDS. (Some business forecasters are now thinking of marketing their quarterly forecasts on diskettes in order to become more self-supporting.) They are thus public goods and, as such, free from public criticisms. Though those forecasts are conveniently put together in the *JERC Bulletin* and Toyo Keizai's *Yearbook*, they are seldom subjected to systematic reviews. In the absence of the market test and the competitive milieu, the survival of the fittest does not work. See Sato (1986) on these points.

References

Amano, Akihiro (1982) 'A Structural Approach to Capital Flows and Exchange Rates', Discussion Paper no. 179, Kyoto Institute of Economic Research, August.

———— (1983) 'Hendo Kawase Reito Seido to Nihon Keizai' [The Floating Exchange Rate System and the Japanese Economy], in Moriguchi *et al.*, pp. 23–44.

———— (1985) 'Wagakuni niokeru Kokusai Renketsu Makuro Keiryo Moderu, Tembo' [Macroeconometric Models of International Linkage in Japan: A Survey], Working Paper 8504, Kobe University School of Business Administration, August.

Amano, Akihiro *et al.* (1973) *Kokusai Shushi Moderu no Kenkyu* [A Balance-of-Payments Model of Japan], Monograph No. 27, Economic Research Institute, Economic Planning Agency (Tokyo: Government Printing Office).

Amano, Akihiro, Kanemi Ban, and Chikashi Moriguchi (1976) 'A Quarterly Forecasting Econometric Model of Japan: KYQ75', Discussion Paper No. 095, Kyoto Institute of Economic Research, Kyoto University, March.

Andersen, L. C. and K. M. Carlson (1970) 'A Monetarist Model for Economic Stabilization', Federal Reserve Bank of St Louis *Review*, 52 (April) pp. 7–25.

Ban, Kanemi (1979) 'A Comparison of Alternative Estimation Methods for Large-Scale Econometric Models: A Case Study of an Econometric Model of Japan', *Economic Studies Quarterly*, 30 (April) pp. 10–20.

Bank of Japan (Special Studies Department) (1981) 'Panel Discussion: Methods of Empirical Analysis – Econometric versus Time-Series Approaches' (in Japanese) *Kin'yu Kenkyu Shiryo*, No. 6 (January).

Bank of Japan (Statistical Department) (1972) 'Nihon Ginko Keiryo Keizai Moderu – sono Kanten to Kosei' [The Bank of Japan Macroeconometric Model: Its Viewpoint and Structure], *Chosa Geppo* (Bank of Japan, September).

Blumenthal, Tuvia (1965) 'A Test of the Klein–Shinkai Econometric Model of Japan', *International Economic Review*, 6 (May) pp. 211–28.

Bronfenbrenner, Martin (1965) 'Formalizing the Shimomura Growth Model', *Economic Development and Cultural Change*, 14 (October) pp. 85–90.

Clark, Colin (1949) 'A System of Equations Explaining the United States Trade Cycle 1921 to 1941', *Econometrica*, 17 (April) pp. 93–124.

Committee for Econometric Model Analysis (Keiryo Iinkai (1967–84) Economic Delibe-ration Council (ed.), *Keiryo Iinkai Hokoku* [Committee Report] (Tokyo: Government Printing Office) – I (1967), II (1968), III (1970), IV (1973), V (1977), VI (1980), VII (1984).

———— (1979) *Econometric Model for the New Economic and Social Seven-Year Plan* (Tokyo: Economic Planning Agency).

Daiwa Securities Co. (1978) 'A Quarterly Econometric Model of Japan, Twelfth Revised Version', Discussion Paper No. 2 (July).

Denken [Central Research Institute for Electric Power Industry], (1983) 'Gen'yu Nesagari no Nihon Keizai ni oyobosu Eikyo' [Effects of the Oil Price Decline on the Japanese Economy], May.

Duesenberry, James, Gary Fromm, Lawrence Klein and Edwin Kuh (eds) (1965) *The Brookings Quarterly Econometric Model of the U.S. Economy* (Chigaco: Rand McNally).

Eckstein, Otto (1983) *The DRI Model of the U.S. Economy* (New York: McGraw-Hill).

Economic Planning Agency (ed.) (1965) *Chuki Keizai Keikaku* [Medium-Term Economic Plan] (Tokyo: Government Printing Office).

———— (ed.) (1966) *Chuki Keizai Keikaku, Keiryo Keizai Moderu niyoru Nihon Keizai Bun-seki, Keiryo Shoiinkai Kenkyu Hokoku* [Medium-Term Economic Plan's Econometric Model Analysis of the Japanese Economy, A Report of the Econometric Subcommittee] (Tokyo: Government Printing Office).

———— (1982) *2000-nen no Nihon* [Japan in Year 2000], vol. 10, *Choki Tembo Technical Report* [Technical Report on Long-Term Projections] (Tokyo: Government Printing Office).

Economic Research Institute (1978) 'A New Short-Term Econometric Prediction Model', mimeo, 15 December.

———— Economic Research Institute (1982, 1984, 1987) 'EPA World Economic Model', Discussion Paper No. 11 (February 1982), No. 16 (February 1984), No. 18 (September 1987).

Ezaki, Mitsuo (1979) 'Linking National Econometric Models of Japan, U.S.A., and the East and Southeast Asian Countries – A Pilot Study', *Tonan Ajia Kenkyu*, 17 (Sept.) pp. 178–200.

———— (1986) 'A Computable General Equilibrium Model of the Japanese Economy', *Kobe Economic and Business Review*, pp. 55–100.

Ezaki, Mitsuo, Mamoru Shibayama and Shin'ichi Ichimura (1984) 'An Econometric Link System for the East and Southeast Asian Countries, Japan and the United States', *Tonan Ajia Kenkyu* [Southeast Asian Studies], 22 (Dec.) pp. 260–83.

Fujino, Shozaburo (1980) '*Keizai Kenkyu* ni okeru Kenkyu Doko' [Major Trends in Studies Published in *Keizai Kenkyu*], *Keizai Kenkyu*, 31 (July) pp. 193–204.

Fujino, Shozaburo and Yoshimasa Kurabayashi (1952) 'Keiki Hendo to Keizai Mokei' [Business Cycles and an Economic Model], *Economic Studies Quarterly*, 3 (April) pp. 159–66.

Hamada, Fumimasa (1978) 'A Quarterly Econometric Model of Japan', *Keio Economic Studies*, 15, pp. 1–51.

———— (1984) *Nihon Keizai no Makuro Bunseki* [Macroeconomic Analysis of the Japanese Economy] (Tokyo: Nippon Hyoron Sha).

Hatanaka, Michio and Shin Saito (1974) 'Nihon Keizai no Makuro Keiryo Moderu ni motozuku Tanki Yosoku no Performance ni tsuite' [On the Performance of Short-Term Forecasts by the Japanese Econometric Models], *Economic Studies Quarterly*, 25 (August) pp. 15–28.

Ichimura, Shin'ichi (1962) 'Kahei no Juyo Kansu to Kyokyu Kansu' [Demand for and Supply of Money Functions], *Economic Studies Quarterly*, 12 (January) pp. 10–20.

Ichimura, Shin'ichi and Mitsuo Ezaki (eds) (1985) *Econometric Models of Asian Link* (Berlin: Springer Verlag).

Ichimura, Shin'ichi, Lawrence R. Klein, Susumu Koizumi, Kazuo Sato and Yoichi Shinkai (1964) 'A Quarterly Econometric Model of Japan, 1952–59', *Osaka Economic Papers*, 12 (March) pp. 19–44.

———— (1977) *An Econometric Analysis of the Japanese Economy* (Kyoto: The Japanese Society for Asian Studies).

Institute of Developing Economies (1984) *Econometric Link System for ASEAN, Overview* (Tokyo: IDE).
_____ (1985) *Econometric Link System for ASEAN*, 2 vols (Tokyo: IDE).
Ito, Kokichi and Yasuhiro Murota (1984) 'Translog kata Hiyo Kansu o fukunda Macro Model no Suikei' [Estimation of a Macro-Model including Cost Functions of the Translog Type], *Nihon Keizai Kenkyu*, No. 13 (March) pp. 31–40.
Ito, Seiichi, Kanemi Ban, *et al.* (1984) 'Daikibo Keiryo Keizai Moderu no Kozo Bunseki, Kaiho, Suikei ni tsuite' [On Structural Analysis of Large-Scale Econometric Models], *Keizai Bunseki*, No. 93 (March).
Japan Economic Research Center (1976) *Nihon Keizai Kenkyu Senta Shin Makuro Moderu* [A New Macroeconometric Model of the JERC] (January).
_____ (1986) *Dai 12-kai Gokanen Keizai Yosoku* [Twelfth Five-Year Economic Projection, 1986–90] (Tokyo: JERC, April).
_____ (1988) *2000-nen no Seikai Keizai* [The World Economy in the Year 2000] (Tokyo: JERC).
Kanamori, Hisao (ed.) (1977a) *Keiki Yosoku Nyumon* [An Introduction to Business Forecasting] (Tokyo: Nihon Keizai Shimbun Sha).
Kanamori, Hisao (1977b) 'Keiki Yosoku no Performance' [The Performance of Business Forecasts], Kanamori (1977a) pp. 351–67.
Kansai Joho Center [Kansai Information Center] (1978) *Sangyo Renkan Bunseki Yo Software no Kaihatsu* [Development of Software for Economic Analysis in Linking Interindustry and Macroeconometric Models] (Osaka: Kansai Joho Center, March).
Kansai Keizai Kenkyu Center [Kansai Economic Research Center] (1980) *Nihon Keizai to Zaisei no Keiryo Bunseki — Chuki Zaisei Moderu no Kaihatsu to Oyo* [Econometric Analysis of the Japanese Economy and its Public Finance – Development and Application of a Medium-Term Public Finance Model] (Osaka: Kansai Keizai Kenkyu Center, July).
_____ (1984) *Nihon Keizai to Zaisei Kin'yu no Keiryo Bunseki Hokokusho* (Report on Econometric Analysis of Public Finance and Financial Sectors in the Japanese Economy] (Osaka: Kansai Keizai Kenkyu Center), March).
Katsumura, Yasuro (1977) 'Dankaiteki Sekkinho ni yoru Keiki Yosoku' [Economic Forecasts by Successive Approximations], Chapter 4 of Kanamori (1977a) pp. 101–17.
Keran, Michael W. (1970) 'Monetary Policy and the Business Cycle in Postwar Japan', in David Meiselman, *Varieties of Monetary Experience* (Chicago: University of Chicago Press) chapter 3, pp. 163–248.
Keynes, John M. (1936) *The General Theory of Employment, Interest and Money* (London: Macmillan); Japanese translation by Tsukumo Shionoya (Tokyo: Toyo Keizai Shimpo Sha, 1941).
Kinoshita, Soshichi (1983) 'Structure and Application of a World Industry and Trade Model', Link Fall Meeting, University of Tsukuba, September.
_____ (1984) 'Takokukan Tabumon Moderu niyoru Hogo Boeki Shugi no Simulation' [Simulations of Trade Protectionism Based on a Multi-Country, Multi-Sector Model], *Keizai Kagaku* (Nagoya University) 31 (March) pp. 1–49.
Kinoshita, Soshichi, Y. Kajino, M. Saito, Y. Shiina and M. Yamada (1982) *Nihon o meguru Kokusai-teki Sangyo Boeki Kozo Bunseki no tameno Sangyo Boeki Moderu no Kaihatsu to Tembo* [Development and Application of a World Industry and Trade Model for the Analysis of International Trade and Industry Structure Focusing on Japan], Economic Research Institute, Economic Planning Agency, Monograph No. 38 (Tokyo: Government Printing Office).
Klein, Lawrence R. (1961) 'A Model of Japanese Economic Growth, 1878–1937', *Econometrica*, 29 (July) pp. 277–92.
Klein, Lawrence R. and Arthur S. Goldberger (1955) *An Econometric Model of the United States, 1929–52* (Amsterdam: North-Holland).
Klein, Lawrence R. and Richard F. Kosobud (1961) 'Some Econometrics of Growth: Great Ratios of Economics', *Quarterly Journal of Economics*, 75 (May) pp. 173–98.

Klein, Lawrence R. and Yoichi Shinkai (1963) 'An Econometric Model of Japan, 1930–59', *International Economic Review*, 4 (January) pp. 1–28.

Koizumi, Susumu (1963) 'Nihon Keizai no Econometric Moderu' [Econometric Models of the Japanese Economy], *Economic Studies Quarterly*, 13 (May) pp. 1–12.

Ministry of International Trade and Industry (MITI) (Research and Statistics Division, Ministerial Office) (1964) *Nihon Keizai no Kyoshiteki Keiryo Keizai Moderu, sono Tembo to Hyoka* [Macroeconometric Models of the Japanese Economy: Survey and Evaluation] (Tokyo: Tsusho Sangyo Chosakai).

Mori, Kei (1963) 'Minkan Zaisei Kongo Moderu niyoru Nihon Keiizai no Kozo Bunseki: 1953IV–1964I, TCER Model V-8-I, II no Sakusei to Simulation Jikken' [A Simulation Model of the Postwar Japanese Economy, 1953–IV–1964-I], *Economic Studies Quarterly*, 13 (May) pp. 45–67.

_____ (1966) 'Simulation Analysis of Fluctuations and Growth of the Japanese Economy: 1955–1960', R. Komiya (ed.), *Postwar Economic Growth in Japan* (University of California Press) pp. 189–205; translation of the Japanese article in Komiya, R. (ed.) (1963) *Sengo Nihon no Keizai Seicho* (Tokyo: Iwanami Shoten).

Moriguchi, Chikashi (1979) 'Makuro Keiryo Moderu nimiru Nihon Keizai no Kozo Henka to Seisakuteki Imi' [Structural Changes in the Japanese Economy in the Recent Decade, from a Macroeconometric Viewpoint], *Keizai Kenkyu*, 30 (January) pp. 20–9.

_____ (1983) 'Nihon Keizai no Makuro Keiryu Moderu Bunseki' [Macroeconometric Analysis of the Japanese Economy], chapter 1 in Moriguchi *et al.* (1983) pp. 5–21.

Moriguchi, Chikashi, Masahiko Aoki and Takamitsu Sawa (eds) (1983) *Nihon Keizai no Kozo Bunseki* [Structural Analysis of the Japanese Economy] (Tokyo: Sobunsha).

Moruta, Yasuhiro (1985) '1995-nen no Enerugi Jukyu Yosoku' [1995 Projections of Energy Demand and Supply], *Japan Economic Research Center Bulletin*, no. 486 (15 April) pp. 8–16.

Muto, Hiromichi (1980) 'Tanki Makuro Keizai Yosoku no Kagakusci to Yuyosei' [Short-Term Macroeconomic Predictions: Being Scientific and Useful], *Nihon Keizai Kenkyu*, No. 9 (March) pp. 52–61.

NEEDS (1984) *Nikkei Macro Moderu* [Nikkei Macro Model], July.

Nerlove, Marc (1966) 'A Tabular Survey of Macroeconometric Models', *International Economic Review*, 7 (May) pp. 127–75.

Nomura Research Institute (1982) *NRI Tanki Makuro Yosoku Moderu* [NRI Short-Term Macroeconomic Forecasting Model], January.

Ohkawa, Kazushi and Miyokei Shinohara (1979) *Patterns of Japanese Economic Development: A Quantitative Approach* (New Haven: Yale University Press).

Okina, Kunio (1985) 'Reexamination of Empirical Studies Using Granger Causality – "Causality" between Money Supply and National Income', Bank of Japan, *Monetary and Economic Studies*, 3 (December) pp. 129–62.

_____ (1986) 'Relationships between Money Supply and Real Output in the Japanese Economy – Survey on the Empirical Tests of the LSW Proposition', Bank of Japan, *Monetary and Economic Studies*, 4 (April) pp. 41–77.

Onishi, Akira (1983) 'North–South Relations: Alternative Policy Simulations for the World Economy in the 1980s', *Journal of Policy Modeling*, 5 (March) pp. 55–74.

Sadahiro, Akira *et al.* (1987) 'Sekai Keizai Moderu ni okeru Nihon Keizai Moderu' [The Japanese Model in the World Economic Model], *Keizai Bunseki*, No. 110 (July) pp. 1–118.

Saito, Mitsuo (1974) *Ippan Kinko to Kakaku* [General Equilibrium and Prices] (Tokyo: Sobunsha).

Saito, Mitsuo and Chikashi Moriguchi (1985) 'Nihon Keizai no Makuro Moderu, Tembo' [A Survey of Macroeconometric Models of Japan], Discussion Paper 8503, Kyoto Institute of Economic Research, October.

Saito, Mitsuo and Takayuki Oono (1985) 'An Energy Model of the Japanese Economy', mimeo, Kobe University Department of Economics.

Sato, Kazuo (1981) 'A Survey of Macroeconometric Forecasting Models of Japan: Development and Current State', *Japanese Economic Studies*, 9 (Spring) pp. 3–60.

_____ (1986) 'Evaluations of Forecasts', *Nihon Keizai Kenkyu*, No. 15 (March) pp. 2–13.

Sawa, Takamitsu (1980) 'Makuro Keizai Moderu no Yukosei' [The Validity of Macroeconometric Models], *Keizai Seminar*, no. 301 (February) pp. 24–31.

Sawa, Takamitsu *et al.* (1987–8) 'Post Kodo Seichoki no Keizai Kozo' [Economic Structure in the Post-Rapid-Growth Period], Parts I & II, *Financial Review* (Ministry of Finance Institute of Fiscal and Monetary Policy), No. 6 (October 1987) pp. 72–123 and No. 7 (March 1988) pp. 21–49.

Shimomura, Osamu (1961) 'Seicho Seisaku no Kihon Mondai' [Basic Issues in Growth Policy], *Economic Studies Quarterly*, 11 (March–April).

Shimpo, Seiji (1980) *Gendai Nihon Keizai no Keimei* [Study of Contemporary Japanese Economy] (Tokyo: Tokyo Keizai Shimpo Sha).

_____ (1985) *Bunseki Nihon Keizai* [Analysis of the Japanese Economy] (Tokyo: Toyo Keizai Shimpo Sha, October).

Shimpo, Seiji, K. Konishi and S. Ohira (1978) 'Monetarist Moderu ni yoru Stagflation no Bunseki' [Stagflation Analysed by a Monetarist Model], *Kenzai Bunseki*, no. 72 (June); English version, 'A Monetarist Model for the Japanese Economy', Discussion Paper No. 20, Economic Research Institute, Economic Planning Agency, March.

Shinjo, Koji (1988) 'The Computer Industry', Ryutaro Komiya *et al.* (eds) *Industrial Policy of Japan* (Tokyo: Academic Press) chapter 13, pp. 333–65.

Shishido, Shuntaro (1984) 'Denshi Mail ni yoru Kokusai Keizai Yosoku Joho no Network to Data Base' [Data Base on International Economic Forecasts Using the Electronic Mail Network], *Statistical Data Bank*, 2 (October) pp. 1–6.

Shishido, Shuntaro, Akio Kohno, Seiichi Nagaya and Shosuke Tanaka (1968) 'Use of National Accounts for a Short-Term Econometric Model, 1954–1966'. *Review of Income and Wealth*, 14 (September) pp. 267–309.

Shishido, Shuntaro, Yo Ichikawa, Tsutomu Noda, Ken'ichi Furuya, Akira Oshizaka and Shunsaku Nishikawa (1970) *Tanki Keizai Yosoku Master Moderu no Kenkyu* [A Master Model for Short-Term Economic Predictions], Monograph No. 21, Economic Research Institute, Economic Planning Agency (Tokyo: Government Printing Office).

Shishido, Shuntaro, H. Fujiwara, A. Kohno, Y. Kurokawa, S. Matsuura and H. Wago (1980) 'A Model for the Coordination of Recovery Policies in the OECD Region', *Journal of Policy Modeling*, 2 (January) pp. 35–55.

Suzuki, Yoshio (1964) *Nihon no Tsuka to Bukka* [Money and Prices in Japan] (Tokyo: Toyo Keizai Shimpo Sha).

_____ (1974) *Gendai Nihon Kin'yuron* (Tokyo: Toyo Keizai Shimpo Sha); English version, *Money and Banking in Contemporary Japan* (New Haven: Yale University Press, 1980).

_____ (1982) 'The Inflation Debate in Japan: A Historical Review', *Japanese Economic Studies*, 11 (Autumn) pp. 3–36.

Takeuchi, Kei *et al.* (1985) 'Soft-ka ni okeru Keizai Tokei no Kadai' [Tasks for Economic Statistics in the 'Softization' Era], *Softonomics Series*, I (March).

Tatemoto, Masahiro (1988) '"A Stabilization Model" After Twenty Years', *Economic Studies Quarterly*, 39 (March) pp. 1–13.

Tatemoto, Masahiro and Mitsuho Uchida (1972) 'Denken Makuro Moderu: 1958–1968IV' [Denken Macro Model], *Denryoku Keizai Kenkyu*, no. 1 (August) pp. 1–18.

Tatemoto, Masahiro, Tadao Uchida and Tsunehiko Watanabe (1967) 'A Stabilization Model for the Postwar Japanese Economy, 1954–1962', *International Economic Review*, 8 (February) pp. 13–44.

Tinbergen, Jan (1939) *Statistical Testing of Business Cycle Theories*, Part II, 'Business Cycles in the United States of America, 1919–1932' (Geneva: League of Nations).

Tsujimura, Kotaro and Masahiro Kuroda (1974) *Nihon Keizai no Ippan Kinko Bunseki* [General Equilibrium Analysis of the Japanese Economy] (Tokyo: Chikuma Shobo).

Tsujimura, Kotaro, Masahiro Kuroda and Haruo Shimada (1981) *Economic Policy and General Interdependence: A Quantitative Theory of Price and Empirical Model Building* (Tokyo: Kogakusha).

Tsukui, Jinkichi and Yasusuke Murakami (1979) *Turnpike Optimality in Input/Output System* (Amsterdam: North-Holland).

Tsukui, Jinkichi, Yasusuke Murakami *et al.* (1973) *Turnpike Moderu – Tabumon Saiteki Moderu* [A Turnpike Model of Multi-Sector Optimization], Monograph No. 28, Economic Research Institute, Economic Planning Agency (Tokyo: Government Printing Office).

Uchida, Tadao and Tsunehiko Watanabe (1959) 'Nihon Keizai no Hendo 1951–1956' [Fluctuations in the Japanese Economy], *Economic Studies Quarterly*, 9 (June) pp. 20–9.

Uchida, Tadao and Kei Mori (1960) 'Nihon Keizai no Simulation Bunseki' [A Simulation Analysis of the Japanese Economy], *Atarashii Keizai Bunseki* (Tokyo: Sobunsha pp. 211–42).

Uchida, Tadao, Sei Kuribayashi, Akira Yajima and Tsunehiko Watanabe (1966) *Keizai Yosoku to Keiryo Moderu* [Economic Forecasting and Macroeconometric Models], Monograph No. 7, Japan Economic Research Centre (Tokyo: Nihon Keizai Shimbun Sha).

Ueno, Hiroya (1961) 'Nihon Keisai no Choki Moderu, 1920–1958' [A Long-Term Model of the Japanese Economy, 1920–1958], *Keizai Kenkyu*, 12 (July) pp. 209–15.

_____ (1963) 'A Long-Term Model of the Japanese Economy 1920–1958', *International Economic Review*, 3 (May) pp. 171–93.

_____ (1980) *Tabumon Moderu no Oyo* [Applications of Multi-Sector Econometric Models] (Tokyo: Nihon Keizai Shimbun Sha).

Ueno, Hiroya and Soshichi Kinoshita (1965) *Nihon Keizai no Seicho Moderu* [A Growth Model of the Japanese Economy] (Tokyo: Toyo Keizai Shimpo Sha).

Ueno, Hiroya and Soshichi Kinoshita (1968) 'A Simulation Experiment for Growth with a Long-Term Model of Japan', *International Economic Review*, 9 (February) pp. 14–48.

Ueno, Hiroya and Hiromichi Muto (1975) 'Nihon Keizai no Sangyokan Rendo Moderu' [A Simultaneous Interindustry Model of the Japanese Economy], in Hiroya Ueno and Yasusuke Murakami (eds), *Nihon Keizai no Keiryo Bunseki* [Econometric Analysis of the Japanese Economy] (Tokyo: Iwanami Shoten).

Ueno, Hiroya, Tatsuo Yagi and Seiji Terui (1971) *Nibumon Seicho Moderu niyoru Senzai Seichoryoku no Sokutei* [Measurement of Growth Potential in a Two-Sector Growth Model], Monograph No. 23, Economic Research Institute, Economic Planning Agency (Tokyo: Government Printing Office).

Uno, Kimio (1978) *Shakai Shihyo Keiryo Moderu* [An Econometric Model of Social Indicators] (Tokyo: Japan Economic Research Center).

Uzawa, Hirofumi and Tadao Uchida (1980) 'Keizaigaku to Keizai no Kiki o Saikento suru' [Crises of Economics and Economy Re-examined], *Kikan Gendai Keizai* [Contemporary Economics], no. 39 (Summer) pp. 3–20.

Valavanis-Vail, Stefan (1955) 'An Econometric Model of Growth: U.S.A., 1869–1953', *American Economic Review*, 45 (May) pp. 208–21.

Watanabe, Tsunehiko (1969) *Gendai no Keizai Seisaku* [Contemporary Economic Policy] (Tokyo: Iwanami Shoten).

_____ (1970) 'National Planning and Economic Development: A Critical Review of the Japanese Experience', *Economic Planning*, 10, pp. 21–51.

Watanabe, Tsunehiko and Tadao Uchida (1969) 'A Quantitative Appraisal of National Economic Policy: The Case of Japan', Discussion Paper No. 015, Kyoto Institute of Economic Research, August.

Yamaha, Isamu (1948) 'Keynes no Dotaiteki Taikei niyoru Nihon Keizai no Bunseki' [The Structural Analysis of the Japanese Economy by a Dynamic Keynesian System], *Hitotsubashi Ronso*, 19, pp. 25–42; reprinted with recomputations in Isamu Yamada, *Keizai no Keiryo* (Measurement of the Economy] (1949) pp. 40–84.

Yoshida, Kazuo, in collaboration with Takamitsu Sawa (1984) 'A Test of the Efficacy of Fiscal Policy in the Japanese Economy', mimeo, Ministry of Finance.

Yoshitomi, Masaru *et al.* (1981) 'Sekai Keizai Moderu niokeru Nihon Keizai no Tanki Yosoku Moderu' [An Econometric Model of Japan for Short-Term Forecasting in the EPA World Economic Model], *Keizai Bunseki*, no. 82 (April) pp. 1–299.

Appendix: A tabular survey of principal macro-models in the 1970s and the early 1980s

No.	Model name	Builder	Size	Time unit	Objective
1A1	Keio Multi-Sector Model	Economic Observatory, Keio University	medium 166 (52B/114D)	annual (inactive)	analysis of general equilibrium interdependence
1B1	EPA Medium-Term Macro-Model	Committee for Econometric Model Analysis	small 72 (43B/29D) (1976 version)	semi-annual (discont.)	policy simulation (replaced by 1B2)
1B2	EPA Medium-Term Multi-Sector Model	Committee for Econometric Model Analysis	large 834 (212B/622D)	semi-annual (active)	medium-term plan projections
1B3/3A3	EPA–Kinoshita Multi-Sector Model	Soshichi Kinoshita (Nagoya University) in association with the EPA Institute	large 390 (314B/76D)	annual (active)	analysis of impacts of shifting comparative advantage
1B4	JERC Medium-Term Projection Model	Japan Economic Research Center	small 62 (43B/19D)	annual (active)	Medium-term projections
2A1	Medium-Term Public Finance Model	Kansai Economic Research Center	large 440 (218B/222D) (only for public finance)	quarterly (inactive)	fiscal policy simulation

No.	Model name	Builder	Size	Time unit	Objective
2B1	BOJ Macro-Model	Research & Statistics Department, Bank of Japan	medium 151 (64B/87/D) (1979 version)	quarterly (?)	analysis of financial behaviour
2B2	KERC Financial Model	Kansai Economic Research Center	medium 200 (88B/112D)	quarterly (inactive)	endogenizing the financial sector; monetary and fiscal simulation
2C1	KIC Econometric Model	Kansai Information Center	small 82 (59B/23D)	annual (inactive)	Evaluating the macro-effects of natural resource constraints
2C2	Kobe University Energy Model	Mitsuo Saito (Kobe University) & Takayuki Oono (Kagawa University)	medium 116 (69B/47D)	annual (active)	energy problem & its medium-term forecasting
2C3	Computable General* Equilibrium Model	Mitsuo Ezaki (Kyoto University)	large 334 equations	annual (active)	simulation of macro-economic effects of oil price changes
2C4	Saitama University Energy Model	Yasuhiro Murota (Saitama University)	small 25 (18B/7D)	annual (active)	long-term projections of energy

No.	Model name	Builder	Size	Time unit	Objective
2D1	Kobe University FLEX Model	Akihiro Amano (Kobe University)	medium 181 (87B/94D) (FLEX 4, 1982)	quarterly (inactive)	endogenous determination of the exchange rate
2E1	JERC Social Indicator Model	Kimio Uno (University of Tsukuba) in association with the JERC	medium 132 (101B/31D)	annual (inactive)	projections of social indicators (demographic & environmental)
3B2	Asian Link Model	Center for Southeast Asian Studies (Kyoto University) – Mitsuo Ezaki & Chikashi Moriguchi	small 57	annual (active)	analysis of economic interdependence & policy simulation in East & Southeast Asia
4A2	EPA–SP Model	Economic Research Institute, Economic Planning Agency	medium 112 (45B/67D) (SP–19, 1979)	quarterly (discont.)	short-term predictions & policy simulation (replaced by 4A3)
4A3/3A1	EPA World Economy Model	Economic Research Institute, Economic Planning Agency	large 235 (59B/176D) (1987 version)	quarterly (active)	short-term predictions & policy simulations in the global framework

No.	Model name	Builder	Size	Time unit	Objective
4A4	BOJ Short-Term Forecasting	Research & Statistics Dept., Bank of Japan	medium 171 (60B/111D)	quarterly (active)	quarterly predictions & policy simulations
4A5I	MOF Macro-Model I	Institute of Fiscal and Monetary Policy, Ministry of Finance	small 16 (9B/7D)	quarterly (active)	testing structural change at 1975
4A5II	MOF Macro-Model II	Institute of Fiscal and Monetary Policy, Ministry of Finance	small 56 (25B/31D)	quarterly (active)	testing structural change at 1975
4B1	Kyoto University Macro-Model (KYQ)	Kyoto University Institute of Economic Research – Chikaski Moriguchi	medium 179 (80B/99D)	quarterly (active)	quarterly forecasting
4B2/3A2	Tsukuba–FAIS Annual Model	Tsukuba University– FAIS – Shuntaro Shishido	small 95 (39B/56D)	annual (active)	annual predictions with international linkage
4B3	Keio University Macroeconomic Model (KOMN 2)	Fumimasa Hamada (Keio University)	medium 117 (60B/57D)	quarterly (active)	quarterly forecasting

No.	Model name	Builder	Size	Time unit	Objective
4B4	Kei Mori's Macro-Model (KS53)	Hirofumi Hayashi (Management Engineering, Keio University)	medium 167 (83B/84D)	quarterly (active)	forecasting & policy simulation
4C1	NEEDS Model	Nihon Keizai Shimbun (Japan Economic Journal)	large 251 (116B/135D) (1984 version)	quarterly (active)	quarterly predictions & simulation analysis
4D2	JERC Short-Term Forecasting Model	JERC Econometric Unit	medium 122 (46B/76D) (1976 version)	quarterly (discont.)	quarterly forecasting
4D3	JERC Simultaneous Inter-industry Model	JERC Econometric Unit – Hiroya Ueno & Hiromichi Muto	large 291	semi-annual (discont.)	Medium-term predictions at the macro & industry levels
4D4	RINE Macro-Model	Research Institute of National Economy	small 28 (13B/15D)	quarterly (active)	quarterly & annual forecasting
4D5	NRI Short-Term Macro Forecasting Model	Nomura Research Institute	medium 152 (66B/86D)	quarterly (active)	quarterly forecasting & simulations

No.	Model name	Builder	Size	Time unit	Objective
4D6	MRI Macro-Model	Mitsubishi Research Institute	medium 180 (120B/60D)	quarterly (active)	annual forecasting
4D7	Daiwa Macro-Model	Daiwa Securities Economic Research Institute	large 283 (91B/1928)	quarterly (active)	quarterly forecasting
4D8	Denken Macro-Model	Central Research Institute for Electric Power Industry	small 64 (35B/29D)	quarterly (active)	quarterly forecasting with emphasis on energy & electricity
5A1	EPA-Shimpo Monetarist Model	Seiji Shimpo, Economic Research Institute, Economic Planning Agency	small 12 (5B/7D)	quarterly (inactive)	Analysis of the 1973–4 inflation
5A2	ELSA Japan Model	Institute of Development Economies	small 7 (5B/2D)	annual (active)	Analysis of economic interdependence in East & Southeast Asia, in a monetarist framework

*Coefficient estimates are either determined by the 1980 input–output table or taken from other studies in the case of behavioural equations.

Notes

1. No.: Identification code.
2. Size: small = less than 100 equations; medium = 100–200 equations; large = more than 200 equations; B = behavioural equations (including regression-estimated statistical equations); D = definitional equations.
3. Time unit: quarterly, annual, etc.; active = the model is kept up; inactive = the model is not kept up but not given up; discontinued (discont.) = the model is abandoned.

355

11 Macroeconometric modelling of South-East Asia: the case of India

1 Introduction

The story of the macroeconometric modelling of the developing countries of South-East Asia directly emerges from the intellectual heritage provided by Jan Tinbergen and Lawrence R. Klein to an early generation of their PhD students. India was the first country in South-East Asia for which a macroeconometric model was constructed, which was done more than three decades ago.[1] In this chapter we trace, with documentation in chronological order, the evolution of macroeconometric modelling of the Indian economy. The modelling of India is of particular interest (especially for Marwah) for an additional reason, namely that it invokes many nostalgic reminiscences going back to its early stages, relating to the story told in other chapters.

Our story begins in 1956, a year after the publication of the Klein–Goldberger Model of the United States (discussed in Chapter 3), when N.V.A. Narasimham published *A Short-Term Planning Model for India*. Narasimham was a student of Tinbergen and he developed this model, outside India, as his PhD dissertation under Tinbergen's guidance. While there already existed two-sector and four-sector models of P.C. Mahalanobis (1953, 1955), which had served as background for the early Five-Year Plans, these models were inherently non-econometric in nature. At the time of writing, in the latest edition (January 1988) of their bibliography of models, Uebe, Huber and Fischer list over 250 models of all genres, including econometric, input–output, linear and non-linear programming, for countries of South-East Asia. About 80 of these listings belong to India, of which close to a dozen that are fully econometric may be recognized as substantive models.

By and large, the econometric models of India have been the outgrowth of PhD dissertations prepared at leading academic institutions outside India.[2] For example, a vast majority of these were either developed at the University of Pennsylvania or were further extensions of the work initiated there. From this point of view the macroeconometric models of India, especially those belonging to the early 'first generation', constitute a unique class. The circumstance of being a PhD student presents a special problem as well as a challenge to the model-builder. Whereas the benefit of any team-work is lacking, the pressures of limited time and scarce resources are tremendous. This situation was made more difficult by the additional considerations that modelling activity in the mid-1950s was in its infancy, India was a less developed country which not too long before had undergone a major political and structural change, data were sparse, and the theoretical underpinnings of models of growth and development were under sharp debate. Thus these PhD students were embarking on new and unchartered waters, and their pioneering efforts seem worthy of special recognition. In comparison, as we have already seen, all early models of the United States, the United Kingdom, Canada and Japan were built by established scholars, and largely as a part of team-work.

The macroeconometric models of India, judged by the current standard, have remained small to medium in size. And, in spite of their prolific growth over the past three decades, they are still basically descriptive of the structure and functioning of the Indian economy. The models have been used to explore interactions between various economic sectors, between market and policy variables, and the details of these interactions at different levels of disaggregation. Although, occasionally, the policy simulations have also been generated from these models, they have not been widely and systematically used in actual practice, either in policy decisions or in forecasting. From this point of view, one may say that macroeconometric modelling in India is still at a learning stage and that it has not yet reached maturity.

It must also be noted that, with regard to the Indian economy, there has been a parallel development of the planning models. These models and their underlying techniques have evolved over a period of time with successive Five-Year Plans and have become fairly sophisticated. For example, beginning with a very simple growth model of Harrod-Domar type used in the First Five-Year Plan (1951–6), they have evolved through two-sector and four-sector models of Mahalanobis and static multisectoral consistency models of Jan Sandee, Alan Manne and Ashok Rudra to dynamic multisectoral models of the type developed by Manne and Weisskopf. An excellent survey of the development of early planning models is found in Section 1 of Bhagwati and Chakravarty (1969).[3] It is these planning models which have been in the focus for long-term policy decisions. However, since we are concerned primarily with econometric models, we shall not include planning models in our survey. Moreover, in presenting their chronological development, we shall only describe their general characteristics and not their structural details.

An excellent, widely-cited, insightful survey of the eight early models is found in Desai (1973). These are (alphabetically): Agarwala (1970), Choudhry (1963), Krishnamurty (1964), Krishnamurty and Choudhry (1968), Mammen (1967), Marwah (1963, 1969) and Narasimham (1956).

In presenting an annotated listing of these models, Desai has also cast them into standardized notations for easy comparison. Five of these models, those of Krishnamurty, Marwah (both models), Mammen and Narasimham, together with UNCTAD (1968), have been further reviewed in Pani (1977). There may be other surveys. Pani's tabular comparison of these models is particularly useful; however, his critique seems partly somewhat out of focus when one considers the time period during which these models were constructed. Some of his comments originate from a much later perspective and therefore could be argued to be less relevant. One must remember that these early models were severely constrained by sparseness of data and by primitive computational and software facilities. They were supposed to be solved in a practical manner on desk calculators, and often in order to make the solutions manageable, linearized approximations of even elementary but inherently non-linear relationships were derived and employed, while block-recursiveness was actively sought or deliberately introduced. More on these simplifications follows in the next section. Our purpose in this chapter is to supplement and not to supplant the analysis of the existing reviews. After these prefatory remarks, let us now examine the historical development of macroeconometric modelling of the Indian economy.

2   The period until the mid-1960s

Shortly after macroeconometric modelling made a giant stride with the landmark publication of the Klein–Goldberger Model, new ground in another area was broken by one of Tinbergen's students, under his guidance. In 1956, when Narasimhan published *A Short-Term Planning Model of India*, it was (in spite of its name) the first econometric model of any developing country. The model was indeed a pioneering and ambitious exercise, given that no consistent national income account series for India were available at that time. The data were sparse and generally very poor. The compilation of data in itself was a challenge and major research exercise. It usually involved making simplified assumptions, splicing various segments, linking truncated series, filling gaps with interpolated values and the like. It was a test of the ingenuity of the model-builder to use most shrewdly whatever data were available in quantifying even the very basic relationships. Since specification of structural relationships was bound to be highly constrained by the availability of data, it meant that many finer details would always have to be sacrificed and left unexplored. Moreover, in order to keep the solution of the entire model from becoming cumbersome, the relationships were generally kept in linear form both in parameters and variables. For example, even an elementary definition that a nominal quantity is a *product* of a real quantity and a price level used to be looked upon as potentially troublesome and would normally be approximated in the linear form; that is, a nominal quantity would be presented as a *linear* function of a real quantity and a price level. It may be parenthetically noted here that Pani's critical comments on the determinacy aspect of some early models seem to reflect a lack of sufficient appreciation of this constraint.

Narasimham's model indeed represented a small and significant step forward in the history of macroeconometric modelling. It was a medium-size model (for the time) of 18 equations, of which 11 were stochastic and seven were definitions. It was based on the annual data for 1923–48, and estimated by ordinary least squares. The variables were generally specified in terms of deviations from the trend measured by a nine-year moving average.

Basically, this model was a demand-determined income model whose general structure belonged naturally to the genre of models built by Tinbergen and Klein. Total real output was disaggregated in terms of consumption goods and investment goods. The equations for individual components of aggregate demand were estimated in nominal terms. These endogenous components were private consumption, private investment and an import demand function. In addition, a labour demand function was also estimated. Government expenditures (including both consumption and investment), exports and indirect taxes were treated as exogenous variables. On the distribution side, total nominal income had five components: corporate and non-corporate profits, farm income, private non-farm wage income and the government salary bill. All except the government salary bill were determined within the model. In addition, there were three price equations, namely for the price levels of consumer goods, investment goods and total output, and there was one equation for the wage rate. Only tax receipts from the non-corporate sector were estimated endogenously.

The consumption function was basically explained by disposable income. However the distributional components of disposable income entered separately as explanatory variables. Thus a distinct effect of the distribution of income as expected was clearly captured in the relative magnitudes of different marginal propensities to consume. Investment demand was jointly driven by corporate and non-corporate profits with a fractional lag of six months. The demand for labour was estimated as a derived demand, as would be expected in a standard demand-driven model. The price equations capture the supply behaviour along the lines suggested by Tinbergen's model for the United Kingdom and the United States. The equation for the wage rate is especially noteworthy; the effects of the price level, the employment rate and a downward trend are all statistically significant. The dynamic aspects of the model are simple; a full lag of one year or a fractional lag of six months appear at few places. Surprisingly, the monetary sector is completely absent and there is no role of interest rate or any other financial variable.[4] The model did contain some fiscal policy variables, which were used later to conduct some policy experiments with the model.

Inside India, Narasimham's model almost went unnoticed; at this time all attention was being concentrated on the Five-Year Plans and their underlying processes, which were generating a great deal of excitement and hope. And, if any modelling was to be relevant, it had to be normative. Once again, it was outside India that, in 1963–4, three graduate students from India, studying in the United States, completed almost contemporaneously three new macro-models of India as part of their PhD dissertations.[5] N.K. Choudhry developed 'An Econometric Model of India, 1930–1955' under the supervision of Arthur Goldberger at the University of Wisconsin; K. Krishnamurty built 'An Econometric Model of India 1948–1961', and Kanta Marwah, 'An Econometric Model of Price Behaviour in India', both under the direction of Lawrence R. Klein at the University of Pennsylvania.[6]

The sample period for *Choudhry's model*, 1930–55, largely overlapped Narasimham's model, except for seven observations. Both models had a few other structural similarities too. For example, Choudhry's model was also an aggregate demand-determined annual model and, like Narasimham, he specified its equations of expenditure flows in nominal values. Moreover his price equation was the same linearized version of the basic identity connecting real and nominal quantities. The nominal income was generated from aggregate expenditure flow and the real income from a simple production function.

The model was presented in three versions, each made successively larger (having 10, 20 and 22 equations, including all identities, respectively) by disaggregating mainly the foreign trade sector into types of commodities. There were also minor differences in specification of some equations. A new equation in the model was the liquidity demand function, but this was also specified in nominal terms. Furthermore the role of monetary sector in income determination was shown through the direct effects of the interest rate and of liquid assets on aggregate expenditure components. The interest rate entered in the investment equation and liquid assets entered both in consumption and investment. However the effect of liquid assets on consumption turned out to be statistically insignificant, and the effects of both interest rate and liquid assets on investment turned out to be theoretically perverse: positive with respect to interest and negative with respect to liquid assets.

There were separate equations for each of the four components (consumption, investment, exports and imports) of aggregate expenditure. Assessed individually from the statistical point of view, these equations were somewhat weak. For example, there were four explanatory variables, namely disposable income, liquid assets, population and lagged consumption, in the consumption function. But only the coefficient of disposable income was statistically significant and the magnitude of the implied marginal propensity to consume was quite high, 0.92 in the short run and almost unity in the long run. Moreover the coefficient of population had a negative sign, although it was statistically insignificant. The perverse effects of interest rate and liquid assets in the investment equation have already been noted above. Some price coefficients in the trade equations, especially for exports, had similar problems.

The model was basically made dynamic by using lagged income, lagged consumption and lagged capital stock in the expenditures equations. It was estimated both by ordinary least squares and by limited-information maximum likelihood estimating techniques. Although some policy experiments using the model were also made, its prime contribution was merely that of exploring some economic relationships of the Indian economy.

Krishnamurty and Marwah were also finishing their models at the same time. Marwah (the present writer) recalls those days of graduate studies with great nostalgia. I had arrived from India with a background of basic training in economics and one full course in statistics. Econometrics and econometric modelling were all very new to me when Klein hired me as his research assistant right at the beginning of my graduate studies. On the very first day of my work, he took me to the library, showed me the data sources and asked me to compile a few series and draw some scatter diagrams. This was to be my initiation to the Postwar Quarterly Model (discussed in Chapter 4), which he had just started building, and to econometrics, the first formal course of which I was to take a term later. My introduction to econometrics was an exhilarating experience, as I was fascinated by it and I became attached to modelling in no time. I also recall the awe and trepidation I felt at the beginning when one day during the first few weeks, as I sat behind a corner desk in an office shared by senior graduate students, I found James Ball (see Chapter 7) and Eugene Smolensky deep in discussion about autocorrelation and heteroscedasticity, or later when Mitsugu Nakamura would talk about multicollinearity in *n*-dimensions. It was Ball who introduced me to the computer room, and I was totally mesmerized by that giant machine.

I had my study and work space in a room across from Klein's office and at times I shared this room with Motoo Abe and Yoichi Shinkai, among others. Whenever I found any puzzling result or a 'real neat result' on the first trial, Shinkai was always the first to see and give me the benefit of his judgement. It was in this room that by working throughout the night we solved the entire Postwar Quarterly Model for the first time in the small hours of the morning, and that on the desk calculators (Munroe and Friedan). What a thrilling feeling! It was also in this office that I computed many 'Doolittle' solutions while pounding on these calculators. To this day, in some corner of my office cabinet, I have kept a souvenir of those yellow (analysis) work-sheets, a step-by-step record of my 'Doolittle' calculations of an inventory investment demand function, which incorporated six explanatory variables plus an intercept and was based on a sample size of 44 quarterly observations. It took me practically two days to estimate this equation.

Around this time, Manoranjan Dutta was finishing his dissertation on the foreign trade sector of India. (Dutta, 1964 was based on this.) Soon after Krishnamurty arrived, followed by Meghnad Desai and then by Thampy Mammen. We had plentiful interactions, youthful disagreements and fights, but it was all in the spirit of research, and part of learning and growing experience. It was from this background that the next two models emerged. Let us now consider briefly Krishnamurty's model.

Krishnamurty's model covered only the post-independence period. It was based on the annual data for 1948–9 to 1960–1.[7] it contained altogether 21 equations: 15 stochastic and six identities. The equations were estimated by ordinary least squares and by two-stage least squares. The model was simulated over a post-sample period covering the Third Five-Year Plan, 1961–2 to 1965–6.

Like the other two models discussed above, Krishnamurty's model was structurally of a simple Keynesian type. Other than assuming implicitly that aggregate supply was infinitely elastic, this model provided no additional explanation for the price level. In fact, it had no price equation. However, unlike the other two, its equations for aggregate demand components were specified in real terms. These components were private consumption, private investment (decomposed into plant and equipment, construction and inventories) and imports. Government expenditures, exports and anything else entering the national income accounting equation (in real terms) were treated as exogenous. These aggregate demand equations determined the real output through the multiplier process. Basically, it was these equations interacting with an endogenously determined population variable that introduced simultaneity in the system. The rest of the model was mostly recursive. The endogenous specification of population growth with birth and death rates was a noteworthy contribution of this model.

Furthermore total output was disaggregated into two sectors: agriculture and non-agriculture. Agriculture output was determined by the production function and the non-agriculture as a residual from the total. There was, none the less, a second production function for non-agriculture output but this was used to derive employment in the non-agriculture sector in the true Keynesian tradition. Following the Postwar Quarterly Model of the US economy, the production function for non-agriculture output had capital stock adjusted for the capacity utilization rate, which was assumed to be known exogenously.[8] Later, in the revised version, this production function was simply dropped in favour of a direct relation expressing employment as a simple linear function of non-agriculture output.[9]

The monetary sector of the model was rather rudimentary, and its linkage to the real sector was unidirectional. The long-term rate of interest entered as an explanatory variable in the investment demand equation for plant and equipment, but there was no feedback effect whatsoever of the real model on the monetary sector. The long-term interest rate was linked to the short-term interest rate by a Koyck distributed lag and the short-term rate was determined by schedule banks' excess reserves over required reserves and by the discount rate set by the Reserve Bank. Thus the long-term interest was essentially a predetermined variable as far as the real part of the model was concerned. There was no equation explaining money demand and no variable measuring the stock of money.

Examining key equations individually, we note that the consumption function was estimated in per capita form using per capita income, the ratio of agriculture to non-agriculture output and a linear trend as main determinants. But only the coefficient of income was statistically significant; moreover the trend coefficient had a negative sign, although it was not significant. Similarly, among all coefficients in the three equations for investment demand, only one was statistically significant.

The wage rate was in no way related to either productivity or employment, it was simply made a function of time and showed a positive trend. The equation for industrial profits indicated negative relationship with wages and a positive one with the capacity utilization rate. The equations for wage rate and industrial profits jointly led to the somewhat awkward implication that, at a given level of capacity utilization rate, profits would fall over time. Furthermore this implication of negative trend was automatically carried over to investment in plant and equipment, which had lagged profits as one of the determinants.

To sum up, by providing some new insights into alternative specifications of economic relationships, Krishnamurty's model represents another step forward in the history of development of macroeconometric modelling of India.

Marwah's model (model 1)[10] was based on the annual data for the sample period 1939–60. The size of the sample did vary for some sectoral equations as a result of data constraints. The model was of fairly medium size (in the context of its time), containing 21 equations in one version. Two more equations were later added as auxiliary equations at the time of simulation. The model was estimated both by ordinary least squares and two-stage least squares. It was applied to make some policy experiments with respect to deficit financing and broad fiscal policy. The values of income, output and inflation multipliers implied by the simulated results over the post-sample period of the Third Five-Year Plan (1961–5) were also presented.

The guiding spirit behind the macro structure of the model was essentially an income–expenditure framework. After analysing the historical development and the general empirical patterns of price movements in India over the past century, the model was developed to determine the behaviour of general price level as well as of sectoral prices. There were four sectors modelled explicitly, namely manufactured goods, semi-manufactures, industrial raw materials and food grains.

The theory of inflation takes alternative forms. The behaviour of the general price level is explained in two versions: the first follows the traditional lines of the quantity theory of money but treats the income velocity as a variable rather than a constant entity; the second is set in the spirit of a Keynesian theory in terms of interaction between aggregate demand and supply. Likewise two competing hypotheses are explored at the sectoral level: a cost-push approach with price mark-ups, and market-clearing behaviour using inventory-output ratios. All of these alternative lines of development are analysed and show up in the model, even to the extent of developing competing models with different price determining equations in each. The price levels of manufactured goods and food grains are described by subsystems of equations but the price level of semi-manufactures and of industrial raw-materials are set in terms of single equation reduced-forms.

Aggregate demand equations pivotal to the entire price analysis are specified in real terms. These are equations for private consumption, investment and (later) for imports. In the consumption function, real income, population and the stock of liquid assets appear as explanatory variables. The liquid assets are also measured in real terms and are used as a proxy for wealth. The lagged stock of liquid assets is deflated by current prices to arrive at a measure of wealth, and also to capture the effect of inflation on consumption. Such a measure of wealth was used to adapt the consumption function to the Indian conditions of a developing country, and also to make the model dynamic. However it must be mentioned that, although both the wealth effect and the population effect were positive as expected, their magnitudes were not statistically significant.

The investment demand equation included government investment expenditure and was simply made a function of income with a Koyck distributed lag. Some evidence suggesting a positive interest elasticity of investment expenditure was also found. It was rationalized by arguing that, in the context of developing countries facing severe resource constraints, the interest rate may indeed serve as a proxy for the availability of domestic savings.

Marwah's model 1 presented a new attempt at integrating the monetary sector with the real sector of the Indian economy. Corresponding to two theoretical specifications for determining the general price level, the money demand equation was estimated alternatively in two forms: in the standard form, using the real money stock as the dependent variable, and by using money-income velocity instead. Both versions produced acceptable results. Money defined narrowly as M (= M1, currency plus demand deposits) was found to perform better than when defined as L (= M2) by adding time deposits.[11] Both interest rate and income variables were statistically significant, and there was found a basic quantitative structure of an LM relationship. There was also one simple equation relating the long-term interest rate to the short-term rate. In comparison with the short-term interest rate, the long-term interest rate, jointly with share prices, was found to perform much better directly in the money demand equation.

Both versions of the price level equation, the integrated income approach and the quantity theoretic version, indicate an inherent stability of the system from static as well as dynamic points of view.[12] In integrating real and monetary sectors together, model 1 indeed represents an attempt towards quantifying the basic parameters of the $IS-LM$ framework and of an aggregate demand function for a developing country.[13]

The general price level provides macro foundations for the movements of sectoral prices, which it influences directly. Itself determined by overall macro conditions, the general price level is seen to be setting a base around which sectoral prices driven by sectoral conditions are shown to move.[14] The sectoral equations appear as satellite submodels in the aggregate system. The manufactured goods sector forms a subsystem of five structural equations in one version, and a single reduced form equation in the other. The version with five equations contains a production function, a wage rate equation, a price equation for manufactured goods and an equation linking the consumer goods prices to the general price level. The manufactured goods prices are determined jointly by mark-ups on average wage cost and import prices, while wages are determined on the basis of average productivity and the change in consumer goods prices. Wages do not move instantaneously, but with a distributed lag. Here we see some basic ingredients of a dynamic Klein–Phillips relationship. The estimated values of both the mark-up factor and the coefficient of wage-price adjustment are substantially less than unity, and thus underscore an inherent stability of the system.

The food grains sector evolves around market-clearing behaviour. It has four equations, three structural and one as identity. The identity which balances the demand and supply quantities is innovatively closed by assuming that imports are a measure of excess demand. The demand for food grains depends upon population and real income, and the supply on total agricultural output and lagged prices. Finally, the price level of food grains adjusts following the level of excess demand in the tradition of the cobweb model. The dummy variable is used to account for the effect of weather conditions.

Of the two remaining sectors, semi-manufactures and raw materials, the price level of semi-manufactures is determined by the unintended level of stocks with a Koyck distributed lag. Both the structural and the lagged effect coefficients are statistically significant and have the expected signs.[15] The raw material prices are explained by the level of industrial production, export prices as adjusted by the fraction of total output exported, and by the general price level. Thus import and export prices, which are exogenous in the model, are transmitted in the system through manufactured goods and raw materials sectors, respectively.

In general, as far as the prices are concerned, the model clearly shows that demand factors are basic to the aggregative analysis, and the cost factors as such are directly more relevant at the sectoral level. In particular, wage and cost factors act as quick intensifiers of forces initially generated by aggregate demand.

Marwah applied her model 1 to test and analyse the implications for deficient financing if the economy were to grow at a certain rate. She also simulated her model by assuming I.M.D. Little's (1959) estimates of the time profile of total investment targetted over the Third Five-Year Plan. Her model predicted quite accurately that an increase in investment allocation over the entire plan period by 20.4 per cent would give rise to a general price level by 20 per cent (using the excess demand/integrated-income version) or 24 per cent (using the quantity theoretic approach). Correspondingly, real output would rise by 14 per cent or 16 per cent and the money value of output by 37 per cent or 44 per cent. The implied value of the dynamic multiplier (distributed over five years) with respect to real output was estimated in the neighbourhood of 3.5 to 4. It was these results which led Desai to note in his survey (1973) that 'the shortfall in growth of real output and the increasing inflationary pressures during the Third Plan are correctly predicted by her model'. (p.183).

The dynamic properties of this model 1 were later investigated by Hickman (1969) in his international comparison study. Macroeconometric models for 10 countries were included in this study, and for India this was the model which Hickman selected.[16] Also, in a new chapter (Chapter IX, 'The Econometrics of the General Theory') in the second edition of his *Keynesian Revolution* (1966), Klein cited estimates for consumption, investment and liquidity preference functions for several countries to illustrate the universality of the Keynesian revolution. For India, as an illustration from developing countries, equations of model 1 were listed.[17]

Finally, the contributions and legacy of these early efforts at macroeconometric modelling for India can best be summarized by what Klein wrote in May 1965 in his foreword to Marwah's unpublished book based on model 1 (see note 6):

> In our subject, problems are never completely solved, but we try to make significant steps towards clarification, understanding and predictability. I doubt that we shall ever understand price index movements with complete certainty, and we are surely far from understanding such movements in a developing country, such as India, where data are sparse and imprecise. Yet I am sure we know more about such movements as a result of [this] study . . .
>
> [It] takes us along the path towards development of more satisfactory models of India. The sample is admittedly small, and many of the underlying series are weak, but first steps must be made in order to pave the way for giant strides later. In this connection, an important issue is considered. Activity in econometric model construction has been largely concentrated in the study of advanced industrial nations such as the U.S.A., Canada, the Netherlands, the U.K., Japan and others. The guiding spirit dominating these efforts has been the Keynesian model of effective demand, but it is far from certain what is the appropriate model for describing aggregate activity in the emergent countries of the world. Miss Marwah's analysis of the appropriate model for India is revealing. With more such studies, we can hope to converge on acceptable models for countries in Asia, Africa and Latin America.

It was from this vantage, one may surmise, that Klein's classic article 'What kind of Macroeconometric Model for Developing Economies?' (1965) was written.

3 Years of steady progress and more explorations, 1966–70

In the second half of the 1960s, four more full models were completed: Thampy Mammen (1967) submitted his dissertation, 'An Econometric Study of the Money Market in India', at the University of Pennsylvania;

UNCTAD (United Nations Conference on Trade and Development) (1968) published a model, 'Trade Projections for India', as a part of its voluminous study, *Trade Prospects and Capital Needs of Developing Countries*; Kanta Marwah (1969) circulated her model 2, *An Econometric Model of India, Estimating Prices, Their Role and Source of Change*; and Ramgopal Agarwala (1970) published *An Econometric Model of India 1948–61*, based on his PhD dissertation submitted to the University of Manchester; thus during the last four years of the 1960s, virtually one model a year emerged.[18]

Mammen's model is basically made of two separate segments: the first is based on real income and elements of aggregate demand and the second on the money market. These two segments are loosely connected by a price equation, but otherwise they operate virtually independently of each other. By one count (see Desai),[19] the model has 23 equations, 19 of which may be considered stochastic. The model covers the annual observations for the sample period 1948–9 to 1963–4. It is estimated by ordinary least squares and two-stage least squares with principal components. The model is simulated over a post-sample period from 1964–5 to 1970–1.

Four equations of the model relate to aggregate demand components, and they are all specified in real terms. Private consumption is explained by income alone, as neither any measure of wealth nor population size enters in this equation. Private investment depends upon profits and capital flows from abroad, with the coefficients of both variables statistically significant. Furthermore foreign capital facilitates total imports; with the marginal coefficient close to unity, there is almost one-to-one matching between the two. Thus the role of foreign capital on the real economy is correctly built into the model, but there is no production function and thus no role of domestic capital is captured directly. Moreover imports are not subject to any competition through domestic price considerations and there is no price substitution effect. Government investment is driven by the difference between the targetted level (assumed to grow at 5 per cent annually) and the actual level of real income. Government consumption expenditures and exports are treated as exogenous variables. Given the level of money stock, the price level can be easily computed, as all needed information is now available.[20] The money stock, however, is independently determined in the monetary segment of the model.

Mammen's model is supposed to be focused on the money market and it is here that its main contribution lies. The demand for current and time deposits, five types of interest rates (including yield on industrial stocks), and commercial banks' portfolio allocation in terms of required reserves, excess reserves and the ratio of loans to investment in securities are all explained in the extended monetary sector. The linkage from the aggregate demand segment is provided by the nominal values of profit and income variables, the former entering to determine the yield on industrial stocks and the latter in money demand components. The five endogenously determined interest rates are directly or indirectly connected to each other by at least one linkage. If we consider three exogenous variables, the direct impact of the bank rate is on the call money rate, the direct impact of government securities is on the bond yield and, finally, currency in circulation affects the three-months commercial paper rate. The stock of money is affected by changes in interest rate, and since the price level is directly determined by money stock, we have some feedback on the real segment.

The parameter estimates of Mammen's model seem to be statistically quite reliable as their *t*-values generally exceed 2.0.[21] In broad terms, we may assert that Mammen's model successfully added further insights, in a continuing process of exploration of statistical relationships into the functioning of the money market of India.

The UNCTAD (1968) model was presented as a part of a larger study containing 30 or so individual country models of the developing countries. This was the first substantive model of India which was not the direct outcome of any PhD dissertation.[22] The larger study was designed and prepared to assess the trade prospects and capital needs of developing countries if they were to achieve more rapid rates of growth than experienced in their past. Each model provided a statistical framework for general discussions of trade and foreign aid needs with regard to that country.

UNCTAD's model of India (in conformity with its other country models) was structured around the two-gap theory popularized by H.B. Chenery to estimate the external resource requirements of a developing country. (See, for example, Chenery and Strout, 1966.) The two-gap conception, including the resource gap and the trade gap, is a simple open-economy extension of the Harrod–Domar Model of long-term growth based on the Keynesian system. The India model was accordingly constructed for the purpose of making long-term projections. It had 32 equations, of which 17 were stochastic and 15 were definitional or identities. It was based on the sample period 1950–1 to 1962–3 and was estimated by ordinary least squares.

The model has one production function, which relates aggregate output to the level of capital stock (cumulative investment) predetermined at the beginning of the period. This production function in fact serves as an investment requirement equation.[23] There is no separate production function for either agriculture or the non-agricultural sector; however the total output is simply split between the two sectors by assuming a linear relationship between agriculture output and total output, and by estimating the non-agricultural component as a residual.

In marked contrast to modelling the behaviour of consumer expenditures from the consumption side, as was done in the previous models, it is the savings side which is the focus of analysis in the UNCTAD models. Savings behaviour is distinguished by three sectors: government, corporate and household. Government savings are made a distributed lag function of tax revenue; corporate savings depend upon the output of the mining and manufacturing sectors; and household savings are determined by income and also by the terms of trade between agriculture and the non-agricultural sector. The difference between the investment requirements derived from the production function and the total level of savings thus generated endogenously is identified as the resource gap.

Total exports are analysed under three groups: tea, jute textiles and others. Tea exports are assumed to grow at a certain constant rate, but jute exports and other exports are determined by demand factors such as total world trade and the level of prices. On the import side there are two groups: food and non-food. Food imports are fixed exogenously by estimating domestic needs, while non-food imports are determined by domestic income and by earnings from exports. The difference between import needs and export earnings, after making adjustments for receipts of invisible items and net factor incomes, is treated as the trade gap.

The resource gap and the trade gap are explicitly shown to be equal only in the nominal terms as implied by the national income accounting relationship, but there is no equilibrium condition used to show their equality in real terms. This generates potential implications for the dynamic process of price adjustment.

With regard to the formation of domestic prices, the agricultural price level is explained by the ratio of agriculture to non-agriculture income, with a declining distributed lag scheme; the general price level is determined by the agricultural price level and by the ratio of cash balances to the real output. The other two prices, namely those of non-food and of non-agriculture, are linearly related to the general price level. There are also two equations showing the formation of export prices. Finally, except for the impact of cash balances on the general price level, there is no role of any other monetary factor in the model.

The model was used (as intended) to project for 1975–6 the foreign capital requirements of India, based on two separate assumptions regarding growth rate in national income: a low one at 4 per cent per year and a high one at 5 per cent annually. The results led to the general conclusion that foreign exchange limitations might entail a serious constraint on the growth of the Indian economy in the 'near-term' future.

In the meanwhile, *Marwah* was finishing her *model 2*, which was initially circulated in 1969 in the form of a working paper. Later, the full model, but with abridged text, was published as Marwah (1972), an application of the model having been already published as Marwah (1970). Our discussion here refers to the published sources.

To our knowledge, *Marwah's model 2* was the first model of India which went through the complete gamut of tests: estimation, post-sample forecasting, multiplier calculations (although rudimentary) and policy simulations. Moreover, structurally, it had several novel features which presented significant advances over existing models. First, the supply side was accorded a special recognition as a new operational meaning was attached to the national income accounting identity in the context of a developing economy. The aggregate demand and aggregate supply identity played a distinct role in closing the system. Second, the real and monetary sectors were more realistically integrated as the money market implicitly recognized hoarding as a special phenomenon of the Indian economy. Third, the foreign trade sector was disaggregated and extraneous information was used in estimating its parameters. In particular, cross-section estimates for developing countries were pooled with time series data for India. Fourth, the interaction between aggregate and sectoral factors was more appropriately recognized. To quote Pani (1977, p. 62), 'A significant feature of Marwah's model is that the domestic exogenous variables which shift the economy from one equilibrium to another are highly simplified as all important variables are endogenized'. Finally, the dynamic responses of prices and output to exogenous shocks were separated and measured distinguishably.

The model had 48 equations, 39 of which were stochastic and nine were identities. It was estimated by ordinary least squares and by 'modified' two-stage least squares, based mainly on annual data for the sample period 1939–65. The dynamic structure of aggregate demand, aggregate supply and prices was as follows. Given the initial level of the inventory stock and of credit availability, the capacity utilization rate was determined first. The existing level of the capital stock, adjusted for the capacity utilization rate, gave the supply of output through the production function. The production function was based on the same assumption as in the UNCTAD model, except that the capital stock was adjusted for the utilization rate. Once the total output was known, the general price level was determined simultaneously with all the entities of money market and the food sector. Total output multiplied by price level yielded the nominal value of aggregate supply. Aggregate demand, on the other hand, was determined by expenditure flows such as private consumption, private investment, government investment, exports and imports. The national income accounting equation was then used to measure the disequilibrium gap between the already determined level of aggregate demand thus generated and the value of aggregate supply. This gap was treated as a 'catch-all slack-variable', a proxy for excess demand or supply shortage. The real value of this gap determined an unintended change in inventory stocks, which, together with the money market conditions, determined the capacity utilization rate in the following period. The rate of capital utilization generated a new level of output and the whole system could be resolved for the succeeding period.

As far as the aggregate demand components are concerned, consumption and investment equations were similar to those developed in model 1 except that investment was now disaggregated into private investment and government investment. The foreign trade sector was extensively modelled. While imports of services were exogenous, merchandise imports were disaggregated in seven SITC (Standard International Trade Classification) one-digit classes. These are food and beverages (0 + 1), raw materials (2 + 4), fuels (3), chemicals (5), manufactured goods (6 + 8), machinery and transport equipment (7), and other imports. The role of income, relative prices, foreign exchange constraints and the size of the market emerged quite significantly in the foreign trade sector.

On the sectoral level, output and price equations were established for four sectors: food grains, raw materials, semi-manufactures and manufactures. As in model 1, the behaviour of the first three sectors followed a market-clearing mechanism, while the behaviour of the last one was, in addition, tested alternatively on a cost mark-up hypothesis. Among the other prices, the price level of fuels, of chemicals and of machinery and transportation equipment were simply related to the general price level. Import prices were transmitted directly to the general price level equation.

The predictive performance of the model was tested by solving the model for the terminal year (1965) of the sample period, and by making *ex post* predictions for 1966 and 1967. The detailed comparison of the actual values with the predicted values led to the broad conclusion that the model represented the structure of the Indian economy reasonably well.

As the model was characterized by both linear and non-linear relationships, only rudimentary calculations of impact multipliers were obtained. These multipliers provided some clear insights on variety of factors, particularly with respect to prices. For example, factors related to a trade-off between monetary policy and fiscal policy in fighting inflation; the nature of the partial and joint impacts of money and the bank rate as instruments of monetary policy; and the impact of investment-oriented deficit-financing versus the government's current expenditures were all highlighted.

On 6 June, 1966, the Indian rupee was devalued by 36.5 per cent and the model was used to measure the impact of this devaluation on the Indian economy. The results appeared in Marwah (1970). The model predicted a reduction in the balance of payments deficit measured in current prices and in terms of the US dollar by 37 per cent in 1966, and 21 per cent in 1967. The corresponding values in constant prices for 1966 and 1967 were respectively 55 per cent and 63 per cent. Similarly, the model predicted that devaluation would have an upward impact on domestic prices across the board, the brunt being borne by manufactured goods prices, followed in turn by the prices of raw materials and semi-manufactures. In retrospect, these predictions turned out to be generally accurate.

Shortly afterwards, Paul Jonas (1970), in his study for the US Agency for International Development, New Delhi, combined this model with the Consistency Dynamic Multisectoral Model of Manne and Weisskopf (1967) to make long-term projections for the Indian economy. These projections related to the period 1969–80. This exercise demonstrated how predictions from an econometric model can be used and integrated with the analysis of a planning model.

A year later, in *1970, Agarwala* published his model of a somewhat different genre. His econometric model was based on the theoretical framework of W.A. Lewis's two-sector growth model with unlimited supplies of labour (see Lewis, 1954). The model was augmented by investment and price equations; by Desai's count, it had 24 equations, which, with some variations for the sample periods 1920–61 to 1948–61, were estimated by ordinary least squares and, in part, by two-stage least squares and limited-information maximum likelihood techniques. The model was simulated over the sample period and the post-sample period up to 1965.

Agarwala was primarily concerned with the question of how output was determined in the two sectors, namely agriculture and industry, and what provided the linkages between them. He showed that output in the agriculture sector was determined (in a log-linear relationship) by the existing level of the capital stock and the amount of rainfall. The model then showed how agricultural output determined the amount of food surplus, and how this food surplus supplemented further by food imports translated itself into industrial employment. Non-agricultural output was then obtained by combining industrial employment with the capital stock through a Cobb-Douglas production function. The demand side of the model was generally underplayed, except for two investment equations, which were needed to explain capital formation in both sectors. The level of import demand was constrained by exports earnings. The terms of trade between the two sectors and the general inflation rate provided an input for the investment equations, while the price equations basically explained the terms of trade and the inflation rate. The general price level was simply determined within the quantity-theoretic framework. The cost of living was shown to adjust slowly with the level of agricultural prices, while wages followed the cost of living. Prices in the non-agricultural sector depended upon wage costs and productivity factors.

Agarwala's model was indeed a simple model, suitable for tracking long-term trends in sectoral outputs; however, surprisingly, with the exception of the level of employment in the non-agricultural sector, there was virtually no role played by demographic factors.

4   The 1970s: more explorations and some indigenous advances

The foundations laid by the pioneering models of the pre-1970s began to be solidified and consolidated during the 1970s as modelling activity continued to grow during this decade. To the extent that model-builders became equipped with better information and improved computing facilities, they could increasingly recognize the institutional characteristics of the Indian economy and place more emphasis on policy analysis.[24] Ironically, it was during the decade of the 1970s, when the usefulness of macroeconometric modelling was coming under sharp and critical review internationally, that this activity expanded into India and thus to some extent became indigenous. But, not surprisingly, a large part of it was aimed at macro analysis of the topical issue of price behaviour in India as in Pandit (1973, 1977), Sreenivas (1974), Brahmananda (1977), Chakrabarti (1977) and Ahluwalia (1979); whereas Bhattacharya (1975) and Pani (1977) were relatively general-purpose models.[25] A few years later both Bhattacharya and Pandit extended their models into new versions, on which we shall comment in the next section.

Among other models, we may briefly note that *Sreenivas* estimated and tested three alternative formulations of a general price equation based on three separate hypotheses: the inflationary gap, the quantity theory of money and the wage-cost approach. In comparing these hypotheses, he made a generous use of the analysis already developed in some earlier models, especially in Marwah model 1. His estimates were mostly obtained from annual observations for the sample period 1950–1 to 1965–6. *Chakrabarti* estimated price equations basically for two sectors: cereals and manufactured goods. The price level of cereals relative to the price level of manufactured goods depended upon exogenously known levels of current and lagged cereal output per capita, the proportion of cereal output procured and per capita income; the manufactured goods price level was explained by unit wage cost, per capita money stock and the prices of industrial raw materials. All the explanatory variables of these two equations were predetermined. The general price level and the consumer goods prices were simply shown as two linear combinations of the price level of cereals and of manufactured goods. The fifth equation explained the wage rate as a function of average productivity and the lagged price level of consumer goods. This model containing five price equations was not a full model and was quite limited in scope. It assumed that neither the goods market nor the money market responded to price changes, as all basic variables such as output, productivity, money stock and even raw materials prices were treated as exogenous. Except for some simple calculations of dynamic multipliers and elasticities, the study made very little advance from a structural point of view over the price equations estimated in the existing models of India.[26] The estimates used in the analysis were based on the annual data for the sample period 1952–66; however a postscript of updated estimates based on the 1952–70 period was also provided.

Let us now look at the two full models of Pani and Ahluwalia in chronological order of their appearance. *Pani's model* was based on annual data for the 20-year period of 1950–1 to 1969–70, and was published in 1977. Altogether it had 80 equations, of which 55 were behavioural. Thus, in size, it was larger than any of the 'first-generation' models. Its structural contributions may be rated as mild in elaborating the supply side, fair in analysing the government sector and extensive in developing the monetary and financial sector. And, although it did quantify successfully some new elements in the foreign sector and in the price equations, these equations on the whole were structurally not as sophisticated as those of some existing models. The model was broadly organized into seven sectors: the first related to production and supply, the next four treated aggregate demand (namely consumption, investment, government operations and foreign trade), the sixth contained the price equations and the seventh described the monetary and financial relations.

The production and supply sector recognized the structural duality of the (agriculture-dominated) unorganized sector and the (market-oriented) organized corporate sector. It had 10 behavioural equations, which described the area under cultivation, the output of the agriculture sector divided into food grains and non-food grains, and the output of the non-agriculture sector, which was divided into manufacturing, non-manufacturing and services. On the demand side, aggregate consumption was estimated by three equations describing, respectively, consumption expenditures of households, corporate savings and the savings of the government sector. Investment demand was described by four categories, namely investment in machinery and equipment by the private corporate sector, construction by the private corporate sector, fixed investment by the private non-corporate sector and investment in inventories. The invest-ment equations were formulated by recognizing constraints imposed by government activity, the supply of domestic savings and the inflow of funds from abroad. Seven behavioural equations were listed under the operations of the government sector, which described direct and indirect tax receipts, and linked money creation to the budgetary deficit. The government investment demand was treated as exogenous, and the gap between its expenditures on capital account and the sum total of its savings, including foreign aid and domestic borrowings, was closed by deficit spending. The deficit spending was in turn financed by additional money creation, which was thus endogenously determined for the first time in a model of India.[27] Foreign trade sector was described by three import equations, one each for food grains, raw materials, and capital goods, and by an equation for aggregate exports. The link between the foreign sector and domestic activity remained weak.

The remaining 29 behavioural equations describe the last two sectors, 13 relating to price formation and 16 to the monetary and financial sector. The price levels for food grains, non-food grains and manufactured goods were described by equations having distinct structural features, and the general price level was simply made a linear function of these sectoral price levels. Similarly, other price levels were linearly related to each other. In the price equations, the model did make some new explorations and presented a few new insights, but the analysis as a whole did not appear to make a major advance. For example, as we have seen above, the price level equation for manufactured goods in Marwah's models was based on broader and stronger theoretical underpinnings compared with the equa-tion of this model.

The principal and most significant contribution of Pani's model appears to be in extensively developing the monetary sector as an integral part of a full model. Separate equations described the demand for currency held by the financial institutions and by the rest of the economy, and the demand for deposits was disaggregated into demand, savings and time deposits. The total supply of currency, as mentioned above, was related to the government budgetary position. The portfolio behaviour of commercial banks was modelled quite extensively.

The model was estimated both by ordinary least squares and two-stage least squares, based on principal components methods. The performance of the model was also tested at the end by both one-period ahead static simulations as well as dynamic simulations, and the results were mixed. The model was not subjected to policy experiments, although it did contain several policy variables.[28]

Ahluwalia's model was a revised version of her PhD thesis completed at

MIT. It became available in 1979, two years after Pani's model was published. It was based on annual observations for the sample period 1951–73, which was almost the same as Pani's. Altogether, it had 67 equations, of which 29 were identities or simple links, and 38 were structural. It advanced the modelling of the Indian economy precisely in the same manner as Pani's model did, that is by consolidating, elaborating and refining in bits and pieces some structural relationships which had been weakly recognized in the earlier models. Its explicit treatment and determination of the marketed surplus of food grains is particularly noteworthy.[29] In this it followed the duality aspect recognized first by Agarwala's model and treated later by Pani. Its monetary and fiscal sectors were also structured in the spirit of Pani's model, although with much smaller detail, especially in tracking the fiscal impact of agricultural activity and thus its implications for the monetary sector. Similarly, in the determination of price behaviour, it moved forward in the spirit of Marwah's models by following an eclectic or integrated approach instead of adhering exclusively to either a Keynesian, a monetarist or a structural framework. As a matter of fact, more of its elements can be linked directly to the heritage of Marwah's model 2 than to any other single model. For example, their affinity can be traced on these counts: an approach towards the general price level and food grains prices; the role of the capacity utilization ratio and its endogenous determination within the model; the impact of the agricultural sector on the manufacturing sector through food prices; the demand for time deposits relative to other components of the money stock; the constraining role of the level and availability of foreign reserves; and finally, the analysis of manufacturing sector. Nevertheless, in the detailed analysis of the foreign trade sector and in the formulation of the price equation for manufactured goods, it did not go as far as Marwah's model 2.[30]

Structurally, in order to recognize the duality aspect of production, the Indian economy was divided into two sectors: agriculture and manufacturing. The agriculture sector was further subdivided into food grains and commercial crops; it included equations determining cultivated acreage, output, marketed surplus and the relative prices of food grains and commercial crops. The equation for marketed surplus was estimated in the reduced form as the food grains savings of the farmers. The demand for food grains consumed on farms was assumed to depend upon total farm income originating from food and (commercial) non-food crops, and on relative prices. Total output less consumption on the farms and (exogenously known) changes in inventories was defined as marketed surplus. The manufacturing sector included equations for a production function, the capacity utilization rate, investment and the money wage rate. It had no price mark-up equation, as the manufactured goods price was simply linked to the GDP deflator for the non-agricultural sector. The linkage from agriculture sector to manufacturing was provided through the wage rate equation, which was partly determined by the price level of food grains; a similar link to the manufacturing sector from the foreign sector was established through the level of investment and the capacity utilization rate. The former was affected by imports of capital and the latter by imports of goods other than food and capital. The entire foreign sector was quite weak in this model. There were only two estimated structural equations, one for imports of capital goods and the other for other imports. Total imports were derived by adding to the two estimated categories the exogenously known imports of food grains. The entire trade in services, all exports, and all flows of foreign capital were considered exogenous. Thus, through the balance of payments identity, international reserves were derived using only two endogenous categories of imports.

The fiscal sector consisted of four tax equations (direct and indirect taxes on agriculture, customs revenue, and revenue from other indirect taxes) and an equation which explained government expenditures on wages and salaries as a function of its non-wage current expenditure and the lagged prices of food grains. The accounting equation then defined the budget deficit, which was subsequently related to the monetary sector.

The monetary sector included equations specifying the behaviour of the private non-banking sector (in terms of the aggregate money demand function, the demand for currency, and the demand for time deposits relative to demand deposits), commercial banks' credit to the private sector and, finally, an equation relating the monetary base to foreign exchange reserves and deficit financing. The equation for the monetary base had some interesting features. It showed that changes in foreign exchange reserves in conjunction with deficit financing tended to have the expected positive effects on the monetary base. And, although this effect is statistically insignificant, it may be compared with Pani's estimate of negative relationship between the money supply and changes in foreign reserves (see note 27).

Several structural equations of the model were estimated in non-linear form. The distribution of the basic 38 structural equations across sectors was as follows: agriculture: nine; manufacturing: eight; foreign sector: four; fiscal sector: six; and monetary sector: 11. The remaining 29 equations were described as other equations, identities or simple link equations. The model was estimated by ordinary least squares and by two-stage least squares for the sample period 1950–1 to 1972–3.

The performance characteristics of Ahluwalia's model were finally tested by obtaining static as well as dynamic simulations. More extensively than any of previous models, it was subjected to multiplier analyses by generating new solutions based on four counterfactual changes, taking one at a time: (a) the drought years of 1965–6 and 1966–7 were converted into normal years by altering the rainfall indices; (b) the level of government investment was assumed to increase (instead of the recorded decline) in 1966–7; (c) imports of food grains were assumed to be zero during the period 1961–2 to 1967–8; and (d) in addition to assuming zero imports of food grains during 1961–2 to 1967–8, government current expenditures were also lowered during this period. The year-to-year solutions thus obtained were compared with the 'no change' solutions. However, since the model was non-linear in structure and the multiplier effects were subject to the initial conditions as well as the amount of change, it was difficult to generalize about the quantitative impact of the above shocks.

In closing this section, it may be mentioned that the first model of Asia as a region was also published in the mid-1970s (see Marwah, 1975). It was basically a growth model for an open economy extended to a large region. It contained 21 equations which showed economic linkages of Asia with the rest of the world, the interactions of the growth process with the dynamics of inflation, the role of foreign assistance and the terms of trade, and the influence of other variables. It was applied to check the overall quantitative consistency of policy recommendations put forward particularly by the Pearson Commission on International Development (1969). The same model was also applied to Latin America.

5 The 1980s and prospects thereafter

The models of 1980s are said to belong to the 'third generation' of macroeconometric models of India. It now appears that this modelling activity has finally come of age, being somewhat mature, more sophisticated and increasingly policy-oriented. These models have tended to be relatively large and more disaggregated; they appear to be emerging from the exploratory watersheds and moving forward to an operational state. Moreover their support is no longer confined to the academic profession, as research teams at other institutions such as the Reserve Bank of India and the National Council of Applied Economic Research are developing their own models. Some are intended to be working models, fully maintained and updated. In what follows we comment on three of the published models, namely Bhattacharya (1984), Krishnamurty (1985) and Pandit (1985), all developed at the Institute of Economic Growth, Delhi.[31] These models have been built by researchers with an experience of early modelling, and with a technical perspective of improved and richer data bases. Moreover these three models emphasize inflation and growth as their focal themes.

Bhattacharya's model covers 25 years of the post-plan era (1951–2 to 1975–6), starting with the First Five-Year Plan.[32] It contains 121 equations, of which 55 are stochastic and 66 are definitional. The framework of the model is developed with the stated purpose of analysing the role of public sector in economic activity in the aggregate as well as at sectoral levels. In particular, the interactions between private and public transactions and their effects on growth and inflation are modelled in detail.

As far as public transactions are concerned, an attempt has been made to distinguish between those transactions which are determined endogenously and those which are policy-based. Endogeneity in this context has been recognized in terms of (a) a functional dependence of the public sector on the level of economic activity and (b) an interdependence of the public sector, such as the dependence of revenues and expenditures arising out of the budget constraint and other policy decisions. The major fiscal instruments are personal and corporate tax rates, government commercial borrowings from abroad and from banks in India, the public sector's fixed and inventory investment, interest payments on government securities and the public distribution of food and fertilizers. Similarly, the primary monetary instruments are the bank rate, the commercial bank minimum advance rate, the ceiling deposit rate, the required reserve ratio, and the level of Reserve Bank credit to cooperative banks and to the non-banking private sector. The budgetary items of the public sector are described by 29 equations, which include a large number of accounting identities and simple link relationships. On the revenue side, these equations describe separately the generation of personal tax revenues, land revenues, and revenues from the corporate tax, the excise tax, import duties and other indirect taxes. On the expenditure side, they describe the current expenditures on wages and salaries, subsidies, transfer payments and interest payments; the public sector's investment expenditure in current prices is treated as an exogenous variable.

Some 27 equations describe the monetary sector that includes demand functions for currency in circulation, demand deposits, time deposits, commercial bank reserves, bank credit and also equations for interest rates. As in the earlier models, the supply of money has been related to the government budget deficit and the stock of foreign exchange reserves, which in turn have been linked to international trade transactions and net borrowings from abroad.

Aggregate production has been disaggregated into three sectors: agriculture, manufacturing and services, which have been further subdivided respectively into food and non-food agriculture, public and private industries, and public and private services. The behaviour of production and employment is described broadly by 14 equations, and prices and wages are tracked by another 13 equations. Following the tradition, for example, of Marwah's and Ahluwalia's models, prices have been explained eclectically by both monetary and non-monetary factors. Agriculture goods prices are determined by relative demand and supply considerations, but the price levels of the manufacturing and service sectors are explained by cost mark-ups. There is also a limited role of price expectations, which add to the dynamism of the model. The remaining equations close the model by describing capital formation, private (household) demand, foreign trade and some other miscellaneous elements.

The model covers relatively more recent data than any of the previous models, and several of its equations are specified in terms of first differences of levels or in terms of the logarithms of the variables. However its parameter estimates remain subject to the simultaneous equations bias, as the model was estimated by ordinary least squares alone.[33] And, in spite of its greater recognition of various economic interactions, several of its structural relationships are either quite weak or remain simple *ad hoc* linkages. As an illustration, the gap between aggregate demand and aggregate supply does explain inventory adjustments, but nowhere are these adjustments shown to have any feedback effect in the system.

The historical validity of the model was tested by simulating it over the sample period, 1951–2 to 1975–6. For the purpose of simulation, the model was cast in an abridged and compact version containing only 36 equations. The first run reportedly turned out to be disappointing: the model failed to converge for several initial and final years, specifically for the Korean War period (1952–4) and for the period of the post-oil crisis (1973–5). It was believed that imports were the problem area; consequently, imports were treated as exogenous and the corresponding equations were suppressed. In this restricted version, the model did converge, although it continued to register some large errors. None the less, this version (which made the model smaller in size than even some 'first-generation' models) was subjected to policy simulations over the last few years of the sample period. In particular, the multiplier responses to monetary policy, to discretionary budgetary transactions in several forms, to capital inflows, to import prices, and, as in Ahluwalia, to rainfall shocks were tracked. The results provided some new insights, especially in the public sector, but at best these could only be described as exploratory in nature. The model needs more experimentation before, if at all, it can function as a working model as originally intended.

The last two models, of *Krishnamurty* and *Pandit*, were motivated by a desire to capture some of the fundamental and substantive issues that have become relevant for the Indian economy over the past three decades, and were not intended to be forecasting models. Among the major avowed

issues are: the rate, structure and sources of sectoral growth, the interdependence of sectors with respect to growth and price stability, the growth–
inflation trade-off with regard to the role of fiscal and monetary policies,
the saving-investment process as related to inflation, the role of public
sector and its regulatory policies, the food sector as a provider of a basic
wage good, and the entire issue of trade and balance of payments in the
short and long runs.

To begin with, Krishnamurty's model consists of 77 equations, compared with Pandit's 58. Both models cover almost the entire decade of the
turbulent 1970s, although the sample period of Krishnamurty's model
(1960–1 to 1979–80) is much shorter than that of Pandit's model (1950–1
to 1977–8). During the period covered by both models, the economy was
subject to a number of exogenous shocks, including three military episodes (the Indo-Chinese War of 1962 and the Indo-Pakistan Wars of 1965
and 1967), political turmoils (1967–70, 1975–7), major crop failures and
droughts (1957, 1965, 1966, 1973 and 1979), and two oil shocks (1973 and
1979). In addition, there were other structural changes, such as special
emphasis placed on industrialization and import substitution in the
Second Five-Year Plan launched in 1956, the new agriculture strategy
adopted in the mid-1960s, the devaluation of the Indian rupee in 1966 and
the bank nationalization in 1969. To build suitably around such shocks is
indeed a challenge for any model-builder.

The agriculture sector, divided into food and non-food subsectors,
occupies a critical place in both models. Whereas Krishnamurty specifies
the determination of agricultural output by first explaining changes in
productivity as an intermediate step, Pandit tackles it directly through a
standard production function by using cultivated area, irrigation and
weather as the major arguments. The allocation of cultivated area between
food and non-food crops is assumed to respond to relative prices in both
models.

The two models follow a similar approach to the growth–inflation
trade-off issue as related to and implied by a resource mobilization
problem, and as integrated with investment in the public sector, deficit
financing and the budgetary constraint. They also deal with inflation and
the general price level as well as with sectoral prices, but their structural
frameworks are not the same. Krishnamurty formulates the general price
level on quantity theoretic lines, although his sectoral prices are mainly
determined by sector-specific factors. His sectoral prices relate to the
agriculture sector, the industrial sector (mining and manufacturing) and
the public sector's infrastructure. The prices of the tertiary sector are
determined as a residual linking the general price level to the other three
sectors. Pandit, on the other hand, formulates the general price level as a

weighted sum of sectoral prices, each determined primarily by sector-specific factors. In his model, the money supply plays a prominent role in determining agricultural prices. Moreover the price equations are generally specified in terms of rates of change in Pandit's model, as compared with the absolute price level in Krishnamurty's. Both models have attempted to arrive at GDP deflators through simple linkages of the sectoral prices levels. There are about 15 price equations in each model.

The two models differ in substantive ways in their treatment of non-agricultural output. Krishnamurty treats it by disaggregation into three sectors: manufacturing, public infrastructure and a tertiary sector, each having productivity and output equations. The output in the tertiary sector is only demand-determined; in the other two, supply is the driving force. Rising prices are shown to be conducive to capital formation in the short run but affect this process adversely in the long run.

In Pandit's model, there is virtually no disaggregated analysis, although three sectors outside agriculture are considered.[34] Aggregate activity is determined by a presumed equilibrium between saving and investment, and since agricultural output is primarily determined by agriculture-specific factors, it is the variations in non-agricultural output which effect an equilibrium between the two. Savings and investment are further disaggregated by sources: households, the private corporate sector and the public sector.[35]

The analysis of the monetary sector is conducted in much greater detail in Pandit's model than in Krishnamurty's, but it stops far short of the earlier models of Pani and Bhattacharya. Similarly, both models do give prominent role to public sector operations, but with a much smaller degree of detail than may be found in Bhattacharya's model. Furthermore Krishnamurty treats the entire foreign trade sector as exogenously known, while Pandit makes it endogenous but treats it very briefly. This is one of the major limitations of these two models.

In short, these two models have attempted to recapture quantitatively some of the patterns of the Indian economy established earlier by using more extended data. Krishnamurty's model is more appropriate to the analysis of long-term issues related to growth and Pandit's to policy analysis of short-term and medium-term problems. By the authors' own assessment and advice, these two models should be simply seen as contributing to a continuing process of 'learning by doing', as embodied in the previous models of India. However it is believed that, soon, under the auspices of Project LINK, a new model should be initiated, using these two models as points of departure.

It is hoped that this new venture, when combined with extensive sectoral analyses developed as part of other independent studies, will eventually produce an acceptable working model for India.[36] In particular, we hope that such a future model would include an extended balance of payments sector. A model of the foreign exchange market of India has recently become available (see Marwah, 1987). We also hope that the 'other' duality, perceived to be rooted deeply in the Indian economy, namely the open versus the 'black' or 'underground' market, would not be ignored as a matter of mere 'white noise'. Such a future macroeconometric model must ideally recognize and measure a structural role for this duality. After three decades of 'thinkful learning', and 'learning by doing', the time is indeed ripe for a good working model to emerge.

Notes

1. India was perhaps the first developing country in the entire world for which a macroeconometric model was constructed. As far as other Asian countries are concerned, we have seen in Chapter 10 that, even for Japan, the first model appeared only in the late 1950s.

2. Occasionally there has been some involvement of the international agencies, especially of UNCTAD (United Nations Conference on Trade and Development), ECAFE (Economic Commission for Asia and Far East) and the World Bank.

3. Some selective landmarks in the early development of these models may be chronologically listed as: Mahalanobis (1953, 1955), Brahmananda and Vakil (1956), Frisch (1960), Sandee (1960), Reddaway (1962), Chakravarty and Eckaus (1964), Chakravarty and Lefeber (1965), Manne and Rudra (1965), Manne and Bergsman (1966), Manne and Weisskopf (1967), and Eckaus and Parikh (1968).

4. This is somewhat surprising as data series might have been more readily available on some financial variables than on some other variables used in the model.

5. The chronological ordering of these dissertations is somewhat ambiguous. For example, Marwah's dissertation was completed in the summer of 1963 (and it is 1963 which appears on the study), but the degree was formally awarded at the next convocation in 1964. Most of the citations of this model, in surveys and otherwise, refer to 1964, the year of the award of the degree.

6. These three dissertations in their entirety have remained unpublished. However the listing of the equations of these models appeared first in Desai's (1973) survey. In this connection one might also note one regrettable instance which testifies to the underdeveloped state of the publishing industry at the time in India. Soon after Marwah's model was completed, Asia Publishing House offered a contract, with the assurance that the book would appear within a year or so. The contract was signed and the press copy was prepared with some minor revisions and with a foreword written by Lawrence R. Klein. However Asia Publishing House failed to keep its terms. It delayed publication of the study year after year, shuttled the manuscript from one printing press to another, and under no condition was willing to release the manuscript and withdraw its property rights. Eventually the company became defunct and the manuscript was either lost or destroyed. From a distance of thousands of miles away in the United States, there was not much that the author could do.

7. There were minor variations in the sample size of few equations. The sample period of equations explaining birth and death rates was extended backwards, and so it started in 1922.

8. The capacity utilization rate was computed by using the same method as used for the Wharton series. The capacity output was first obtained by interpolating linear trends between peaks. The utilization rate was then computed as a ratio of actual output to the capacity output.

9. It may, however, be noted parenthetically that, by specifying the original production

function in terms of capital stock adjusted for capital utilization rate, Krishnamurty was able to derive an estimable equation for which the initial capital stock as a benchmark value was not needed. In fact this value was estimated as a parameter in the equation.

10. A few years later Marwah presented another model which is discussed in the next section. We shall call it model 2.

11. This is not an unexpected result for a developing country such as India, where time deposits are most commonly used to hold small savings over long periods.

12. The same quantity theoretic specification was later used by Marwah in model 2, in a model of Colombia (discussed briefly in Chapter 12), and in her regional growth models for Asia and Latin America (1975), with even greater success.

13. Although the slope of the *IS* curve in the model is somewhat uncertain, it does incorporate the wealth effect.

14. Alternatively, one might reverse the approach and seek to explain aggregate price level by sectoral price levels. Such an approach would necessitate a multisectoral analysis with Walrasian details, an unrealistic task, given the state of data availability. Moreover a methodological globalist would question such an approach on philosophical grounds.

15. In quoting any results, the reader is advised to check the listing from the original source. In the listing of equations in survey articles, some printing errors were noted. For example, in the equation for semi-manufactures listed as (6.16) in Desai (1973), the correct sign of the coefficient of the stock variable is negative (the correct value of the coefficient is − 11.25). The same remains true in the equation listed as (6.15a).

16. The 10 countries included in Hickman's study were: Australia, Canada, Federal Republic of Germany, Greece, Holland, India, Italy, Japan, the United Kingdom and the United States. Altogether, 13 models were reviewed. There were two models for Australia and three for the United States.

17. The other countries were Japan, Israel, the Netherlands and the United Kingdom.

18. It may also be noted that Krishnamurty and Choudhry (1968) attempted to merge the equations from their two separate models into a joint model containing 31 equations. Their new model was estimated by ordinary least squares for the sample period 1948–61 and was circulated in the form of a working paper. However the model was neither tested nor subjected to any policy experiments, nor did they undertake (to our knowledge) any follow-up work.

19. With a different count of identities, Pani lists 26 equations for this model.

20. Actually the role of prices is very minor in the entire model. As Desai has pointed out, the price equation acts simply as an implicit supply equation introduced to bring about an adjustment in real and nominal values of some (minor) aggregate demand components assumed to be known exogenously.

21. The technique of principal components used to estimate the model provided a strong safeguard against the adverse effect of multicollinearity.

22. The group, led by V.K. Sastry, which prepared this study at UNCTAD, had a close association with Klein, who at times also acted as their official consultant.

23. In contrast to the Keynesian model for advanced economies where it is generally used to derive the demand for labour, the production function is used in the UNCTAD model to derive investment needs, on the assumption that capital rather than labour is the scarce factor.

24. The models of the 1970s have been generally regarded as the 'second-generation' models of India. As longer, better and more disaggregated data became available, the new model-builders could presumably expand on the insights provided by the first generation of models.

25. It may be pointed out that these citations are not intended to make an exhaustive listing. We have simply attempted to include some distinguished and substantial contributions.

26. These equations can be simply interpreted as truncated versions of the price equations of the two corresponding sectors (namely food and manufactured goods) of Marwah's

full models, model 1 and model 2. Surprisingly, Chakrabarti refers to both Narasim-ham's and Agarwala's models but makes no reference to Marwah. Unfortunately there was a long lag between the completion of the study and its publication. The model was based on his PhD thesis, completed in 1970, under Alan A. Walters at the London School of Economics.

27. Interestingly, one may note that the money supply multiplier with respect to net foreign assets was negative, which is contrary to *a priori* expectations for any fixed exchange rate regime, which characterized India during the period under study.

28. For example, in addition to the standard monetary and fiscal policy variables, there were public investment, capital imports, and food grains stocks, as exogenous variables all controlled by the central authorities.

29. The question of marketable surplus was handled implicity (for lack of data) by Marwah. In her models, the market equilibrium condition was used in such a way that total demand included (own) consumption at the farm and supply included availability from all sources. Imports of food grains were used as a proxy for excess demand. Thus, without computing the marketed surplus, the demand and supply equations were identified and estimated separately.

30. It may be mentioned that, although Marwah model 2 had become available, even in the published form, in 1972, there is no reference to it in Ahluwalia's study. Ahluwalia's model might have represented a greater advance had she also been able to build on the results of Marwah's model 2.

31. The last two models appear in a joint volume by Krishnamurty and Pandit (1985) on inflation and growth.

32. Unfortunately, by the time (1984) that the model became available in published form, it had already become outdated. It is not clear whether a more recent version has been produced.

33. The various earlier models, we may recall, did deal in a limited way with the simultaneous equation aspect of parameter estimation.

34. These three sectors are manufacturing, services and mining, and forestry and fisheries. The forestry and fisheries sector is treated as exogenous; the output of services and mining is linearly related to that of agriculture and manufacturing, and manufacturing is obtained as a residual from the GDP accounting equation.

35. The difference between household savings and household investment is unclear, and seems not to be adequately identified.

36. There has been a prolific growth in sectoral models of the Indian economy, in parallel with models of the full economy. Two early examples are Dutta (1964) and Sastry (1965). However, in this chapter, we have generally not been concerned with sectoral models for India.

References

Agarwala, R. (1970) *An Econometric Model of India, 1948–61* (London: Frank Cass).

Ahluwalia, I.J. (1979) *Behaviour of Prices and Output in India: A Macroeconometric Approach* (Delhi: Macmillan Company of India).

Bhagwati, J.N. and S. Chakravarty (1969) 'Contributions to Indian Economic Analysis: A Survey', *The American Economic Review*, vol. 59, no. 4, part 2, Supplement, September, pp. 2–73.

Bhattacharya, B.B. (1975) *Short-Term Income Determination* (Delhi: Macmillan Company of India).

———— (1984) *Public Expenditure, Inflation and Growth: A Macroeconometric Analysis* (Delhi: Oxford University Press).

Brahmananda, P.R. (1977) *Determinants of Real National Income and Price Level in India* (Bombay: Bombay University Press).

Brahmananda, P.R. and C.N. Vakil (1956) *Planning for an Expanding Economy* (Bombay: Vora and Company).

Chakrabarti, S.K. (1977) *The Behaviour of Prices in India 1952–70, An Empirical Study* (Delhi: Macmillan Company of India).

Chakravarty, S. and R.S. Eckaus (1964) 'An Approach to a Multi-Sectoral Intertemporal Planning Model', in P.N. Rosenstein-Rodan (ed.), *Capital Formation and Economic Development* (London: George Allen and Unwin Limited) pp. 110–27.

Chakravarty, S. and L. Lefeber (1965) 'An Optimizing Planning Model', *The Economic Weekly*, February, 17, pp. 237–52.

Chenery, H.B. and A.M. Strout (1966) 'Foreign Assistance and Economic Development', *American Economic Review*, vol. 56, no. 4, September, pp. 679–733.

Choudhry, N.K. (1963) 'An Econometric Model of India, 1930–1955', PhD dissertation (unpublished), University of Wisconsin.

Commission on International Development (Chairman, Lester B. Pearson) (1969) *Partners in Development* (New York: Praeger).

Desai, M.J. (1973) 'Macro Econometric Models for India: A Survey', *Sankhya*, series B, vol. 3, part 2, pp. 169–206.

Dutta, M. (1964) 'A Prototype Model of India's Foreign Sector', *International Economic Review*, vol. 5, no. 1, January.

Eckaus, R.S. and K.S. Parikh (1968) *Planning for Growth: Multisectoral Intertemporal Models Applied to India* (Cambridge, Mass: MIT Press).

Frisch, R. (1960) *Planning for India: Selected Explanations in Methodology* (Calcutta: Asia Publishing House for Statistical Publishing Society).

Hickman, B.G. (1969) 'Dynamic Properties of Macroeconometric Models: An International Comparison', in M. Bronfenbrenner (ed.), *Is the Business Cycle Obsolete?* (New York: John Wiley) pp. 393–435.

Jonas, Paul (1970) 'Projections and Forecasts for the Indian Economy 1969–80' (unpublished report), US Agency for International Development, New Delhi.

Klein, L.R. (1965) 'What Kind of Macroeconometric Model for Developing Economies?', *Econometric Annual of the India Economic Journal*, vol. 13, no. 3, pp. 313–24.

———— (1966) *The Keynesian Revolution*, 2nd edn. (New York: Macmillan).

Krishnamurty, K. (1964) 'An Econometric Model for India, 1948–61', PhD dissertation (unpublished), University of Pennsylvania.

Krishnamurty, K. and N.K. Choudhry (1968) 'Towards a Post-War Econometric Model of India', Working Paper No. 6814, Institute of Quantitative Analysis of Social and Economic Policy, University of Toronto, June.

Krishnamurty, K. and V. Pandit (1985) *Macroeconometric Modelling of the Indian Economy: Studies on Inflation and Growth* (Delhi: Hindustan Publishing Corp.).

Lewis, W.A. (1954) 'Economic Development with Unlimited Supplies of Labour', *The Manchester School*, vol. 22, May, pp. 139–92.

Little, I.M.D. (1959) *Public Finance and The Third Plan* (New Delhi: unpublished memorandum).

Mahalanobis, P.C. (1953) 'Some Observations on the Process of Growth of National Income,' *Sankhya*, vol. 12, September, pp. 307–12.

———— (1955) 'The Approach of Operational Research to Planning in India', *Sankhya*, vol. 16, December, pp. 3–130.

Mammen, T. (1967) 'An Econometric Study of the Money Market in India', PhD dissertation (unpublished), University of Pennsylvania.

Manne, A.S. and A. Rudra (1965) 'A Consistency Model of India's Fourth Plan', *Sankhya*, series B, vol. 27, February, pp. 57–144.

Manne, A.S. and J. Bergsman (1966) 'An Almost Consistent Intertemporal Model for India's Fourth and Fifth Plans', in I. Adelman and E. Thorbecke (eds), *The Theory and Design of Economic Development* (Baltimore: Johns Hopkins Press) pp. 239–56.

Manne, A.S. and T.E. Weisskopf (1967) 'A Dynamic Multisectoral Model for India: 1967–1975', December (mimeo).

Marwah, K. (1963) 'An Econometric Model of Price Behaviour in India', PhD dissertation (unpublished), University of Pennsylvania.

———— (1969) 'An Econometric Model of India, Estimating Prices, Their Role and Sources of Change', Carleton Economic Papers, No. 69–04, published with abridged text in *Indian Economic Review* (New Series), vol. 7, April 1972, pp. 53–91.

_____ (1970) 'Measurement of Devaluation Impact: Indian Case Study', *Econometric Annual of the Indian Economic Journal*, vol. 70, pp. 737–45.

_____ (1975) 'Econometric Explorations in Growth: Partners, Assistance and All That', *Indian Economic Journal*, vol. 22, no. 3, January–March, pp. 215–38.

_____ (1987) 'On Managing the Exchange Rate of the India Rupee: Modelling Post-Bretton Woods Experience', *Journal of Quantitative Economics*, vol. 3, no. 1, pp. 137–61.

Narasimham, N.V.A. (1956) *A Short-Term Planning Model for India* (Amsterdam: North-Holland).

Pandit, V. (1973) 'National Income and the Price Level in India, 1950–51 to 1965–66: A Macroeconometric Analysis', *Sankhya*, series B, vol. 35, pp. 451–66.

_____ (1977) 'Multiplier, Velocity and Underdevelopment', *Manchester School*, vol. 45, pp. 112–26.

Pani, P.K. (1977) *A Macroeconomic Model of the Indian Economy* (Delhi: Macmillan Company of India).

Reddaway, W.B. (1962) *The Development of the Indian Economy* (London: George Allen and Unwin Ltd.).

Sandee, J. (1960) *A Demonstration Planning Model for India* (Calcutta: Asia Publishing House for Statistical Publishing Society).

Sastry, V.K. (1965) 'Dividends, Investment and External Financing Decisions of the Corporate Sector in India', PhD dissertation (unpublished), University of Pennsylvania.

Sreenivas, M.A. (1974) *Price Behaviour in India–1948–49 to 1965–66 (A Comparative Study of Three Macro-Approaches)* (Bangalore: M.A. Sreenivas).

Ucbc, G., G. Huber and J. Fischer (1988) *Macro-Econometric Models – An International Bibliography* (Aldershot: Gower).

United Nations Conference on Trade and Development (UNCTAD), 'Trade Projections for India', *Trade Prospects and Capital Needs of Developing Countries* (New York: United Nations) pp. 298–317.

12 Macroeconometric model-building of Latin American countries, 1965–85

Abel Beltran-del-Rio＊

Macroeconometric or nationwide model-building started before the mid-1960s. Our selection of 1965–85 for the focus of this historical sketch was based on our perception that these two decades contain a good sample of our subject and that they constitute a period of first-hand knowledge on the part of the author. Earlier work in macroeconometric modelling was directed mainly to the advanced industrial economies, and there were in any case few efforts in Latin America (herein LA) before 1965.

We also made another selective decision. Our main concentration is on structural models of full accounting coverage (multisectoral) which can be used in both forecasting and simulation analysis. We also felt that models with longer histories deserved more space. In fact we tried to use a classificatory framework to provide us with perspective in going over the now large and varied listing of models constructed during this period.

As the bibliography grew and the time shortened, we were unable to analyse the universe. Thus, we sampled it, and we have limited ourselves to paying more attention to those models that have longer histories of continuous utilization. Thus we start by explaining the taxonomy applied to some of the items of the bibliography listed in the Appendix at the end of this chapter. There is also a short list of other references explicitly cited in the body of the text. Dates refer to items in the short list; numbers to the taxonomic bibliography.

1 Taxonomy

Although the main classificatory scheme was based on the purpose and size of the macro-models, we also classified them by author, year and country or region modelled. Since our main taxonomic headings, purpose

＊I would like to acknowledge and to extend my appreciation for the constructive criticism and corresponding suggestions which I received in writing this chapter. My main debts are to Professor Lawrence R. Klein, for ideas and for corrections and additions to the first two drafts of the text and of the bibliography. I also wish to acknowledge Professor F. Gerard Adams, for suggestions and for shaping the survey of Latin American models and for additions and corrections to the extended bibliography. Finally, I wish to thank Professor Ronald G. Bodkin, who took on the task of transforming the working drafts into the final product, through substantial editing of some sections, completing key references and notes, and also by some educated 'guess-estimation'. Despite the efforts of all three individuals, I have to accept final responsibility for any remaining deficiencies.

and size, are not as self-evident as the three last criteria, we devote a few paragraphs to explain them.

Ideally, applied macro-econometricians ambitiously working on an LA economy would like their model:

1. To be an accurate forecasting tool. If they can trust their model to provide them with realistic projections (small prediction errors) after feeding it with precise exogenous assumptions, they will presumably feel more comfortable using it for alternative policy simulations. Forecasting is the harshest test, and the more demanding kind of simulation.
2. To have a wide coverage. The more pieces of the basic macroeconomic accounting the model can project, the more useful this tool will be for their business, government and academic users.
3. To have frequent use and extended life. The more the model is applied in forecasting, simulation and normative uses, the more their professional satisfaction. Their understanding of the economy and of their model as a quantitative representation will increase potentially. Their ability to give better maintenance to the model, via respecification and re-estimation, will improve accordingly.

If we take these three criteria – accuracy, completeness and permanency – as the desiderata of our econometrician, we can set one extreme, ideal point in our classificatory scheme. In the other extreme, we can define, by contrast, the minimum features in macro-modelling: less accuracy, partial coverage and a single utilization of the model.

This minimum means that our econometrician, confronted with limited time and/or resources, will settle for building a model which will be a first approximation, a quantitative sketch, to derive from it rough estimates of the trend and cycle of the future evolution of the economy. This model will not try to cover all the sectors or markets of the economy available in the statistical accounts of the country, but only a few of them. Finally, the econometrician will use it for only one or a few applications, with no intention of maintaining it continuously.

The following brief tabulation clarifies the taxonomy:

Kinds of LA macro-models
(1) Principal purpose
    (1.1) Forecasting
    (1.2) Non-forecasting
        (1.2.1) Simulation of policy effects
        (1.2.2) Normative use: resource or policy requirements, optimization

(2) Size
    (2.1) Full accounting coverage: macro-models
    (2.2) Partial coverage: sectoral models
(3) Length of service
    (3.1) Continuous or repetitive utilization
    (3.2) Discontinuous or irregular utilization

This simple classification helps to interpret the historical record of model-building. All the models in the list fall between the extreme points defined. The space allotted to some of them has been in proportion to their location with regard to the maximum point defined.

Some further clarifications are in order here. First, a model is a multi-purpose instrument. A *forecasting model* can be utilized for normative, planning purposes and vice versa. A *policy simulation model* can be tried in forecasting. The fact is, however, that model-builders usually have a primary purpose in mind when they construct their models. They want it mainly for prediction, for policy analysis or for planning. This purpose is normally easy to detect in the statements of the authors, in the type of model built, or in the most frequent kind of applications. We call this the main purpose.

Nevertheless we submit the hypothesis that a realistically constructed forecasting model is, in principle, also a good policy simulation model and a good planning model; but this is not necessarily true the other way around. Our classification is based on this likely, but unproven, view.

Second, forecasting accuracy is the result of two different factors, the instrument and its user, exactly as with accuracy of bow and arrow or rifle marksmanship; part depends on the quality of the instrument, part on the ability of the user. What we have in mind here is instrument accuracy, not user accuracy. An accurate model, properly defined, is one which generates smaller 'predictive' errors in back-casting the historical period and in *ex-post* forecasting, once the actual values of the exogenous inputs are known. An accurate forecaster is the one who can predict the *ex-ante* exogenous variables and also the endogenous variables, which are the ultimate objectives, with smaller predictive errors, more frequently than can her/his colleagues, in repeated forecasting applications.[1] In going over the literature of LA models, however, this separation of an accurate instrument as contrasted to an accurate forecaster was impossible to make. Thus we gave the term 'accuracy' a connotation applicable to our purpose. We mean by it the incorporation into the model of the characteristic traits of the economy being modelled.

These traits are those of the economy of a less developed country (LDC), as found in the particular country in question, plus those specific to the country itself. A Mexican model, for example, has to include not only the productive constraints typical of an LDC, such as the capital formation process that tries to lift those constraints, the imbalances that this process generates in the external sector, the price system (inflation), the external debt and the foreign exchange markets, but also (since 1977) the oil sector, as well as the huge demographic expansion characteristic of that country.

Third, regarding the size of the model, a list of the bodies of data available for modelling helps to understand what we mean by completeness. Ideally, a complete national model incorporates the following accounts:

1. the national product and income: both demand and supply;
2. the balance of payments: current and capital accounts;
3. the fiscal accounts: taxes and expenditures, and government finance;
4. the monetary and financial accounts: flow-of-funds, statements or tables of indebtedness;
5. the input–output table; and
6. the main demographic statistics.

We are aware that these are very ambitious requirements and that, for some LA countries, some of these accounts are unavailable, but the literature provides us with some examples that approximate this ideal of completeness.

Fourth, this taxonomy, despite its limitations and evaluative shortcomings, helped to guide us in roughly interpreting and classifying some of the LA modelling work of the period 1965–85. We hope that it also helped to unify (and to enliven) the exposition.

Fifth, in the bibliography we did not confine ourselves strictly to macro-models within the range defined by the maximum and minimum just established. We included some modelling work done outside the range. In the bibliography there are sectoral and micro (firm) models, as well as models of agricultural crops and primary goods.

2   Model designs

The underlying or basic model design merits a final introductory comment. By basic design we mean the more aggregative identities of a model – its theoretical backbone. It seems that the large forecasting modelling of an LA country has fundamentally designed the determination of real, value-added output (gross domestic product or GDP) on the basis of a demand-driven, Keynesian blueprint. Typically, GDP results from addition of consumption and investment (usually divided into private, public and inventory change) plus net exports of goods and services. This 'vertebral' demand identity is usually complemented with a demand-driven supply determination of sectoral value-added outputs, adding also to GDP. The link is forged through the basic input-output identity (or its approximation) connecting each sector's net production to the demand components that drive them.[2]

In this branch of large modelling, the financial sector has been specified using the flow-of-fund identities or their simplified versions, when data limitations have not permitted otherwise. The quantity of money equation is usually included to link the monetary sector with price determination.

The generalization that seems to suggest itself is that the large forecasting model for LA started as a branch of the applied econometric work done in the United States and concretely from the work of L.R. Klein, whose fundamental design was an extension of the original Keynesian model.[3] Beyond this exposition of the basic 'blueprint' of model construction as a Keynesian prototype, there is the fundamental fact of a model as a set of *simultaneous* equations, which allow the interplay of the Keynesian part of the model with other parts, which may conceivably be strictly monetarist or even of Marxist origin (if they fit and explain the data well). A simultaneous model, like a big house, can have 'rooms' of different décors and still function as an interlinked unit. In other words, it can be eclectic. A Keynesian–Leontief–Friedman model is perfectly feasible, given the interconnections of the different groups of equations of a large-scale model, with the use of several explanatory variables in the estimated equations of a model.

Smaller, normative modelling has used other architectural blueprints. The two-gap conception of Chenery has been the foundation of some of the work done.[4] The Chenery open economy approach derives from the Harrod-Domar extension of the Keynesian system to long-term growth. When capital requirements are to be estimated, the two-gap approach provides a direct way of going about it. The United Nations Conference on Trade and Development (UNCTAD) follows this identity in its studies. It can be claimed, however, that this is also a Keynesian-inspired design, since the two-gap equation is a transformation of the GDP demand identity (Q). Thus we have:

$$Q = C + I + E - M \text{ (Keynesian identity); and}$$
$$S - I = E - M \text{ (two-gap identity);}$$

where C is consumption (public and private), I investment (public and private), E exports, M imports, S domestic savings (public and private), and Q has been defined above. The difference is, however, that the

Chenery modelling estimates the two gaps directly, whereas the Klein model does it indirectly.

Monetary theory has been another theoretical foundation, although less common than the two previously discussed. Some 'mini-' or 'midi-' size modelling has used this approach. One interesting example is the monetarist model of Mexico, constructed by Gilberto Escobedo (82), using St Louis Federal Reserve Bank specifications, where nominal output (GNP) was regressed directly on money supply (M1), employment, government revenue and expenditure.

With regard to partial model-building, the fundamental identities have varied according to the sector in question. A version of the equation for the quantity of money usually finds its way as the key element in modelling the financial sector or the monetary sector alone, usually with links to price formation. There is, however, great diversity in underlying designs in sectoral modelling.

In some cases we can discover in some regressions empirically introduced explanatory variables whose legitimacy may be questioned from a doctrinal viewpoint. And, also, we can find examples of 'measurement without theory'. Normally this is not the case in best practice modelling done in LA. Quite often, the opposite is the case: the complexities of the typical LA economy have been forced onto the Procrustean bed of too narrow a theory.

In countries where hyperinflation takes hold, Brazil, Argentina, Chile, Bolivia and, more recently, Mexico, the nominal figures are so large that the relationship between money supply and nominal GDP swamps everything else from the point of view of empirical correlation.

The countries
Since our task, in principle, is to cover macro-modelling of the developing economies of LA, it is convenient to specify the countries (and regions) involved. The Organization of American States' list of members, with Puerto Rico added, helped us to try to uncover historical examples of modelling work on the countries included:[5]

Latin America (LA)
   (a)   Continental
         (1) North America: Mexico
         (2) Central America: Costa Rica, Guatemala, El Salvador, Honduras, Nicaragua, Panama
         (3) South America: Argentina, Bolivia, Brazil, Chile, Colombia, Ecuador, Paraguay, Peru, Uruguay, Venezuela

(b)   Non-continental   (Caribbean):   Barbados,   Cuba,   Dominican Republic, Haiti, Jamaica, Puerto Rico, Trinidad and Tobago

3   Model-building institutions

Macroeconomic model-building for LA started in the universities during the early 1960s. International or government institutions came to support this work during the second half of that decade. Commercial institutions, specializing in applied econometrics, came into the field at the end of the 1960s and the beginning of the 1970s.

This institutional evolution can be exemplified by the cases of Brazil and Mexico. The first Brazilian large forecasting model was constructed in 1967–8 at the University of Pennsylvania by two PhD students of Lawrence R. Klein, Denise De Souza and Mahmoud S. Marzouk. (See Marzouk's doctoral dissertation (123). In 1974, another version of the Brazilian model was developed at Pennsylvania by a student of Professor F. Gerard Adams, Ana Maria Jul. This model became a forecasting tool in Wharton Econometric Forecasting Associates (WEFA), servicing the company's subscribers to Latin American services. In 1968, UNCTAD developed its own version of the Brazilian model, for estimating capital and export requirements.

The case of Mexico is similar. Forecasting models of the country were developed first at the University of Pennsylvania, by this author, as part of his PhD requirements, under the direction of L.R. Klein and F.G. Adams (42). This model served as the basis for the start of the Mexican Project in 1969 (known now as CIEMEX) of WEFA, now a commercially oriented service corporation. UNCTAD also built in 1968 Mexican and Brazilian models for its monumental study, *Trade Prospects and Capital Needs of Developing Countries*, included in our bibliography (182). Klein and Adams were consultants of UNCTAD during the period of the preparation of those models.

The housing of model-building in these three different types of institution influenced the size and purpose of the models. The university built large, ambitious forecasting models, which the commercial institutions took over. Some of the size, theoretical complexity and simultaneity of academic model-building diminished under the rigours of a commercial orientation and the pressures of periodic forecasting for a large set of customers. Model continuity, however, was enhanced. The official, international institutions favoured normative or planning modelling and smaller-sized structures, except for input–output components.

In reviewing the econometric work done on LA over the period 1965–85, at least three main strands can be detected: first, the origin and evolution of the large, forecasting macroeconometric models; second, the work on smaller, normative or planning macro-models; and third, the modelling done on sectors or specific markets of LA countries (micromodelling). Each of these developments had its specific source. The large, forecasting model-building originated mainly in L.R. Klein's Wharton workshops, at the University of Pennsylvania. The smaller, normative modelling took place mainly under the auspices of some international organizations (the International Development Bank or IDB, the World Bank or IBRD, UNCTAD). Sectoral or micro-modelling has had more diversified origins and cannot be identified, even broadly, with one or two main sources, either academic, official or commercial.

4   Large macroeconometric forecasting modelling: the Klein–Wharton branch

The initial work dates from 1965. Lawrence R. Klein, of the Graduate Economics Department and the Wharton School of the University of Pennsylvania, provided the inspiration and guidance for this pioneering work done by his colleagues and by his PhD economics students. Since these models have become known as the Wharton models, we shall refer to them generically as the Klein, Wharton or Klein–Wharton models.

This work in applied econometrics can be considered a branching out of Klein's previous work in the MDC (more developed country) economies, especially his series of models of the USA.[6] Klein's innovations and derived methodology of model-building have been very fruitful. His Latin American students and associates have generated an extensive and varied crop of models, some of which have become continuous, client-supported, non-commercial and commercial forecasting projects. Most of them utilize large forecasting models that are empirically based. As already noted, we put the emphasis on continuous models, that is models that have turned into projects.

Of all the Klein–Wharton models built during the 1965–80 period, three deserve special mention, owing to their continuity and evolution: the Mexican (1969), the Venezuelan (1978) and the Puerto Rican (1979) models. These models have enjoyed independent, uninterrupted forecasting lives since their inception and have evolved in response to changing economic conditions and data availability. The three models have turned into projects with a subscriber or client base that has assured their financial viability.

The Brazilian Model, the first one to be constructed (1967), has survived, although it has not enjoyed the independent evolution of the three above.

5   The Mexican Model: the CIEMEX–Wharton project

Of the three Klein–Wharton inspired models, the Mexican Model is the oldest in continuous existence. Its origin dates from a grant given to Professor L.R. Klein in 1968 by the DuPont Corporation to develop econometric models for the three largest LA economies, Argentina, Brazil and Mexico. Klein channelled the grant through the Wharton Econometric Forecasting Unit (WEFU) of the Department of Economics of the University of Pennsylvania, headed by Professor F. Gerard Adams. DuPont agreed, following academic requirements, to leave the models at the disposal of WEFU for their further use as PhD dissertation topics and for other research applications. DuPont not only provided the funding, but also an enthusiastic support for the initial data-gathering and formulation of the models, utilizing the help of its staff in the selected countries.

Out of this initial effort, the first version of the Mexican Model was finished during the summer of 1968 by Abel Beltran-del-Rio and Hunt Howell, both PhD students working at WEFU. During 1969–70, a group of large Mexican firms in Monterrey and Mexico City, plus two Mexican government agencies and the Inter-American Development Bank constituted the founding group of subscribers of the Mexican Center of Econometric Research (CIEMEX) of Wharton EFA. These 19 subscribers (with DuPont of Mexico among them) were interested in financing the exploration and the usefulness of the new Mexican Model as a tool for economic forecasting and business planning.

The original goal was two years of experimentation (1969–70) to determine the worthiness of the effort. The continued support for the Mexican Center since 1971 represents a confirmation by its users (now close to 100 in Mexico and 25 in the United States) of the practical value they place on CIEMEX's regular forecasting work. An additional benefit of CIEMEX activity was the funding (total or partial) of the doctoral dissertations on Mexico by some of the group's original analysts, including the author of this chapter, Dr Rogelio Montemayor and Dr Oscar A. Rufatt.[7]

Through an applied training programme created since 1972, CIEMEX has trained economists from different Spanish-speaking countries in model-building and forecasting techniques adapted to developing economies. As a result, three econometric forecasting centres have evolved: in Venezuela (Metroeconomica, 1978), Puerto Rico (Universidad Interamericana, 1977) and Spain (Universidad Autonoma de Madrid, 1980). Government economists from Peru (1973) and Panama (1976) were also trained in this one-year programme.

CIEMEX operates by producing quarterly forecasts of Mexico (using annual data) for more than 500 variables. These forecasts are presented to the users in quarterly meetings held in Mexico (semi-annually with US subscribers) for their feedback and suggestions in order to minimize forecasting errors. The distribution of the Mexican users across the entire economic spectrum (public, private and international agencies, including most productive activities: primary, secondary and tertiary) permits valuable exchanges of information for improving the forecasting effort. Out of these discussions, the CIEMEX staff gathers quantitative corrections, suggestions for alternative scenarios and microeconomic detail to fill the gaps of macro-forecasting.

Between meetings, through frequent telephone consultations with the users, the CIEMEX staff keeps abreast of daily developments in the Mexican economy, to confirm or correct its estimates for the current year and the economic policy assumptions incorporated exogenously in the model.

Over the period 1969–85, CIEMEX has built 11 versions of the Mexican Model. The main objective has been to construct a complete and accurate forecasting tool. In practice, the following specification goals have become the guiding principles:

1. To utilize the macroeconomic accounting available in Mexico. This has meant using the national accounts, the balance of payments, and fiscal and monetary accounts, plus the input–output tables. Some demographic statistics have also been regularly included (total population and also urban and rural components). CIEMEX has sought to establish the links among these groups of variables through the main accounting identities (for example, GDP demand and supply identities, the Leontief identity, the quantity equation for money, and the monetary base-money supply, plus monetary base-public deficit-international reserves identities).
2. To specify the behavioural or estimated equations with suitable right-hand side (RHS) explanatory variables, which minimize and randomize the 'forecasting' errors during the period of estimation. CIEMEX has selected and supplemented the RHS variables from the theoretical menu available, to approximate the institutional or historical behaviour of the Mexican economy.
3. To maintain the model in top condition by re-estimating it annually and by changing the behavioural and institutional (taxes, oil, debt, prices) equations, following developments in the economy.

Table 12.1 presents a condensed view of the 11 versions constructed during this period, indicating the size of each model, its main features, the principal CIEMEX model-builder, and other pertinent features.

6 The Venezuelan Model: Metroeconomica

The Venezuelan Model originated with the PhD dissertation of Pedro Palma Carillo at the University of Pennsylvania (150) in 1976 under the supervision of L.R. Klein. Cristina Cerboni (58) did additional work in developing the monetary sector of the model with a grant provided by the Central Bank of Venezuela. This work was done at WEFA, under the supervision of Abel Beltran-del-Rio, in 1977–8.

The establishment of the enterprise Metroeconomica by Pedro Palma, in 1978, led to the linkage of the real sector, developed by Palma, with the monetary sector, developed by Cerboni. Since then, the integrated version has been used for regular forecasting applications, which are utilized by Caracas business firms and some of the Venezuelan government agencies.

The Venezuelan Model has evolved in successive re-estimations and respecifications, paying attention to the crucial role of the oil sector and more recently to external financial aspects. The Venezuelan Model has been used extensively in policy simulation.

7 The Puerto Rican Model: Applied Research, Inc.

The first version of this forecasting model was built by Jorge F. Freyre, Professor of Economics at the Interamerican University of Puerto Rico and economic consultant to business and government in San Juan. The original model is described in Freyre's book (89), published in 1979.

In a subsequent version of the model, Freyre integrated an input–output table, following the Klein–Wharton technique. This model has been in continuous forecasting use, and with its transfer to the Freyre's consulting firm (Applied Research, Inc.) and with the utilization of micro computers, the model has begun a new phase of development. Applications have been made at the request of its commercial users.

8 The Brazilian Model: Wharton EFA LA Project

Although not enjoying the independent life and development of the three models just described, the oldest Latin American Wharton Model, the Brazilian Model, has been the subject of PhD dissertations: Marzouk (123) in 1969 and Jul, Roldan and Priovolos in the 1970s. Most of this work has been done under the guidance of Professor F.G. Adams.

The conversion of this academic work into a project at WEFA was done by Adams and his students, specially Jul, Roldan and Priovolos, mentioned above. The Brazilian Model in condensed version is now part of the Latin American Project, along with models of the main South American economies.

Table 12.1   Evolution of the CIEMEX Mexican Model

Version	Endogenous variables	Size of model		Coef-ficients	Original sample period use	Period in use
		Behavioural equations	Exogenous variables			
I–II	40–50	15–20	15–20	50–60	1950–66	1969–
III	61	28	26	88	1950–68	1971
IV	76	34	40	128	1950–70	1972
V	143	40	46	143	1950–70	1972–
VI	203	67	59	245	1950–70	1974
VII–VIII	359	81	107	n.a.	1960–78	1976–
IX	476	123	115	n.a.	1950–78	1979–
X	676	189	85	801	1960–80	1982–
XI	652	83	156	480	1965–84	1985–

' of on	Main features	Main publication	Principal modeller
	Preliminary learning models of the real sector; highly theoretical	Articles published in *Comercio Exterior*, monthly issues.	Abel Beltran-del-Rio
	More empirically based specifications	,, ,,	Abel Beltran-del-Rio
	Incorporated embryonic monetary sector and more extensive lags	,, ,,	Abel Beltran-del-Rio
	Successfully incorporated a limited monetary sector and polynominal lags; based on better institutional understanding	PhD dissertation, Penn., 1973.	Abel Beltran-del-Rio
	Full monetary and input– output sectors	PhD dissertation, Penn., 1974.	Rogelio Montemayor S.
	First models of Mexican instability period (1973–?); incorporated exchange rates and more detailed price formation equations; used for optimal control purposes	PhD dissertation, Penn., 1981.	Oscar A. Ruffat
	Incorporated new monetary and fiscal sectors	– – – – –	Manuel Lasaga
	Incorporated oil and debt sectors; transition to new official statistics, includes bridge equations between new and old national accounts	– – – – –	Vaughn Montes F.
	Based on new national accounts; enlarged some sectors; added saving sector; restructured the financial sector after nationalization of banks	– – – – –	Jonathan Heath C.

9   The non-continuous Klein–Wharton models: Central and South America

The Klein–Wharton branch of model-building was extended to several other LA economies, besides the three largest. This set of models, developed by Klein and Adams and their colleagues or students at the University of Pennsylvania, has, in general, the same physiognomy as the Klein school of modelling: large models, a forecasting emphasis, heavy use of data (empirically grounded) and frequent applications. However they have not been able to enjoy as long and as continuous lives as has been the case with the models mentioned in the previous section.

In this category, among others, we find the following models:

Argentina: Joaquin P. Pujol (154), PhD work; advisers: L.R. Klein and F.G. Adams.
Chile: Jere R. Behrman (28–30).
Central America: Gabriel Siri (162), advisers: F.G. Adams and J. Behrman.
Costa Rica: Fernando E. Naranjo-Villalobos (135,137), PhD dissertation, Pennsylvania, 1974; adviser: Albert Ando.
Panama: J.R. Behrman and J.R. Vargas (38).
Colombia: Diego Otero, PhD work at University of Pennsylvania; adviser: F.G. Adams.
Venezuela: Mario Cantu-Suarez (53), 1983.
Venezuela: Cristina Cerboni (58), 1975.
Colombia: Kanta Marwah (122), 1969.
Chile: Ricardo Lira (117).
Honduras: Fernando E. Naranjo-Villalobos (138).
Peru: Walter Reinafarje and M.A. Yepez (1972).

The main purpose of some of these models has been to do mainly policy simulations rather than economic forecasting. Thus the Colombian Model of Kanta Marwah was focused on the issue of a possible devaluation of the Colombian peso, with the ensuing effects that it would have on the Colombian economy. (Marwah's model suggested that the principal gains to such a policy would be a slackening of balance-of-payments pressures, but that there would be negative effects on real output eventually, to say nothing of the usual inflationary forces unleashed by the devaluation.) Incidentally, it may be noted that Marwah's model contains an interesting behavioural relationship explaining the free exchange rate (the market-determined peso–dollar ratio) in terms of net foreign assets available at the beginning of the period and also in terms of an average of the controlled rates for both buying and selling purposes. We believe that this is the first equation for explaining exchange rates in the context of LDC macroeconometric models.

10 The Klein–Wharton modelling ramifications outside LA: Spain
Although this is outside our assigned geographical area, it is nevertheless within the cultural bounds of the Hispanic world. It is interesting to observe that the Klein–Wharton modelling method has taken hold in Spain.

From 1977 a group of economists, headed by Professor Antonio Pulido Sanroman of the Universidad Autonoma de Madrid, became interested in developing a Spanish model. Adolfo Castilla, a former student of the University of Pennsylvania, was the main promoter of the contact between the Spanish academic team and the Klein group in the United States.

The prototype version of the Spanish model was provided by Jean Marie Viane (formerly of Namur), who estimated a system in order to study, by means of simulations, the effects of Spain's entry into the Common Market. Viane's research was for a PhD dissertation at the University of Pennsylvania, under the supervision of L. R. Klein.

In 1980, the joint effort of Pennsylvania and Madrid led to the establishment of CEPREDE (Centro de Prediccion Economica). In turn, CEPREDE served to house the Spanish model, which has since been employed for regular forecasting purposes, in particular for a group of Spanish private and public institutions that partially finance this effort. Research grants from counterpart funds of the US government have been crucial in allowing the model to be built and developed.

With the establishment of the *Centro de Investigacion Econometrica Lawrence R. Klein* at the Autonomous University of Madrid in 1981, the Spanish model gained additional academic support.

11 Conclusions on the Klein–Wharton branch
The history of the Klein–Wharton models shows some common patterns:

1. All of them are the result of a process of 'diffusion' which, as we mentioned before, started with the pioneering work for the developed countries of L. R. Klein and his main associates in the early 1960s. The diffusion took place principally through the LA graduate students of Klein and Adams at the University of Pennsylvania.
2. The process of diffusion consisted of two phases: imitation and adaptation. In the second phase a host of changes were introduced in the methodology of model-building. Some of them were related to paucity of data, while others derived from the differences in the structure

of actual behaviour of the LA economies, as well as from their sensitivity (vulnerability) to internal political events and external trade conditions (dependence), reflecting in part the presence of long-term disequilibria.

3. The 'migration' from an academic to a commercial setting took place perhaps earlier than in the Klein-inspired models of more developed countries. Their shorter period in incubation in the 'University' derived from the scarcity of academic research funds common in LA. LA modelling, then, found a home in government planning agencies, consulting firms or large corporations. In some cases, the local university provided partial assistance, by contributing computer facilities or research staff on a voluntary basis.

12   The indigenous branch of LA modelling: Argentina, Brazil, Chile, Mexico and others

Although it is difficult to make watertight distinctions in these last two decades of the 'collapse of national frontiers' and the internationalization of knowledge, for the purpose of categorization we include here a list of macroeconometric modelling work done during our period of analysis by economists working for LA national institutions (universities, governments or private foundations) in the countries modelled. For lack of a better name, we call them 'indigenous models'. A sample from our bibliography follows:

Chile: Alejandro Foxley (88), a 1970 PhD thesis at the University of Wisconsin.
Mexico: David Ibarra and Ifigenia M. de Navarrete (105); Gilberto Escobedo (82).
Ecuador: O. Davila (71); M. E. Deprano and J. B. Nugent (72).
Colombia: Carlos Diaz-Alejandro (74).
Puerto Rico: M. Dutta and V. Su (81).

Using our taxonomic guidelines, we can characterize such models broadly as policy analysis or normative models, the main intent of their authors *not* being regular forecasting work. Their coverage of the macroeconomic accounting is partial (usually they are models of the demand or supply sectors, measured in real terms, or models of the fiscal or financial sector). Their life has been generally short.

The fact that some of these models have been built *in situ* by economists experienced in the actual workings of these economies has given their models a structural design (which is noticeable in the selection of explanatory variables and in the chains of casuality) which is thus more representative of the institutional realities of the country being modelled. This fact leads us to reflect on the desirability of joint efforts between the national economists and US-based econometricians, to generate models designed to portray more accurately the actual 'anatomy and physiology' of the different LA economies. It is to be hoped that this will help to generate smaller *ex ante* predictive errors.

13 Smaller normative models

This work was done mainly by and at international institutions, as part of their effort to determine external and internal economic requirements for growth and stability in the LDCs, and particularly in LA. During 1965–85, these planning or normative studies led to the construction of smaller models, as compared with the size and coverage of the Klein–Wharton forecasting structures. As far as we know, none of these models has become instruments of continuous utilization. The most notable work has been by the applied econometricians at UNCTAD, the IDB and the World Bank. The influence of the methodology of Klein has also been felt in the work of these institutions. Some of the modelling attempted full coverage, with a demand-driven, Keynesian-type, basic design, although simultaneous supply determination has been used via the Leontief input–output identities.

A partial alphabetical country listing follows, extracted from the bibliography:

Argentina, Brazil, Chile and others: UNCTAD (182).
Mexico: L. E. Barraza, Tecpatl I, Banco de Mexico (24).
Mexico: Fernando Clavijo, Secretaria de Programacion y Presupuesto (60).
Argentina: S. Gupta, IBRD (95).
Nicaragua: Instituto Centroamericano de Administracion de Empresas (106).
Chile: C. Molina and P. Mellor (127).
Brazil: Thomas H. Naylor *et al.* (139, 140).
Costa Rica, El Salvador, Guatemala, Honduras, Nicaragua: J. B. Nugent (141, 143–7).
Central America: SIECA (160); Gabriel Siri (161–2).

14 The input–output approach in LA modelling: A. Manne

One of the first extensive efforts to utilize the input–output approach to model a Latin American economy was made by Professor Alan Manne of Stanford University. His paper, *Key Sectors of the Mexican Economy*

(121), published in 1966, constituted a major step forward in the application of the Leontief inter-industry analysis.

Using an algebraic formulation of Chenery and Kretschmer, and concentrating on 12 key sectors of interest to Nacional Financiera, the Mexican government development bank, Manne addressed the question of whether to 'make or import' capital goods. The calculation from this model led him to conclude that, by the mid-1970s (the study was done in 1963), Mexico was ready to produce, at comparable US plant sizes, in nine out of the 12 key sectors examined.

15   The MIT branch of LA models: L. Taylor

Under the leadership of Professor Lance Taylor, a panoply of LA models have been built during the 1960s and 1970s. They constitute, along with the Klein–Wharton models, an identifiable branch of modelling of the economies of the region.

In contrast with the Wharton philosophy, the MIT (Massachusetts Institute of Technology) models can be characterized by their emphasis on simulation uses, rather than forecasting, their meticulous theoretical designs, rather than data accommodation, and their discontinuous utilization. They also tend to be more compact than the Wharton versions.

The difference in the methodology of model-building is the result of philosophical differences regarding the accuracy of macroeconomic data and the relevance of statistical estimation methods in view of the softness of the 'raw material'. Klein and his associates are more ready to work with the available information and, by so doing, to generate a demand for data improvement. Accordingly, they are ready to re-estimate and respecify their models as soon as new data releases require and facilitate the process of a continuing search for precision. Taylor (170–2), on the other hand, prefers to rely less on the data, to trust more the theoretical structures, and use the data with a grain of salt. So one is an optimist and the other a pessimist regarding the status of economic measurement.

To carry this point forward slightly, we note that, in LA model-building, one finds essentially two ways of estimating behavioural coefficients. One is through regression methods, while the other is through an inspection of key coefficients in the time series of the country in question and a selection of their 'reasonable values' by the model-builder. These coefficients are then used as constants. The regression method has been systematically used by the Klein–Wharton model-builders. Their forecasting purpose makes them favour periodic re-estimation of coefficients (recalibration) in trying to reduce predictive errors, in order to be as close as possible to the estimates of the national income accounts.

The non-regression estimates have been used by model-builders in planning. Their normative or policy-decision purpose, added to their view of the 'softness' of the data, leads them to prefer a simpler and less costly method. The modelling work of Lance Taylor of MIT provides examples of this approach.

16   Recent developments: 1980–5
The evolution of macro-modelling in LA in the last half-decade has seen the strengthening of some lines of development already implicit in the 1970s. We will survey them under the headings of (a) modelling trends, (b) computational trends and (c) LA economic developments which are capable of being modelled.

Modelling trends
Regionalization, optimization and the adoption by corporations of modelling are some of the developments one can detect in the recent econometric work on LA. Another is the impact of micro computers in the diffusion of model-building techniques and the consequent impact in the specification of the constructed models.

As part of the natural propensity to go from the whole to the component parts, supported by improvement in data availability, regionalization is perhaps one clear trend in LA Model building.[8] Having reached a saturation of general (national) economic models, in some countries one can detect efforts to build particular (regional) models. One example, in the case of Mexico, is the joint efforts of scholars from Monterrey Institute of Technology, headed by Alejandro Ibarra, with the support of Norman Glickman of the University of Texas at Austin, in developing the state model of Nuevo Leon, the industrial north-eastern Mexican state. Ibarra's efforts include an ambitious scheme of industrial statistical data-gathering in Monterrey, the capital city of Nuevo Leon. He was planning (at the time of writing) to use the CIEMEX–Wharton national model as a basis of some of the national or world forecasting inputs. If successful, this would be the first case in LA of modelling and forecasting of a region in parallel with national forecasting.

This regionalization can be seen as a natural evolutionary process in model-building. It is part of the effort to enlarge the coverage of the models to include not only functional economic sectors but also geographical sectors.

Another development, implicit since the early phases, is the establishment of models in corporations for use in their internal planning. This means the adoption of econometrics as part of the analytical work done inside or financed on the outside by the business enterprises.

Two cases, one in South America and the other in Mexico, exemplify this trend. Bunge and Born, one of the largest grain traders in the world, established a full econometric research centre (Serfina), with headquarters in São Paulo, Brazil, whose task includes the building of econometric models for the LA countries where the company has interests and does regular forecasting. Economic policy recommendations are also part of the job of the centre's econometricians. One of the more recent efforts has been their exploration of a policy package that deals with growth for LA countries in a non-inflationary environment. They are offering alternatives to the general lines of austerity and restraint that are being recommended by outsiders for dealing with the present economic crisis.[9] Serfina is one of the most ambitious macroeconometric efforts undertaken by a corporation in LA. They maintain and utilize models of Argentina, Brazil, Uruguay and Peru.

Another case of a corporate econometric undertaking is the one of Grupo Vitro, the largest glass corporation of Mexico, with headquarters in Monterrey City. The interesting aspect of the Vitro work consists in the vertical integration of its modelling, as well as its incorporation in the overall business planning of the corporation. Vitro's head economist, Baltazar Ponguta H., has built in hierarchical fashion a constellation of models that start with national variables, then go to variables of the whole glass industry and end with specific Vitro products. The continuous utilization of econometric modelling in an integrated fashion makes Vitro's work a trend-setting case of corporate econometrics.

A third trend of the 1980s, which was only beginning in the previous decade, is the use of optimization models of LA countries. Professor David Kendrick and his students at the University of Texas at Austin are leaders in this development. (See, for example, 93 in the bibliography.)

The Cartagena Group (Junta del Acuerdo de Cartagena) maintains models for forecasting and policy analysis in Lima, Peru for the Andean Pact countries. Regular reports are issued at quarterly intervals. Their materials are being used by Project LINK, the cooperative system for world modelling, discussed in Chapter 14 below. It should also be noted that economists at the Universidad de Chile maintain a Chilean model for use in LINK, and Pedro Palma's model of Venezuela (149) is also incorporated in the system.

Computational trends[10]

As in North America and other advanced industrial areas, the micro computer has begun to revolutionize the process of model-building in LA. Its main impact has just begun to be felt in Brazil, Venezuela and Mexico.

The availability of inexpensive computational power, the proliferation of software and the easy personal access to the machine are also generating an explosive phase of model-building, both at macro and at micro levels (industrial, corporate). In fact, the trend towards the use of models in corporations is being supported or strengthened by the micro computer. It is very likely at present that the increasing use of the personal computer will be a powerful factor in the diffusion of econometric modelling in LA, both in the corporation and at the university. The same process would appear to be taking place in the public sector, too.

The micro computer is also stimulating or strengthening the use of models in commercial economic consulting. In Puerto Rico, for example, Jorge F. Freyre, head of Applied Research, Inc., has found extensive and cheaper application of the micro computer and the new WEFA software (AREMOS) in transporting his Puerto Rican Model from the main-frame to the micro computer. In fact, the computational economies provided by these micro computers have generated a new lease on life in the Puerto Rican Model applications, which were in jeopardy because of computational expenses of using a main-frame computer located in the United States, accessible only through telephone lines.

In Venezuela we find another case of econometric consulting strengthened by the new technology. Pedro Palma, founder of Metroeconomica, in Caracas, has had a similar experience and has developed his own software for these purposes.

It is interesting to note the effects that micro computers are having on the size and design of LA modelling. Some of the models built with the micro computers tend to be smaller and more recursive than those built with the main-frame during the 1970s, but this will probably change as the micro computers become even more powerful. Another trend seems to be a looser connection with theory and a greater readiness to experiment with explanatory variables of interest only to the model-builder. In our view, this improvization has led, in some cases, to excesses and to a lowering of the quality of model specification, where anything goes. One has to recognize, however, that the boom in model-building, generated by the micro computer, is inevitable and we suspect that the empirically based models will become more realistic and precise because they will have to survive the harsh test of repeated forecasting applications.

Modelling of developments in LA economies
While modelling has evolved in the manner broadly described in the previous section, the LA economic reality has evolved in some directions that have fallen within the representational capacity of the models, while other developments have tended to escape it and call for model improvements to try to capture the new realities. Some of these new 'modellable' economic developments in LA are the following:

1. The rise (1973–85) in the terms of trade for oil, affecting Mexico, Venezuela and Ecuador on the export supply side and others, notably Brazil, on the import demand side. The more recent fall and its reverse effects for suppliers and importers have already been captured by the 'continuous' forecasting models of the region.
2. The LA debt crisis, signalled in August 1982 by Mexico's temporary suspension of servicing payments. In 1986–7 some of the proposals to alleviate the debt-servicing burden have been simulated with the Mexican CIEMEX–WEFA Model.
3. The phenomenon of capital flight, which has reached enormous size in LA and most conspicuously in the case of Mexico. This phenomenon is, of course, not unrelated to the previous one.
4. Emigration to the United States from all over LA, and especially from Mexico and Central America. In both its legal and illegal dimensions, this development is having important economic consequences for the United States and for the LA countries where these human flows originate. For the LA nations, it means labour exports and the corresponding remittances. It also means a reduction of their unemployment levels.[11]
5. The expansion of the underground economy and the strengthening and integration of illegal revenue-producing activities, particularly the production of non-medical drugs.
6. The radical stabilization (anti-inflationary) programmes of Argentina, Brazil and Mexico.

The emergence of the extreme importance of oil led to more elaborate detail in the energy and the related trade sectors. The next two phenomena, external debt and capital flight, confirm the previous conclusion of the crucial importance of modelling the financial sector of the LA economies. Migratory flows and labour remittances are captured in the Mexican external current account balance and have been components of the CIEMEX–WEFA Model. But their fuller ramifications still pose a challenge to the statistician and consequently to Mexican econometricians. The most intractable development is the expansion of the underground economy. Its very measurement represents a serious limitation to the representational ability of the LA models, because activities for which the accounts are not available represent a high ratio to those captured by the statisticians. (One example is the sudden or sustained presence of consumption based on disposable income generated outside the national accounts.) The Cruzado and Austral plans of monetary reform and stabilization have had a temporary structural impact on Brazilian and Argentinian models, but, after two years, it appears that established patterns of behaviour dominate these two economies once again. The more recent Mexican (December 1983) anti-inflationary plan, with its rapid opening of the economy, among other elements, has led to respecification of the external sector of the CIEMEX Model.

In conclusion, we may say that the LA models have had a number of successes, although a number of challenges remain for the young researcher in this field. We have also tried to indicate the usefulness of a multiplicity of modelling approaches, in attempting to capture the essence of this intriguing portion of our world.

Notes

1. For simplicity, we are leaving out the consideration of forecasting the errors (the add-factors) of the behavioural equations. They can, however, be included in defining a good forecaster.
2. This imaginative solution, started in the Brookings Model, has been taken up by Latin American econometricians, generally colleagues or students of L. R. Klein with his Wharton methodology. An example, among many possible, is the Puerto Rican Model of Jorge F. Freyre (89).
3. L. R. Klein, *The Keynesian Revolution*, 2nd edn (1966), Chapters 8 and 9, especially pp. 217–26.
4. For instance, see Chenery and Strout (1966). See also the discussion in the preceding chapter.
5. As noted in Chapter 11 above, there exists also an econometric model for the region of Latin America as a whole; see Marwah (1975). This small-scale model of LA as a whole, constructed jointly with a small-scale model of Asia (excluding Japan) as a whole, was oriented towards policy simulations of varying levels of development assistance from the developed countries, directed towards these two regional aggregations of LDCs.
6. L. R. Klein and A. S. Goldberger, *An Econometric Model of the United States, 1929–1953* (1955); Klein (1964); Evans and Klein (1968). These models have been discussed in Part II of this work.
7. Abel Beltran-del-Rio (42) in 1973; Rogelio Montemayor-Seguy (132) in 1974; and Oscar A. Rufatt (158) in 1981.
8. See also the discussion of regional macroeconometric modelling in the following chapter.
9. See J. B. Campodonico and J. A. Welsh Miguens (1986), as well as the references to the specific models of Argentina (1985), Brazil (1988), and Peru (1987).
10. See also Chapter 15 below.
11. Professor Clark W. Reynolds of Stanford University has been a leading student of the quantitative impact of these human flows in the two groups of nations. See, in particular, Reynolds and McCleery (1985). He has used econometric methods for his investigations.

Appendix: Bibliography of Latin America macro-model-building, 1965–85

No.	Author	Title	Editors (where relevant)	Reference
1	Abarca, Roberto, Castro, Antonio, Clavijo, Fernando and Esperon, Maria L.	'Aspectos Dinamicos de la Economia Mexicana'	D.G.P.H. de la S.H.C.P.	mimeo
2	Adams, F. Gerard, Behrman, Jere R. and Lasaga, Manuel	'Commodity Exports and NIEO Proposals for Buffer Stocks and Compensatory Finance: Implications for Latin America'	W. Baer and M. Gillis	*Export Diversification and the New Protectionism*
3	Adams, F. Gerard, Roldan, Romualdo A. and Behrman, Jere R.	'Measuring the Impact of Primary Commodity Fluctuations on Economic Development: Coffee and Brazil'		*American Economic Review*, 69, no. 2 (pp. 164–8)
4	Adams, F. Gerard, Adams, Mark E. and Sanchez, Enrique P.	'Can Latin America Carry its International Debt? A Prospective Analysis Using the Wharton Latin American Debt Simulation Model'		*Journal of Policy Modeling*, 5, no. 3
5	Adams, F. Gerard and Roldan, Romualdo A.	'An Econometric Approach to Measuring the Impact of Primary Commodity Price Fluctuations on Economic Development: Coffee and Brazil'	W. C. Labys, M. Ishaq Nadiri and Jose Nunez del Arco	*Commodity Markets and Latin American Development: A Modeling Approach*
6	Adams, F. Gerard and Priovolos, Theophilos	'Commodity Exports, Economic Development and Policy: Coffee and Brazil'		Unpublished report to US AID
7	Adams, F. Gerard and Roldan, Romualdo A.	'Econometric Studies of the Impact of Primary Commodity Markets on Economic Development in Latin America'		Conference of Commodity Markets, Models and Policies in Latin America
8	Adams, F. Gerard and Priovolos, Theophilos	'The Commodity Problem and Goal Attainment in Brazil: An Integrated Econometric Investigation'		mimeo

412

Publisher/Source	Year	Coverage	Purpose	Continuity	Country/Region
Mexico, D. F.: Secretaria de Hacienda y Cazerio Publico	1979	full	forecasting	continuous	Mexico
Illinois: Bureau of Economics and Business Research, University of Illinois	1981	partial	non-forecasting policy	discontinuous	Latin America
	1979	partial	non-forecasting simulation	discontinuous	Brazil
	1983	partial	non-forecasting policy	discontinuous	Latin America
Cambridge, Mass.: Ballinger, for the National Bureau of Economic Research	1980	partial	non-forecasting simulation	discontinuous	Brazil
Philadelphia: Wharton Econometric Forecasting Associate Inc.	1981	partial	non-forecasting simulation	discontinuous	Brazil
Lima, Peru	1978	partial	non-forecasting	discontinuous	Latin America
Philadelphia: Wharton-EFA	1980	partial	non-forecasting simulation	discontinuous	Brazil

413

Appendix: Bibliography of Latin America macro-model-building, 1965–85

No.	Author	Title	Editors (where relevant)	Reference
9	Adams, F. Gerard and Roldan, A.	'Econometric Studies of the Impact of Primary Commodity Markets on Economic Development in Latin America'		Conference on Commodity Markets, Models and Policies in Latin America
10	Adams, F. Gerard and Behrman, Jere R.	*Commodity Exports and Economic Development: The Commodity Problem and Policy in Countries*		
11	Added, Abdalla	'An Econometric Interpretation of the Relationships of Prices and Money Supply in Selected Latin-American Countries, with Special Reference to Brazil'		PhD dissertation
12	Albertelli, O.	'A Macroeconometric Model of Mexico'	IMF	mimeo
13	Alejandro, F., P. Clark and Jul, A.	'Projecting the Optimal Level of Copper Production in Chile'	Richard Eckaus and Paul Rosenstein-Rodan	*Analysis of Development Problems: Studies of the Chilean Economy*
14	Alves, Eliseu Roberto de Andrade	'An Econometric Study of the Agricultural Labor Market in Brazil: A test of Subsistence and Commercial Family Farm Models'		PhD Thesis
15	Amieva Huerta, Juan	'Aspectos Teoricos de un Modelo Macroeconometrico para la Economia Mexicana'		*El Trimestre Economico*, 52, no. 205
16	Ason, Elias Raul	'An Econometric Model of the Puerto Rican Banking Sector'		PhD thesis
17	Aspe, Pedro and Jarque, Carlos	'Expectativas Racionales: Un Modelo Trimestral para la Economia Mexicana'		*El Trimestre Economico*, 52, no. 207
18	Assis, C.	'A Mixed Integer Programming Model for the Brazilian Cement Industry'		PhD thesis

Publisher/Source	Year	Coverage	Purpose	Continuity	Country/Region
Lima, Peru	1978	partial	non-forecasting	discon-tinuous	Latin America
Lexington Mass.; D. C. Heath	1982	book			general
Purdue University	1963	partial	non-forecasting	discon-tinuous	Latin America/Brazil
Washington DC	1967	full	forecasting	discon-tinuous	Mexico
Amsterdam: North Holland	1973	partial	non-forccasting policy	discon-tinuous	Chile
Purdue University	1972	partial	non-forecasting simulation	discontin-uous	Brazil
	1985 (Jan.–Mar.)	full	non-forecasting simulation	discon-tinuous	Mexico
University of California, Berkeley	1970	partial	forecasting	discon-tinuous	Puerto Rico
	1985 (Jul.–Sept.)	full	forecasting	continuous	Mexico
Johns Hopkins University	1977	partial	non-forecasting programming	discon-tinuous	Brazil

Appendix: Bibliography of Latin America macro-model-building, 1965–85

No.	Author	Title	Editors (where relevant)	Reference
19	Baby, V. J.	'An Analysis of Economic Fertility and Recommendations For Increased Sorghum Production and Utilization in Colombia'		PhD thesis
20	Bacha, Edmar Lisboa	'An Economic Model for the World Coffee Market. The Impact of Brazilian Price Policy'		PhD thesis
21	Balassa, Bela	'Policy Responses to External Shocks in Selected Latin American Countries'	W. Baer and M. Gillis	*Export Diversification and The New Protectionism*
22	Banco de Mexico	'A System of Short-Run Projections'		mimeo
23	Barraza Allende, L. E.	'A Three-Sector Model of Growth in Mexico'		PhD thesis
24	Barraza Allende, L. E.	'Tecpatl l, Short-Run Econometric Model of Mexico'		Banco de Mexico, mimeo
25	Barro, Robert J.	'Money and Output in Mexico, Colombia and Brazil'	Jere Behrman and James A. Hanson	*Short-Term Macroeconomic Policy in Latin America* (pp. 177–200)
26	Barro, Robert J.	'Money and Output in Mexico'		Paper presented at the ILPES/National Bureau of Economic Research Conference on Short-Term Macroeconomic Policy in Latin America
27	Bateman, M.	'Analyzing and Forecasting World Sugar Prices'		Conference on Commodity Markets, Models and Policies in Latin America
28	Behrman, Jere R.	Aggregative Market Responses in Developing Agriculture: The Postwar Chilean Experience'	Richard Eckaus and Paul Rosenstein-Rodan	*Analysis of Development Problems: Studies of the Chilean Economy*, Ch. 2
29	Behrman, Jere R.	'Cyclical Sectorial Capacity Utilization in a Developing Economy'	Richard Eckaus and Paul Rosenstein-Rodan	*Analysis of Development Problems: Studies of the Chilean Economy*, (pp. 251–68)

Publisher/Source	Year	Coverage	Purpose	Continuity	Country/Region
University of Nebraska	1973	partial	non-forecasting policy/analysis	discontinuous	Colombia
Yale University	1968	partial	non-forecasting simulation	discontinuous	Brazil
Illinois: Bureau of Economics and Business	1981	partial	non-forecasting simulation	discontinuous	Latin America
	n.d.	full	forecasting	discontinuous	Mexico
University of Wisconsin, Madison	1968	partial	non-forecasting	discontinuous	Mexico
	1974	full	forecasting	discontinuous	Mexico
Cambridge, Mass.: National Bureau of Economic Research Inc.	1979	partial	non-forecasting simulation	discontinuous	Mexico, Brazil and Colombia
	1975	partial	non-forecasting	discontinuous	Mexico
Lima, Peru	1978	partial	forecasting non-forecasting	discontinuous	Latin America
Amsterdam: North Holland	1973	partial	non-forecasting	discontinuous	Chile
Amsterdam: North Holland	1973	partial	non-forecasting	discontinuous	Chile

Appendix: Bibliography of Latin America macro-model-building, 1965–85

No.	Author	Title	Editors (where relevant)	Reference
30	Behrman, Jere R.	'Econometric Modeling of National Income Determination in Developing Countries, with Special Reference to the Chilean Experience'		*Annals of Economic and Social Measurement* 4 no. 4 (p. 461–88) Spanish Translation in *Demografia y Economia* 9 no. 3 (pp. 287–323)
31	Behrman, Jere R.	'Macroeconomic Policy in a Developing Country, an Econometric Investigation of the Postwar Chilean Experience'		unpublished paper
32	Behrman, Jere R.	'Price Determination in an Inflationary Economy: The Dynamics of Chilean Inflation Revisited'	Richard Eckaus and Rosenstein-Rodan, Paul	*Analysis of Development Problems: Studies of the Chilean Economy*, (pp. 369–98)
33	Behrman, Jere R.	'Proposed Specification of Quarterly Panamanian Econometric Model'	ILPES	Ministerio de Planificacion y Politica Economica, Project Working Paper #3, Panamanian Volume
34	Behrman, Jere R.	'Sectorial Elasticities of Substitution Between Capital and Labor in a Developing Economy: Time Series Analysis in The Case of Postwar Chile'		*Econometrica*, 40 no. 2 (pp. 311–27)
35	Behrman, Jere R.	'Short-Run Flexibility in a Developing Economy: The Postwar Chilean Experience'		*Journal of Political Economy*, 80, no. 2 (pp. 292–313)
36	Behrman, Jere R. and Hanson, James A.	'The Use of Econometric Models in Developing Countries'	Jere R. Behrman and James A. Hanson	*Short-Term Macroeconomic Policy in Latin America* (pp. 1–38)
37	Behrman, Jere R.	'Variable Definitions and Data Sources for Panamanian Quarterly Econometric Model'	ILPES	Ministerio de Planficacion y Politica Economica Project Working Paper #3, Panamanian Volume

Publisher/Source	Year	Coverage	Purpose	Continuity	Country/Region
	1975	partial	forecasting	discontinuous	Chile
University of Pennsylvania, Graduate Group in Economics	n.d.	full	non-forecasting	discontinuous	Chile
Amsterdam: North Holland	1973	partial	non-forecasting	discontinuous	Chile
Panama: Panama City	1975				Panama
	1972	partial	non-forecasting	discontinuous	Chile
	1972	full	non-forecasting	discontinuous	Chile
Cambridge, Mass.: Ballinger	1979	partial	non-forecasting	discontinuous	Latin America
Panama: Panama City	1975				Panama

Appendix: Bibliography of Latin America macro-model-building, 1965–85

No.	Author	Title	Editors (where relevant)	Reference
38	Behrman, Jere R. and Vargas, J. R.	'A Quarterly Econometric Model of the Panamanian Economy'	Jere R. Behrman and James A. Hanson	*Short-Term Macroeconomic Policy in Latin America* (pp. 39–82)
39	Behrman, Jere R. and Tinakorn, P.	'The Impact of the UNCTAD Integrated Program on Latin American Export Earnings'		Conference on Commodity Markets, Models and Policies in Latin America
40	Behrman, J. R. and Klein, L. R.	'A Tentative Model of Brazil'		unpublished
41	Bello, I.	'A Simple Macroeconomic Model for the Chilean Economy'		PhD thesis
42	Beltran-del-Rio, Abel	'A Macroeconometric Forecasting Model for Mexico: Specification and Simulations'		PhD thesis
43	Beltran-del-Rio, Abel	'Econometric Forecasting for Mexico: An Analysis of Errors in Prediction'	Jere R. Behrman and James A. Hanson	*Short-Term Macroeconomic Policy in Latin America* (pp. 115–32)
44	Beltran-del-Rio, Abel and Klein, Lawrence R.	'Macroeconometric Model Building in Latin America: The Mexican Case'	N. Ruggles	*The Computer in Economic Social Research in Latin America* (pp. 161–90)
45	Beltran-del-Rio, Abel	'The Mexican Oil Syndrome: Early Symptoms, Preventive Efforts and Prognosis'	W. Baer and M. Gillis	*Export Diversification and the New Protectionism*
46	Betancourt, Roger Rene	'An Econometric Analysis of the Household's Intertemporal Allocation Under Additive Preferences: A Test of the Normal Income Hypothesis with Chilean Cross-Section Data'		PhD thesis
47	Borts, George H. and Hanson, James A.	'The Monetary Approach to the Balance of Payments with Empirical Application to the Case of Panama'	Jere R. Behrman and James A. Hanson	*Short-Term Macroeconomic Policy in Latin America* (pp. 257–88)

Publisher/Source	Year	Coverage	Purpose	Continuity	Country/Region
Cambridge, Mass.: Ballinger	1979	full	forecasting	continuous (?)	Panama
Lima, Peru	1978	partial	non-forecasting	discontinuous	Latin America
University of Pennsylvania	1965	full	forecasting	discontinuous	Brazil
University of Southern California	1969	full	non-forecasting	discontinuous	Chile
University of Pennsylvania	1973	full	forecasting	continuous	Mexico
Cambridge, Mass.: National Bureau of Economic Research Inc.	1979				Mexico
New York: Columbia University Press	1974	full	forecasting	continuous	Mexico
Illinois, Bureau of Economic and Business Research, University of Illinois	1981	partial	non-forecasting	discontinuous	Mexico
University of Wisconsin	1970	partial	non-forecasting simulation	discontinuous	Chile
Cambridge, Mass.: Ballinger	1979	partial	non-forecasting	discontinuous	Panama

Appendix: Bibliography of Latin America macro-model-building, 1965–85

No.	Author	Title	Editors (where relevant)	Reference
48	Brodersohn, Mario S.	'The Phillips Curve and the Conflicts Between Full Employment and Price Stability in the Argentine Economy, 1964–1974'	Jere R. Behrman and James A. Hanson	*Short-Term Macroeconomic Policy in Latin America* (pp. 201–225)
49	Caceres, Luis Rene	'Integracion Economica e Inflacion en Centro America. Un Modelo Espacias?'		*El Trimestre Economico* No. 180 (pp. 811–841)
50	Campos, Roberto de Oliveira	'Economic Development and Inflation with Special Reference to Latin America'		*Development Plans and Programmes*
51	Campos, Roberto de Oliveira	'Monetarism and Structuralism in Latin America'	Gerald M. Meier	*Leading Issues in Economic Development: Studies in International Poverty* (pp. 241–7)
52	Cantu Suarez, Mario and Sanchez, Enrique	'Modelo Econometrico de Argentina'		
53	Cantu-Suarez, Mario	'Venezuelan Econometric Model'		
54	Cardoso, Eliana A.	'The Burden of Exchange Rate Adjustment in Brazil'	W. Baer and J. Gillis	*Export Diversification and the New Protectionism*
55	Cardoso, Eliana A. and Dornbusch, Rudiger	'An Equation of Brazilian Exports of Manufactures'		*Revista Brasileira de Economia*, vol. 34
56	Cardoso, E. and Taylor, L. J.	'Identity-Based Forecasts of Prices and Quantities: Some Medium-Term Projections for Brazil'		mimeo
57	Carter, N. G.	'A Macroeconomic Model of Jamaica, 1959–1966'		*Social and Economic Studies*, 19 (pp. 178–201)
58	Cerboni, Cristina	'A Model of the Venezuelan Economy'		mimeo

Publisher/Source	Year	Coverage	Purpose	Continuity	Country/Region
Cambridge, Mass.: Ballinger	1979	partial	non-forecasting	discontinuous	Argentina
	1978 (Oct.–Dec.)				Central America
Paris: OECD Development Centre	1964	partial	non-forecasting	discontinuous	Latin America
New York: Oxford University Press	1970	partial	forecasting	discontinuous	Latin America
Wharton Econometrics Forecasting Associates	1983	partial	forecasting	continuous	Argentina
Wharton Econometrics, Philadelphia, PA	1983	full	forecasting	continuous	Venezuela
Illinois, Bureau of Economic and Business Research, University of Illinios	1981	partial	non-forecasting	discontinuous	Brazil
	1980	partial	non-forecasting	discontinuous	Brazil
Department of Economics, Massachusetts Institute of Technology	1975	partial	forecasting	discontinuous	Brazil
	1970	full	forecasting	discontinuous	Jamaica
Wharton Econometric Forecasting Associates	1977–8	full	forecasting	continuous (?)	Venezuela

Appendix: Bibliography of Latin America macro-model-building, 1965–85

No.	Author	Title	Editors (where relevant)	Reference
59	Ciorolo, Luis O.	'An Econometric Analysis of the Beef-Cattle Industry of Uruguay'		PhD thesis
60	Clavijo, Fernando	'Desarrollo y Perspectivas de la Economia Mexicana en el Corto Plazo. Un Modelo Econometrico Trimestral'		*El Trimestre Economico*, no. 172 (pp. 845–79)
61	Cole, S.	'A Case Study of A Normative Model: The Latin American World Model as a Tool of Analysis in Integrated Planning at a National and Regional Level in Developing Countries'		Working Paper, Department of Social Statistics, UNESCO and Science Policy Research Unit
62	Cole, W. E.	'The Mexican Steel Industry and its Impact on the Mexican Economy'		PhD thesis
63	Condos, A.	'The Application of Macroeconomic Models to Development Planning: Peru'		PhD thesis
64	Corbo, Lioi Vittorio	'An Econometric Study of the Chilean Inflation'		PhD thesis
65	Corbo, Lioi Vittorio	'An Econometric Study of the Chilean Inflation'		Published as: *Inflation in Developing Countries: An Econometric Study of Chilean Inflation*
66	Crocomo, Doraci Eloisa	'An Econometric Simulation Study of the Effect of Exchange Rate Overvaluation on Brazilian Agriculture'		PhD thesis
67	Dagum, Camilo	'Un Modelo Econometrico de la Oferta y la Demanda de Energeticos (Estudio de un Caso: Mexico)'		*El Trimestre Economico*, no. 150 (pp. 275–301)
68	Dagum, Camilo	'Un Modelo Econometrico sobre la Inflacion Estructural'		*El Trimestre Economico*, no. 145 (pp. 39–59)
69	Dagum, Camilo	'Un Modelo no Lineal Generalizado de la Distribucion Funcional del Ingreso'		*El Trimestre Economico*, no. 163 (pp. 483–521)

Publisher/Source	Year	Coverage	Purpose	Continuity	Country/Region
Michigan State University	1980	partial	non-forecasting simulation	discontinuous	Uruguay
	1976 (Oct.–Dec.)				Mexico
University of Sussex, England	1977	partial	non-forecasting planning	discontinuous	Latin America
University of Texas	1965	partial	non-forecasting	discontinuous	Mexico
Iowa State University	1966	partial	non-forecasting simulation	discontinuous	Peru
MIT	1971	partial	non-forecasting	discontinuous	Chile
Amsterdam: North Holland	1974	partial	non-forecasting	discontinuous	Chile
Michigan State University	1982	partial	non-forecasting simulation	discontinuous	Brazil
Universidad Nacional Autonoma de Mexico	1971 (Apr.–June)				Mexico
Fondo de Cultura Economica Mexico D. F.	1970 (Jan.–Mar.)				Latin America
	1974 (July–Sep.)				Latin America

Appendix: Bibliography of Latin America macro-model-building, 1965–85

No.	Author	Title	Editors (where relevant)	Reference
70	Dagum, Estela Maria Bee de	'Un Modelo Econometrico del Multiplicador Dinamico de Exportacion: Un Calculo para la Argentina'		*El Trimestre Economico*, no. 141 (pp. 53–69)
71	Davila, O.	'A Small Econometric Model of Ecuador'		*Essays in Economics*
72	Deprano, M. E. and Nugent, J. B.	'A Global Financial Model of Ecuador'		mimeo
73	Derbez, Luis Ernesto	*Econometric Modeling and Decision Support Systems: An Applied Exercise for a Mexican Firm*		PhD thesis
74	Diaz-Alejandro, Carlos	*Foreign Trade Regimes and Economic Development, Columbia*		
75	Dieguez, Hector L	'Un Ejercicio Econometrico en Torno a los Problemas de Multicolinearidad y Autocorrelacion'		*El Trimestre Economico*, no. 159
76	Direccion General de Politica Economica y Social de la SPP	'Modelo Econometrico "Programma"'		Plan Global De Desarrollo, 1980–1982, mimeo
77	Diz Cesar, Adolfo	'Money and Prices in Argentina'	Matthew Edel	*Food Supply and Inflation Latin America*
78	Diz Cesar, Adolfo	'Money and Prices in Argentina'	David Melselman	*Variety Monetary Experience*
79	Duarte, Adriano Romariz	'Current Brazilian Cocoa Expansion Policy and the Issue of Foreign Exchange Earnings: An Econometric Analysis'		PhD thesis
80	Duran Downing, L. and Solis, Felix J.	'An Econometric Model of Nicaragua Dusol'	Jere R. Behrman and Hanson, James A.	*Short-Term Macroeconomic Policy in Latin America* (pp. 83–113)
81	Dutta, Manoranjan and Su, Vincent	'An Econometric Model of Puerto Rico'		*The Review of Economics Studies*
82	Escobedo, Gilberto	'Formulating a Model of the Mexican Economy'		*Federal Reserve Bank of St Louis Review*, no. 55

Publisher/Source	Year	Coverage	Purpose	Continuity	Country/Region
	1969 (Jan.–Mar.)				Argentina
Quito, Ecuador	1966	full	forecasting	discontinuous	Ecuador
Junta Nacional de Planificacion, Quito, Ecuador	1966	partial	forecasting (?)	discontinuous	Ecuador
Iowa State University	1980	partial	forecasting	continuous (?)	Mexico
New York: NBER and Columbia University Press	1977	partial	non-forecasting simulation	discontinuous	Colombia
	1973 (July–Sep.)				
Secretaria de Programacion y Presupuesto	1980 1982	full	forecasting	continuous	Mexico
New York: Praeger	1969	partial	non-forecasting	discontinuous	Argentina
Chicago: University of Chicago Press	1970	partial	non-forecasting	discontinuous	Argentina
Ohio State University	1982	partial	non-forecasting simulation	discontinuous	Brazil
Cambridge: National Bureau of Economic Research Inc.	1969	partial	forecasting	continuous (?)	Nicaragua
	1979 (July)	full	forecasting	continuous (?)	Puerto Rico
	1973	full	forecasting	discontinuous	Mexico

Appendix: Bibliography of Latin America macro-model-building, 1965–85

No.	Author	Title	Editors (where relevant)	Reference
83	Escuela Nacional de Economia	'Un Modelo de Politica Economica para Mexico'		mimeo
84	Fayissa, Bichaka	'An Econometric Analysis of Male and Female Interstate Migration in Mexico'		PhD thesis
85	Fernandez, Roque B.	'Short-Run Output–Inflation Tradeoff in Argentina and Brazil'	Jere R. Behrman and Hanson, James A.	*Short-Term Macroeconomic Policy in Latin America* (pp. 133–76)
86	Figueroa, Adolfo	'Effects of Changes in Consumption and Trade Patterns on Agricultural Development in Latin America'	Werner Baer and Malcolm Gillis	*Export Diversification and the New Protectionism*
87	Fletcher, L. P.	'Some Aspects of Economic Development in Trinidad 1951 to 1959'		PhD thesis
88	Foxley, Alexandro	'Structural Disequilibrium and Alternative Growth Patterns for the Chilean Economy, 1970–80'		PhD thesis
89	Freyre, J. F.	*El Modelo Economico de Puerto Rico*		
90	Furtado, Celso and Maneschi, Andrea	'Un Modelo de Simulacion del Desarrollo y el Estancamiento en America Latina'		*El Trimestre Economico*, no. 138 (pp. 181–205)
91	Geithmann, D. T.	'Money and Income in Colombia, 1950–1960'		PhD thesis
92	Gomez, J.	'Trade Projections for Argentina'		mimeo
93	Gonzalez Villa, Felipe	'An Optimal Control Model for Policy Analysis of the Mexican Economy'		PhD thesis
94	Griffiths, B.	*Mexican Monetary Policy and Economic Development*		

Publisher/Source	Year	Coverage	Purpose	Continuity	Country/Region
Mexico: Universidad Nacional Autonoma de Mexico	1970	partial	non-forecasting policy	discontinuous	Mexico
The University of Tennessee	1982	partial	non-forecasting simulation	discontinuous	Mexico
Cambridge: National Bureau of Economic Research Inc.	1979	partial	non-forecasting simulation	discontinuous	Brazil Argentina
Illinois, Bureau of Economic and Business Research, University of Illinois	1981	partial	non-forecasting simulation	discontinuous	Latin America
Brown University	1965	partial	non-forecasting simulation	discontinuous	Trinidad
The University of Wisconsin	1970				Chile
San Juan, Puerto Rico: Interamerican Press	1979	full	forecasting	continuous	Puerto Rico
	1968 (Apr.–June.)			discontinuous	Latin America
University of Florida	1964	partial	non-forecasting simulation	discontinuous	Colombia
UNCTAD	1968	partial	forecasting	discontinuous	Argentina
University of Texas, Austin	1983	partial	non-forecasting policy	discontinuous	Mexico
New York: Praeger	1972	partial	non-forecasting policy	discontinuous	Mexico

Appendix: Bibliography of Latin America macro-model-building, 1965–85

No.	Author	Title	Editors (where relevant)	Reference
95	Gupta, S.	'Econometric Model for Argentina'		mimeo
96	Halperin, Ricardo Alberto	'The Behavior of the Argentine Monetary Sector – An Econometric Study'		PhD thesis
97	Hanson, James A.	'The Short-Run Relation Between Growth and Inflation in Latin America: A Quasi-Rational Expectations Approach'		Working Paper No. 67–3
98	Harberger, Arnold	'The Dynamics of Inflation in Chile'	Carl Christ	*Measurement in Economics: Studies in Mathematical Economics. (In Memory of Jehuda Grunfeld)* (pp. 219–50)
99	Harberger, Arnold C. and Selowksy, Marcelo	'Key Factors in the Economic Growth of Chile: An Analysis of Sources of Past Growth and of Prospects for 1965–1970'		Paper presented at Conference on the Next Decade of Latin American Economic Development
100	Harris, D. J.	'Saving and Foreign Trade as Constraints in Economic Growth: A Study of Jamaica'		*Social and Economic Studies*, 19 (pp. 147–77)
101	Harris, W. G.	'The Impact of the Petroleum Industry on the Pattern of Venezuelan Economic Development		PhD thesis
102	Hernandez, R.	'National Regional Macroeconometric Model for Argentina'		Paper presented to the NBER-Colegio de Mexico Conference
103	Hernandez-Cata, Ernesto	'International Movements of Private Financial Capital: An Econometric Analysis of the Mexican Case'		PhD thesis
104	Hughes, H. G.	'Economic Analysis of Sugarcane Production in Brazil'		PhD thesis
105	Ibarra, D. and de Navarette, I. M.	'Un Modelo de Politica Economica para Mexico'		mimeo

Publisher/Source	Year	Coverage	Purpose	Continuity	Country/Region
IBRD: Washington, DC	1974	full	forecasting	continuous (?)	Argentina
Columbia University	1968	partial	non-forecastng simulation	discontinuous	Argentina
Brown University	1976 (Oct.)	partial	non-forecasting simulation	discontinuous	Latin America
Palo Alto, California: Stanford University Press	1963	partial	non-forecasting simulation	discontinuous	Chile
Cornell University	1966 (April 20–22)	partial	non-forecasting simulation	discontinuous	Chile
	1970	partial	non-forecasting simulation	discontinuous	Jamaica
University of Oregon	1967	partial	non-forecasting simulation	discontinous	Venezuela
Mexico City	1974	full	forecasting	continuous (?)	Argentina
Yale University	1974	partial	non-forecasting simulation	discontinuous	Mexico
University of Missouri at Colombia	1971	partial	non-forecasting analysis	discontinuous	Brazil
Mexico: Universidad Nacional Autonoma de Mexico	1970	partial	non-forecasting policy	discontinuous	Mexico

Appendix: Bibliography of Latin America macro-model-building, 1965–85

No.	Author	Title	Editors (where relevant)	Reference
106	Instituto Centroamericano de Administracion de Empresas: Centro de Asesoramiento	'Modelo Macroeconomico de Nicaragua'		mimeo
107	Kelso, C. M. Jr.	'An Econometric Study of the Peruvian Economy'		mimeo
108	Khan, M. S.	'Experiments with a Monetary Model for the Venezuelan Economy'		*IMF Staff Papers*, 21 (pp. 389–413)
109	Khatkhate, Deena R., Galbis, Vincente G., and Villaneuva, Delano P.	'A Money Multiplier Model for A Developing Economy: The Venezuelan Case'		*IMF Staff Papers* 21 (pp. 389–413)
110	Kohout, J. C.	'A Price and Allocation Model for the Beef Economy in Argentina'		PhD thesis
111	Labys, Walter C.	'Commodity Models and Their Potential for Latin American Planning'	Walter C. Labys, M. Ishaq Nadiri, and Josc Nunez del Arco	*Commodity Markets and Latin American Development: A Modeling Approach* (pp. 9–40)
112	Labys, Walter C., Nadiri, M. Ishaq and del Arco, J. Nunez			*Commodity Markets and Latin American Development: A Modeling Approach*
113	Lasaga, Manuel	'The Commodity Problem and Goal Attainment in Chile: An Integrated Econometric Investigation'		mimeo
114	Lattimore, Ralph Gerard	'An Econometric Study of the Brazilian Beef Sector'		PhD thesis
115	Laursen, K.	'Macroeconomic Relationships in Colombia'		mimeo
116	Leite, Jose Alfredo Americo	'A Econometric Analysis of the Brazilian Money Supply Process and its Implications for Monetary Policy'		PhD thesis

Publisher/Source	Year	Coverage	Purpose	Continuity	Country/Region
Managua, Nicaragua	1973	full	forecasting	discontinuous	Nicaragua
	1973	full	non-forecasting	discontinuous	Peru
	1974	partial	non-forecasting	discontinuous	Venezuela
	1974 (Nov.)	partial	non-forecasting	discontinuous (?)	Venezuela
University of Illinios	1968	partial	non-forecasting policy	discontinuous	Argentina
National Bureau of Economic Research: Ballinger, Cambridge, Mass.	1980	partial	non-forecasting simulation	discontinuous	Latin America
Cambridge, Mass.: Ballinger, for the National Bureau of Economic Research	1980				
	1980	partial	non-forecasting	discontinuous	Chile
Purdue University	1974	partial	non-forecasting	discontinuous	Brazil
Bogota, Colombia	1967	full	non-forecasting	discontinuous	Colombia
University of Oregon	1976	partial	non-forecasting simulation	discontinuous	Brazil

Appendix: Bibliography of Latin America macro-model-building, 1965–85

No.	Author	Title	Editors (where relevant)	Reference
117	Lira, Ricardo	'Un Modelo Macroeconometrico de Corto Plazo y de Dos Sectores para la Economia Chilean'		*Cuadernos de Economia*
118	Liu, J. C. and De-Vires, B. A.	'An Econometric Model of Inflation and Growth in Brazil'		Paper presented at the Econometric Society
119	Maneshi, Andrea and Reynolds, C. W.	'The Effect of Import Substitution on Foreign Exchange Needs, Savings Rates and Growth in Latin America'		Economic Growth Center Discussion Paper No. 18
120	Manhertz, H.	'An Exploratory Econometric Model for Jamaica'		*Social and Economic Studies*, no. 20 (pp. 198–226)
121	Manne, A.	'Key Sectors of the Mexican Economy'	I. Adelman and E. Thorbecke	*The Theory and Design of Development*
122	Marwah, K.	'An Econometric Model of Colombia: A Prototype Devaluation View'		*Econometrica*, vol. 37, no. 2 (pp. 228–51)
123	Marzouk, Mahmoud S. H.	'The Predictability of Predetermined Variables in Macroeconometric Models for Developing Economies'		PhD thesis
124	Maynard, G. and Van Rijckehem, W.	'Stabilization Policy in an Inflationary Economy, Argentina'	G. Papanek	*Development Policy, Theory and Practice* (pp. 207–35)
125	Menezes, Jose Marcos Cavallanti de	'A Structured Approach to Econometric Forecasting Brazil's Future Energy Management Profile'		PhD thesis
126	Merrill, W. C., Fletcher, L. B., Hoffman, R. and Applegate, M.	*Panama's Economic Development: The Role of Agriculture*		
127	Molina, C. and Mellor, P.	'A Short-Run Macroeconomic Model of the Chilean Economy'		mimeo

Publisher/Source	Year	Coverage	Purpose	Continuity	Country/Region
	1975	partial	forecasting	discontinuous	Chile
New York	1969	full (?)	forecasting	discontinuous	Brazil
Yale University	1964	partial	non-forecasting	discontinuous	Latin America
	1971	full	non-forecasting	discontinuous	Jamaica
Baltimore: Johns Hopkins Press	1966	partial	non-forecasting	discontinuous	Mexico
	1969 (Apr.)	full	forecasting	discontinuous	Colombia
University of Pennsylvania	1969		forecasting	discontinuous	Brazil
Boston: Harvard University Press	1968	partial	non-forecasting policy	discontinuous	Argentina
Tulane University	1980	partial	forecasting policy	discontinuous	Brazil
Ames: Iowa State University Press	1975	partial	forecasting	discontinuous	Panama
Santiago, Catholic University of Chile	1974	full	forecasting	discontinuous	Chile

Appendix: Bibliography of Latin America macro-model-building, 1965–85

No.	Author	Title	Editors (where relevant)	Reference
128	Montague, Lord J.	'Comment on Commodity Exports and NIEO Proposals for Buffer Stocks and Compensatory Finance'	Werner Baer and Malcolm Gillis	*Export Diversification and the New Protectionism*
129	Montague, Lord J.	'Commodity Export Instability and Growth in the Latin American Economies'	W. Labys, M. Ishaq Nadiri, and J. Nunez del Arco	*Commodity Markets and Latin American Development: A Modeling Approach*
130	Montague, Lord J.	'Modeling Commodity Exports of the Latin American Economies'		Presented at the First Latin American Meeting of the Econometric Society
131	Montague, Lord J.	'The UNCTAD Integrated Program: Export Stabilization and Economic Growth in Latin America'	W. Labys, M. Ishaq Nadiri, and J. Nunez del Arco	*Commodity Markets and Latin American Development: A Modeling Approach*
132	Montemayor-Seguy, Rogelio	'An Econometric Model of the Financial Sector: The Case of Mexico'		PhD thesis
133	Monterio, J. V.	'Uma Analise de Macromodele da Economia Brasileira, PUC-RJ'		mimeo
134	Mueller, Marnie W.	'Structural Inflation and the Mexican Experience'		*Yale Economic Essays*, vol. 5, no. 1
135	Naranjo-Villalobos, F. E.	'A Macroeconometric Model of Fiscal Policy for Costa Rica'		mimeo
136	Naranjo-Villalobos, F. E.	'An Econometric Model for Honduras'		mimeo
137	Naranjo-Villalobos, F. E.	'Macroeconomic Policy in Costa Rica		PhD thesis
138	Naranjo-Villalobos, F. E.	'Un Modelo Mecroeconometrico de Politica Fiscal para Costa Rica'		mimeo
139	Naylor, T. H. *et al.*	'A Simulation Model of the Economy of Brazil'		Social System Simulation Programs, Working Paper No. 65
140	Naylor, T. H., Shubik, M., Floravante, M. and Ibrahim, I. A.	'A Simulation Model of the Economy of Brazil'	N. Ruggles	*The Role of the Computer in Economic Social Research in America*

436

Publisher/Source	Year	Coverage	Purpose	Continuity	Country/Region
National Bureau of Economic Research: University of Illinois	1981				
Cambridge, Mass.: Ballinger, for the National Bureau of Economic Research	1980	partial	non-forecasting policy	discontinuous	Latin America
Buenos Aires, Instituto Torcuato di Tella	1980 (July)	partial	non-forecasting	discontinuous	Latin America
Cambridge, Mass.: Ballinger, for the National Bureau of Economic Research	1980	partial	non-forecasting policy	continuous	Latin America
University of Pennsylvania	1974	partial	forecasting	discontinuous	Mexico
Department of Economics, Catholic University of Rio de Janeiro	1971	full	non-forecasting	discontinous	Brazil
Yale University	1965 (spring)	full	non-forecasting	discontinuous	Mexico
University of Costa Rica, San José, Costa Rica	1974	partial	non-forecasting policy	discontinuous	Costa Rica
University of Costa Rica, San José, Costa Rica	1974	full	forecasting	discontinuous	Honduras
University of Pennsylvania	1972	partial	forecasting	discontinuous	Costa Rica
San José, Costa Rica	1970	partial	non-forecasting policy	discontinuous	Costa Rica
Duke University	1971 (1 Aug.)	full	forecasting simulation	discontinuous	Brazil
New York, Columbia University Press	1974	full	forecastin simulation	discontinuous	Brazil

Appendix: Bibliography of Latin America macro-model-building, 1965–85

No.	Author	Title	Editors (where relevant)	Reference
141	Nugent, J. B.	*Economic Integration in Central America: Empirical Investigations*		
142	Nugent, J. B.	'Country Study, Argentina Summer Research Report Series'		
¡43	Nugent, J. B.	'A Small-Scale Model of Costa Rica'	J. B. Nugent	*Economic Integration in Central America: Empirical Investigations*
144	Nugent, J. B.	'A Small-Scale Model of Honduras'	J. B. Nugent	*Economic Integration in Central America: Empirical Investigations*
145	Nugent, J. B.	'A Small-Scale Model of Guatemala'	J. B. Nugent	*Economic Integration in Central America: Empirical Investigations*
146	Nugent, J. B.	'A Small-Scale Model of El Salvador'	J. B. Nugent	*Economic Integration in Central America: Empirical Investigations*
147	Nugent, J. B.	'A Small-Scale Model of Nicaragua'	J. B. Nugent	*Economic Integration in Central America: Empirical Investigations*
148	Otrera, Wylian Rolando	'An Econometric Model for Analyzing Argentina Beef Export Potentials'		PhD thesis
149	Palma Carrillo, Pedro Augustin	'A Macroeconometric Model of Venezuela With Oil Price Impact Applications'		PhD thesis
150	Pandit, V.	'Sources of Inflation in Developing Economies: Case Studies of Colombia, India, Korea and Taiwan'		PhD thesis
151	Penaloza, Tomas	'Un Modelo Dinamico de Economia Abierta: Instrumento para las Decisiones de la Politica Respecto a los Equilibrios "Interno" y "Externo" '		*El Trimestre Economico*, no. 186 (pp. 303–35)
152	Perez-Mata Cervantes, Antonio Miguel	'An Econometric Model for Wages and Enrollment in Education in Mexico with Forecasting'		PhD thesis

Publisher/Source	Year	Coverage	Purpose	Continuity	Country/Region
Baltimore: Johns Hopkins Press	1974				Central America
Washington DC, Agency for International Development	1965	full	non-forecasting simulation	discontinuous	Argentina
Baltimore: Johns Hopkins Press	1974	full	forecasting	discontinuous	Costa Rica
Baltimore: Johns Hopkins Press	1974	full	forecasting	discontinuous	Honduras
Baltimore, Johns Hopkins Press	1974	full	forecasting	discontinuous	Guatemala
Baltimore, Johns Hopkins Press	1974	full	forecasting	discontinuous	El Salvador
Baltimore, Johns Hopkins Press	1974	full	forecasting	discontinuous	Nicaragua
Texas, A & M University	1966				Argentina
University of Pennsylvania	1976	full	forecasting simulations	continuous	Venezuela
University of Pennsylvania	1971	partial	non-forecasting	discontinuous	Colombia
	1980 (Apr.–Jun.)				
University of Pittsburgh	1982	partial		discontinuous	Mexico

Appendix: Bibliography of Latin America macro-model-building, 1965–85

No.	Author	Title	Editors (where relevant)	Reference
153	Perez-Castillo, J. P. *et. al.*	'Dynamic Models for Simulating The Venezuelan Economy'		unpublished
154	Pujol, J. P.	'An Econometric Model of Argentina'		unpublished paper of Wharton EFA
155	Quadri de la Torre, G. R.	'Efectos Intersectoriales del Manejo de la Deuda Externa en un Modelo de la Teoria del Control para Mexico'		*El Trimestre Economico,* vol. 49, no. 196
156	Reichmann, Thomas	'Persistent Inflation and Macroeconomic Equilibrium: The Case of Chile'		PhD thesis
157	Reinafarje, W. and Yepez, M.	'An Econometric Model of Peru'		mimeo
158	Rufatt, Oscar Adolfo	'Mexico: Economic Policy Analysis 1978–1983: A Macroeconometric Model of Mexico and Control Theory Applications'		PhD thesis
159	Schydolowsky, Daniel M.	'Capital Utilization, Growth, Employment, Balance of Payments and Price Stabilization'	Jere Behrman and J. Hanson	*Short-Term Macroeconomic Policy in Latin America* (pp. 311–55)
160	SIECA (Secretaria Permanente del Tratado General de Integracion Economica Centro Americana)	'Evolucion 1960–1970, y Perspectivas 1970–1980'		*El Desarrollo Integrado de Centroamerica en la Presente*
161	Siri, Gabriel	'A Minimodel of External Dependence of the Central American Economies'	Jere Behrman and J. Hanson	*Short-Term Macroeconomic Policy in Latin America*
162	Siri, Gabriel	*El Salvador and Economic Integration in Central America: An Econometric Study*		Wharton Econometric Studies Series
163	Siri, Gabriel	'The Commodity Problem and Goal Attainment in Central America: An Integrated Econometric Investigation'		unpublished manuscript

Publisher/Source	Year	Coverage	Purpose	Continuity	Country/ Region
Washington DC, Simulatics Corp.	1963	full	non-forecasting simulation	discon-tinuous	Venezuela
University of Pennsylvania	1970	full	forecasting	continuous	Argentina
	1983 (Oct.– Dec.)	partial	non-forecasting simulation	discon-tinuous	Mexico
Harvard University	1973	partial	non-forecasting	discon-tinuous	Chile
University of Pennsylvania	1972	full	forecasting	discon-tinuous	Peru
University of Pennsylvania	1981	full	forecasting non-forecasting	discon-tinuous	Mexico
Cambridge, Mass.: National Bureau of Economic Research Inc.	1979	partial	non-forecasting policy	discon-tinuous	Latin America
	1973	full	forecasting/ non-forecasting	discon-tinuous	Central America
Cambridge, Mass.: National Bureau of Economic Research Inc.	1979	partial	non-forecasting simulation	discon-tinuous	Central America
Lexington, Mass: D. C. Heath	forth-coming	partial	non-forecasting policy	discon-tinuous	Central America, El Salvador
	1980	partial	non-forecasting policy	discon-tinuous	Central America

Appendix: Bibliography of Latin America macro-model-building, 1965–85

No.	Author	Title	Editors (where relevant)	Reference
164	Slooten, R. V.	'A Macroeconomic Analysis of the Medium-Term Economic Development Prospects of Peru'		PhD thesis
165	Stahl, J. E.	'An Application of a Klein Growth Model to Puerto Rico, 1947–1961'		*Economic Development and Cultural Change*, 13 (pp. 463–71)
166	Staurou, J. and Arboleda, M.	'An Econometric Model of the Panamanian Economy'		Wharton Econometric Forecasting Associates, unpublished
167	Steed, Leonardo Douglas	'The Nature of Economic Fluctuations in Argentina, An Econometric Study'		PhD thesis
168	Stewart, G. T	'The Economic Development of Uruguay 1936–1961'		PhD thesis
169	Sutton, D. S.	'A Model of Self-Generating Inflation: The Argentina Case'		PhD thesis
170	Taylor, Lance	'Detailed Specification of the Cambridge and Neoclassical Growth Models for Brazil'		*Macro Models for Developing Countries* (pp. 99–118 and 224–30)
171	Taylor, Lance D.	'A Small Econometric Model of Colombia'		Harvard Development Advisory Service, mimeo
172	Taylor, Lance D.	'Macroeconomics and Fiscal Policy in an Import-Constrained Underdeveloped Economy: The Case of Colombia'		*Revista de Planeacion y Desarrollo* 1 (pp. 1–30)
173	Taylor, Timothy Gordon	'A Bio-Econometric Analysis of the Gulf of Mexico Commercial Reef Fish Fishery'		PhD thesis
174	Thorbecke, E.	'Structure and Performance of The Guatemalan Economy, 1950–1966'		mimeo
175	Thorbecke, E. and Condos, A.	'Macroeconomic Growth and Development Models of the Peruvian Economy'	I. Adelman and E. Thorbecke	*The Theory and Design of Economic Development* (pp. 181–209)

Publisher/Source	Year	Coverage	Purpose	Continuity	Country/Region
Iowa State University	1968	partial	non-forecasting simulation	discontinuous	Peru
	1965	partial	non-forecasting simulation	discontinuous	Puerto Rico
University of Pennsylvania	1975	full	forecasting	continuous	Panama
Columbia University	1969	full	non-forecasting simulation	discontinuous	Argentina
University of Alabama	1966	full	non-forecasting simulation	discontinuous	Uruguay
Michigan State University	1968	partial	non-forecasting simulation	discontinuous	Argentina
New York: McGraw-Hill	1979	full	non-forecasting	discontinuous	Brazil
Bogota, Colombia	1969	full	forecasting	discontinuous	Colombia
	1969	partial	non-forecasting simulation	discontinuous	Colombia
The University of Florida	1980	partial	non-forecasting simulation	discontinuous	Gulf of Mexico
	1969	full	non-forecasting simulation	discontinuous	Guatemala
Baltimore: Johns Hopkins Press	1966	full	non-forecasting policy	discontinuous	Peru

Appendix: Bibliography of Latin America macro-model-building, 1965–85

No.	Author	Title	Editors (where relevant)	Reference
176	Tintner, G., Consigliere, I. and Carneiro, J. T. M.	'Un Modelo Econometrico Applicado a la Economia Brasileira'		*Revista Brasileira de Economia*, 24, no. 5–29
77	Tintner, G., Den Hertog, W., Bello, I. and Carreno, M. T.	'Un Modelo Econometrico Applicado a la Economia Mexicana'		mimeo
78	Trejo Reyes, Saul	'Un Modelo de Politica Economica: Promocion de Exportaciones y Crecimiento Optimo de la Economia'		*El Trimestre Economico*, no. 152 (pp. 1041–69)
179	UNCTAD	'The UNCTAD Integrated Program: Earnings Stabilization Through Buffer Stocks for Latin American Commodities'	Walter Labys, M. Ishaq Nadiri and J. Nunez del Arco	*Commodity Markets and Latin American Development: A Modeling Approach*
180	UNCTAD	'Developing Countries in Project Link'		unpublished manuscript
181	UNCTAD	'Models for Developing Countries'	R. J. Ball	*The International Linkage of National Economic Models* (pp. 109–76)
182	UNCTAD	'Trade Prospects and Capital Needs of Developing Countries'		UN Document TD/34/ REV. 1

Publisher/Source	Year	Coverage	Purpose	Continuity	Country/Region
	1970	full	forecasting	discon-tinuous	Brazil
	1970	full	forecasting	discon-tinuous	Mexico
	1971 (Oct.–Dec.)				
Cambridge, Mass.: Ballinger, for the National Bureau of Economic Research	1980	partial	non-forecasting	continuous	Latin America
	1972	(?)	(?)	(?)	Argentina, Brazil, Mexico, Venezuela
Amsterdam: North Holland	1973	full	forecasting	discon-tinuous	Argentina
	1968	partial	non-forecasting	continuous (?)	Argentina, Bolivia, Brazil, Chile, Colombia, Dominican Republic, Ecuador, Jamaica, Mexico, Panama, Paraguay, Peru, Uruguay, Venezuela

Appendix: Bibliography of Latin America macro-model-building, 1965–85

No.	Author	Title	Editors (where relevant)	Reference
183	Vogel, Robert	'The Dynamics of Inflation in Latin America, 1950–1969'		*American Economic Review*, vol. 64, no. 1 (pp. 102–14)
184	Von Rijckeghem, W.	'A Model of Inflation in the Argentine Economy,1950–1963'		unpublished, Consejo Nacional de Desarrollo, Harvard Development Advisory Service, Buenos Aires
185	Von Rijckeghem, W.	'A Stabilization Model for the Argentine Economy'		mimeo, Consejo Nacional de Desarrollo, Harvard Development Advisory Service, Buenos Aires
186	Von Rijckeghem, W.	'An Econometric Model of a Dual Economy: The Case of Puerto Rico'		Paper presented to the European Meeting of the Econometric Society, Brussels
187	Wachter, Susan M.	'Structuralism vs. Monetarism: Inflation in Chile'	Jere R. Behrman and James A. Hanson	*Short-Term Macroeconomic Policy in Latin America* (pp. 227–55)

Publisher/Source	Year	Coverage	Purpose	Continuity	Country/Region
	1974 (March)	partial	non-fore-casting simu-lation	discon-tinuous	Latin America
	1965	partial	non-forecasting simulation	discon-tinuous	Argentina
	1965	partial	non-forecasting policy	discon-tinuous	Argentina
	1969	full	forecasting	discon-tinuous	Puerto Rico
Cambridge, Mass.: National Bureau of Economic Research Inc.	1979	partial	non-forecasting simulation	discon-tinuous	Chile

References

Campodonico, Jorge Baca and José Alfredo Welsh Miguens (1985) 'Annual Econometric Model of Argentina', Internal Memorandum, Serfina, Buenos Aires, Argentina, November.

―――― (1986) 'Alternatives to Austerity in Latin America', Internal Memorandum, Serfina, São Paulo, Brazil.

―――― (1987) 'Annual Macroeconometric Model of Peru', Internal Memorandum, Serfina, Lima, Peru, August.

―――― (1988) 'Small-Scale Econometric Model Based on a General Equilibrium Model for the Brazilian Economy (MODBRAS)', Internal Memorandum, Serfina, São Paulo, Brazil, July.

Chenery, Hollis B. and Alan M. Strout (1966) 'Foreign Assistance and Economic Development', *American Economic Review*, vol. 56, no. 4 (September) pp. 679–733.

Evans, Michael K. and Lawrence R. Klein (1968) *The Wharton Econometric Forecasting Model*, 2nd, enlarged edn (Philadelphia: Economics Research Unit of the University of Pennsylvania).

Klein, Lawrence R. (1964) 'A Postwar Quarterly Model: Description and Applications', pp. 11–30 in *Models of Income Determination*, Studies in Income and Wealth, vol. 28 (Princeton, NJ: Princeton University Press, for the NBER).

―――― (1966) *The Keynesian Revolution*, 2nd edn (New York: Macmillan Company).

Klein, L. R. and A. S. Goldberger (1955) *An Econometric Model of the United States, 1929–1952* (Amsterdam: North-Holland).

Marwah, Kanta (1975) 'Econometric Explorations in Growth: Partners, Assistance and all that', *Indian Economic Journal*, vol. 22, no. 3 (January–March) pp. 215–38.

Reynolds, Clark W. and Robert K. McCleery (1985) 'Modeling U.S.–Mexico Economic Linkages', *American Economic Review, Papers and Proceedings*, vol. 75, no. 2 (May) pp. 217–22.

PART IV

SYSTEMS OF MODELS

13 Regional econometric models
*Roger Bolton**

1 Introduction

Regional econometric models are especially interesting products of research, data collection, forecasting and policy analysis in regional economics and regional science. In this chapter I present a survey of the contemporary regional econometric modelling field, originally aimed at an audience of regional scientists in regional modelling.

A regional econometric model is a set of equations, perhaps highly simultaneous, describing the economic structure of a regional economy, usually a state or province or metropolitan area. The parameters of the equations are estimated econometrically, largely by regression equations, as distinct from an input–output model in which parameters are based on single-point observations. As will be seen, the equations are arranged in a certain logical grouping, which reflects economic theory as applied to product markets, labour markets, firm behaviour, government behaviour, migration and so forth.

The field has evolved and changed greatly since its early days in the 1950s and 1960s when it was dominated by ideas originating in national econometric modelling and also by the export-base framework. As will be seen, the field has developed in ways quite independent of national modelling, largely because of data limitations and regional government policy concerns. Of necessity, regional modelling has had to handle some theoretical and data problems of less concern in national macroeconomics, such as interregional trade and migration. On the other hand, data problems impose certain limitations that a national macroeconomist need not face.

The field is so vast that I must be selective and personally biased in a short discussion. I want to make clear at the start the basis for selectivity and at the same time explain how the reader can fill in the gaps in my treatment. First, I concentrate on large operational econometric models of single regions. There are surveys on multiregional models (Bolton, 1980a, 1980b, 1982a; Rietveld, 1982; Lakshmanan, 1982, 1983; and other papers

*The author is grateful to Ronald Miller, Norman Glickman and Frank Giarratani for helpful comments, while retaining responsibility for any errors of description and interpretation. Apart from some editorial changes, this chapter is essentially the article of the same title, reprinted by permission, from the *Journal of Regional Science*, vol. 25, no. 4 (November 1985) pp. 495–520. The chapter author took advantage of the reprinting to correct one error and add one reference.

in Issaev, 1982), so my few comments on them arise naturally from a discussion of single-region models. I do not cover shift-share techniques or economic-base models; again, there are other surveys (see other articles in Volume 25 of the *Journal of Regional Science*, and Stevens and Moore, 1980).

Second, I provide little detail on any one model. Rather, I summarize the salient characteristics of models in general and give details from some of them as examples. I believe that what is most interesting about a model is its unusual treatment of one or two aspects, so my examples are more often of atypical rather than typical features. Furthermore I concentrate on theoretical specifications and do not review the important areas of relative performance, evaluation, and analysis of sources of error (for excellent discussions of these points, see Glickman, 1976, 1977; Treyz, 1981; Taylor, 1982; Charney and Taylor, 1984b; and Shapiro and Fulton, 1985).

Third, most of my examples are from a small number of very recent models. I believe that allows a contemporary treatment which is more useful to the generalist. Comprehensive surveys of older models are available (Knapp *et al.*, 1978; Glickman, 1977; Shapiro and Fulton, 1985; the last is excellent on the whole field, including older and newer models, data, and econometric aspects). Thus this chapter is not an historical survey, in the conventional sense, and I almost totally ignore many important, even seminal models, from the early and mid-1970s. I generally consider models described in the literature after Norman Glickman's influential book (1977), which provides extensive historical material. One troubling implication is that I omit the improved version of Glickman's Philadelphia model contained there and also the Mississippi model by Adams, Brooking, and Glickman (1975). Both were influential. But they have been described many times, and it seems best to concentrate on more recent efforts.

Fourth, I confine myself to models described in the academic literature, and pay little attention to the many proprietary models that, while valuable, have not been publicized outside the community of builders and users.

Finally, I confine myself to models of the United States. I simply am not able to do justice to other countries. There are interesting examples in other countries, but they are less numerous. There are important multiregional models of other countries, and Courbis's of France has influenced the field (Courbis, 1979, 1980, 1985; see also Bolton, 1982a, on Canada, and the papers on Europe and Japan in Issaev, 1982).

It is both hard and easy to generalize about the scores of models. Every generalization of practice has important exceptions. I try to identify the important exceptions to my generalizations, but undoubtedly have not completely succeeded.

The organization of the chapter is as follows: Section 2 is a general introduction to single-region and multiregional models; Section 3 is an overview of model structure, especially the differences between regional and national models; Section 4 is on origins and purposes of models; Sections 5–12 are on specific sectors, or equation blocks, and linkages between them; Section 13 is on econometric considerations. Section 14 is a brief conclusion.

I sometimes refer to a model by its author, sometimes by the name of the region. In the list of references, I list both names, with a cross-reference from region to author.

2 National models, regional models, and multiregional models

The bigger national econometric models are elaborate extensions of a Keynesian general equilibrium model of product markets, labour markets, government financial operations, and money and financial markets. Figure 13.1 describes such a model (Bolton, 1978). There are one, several, or many mathematical equations for each box (depending on industrial detail and other disaggregation). The equations include behavioural ones, definitions and identities. Figure 13.1 can be only suggestive (see Klein and Burmeister, 1976, for discussion and references).

A regional model must be combined with a national model, because the region is affected by the surrounding nation. Many regional models are 'driven by' a national model that was built for national forecasting and policy analysis purposes. The national model estimates variables that are exogenous to the region. The Wharton, Chase, DRI and INFORUM national models have all been used in that way; the University of Michigan Research Seminar in Quantitative Economics (RSQE) national model drives RSQE's models of Michigan and its metropolitan areas. If the regional model is simple, the national model might be only a few independent projections by some expert. However larger regional models have extensive industrial detail, because regions specialized in a few industries that sell in national and international markets; that suggests the national model should also have industrial detail. For example, the RSQE national model had to be augmented with industrial detail to fit RSQE's model of Michigan.

What of direct links between the 'rest of the world', outside the nation, and the region? Where there is a large national model, those links are almost universally channelled through the national model. That may not be completely satisfactory in some cases, and some possibility for improvement is suggested.[1]

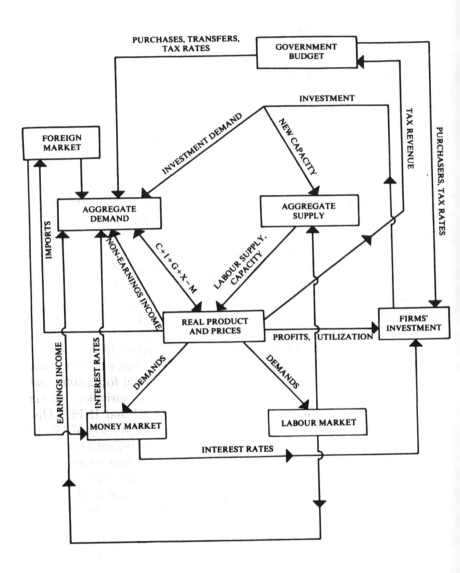

Figure 13.1   A national model

What of feedbacks from the region to the nation? They would seem to be relevant if what happens in the region significantly affects the nation, but single-region modellers have ignored such reverse links. Theoretically, the links are important in any of these cases: (a) a region's labour market is large enough to affect national labour costs (Milne, Glickman, and Adams, 1980), as with, for example, California, south-east England, the Paris Basin (Courbis, 1979) or Stockholm (Bolton, 1985); (b) a region is a dominant producer of one or more products, the exports or imports of which affect the national balance of payments and thus affect financial markets and endogenous policy reactions; (c) a region's governmental policies affect national product markets. Some regions' position in energy production raises possibilities under (b) and (c).

Because the reverse feedback is ignored, single-region models are often termed 'top-down' models or 'recursive satellite models'. There are links from nation to region. One might think there would be links from selected other regions (such as close 'trading partners') to the region being modelled, but they are not common.

Multiregional models
If we are concerned with more than one region, as when we analyse differential regional effects of a national policy or event, we need a multi-regional model, as shown in Figure 13.2 (adapted from Bolton, 1982b). There are links from nation to region, connections between regions, and, in principle, feedbacks from regions back up to the nation. As one would expect, operational multiregional models more often include such feedbacks than do single-region models.

One can conceive of a multiregional model in which the reverse feedbacks are modelled so completely that all national model variables are completely endogenous (sums or averages of regional variables). Such a model is called a 'bottom-up' or 'regional national' model. The first term is self-explanatory; the second, used by Courbis (1979, 1980), is useful because the national and regional results are determined simultaneously. One cannot model the nation independently of the regions; there is no national model apart from the set of regional models.

If the model has no reverse feedbacks, it is called a top-down multiregional model. The national model is run first to produce control totals to be allocated to regions by equations in the regional models. The regional models are models of regional shares of national totals or of regional variables relative to the nation. Top-down has the advantages of consistency and better data. Bottom-up is obviously better in theory. In practice, operational multiregional models are either purely top-down or are 'hybrid' cases, with some national variables being exogenous and others

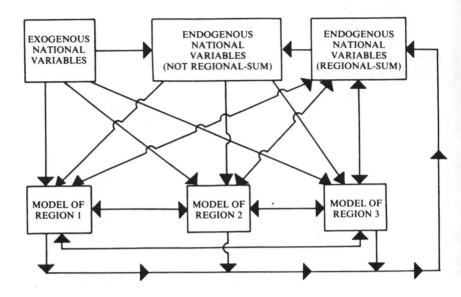

Figure 13.2   A multiregional model

being endogenous sums or averages of regional variables. In the hybrid, as in the pure bottom-up case, regional and national variables cannot be determined independently of each other.

The National-Regional Impact Evaluation System (NRIES) (Ballard, Gustely and Wendling, 1980; Ballard and Wendling, 1980) is an important recent hybrid multiregional model. The continuing effort at the Boston College Social Welfare Research Institute (1981, 1984) holds promise of incorporating bottom-up principles with microdata sets in a combined econometric and multiregional input–output model. It also includes very interesting labour market models featuring non-wage clearing and labour queues. A group headed by Walter Isard, which includes the author, has proposed an elaborate new multiregional model that would also be a hybrid. It would combine input–output with econometric models of industry demand, factor use, and migration and labour force (with equations estimated from microdata bases), and it would also have an optimizing model of inter-regional transportation. (Isard and Anselin, 1982, show the basic outline.)

It is more relevant to this chapter that there are some multiregional models of single states. Ballard and Glickman (1977) pioneered this kind of work with their bottom-up model of the 12 counties in the Delaware Valley region. Their work influenced the later NRIES hybrid model of the United States. Gindra (1977) developed a four-region model for California, testing some bottom-up specifications; he concluded that top-down was superior. The most impressive current example is one for Michigan that produces quarterly forecasts and analyses for Michigan for 12 SMSAs (standard metropolitan statistical areas) and for the rest of the state (Shapiro and Fulton, 1985). It combines a national model, a state model and separate models for each SMSA. Most national effects flow directly to the SMSA, bypassing the state model. The structure is entirely top-down: Michigan does not affect the nation, and no labour market area (not even Detroit) affects the state. The subregions are not connected with each other in any way. Detroit affects Flint no more than it affects Michigan as a whole. The authors admit that inter-regional and bottom-up forces operate – who would deny it? – but justify neglecting them as of minor importance in the short- and medium-term outlook they are concerned with. Also they cannot achieve both a quarterly model and accurate modelling of all the relevant interactions. They acknowledge that their system is not the best long-term model: 'If one were primarily concerned with the long-term shifts in employment and Michigan and the rest of the nation ... these models would not provide the most useful framework for analysis' (Shapiro and Fulton, 1985, p. 169).

Baird (1983) developed an interesting and important multiregional model of Ohio. It has inter-regional links and simultaneous determination of income and personal income among six areas (five SMSAs plus rest of the state). It is also quite detailed, having most two-digit manufacturing industries and seven non-manufacturing sectors. I mention other features of it below as examples of recent work in the field.

Charney and Taylor's model of Arizona and three major areas (Tucson, Phoenix, rest of state) is especially designed to analyse state taxes and expenditures (1984b). It is bottom-up and has intra-area, inter-area, and area–state interactions. Treyz has developed a model of 13 subregions in Colorado somewhat based on his theoretical design of 1980 (Regional Economic Models, Inc., 1984; Treyz, 1980).

3 The general structure; differences from national models

With this background, consider Figure 13.3, which shows the detail within a regional box of Figure 13.2. It is important to see some differences from the national model of Figure 13.1.

To provide a bit of history, it is useful to refer to an often cited paper by Lawrence Klein (1969), who of course came to the question from the perspective of national modelling. He recommended the strategy of linking a regional model to a national econometric model. The problem of specifying regional structure is similar to specifying industrial detail; for example, in neither industries nor regions do we have separate observations on supply of factors. Klein foresaw both regional models and industry models as the sector models consistent with a national econometric model.

He suggested that regional models have aggregate demand components like national models: consumption as a function of income; investment as a function of output, interest rate, and lagged capital stock; state and local government purchases as functions of tax receipts, population and interest rate, with tax receipts in turn a function of regional income, employment, production and so forth; exports as a function of gross product and relative prices; and imports also as a function of gross product and relative prices. Relative prices would be a function of national prices, local wages and an index of prices of imports into the region. Finally, regional wage rates would be functions of national and local unemployment rates and local consumer goods prices.

He chose not to recommend an explicit production function approach for determining factor demand. Indeed, in his scheme, employment is not determined in the model. Income is determined through the aggregate demand approach, not as the sum of labour and other factor incomes.

Model-builders have followed some but not all of Klein's suggestions. Without good data to estimate Keynesian demand components, they build up regional income as the sum of industry outputs or labour earnings. They use national models to forecast national industry outputs which drive output and/or employment in regional industries. On the other hand, regional modellers have been developing more and more sophisticated labour demand functions; the recent Michigan system is a notable example. (See Glickman, 1977, and Klein and Glickman, 1977, for further discussion of Klein's paper and subsequent history.)

The lack of investment, export and import data is almost always an insurmountable obstacle to estimating the same components as in national models.[2] The overwhelming practice is to use not a Keynesian breakdown of output by user, but one by geographical location of buyers: those located inside and those outside the region, or 'export market' and 'local market'. Following Glickman's (1971) Philadelphia model path, the models recognize that many industries sell in both markets and thus have abandoned rigid export base assumptions. Nor is export demand strictly exogenous; there are feedbacks from the labour market and other regional conditions to the region's competitiveness.

Regional output data are weak or missing outside manufacturing, so

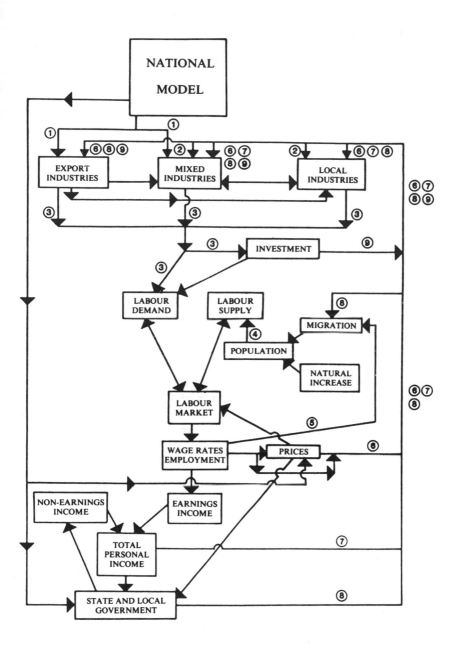

Figure 13.3 A regional model

one must resort to controversial methods if one wants a model to predict total gross regional product (GRP). Modellers who have made attempts in this way include L'Esperance (1981) and Baird (1983) for Ohio, Duobinis (1981) for Chicago and Plaut (1984) for Texas. Some model-builders include manufacturing industries' output in order to incorporate production function and labour demand theories, but then adopt short-cut approaches to labour demand in non-manufacturing. Some ignore output even in manufacturing. On this question, Engle argues, for Boston: 'forecasts of measurable employment are of more interest than forecasts of unmeasurable output. The relation between employment, wages and value added is introduced as an identity rather than generating artificial data to be used in the estimation' (Engle, 1980, p. 125).

If there are no output variables, total regional income is personal income, including non-labour income received from other regions and excluding income produced in the region but remitted to land and capital owners elsewhere. Here model-builders use the detailed and high-quality personal income data of the Bureau of Economic Analysis. Labour earnings are modelled in a more detailed and theoretically defensible way than the rest of income (see Section 10).

The quality-of-data argument for emphasizing personal income is reinforced by other considerations. Regional policy-makers are less concerned with gross product than national policy-makers are. The non-labour income part of GRP, for example, loses some significance when national businesses transfer capital income from region to region, financing investments in one place with profits earned in another. Then, too, labour has usually been regarded as the only significant supply constraint. Models are short run oriented and, even if they are long-run, capital is assumed to flow easily. In addition, the employment, unemployment and personal income data available for even small regions contrast with the scarcity of good data on capital stocks, utilization, and returns to capital. Labour income is more likely to be received in the region where it is produced. Because so many residents of the region depend on labour for income, and because labour is less mobile than capital, regional policy-makers have worried much more about measuring and analysing employment and labour income.[3]

There is a great variation from model to model in the handling of investment. In many models, investment is totally absent: capital stock may be relevant in manufacturing industry labour demand functions, but it is usually exogenous rather than being the accumulation of endogenous investment; and neither investment nor capital stock appears for non-manufacturing industries, owing to lack of data. Sometimes manufacturing investment is endogenous but feeds only into a construction employment equation, not into any capital stock variable. Public investment is even more often absent, even though there are fairly good data on government construction and, for some regions, on non-construction investment as well. Thus an essential public policy handle is missing.

A slightly different way of saying this is that models are short-run and demand-oriented. In saying that, I repeat a point made by many observers, including modellers themselves. Models are not well equipped to handle long-run changes in regional structure, capital stock, and productivity. The key explanation is the problem of data on investment and capital stock, but it is also the case that the funders are often quite satisfied with a short-run model.

The supply-side model of Texas built by Plaut (1984) is a major exception, so it receives some attention below. Plaut argues that the usual demand model is useful for forecasting fluctuations in slow-growing, highly-industrialized regions, but if one wants to forecast a fast-growing region like Texas, one must explicitly model the growth in manufacturing capacity. Plaut criticizes others for leaving capacity expansion implicit when they model a link between national output (employment) and regional output (employment).

One major difference between national and regional models is increasingly under attack by regional economists, although few model-builders have yet responded effectively to the criticism. There are seldom any money markets or financial markets in regional models. Explicitly or implicitly, the supply of liquid capital is assumed to be infinitely elastic at the national rate of return (physical capital, of course, may be fixed in the short run, as discussed later under labour demand). This is justified by saying that inter-regional mobility of liquid capital keeps inter-regional differentials in the *ex ante* rate of return small. If a regional financial market cannot sustain differentials in interest rates, then that market need not be modelled – the national model will produce any interest rates one needs.[4]

However regional economists have begun to discuss financial markets, interest rate differentials and region-specific bank behaviour. Thus far, work has been largely theoretical and not much incorporated into models. Moore and Hill (1982) discuss the issues. Roberts and Fishkind (1979) report interesting econometric estimates of money supply elasticities in different regions. They also revised a Florida model to allow savings flows into banks to affect housing starts and thus construction. The revised model did much better with those improvements, but the comparison is not convincing, because the model was revised in various other desirable ways as well.

To close this section, I note that some regional and multiregional economic models have been augmented by submodels that predict various environmental effects of economic activity and also demands for various kinds of energy resources. For surveys see Solomon (n.d.), Lakshmanan (1982) and Lakshmanan and Ratick (1980).

4   Why does one get started? The origins and purposes of regional models
People build regional models for various purposes; the four main ones seem to be pure economic science, economic forecasting, government revenue forecasting and policy analysis (including impact analysis). Often one purpose dominates. Indeed one of the most obvious and significant characteristics of the field is the tendency for a model to have elaborate detail in one or more sectors, motivated by the special interest of the model-builder, but then have a disappointing and outright simplistic treatment of other sectors. This characteristic will be evident after the discussion of specific sectors and links below. The highly uneven treatment (along with varying quality of data) helps explain why a model's ability to track the economy (as measured, say, by mean absolute percentage errors or root mean square percentage errors) varies so greatly from one variable to another.

Some models designed primarily for forecasting do not have many 'policy handles', that is, variables which governments can manipulate directly, such as public investment in infrastructure, business and household tax rates and subsidies, worker training and so forth. A forecasting model may include very aggregate variables and reduced forms that are not easily affected by government policies. In that case policy analysis must be accomplished by so-called constant term manipulations; that is, the constant term in an equation is raised or lowered by an amount representing a best guess of how much a policy will affect the variable. Many multiplier analyses are done in that way. A forecasting model might do well by the usual econometric tests even if it has an underlying structure that is incomplete or illogical, simply because it captures correlations in the historical period. Fortunately the tests of a model usually include the ability to replicate historical experience outside the period of fit. But even that is a test of forecasting ability, not policy analysis ability, and the prevailing practice of doing so only for a few out-of-sample periods may be inadequate (see Charney and Taylor, 1984a).

Pure science is sometimes one of the motives, but it actually seems rather limited. The development and testing of major innovations in regional economic theory is not a common goal. The statement by Shapiro and Fulton (1985), the builders would agree: 'If we have been successful, we have been skillful bricklayers rather than the manufacturers of new bricks in the sense that we have assembled, largely through the use of exisiting techniques, a new structure rather than created new building materials' (p. xi).

If new theory is not a common goal, neither is it a common result. One who follows both regional models and the general scientific literature will probably notice a gap between the two. The partial, focused analyses in the latter are typically much more sophisticated; examples are found in regional competitiveness, transportation cost, labour and other factor demand, migration, unemployment and so forth. Building and operating a model requires data collection and econometric analyses of so many different economic processes that the persons involved cannot spend the time required to investigate many partial equilibrium phenomena in depth. The trade-off is clear. Degrees of freedom vanish fast when good time series are so short. There are few adequate samples of micro-data for a single region. The trade-off is present even in the Michigan system, and the builders' resolution of the conflict bears their stamp: the model draws on the advanced theoretical and econometric work on labour demand done by macroeconomists, but in many other sectors of the model the specifications are quite simple and ordinary.

Thus the originality of research in the field lies, not in forging totally new tools, but rather in the following: packaging existing theory into a useful forecasting and policy analysis machine; doing so in a way that captures the special features of some region; developing and evaluating data adequate for the testing and subsequent use of the model.

Many models are built by solitary individuals, and indeed many are born in PhD dissertations. Many do not survive long, if by survival we mean continued development, regular use in forecasting, and support of users through software and up-to-date data bases. Generally speaking, that sort of survival depends on the continued use and support by a consulting firm or by a state or local government agency (Renfro, 1984). But there are some impressive examples to show how a model is a special creature of its region. Excluding the numerous multiplier exercises (new plants, new dams, new markets, higher budgets), some interesting applications include the effect of:

1. a change in new car sales in the United States (Michigan, Detroit, Delaware);
2. an increase in defence contracts (Ohio);
3. state government countercyclical policy, including a rudimentary optimal control analysis (Ohio);
4. alternative state government rules on use of an oil royalty fund, including effects on migration and income distribution by detailed demographic group (Alaska);

5. an initial decline in manufacturing and an equal increase in non-manufacturing output (Pittsburgh);
6. a temporary deficit in city government finances, causing immediate demand stimulus but requiring higher taxes in later years to service debt (Boston);
7. a change in the formula for local government sharing of state income tax revenue (Arizona); and
8. a social contract under which high-technology firms, in exchange for favourable state policies, declare an intention to create 10 000 new jobs per year (Massachusetts).

Finally, we have the interesting situation in Tennessee, where the constitution prohibits appropriations rising faster than the estimated growth of state personal income and requires legislators to use the state university's model's forecast of personal income growth as one piece of evidence on growth of income (Hake, 1983).

5 Industry demand and output[5]
In Figure 13.3, links 1 and 2 are of concern here. In theory, one should not discuss them independently of the labour market. Ideally, industry output depends on both demand and supply, and supply depends on factor prices, labour use and capital use. Even if we assume capital services are fixed, it is still the case that labour demand, output and product price are all determined simultaneously. Many regional industries are not competitive, so product price should be endogenous. The wage rate is the major influence on product price, and it may have to proxy for product price in a model. 'The price of labour is often seen as the basic price level in macroeconomic models, and the same is reasonable for a metropolitan model' (Engle, 1980, p. 138). Figure 13.3 allows for all this, by including link 6. However I discuss links 1 and 2 separately, assuming that the reader will remember that the equations may include endogenous wage rates.
On the other hand, some models are actually incomplete enough for labour demand really to be an independent step. Indeed some contemporary models (and many older ones) skip the output stage altogether, and simply link industry employment in the region directly to national output or employment. Boston is an example. The older Michigan state model is another, but in the new multilevel system the Detroit SMSA (but not the 'outstate' SMSAs) has industry output. Even the very sophisticated Massachusetts model and others in Treyz's system skip the output stage. Employment is the key variable, because the authors believe employment

data are so much better (Treyz and Stevens, 1985; Regional Economic Models, Inc., 1984).

It is useful first to describe the industries classified in each of my three categories of market orientation: export, mixed, local (see Figure 13.3). As shown, national demands are relevant for the first and second (link 1), but not the third; regional personal income is relevant for the second and third (link 2), but not the first. The average model has about 12–22 different private industries, with perhaps 5–15 of them in manufacturing. A few models achieve close to two-digit SIC (Standard Industrial Classification) detail in manufacturing, but outside it much broader groups are the rule (agriculture; mining; construction; transportation and utilities; wholesale and retail trade; finance; services; or combinations of these). Proprietary models usually have much more detail, perhaps 50 or more industries, including many two-digit ones outside manufacturing. In the real world, all industries should be mixed, in the sense that all sell in national and in local markets. The Massachusetts model achieves this, but it is more often found that many manufacturing industries are put only in the export group and most services only in mixed or local. Engle (1980) put Boston financial and business services in the export block and included lagged non-profit services as an explanatory variable, to reflect the effect of the education and medical industries on skilled labour force. One finds a few other examples of export or mixed services. But in the Detroit model, all nonmanufacturing industries are local: 'Unlike Chicago, Detroit cannot be considered an important regional service or financial center for the midwestern section of the country' (Shapiro and Fulton, 1985, p. 228).

Construction is a mixed industry; manufacturing investment and housing starts may be included as explanatory variables. Agriculture and mining are difficult cases, but if they are endogenous, the national prices are prominent variables.[6] In the government category, federal, state and local government are usually separated; the first is export, the third is local, and the second is usually export in an SMSA model and local in a state model.

Consider a more typical industry. If output is modelled, there is a demand function in which industry output is a function of some of the following, incorporating links 1 and 2: national output variables (industry-specific or GNP); output or income of nearby regions; regional price or cost relative to other regions or the national average; other variables affecting the region's share of national output (for example, transportation cost proxies); regional personal income. Which ones are included depends on the industry (export or not), on the completeness of the model and available data, and on the preferences of the model-builder.[7]

General equilibrium effects are usually ignored. If not, they are very weakly proxied by including the output of a few other regional industries assumed to be major buyers from the industry in question, as identified by expert judgement or a regional input–output table. Glickman (1977) included quite a few selected input–output links in his influential model of Philadelphia. The Chicago model also has them; for example, electrical machinery output depends in part on Chicago output in paper products, stone, clay and glass products, primary metals and fabricated metals. The Milwaukee modellers, however, found such links insignificant; they suggested as a reason Milwaukee's greater openness and trade with Chicago (Rubin and Erickson, 1980). The model of the State of Washington is a major exception, combining a detailed input–output model of industry gross output with an econometric model of industry final demands (see Bourque, Conway and Howard, 1977). The Massachusetts model also specifies many input–output links, as described in the section on labour demand below.

Next, consider the supply curve. It should be based on a production function, factor prices, assumptions about speed of adjustment and so forth. The supply curve, however, is very seldom found: the major stumbling-block to implementing the whole demand and supply framework is the lack of industry price indexes at the regional level.

Baird's Ohio model (1983) is one of the best in specifying demand and supply. The industry block determines industry output and price simultaneously for two-digit manufacturing industries and for six non-manufacturing ones, in each of six subregions in Ohio. Demand in a manufacturing industry is determined by output price, industry output in the six regions combined, and industry output in the rest of the United States. Non-manufacturing industries' demands are functions of output price and total personal income in the six regions. Supply price is determined by a Cobb-Douglas cost function of output, the wage rate (sector-specific) and the national price of capital. The wage rates, however, are exogenous; this is justified by a quantity-adjustment theory of the Ohio labour market, affected as it is by national trends and collective bargaining.

What makes Baird's treatment so unusual is the special work required, and done, to estimate a 'synthetic' price for a regional industry's output. While certainly not satisfactory to everybody, the effort does contrast with the prevailing practice when there are no regular data on prices: use a national industry price, or the local industry wage rate or even the average wage in all regional industries. The Chicago model, for example, has the same industry demand and supply framework with a translog production function, but it uses national industry prices.

The Pittsburgh model (Pittsburgh Modeling Project, 1985; Cassing and Giarratani, 1986) has a supply and demand framework. It does not assume competitive markets but rather mark-up pricing behaviour, which makes the industry price proportional to marginal cost, which in turn is calculated from a translog function. Others implicitly assume competitive markets by employing a national price as a proxy for the regional industry price.

The gap between theory and practice is seldom as graphic as in the Detroit model (Shapiro and Fulton, 1985). For export industries, it uses a venerable framework:

$$X_i = GNP(N_i/GNP) \ (X_i/N_i) \qquad\qquad (13.1)$$

where X_i is output in Detroit's industry i and N_i is national output in industry i. The last term, the regional share, is what must be modelled: it adjusts gradually towards a desired level, which is in turn theoretically a function of relative wage differentials, productivity differentials and time trend. But only the time trend survived the rigours of econometrics, so no competitiveness variables appear. Output in selected other industries is included, and the share of small-car sales in total automobile sales proved significant in the transportation equipment industry case.

6   Labour demand and the role of capital

Link 3 in Figure 13.3 concerns us here. A major development in the 1970s was the wider use of explicit production functions in labour demand model-building. Bell (1967), Glickman (1977), Adams, Brooking and Glickman (1975), and Friedlaender, Treyz and Tresch (1975) were leading proponents. The production function, plus an assumption of optimizing behaviour, determines desired labour use measured in hours or employment. If labour is measured in hours, a separate equation converts the hours to employment. The industrial detail here will, of course, be the same as for output. The production functions used are varied: CES (constant elasticity of substitution), Cobb-Douglas, translog, or even simpler linear forms.

Partial analysis is even more frequent here than for demand, and it is short-run: in manufacturing, capital stock is fixed in each period (most often a year), and then labour demand (employment, hours, or both) is determined by solving the equation making the marginal value product equal to the wage rate. This demand, which is desired labour use, is thus a function of output, wage rate, capital stock and product price. The last is often omitted, or replaced by a national price; capital stock is also often omitted, especially in non-manufacturing. The wage may be exogenous or endogenous; if the latter, the wage rate feeds back into the industry output equation (sometimes only in the form of an influence on the region's average wage rate, so that no one industry has a very strong effect). The capital stock is usually adjusted from period to period exogenously (Pittsburgh and Boston are exceptions). If capital is omitted, labour demand may thus be simply a function of industry output or lagged output (as in Chicago's non-manufacturing) or of the wage and national price of capital and industry output (as in Baird's Ohio model).

That is the theory of desired labour use. For actual labour use, lagged adjustment models are nearly universal. Employment or hours are adjusted gradually towards the desired level. Some details are worth noting. The Detroit model has unusually elaborate labour demand, and my brief comment cannot do justice to the specification or to the excellent discussion of the issues. Hours and employment are determined interdependently, with average weekly hours one determinant of employment adjustment. The underlying theory for manufacturing is one of labour reserves, with hiring costs inducing firms to hoard labour. The national unemployment rate affects the speed of adjustment: a lower unemployment rate raises firms' expected hiring costs, so they adjust faster to an increase in desired labour use and more slowly to a decrease. In each non-manufacturing industry, employment is a function of total regional employment, the change in the unemployment rate, and some special factors affecting the industry's share of total regional employment, such as building permits and a time trend (See Shapiro and Fulton, 1985).[8]

Yet, as mentioned above, the output demand functions in the Detroit model are relatively simple, and not nearly as convincing as in other models. Another useful example of unevenness is the Chicago model. It uses a translog production function, but has exogenous wage rates; optimal labour use is in hours, but a simple linear function converts hours to employment. Capital stock is exogenous in manufacturing, and in other industries capital is assumed to adjust rapidly to output changes and is in fact proportional to lagged output, so that labour demand is a function only of wage rate and lagged output.

The Delaware approach is also interesting. The economy is small and its manufacturing very specialized, so there are only eight national variables, including GNP. The only one of them remotely industry-specific is 'new car sales'. These national variables affect employment in each of 17 Delaware industries directly, with no output step. Thus the regional model can be run without an elaborate national model. The industry wage rate relative to a national industry price is also important. Employment and hours are determined simultaneously, with average hours determining the speed of adjustment of employment.

The Massachusetts model and the TFS multiregional modelling system
The Massachusetts model is a world apart in complexity, reliance on inter-industry linkages and modelling philosophy. It skips the output stage and combines links 1, 2 and 3. It is the origin of the TFS system of multiregional modelling. (TFS stands for Treyz, Friedlaender and Stevens, all of whom helped develop the Massachusetts model; see Friedlaender, Treyz and Tresch, 1975; Treyz *et al.* 1980; Treyz, Friedlaender and Stevens, 1980.) Treyz and Stevens (1985) adapted the model for every other state as well.

Treyz and Stevens articulate the beliefs that: the same theoretical framework is useful in every state; some behaviour is uniform across the nation ('there is little reason to believe that economic units in one region of the country have measureably [*sic*] different behavioral characteristics from those in another' p. 24); given short time series and other data problems, *a priori* non-regression information and estimates from pooled regressions of all states should be used and their advantages outweigh the disadvantages of imposing the same specification on all states. Thus they reject the traditional approach of tailoring the model's basic specifications to the region. This philosophy is used in the TFS system (one assumes that the Massachusetts model departs from the models for other states in some respects, because it has a longer history of research and better data).

Even industry is assumed to sell in both export and local markets. Employment stimulated by export demand on an industry is a function of national industry employment, modified by relative cost variables (wage rates, fuel prices, local cost of capital as affected by business tax rates) and also by the labour intensity in the state relative to the nation. Relative labour intensity is determined by relative costs, according to a Cobb-Douglas production function, the parameters of which are estimated from national data and assumed to be the same in Massachusetts. Actual labour use moves toward the optimal in a lagged adjustment process.[9]

In any given industry the elasticity of its share of the national market with respect to an index of relative costs is assumed to be identical in every state. Recent estimated elasticities from pooled data are consistent with location theory: lumber, stone products, food, paper and chemicals all have negative elasticities less than one in absolute value; instruments, apparel, petroleum products, machinery have very high elasticities (Treyz and Stevens, 1985).

Each industry also has local demand, both final and intermediate. It is a function of: total employment in the region; population; inter-industry labour requirements as estimated by the coefficients from a non-survey input–output model for the state; relative labour intensity; and the ability of local firms to compete against imports in the region. A major variable here is the regional purchase coefficient, the fraction of regional demand satisfied by local firms; it is a non-linear function of proxies for transportation cost (weight/value, and land area of state) and supply/demand ratios (the last makes the coefficient endogenous). The use of inter-industry requirements requires simultaneous determination of employment in all the industries (currently over 50).

The Texas supply-side model
Having moved through links 1, 2 and 3, we should look at the Texas supply-side model, another world apart (Plaut, 1982, 1984). The manufacturing industries are the most interesting. In them, the model moves recursively to accomplish the following:

1. Industry investment is determined first, as a function of national investment in the industry, industrial energy costs in Texas relative to the United States, and real personal income in Texas relative to the United States. The latter term reflects market pull. How can the cost of capital be omitted? Plaut adopts Crow's view of investment: a national pool of capital formation is determined by national factors and then allocated to regions according to production cost and access to markets (Crow, 1979; sees also Engle's point on the cost of capital, below).
2. Capital stock is determined by cumulating investment. But capital services are a function of the utilization rate, in turn a function of the national utilization rate and the average age of Texas capital.
3. Man-hours are determined, assuming a CES production function and lagged adjustment.
4. Output is determined last, according to the CES function of hours and capital services. The model determines output solely by supply factors: there is no industry demand function.

This manufacturing sector is embedded in a much larger model; I mention the migration sector later. By the usual tests, the model works quite well. The root-mean-squared percentage errors are high for investment (nearly 12 per cent for total manufacturing investment), but they are low for manufacturing output (2.36 per cent) and gross state product (1.20 per cent).

Harris's model
A final atypical model, and one that also incorporates supply-side characteristics, is Curtis Harris's multiregional model (1973, 1980).[10] It is a top-down model of the 1973 Bureau of Economic Analysis economic areas (a

county version also exists). There are output and employment variables for 99 industries (62 in manufacturing); equipment investment for 69. Many of the data are created by multiple assumptions about unobserved relationships, and parameters in regional share equations are estimated by cross-section regressions across regions, a procedure that is somewhat controversial. The model is annual and recursive, no variables for a region entering directly into the equations for another region. However explanatory variables include lagged transportation costs of inputs and outputs, estimated in a separate complicated demand- and supply-balancing linear programming transportation model. Transportation costs, along with relative labour and land prices, determine location rent, and location rent in an industry helps determine a region's share of that industry's national output. Investment is endogenous, responding to location rent. Lagged investment affects some regions' output shares and employment, acting as a proxy for size and newness of capital stock, which is not calculated. Harris also assumes that the ratio of capital to capacity output in all regions is equal to the national ratio.

7 Labour supply and the labour market

Here is a critical difference between the econometric model and both the economic base model and the input–output model. Wage rates (other terms of the wage bargain are not modelled) affect the region's ability to compete in export, mixed, and local industries (link 6). Wage rates and employment also determine the wage bill, the major part of personal income, which is important in itself and which also affects demands for local and mixed industries (link 2).

In a large model, wage rates may be industry-specific. The Klein–Phillips curve is widely used, and common variables are unemployment rate (level and/or change), employment change, national wage rates, and national and local consumer price indexes. The Massachusetts model produces wage rates for occupations (functions were estimated with micro-data and industry–occupation matrices) and the industry wage is a function of its occupational mix.

Figure 13.3 shows that labour force participation rate is a crucial variable. It may be a function of lagged wage (relative to the nation) and employment. A short-cut is to link labour supply directly to net migration, on the grounds that, in the short run, it is only migration that changes fast enough to affect wage rates.

The unemployment rate is a major output of this block: it is a major performance variable and can dampen wage increases, with many follow-on effects. In some large-scale models, unemployment has an automatic stabilizing effect on personal income through unemployment insurance payments. In the typical case, unemployment is defined as the residual of population or labour force less endogenous employment. But in some models there is an independent stochastic equation. In the Michigan system, for example, the unemployment rate is a function of the national rate and the change in employment. This allows the Michigan system to dispense completely with labour force and population. In the Boston model, the rate is a function of potential work force (the working age population that would result if there were no migration, constructed using standard demographic cohort survival methods), the change in employment, the real wage relative to the United States, and the US unemployment rate. Engle points out that the model cannot separate migration from participation rate changes as labour force adjustments.

8　Migration and population

Population seems not to be an important variable in itself, because few models are used for long-term simulations. But this block is important because of the effects it has on other variables through the labour market. Population is sometimes exogenous: Delaware, where it is 'tolerable in a quarterly model designed for short-term forecasts' (Latham *et al.*, 1979, p. 7), and Pittsburgh, where exogeneity was settled for after a Harris-Todaro approach and a job vacancy index did not work well. It is not a part of the Michigan system at all, and it is only an implicit factor in Boston. If population is exogenous, unemployment can still be an important variable, but it is not as fully endogenous as one might like.

Natural increase is usually exogenous (but see Alaska and Texas, below). Net migration may depend on wage rates, personal income and unemployment, relative to the nation (weighting of nearby regions is not common, except in some multiregional models). There are few region-to-region migration data, but one might consider defining a labour supply potential variable, just as many do a demand potential variable. For example, as many of the immigrants to New England in recent years have come from the Mid-Atlantic region, such a weighting might be useful in modelling New England. Treyz (1980), by the way, proposed a multi-regional model that would make migration flows among states endogenous, and proposed to estimate the equations from Continuous Work History Sample data. The Chicago model uses a Harris-Todaro approach: net migration is a linear function of expected wage in Chicago and expected wage in the United States; each variable is a wage rate times the employment rate (but neither is significant).

The Alaska model is an exception, as befits a region with rapid natural resource development. It is unusually detailed in migration and labour supply. A submodel with many age–sex–race cohorts is used for migration and income distribution analysis. Natural increase depends on exogenous cohort-specific birth and death rates. Occupational participation rates are cohort-specific. The labour demand side of the market is also unusual, in having industry-specific skill requirements. Migration is a function of increase in employment and per capita income relative to the United States, and is distributed to occupations so as to reduce excess demand or supply in occupations. Migration is modelled separately for natives, non-native civilians and military personnel.

The Texas model is also detailed, with 32 age–sex groups (Plaut, 1981). Migration, under a modified Harris-Todaro approach, depends on the ratio of job vacancies to the number of unemployed and on the real wage rate (both relative to the United States), and also on US per capita income, to reflect the fact that rising incomes make people more responsive to the favourable environmental conditions in Texas.

9 Investment

Investment and capital have been discussed frequently above, but only because they are so often absent. Link 9 is very weak in operational models. Data problems are enormously influential in shaping the usual approaches. Manufacturing is modelled in a more satisfactory theoretical way than other industries. Investment is sometimes endogenous, but capital stock and capital services are less often so. Plaut's point that more attention to investment and capital are essential to model fast-growing regions is very important. Nadji and Harris (1984) argue that expected profit is the true determinant of investment and that the common proxy of lagged output is less and less satisfactory in smaller and smaller regions. In a small region, the proxy is poor because new plants are lumpy investments; in a large region, aggregation alleviates the problem and makes functions based on historical data for lagged output look better.

On a related point, Engle (1980) points out that the cost of capital is a relevant opportunity cost for national investment, but the cost of capital in the region is not very relevant. The firm must compare expected rate of return to the expected marginal rate of return in other regions. It is that comparison that is imperfectly proxied by Plaut in the Texas model. Engle also notes that data problems are eased in a Cobb-Douglas framework, because marginal value product is proportional to average return to capital, which is proportional to the ratio of payroll to capital stock.

On data, Rubin and Erickson (1980) usefully point out that the available capital expenditure data do not allow one to distinguish between replacement, expansion and pollution control investment.

Residential construction expenditures do not often appear in models, although housing starts are a proxy for some purposes. The Pittsburgh and Massachusetts models are exceptions. The first makes housing investment a function of regional income, a credit availability variable, population and a construction cost index. The second makes the actual stock gradually approach the desired stock, taken to be the ratio of state-to-USA (smoothed) real disposable income times the national stock.

10   Non-earnings income

Non-earnings income is an extremely (quantitatively) important part of any regional economy, and there are a lot of data, but models are surprisingly rudimentary. In the Chicago model, for example, it is all exogenous, and in some models it is a simple function of the national counterpart, or of local earned income. But then, generally, non-earnings income is relatively neglected in regional economics, for reasons that are unclear. Perhaps the heavy hands of location theory and inter-regional trade theory are responsible.

The main components are: fringe benefits, unemployment insurance, other transfer payments, dividends, rent and interest. The first can be incorporated into the wage rate or made a function of earnings. The second is usually a relatively simple function of the unemployment rate and some national policy variables. The last three are components of property income, which is unsatisfactorily handled in these models – mainly because property is not well handled! Much of property is capital and, therefore, is a familiar problem.

One general shortcoming of these models that is especially important in some regions and applications is that business profits are not included. Profits are an important determinant of residents' property income and also are an important tax base in some states. The Boston model makes property income a function of total value added in the region minus corporate taxes minus earned income, and also of national property income.

11   Regional government

The state or local government block is often one of the most developed in a model, owing to a desire for revenue forecasting. Especially for local government, expenditures are often assumed to be equal to receipts. Tax receipts are often detailed, in each case with an exogenous tax rate (which is a potential policy handle) and an endogenous tax base that is a component of income or of retail sales. The Michigan state model has three separate income tax functions (one for withholding, one for quarterly payments, one for payments with annual returns), and two retail sales tax functions (automobile and other). As long as there are endogenous variables reasonably proxying the tax bases, this sort of detail is fairly straightforward; tax collection is not as stochastic as most other behaviour in a region. However Latham *et al.* (1979), who have 14 Delaware revenue sources, usefully remind us that modelling revenue is difficult because of frequent legislative changes in rate structures, bases, filing dates and tax base definitions; they suggest using dummy variables or adjusting official data to levels that would be observed under the most recent provisions.

Arizona relies heavily on sales-based taxes, and Charney and Taylor (1984b) point out that revenue estimation and tax policy analysis must model tax bases so that they respond appropriately to relative prices as well as to income. They make tax rates affect relative prices. Such attention to relative prices is not usual in government sectors of models. The Arizona model is also very unusual in having federal and state income taxes interrelate: they share bases, each is a deduction from the other's base, and both bases are endogenously affected by changes in other state and local taxes that are deductible.

In a metropolitan area, property taxes are important. The lack of endogenous business capital and housing property value variables is a problem. The Pittsburgh model estimates housing stock by cumulating recent housing construction and estimating survival from earlier construction and then makes assessed value a linear function of the stock. The assessed value is then a variable in the tax receipts equation. But that model is an exception. In Chicago, all local government revenue is a linear function of personal income: 'local government revenue is assumed to take the form of a proportional income tax' (Duobinis, 1981, p. 302). Engle has only one stochastic equation for the entire local government sector; it relates government employment to local income, to a tax rate that is simply total taxes divided by personal income (so that he too assumes local government tax revenue comes from a proportional income tax), and to non-payroll expenditures (exogenous). The latter has a negative effect, but it is expected *a priori* because such expenditures use up taxing capacity and revenue-sharing receipts but require little employment.

Detailed government expenditure components are less often of interest to users. For example, they are exogenous in the Delaware model. An occasional exception is government construction, which feeds into a mixed or local construction industry via a link of type 2. Federal government expenditures are usually exogenous and, it is hoped, a policy handle. Generally government expenditures feed into labour demand by a function relating government employment to them.

In the real world, state and local government effects that flow through type-8 links are not limited to tax rates and expenditures. Regulations, especially in the labour market, are potentially very important. These are seldom modelled, however, even in policy simulations. Simulations of government policy have overwhelmingly concentrated on tax rate and expenditure policy.

12   Local prices

As noted, industry-specific prices are not generally available, but a consumer price index (CPI) may be. CPIs are published for cities, and some state models adopt one as the state index (Michigan uses Detroit's). If the index is endogenous, it tends to be a function of the national index, average wage rates and other labour market variables. In the Boston model, commodity prices are national ones, housing prices are exogenous and services prices are functions of wage rates. As discussed earlier, a regional price index may feed into migration, labour supply and some industry demand equations, and of course it is necessary if total regional income is in real terms.

13   Econometric methods

This is a major subject that is very hard to summarize. I only want to stress that the typical model has some blocks that are highly simultaneous, yet ordinary least squares is very often used. The model is usually block-recursive, and some blocks may not have enough simultaneity to make one abandon ordinary least squares (OLS). Even within highly simultaneous blocks, other methods do not have advantages that are convincing, given the small samples that modellers must work with, and they are complicated and more costly. Many Monte Carlo comparisons – of error statistics in simulations with parameters estimated by different methods – show that it gives similar results. OLS seems to have some advantages when there is multicollinearity in exogenous variables. The problems of creating and working with artificial data and dealing with missing observations absorb a lot of time, and using an alternative estimator may seem too high an additional price to pay. It is not surprising that many model-builders continue to use OLS even when there is simultaneous equation bias. (For further discussion see Johnston, 1972; Baird, 1983; Glickman, 1976, 1977.)

14   Conclusion

One is impressed with the tremendous variety. The nature of the regions and the interests of the builders show up in this variety, and also in the great unevenness of detail within most of the models. A builder may lavish great care on one or two sectors, applying interesting and up-to-date theory, but then use unexciting, off-the-shelf specifications in the other sectors. (Of all the models, the Massachusetts one perhaps shows the least unevenness, and its builders have a definite philosophy behind the omission of some features found in other models.) In retrospect this is understandable, considering the very varied origins and purposes of models. To some extent, the variety of models reflects the decentralized nature of research and the decentralized nature of regional policy-making in a federal political system. Part and parcel of the variety is the general pattern that models have largely applied standard theory and have not forged new theory. Some observers might say that that is an inefficient result, but, after all, one wholly expected from what is essentially a monopolistically competitive industry. Certainly there is abundant product differentiation. Others would, of course, disagree that the variety is excessive, given the nature of the regions being modelled and of the nation.

Notes

1. If the national model is merely a handful of projections, international effects can be entered directly into the regional model, as is done for Alaska (Kresge *et al.*, 1984).
2. Models for Puerto Rico and Hawaii are partial exceptions (see Ghali and Renaud, 1975, and Dutta and Su, 1969, and, for comments, Glickman, 1977, and Shapiro and Fulton, 1985). Some earlier models of inland regions also had demand components, with net exports estimated as a residual in the absence of direct data (see Crow, 1973, and comments by Glickman, 1977).
3. L'Esperance (1981) believed strongly that an output measure is preferable, and that it is possible to estimate it acceptably. His book contains a good discussion of the various estimation methods applied to Ohio. His Ohio model even has four aggregate demand components: auto consumption, other consumption, manufacturing investment in structures, and manufacturing investment in equipment (the latter two interdependent). The specifications are very simple and, as some demand components are missing, it is necessary to determine regional income as the sum of industry outputs (there are six broad industry groups). Equipment investment is a function of an interest rate, investment in structures, and internally generated funds in manufacturing, and the latter in turn is a function of the level and change in total gross product in manufacturing.
4. Some regional models do include the effects of regional taxes or subsidies on the supply price of capital, but even then the supply is assumed to be perfectly elastic at the national rate plus or minus the regional tax/subsidy.
5. Good general references on the theory of the various linkages in Figure 13.3 and on specification in general are: Glickman (1977); Engle (1980); Plaut (1984); Baird (1983); Shapiro and Fulton (1985). The last is also an excellent reference on data and econometric techniques. In the following discussion, I often do not distinguish between linear and non-linear forms or mention the many examples of time trends or lagged dependent variables.
6. In some states there are elaborate sector models of agriculture and mining, and they may be run in tandem with a more general state model.
7. In Alaska, earnings in 'enclaves' (isolated construction sites) and the rest of regional income are two separate explanatory variables for local industries, owing to the different consumption habits of the construction workers.
8. In the Michigan model, outstate regions' manufacturing labour demand is much simpler than in Detroit. Hours are not modelled, and the basic production function is a fixed labour coefficients model. However the optimal output–labour ratio changes over time, and the model-builders devote considerable attention to estimating it as a function of prices or interest rates, wage rate and a time trend (for technological change).

9.   Capital does not appear in labour demand functions, but manufacturing investment is endogenous; it is determined by a lagged adjustment to an optimal capital stock that is determined by the same basic framework as labour; that is, the relative capital intensity in a state depends on region-specific relative factor prices and a Cobb-Douglas production function that is uniform across states.
10.   This summary draws on Bolton (1980b, 1982a).

References

Adams, F. Gerard, Carl G. Brooking and Norman J. Glickman (1975) 'On the Specification and Simulation of a Regional Econometric Model: A Model of Mississippi', *Review of Economics and Statistics*, 57, pp. 286–98.

Alaska (see Kresge *et al.*).

Baird, Catherine (1983) 'A Multiregional Econometric Model of Ohio', *Journal of Regional Science*, 23, pp. 501–16.

Ballard, Kenneth and Norman Glickman (1977) 'A Multiregional Econometric Forecasting System: A Model for the Delaware Valley', *Journal of Regional Science*, 17, pp. 161–77.

Ballard, Kenneth and Robert Wendling (1980) 'The National–Regional Impact Evaluation System: A Spatial Model of US Economic and Demographic Activity', *Journal of Regional Science*, 20, pp. 143–58.

Ballard, Kenneth, Richard Gustely and Robert Wendling (1980) *NRIES: Structure, Performance, and Application of a Bottom-Up Interregional Econometric Model* (Washington, DC: Bureau of Economic Analysis, US Department of Commerce).

Bell, Federick W. (1967) 'An Econometric Forecasting Model for a Region', *Journal of Regional Science*, 7, pp. 109–27.

Bolton, Roger (1978) 'Review of the Literature on Regional Econometric Models and Regional Business Cycles', unpublished paper.

_____ (1980a) 'Multiregional Models; Introduction to a Symposium', *Journal of Regional Science*, 20, pp. 131–43.

_____ (1980b) 'Multiregional Models in Policy Analysis: A Survey', in F. Gerard Adams and Norman Glickman (eds), *Modeling the Multiregional Economic System* (Lexington, MA: Lexington Books) pp. 225–83.

_____ (1982a) 'The Development of Multiregional Economic Modeling in North America: Multiregional Models in Transition for Economies in Transition', in Boris Issaev *et al.* (eds), *Multiregional Economic Modeling: Practice and Prospect* (Amsterdam: North-Holland) pp. 157–70.

_____ (1982b) 'Industrial and Regional Policy in Multiregional Modeling', in Michael Bell and Paul Lande (eds), *Regional Dimensions of Industrial Policy* (Lexington, MA: Lexington Books) pp. 169–94.

_____ (1985) 'Review of The Swedish Case Study', in T. R. Lakshmanan and Borje Johansson (eds), *Large-Scale Energy Projects: Assessment of Regional Consequences* (Amsterdam: North-Holland) pp. 163–73.

Boston (see Engle).

Boston College Social Welfare Research Institute (1981) *MRPIS: A Research Strategy* (Boston: Boston College Social Welfare Research Institute).

_____ (1984) *MRPIS 2.0* (Boston: Boston College Social Welfare Research Institute).

Bourque, Phillip, Richard Conway and Charles Howard (1977) *The Washington Projection and Simulation Model* (Seattle: Graduate School of Business, University of Washington).

Cassing, S. and F. Giarratani (1986) 'A Simulation-Oriented Regional Econometric Model', *Environment and Planning A*, 18, pp. 1611–28.

Charney, Alberta and Carol Taylor (1984a) 'Decomposition of Ex Ante State Model Forecasting Errors', *Journal of Regional Science*, 24, pp. 229–48.

_____ (1984b) 'State Tax Policy Analysis with a State-Substate Econometric Model', paper at Regional Science Association meeting, Denver.

Chicago (see Duobinis).

Courbis, Raymond (1979) 'The REGINA Model: A Regional-National Model for French Planning', *Regional Science and Urban Economics*, 9, pp. 117–39.

―――― (1980) 'Multiregional Modeling and the Interaction between Regional and National Development: A General Theoretical Framework', in F. Gerard Adams and Norman Glickman (eds), *Modeling the Multiregional Economic System* (Lexington, MA: Lexington Books) pp. 107–30.

―――― (1985) 'The Time Factor in Multiregional modeling: Some Conceptual Remarks', paper at International Institute for Applied System Analysis and USSR Academy of Sciences conferences, Tbilisi, USSR.

Crow, Robert (1973) 'A Nationally Linked Regional Econometric Model', *Journal of Regional Science*, 13, pp. 187–204.

―――― (1979) 'Output Determination and Investment Specification in Macroeconomic Models of Open Regions', *Regional Science and Urban Economics*, 9, pp. 141–58.

Delaware (see Latham *et al.*).

Detroit (see Shapiro and Fulton).

Duobinis, Stanley (1981) 'An Econometric Model of the Chicago Standard Metropolitan Statistical Area', *Journal of Regional Science*, 21, pp. 293–320.

Dutta, M. and V. Su (1969) 'An Econometric Model of Puerto Rico', *Review of Economic Studies*, 36, pp. 319–33.

Engle, Robert (1980) 'An Exploratory Policy-Oriented Econometric Model of a Metropolitan Area: Boston', in Lawrence Klein *et al.* (eds), *Quantitative Economics and Development: Essays in Memory of Ta-Chung Liu* (New York: Academic Press) pp. 123–56.

Friedlaender, Ann, George Treyz and Richard Tresch (1975) 'A Quarterly Econometric Model of Massachusetts and Its Fiscal Structure', unpublished.

Ghali, Moheb and Bertrand Renaud (1975) *The Structure and Dynamic Properties of a Regional Economy: An Econometric Model for Hawaii* (Lexington, MA: Lexington Books).

Gindra, Arthur (1977) 'A Regional Econometric Model of the California Economy', unpublished PhD dissertation, University of California at Los Angeles.

Glickman, Norman (1971) 'An Econometric Forecasting Model for the Philadelphia Region, *Journal of Regional Science*, 11, pp. 15–32.

―――― (1976) 'A Note on Simultaneous Equation Estimation Techniques: Applications with a Regional Econometric Model', *Regional Science and Urban Economics*, 6, pp. 275–87.

―――― (1977) *Econometric Analysis of Regional Systems* (New York: Academic Press).

Hake, David (1983) 'Advising State Government: The Case of Tennessee', paper at meeting of Association for Public Policy Analysis and Management, Philadelphia.

Harris, Curtis, Jr (1973) *The Urban Economies, 1985: A Multiregional Multi-Industry Forecasting Model* (Lexington, MA: Lexington Books).

―――― (1980) 'New Developments and Extensions of the Multiregional Multi-Industry Forecasting Model', *Journal of Regional Science*, 20, pp. 159–72.

Isard, Walter and Luc Anselin (1982) 'Integration of Multiregional Models for Policy Analysis', *Environmental and Planning A*, 14, pp. 359–76.

Issaev, Boris (ed.) (1982) *Multiregional Economic Modeling: Practice and Prospect* (Amsterdam: North-Holland).

Johnston, J. (1972) *Econometric Methods*, 2nd edn (New York: McGraw-Hill).

Klein, Lawrence (1969) 'The Specification of Regional Econometric Models', *Papers, Regional Science Association*, 23, pp. 105–15.

Klein, Lawrence and Edwin Burmeister (eds) (1976) *Econometric Model Performance* (Philadelphia: University of Pennsylvania Press).

Klein, Lawrence and Norman Glickman (1977) 'Econometric Model-Building at Regional Level', *Regional Science and Urban Economics*, 7, pp. 3–23.

Knapp, John *et al.* (1978) *A Survey of State and Regional Econometric Models* (Charlottesville, Virginia: Colgate Darden Graduate School of Business Administration, University of Virginia).

Kresge, David T., Daniel A. Seiver, Oliver S. Goldsmith and Michael O. J. Scott (1984) *Regions and Resources: Strategies for Development* (Cambridge, MA: MIT Press).

Lakshmanan, T. R. (1982) 'Integrated Multiregional Economic Modeling for the USA', in Boris Issaev *et al.* (eds), *Multiregional Economic Modeling: Practice and Prospect* (Amsterdam: North-Holland) pp. 171–88.

―――― (1983) 'A Multiregional Model of the Economy, Environment, and Energy Demand in the United States', *Economic Geography*, 59, pp. 296–320.

Lakshmanan, T. R. and Samuel Ratick (1980) 'Integrated Models for Economic-Energy-Environmental Impact Analysis', in T. R. Lakshmanan and Peter Nijkamp (eds), *Economic-Environmental-Energy Interactions: Modeling and Policy Analysis* (Boston: Martinus Nijhoff) pp. 7–39.

Latham, William R., Kenneth A. Lewis and John H. Landon (1979) 'Regional Econometric Models: Specification and Simulation of a Quarterly Alternative for Small Regions', *Journal of Regional Science*, 19, pp. 1–14.

L'Esperance, Wilford (1981) *The Structure and Control of a State Economy* (London: Pion).

Massachusetts (see Friedlaender *et al.*; Treyz and Stevens; Treyz, Friedlander, and Stevens; Treyz *et al.*).

Michigan (see Shapiro and Fulton).

Milne, William, Norman Glickman and F. Gerard Adams (1980) 'A Framework for Analyzing Regional Growth and Decline: a Multiregional Econometric Model of the United States', *Journal of Regional Science*, 20, pp. 173–90.

Milwaukee (see Rubin and Erickson).

Moore, Craig and Joanne Hill (1982) 'Interregional Arbitrage and the Supply of Loanable Funds', *Journal of Regional Science*, 22, pp. 499–512.

Nadji, Mehrzad and Curtis Harris, Jr (1984) 'A Note on Regional Investment Functions', *Journal of Regional Science*, 24, pp. 271–6.

Ohio (see L'Esperance: Baird).

Philadelphia (see Glickman, 1977).

Pittsburgh Modelling Project (1985) *Modeling Economic Activity in the Pittsburgh Region* (Pittsburgh: Department of Economics, University of Pittsburgh).

Plaut, Thomas (1981) 'An Econometric Model for Forecasting Regional Population Growth', *International Regional Science Review*, 6, pp. 53–70.

―――― (1982) 'A Supply-Side Model of the Texas Economy', *Texas Business Review*, March–April, pp. 49–55.

―――― (1984) 'A Supply-Side Model of Texas Manufacturing Growth', *Journal of Regional Science*, 24, pp. 373–90.

Regional Economic Models, Inc (1984) *The FS-53 Forecasting and Simulation Models* (Amherst, MA: Regional Economic Models, Inc.)

Renfro, Charles (1984) 'A Survey of Regional Models', unpublished paper.

Rietveld, Piet (1982) 'A General Overview of Multiregional Economic Models', in Boris Issaev (ed.), *Multiregional Economic Modeling: Practice and Prospect* (Amsterdam: North-Holland) pp. 15–34 and Appendix in same volume, pp. 231–331.

Roberts, R. Blaine and Henry Fishkind (1979) 'The Role of Monetary Forces in Regional Economic Activity: An Econometric Simulation Analysis', *Journal of Regional Science*, 19, pp. 15–30.

Rubin, Barry and Rodney Erickson (1980) 'Specification and Performance Improvements in Regional Econometric Forecasting Models: A Model for the Milwaukee Metropolitan Area', *Journal of Regional Science*, 20, pp. 11–36.

Shapiro, Harold and George Fulton (1985) *A Regional Econometric Forecasting System* (Ann Arbor, MI: University of Michigan Press).

Solomon, Barry (n.d.) 'Regional Econometric Models for Environmental Impact Analysis', working paper no. 86, Morgantown, WV, West Virginia University, Department of Mineral, Energy and Resource Economics.

Stevens, Benjamin and Craig Moore (1980) 'A Critical Review of the Literature on Shift-Share as a Forecasting Technique', *Journal of Regional Science*, 20, pp. 419–38.

Taylor, Carol (1982) 'Econometric Modeling of Urban and Other Substate Areas: An Analysis of Alternative Methodologies', *Regional Science and Urban Economics*, 12, pp. 425–48.

Texas (see Plaut).

Treyz, George (1980), 'Design of a Multiregional Policy Analysis Model', *Journal of Regional Science*, 20, pp. 191–206.

———— (1981), 'Efficient Information Use in Regional Policy Analysis and Forecasting Models', Regional Science Research Institute Discussion Paper No. 123, Amherst, MA.

Treyz, George and Benjamin Stevens (1985) 'The TFS Regional Modeling Methodology', revised version of paper at Regional Science Association meeting, Chicago.

Treyz, George, Ann Friedlaender and Benjamin Stevens (1980) 'The Employment Sector of a Regional Economic Policy Simulation Model', *Review of Economics and Statistics*, 62, pp. 63–73.

Treyz, George, Roy Williams, Gerry DuGuay, Benjamin Stevens and Ann Friedlander (1980) 'An Overview of the Massachusetts Economic Policy Analysis (MEPA) Model', paper at Harvard–MIT Joint Center for Urban Studies conference on The State of the Art in Regional Modeling, Cambridge, MA.

14 Project LINK and multi-country modelling

Bert G. Hickman

The efflorescence of national econometric models following the Second World War has been delineated in Parts II and III of this volume. By the late 1960s, econometric modelling was a flourishing enterprise in Europe, Japan and North America, and the foundation had been laid for the international linkage of national economic models. This was the genesis of Project LINK, the pioneering global multi-country model. Although the evolution of global modelling is chronicled primarily from the viewpoint of the LINK system in the following pages, additional perspective is provided by briefer consideration of important antecedents and newer models.

1 Antecedents

As early as 1939, J. J. Polak published a paper on 'International Propagation of Business Cycles', perhaps the pioneering attempt at a quantifiable world model. Using multiple correlation analysis, he 'explained' the national cycles of industrial production in each of eight countries during 1920–36 as a function only of the world cycle in industrial production and the exchange rate of each country against the world, illustrated the transmission process in some detail with estimated structural equations for Holland, and argued that the world cycle was itself largely induced by an endogenous cycle in the US economy.

In 'Underemployment Equilibrium in International Trade' (1942), Lloyd A. Metzler generalized the Keynesian income–expenditure theory to a simplified two-country 'world' model with endogenous trade, and presented a theoretical analysis of stability conditions and the signs of the domestic and foreign responses to various shocks.

In 1947 Ragnar Frisch published 'On the Need for Forecasting a Multilateral Balance of Payments', calling attention to the multilateral impacts of exchange operations or import restrictions by individual countries. The discussion was couched in terms of a merchandise trade matrix in which the rows represented exporting countries and the columns importing countries, with each cell giving the value of exports from country i to country j. In such a matrix the row sums represent the total exports of each country, the column sums the corresponding import totals, and the sum of either the total export column or total import row the volume of world trade. By adding a marginal column to contain the net surpluses of those countries where exports exceed imports and a marginal row for the corresponding entries for the deficit countries, Frisch was able to display the individual trade imbalances, with the export surpluses summing to the same figure as the import deficits. The matrix was used to discuss feasible procedures for the simultaneous achievement of balanced trade in all countries. The paper ended with a call for the continuous study and worldwide dissemination of trade matrices by international agencies. Fortunately the call was heeded, since empirical trade matrices are not only indispensable for multilateral trade modelling but also provide the central linkage mechanism for Project LINK and other large multi-country models.

Another seminal article appeared in 1950 when Lloyd A. Metzler published 'A Multiple-Region Theory of Income and Trade', generalizing his earlier two-country model. The paper set forth a multilateral income–expenditure model of open economies linked by trade flows and derived the analytical own and cross multipliers relating the income changes induced at home and abroad to an investment shock in a given country. Metzler showed that the stability of the system depended on the marginal propensities to spend of the various countries, with stability guaranteed if all the propensities were less than unity and possible if countries with low propensities dominated those with propensities exceeding unity. He also analysed the impact of an investment shock at home on the trade balances of other countries, and demonstrated that the effects would be favourable for all countries with spending propensities less than unity and conversely for the other countries. His model was a rudimentary but elegant theoretical version of the general structure of trade-linked multi-country models even as they exist today, and his theoretical applications of multiplier analysis foreshadowed the methodology employed to study the international transmission mechanism in today's large-scale empirical system.

In *An International Economic System* (1953), J. J. Polak presented a theoretical model of linked economies and estimated a simplified reduced form version of the system for 25 countries on data for the period between the First and Second World Wars. The income multiplier model was augmented to include exogenous terms-of-trade effects, and imports were responsive to exogenous changes in the relative price of domestic and foreign goods as well as to endogenous changes in national income. Exports were made a function of world trade (defined as the sum of individual country imports) and an exogenous index of the relative price of exports for each country. Empirical results were presented for own-country income multiplier equations, in most cases estimated only for shocks to foreign trade, and for the world trade multiplier.

The reduced form approach was adopted by Polak because of the paucity of national models at that time. Thus he stated (p. 14):

> For a few countries dynamic economic models exist which describe the mechanism of fluctuation of the domestic economies of these countries. One might conceivably arrive at an international economic model by pushing further along this road, constructing for one country after another a similar dynamic economic model. Through the foreign trade relationships in each such model, these various country models could then ultimately be tied together into an international model.

He went on to observe that it would take years to build such a set of models and that for a great majority of countries the necessary data base did not exist, although interwar trade statistics were available to construct directly the reduced form system presented in his study.

Ten years later he repeated the lament (Polak and Rhomberg, 1962):

> With respect to the construction of what is in effect a world economic model we are, however, still in the impasse about which one of us complained ten years ago ... [W]e lack the national economic models that could be hooked together into a world model by linking their international trade connections.

Nearly another decade was to pass before enough national models were in existence to start Project LINK. Meanwhile Polak and Rhomberg constructed a three-region world model in structural form aggregating North America, other industrialized countries, and less developed countries, and estimated this system from annual data for the period 1948–60.

This pioneering structural model was limited on the income side, with only consumption and imports endogenous for each region, and the domestic price level was exogenous. Trading relationships were treated in detail, however, using bilateral import functions to determine world trade and its regional distribution and incorporating endogenous equations for services and investment payments on current account and for export supply price in each region. Exchange rates were exogenous. There were 26 stochastic equations and three identities in the complete model.

Static own and cross multipliers were computed for the principal endogenous variables and for shocks to investment, domestic prices, and OEEC (Organisation for European Economic Co-operation) countries' exchange rate against the dollar, and net capital imports into the less developed region. The own and cross income multipliers were respectively 1.45 and 0.04 for a domestic demand disturbance originating in North America and 1.45 and 0.12 for one originating in Japan and Western

Europe, implying substantial damping in the mechanism by which fluctuations in economic activity are transmitted between the two industrial regions. The authors observe that this is 'fully in accordance with the observations made during the last decade about the virtual independence of cyclical developments in Europe and the United States'. Later multiplier studies of the LINK system and other multi-country models have generally confirmed the finding of weak transmission effects except between close trading partners, but synchronized shocks have sometimes induced highly synchronized fluctuations in the industrialized countries since the 1950s.

2 Project LINK: the formative years, 1968–72
The project was launched in 1968 when the Committee on Economic Stability and Growth of the Social Science Research Council decided to adopt a suggestion of Rudolf R. Rhomberg to study the international transmission mechanism. An exploratory meeting was held at Stanford University in July 1968 to assess the feasibility of integrating existing national econometric models into a world system. Attending were four members of the SSRC Committee – R. A. Gordon (University of California, Berkeley), Bert G. Hickman (Stanford University), Lawrence R. Klein (University of Pennsylvania) and Rudolf R. Rhomberg (International Monetary Fund), as well as R. J. Ball (London Graduate School of Business Studies), Hidekazu Eguchi (Bank of Japan), John A. Sawyer (University of Toronto), Petrus J. Verdoorn (Central Planning Bureau of the Netherlands), Jean Waelbroeck (Free University of Brussels) and Tsunehiko Watanabe (Kyoto University). Wilhelm Krelle (Bonn University) was unable to attend the meeting, but otherwise participated from the outset of the project. The outcome of the two-day meeting was a research strategy founded on four principles:

1. Each national model would be included in the form put forward by its resident econometric team, subject to group critique and the provision of necessary linkage elements.
2. The principal linkages would come initially through merchandise trade flows and prices, with services and capital flows to be added later.
3. Imports would be determined endogenously in each national model and exports would be allocated through a central trade matrix, with the world trade identity satisfied in the global solution.
4. The first group of models would include Belgium, Canada, West Germany, Japan, the Netherlands, the United Kingdom and the United States. Other countries with continuing model projects would

be invited to join as the system evolved. Group meetings would be held periodically to prepare forecasts, discuss research carried on by the various model-building centres, and establish plans and priorities for future work.

The Committee on Economic Stability and Growth took responsibility for organization and administration of the project. Financial support for a three-year period beginning in 1969 was secured from the International Monetary Fund and the National Science Foundation, with supplemental support from the Japan Economic Research Center and the Bank of Japan, the Belgian National Science Foundation, and the United Nations Conference on Trade and Development. A Coordinating Center (later known as LINK Central) was established at the University of Pennsylvania, under the direction of Lawrence R. Klein, to manage the central file of national models and solution programmes and the data bank for LINK forecasts and simulations. Regional working teams were organized for North America and Japan (under the chairmanship of Rhomberg) and Western Europe (chaired by R. J. Ball). An executive committee, consisting of Robert A. Gordon, Bert G. Hickman (chair), Klein and Rhomberg, was set up to oversee the general course of the project.

The decisions taken at the 1968 planning meeting set the general boundaries for the first few years of LINK research. Merchandise trade was disaggregated into four categories: food, beverages and tobacco; other basic materials; mineral fuels (mainly oil); and manufactures. To prepare the models for linkage, each national modelling centre undertook to re-estimate its own import demand functions according to this classification. The group was persuaded that estimating bilateral import functions among all pairs of trading countries was impractical on a project of this scale, and opted instead to determine exports through a central matrix of trade shares. Since the export shares approach would involve difficult theoretical and empirical problems, however, it was also decided to experiment with simpler methods for obtaining a consistent world trade solution while development of the data base and methodology for the shares approach progressed. The simpler method, Mini-LINK, was used in the first *ex ante* world trade forecasts prepared by the project in 1970. Meanwhile programming of the entire set of national models for solution at LINK central was proceeding apace, and by the spring of 1971 Maxi-LINK solutions were being obtained by the export shares approach.

Mini-LINK was based on the accounting identity giving total world trade as the sum of the imports of all countries or regions and it did not require simultaneous solution of the entire set of models on a central computer. In each national model it was possible to express exports as a function of world trade and other variables. In Mini-LINK, each national model was solved four times at its home centre with a single set of its own predetermined domestic policy variables but with four alternative levels of world trade specified as exogenous inputs. The summed import predictions for each assumed trade level were then plotted on a chart with the import total as ordinate and the corresponding world trade level as abscissa. The four points lay virtually on a straight line, with slope smaller than unity. The intersection of this aggregate import demand function with a 45-degree line through the origin, representing aggregate export supply, gave the solution as that level of world trade which was supportable in the sense that the resulting income and import levels in the various countries would be sufficient to absorb total world exports. The equilibrium was stable, since demand quantity exceeded supply quantity to the left of the equilibrium point and fell short to the right. Conceptually, equilibrating movements would be induced by unintended accumulation or depletion of inventories of export commodities, since trade prices were fixed exogenously in the Mini-LINK solution.

The Mini-LINK method was fast, did not require expensive centralized computations, and provided consistent estimates of world trade and the associated domestic activity levels in each country. It did not, however, allow for equilibrating price movements as part of the adjustment process by which excess import demand is eliminated, nor did it ensure that the export predictions of the individual models summed to the same level of world trade as did those for imports. These deficiencies were eliminated in Maxi-LINK.

The heart of the Maxi-LINK system is an export shares matrix, with exporting countries in the rows and importing countries in the columns. Each cell in a column contains the export share of the ith country in the total imports of the jth country. Given the solution for imports in each national model, the shares matrix is used to allocate the total exhaustively among that country's suppliers, guaranteeing that exports as well as imports sum to world trade. A consistent solution is obtained by iterating between the national and trade models until the predicted exports to each country from the trade matrix, along with the given values of the domestic predetermined variables, yield a solution vector of country imports satisfying the adding-up constraint.

Another striking advance over Mini-LINK was the endogenization of trade prices in the Maxi-LINK solution. Export prices and import volumes are endogenous variables in the national models. Import prices are exogenous to the national models, but they are themselves weighted averages of export prices, with weights given by the same market share matrix used to allocate imports among exporting countries. The simultaneous solution determines a set of national export prices and import quantities which are converted to a set of import prices and export quantities by the trade matrix, and these import prices and export quantities are in turn the predetermined external variables in the national model solutions. Thus, in Maxi-LINK, trade prices as well as quantities adjust to equilibrate international markets.

The theoretical structure of model linkage is developed in three contributions to *The International Linkage of National Economic Models* (Ball, 1973). In 'Towards a General Trade Model', Rhomberg outlines an ideal Walrasian trade model and discusses practical simplifications to reduce the dimensions of the system through the use of a trade matrix for allocating imports and aggregating prices of tradables. 'A General Linear Model of World Trade' by Hickman presents a mathematically explicit approach to the linkage of national models through an endogenous trade matrix with additivity constraints automatically satisfied. Finally, Waelbroeck discusses the practical problems of empirical implementation of theoretical linkage schemes in 'The Methodology of Linkage'.

The same volume includes a description of the initial empirical implementation of Maxi-LINK in 'Forecasting World Trade within Project LINK' (Klein and Alain van Peeterssen) and of the IMF trade model, which provided the template for the linkage system in 'A Model of World Trade' (Grant B. Taplin).

Three specific approaches to the endogenous determination of trade shares and exports in the central trade model were formulated by LINK researchers during 1972. The first was a modified version of a linear expenditure system (LES) by Klein and van Peeterssen, which related the total exports of each country to a weighted average of partner country imports, with weights given by the known pre-forecast matrix of trade shares, and to the price of the exports of the country relative to a trade-weighted average of competitors' prices. The second, developed by Chikashi Moriguchi, modified the trade share matrix by relative price changes among export competitors and assumed the same elasticity of substitution of a particular exporter in any country's import market. These two approaches are compared in papers by Moriguchi (1973) and Klein, Moriguchi and van Peeterssen (1975). The third approach, authored by Hickman and Lawrence J. Lau (1973), also explains changes in the shares by relative price movements, but it assumes the same elasticity of substitution among all exporters in a given import market, building on the theoretical model of a constant elasticity of substitution (CES) demand system for products distinguished by place of origin in Armington (1969). (The methodological assumption of the same elasticity of substitution was later relaxed in a similar but somewhat more intricate approach undertaken by Kanta Marwah (1976) for a regional Mini-Link system at the United Nations Conference on Trade and Development.)

The LINK model was put to two main uses in 1971–2. First, *ex ante* forecasts were prepared each year for that and the subsequent year. Second, simulation studies were undertaken of the impact of the New Economic Policy of the United States on the rest of the world, by comparing the predicted outcomes with and without the suspension of official gold trading, the import surcharge, and the currency realignments of the Smithsonian Accord (Klein, Moriguchi and van Peeterssen, 1972).

Thus, by the end of the first three years of research, the project had not only developed the methodology for the solution of a large-scale system of linked national models satisfying world trading constraints but had also proven its worth as an operating system for forecasting world activity and trade and for undertaking realistic policy simulations in the global context for which it had been designed. The practicality of effective international modelling in a multi-country framework had been conclusively demonstrated, laying the groundwork for further improvements within LINK itself and encouraging new efforts by other model-building groups.

The basic content of the system had been foreshadowed in the seminal writings of Frisch, Metzler and Polak in the early postwar years, but LINK expanded on these ideas in significant ways. A trade matrix is central to the linkage mechanism, as in the Frisch and Metzler papers. It is used not only to allocate real exports among trading countries, however, but also to endogenize import prices. Moreover the trade shares are endogenous variables instead of fixed parameters, so that the structure of world trade changes endogenously over time in model simulations and forecasts. The linkage is implemented using the Klein–van Peeterssen linear expenditure approach.

With regard to the national models, they go far beyond the simple multiplier schemes of Metzler and Polak, not only in the modelling of aggregate demand but in endogenizing wages and prices and incorporating the instruments of fiscal and monetary policy. Thus LINK can be used to study the transmission of inflation as well as real disturbances and to investigate the impact of unilateral and coordinated policy initiatives.

Other organizations were also making important contributions to world trade modelling in the early 1970s. The work at the IMF of Taplin, who was an active participant in Project LINK, has already been cited. The Secretariat of the Organisation for Economic Co-operation and Development (OECD) was another early leader in the field (Adams *et al.*, 1969; Meyer-zu-Schlochtern and Yajima, 1970; and Samuelson, 1973). In Samuelson's implementation, the OECD trade model included a number of the same attributes as LINK – endogenous determination of trade quantities and prices and of market shares – and featured an alternative approach to the implementation of a CES demand system to that offered by Hickman and Lau. The trade model was not a device for linking structural models of individual countries at this time, however, but rather was used to achieve a consistent solution for the foreign accounts of the various OECD countries, for given exogenous inputs on domestic demand, capacity output and domestic prices.

The original coverage of seven industrial countries in the LINK system was broadened during these early years by the addition of structural models for Austria, Finland, Italy and Sweden (Ball, 1973, Chapter 5). Moreover Project LINK, which had begun as a study of the trade and transmission mechanism among the main industrial market economies, was already expanding in two significant new directions. First, economists at the United Nations Conference on Trade and Development (UNCTAD) were constructing structural models of four major developing regions – Latin America, Africa, West Asia and South-East Asia – to replace the reduced-form trade equations used initially to close the world trade model (Ball, 1973, Chapter 6). Second, at the annual meeting of LINK in 1971, UNCTAD economists presented a statistical model for trade of the socialist countries in the Council of Mutual Economic Assistance (CMEA), namely the Soviet Union, Bulgaria, Czechoslovakia, East Germany, Hungary, Poland and Romania. This system was programmed into the central LINK files and used to indicate some of the effects of the burgeoning trade flows from West to East. The total system then included about 1500 equations.

From the outset the project encompassed research on general aspects of the international linkage mechanism, apart from direct contributions to the construction of the LINK system itself. In Ball (1973) these contributions included critiques of the commodity trade equations in the LINK models by Giorgio Basevi and of the equations for invisibles by John A. Sawyer, a paper on the theory and estimation of international capital flows by Akihiro Amano, and applications of bilateral linkage between large models of Japan and the United States, by Moriguchi and Tatemoto, and between Canada and the United States, by J. F. Helliwell, F. W. Gorbet, G. R. Sparks and I. A. Stewart.

3   The tumultuous 1970s

Project LINK began during the waning years of fixed exchange parities and relatively steady growth in the late 1960s. The breakdown of the Bretton Woods system in 1973 ushered in an era of flexible exchanges, however, and the world economy was also subjected to a series of powerful shocks from commodity and oil prices. Much of the evolving LINK research agenda was accordingly oriented towards the modelling of capital flows and exchange rates and the analysis of the impact of supply shocks, especially from oil prices. The coverage of national models increased apace and further improvements were made in the trade linkage system and in the forecasting horizon. Major programming advances occurred in the data bank and model simulation programmes. Finally, the international transmission mechanism was investigated in a series of scenario analyses and multiplier simulations.

By 1973, the number of full-size national models included in LINK had grown to 13 (Australia, Austria, Belgium, Canada, Finland, France, West Germany, Italy, Japan, the Netherlands, Sweden, the United Kingdom and the United States) and the UNCTAD models of major developing regions had been installed. These models are fully documented in Waelbroeck (1976). The same volume includes a report, by Keith N. Johnson and van Peeterssen, updating and documenting the programming structure for solving the LINK system.

Applications at this time included forecasts of world trade by Moriguchi (1973) and Klein, Moriguchi and van Peeterssen (1975), using the new Maxi-LINK methodology. In 1974 the LINK Central staff also undertook simulations of scenarios concerning higher import absorption by Middle East oil exporting countries, the introduction of inventory recessions in the United States, the United Kingdom and Italy, higher commodity export prices for developing countries, and the sensitivity of the world inflation rate to alternative patterns for the price of crude oil (Waelbroeck, 1976, Chapter 1). Another paper by Johnson and Klein (1974a) evaluated the effects of the second, post-Smithsonian wave of currency realignments in early 1973. These studies, which dealt with crucial economic problems as they were unfolding, are early examples of the sort of timely analyses of contemporary disturbances for which the LINK system was originally designed (without, of course, foreknowledge of the specifics of future shocks) and for which it has continued to be employed.

Analytical simulations were undertaken at about the same time to evaluate general aspects of the international transmission mechanism in the LINK system. One contribution, by Johnson and Klein (1974b), investigated the differential responses of individual countries to exchange rate shocks with and without international linkages and also studied the amplification effects of synchronized real (expenditure) and nominal (wage) shocks in the various country models when linked. It was shown that linkage has a moderate effect on the world economy and that synchronized real shocks amplified the country responses to individual shocks by about 50 per cent. As the authors observed, to many people this kind of calculation indicated great stability in the world economy.

Another study, by Hickman (1974), presented own and cross-multipliers for real incomes and prices over a three-year period. They were calculated for independent expenditure shocks equal to 1 per cent of real GNP in each of 11 industrial countries in the LINK system, and led to the general finding of rather weak spillover effects to other countries from disturbances originating even in large countries. These results confirmed the earlier findings by Polak and Rhomberg (1962) of weak cross-multipliers for income between the North American and the Japan and European regions as aggregates, and broadened the analysis to include the transmission of inflation from real demand shocks and to cover a three-year horizon in a dynamic simulation. In another, contemporaneous study influenced by LINK research, Waelbroeck and Dramais (1974) used their linked DESMOS model of nine European Economic Community (EEC) countries to investigate the international transmission mechanism, again finding weak cross-multipliers among countries, albeit differing in detail from the LINK results.

An achievement during 1974–5 was the change-over to an entirely new computer program for data management, estimation and pre- and post-linkage simulations. By 1974, the system had grown to over 3000 equations and calculations of increasing complexity were the rule. The project commissioned Morris Norman to design a new program from scratch, and this was subsequently adapted and improved by Jorge Gana of the LINK Central staff.

The principal themes of LINK research during 1975–7, as documented in *Modelling the International Transmission Mechanism* (Sawyer, 1979), included applications and tests of the forecasting system, preparation of analytical and policy scenarios, model-building improvements for the developing economies and socialist countries, and research on monetary factors and capital flows in particular countries. Related work published elsewhere will be cited where appropriate.

Three papers in the Sawyer volume dealt with forecasting world trade. An error analysis of four alternative methods of forecasting market shares in the stand-alone trade model – constant value shares, constant quantity shares, the LES method of Klein and van Peeterssen, and the CES method of Hickman and Lau – was undertaken in 'Alternative Approaches to Linkage of National Econometric Models' by Jorge L. Gana, Hickman, Lau and Laurence R. Jacobson. Errors in forecasting world trade with the complete LINK system over the sample period beginning in 1965 and in *ex ante* mode for 1970–4 were examined in 'Error Analysis of the LINK Model' by Johnson and Klein. In 'Long-Run Projections of the LINK

World Trade Model', Klein and Asher Tishler presented a new methodology for extrapolating the world trade forecasts for 1976–8, made with the full-blown LINK model in mid-1976, by an additional six years up to 1984. The computational burdens of a long-term forecast with the complete LINK system were too large to be feasible at the time, so the short-cut method was employed of estimating (by model simulation or regression) compact reduced forms for export price and import quantity for each country in the system, in order to complete the linkage for the extrapolation through the world trade model.

It was vitally necessary to maintain a series of updated trade matrices in order to implement Maxi-LINK, especially after the introduction of floating exchange rates and oil shocks induced large movements in relative prices of tradeable goods. The statistical work was done initially under the supervision of Taplin at the IMF and later taken over by Project LINK. These data were used to analyse the redirection of world trade between 1970 and 1975 in a paper by Paul Beaumont, Ingmar Prucha and Victor Filatov (1979).

The first simulations of coordinated economic policies in the LINK system, made during 1977 for the period 1977–9, were published in the Sawyer volume by Klein, Vincent Su and Paul Beaumont (Chapter 7). Various combinations of fiscal stimulus by the 'Big Three' (Japan, Germany and the United States) were examined alone and in combination with exchange revaluations of their currencies, and in other cases the fiscal stimulus was extended to six or seven countries with and without revaluation of the big three currencies. The results indicated modest gains in world trade from either a coordinated fiscal stimulus or coordinated revaluation of the major currencies, with the individual results additive if both policies were combined, indicating the fundamental linearity of the total system. The major gains from a fiscal stimulus accrue to the countries undertaking the stimulus, with small spillover effects to other countries. Similar results are reported by Carl Weinberg (Chapter 6) in another set of simulations of exchange revaluations and fiscal coordination among the big three trading nations.

Matrix multipliers for own- and partner-country responses were analysed for independent wage shocks in nine of the national models in 'Price Determination and Transmission of Inflation in the LINK System' by Hickman and Anthony Lima (Chapter 5 of the Sawyer volume).

In a related paper, Hickman and Stefan Schleicher (1978) summarized the cumulative findings from LINK multiplier experiments, noted that spillover effects to other countries from local disturbances are generally small, examined diffusion indexes for evidence of synchronization of international growth cycles during 1950–76, and concluded that synchronized worldwide fluctuations result from synchronized shocks, rather than the international propagation of independent impulses from major trading countries. These conclusions parallel the early insights and empirical findings of Polak and Rhomberg.

A significant increase in the number and quality of the country models of LINK was achieved during the mid-1970s. In 1975–6 short-term models of six centrally-planned Eastern European countries were constructed by the Centre for Development Planning, Projections and Policies of the United Nations Secretariat, specifically for incorporation in Project LINK (see the paper in the Sawyer volume by Antonio M. Costa and Stanislav M. Menshikov, with assistance by Saturnio Franco). These structural models replaced the trade flow model of the CMEA countries developed by UNCTAD and used in LINK for several years. The USSR was represented in LINK by a model built by Wharton Econometric Forecasting Associates. Improvements were made in the regional less-developed country (LDC) models of UNCTAD, especially with regard to a new breakdown between oil-producing and other regions and the incorporation of a satellite system for commodity price determination, as described in Sawyer, Chapter 9, by J. Glowacki and Kenneth G. Ruffing. Finally, Keith N. Johnson estimated compact structural models for the 13 OECD nations not represented by resident model-building centres, for use until such time as they could be replaced by home-based model (Chapter 10).

The mid-1970s also saw experimentation with the introduction of a set of 23 worldwide commodity models into the system. The COMLINK models and their linkages to the country models are described in 'Integrating Commodity Models into LINK' by F. Gerard Adams in the Sawyer volume and in Adams (1978), 'Primary Commodity Markets in a World Model System' (Adams and Sonia A. Klein, eds). Another example of LINK research on commodity models is to be found in the paper by Sawyer and Chukwuma Obidegwu on 'Incorporating Commodity Models into National Models: a Copper Model' (Sawyer, 1979).

The Sawyer volume concludes with articles concerning aspects of current research to improve the modelling of financial sectors and capital flows in some of the LINK country models: 'Long-Run Portfolio Equilibrium and Balance-of-Payments Adjustment in Econometric Models', by R. J. Ball and Terrence Burns, 'The Effects of Foreign Monetary Impulses and of Fiscal and Monetary Policy Changes on the German Economy: Simulations with the Bonn Forecasting System', by Wilhelm Krelle, Klaus Conrad, Gerald Grisse and Jorn Martiensen, and 'An Empirical Comparison of Four Models of Capital Flows: OLS and 2SLS Estimations of the

Branson, Genberg, Kouri and Lybeck Models', by Johan A. Lybeck, Jan Haggstrom and Bjorn Jarnhall.

These last papers are indicative of the continuing process then under way of extending the country models for determination of capital flows and exchange rates. Meanwhile Klein and J. J. Sztaudynger at LINK Central built a pooled cross-sectional model of capital flows and exchange rates for the 13 LINK OECD countries and tested it in Maxi-LINK simulations in October 1978. Earlier, in work begun in 1974 and published in 1979, Johnson had used another system-wide approach to exchange rate determination in an instrument-and-target formulation with exogenous trade balance targets and endogenous exchange rates, solving the large-scale computational problem on a reduced version of the LINK system.

In 'Disturbances to the International Economy' (1978), Klein examined LINK scenarios for hypothetical increases in commodity prices in 1975–6 and of oil prices in 1978–9. These show that such price or supply shocks induce stagflations in oil-importing countries, with domestic price levels increasing and real income declining in response. In his comment on the Klein paper, Helliwell (1978) evaluates the *ex ante* forecast errors for real GNP, consumer prices and wage rates for the 13 LINK industrial countries from the Maxi-LINK forecast for 1974–6 as published in Chapter 1 of the Waelbroeck volume (1976).

A final example of LINK research in the late 1970s is provided by two hypothetical or contingency studies: 'Scenario of a World Wide Grain Shortage' by Klein, Politi and Su (1978) and 'Protectionism: An Analysis from Project LINK' by Klein and Su (1979). The latter was prompted by the growth of protectionist sentiment and demonstrated the serious losses to be expected from a spread of restrictive trade policies.

By the end of the 1970s, the LINK system had expanded substantially. The number of full-blown OECD country models had increased from six to 13, small models had been estimated at LINK Central for the remaining OECD economies, and seven socialist countries and four developing regions were now represented by structural models. Exchange rates and capital flows among the developed countries were determined endogenously, along with trade flows and prices. The complete system numbered in excess of 5000 equations.

The mid- and late 1970s were also a period of active multi-country modelling under other auspices. Work was begun in 1976 at the OECD Secretariat to expand the existing OECD trade model into a linked system of national models, christened INTERLINK (Llewellyn and Samuelson, 1979). Initially the country models consisted largely of reduced-form equations, derived from the simulation properties of large structural models used by national administrations. In subsequent years the reduced-form relations were progressively replaced by in-house structural systems, which by 1985 numbered 23 models of approximately 50 behavioural equations and 100 identities each for the OECD member countries. Reduced-form modules for eight non-OECD regions complete the system, together with world trade and financial linkage models. The principal features of INTERLINK are documented and its role in the preparation of the internationally consistent forecasts for all member countries in the *OECD Economic Outlook* is described in Llewellyn *et al.* (1985).

Both Project LINK and INTERLINK were originally conceived to emphasize trade linkages in the transmission mechanism, although both were broadened over time to determine capital flows and exchange rates endogenously. From the outset of the project in 1975, however, the authors of the Multi-Country Model (MCM) of the Board of Governors of the Federal Reserve System focused their attention primarily on improved modelling of financial linkages and exchange rates and the quantitative analysis of the domestic and international effects of monetary and intervention policy (Stevens *et al.*, 1984). In the interest of these objectives, MCM includes only five country models (for Canada, Germany, Japan, the United Kingdom and the United States) and an abbreviated model for the rest of the world, sacrificing geographical coverage in order to concentrate on important actors in international financial markets. Trade linkage is accomplished with bilateral import functions instead of an import allocation model, although the world trade constraint is none the less honoured in linked solutions. Supplies and demands for domestic and foreign assets are specified along portfolio-balance lines and the model incorporates the balance sheet and budget constraints of the central bank, the rest of government, commercial banks and the private non-bank sector. The system can be operated under fixed exchange rates or in a regime of managed floating. All the component models were constructed and are maintained in-house, and the authors note that the stucture of MCM relies heavily on the path-breaking work embodied in Project LINK, the Multilateral Exchange Rate Model (MERM) at the IMF, the RDX2 Model for Canada (discussed in Chapter 9) and the London Business School Model for the United Kingdom (see Chapter 7).

4   LINK in the 1980s

The evolution of the project proceeded apace in the 1980s. The incorporation of exchange rates and capital flows as endogenous variables in Maxi-LINK forecasts and simulations continued to be the principal modelling thrust. New investigations of the transmission mechanism were undertaken. The eruption of the Iranian crisis in 1979 again highlighted research on the impact of oil shocks on the world economy. The system was further enlarged by the introduction of models of individual developing economies – a long-standing goal, which assumed augmented importance owing to the depressing effects of slower growth in the developed world and the emergence of LDC debt problems. Programming improvements were made and the forecast horizon was extended routinely to five years. Outside participation of international economists and model-builders in LINK meetings was actively encouraged and special sessions were arranged on comparative model simulations, exchange rates, monetary stabilization and foreign debt problems.

A survey of the way in which exchange rates were determined endogenously in several LINK country models and in a multinational system of exchange rate equations, estimated by Victor Filatov and Klein in 1981, is presented in Hickman (1983a). In the Filatov–Klein specification the spot rate follows purchasing power parity for export goods, the inflation differential and the ratio of the current balance to current GNP. The Hickman survey also summarizes the study, 'Purchasing Power Parity in Medium-Term Simulation of the World Economy' by Klein, Fardoust and Filatov (1981). Finally, it reports on exchange rate dynamics in the current account and J-curve effects from simulation studies of the unlinked country models for Japan, Germany, the United Kingdom, France, Canada, Austria, Denmark, Italy, the Netherlands, Switzerland and the United States.

A special session on capital flows and exchange rate determination was organized at the Bundesbank, Frankfurt, in connection with the LINK meetings in September 1982. The proceedings, edited by Klein and Krelle (1983), include: 'A Model of Foreign Exchange Markets: Endogenizing Capital Flows and Exchange Rates', written at LINK Central by Kanta Marwah and Klein and presenting empirical estimates for Canada, France, Germany, Japan, the United Kingdom and the United States. 'A Structural Approach to Capital Flows and Exchange Rates' by Amano describes his FLEX model of the balance of payments and exchange rates as implemented in the EPA World Economic Model of the Economic Planning Agency, Japan. (See also Chapter 10 above.) In 'Alternative Approaches to General Equilibrium Modeling of Exchange Rates and Capital Flows: The MCM Experience', Hooper, Haas, Symansky and Stekler report on research endogenizing capital flows and exchange rates for six countries in the multi-country model of the Federal Reserve Board. A paper by Krelle and Sarrazin sets forth the theoretical structure and estimated equations for determining capital flows and exchange rates in the Bonn model of the German economy. The volume also includes several papers on special topics in exchange rate modelling by Mitsuhiro Fukao; Gordon Hacche and John C. Townend; and Jean-Pierre Beguelin, Hans-Jurg Buttler and Kurt Schiltknecht.

Additional studies of exchange rate determination were reported to another joint meeting in 1983 at the Bank of Japan and are published in the *European Economic Review*, February 1986. The format called for comparative exchange rate simulations using the LINK, MCM, EPA and OECD multi-country models. The LINK simulations are analysed in 'Exchange Rate Responses in the LINK System' by Peter Pauly and Christian E. Petersen (1986). This paper describes the exchange rate subsystem currently in use in Maxi-LINK. It is an eclectic portfolio-balance asset market model relating the spot rate to relative money supplies, interest rate differentials, relative incomes, relative inflation rates, net foreign assets of the home country, total home country wealth and relative current account balances.

A third joint conference on *International Monetary Stabilization and the Foreign Debt Problem* (Hickman, 1984a) was co-sponsored by Project LINK and the Federal Reserve Bank of San Francisco on 29 August 1984. In 'The Case for Internationalizing American Monetary Policy', Ronald I. McKinnon discusses the theoretical foundation and empirical support for his proposal that Japan, Germany and the United States stabilize exchange rates through coordinated monetary policies. In their complementary paper, 'An Empirical Evaluation of the McKinnon Proposal', Pauly and Petersen treat the proposal as a control theory problem in the Maxi-LINK system. They conclude from the empirical implementation that the proposal had the potential to contribute to a reduction of world inflation without major effects on aggregate economic activity, but not without sacrifices in the appreciating countries (Japan and Germany). It should be noted that this study was possible only because the authors successfully programmed the solution to the instrument-target problem in a much expanded LINK system 10 years after Johnson began his seminal effort.

The afternoon session of the joint meeting in San Francisco was devoted to LDC debt problems. In 'World Recovery and Debt Prospects', Klein used quantitative evidence from LINK forecasts and simulations to criticize the view that world recovery would enable debtor countries to make economic progress while still servicing their external debts. Another LINK participant, Pedro A. Palma, presented a paper entitled 'The Debt Problem: A Debtor's Point of View', in which he examines the origin of the problem and concludes that errors were made on all sides and that the burdens and benefits of the solution must similarly be shared by all parties.

In 1981 the Eighth Global Modeling Conference of the International Institute of Applied Systems Analysis was devoted to the subject of Global International Economic Models. The conference volume (Hickman, 1983b) includes a paper by Filatov, Hickman and Klein on 'Long-Term Simulations with the Project LINK System'. This paper describes the methodology for extrapolating the standard, three-year Maxi-LINK forecast made in the spring of 1979 for 1979–81 by an additional four years to 1985. The resulting baseline forecast is used as the control solution for simulations of the effects on world productivity of a synchronized fiscal policy stimulus to investment demand and of the effects on growth, trade balances and inflation rates of an increase in oil prices greater than that assumed in the forecast itself. Dynamic international income multipliers, spanning seven years for unsynchronized fiscal shocks to each of the 'Big Seven' countries, are also analysed. The responses are shown for the 13 LINK OECD countries, for their combined GNP, and for the unweighted sums of the individual country responses. An analytical decomposition of international income multipliers into impulse and response components, based on these same simulations, was subsequently presented in Hickman and Filatov (1983).

The same conference volume includes brief descriptions and simulation results for the MCM, Tsukuba–FAIS, and Project FUGI multi-country models. The Tsukuba model (Shishido, 1980) is similar in structure and purposes to Project LINK, although all of the component country and regional models were built for the Tsukuba system and are maintained at Tsukuba University in Japan. Project FUGI is a hybrid system comprising separately constructed and loosely interrelated input–output, metal-resource, and multi-country macroeconomic models. One of the three components, the FUGI Macroeconomic Model (Onishi, 1981) is again similar in structure to LINK, but it is maintained at one research centre (Soka University, Japan) and is oriented primarily to long-term analysis of North–South relationships. (Again, see Sato's related discussion in Chapter 10.)

Other LINK applications at the outset of the 1980s included 'Coordinated Monetary Policy and the World Economy' (Klein, Simes and Voisin, 1981) and 'Industrial Policy in the World Economy: Medium-Term Simulations' (Klein, Bollino and Fardoust, 1982).

During 1982–3, Project LINK and the MCM group participated in a joint study of the macroeconomic impacts of energy shocks and policy responses, sponsored by the Energy Modeling Forum at Stanford University, involving comparative simulations from 13 models of the United States and one for Canada. Thus the focus was on the US economy and, except for LINK and MCM, the results are for unlinked national models.

A contribution by Bollino, Pauly and Petersen (1983) discusses the general results for the US module of LINK and another by Pauly and Hooper (1984) appraises the international repercussions in the LINK and MCM systems, whereas the EMF7 Working Group Report (1984) and a paper by Hickman (1984b) compare and analyse the simulations for all the models. The scenarios include positive and negative oil shocks and an increase in gas prices, plus alternative fiscal and monetary policy responses to the base case of an oil shock, and are standardized as much as possible in order to isolate differences due to model structures rather than for ancillary assumptions.

At its annual meeting of 1983 in Tsukuba, Japan, the project organized a session on comparative simulations of oil price reductions and development assistance, jointly with the FUGI world macroeconomic modelling group at Soka University and the Tsukuba–FAIS team (see Bollino, Onishi, Pauly, Petersen and Shishido, 1984).

Unemployment prospects in the OECD area were the focus of alternative LINK scenarios in a paper by Pauly (1984). The LINK models for Canada, France, Germany, Japan, the United Kingdom and the United States were used to investigate wage and price responses to demand (fiscal) and supply (oil) shocks in Hickman and Klein (1984). The problems of the developing economies were addressed in 'World Recovery Strategies in the 80s: Is World Recovery Synonymous to LDC Recovery?' (Bollino and Klein, 1984), and Klein (1985) revisited the still timely theme of 'Empirical Aspects of Protectionism: LINK Results'.

Project LINK participated in the Brookings Institution Conference on Empirical Macroeconomics for Interdependent Economies, 10–11 March 1986. Comparative simulations of the effects of fiscal and monetary shocks originating in both the United States and OECD were undertaken for 12 multi-country models: Project LINK, MCM, INTERLINK, EPA, the Data Resources, Inc (DRI) International Model, the Wharton Econometric Forecasting Associates (WEFA) World Model, the 'New Classical' world model developed at the University of Liverpool, the COMPACT model of the Commission of the European Economic Community (EEC), the McKibbin–Sachs Simulation Model, the MINIMOD system at the International Monetary Fund, the Taylor Multicountry Econometric Rational Expectations Model, and the Minneapolis World VAR Model. Comparisons and evaluations of these simulations, which highlighted the importance of exchange rate variations and relative price adjustments in a regime of floating rates, were made at the conference in papers by Jeffrey Frankel, Hooper, Hickman and Helliwell. (For details and further evaluations, see Ralph Bryant, Dale W. Henderson, Gerald Holtham, Peter Hooper and Steven A. Symansky (eds, 1988).)

The LINK system underwent another wave of expansion in the early 1980s. A model for China was constructed for LINK by Lawrence J. Lau at Stanford University. With a few exceptions (Iceland, Portugal, Turkey and Yugoslavia), every OECD country was represented by home-based models by 1985. Some 35 new models for developing countries were built at LINK Central with the advice and encouragement of LINK participants from third-world countries, the research staffs at the United Nations and the Asian Development Bank, and Shin'ichi Ichimura, who had pioneered a sublinkage system of Pacific Basin models at Kyoto University. A few LDC models are already being supplied directly by groups which maintain them locally in Chile, India, the Philippines, Taiwan and Venezuela. It is noteworthy that models for two centrally planned economies are already maintained on site, at the University of Lodz in Poland and at the International Market Research Institute in Hungary. A model for China, constructed jointly by a team from the Chinese Academy of Social Sciences, the State Planning Commission and Fudan University, was added to the LINK system in 1987. As of this date, fresh models were scheduled to be maintained as part of the system in Nigeria, Pakistan, Portugal and South Korea.

The incorporation of numerous developing countries became feasible when UN economists undertook the formidable task of constructing highly disaggregated bilateral trade statistics. By 1986, 79 × 79 trade matrices were available for nine commodity groups, accommodating bilateral linkages for 79 countries and areas with interactive feedbacks.

The enlarged system requires sophisticated management of data-files and simulation routines. During 1982–5 the LINK software was completely revised by Christian Petersen (1985). Although the expanded system comprises about 20 000 equations, computer response is rapid and a complete Maxi-LINK simulation for five years can be run in five minutes. Further reductions in processing time can certainly be achieved, and experiments are under way to use the parallel processing abilities of a 'supercomputer' for solving the individual country models simultaneously instead of serially. (See also the discussion of the following chapter.)

An historic telecommunications experiment was undertaken by LINK on 27 April 1984. Teams of LINK participants in London and Virginia were linked by satellite TV audio-visually and two groups with audio service alone were assembled in Geneva and Los Angeles. The teams of participants made live criticisms of a baseline forecast and a policy-mix scenario, a new policy simulation with revised country inputs was run on line, and the new results were viewed for live discussion on computer screens visible to participants in all four locations. A similar teleconference was held on 3 May 1986, this time involving LINK participants at sites in Japan, the United States and Switzerland. (Again, see the related discussion in Chapter 15.)

An advantage of these two teleconferences was that they used an audio-visual medium by satellite, but they were fairly expensive. An inexpensive alternative was tested in March 1986, when Project LINK members meeting at the computer centre of the City University of New York were in contact via the BITNET computer network with colleagues in Madrid, Rome, Bologna, Paris and London. Message transmission was quick and could be readily observed on a large projection screen. A protectionist scenario involving a unilateral import surcharge by the United States was transmitted abroad. After a spirited 'discussion' among the European teams, they decided to retaliate by a move towards lower interest rates in each country, and the retaliatory monetary policy was then implemented in a Maxi-link simulation at LINK central in Philadelphia while all participants remained on line.

Although there is obviously an advantage to be gained from having audio-visual contact, the BITNET message system worked well and was quite inexpensive for participants. It was found that a meaningful economic scenario could be designed, executed and discussed internationally in about one hour. Contemporaneous communication via a BITNET type network is clearly a viable and economical method for international teleconferencing by research and policy groups.

5   The evolution of Project LINK and global modelling

Project LINK is at once a global multinational model, a cooperative international research project, and a forum for research on econometric methods and applications to the world economy. Since its inception in 1968 it has expanded from a nucleus of 11 econometricians and seven country models to more than 100 participants and 79 models in 1987. It has grown not only in geographic detail but in the scope of endogenous international linkages, which now include invisibles in the current account, capital flows, and interest and exchange rates in addition to trade flows and prices. A parallel evolution has occurred in the specifications of the constituent national models, stimulated by the need for new linkages and the exchange of ideas among the participating model-building groups and between them and outside experts invited to the LINK meetings. Many of the country models presently included were directly inspired or assisted by the project in their formative stages, and others have been estimated at LINK Central (University of Pennsylvania) for incorporation in the system, pending the development of locally-based models. Substantive results include multi-year forecasts of the world economy prepared annually in the spring and summer, simulation studies of the international transmission mechanism, control theory applications to exchange rate determination and numerous scenarios of the effects of international disturbances and of international policies and policy coordination.

Over the years since LINK's founding, numerous multi-country models have been built in the United States, Japan and Europe. (See Hickman, 1983b and Bryant *et al.*, 1988.) Some have emphasized trade; others, financial flows. Some highlight relationships among the developed OECD countries; others focus on North–South interdependencies. Some distinguish among many countries; others aggregate important regional blocs. Some are econometric models, some 'calibrated' general equilibrium models, some input–output models, and some mixed systems. Most were built by teams at a single research centre.

Apart from its comprehensive scope and size, the most characteristic feature of Project LINK is the cooperative nature of the undertaking. From its inception, the project has been based on the principle that each resident modelling group knows its own economy best, and that uniform specification of country models is unnecessary and even undesirable if local institutions, industrial structures and policy stances are not to be subordinated to analytical convenience. A contrary approach emphasizing the virtues of common structural specifications is a feature of other, more tightly constructed systems, such as the MCM model. There are sound arguments for both approaches, but, apart from the substantive issues of modelling strategy, in-house maintenance is desirable and probably mandatory for effective use of multi-country models by international or governmental agencies, and this will tend naturally to more uniformity of model structure. On the other hand, the international character and basic research orientation of Project LINK has fostered the diffusion of model-building activities throughout the world and has served as a powerful catalyst for research on many aspects of the international economic system and the functioning of the world economy.

References

Adams, F. Gerard (1978) 'Primary Commodity Markets in a World Model System', in F. Gerard Adams and Sonia A. Klein (eds), *Stabilizing World Commodity Markets* (Lexington: Lexington Books).

Adams, F. Gerard, Hidekazu Eguchi and F. J. M. Meyer-zu-Schlochtern (1969) *An Econometric Analysis of International Trade* (Paris: OECD).

Armington, Paul S. (1969) 'A Theory of Demand for Products Distinguished by Place of Production', *IMF Staff Papers*, March.

Ball, R. J. (ed.) (1973) *The International Linkage of National Economic Models* (Amsterdam: North-Holland).

Beaumont, Paul, Ingmar Prucha and Victor Filatov (1979) 'Performance of the LINK System: 1970 versus 1975 Base Year Trade Share Matrix', *Empirical Economics*, 4, pp. 11–42.

Bollino, C. Andrea and Lawrence R. Klein (1984) 'World Recovery Strategies in the 80s: Is World Recovery Synonymous to LDC Recovery?', *Journal of Policy Modeling*, 6(2), pp. 175–207.

Bollino, C. Andrea, Peter Pauly and Christian E. Petersen (1983) 'National and International Aspects of the EMF7 Scenarios: Results from Project LINK', EMF 7.13, Energy Modeling Forum, Stanford University, December.

Bollino, C. Andrea, Akira Onishi, Peter Pauly, Christian E. Petersen and Shuntaro Shishido (1984) 'Global Impact of Oil Price Reductions and Official Development Assistance: Medium-Term Comparative Simulations with Alternative Global Econometric Models', *The Developing Economies*, 22, pp. 3–26.

Bryant, Ralph, Dale W. Henderson, Gerald Holtham, Peter Hooper and Stephen A. Symansky (eds) (1988) *Empirical Macroeconomics for Interdependent Economies* (Washington, DC: The Brookings Institution).

EMF7 Working Group (1984), 'Macroeconomic Impacts of Energy Shocks: An Overview', EMF 7.2, Energy Modeling Forum, Stanford University, September.

Frisch, Ragnar (1947) 'On the Need for Forecasting a Multilateral Balance of Payments', *American Economic Review*, 37, September, pp. 535–51.

Helliwell, John F. (1978) 'Discussion of "Disturbances to the International Economy"', in Robert M. Solow (ed.), *After the Phillips Curve: Persistence of High Inflation and High Unemployment* (Boston: Federal Reserve Bank of Boston).

Hickman, Bert G. (1974) 'International Transmission of Economic Fluctuations and Inflation', in Albert Ando, Richard Herring and Richard Marston (eds), *International Aspects of Stabilization Policies* (Boston: Federal Reserve Bank of Boston).

_____ (1975) 'Project LINK in 1972: Retrospect and Prospect', in G. A. Renton (ed.), *Modelling the Economy* (London: Heinemann).

_____ (1983a) 'Exchange Rates in Project LINK', in Paul DeGrauwe and Theo Peeters (eds), *Exchange Rates in Multicountry Econometric Models* (London: Macmillan).

_____ (ed.) (1983b) *Global International Economic Models* (Amsterdam: North-Holland).

_____ (ed.) (1984a) *International Monetary Stabilization and the Foreign Debt Problem* (San Francisco: Federal Reserve Bank of San Francisco).

_____ (1984b) 'Macroeconomic Effects of Energy Shocks and Policy Responses: A Structural Comparison of Fourteen Models', EMF 7.4, Energy Modeling Forum, Stanford University, September.

Hickman, Bert G. and Lawrence J. Lau (1973) 'Elasticities of Substitution and Export Demand in a World Trade Model', *European Economic Review*, 4, pp. 347–80.

Hickman, Bert G. and Stefan Schleicher (1978) 'The Interdependence of National Economies and the Synchronization of Economic Fluctuations: Evidence from the LINK Project', *Weltwirtschaftsliches Archiv*, 114(4), pp. 642–708.

Hickman, Bert G. and Lawrence R. Klein (1979) 'A Decade of Research by Project LINK', *Social Science Research Council Items*, vol. 33, nos 3/4, pp. 49–56.

Hickman, Bert G. and Victor Filatov (1983) 'A Decomposition of International Income Multipliers', in F. Gerard Adams and Bert G. Hickman (eds), *Global Econometrics: Essays in Honor of Lawrence R. Klein* (Cambridge, Massachusetts: MIT Press).

Hickman, Bert G. and Lawrence R. Klein (1984) 'Wage-Price Behavior in the National Models of Project LINK', *American Economic Review, Papers and Proceedings*, May, pp. 150–4.

Hickman, Bert G. and Lawrence R. Klein (1985) 'Recent Developments in Project LINK', *Social Science Research Council Items*, vol. 39, nos 1/2, pp. 7–11.

Johnson, Keith N. (1979) 'Balance of Payments Equilibrium and Equilibrating Exchange Rates in a World Economic Model', PhD dissertation, University of Pennsylvania.

Johnson, Keith N. and Lawrence R. Klein (1974a) 'LINK Model Simulations of International Trade: An Evaluation of the Effects of Currency Realignment', *Journal of Finance, Papers and Proceedings*, 29, pp. 617–30.

Johnson, Keith N. and Lawrence R. Klein (1974b) 'Stability in the International Economy: The LINK Experience', in Albert Ando, Richard Herring and Richard Marston (eds), *International Aspects of Stabilization Policies* (Boston: Federal Reserve Bank of Boston).

Klein, Lawrence R. (1973) 'Project LINK: Entering a New Phase', *Social Science Research Council Items*, 27(2), pp. 13–16.

_____ (1978) 'Disturbances to the International Economy', in Robert M. Solow (ed.), *After the Phillips Curve: Persistence of High Inflation and High Unemployment* (Boston: Federal Reserve Bank of Boston).

_____ (1985) 'Empirical Aspects of Protectionism: LINK Results', *Journal of Policy Modeling*, 7(1).

Klein, Lawrence R. and Vincent Su (1979) 'Protectionism: An Analysis from Project LINK', *Journal of Policy Modeling*, 1, pp. 5–35.

Klein, Lawrence R. and Wilhelm Krelle (eds) (1983) *Capital Flows and Exchange Rate Determination*, Zeitschrift fur Nationalokonomie, Supplementum 3 (Vienna and New York: Springer-Verlag).

Klein, Lawrence R., Chikashi Moriguchi and Alain van Peeterssen (1972) 'NEP in the World Economy: Simulation of the International Transmission Mechanism', Project LINK Working Paper 2.

Klein, Lawrence R., Chikashi Moriguchi and Alain van Peeterssen (1975) 'The LINK Model of World Trade with Applications to 1972–73', in Peter Kenen (ed.), *International Trade and Finance* (New York: Cambridge University Press).

Klein, Lawrence R., M. Politi and Vincent Su (1978) 'Scenario of a World Wide Grain Shortage', LINK Memorandum, July.

Klein, Lawrence R., Shahrokh Fardoust and Victor Filatov (1981) 'Purchasing Power Parity in Medium-Term Simulation of the World Economy', *Scandinavian Journal of Economics*, 4, pp. 479–96.

Klein, Lawrence R., Richard Simes and Pascal Voisin (1981) 'Coordinated Monetary Policy and the World Economy', *Prévision et analyse économique*, 2(3), pp. 75–105.

Klein, Lawrence R., C. Andrea Bollino and Shahrokh Fardoust (1982) 'Industrial Policy in the World Economy: Medium-Term Simulations', *Journal of Policy Modeling*, 4(2), pp. 175–89.

Llewellyn, John and Lee Samuelson (1979) 'The OECD International Linkage Model', *OECD Economic Outlook, Occasional Studies*.

Llewellyn, John, Stephen Potter and Lee Samuelson (1985) *Economic Forecasting and Policy – the International Dimension* (London: Routledge & Kegan Paul).

Marwah, Kanta (1976) 'A World Model of International Trade: Forecasting Market Shares and Trade Flows', *Empirical Economics*, 1(1), pp. 1–39.

Metzler, Lloyd A. (1942) 'Underemployment Equilibrium in International Trade', *Econometrica*, 10, pp. 97–112.

_____ (1950) 'A Multiple-Region Theory of Income and Trade', *Econometrica*, 18, pp. 329–54.

Meyer-zu-Schlochtern, F. J. M. and Akira Yajima (1970) 'OECD Trade Model: 1970 Version', *OECD Economic Outlook, Occasional Studies*, December.

Moriguchi, Chikashi (1973) 'Forecasting and Simulating the World Economy', *American Economic Review, Papers and Proceedings*, 63, May, pp. 402–9.

Onishi, Akira (1981) 'Projections of Alternative Paths of Development of the ESCAP Countries in the Third United Nations Development Decade, 1981–1990', *Soka Economic Studies Quarterly*, March, pp. 175–227.

Pauly, Peter (1984) 'Unemployment Prospects for the OECD Area: Alternative Scenarios with the LINK System', in *Forecasting Models and the Employment Problem* (Geneva: International Labour Organisation).

Pauly, Peter and Peter Hooper (1984) 'Impact of an Oil Price Shock on the U.S. Economy: International Repercussions', Federal Reserve Board, International Finance Discussion Paper 262 (Washington: Federal Reserve Board).

Pauly, Peter and Christian E. Petersen (1986) 'Exchange Rate Responses in the LINK System', *European Economic Review*, 30(1), pp. 149–70.

Petersen, Christian E. (1985) *Simnew User's Guide*, Project LINK, University of Pennsylvania.

Polak, J. J. (1939) 'International Propagation of Business Cycles', *Review of Economic Studies*, 6(2), February, pp. 79–99.

_____ (1953) *An International Economic System* (Chicago: University of Chicago Press).

Polak, Jacques J. and Rudolf R. Rhomberg (1962) 'Economic Instability in an International Setting', *American Economic Review: Papers and Proceedings*, 52, May. Reprinted with model appendix added in Robert Aaron Gordon and Lawrence R. Klein (eds) (1965) *Readings in Business Cycles* (Homewood, Illinois: Richard D. Irwin).

Samuelson, Lee (1973) 'A New Model of World Trade', *OECD Economic Outlook, Occasional Studies*, December.

Sawyer, John A. (ed.) (1979) *Modelling the International Transmission Mechanism* (Amsterdam: North-Holland).

Shishido, Shuntaro (1980) 'A Model for the Coordination of Recovery Policies in the OECD Region', *Journal of Policy Modeling*, 2(1), pp. 33–55.

Stevens, Guy V. G., Richard B. Berner, Peter B. Clark, Ernesto Hernandez-Cata, Howard J. Howe and Sung Y. Kwack (1984) *The U.S. Economy in an Interdependent World* (Washington, DC: Board of Governors of the Federal Reserve System).

Waelbroeck, Jean L. (ed.) (1976) *The Models of Project LINK* (Amsterdam: North-Holland).

Waelbroeck, Jean and A. Dramais (1974) 'DESMOS: A Model for the Coordination of Economic Policies in the EEC Countries', in Albert Ando, Richard Herring and Richard Marston (eds), *International Aspects of Stabilization Policies* (Boston: Federal Reserve Bank of Boston).

PART V

SUMMING UP

15   A history of computation in econometrics

Throughout this book we have made oblique references to problems of computation, particularly in the early days of the discipline of macroeconometric model-building. It is now time to tie some of these strands together. This chapter, originally prepared by Lawrence R. Klein on the occasion of a symposium in 1972 at the Institute of Advanced Study (Princeton University) honouring the contribution of John von Neumann to the development of the electronic computer, and which has subsequently been brought up to date, has somewhat broader coverage than the rest of this work. Nevertheless the original text has only been modified slightly, as it is felt that this extended coverage forms a valuable background and serves as contrast.

On the occasion of this symposium, Klein was struck by the contrast between the perceptions of the computer's impact in economics and in most other fields – mathematics, natural science, psychology and general social science. It was argued that the growing use of the computer radically changed the way that research is done in economics. Moreover it also affected the outcome of research. Naturally the contribution of computing to econometrics was emphasized. By contrast, most, if not all, speakers from other fields argued that the role of the computer was not decisive for scholarly development. Some speakers not only played down the role of the computer but thought that it was either not important or even harmful.

Ideas concerning other fields may have changed significantly in roughly two decades since the time of the symposium, and there has been considerable improvement in computer power or versatility since then, but there is no doubt (in our view) where economics should stand on the issue. The face of econometric and all quantitative economic research has been radically altered by the advent of the computer. We feel advances in computation have had an extremely large influence on econometrics and have utterly transformed our subject. A recent interview with T. W. Anderson in *Econometric Theory* is filled with references to the restraining influence of older computational facilities.[1] When asked to single out particular areas for further research, Anderson replied, 'I think that one of the major aspects of current research in any statistical field is how to exploit the use of the computer. That is, not only, in effective computation

[of] methods that have been developed on the basis of some theory, but methods that use the computer in a more creative fashion.' When asked to place himself in the role of a new PhD student choosing a topic for research, Anderson responded, 'It's hard to answer that question because, for example, a Ph.D. student now would have a lot more background in computation than I would.'

Computation has been of great importance for our subject, and research achievement was considerably retarded for a number of years because computer facilities were not powerful, yet computational demands were heavy. Anderson cites the way research and problem formulation were considerably changed ('bent') to fit the rudimentary computer facilities available. In the pages below, we shall follow up that concept and see the processes by which efficient and available computation changed the nature of our findings and research activities.

1   Statistical calculations in the pre-computer era

By 'computer' we mean the electronic computer, which is essentially a facility that became generally available after the Second World War. Statistical research had been implemented through the use of a variety of devices: hand-plotted diagrams, hand operations ($+$, $-$, $\div$, $\times$), slide rules, the abacus, adding machines, manually operated desk-top calculators, electrically operated desk-top calculators (electro-mechanical), analog devices, punched card tabulators (electro-mechanical), and sundry other devices.

Short-cut formulas were used to the fullest extent possible. For example, to compute:

$$\sum_{i=1}^{n} (x_i - \overline{x})^2, \ \overline{x} = \frac{1}{n}\sum_{i=1}^{n} x_i,$$

researchers formed the identity

$$\sum_{i=1}^{n} (x_i - \overline{x})^2 = \sum_{i=1}^{n} x^2_i - n\overline{x}^2$$

and computed each of the two right-hand expressions, without ever subtracting $\overline{x}$ from each x_i, squaring and summing. Simplifying identities were used wherever possible.

When large-scale calculations were needed, systematic checking devices were introduced so that intermediate errors could be detected and eliminated along the way. One of the most intricate calculations was matrix inversion or the solution of linear simultaneous equations. The estimation equations of linear regression theory (least-squares equations) were laid out systematically according to the 'Doolittle' method in a way that took advantage of the symmetry of the calculations, and carried along an extra *sum* column for row checks at each stage of the operation. Regressions involving fewer than 10 unknown parameters could be estimated routinely in a fraction of a working day, varying with the skill and speed of the machine operator. Bigger regressions were formidable and non-linear transformations of data into logarithms, trigonometric functions, ratios, products and so on also required individual treatment, either from consulting special tables or from arithmetic operations. In regression problems the formation of

$$\sum_i y_i, \ \sum_i y_i^2, \ \sum_i y_i x_{ij}, \ \sum_i x_{ij}, \ \sum_i x_{ij} x_{ik}$$

formed separate steps. After these sample moments were obtained, the 'Doolittle' process could be initiated. Sometimes, special equipment, such as an analog device, was used for one part of the problem, say the moment evaluation problem, and the 'Doolittle' method was used for the next step, by hand with a desk-top calculator. Punched-card tabulating machines were used in a technique called 'progressive digiting', which involved repeated summation by digital columns, one at a time, in order to evaluate large masses of data in the form of sample moments.

There was much advance screening of data by quick graphical methods. The technique of subgroup averages was often used to get a quick picture of the stochastic relation:

$$y_i = f(x_i) + e_i, \quad i = 1,2,...n.$$

The data were classified by size distribution of x_i, and mean y_i and mean x_i were computed for each class. Then class means were plotted in two dimensions in order to get a quick visual impression of the parametric structure of f. These ideas were often taken much further and were used to make graphical estimates of multiple correlation equations. A serious debate was carried on in the *Quarterly Journal of Economics* on the virtues or defects of graphical versus numerical fitting procedures.[2]

The problem of estimating economic relationships, carried out on the basis of regression for a single equation until the 1940s, was a central computing issue for data management, the computation of sample moments, and the solution of the estimation equations. There were, however, other important computational barriers. The National Bureau of Economic Research carried out extensive time-series analyses by identifying cyclical stages of many individual series and summarizing their cyclical behaviour, particularly for timing. They did not use many formal mathematical methods and relied mainly on non-parametric data classification analysis. There was, however, need for extensive data management and computation. Graphical methods were used quite extensively. Standardized forms, many clerical workers and conventional desk-top calculators were the main facilities used.

The major econometric problem centred around the analysis of single equations and estimated parameter properties. Little attention was paid to numerical dynamic system performance, except in Professor Tinbergen's work, where, as we saw in Chapter 2, he dealt with cyclical characteristics of linear systems of finite difference equations. While now we are primarily interested in forecasting and simulations analysis for the study of multipliers, policy simulations and dynamic response characteristics, Tinbergen and his contemporaries in the 1930s paid a great deal of attention to the eigenvalues of linear dynamic systems. For small models, explicit solutions in closed form could readily be derived, but Tinbergen's models were larger, containing 10 to 50 equations, and required some special approximations. In today's environment, we would simply make computer-generated solutions of such systems over specified horizons from given initial conditions. While it is routine to do such things now, they presented a considerable computing burden to Tinbergen. Klein remembers that, at the time, he personally could solve equations systems of 10–20 linear relations with lags in a day or less. However it was an effort to obtain each solution, and there was little thought of exploring alternatives. Everything was held to the most usable set of calculations.

By approximation and substitution, Tinbergen reduced his systems to a final autoregressive form of up to four lags, formed a characteristic equation and extracted roots from the associated polynomial expression. The computed roots were examined for stability conditions and periodicity. This approach is not generally applicable to non-linear systems, except in a neighbourhood of some initial values. In linear systems, the homogeneous part of the characteristic equation is the same for *all* variables; therefore this exercise need be done only once, and one set of eigenvalues serves the whole system.

Another area of econometric investigation was in the field of input–output analysis. Here there was a large problem of data management, but also the analytical problem of evaluating the inverse matrix:

$(I - A)^{-1}.$

Professor W. Leontief, the primary architect of input–output analysis, was an early user of the computer after the Second World War, but he used various analog devices and took advantage of the sparseness of the well-known interindustry-flow matrix A in order to estimate the required inverse. Since matrix multiplication is a 'forward' and relatively easy calculation to implement, the possibility of using the expansion

$$(I - A)^{-1} = I + A + A^2 + A^3 + \ldots .$$

was explored.[3] This was in step with other branches of econometrics, where tricks, transformations or identities were used wherever possible in order to ease the burden of computation. During the 1930s or 1940s, a 50 × 50 input–output matrix posed significant computation problems. This kind of problem is far removed from present-day concerns.

A branch of econometrics–broadly construed as 'measurement in economics' – is *Activity Analysis*, in which linear programming plays a large role.[4] The linear programming problem is to find values of the variables λ_j which maximize the linear function

$$\sum_{i=1}^{n} \lambda_i c_i,$$

subject to:

$$\lambda_j \geq 0, j = 1, 2, \ldots n,$$

and

$$\sum_{j=1}^{n} a_{ij}\lambda_j = h_i \quad i = 1, 2, \ldots m.$$

The a_{ij}, b_i, and c_i are constants. The linear constraint system resembles an input–output model, but is not necessarily square, as is the input–output system.

When Tjalling Koopmans reached a certain stage in research on macroeconometric model-building at the Cowles Commission, he turned his attention principally to activity analysis, to which he had been earlier attracted by the shipping problem, namely how to route freighters among ports and voyages so as to optimize their use (for example, minimize their movement with empty cargo space). Essentially, he turned from large-scale computing problems associated with estimation of equation systems in econometrics to equally large-scale computing problems associated with activity analysis.

George Dantzig proposed the simplex method to handle the complicated computational problems involved in solving the linear programming problem stated above. To provide the flavour of the computational problem, Dantzig noted,

> Because of the special form of the equations [in the Hitchcock–Koopmans transportation problem] simplified computational procedures are possible. For example, a large-scale problem involving about 25 origins and 60 destinations was solved recently in 9 man-days by hand computation techniques.[5]

Another typical problem, introduced by George Stigler, was called the diet problem. This problem was to find the minimum cost of a diet (which in practice could be quite unpalatable) meeting certain nutritional standards. 'A problem involving 9 dietary elements and 77 foods took 120 man-days to compute by hand.'[6]

Problems like these were solved during the 1940s by what would now be considered as very laborious methods. The linear programming problem eventually became the quadratic programming problem. The general terms *Activity Analysis* and *Programming* raised similar computational problems and generally concerned the finding of constrained optimal solutions to economic problems.

Family budget sample surveys, censuses and other studies requiring large-scale data handling were awkward but manageable by hand methods with large numbers of clerical workers. Complicated cross-tabulations or variance analyses were major problems. Electro-mechanical tabulators were helpful in this respect. Intricate mathematical calculations were not the issue, simply the handling and storage of large data files. The study and examination of the findings, listed by hand on detailed questionnaires, were limited, but the primary analyses were carried out by the 'brute force' of hand work.

2 The computer era

After the Second World War, the electronic computer became available, but at first econometricians gained only limited access. Leontief used early versions for his problems in input–output analysis. Survey statisticians used tabulators and other punched-card equipment, and generally shifted more basic data analysis to electronic machines during the early 1950s. Linear programming problems were solved by computers in the 1950s, as well.

H. Houthakker, then in England, was an early user of large-scale computers for the management of data and the estimation of demand relations in both family budgets and time-series samples. He used the EDSAC facility in Cambridge and had to do the original programming for econometric applications. The macro-models built at the Cowles Commission were estimated and solved with desk-top calculators. The Klein–Goldberger Model, discussed at some length in Chapter 3, at the University of Michigan, was first estimated and solved in the same way, but by 1954 was partially shifted to electronic computers for the estimation of moments in preparation for parameter estimation. A general simulation program was being developed at Michigan for this model but was never completed. The Oxford model built a few years later in England (see Chapter 7) was handled in the same mixed way – it was estimated partially by desk-top calculator and partially by electronic computer. By the end of the 1950s, however, this work was completely shifted to the new modern computers. Pioneering work by Edwin Kuh, Morris Norman, Robert Hall and others produced comprehensive programs that started with sample data (provided already at that time in *machine-readable form*) and moved on to data transformation, equation estimation, system building, system testing and system use. Equation estimation could be done in simple form (single-equation least squares, for example) or by more complicated procedures applicable either to partial systems or individual equations, or by complete systems methods (FIML, SLS, IIV and others). These methods took up the direct estimation of the separate equations and systems of equations that the Cowles Commission found to be such heavy burdens. They and subsequent mathematical statisticians worked out the algorithms. It was only a question of how to handle the intricate, usually non-linear, equations that are implied by the algorithms which were developed separately.

The solution of dynamic systems for simulation purposes in forecasting, multiplier evaluation, scenario analysis and the general study of response characteristics involved an entirely new set of computational problems.

The solution of large equation systems provides an interesting glimpse of progress in using the computer. Researchers used to prepare solutions to their models by the laborious hand procedures of substitution and elimination, down to the last variable. The early models of the 1960s harnessed the computer and worked particularly well for the purely linear case or for linear approximations to non-linear systems.

The Brookings Model of the 1960s (see Chapter 4) was not completely linear and consisted of 300 or more simultaneous equations, which at the time was considered to be very large. Klein and others found that one block of equations was linear in quantities if prices were given; that is, this could be represented as:

$L_1(q|p) = 0.$

In addition, a second block was linear in prices if quantities were given: the representation was:

$L_2(p|q) = 0.$

An iteration procedure was established by guessing at a vector of prices (the p_i's) and solving $L_1 = 0$, by linear methods. The computed values of the q vector were read into L_2 as givens, and the model generated a solution for p. The problem was then iterated between $L_1 = 0$ and $L_2 = 0$. Good results were obtained, but it was a fairly laborious procedure – certainly data-intensive. In the late 1980s it is no problem at all to solve 300 simultaneous equations, but that was considered to be a very difficult problem some 20 years ago. Also the solution was presented, as a final result, simply as a set of values obtained by solving simultaneous equations.

For some model specifications, it was necessary to introduce more than two main blocks, and Edwin Kuh observed that, if the blocks were to be subdivided to the limit – one equation per block – a much faster solution was obtained. The block procedure used matrix inversion for a set of simultaneous linear equations, and this was much more time-consuming than simply iterating the evaluation of single equations, in direct solutions without inversion. The well-known methods of Gauss-Seidel iteration were thus introduced to econometrics and have been used for decades now, all over the world, in practically every centre faced with the computational problem of solving simultaneous equation systems.

It was not only the speed and simplicity of the Gauss-Seidel algorithms that were ideally designed for the electronic computer where repeated iteration is efficient; the programmed computer was also efficient in constructing tables and graphics for the final results. Now the solutions are not presented to a user community as a listing of values that satisfy a system of simultaneous equations, but in standardized tables like those produced by the official government agencies. The user community are generally aware of the official tables and know immediately how to interpret them. Widely available graphic routines that handle the data as soon as simulations are completed enable the findings to be dramatically displayed for the users. The generation of solutions in the form of neat accounting tables was completed in the mid-1960s, while graphics have been most rapidly developed in the late 1970s and 1980s.

A difficult problem for almost all econometricians is to deal with a proper probabilistic treatment of small sample theory applied to econometric inference. Asymptotic theory can, in many cases, be worked out in closed mathematical form, and the computer can be used for the evaluation of complicated expressions. This is, indeed, an important use for the computer, but it is not as computer-intensive as the design and use of constructed sampling experiments, using the computer for so-called Monte Carlo methods. Not only small-sample problems but generally intractable problems such as specification changes, unusual non-linearities and other complications can be expressed or studied by the use of the computer. Usually the investigator sets out plausible values for unknown parameters, even exploring a good portion of the parameter spaces, and disturbs the system with appropriately bounded random drawings. The disturbed solutions can be replicated so that experimental sampling distributions, for whatever sample size, can be generated. Confidence intervals and other measures associated with the sampling distributions can then be studied. All such experiments have their limitations in not being general, but ever more powerful computers are facilitating the exploration of wider and wider regions in the parameter space.

Early uses of computer experiments by Harvey Wagner, Robert Summers and many others threw light on finite sample distributions of simultaneous equation estimators.[7] Irma and Frank Adelman cleverly designed computer experiments to study model-generated business cycles under conditions of applied random shocks.[8] Their results gave a beautiful display of stochastic cyclical components discovered earlier by Yule, Frisch and Slutsky. Subsequent to these pioneering studies, there have been scores of Monte Carlo exercises for generating sampling distributions and stochastic simulations. Obstacles to the evaluation of complicated formulas for the standard error of forecast have been overcome through computer use.[9]

While the computer has been indispensable for studying finite sample methods in a wide variety of applications, there are also large-sample situations which do occur, and the computer has provided a breakthrough in enabling the researcher to manage large masses of data professionally for statistical purposes in econometrics. Large samples are found in cross-section data, such as household samples for the study of family budgets and labour market choices. Also large-scale distributions of productive establishments generate large masses of data. Computers with large memories can store large amounts of data, which are then processed and used in econometric inferences. Not only single cross-sections, but also time series of cross-sections are being used a great deal in econometric research. Each sample may contain thousands of household or firm data listings, which are then processed in the form of 'moments' to be used in further computation.

Heavy use of computer memory extends beyond cross-section data collection; it occurs in data banking or data management. One of the first computer data banks was constructed at Brookings by James Craig in the early 1960s for maintenance of the thousands of series used in the econometric model. This was perhaps the point at which the large data bank, as we know it now, was first conceived. The Brookings Model was then so large that the central research team had to develop systematic, uniform, and comprehensive methods in order that the data could be managed: transformed when necessary, kept up to date as new releases produced new observation points every week, and maintained in storage so that series could be retrieved when needed for whatever purpose in model analysis. The computer allowed the refinement of this approach to the point at which primary data collection agencies transmit data, in relatively unprocessed form, to large banks in storage. This enables data to be ever ready for selective downloading for the purposes of econometric investigation, centralizes the creation of uniformly processed series brought up to date, with historical corrections, and provides economists at all levels – teachers, students, researchers – with data that are ready for immediate use. The delivery of data, from both the public and the private sectors, to econometrician users has been vastly simplified and enhanced to the point at which the most ordinary researcher or teacher has access to almost all the data ever available for work on econometric problems.

The computer made the burdensome problems of solving linear programming systems very quick and routine. Non-linear programming, as well as non-linear methods in general, could be handled with comparative ease. In place of the many man-days of work, cited above by George Dantzig, such problems could be treated in minutes or possibly seconds. Given the practical applicability of linear programming methods to defence problems, the operation of refineries, the preparation of animal feed mixes, and similar commercial uses, it is not surprising that the adaptation to the electronic computer took place in this application sooner than in macroeconometrics during the 1950s.

Methods of control engineering were known for some time to be suitable for use with econometric models. During the latter part of the 1960s and early 1970s, a close collaboration between control engineers and economists developed. At first the computational problems looked formidable, but the interest grew just at the time that econometric models of simultaneous equation systems were being solved by iterative methods on the computers that were then available. These first comprehensive computer programs for dynamic solutions of models using simulations were rapidly extended to include the optimization of objective functions as posited in control theory, so that large systems were being solved within a few years according to the principles of control theory. A typical forerunner in this development was implemented by Benjamin Friedman.[10] He used the Wharton Model, vintage early 1970s, as the large-scale vehicle, but much larger systems with more complicated objective functions were subsequently dealt with as computer power increased.

An important feature of computer development was (and remains) fast turn-around. Problems that took days were reduced to minutes or less, and this has had a great impact on econometric research. In the first place, search techniques and iterative techniques that were previously time-consuming became possible to implement for the first time. Econometricians had long known how to specify complicated routines, either for estimating systems, testing them, or using them in applications. The fast computer made exploration much more possible. Where researchers used to look at one or two system multipliers, at present dozens are scanned. Accompanying 'baseline' forecasts for many periods into the future, there are alternative forecasts, both more and less optimistic. External contingencies can be taken into account in alternatives. Different methods of estimation applied to the same specified system are searched for the 'best' set.

A great deal of 'latest information' goes into the making of forecasts from econometric models. Nearly every day in the United States new statistical reports are made available, and the fast turn-around facility enables the researcher to keep incorporating new information into an evolving forecast exercise up to the last minute prior to release time.

3 The computer and telecommunications

As early as the mid-1960s, computers were being used for the immediate solution of econometric models in conjunction with a conference of experts. As users of model-based projections assembled together for face-to-face discussions of forecasts and policy scenarios, new ideas were generated on the spot for considering changed inputs into the model. It was possible to collect ideas in the morning and have results by afternoon, or even sooner, for the assembled gathering. This concept has been taken further with the use of teleconferences. People in different geographical locations have been brought into audio-visual contact and have looked simultaneously at the same model simulations. Different parties suggested changes in the simulations; these were instantly programmed into new solutions that were executed at some other location and routed back into printers or display screens for study by the conferees at their respective locations. In this kind of exercise, fast turn-around is of the utmost importance. Such procedures for using econometric models would never have been possible in the pre-computer era.

Teleconferencing with computers and econometric models has been taken far with international systems. In the first place, an international system involves a new set of computer problems. It is one thing to construct international economic relationships in one central location; that is hardly different from studying national systems by econometric methods in the same place. It is, however, an interestingly different approach to combine national econometric systems from around the world and to coordinate them in a consistent way in a single computer. This is the approach of project LINK. Nationally maintained models from more than 35 different centres, encompassing 80 countries or regions, are put together into a world trade model at the University of Pennsylvania in Philadelphia. Telecommunications techniques are used for the transmission of data from practically every part of the earth.

At the beginning of the actual working of the LINK system, data were transported manually from participating countries to the research centre at the University of Pennsylvania. Boxes of punched cards or lengthy listings of data and equations in hard copy were sent by mail or freight between continents. This was very clumsy and awkward. Gradually, punched card distribution gave way to magnetic tape distribution, but there were numerous problems in reading tapes from elsewhere, especially when they were taken from different computer configurations or operating systems. In addition, the portability of LINK software for solving simulations of an entire international system was limited and the system would not readily function in strange or unfamiliar environments. The objective was to have the large, internationally-linked system solvable anywhere in the world. This was possible, but not easily implemented.

During the past decade, however, telecommunications technology has changed radically. The concepts are much older than 10 years, but the ready availability of facilities at nominal cost is not. Now different centres all over the world – in all continents, in developing as well as developed countries – can communicate well and use common software. The ultimate in data transmittal has not yet been achieved at the practical level, but participants in the LINK project are able to transmit data from many countries over special networks to Philadelphia and to access the central main-frame unit. The present LINK system of approximately 20 000 equations is, in fact, solved in different parts of the world. Complete flexibility, accessibility and portability are all achievable but, so far, practised on a limited scale. None the less accomplishments grow year by year and the ideal goal is in sight.

An interesting aspect of modern computing, learned in the internationally coordinated LINK project and in many other individual exercises, is that the computing technology of econometrics is fully transferable. In one developing or remote-controlled (socialist) country after another, common hardware, common programs, and common data files are being used for econometric calculations every day. The same tabular displays of results for academic and non-academic users are now commonplace in many remote, developing areas.

In some interesting teleconferences, participants in project LINK have been stationed in different areas, the most elaborate one using Tokyo, Bedminster (New Jersey) and Zurich. Audio-visual connections enabled conference participants in the different sites to converse about a problem and suggest fresh calculations, in the form of a dynamic model scenario, which was then executed in Philadelphia, printed at the Bedminster site and transmitted by facsimile to the other sites. All this took place during a four-hour session, but the computing turn-around took only 15–20 minutes. Execution took only about five minutes for solving 20 000 equations over a five-period horizon. These are only first attempts at using teleconferencing facilities with real-time computing, but it is something that was not even being contemplated in the early days of econometrics. A repeat experiment at the Toronto Economic Summit (in 1988) linked together Tokyo, Toronto and Hamburg, with the computing being done in Philadelphia, in an even shorter time period (a three-hour session).[11]

4 Prospective future developments in computation

The computing for project LINK can be viewed for econometrics as the multiple-model problem, in which computing for several interrelated models is handled in parallel. The optimal control problem first seemed to pose non-trivial computational burdens for econometric application, which were overcome without too much difficulty for the single-model case. International optimality of coordinated economic policies among countries poses new issues for computation, and first results for the 80-model system of LINK involving 20 000 equations are being obtained.

A similar computing obstacle occurs in the case of stochastic simulations. These techniques, as indicated above, were used in the 1950s for computer experiments in statistical inference, but the econometric systems were quite simple – mainly pedagogical. The Adelman–Adelman study of stochastic simulations moved from use of a very small system of two or three equations, in previous studies, to the moderate-size Klein–Goldberger Model, modified to contain about 15–20 equations. Larger and larger models were used in subsequent computations for stochastic simulations. A. Nagar first applied general stochastic simulation to the large-scale Brookings Model during the late 1960s, and his techniques were extended by Michael McCarthy of the Brookings Model Team to handle still more general systems. Just as the Gauss-Seidel iteration techniques developed for that project in order to simulate models were taken over by nearly every macroeconometric centre for solution algorithms, so was the McCarthy method adopted in near-universal form by most analysts using stochastic simulations. George Schink made use of it for evaluating the standard error of forecast, a very complicated calculation, in a large-scale model, the Wharton Model.[12]

The multiple-model problem, however, under stochastic simulation, poses new computational burdens. Again, with small, simplified systems of equations, stochastic simulation across interrelated models has been implemented.[13] Stochastic simulation for a system as large as the multiple LINK models, taken as a coordinated set, has not yet been fully implemented, but, in principle, it is undoubtedly a soluble problem.

At the present time, econometric computing is moving in two polar directions. At one extreme the supercomputer is being used, in both vector and parallel architecture, for truly large-scale or very complicated calculations, as in extreme conditions of non-linearity. The supercomputer handles problems with very large storage, lengthy programming codes (100 000 or more lines) or problems that are highly repetitive, as in stochastic simulation. In some respects, the supercomputer is the logical outcome of a popular computing mode that developed in econometrics during the 1970s, namely the use of time-sharing systems. Large data files are stored in a main-frame computer and are accessed by remote terminals in a network. The terminal operator can simply access data or implement econometric software to produce local results, either on terminal screens or in printed form.

At the other extreme, the micro computer (in contrast to the supercomputer) is being used for self-contained econometric computation. The large main-frame computer with extensive storage capability is still used for maintaining data banks, but data can be downloaded for use on the micro computer on a self-contained basis. Conversely, results derived from micro computer calculation can be uploaded to the mainframe; so the two systems can be used interactively. But the power of the micro computer has grown so fast that the large main-frame software programs of a few years ago can now be made operable on micro computers. System estimation, non-linear estimation, large-model simulation, and many other econometric computations can now be done on micro computers. Individual econometricians now have immense computer power at their fingertips, and for most problems computation is no longer the obstacle that it was some 40 or 50 years ago. Also, from a pedagogical point of view, the micro computer can be brought directly into the classroom for demonstration purposes in teaching econometrics; and students can be assigned problems requiring computing because micro computer facilities are now so widely available.

5 Retrospective thoughts as guides for the future

There can be no doubt that the computer has had a very important impact on the historical development of econometrics. The substantive subject is little more than 60–70 years old, and the last 20 years of that history is strongly influenced by the development of the computer tool. The tool is rapidly changing, so the full impact of its effect is yet to be assessed. In this presentation, one of us (Klein) has been looking retrospectively over the 45 years during which he has been directly involved.

It is not only an important thing; it is surely a good thing for econometrics, yet the computer may induce side-effects and not realize its full potential. The problems can, perhaps, best be summed up by Robert Summers's cute, but deep, diagram showing a trade-off between *THINK* and *think*.[14] In his pioneering Monte Carlo (sampling experiment), which was an early computer-intensive investigation of sampling distributions for estimates in equation systems, Summers made significant gains by applying *think* to his problems before he used the full power of the computer (*THINK*).

In the pre-computer era, researchers examined their data series carefully, partly because they had to assemble the data themselves and partly because they wanted to have the relationships to be estimated as well specified as possible in advance of getting involved in heavy computational burdens. Data series were scanned side by side; scatter diagrams were examined; time-series diagrams or average Engel curves were studied; researchers tried to anticipate the computed outcomes as well as they could. In a sense, researchers lived with their data samples and understood them well from many angles.

The modern researcher may simply retrieve data from computer files and execute many regression-type estimates in a loose search process. This investigator may not fully appreciate data limitations or singularities. Special considerations for outliers, structural change (temporary or permanent), unusual factors, conceptual difficulties and the like tend to be bypassed. In many cases, it becomes a heavy-handed substitution of *THINK* for *think*. Model-building and estimation become too exploratory, bordering on the practice of data-mining.

Of course it is a technical gain that we can, indeed, be exploratory. That widens our horizons and often leads to discovery, but data-mining can cause seriously misleading conclusions; therefore it is important to keep to limits of prudent combinations of *THINK* and *think*.

If the new generations of econometricians can, in fact, stay closely in touch with their data, even though they are automatically retrieved from a data bank, and if they can stay in close touch with the pictorial shapes of the relationships they are handling, then all the new computer facilities can be of enormous benefit. The computer devices, and associated pieces of hardware in telecommunications, can be of immense pedagogical use and can enable succeeding generations to do more. They must remember, however, that more will be expected and demanded of them in this new era; so they have to keep refining and honing their estimates.

The coming generation will have very powerful micro-devices that they control personally and also the power of future vintages of main-frames – supercomputers. The supercomputer permits the handling of very large masses of data. That helps the single-handed investigator, but, to keep order in such large data files and among so many variables, more than one mind (and one pair of eyes) are important. There will be continuing need for team research on large problems, even though individuals will be able to go further than we had ever thought possible.

These final remarks serve as a suitable introduction to Chapter 16, where we attempt to distil at somewhat greater length the lessons to be learned from macroeconometric model-building.

Notes

1. 'The ET Interview: Professor T. W. Anderson', (by Peter C. B. Phillips) *Econometric Theory*, vol. 2, no. 2, August 1986, pp. 249–88.
2. W. Malenbaum and J. D. Black, 'The Use of the Short-cut Graphic Method of Multiple Correlation', *Quarterly Journal of Economics*, 52 (November 1937) pp. 66–112; 'The Use of the Short-Cut Graphic Method of Multiple Correlation: Comments', by Louis Bean; 'Further Comment', by Mordecai Ezekiel; 'Rejoinder and Concluding Comments', by W. Malenbaum and J. D. Black, *Quarterly Journal of Economics* 54 (February 1940) pp. 318–41, 346–58, 358–64.
3. Frederick V. Waugh, 'Inversion of the Leontief Matrix by Power Series', *Econometrica* 18 (April 1950) pp. 142–54.
4. *Activity Analysis of Production and Allocation*, ed. by T. C. Koopmans (New York: John Wiley, 1951).
5. George B. Dantzig, 'The Programming of Interdependent Activities: Mathematical Model', *Activity Analysis of Production and Allocation*, p. 18.
6. Ibid.
7. Harvey Wagner, 'A Monte Carlo Study of Estimates of Simultaneous Linear Structural Equations', *Econometrica* 26 (January 1958) pp. 117–33; Robert Summers, 'A Capital-Intensive Approach to the Small Sample Properties of Various Simultaneous Equation Estimators', *Econometrica* 33 (January 1965) pp. 1–41.
8. Irma and F. L. Adelman, 'The Dynamic Properties of the Klein–Goldberger Model', *Econometrica* 27 (October 1959) pp. 596–625. See also the summary of their study in Chapter 3 above.
9. George Schink, 'Small Sample Estimates of the Variance–Covariance Matrix of Forecast Errors for Large Econometric Models: The Stochastic Simulation Technique', PhD thesis, University of Pennsylvania, 1971.
10. Benjamin M. Friedman, *Economic Stabilization Policy: Methods in Optimization* (Amsterdam: North-Holland, 1975).

11. See also the discussion of this point in the preceding chapter, where the LINK system is discussed.
12. George Schink, *Small Sample Estimates*.
13. Frederick Sterbenz, 'Stochastic Simulation of the Linkage of Macroeconomic Models and Techniques for Generating Pseudo-Random Vectors with Desirable Properties', PhD thesis, University of Pennsylvania, 1981.
14. Robert Summers, pre-publication presentations of his paper cited above. THINK is an IBM Logo-slogan.

16 Lessons from half a century of macroeconometric modelling*

We have now largely arrived at the end of our story, and the following chapter – our final chapter – presents our necessarily speculative look into the future of macroeconometric modelling. Before we do this, it is probably well to take stock and discuss some of the things that have been learned as a result of the macroeconometric model-building experience. It has now been well over a half a century since Jan Tinbergen built, in the mid-1930s, the first macroeconometric models for the Dutch economy. Reflecting upon this experience, we feel that we can distil 12 major lessons or summary principles that we (as a profession) have learned from this experience. Some of these generalizations will be controversial, but (like the proverbial umpire in the grand American game of baseball), we shall 'call them as we see them'. Because most of the underlying material has been discussed and cited in preceding chapters, our references in this chapter will be sparse, with only genuinely new material appearing in the short bibliographical list at the end of this chapter.

The first generalization (and one of the most important, in our view) is that there does not appear to be a 'Law of Parsimony' in macroeconometric modelling. Simple generalizations, such as a crude quantity theory (or even a more refined one, such as the St Louis macroeconometric model) simply do not stand up to the cruel facts of economic experience. The world is complicated, not simple, and we need large, detailed, complicated systems to interpret this universe, even in approximation. In general, simple formulas, particularly linear and/or bivariate ones, will simply not work. If they appear to do so in some fairly limited set of circumstances, they are bound to fail at some critical point of extrapolation beyond sample limits.[1] For this reason, we need a system – a macroeconometric model – that is as large as we can comfortably manage.[2] The preceding chapter has already indicated that modern computational instruments have greatly extended the size and scope of the macroeconometric model that can be manipulated conveniently.

A second lesson, which is closely related to the first, might be termed the importance of the generalizability of the paradigm. One example of this

*This chapter is in large part a reworking of Lawrence R. Klein's, 'Carrying forward the Tinbergen Initiative in Macroeconometrics', an address (The Tinbergen Lecture) to the Royal Netherlands Economic Society, at the Hague, 24 October 1987; this address has subsequently been published.

lesson concerns the 'cobweb' theory of demand and supply interaction in individual commodity markets, particularly agricultural markets. Broadly and generally speaking, we observe that this hypothesis asserts that the supply of a commodity depends upon historical (lagged) prices that are known up to the time of making a commitment, such as planting a crop. It then asserts that actual market price is determined so that market-clearing occurs and supply and demand quantities are brought into balance.[3] Now if one stands strictly by a crude cobweb hypothesis, one will in general find little statistical support, although there are a few unusual markets where a crude cobweb model does appear to be reasonably accurate. Nevertheless most observable data reject this version of the cobweb model. However, if one formulates an extended cobweb system in which a general lag distribution of prices appears in the supply equation; in which other supply factors (costs, subsidies, natural conditions) are also included; in which other demand factors (income, taxes) besides current prices are introduced; and in which the market-clearing assumption is relaxed by permitting inventory accumulation, then we have the framework of a more elaborate system that appears to fit the facts quite well.[4] Similarly, although the crude accelerator, as formulated by Aftalion or John Maurice Clark, does not appear to explain capital formation very well, a version of the flexible accelerator is often useful in a number of contexts. Another example is the crude liquidity preference hypothesis, which in itself has not held up well to half a century of macroeconometric testing; nevertheless, considered as an element in a more general theory of financial portfolio balance, this approach has been a useful starting-point.

Thirdly, we may observe that the history of macroeconometric model-building is one of slow, steady progress, rather than quantum leaps or paradigm changes. Near the end of a book of this length, it would be otiose to cite examples; in a real sense, we feel that the preceding 15 chapters illustrate this assertion. As we shall indicate below, we feel that this progress has been fuelled principally by four developments: the improvement in computational capacity, improvements in the quality and availability of economic data,[5] developments in econometric theory, and the virtuous circle of improvements in macroeconomic theory and the evolution of macroeconometric models. By contrast, fads come and go, and many ideas that looked extremely promising when they were first presented have turned out either to be a flash in the pan (quite unimportant) or else a modest addition to the macroeconometric model-builder's intellectual capital. It would be ungracious to cite particular examples here, although the reader will doubtlessly have her/his particular illustration of this proposition. By contrast, it is our view that genuine, major breakthroughs are extremely rare.

A fourth lesson is the importance of financial factors, with their repercussions on the real economy. As we recall from Chapter 2, Tinbergen's League of Nations model of the prewar US economy had an endogenous explanation of the level of stock market prices, which had important effects on the consumption function and hence on the stability of the US economy. For a time (in the 1950s and 1960s), we appeared to be moving away from this approach, but recent vintages of US macroeconometric models have returned to this seminal insight of Tinbergen's concerning the importance of financial factors; one may cite the recent Wharton Models, the MPS Model, and especially the DRI Model with its complete financial submodel of the flow of funds. In the field of world models constructed on the basis of systems of national and regional models, we note that a satisfactory modelling of the determination of exchange rates will require an accurate modelling of capital flows.[6] At present, there is a particularly great challenge in this area because of the current importance of financial innovations. The technical changes that are taking place in telecommunications and the use of computers in international financial markets pose challenging problems for econometricians. In turn, this calls for new econometric work at the international level because the instruments have such a high degree of substitutability that what happens in any one market quickly spreads to others. As the problem and its manifestations in the form of capital flows are truly global, they must be modelled on a global (that is, international) basis. In turn, this has important implications for possible major disturbances such as world debt crises, which conventional modelling of the real side of the world's national economies cannot encapsulate.

Fifthly, we should argue that, in macroeconometric model-building, as in macroeconomic theory generally, critical tests are extremely rare. (This point of course is not unrelated to our third generalization above, namely the predominance of slow, steady progress, and the usual absence of quantum leaps or paradigm changes.) In general, nature is not kind enough to present us with data that approximate a controlled experiment, to permit us to distinguish easily between (among) two (or more) competing theories. Our own preference is for forecasting (particularly *ex ante* forecasting, which is the type that is used in practical applications of the macroeconometric models) as a basis for attempting to weed out inferior (that is, less accurate) models. Indeed, we firmly believe that forecasting, because it provides a severe testing ground for models and their uses,[7] is the ultimate test for our subject, the 'bottom line' in the parlance of the business community. We believe that, if a disinterested party looks at all the evidence that has become available over the years, he or she will find that the best (in the sense of the most accurate) forecasts have been made on the basis of models in the Main Stream tradition. Until the challengers – the exponents of rational expectations, the time-series analysts, or the consensus surveyors – can produce a better record under a number of replications, we feel that the tentative verdict has to be on the side of the Main Stream model.[8] Two recent studies of American macroeconometric models and their forecasting performances tend to bear this out. Charles Wolf's study (1987) suggests that two Main Stream American models, those of Data Resources, Inc. and of Wharton Econometrics, score very highly for the first half of the 1980s and certainly well above repetitive forecasts that use different approaches, such as personal judgement or consensus among many independent forecasters. By contrast, the recent results of Stephen McNees of the Federal Reserve Bank of Boston (1987) are not quite so unequivocal. McNees finds that the model-based forecasts are mixed in comparison with the consensus forecasts, but certainly not worse. He also finds that the time-series forecasts by either single equation ARIMA methods or multivariate autoregression (sometimes called VAR) methods both have mixed forecast performance records in comparison to those of the structural models. After a brief history of comparatively favourable results, the time-series methods have recently had much more difficulty in reproducing the measured data. These methods have been particularly weak recently (late 1980s) in forecasting inflation and interest rate movements. And the lack of structure in the system has interfered with the improvement of the inflation and interest rate forecasts, because, when systems are built that attempt to correct for defects in the treatment of these variables, such corrections bring down the effectiveness of the handling of the real variables.

A sixth lesson is the consideration that linearity is usually at best only a helpful approximation. Linearity is a very helpful assumption in many estimation problems, and the solution of a system of linear equations is obviously much easier than when some important non-linearity is introduced into the system.[9] Nevertheless one can progress only so far with hypotheses of linearity. Often some key relationships which are approximately linear over some range of experience become non-linear in a critical interval. Some early examples of this include the various business cycle models of Hicks, Goodwin, Kaldor, Kalecki and others. Another example, which appears to have more importance in the contemporary scene, is the issue of the point at which there is a regime change so that a dynamic system moves from stable (non-accelerating) inflation into accelerating inflation.

A seventh generalization is the importance of the computer, as discussed in the preceding chapter. At the outset of our story, rapid computation was impossible, and many ingenious tricks of computation were necessary to calculate regression coefficients, to obtain approximate solutions and to make truncated forecasts. The arrival of the electronic computer changed all that. At present, searching, testing, experimentation and repetitive policy analysis have become much richer and more informative than they were during the first quarter-century of macroeconometric modelling. For instance, many of Professor Tinbergen's approximations and linearizations (see Chapter 2 above) would not have been necessary in the computer age. This marvellous tool of research has itself developed considerably in the past decade. While the main-frame computer still has its uses (for medium to large macroeconometric models), the increasing sophistication of the computer chip has led to a branching in two directions. Personal computers (or mini- or desktop computers) are useful for solving small macroeconometric models, or even for making calculations with peripheral or satellite models driven by a general purpose macroeconometric model. On the other hand, the use of the supercomputer to solve large systems of linked national macroeconometric models has also been mentioned in the preceding chapter.

An eighth generalization is the importance of the continuing development of econometric theory. To take two examples, the problem of simultaneous equations biases, first stated with great clarity by Haavelmo in the 1940s, was first overcome (in general) in the late 1940s and early 1950s by the maximum likelihood estimators (either full information or limited). In the late 1950s, Theil's two-stage least squares technique added a considerable computational simplicity, and often was found to be superior in the small sample on the basis of Monte Carlo experiments. However refinements of the simultaneous equations estimators continue to be made, often to take account of special problems. In recent years, Amemiya, Fair and others have developed simultaneous equations estimators that handle simultaneously the problem of first-degree autocorrelation in the disturbance terms of the structural equations.

Another example is the problem of distributed lags. Some of Tinbergen's techniques pointed up in Chapter 2 (fractional lags) can be thought of as an approximation to distributed lags. In the 1950s, the development of the Koyck technique (either in standard form or, later, with a slight modification) revolutionized the field. The Almon or polynomial lag in the 1960s was a quantum improvement, and technical improvements in this area have continued to take place. Indeed the rise of the theory of rational expectations has given added impetus to the study of distributed lags, on the one hand, and to the development of suitable econometric methods to handle models with these characteristics, on the other.[10]

A ninth generalization is the mutually reinforcing role, from the outset in the 1930s to the present time, of macroeconometric model-building and macroeconomic theory. We shall not attempt to buttress this assertion with examples; rather, we trust that the preceding 15 chapters contain numerous illustrations of these assertions. Instead, we should like to highlight our interpretation of the history. In general, macroeconomic theory, which preceded macroeconometric modelling historically, has provided a very solid foundation for the macroeconometric model-building. This has been true as macroeconomic theory was being reconstructed during the 1930s, during the days of the dominance of Keynesian theory, and also during recent years, when there has been less of a consensus about the appropriate type of macroeconomic theory to employ. However, conversely, the lessons from macroeconometric model-building have served to refine macroeconomic theory and at times even to call into question some of its accepted propositions. For instance (a single exception to our refusal to provide examples), our knowledge of the time path of the standard expenditures multiplier of Main Stream Keynesian theory has benefited greatly from the decades of work that macroeconometric model-builders have accomplished in this regard.

A tenth lesson (one that we are still in the process of learning) concerns the possibility of improving our *ex ante* forecasts by combining the model-based forecasts with time-series methods. As noted above (point 5), we have argued that the model-based forecasts dominate their rivals (judgement forecasts, simple consensus methods based on these, and time-series techniques) for any reasonably long period of time. While this is true, it must be admitted (see Malinvaud (1981) or Gordon (1987), especially pp. 373–7) that at times model-based forecasts in themselves may not be accurate enough for all users.[11] Now it has long been known by many applied economists that the combination of model forecasts in itself can reduce the risk of error. In particular, the variance of forecasts can be reduced in this way. This is very much like the investment principle of portfolio diversification in order to reduce risks (lower the variance) of anticipated returns. In addition to the reduction of risk, there is the possibility that even the absolute levels of accuracy may be improved, in this manner.

Similarly, we are suggesting the combination of forecasts for high frequency intervals (such as monthly, weekly or even daily) from time-series models with quarterly predictions from the structural macroeconometric models. The time-series models could be either VAR or single-equation ARIMA types. Various research centres are pursuing this path in their individual ways, but our suggestion is to use the time-series methods for very short-run forecasts, say up to six months duration. It has been observed that ARIMA methods, by capturing the details of serial dependence inherent in an economy, do well in forecasting for very short periods ahead. (Although they do not do uniformly better than the structural models, they do approximately as well, and for selected variables even better.) In particular, an advantage of using ARIMA methods is that they can capture the very latest pieces of information as these become available in reports which are released daily. One day it is orders, then inventories, then prices, then foreign trade, then retail sales and so on. Of course, there are always daily financial reports. These high-frequency data are published rapidly, often with little more than 30 days' delay in reporting time. Hence, early in a given quarter, the overall patterns of economic activity begin to build up and can be gauged on the basis of these reports. Now this 'latest news' is not neglected by model-builders' forecasts, but it is not systematically assimilated. We are suggesting that such information be incorporated in the estimated values of the disturbance terms.[12] In the past such constant adjustments have been made in *ex ante* forecasting, but generally subjectively and approximately, a practice that has been severely criticized by non-model-builders.

Instead of assigning estimated values to the disturbance terms in the usual way, we might choose such adjustments (ideally, as few as possible) to force the model solution to agree with the ARIMA predictions from high-frequency data over the coming three to six months (that is, the next quarter or two). These adjustments should then be left in the equation system for the operation of the model over the entire forecast horizon. Such a procedure has the advantage of making the adjustments more objective and (in principle) scientifically replicable. If more and better high-frequency data are studied carefully, we may incorporate so much more new information that forecast accuracy can only be improved. Indeed, this is one promising line of attack on the problem of prediction error that seems appropriate to the information age, in which data are available with greater speed and wider coverage. Computer and telecommunications facilities enable us to process and use this information to advantage; herein lie the potential gains to be realized.

An eleventh generalization refers to the importance of the stochastic element in macroeconometric models, which of course is the basis for stochastic simulations of these models. Even before the era of macroeconometric models, Slutsky had shown that the process of drawing random perturbations, combined with an economic process that was something like the procedure of taking moving averages, could generate cycles. As we noted in Chapter 1, Ragnar Frisch expanded on this insight, to produce a complete model of the business cycle based on stochastic disturbances striking the system, which then responded in a cyclical manner (the rocking horse analogy). In Chapter 3, we reviewed the Adelmans' classic study with the Klein–Goldberger Model; an important lesson that was learned from this study would appear to be that stochastic disturbances play an essential role in the explanation of the business cycle. Over the years, one of us (Lawrence R. Klein) has come to appreciate this problem more and more. Although the pre-computer age focused principally on the characteristic roots of linear systems (the propagation problem, in Frisch's terminology), we feel that the stochastic aspect of the problem is even more interesting. The theoretical work was outlined by Slutsky and Frisch (as noted above), as well as by Yule and Kalecki, but statistical investigations became possible during the computer age, under the heading of stochastic simulation. Some cycle properties that are peculiar to economics need a non-linear explanation, but we feel that a damped system, or a stable non-linear limit cycle, in conjunction with a random perturbation with suitable properties, gives an excellent approximation to reality. Again, we cannot rule out all competing views, but some simple deterministic models of the cycle do appear to be inferior to those associated with stochastic simulation of the large-scale macroeconometric models. In this connection, an area of great interest is the possible stochastic simulation of the large, internationally linked systems of macroeconometric models. For this problem, the covariances of the disturbances across countries make the calculations difficult but highly realistic. While stochastic simulations of internationally linked models in small, simplified systems have been carried out, it is only recently, with the power of the supercomputer, that it has become feasible to consider this problem in the context of full-size world models, like project LINK.

A final generalization is the point that, in practice, macroeconometric model-building proceeds iteratively.[13] In practice, we do not know enough simply to estimate the parameters of a fully specified model; in consequence, we start with an initial model, test its properties against theoretical and statistical desiderata (for either a single equation or for a full system), and then respecify the system.[14] Usually, several rounds of iteration are required before the model-builder is (for the moment) satisfied, but refinement of the model is a never-ending process for the large model-building projects, such as Wharton or DRI, Inc. In any case, it can readily be conceded that, in the present state of the discipline, macroeconometric model-building is at least as much of an art as it is a set of scientific procedures.

In conclusion, we find that many interesting lessons have been absorbed in the course of over half a century of macroeconometric modelling. Of course, this is not to imply that progress in macroeconometric model-building has been linear, or even monotonic or continuous. Some setbacks have occurred and, with the wisdom of hindsight, many things might have been done differently. But progress there has been, and we feel that our knowledge of the 'real world' macroeconomy is considerably greater today than it was half a century ago. In the final chapter, we engage in some non-econometric forecasting and project our views of the likely future of this discipline, as well as considering some of the criticisms to which this approach has been subjected in recent years.

Notes

1. Thus the St Louis Model of the US economy predicted price level experience reasonably well in the tranquil 1960s, but missed almost completely the inflation explosions associated with the supply shocks of the 1970s, to the point where the principal builders of this model asserted that theirs was not a model for forecasting price level developments. This was readily admitted by Andersen and Carlson (1974, p. 324) after a few years of experience with their model.

2. Michael D. Intriligator (1978, pp. 458–9) has a nice discussion of the optimal scale of a macroeconometric model, applying the marginal principle (abstractly) to this question. Intriligator argues that if the marginal cost of model-building falls (say, as a result of lower computational or data-management costs), then (with an unchanged relationship of benefits to scale), the optimal size of the macroeconometric model would become larger. In fact, this appears to have been the case, at least over the past quarter-century and perhaps throughout the history of macroeconometric modelling.

3. Parenthetically, we may note that some modern theorists, following a rational expectations or efficient markets approach, have argued that the (simple) cobweb model cannot possibly prevail because economic agents will be able to work out in advance the results of such price-quantity interactions and will take profitable actions that would eliminate the oscillations in question.

4. Again parenthetically, we may note that the statistical forecasts of such an extended cobweb model, if also adjusted by the results of a short-run time-series model such as an ARIMA system (as explained below), are at least as good as (and probably better than) predictions generated by an alternative model incorporating both the efficient markets hypothesis and rational expectations (model-consistent predictions).

5. In particular, the current generation of model-builders has much longer runs of consistent data (often in machine-readable form), owing to the patient efforts of data gatherers over the past half-century.

6. In particular, one of the great simplifications of the first half of the twentieth century, Gustav Cassel's purchasing power parity theory of the various national exchange rates, abstracted from financial factors in general and capital flows in particular. Today we know that this is a grievous oversimplification. For instance, the overvaluation of the US dollar during the first half of the 1980s cannot be explained in the absence of a reasonable theory of capital flows.

7. For simple or even complex goodness-of-fit tests (such as full-model simulation within the sample period), there is always some forcing of the fit. For this reason, confronting the model with a sample of data that is virtually independent of the period to which it has been fitted obviously requires the model to be more 'robust', in the sense of accurately describing a wider range of experience.

8. Of course, one can learn much from the critiques of the conventional approach to macroeconometric model-building. Thus (as we develop in the tenth lesson below), autoregressive corrections applied to the disturbance terms of the structural equations can improve forecasts, sometimes markedly, and the rational expectations critique has raised, at a minimum, the entire question of the optimal incorporation of lags into the modelling process. (The rational expectations critique of Main Stream macroeconometric modelling is further discussed, in slightly more detail, in the concluding chapter.) Nevertheless, at present the central approach to forecasting is the use of Main Stream models, with the other approaches making only peripheral contributions.

9. The development of a general algorithm (usually based on the Gauss-Seidel technique) for solving a system of equations with standard non-linearities has been one of the major breakthroughs of the past quarter-century.
10. A seminal article in this area has been the paper by Kenneth F. Wallis (1980), in which (among other things) the statistical properties of models incorporating rational expectations are explored and some suitable estimators (in this context) are suggested.
11. Gordon (1987) even goes so far as to speak of 'the failure of forecasting'!
12. It is interesting to note that Arnold Zellner, in a piece (1979) that is generally critical of macroeconometric model-building, argues that there are great possibilities for improving forecast accuracy by combining traditional econometric modelling with the newer time-series analysis. He calls this approach SEMTSA (for Structural Econometric Modeling Time-Series Analysis) and appears to feel that this is the route to take, in order to remedy most of the defects of (then) existing macroeconometric models.
13. This is another one of Zellner's major points, in the 1979 article already mentioned.
14. As David A. Belsley and Edwin Kuh state, in a comment (1979) on the Zellner article, 'Econometricians have long been classroom theorists and closet pragmatists' (p. 644).

References

Anderson, Leonall C. and Keith Carlson (1974) 'St. Louis Model Revisited', *International Economic Review*, vol. 15, no. 2 (June) pp. 305–27.

Belsley, David A. and Edwin Kuh (1979) 'Comment' [on an article by Arnold Zellner], *Journal of the American Statistical Association*, vol. 74, no. 367 (September) pp. 643–5.

Gordon, Robert J. (1987) *Macroeconomics*, 4th edn (Boston and Toronto: Little, Brown and Company).

Intriligator, Michael D. (1978) *Econometric Models, Techniques, and Applications* (Englewood Cliffs, New Jersey: Prentice-Hall).

Klein, Lawrence R. (1988) *Carrying Forward the Tinbergen Initiative in Macroeconometrics*, Tinbergen Lecture to the Royal Netherlands Economic Association, 24 October 1987 (The Hague: The Royal Netherlands Economic Association, 1987). (This paper, on which this chapter is largely based, has also been reprinted in *De Economist*, vol. 136, no. 1 (1988) pp. 3–21.)

Malinvaud, E. (1981) 'Economics Faced with the Needs of Macroeconomic Policy', *Econometrica*, vol. 49, no. 6 (November) pp. 1363–75.

McNees, S. K. (1987) 'The Accuracy of Two Forecasting Techniques: Some Evidence and an Interpretation', *New England Economic Review*, March/April, pp. 20–31.

Wallis, Kenneth F. (1980) 'Econometric Implications of the Rational Expectations Hypothesis', *Econometrica*, vol. 48, no. 1 (January) pp. 49–73.

Wolf, Charles (1987) 'Scoring the Economic Forecasters', *The Public Interest*, no. 88 (Summer) pp. 48–55.

Zellner, Arnold (1979) 'Statistical Analysis of Econometric Models', *Journal of the American Statistical Association*, vol. 74, no. 367 (September) pp. 628–43.

17 Prospects for macroeconometric modelling

In the past 16 chapters, we have looked at the history of macroeconometric model-building, both in terms of individual developments and also in terms of more general developments. It is now time to look at prospective future developments, for the remainder of the current century and into the next. Of course, some of the discussion of the preceding chapter contained implicit forecasts of prospective future developments; but it is time to be more explicit. One point should be made clear: we have no explicit 'model' of the development of technology in the subdiscipline of macroeconometric modelling, so our 'forecasting' in this chapter is definitely of the impressionistic variety (and hence contrary to what we should recommend in the case of a 'real-world' national economy!).

1 A growth sector

During the great build-up of constructive applications of econometric models of the macroeconomy during the 1960s and 1970s, which coincided with the rapid introduction of the electronic computer, econometrics, in a commercial sense, became known as a growth industry. An entire industry was founded in the form of econometric consulting firms, but the growth concept extended beyond the expansion of sales of econometric services in the market place. Scholarly econometric activity also expanded commensurately with the growth of the industry. Scholarly journals (such as the *Journal of Econometrics, Empirical Economics, Journal of Quantitative Economics, Economic Modelling* and *Journal of Policy Modeling*) were founded, and the econometric content of other, more general journals expanded.

The recession of the early 1980s, the election of a government in the United States that appeared hostile to the modelling concept and the spread of competition in the market-place gave the impression to some observers that the expansion curve had levelled off. But the seeming slowdown of growth was only temporary. As far as commercial activity is concerned, significant growth remains to be captured in international modelling, in areas outside the United States (especially Europe, Japan and the developing countries) and in new areas of research, the market for foreign exchange being a notable case. Good samples of data, the grist for the econometrician's mill, are just becoming available in the field of exchange rate estimation, since the period of floating rates dates only from 1973. After the recession of 1981–2, commercial activity in econometrics resumed its strong upward course again (up to the present time: autumn 1989).

Scholarly activity is also growing, especially in developing and centrally-planned economies. Model-building is a natural tool for development planning in these countries. A misleading opinion that there was too much exogeneity and too little market influence for the successful application of econometric models, let alone their meaningful construction, in such economies has been refuted by the preparation of models for most of the centrally-planned and developing countries. Two bottlenecks have been the lack of availability of usable statistical samples and the shortage of trained personnel. Over a time-span of some 20 or more years, both these obstacles have been overcome. There is now a fair, though far from adequate, data base and a good cadre of econometricians – some self-educated and some trained in institutions of North America, Japan, Europe, Australia and elsewhere. This growth area may prove to be very large in the years to come.

A reason why some people may have thought that they detected a levelling-off in the growth rate of activity in macroeconometrics is that the methodology is becoming so widely accepted. In earlier days, when the econometric approach was struggling for attention, its take-off was quite apparent. Now this approach is taken for granted. The current generation of students is almost completely computer-oriented and, with the computer, the building of models is a natural, straightforward step. It is almost second nature for them to formulate a problem in a quantitative mould, program its analysis on the computer (either the main-frame or the personal computer), and try to work out a solution. Facilities are now so favourable for the econometric approach that it is almost effortlessly implemented. People do an accepted and expected thing; so the growth aspect goes unnoticed.

The econometrics industry achieved greatest commercial growth through the delivery medium of time-sharing, that is, by remote terminal access to a large main-frame computer. In the present era and the period ahead, time-sharing will continue to be used for some problems but probably not as a commercial growth sector. Instead, there is already a marked shift to distributed processing through the medium of microprocessors, used either in a self-contained fashion or in a down-loading and up-loading relationship with large main-frame computers.

The spread of commercial growth will be different because microprocessing is much less expensive. But in terms of econometric activity there is bound to be enormous growth because the micro-processor opens so many easily accessible horizons to the model-builder.

2   Two extremes

Tinbergen's first model of the United States (not his first model, as indicated in Chapter 6) was bigger than textbook models, although not large by modern standards. Klein's early models, reverting to the Keynesian paradigm, tended to be smaller. Then models expanded greatly in size. As we noted in the preceding chapter, the computer made this possible.

There will be a continuing tendency for econometricians to build large models – larger and larger to meet the highly diversified needs of the user community, where specificity together with the macro picture is very demanding. But at the same time a new development in computation has occurred, and it is having some effect on the scope of model-building. There is a distinct tendency to prepare small models, of approximately 10 equations (or fewer) for treatment on a micro computer. Management of data files, sophisticated estimation methods, simulation and many other analytical statistics for the behaviour of models can be readily and speedily implemented. The inexpensive, accessible and self-contained nature of this process is very attractive for the complete econometric treatment of small models, with ever-informative graphic and tabular displays.

While the micro computer is ideal for the study of small models in both research and teaching, it should be noted that it is getting more and more powerful, but not necessarily larger – in size or in cost. The significance of these facts is that fairly large models can also be handled well on the personal computer. It is fully recognized that the models of 50 or more equations tend to become 'black boxes' and not readily understood visually. Intensive personal use on the small computer with good graphics can lend transparency to the 'black box', and so promote understanding through experience. The computer power of the micro-processor is enlarging the capability of model analysis to systems of up to 1000 equations.

There are these reasons to look for more work to be done with small systems and continuing work with conventionally sized systems. But there are also arguments for going to the other extreme, namely the construction and use of the very large system, now considered to be a model of some 10 000 or more equations. A major case of such a large system is an international model like that of project LINK, consisting of many standard-sized models of individual countries.[1] It is called the multi-model system. This is not the only large-scale computing problem that goes with a large model; systems that make extensive use of input–output relations tend to be quite large and impose heavy computer requirements. At the same time, their large size is primarily associated with the need to provide industry detail with overall economic performance, and this need is both continuing and growing. Computer developments are expected to be accommodating.

The multi-model problem for international and interregional systems, as well, has been handled progressively over the past few years with conventional main-frame computers. However more can be done with large multi-model systems if an order of magnitude improvement in computer analysis takes place. At the other extreme from the micro-processor we have the supercomputer. Many versions of the supercomputer have an architecture that is well suited to the multi-model problem; it is an architecture of parallel processing. Each model, in the multi-model system, can be simultaneously processed, instead of being done in a serial fashion; this is a key for speeding up the calculation of the world system, on the basis of the individual country components.[2]

3 Errors of forecasting

In connection with large-scale computer needs, the problem of error in the presentation of forecasts was mentioned and briefly discussed. This problem deserves lengthier consideration in its own right.

It is now routine to have probability limits accompany weather forecasts, and public opinion results often have measures of statistical significance of the point spread presented. In a close election contest, the pollster will frequently say that the estimated outcome is 'too close to call', meaning that the point spread between candidates is less than the width of the associated error band. Political pollsters have had their 'knuckles rapped' so severely in cases of large mistakes in US elections (for example, Landon v. Roosevelt, 1936; Dewey v. Truman, 1948) that they have found it essential to report the error band associated with a forecast. This error band may be substantially widened by the fact that a non-trivial number of the respondents may be unable or unwilling to state a preference, and there is no guarantee that these non-respondents mirror at all the committed portion of the population.

Results from macroeconometric model simulations should be routinely presented as

$$\hat{y}_{T+F} \pm k\hat{S}_y$$

where $\hat{y}_{T+F}$ is the forecast value of y in period F, after the end of the sample T, and k is a multiple associated with a given degree of probability (the higher the probability of enclosing the 'true' value, the larger the value of k). $\hat{S}y$ is an estimate of the standard error or forecast.

The formulas for estimated standard errors of forecast are formidable for large systems. In principle they take into account the errors associated with (1) random disturbances, (2) sampling variability of the system's parameter estimates (variance and covariance), and (3) the magnitude of exogenous or lagged endogenous variables. For small systems, it is possible to use the formulas developed by Goldberger, Nagar and Odeh (1961). For large systems, it seems best to use the Monte Carlo approach of George Schink (1971). In any event, non-linearity would suggest a Monte Carlo approach.

From time to time, forecast errors have been evaluated for main magnitudes of individual models; this is helpful in an indicative sense, but it would be more satisfactory to have all forecast error estimates of all the endogenous variables and an appropriate degree of probability.

The ability to do this, at least in principle, is one of the great advantages of the econometric modelling approach. Some other methods of forecasting or policy analysis are not well suited to the presentation of error bands. The formula for the variance of forecast error for a projection of an endogenous variable from a linear model is:

$$Var \, \hat{y}_{T+F} = F_{T+F} \, \Omega_\pi \, F'_{T+F} + \sum_v$$

where F_{T+F} is an $n \times mn$ matrix display of exogenous variables at forecast period $T+F$, $\Omega\pi$ is an $mn \times mn$ covariance matrix of derived estimated reduced form coefficients ($\pi = A^{-1}B$), and $\sum_v$ is an $n \times n$ covariance matrix of reduced form disturbances ($A^{-1}e_t$). The associated model is $Ay_t + Bx_t = e_t$. There are n endogenous variables (y_t) and m exogenous variables (x_t). (It is assumed that there are no lagged endogenous variables appearing in the model, which is an obvious limitation, but one that could be taken into account.)

The system may be approximated linearly in the neighbourhood of the solution value, and then the formula can be evaluated for that approximate system, or replicated stochastic simulation techniques can be used to generate a whole distribution of forecasts, and the variance of this distribution can be computed. Either approach will be very computer-intensive, but this should be done with every forecast in the future in order to know what is expected with regard to accuracy.

At the same time, a comprehensive record has been compiled by Stephen McNees and associates for a wide variety of variables and models covering the period (by quarters) since 1970.[3] From these tabulations we can compute absolute and squared deviations from actual values, appropriately averaged. This gives experienced error, not expected error based on estimated distributions of stochastic elements. Probability measures to be associated with McNees's tabulations are not known, but his records are extremely valuable in showing what can be learned from experience.

4   Control theory applications

Control theory applied to economic systems is, like error analysis, interesting in its own right, quite apart from the computational issues involved. It is not necessarily the case that control theory will be used to try to control the actual economy or make policy directly, in an optimal way. The principal contribution of control theory to macroeconometric modelling is to teach us something about the properties of estimated systems. By pushing a system towards stringent target values, we learn whether or not it behaves well under stress and whether the optimal values of instrument variables make sense. If the system produces unacceptable results, in terms of extreme values for instruments, or if it is pushed into forbidden territory (violating limits of non-negativity, for example), we may have reason to question the specification or estimated structure of the system.

Also, we have little guidance for the choice of exogenous inputs into the medium (five year) or long-run (ten or more years) forecasts. Control theory methods can be used to find *baseline* values of the inputs (exogenous instrument variables) which will bring the system towards *balanced growth paths* or paths with well established long-run properties, such as:

1. real growth rate = real interest rate;
2. labour's share = constant;
3. personal saving rates = constant.

In connection with the multi-model problem for the LINK system, an interesting application of control theory was used in order to determine numerically the degree of perceived 'overvaluation' of the US dollar in 1984. During the closing years of the Bretton Woods system of fixed parities among currencies, the exchange rates for each country were taken as exogenous variables – fixed by international agreement. An approach for estimating exchange rates is to set a series of targets for current account or trade balances for each country and to ask, through the methods of control theory, what estimated exchange rate values would bring the countries of the world to their balance of payments targets simultaneously over a period of two years. This is the special case, first pointed out by Jan Tinbergen (1956), where the number of targets and instruments are equal. If the control theory calculation is done appropriately, we should find a zero value for the loss function

$$L(y_1 - y_1{}^*, y_2 - y_2{}^*, \ldots, y_n - y_n{}^*)$$

where $L(0, 0, \ldots, 0) = 0$ and $y_i{}^*$ is the target for the ith variable y_i, $i = 1, 2,$ $\ldots, n$. Calculation of this problem was done in 1984, and existing trade balances were modified by reducing the surplus positions of Japan and West Germany considerably and by allocating about one-half of this reduction towards the improvement of the US balance and the remaining portion to the remaining trading partners. The control theory calculation seemed to suggest that the US dollar was overvalued by roughly 30 per cent in 1984, a very plausible result, given the large number of other independent calculations which also came to this approximate value.[4]

When these and other control theory applications have been made routine in model testing, estimation and use (application), we shall have made an important step forward. There is every reason to expect this to happen in the near future.

5 Lags and expectations

Of all the refinements in econometric methodology, none is more important in contributing to better results than the elaborate and sophisticated use of economic dynamics in specifying the structure of economic systems. Deep and extensive exploration of lag structure has done at least as much, and probably more, good in improving econometric model performance than all other refinements in estimation procedure or methodology.

Over the years we have progressed from using one, two or three period lags, freely estimated, to using geometric lags (applying Koyck transformations), to Almon polynominal lag distributions, Shiller lag distributions, Pascal lag distributions, and rational polynomial lag distributions. These are all important steps, some more general than others, but each contributing to our better understanding of dynamic structure.

The advances were made possible through the exploitation of the computer because search or iteration is usually involved. The most important aspect of the advance has been the freeing of our ability to estimate lags in several variables simultaneously. The general expression for a single equation (the ith equation of a system) is:

$$\alpha_i(L)\, y_t + \beta_i(L)\, x_t = \gamma_i(L)\, e_t$$

where:

α_i, β_i and γ_i = row vectors of parameters associated with equation i;
y_t = column vector of endogenous variables;
x_t = column vector of exogenous variables;

e_t = column vector of lagged values of the scalar variable e_{it}, the error
  term associated with equation i at time t; and
L = lag operator, that is, $L^j z_t = z_{t-j}$.

In a sense, if we can search, with the computer, for the best Box-Jenkins estimate of the ith relation, in the sense that the *equilibrium* or steady-state form of the equation satisfies *a priori* economic restrictions, then we shall have good system dynamics.

Economic theory is often fairly explicit about the foundations for the equilibrium form of the equation but offers practically no guidance about the underlying dynamics. That part is empirical and therefore computer-intensive. The importance of lag distribution specification is that it restricts the parameter space for the feasible set of estimates and therefore conserves degrees of freedom, as well as offering some protection against multicollinearity.

A school of thought about the structure of lag distributions is the so-called 'rational expectations' school, who assert that economic agents use the dynamic model solution to project their own expected values, thus implying a specific lag distribution. As suggested in the preceding chapter, however, there is an identification problem, which makes it unlikely that we shall be able to discriminate in specification between the lag distributions generated by 'rational expectations' and those generated by assuming one of the well-known *a priori* distributions.

To the extent that economic behaviour establishes agents' reactions to *expected* values, we might try to estimate explicitly, rather than implicitly, the lag distributions associated with the formation of expectations. In this respect, a promising area of research is the collection of agents' stated expectations from sample surveys, and the estimation of the relevant equations for relationships of reaction as well as the relationships showing how the stated expectations are determined by empirical equations containing lag distributions.

In a simple case, we should have:

$$y_{1t} = f(y^*_{2t}) + e_t$$
$$y^*_{2t} = g\,(y_{1,t-1}, y_{1,t-2}, \ldots, y_{2,t-1}, y_{2,t-2}, \ldots, y_{3,t-1},$$
$$y_{3,t-2}, \ldots, y_{n,t-1}, y_{n,t-2}, \ldots) + u_t,$$

where y^*_{2t} is expected value of y_{2t}. In this illustrative example, y^*_{2t} is made to depend on the chronological evolution of many variables, not simply on its own history.

A great deal of effort has been spent on estimating such equations from consumer and business surveys. Expectation equations generated from such sources are used in some macroeconometric models, and future exploitation of these ideas is likely to be one of the coming developments of our subject.

6   Use of cross-section data

In a broader sense the collection of stated expectations from individual agents can be used in cross-section as well as time-series variation. There is all too little use of cross-section data in the construction of macroeconometric models.

There is a long history of the use of family budget data to estimate Engel curves and associated elasticities. Similarly, inter-establishment or inter-industry data have been used extensively to estimate production functions. These microeconomic relationships may, under some simplifying assumptions, be used for the estimation of aggregative relationships. The key bridging relationship in the aggregation procedure is the underlying distribution function, such as the distribution of income among households or the size distribution of firms.

New advances in understanding and estimating the distribution functions can lend great richness in the specification of macro-models because it enables one to go behind the aggregates and make some estimates of distribution factors. Further work in this direction has the potential of enabling us to build better and more useful models.

The supplementation of aggregative time-series samples with data from cross-sections can lead to a significant improvement in our understanding of behaviour and in developing model structure, but it cannot be a breakthrough. It will simply be incremental. These types of data have been used frequently in the past; so we are not entering an unexplored field of statistical analysis. It is simply a case of not having fully integrated cross-section samples and the associated relationships estimated from them into macroeconometric models as fully as possible.

Every new piece of information helps, and a few pieces may be picked up through our carefully considering micro data from individual economic agents.

7   Flow-of-funds models

A good deal of progress has been made in adding financial detail to macro-models. As we saw in part in Chapter 2, the earliest attempts by Tinbergen put much effort into financial modelling for the United States (and for the United Kingdom). In particular, he investigated the boom–bust cycle of the stock market in the United States during the 1920s and 1930s. He also looked at the development of the UK economy in the era of the gold standard.

Preoccupation with the fiscal structure of Keynesian models diverted some attention from financial aspects, but, in the past quarter-century, when credit crises (or crunches) have had such visibly large effects on macroeconomic performance, it has become imperative to pay more attention again to the financial side of economic structure.

Keynesian models always had a financial sector, and Keynes was personally occupied with financial transactions of a sophisticated nature, but some of the early models, apart from Tinbergen's study of the United States in the 1920s and 1930s, had loosely connected financial and real sectors.

In the reconstruction period following the Second World War, the real economy dominated the situation through the process of demobilization, implementation of the Marshall plan in Europe, and the waging of war in Korea. Once the reconstruction period was completed, interest rates moved in a wide range, and financial markets assumed greater importance.

Many models with elaborate financial content have been built for the Federal Reserve System, for other central banks outside the United States and for non-banking institutions also. Mention must be made of the DRI contribution (Eckstein, Green and Sinai, 1974; Eckstein, 1983), which employed the data in the flow-of-funds accounts. These accounts serve as an elaborate data base for financial models in the same sense that national income accounts and input–output accounts serve real sector models, including real sector models with moderately detailed production sectors.[5]

The flow-of-funds accounts do not have as long a history as do the national income accounts and they contain more data gaps. In general, they are less accurate and less well developed than the national income accounts; nevertheless they are very important and play a strategic role in gaining an understanding of financial behaviour. These accounts attempt to show the flow of transactions involving financial instruments on a 'from-whom'/'to-whom' basis. Financial instruments have issuing agents and holding agents, in stock or level form. The first differences of these stocks are the flows of financial assets and liabilities among the main groups of the domestic macro economy:

commercial banks,
thrift institutions,
the central bank,
the treasury,
insurance companies,
other financial businesses,
non-financial businesses,

households, and
rest-of-the-world.

The process of equating supplies and demands for all instruments determines a set of asset prices. These, in turn, determine interest rates. The 'perpetuity' asset has a simple reciprocal relationship to interest rates:

$$p = 1/r.$$

Finite length bonds and other instruments are related to interest yields in more complicated formulas. But the important issue is that the spectrum of interest rates is determined by the spectrum of instrument prices. This is more specific, and more complicated, than the usual procedure of explaining only a key rate by market equations and spinning off the spectrum of rates through equations of the term structure.

It is more fundamental and ultimately easier to take account of specific institutional features of the financial system to determine rates on mortgages, commercial paper, broker loans, certificates of deposits, retirement accounts, municipal bonds, corporate bonds, bank loans and other instruments by employing supply and demand equations in each of these markets than by doing it in only one (short-term) market and relating other rates to such a key rate.

A full flow-of-funds model is not complete by itself. It needs to be integrated with both national income and input–output models. It appears from the writings of Eckstein and associates (cited above) that this is precisely what has been done in the DRI Model of the US economy, although it has been somewhat difficult to judge, as the description of the individual sectors is sometimes sketchy. In any case, it may be asserted that a complete treatment of the financial sector by means of a flow-of-funds submodel may well be one of the most important contributions that has been made in macroeconometric modelling.

It is worth elaborating a special aspect of the flow-of-funds accounts. Record-keeping has been generally good for international transactions, especially in current price terms. Often it is hard to obtain the associated real and price series that accompany the current value flows. But model-building for the balance of payments is perhaps better known and established.

First, we must account for the flows of imports and exports. This is routine in mainstream macroeconometric models. In world trade or multi-country models, such as Project LINK, the additional detail of bilateral trade flow estimates is also generated by the model. The new feature, however, is the modelling of exchange rates. These rates have been (largely) market-determined for more than a decade; before then, the Bretton Woods system of fixed parities determined exchange rates.

Many of the relevant variables for explaining exchange rates are readily available from macro-models of the real economy and for world trade. But large and volatile capital flows between pairs of countries are not yet very well understood. Why does financial capital leave some shores and enter others? This is inherently a difficult question and we do not have good answers yet. We do not even have good data on bilateral capital flows between nations.[6]

Special modelling of international capital flows and estimation of exchange rates from the equating of supply and demand for currencies are problems that are attracting a great deal of attention from econometricians and are sure to result in some new knowledge.[7] A partial filling of the gaps remaining in flow-of-funds modelling will be taken care of by this research, and the solution of problems of building international macro-models will be advanced. In a limited way, it is possible that a breakthrough could occur here.

8 International modelling

The capital flow/exchange rate problems discussed in connection with flow-of-funds model-building represent but one of several different directions being followed in international model-building. Work will continue in project LINK, the OECD Interlink Model, the Japanese EPA model of the world economy, the Federal Reserve Multi-Country Model, and others with much attention focused on the OECD (industrial market) economies. Two other groups of countries will also be the subject of both national model-building efforts and internationally linked efforts. These are the developing countries (LDC) and the centrally-planned economies (CPE).[8] In the case of China, there are joint aspects of LDC and CPE model-building.

For the most part, data for the LDCs and the CPEs are less available and less reliable. The usual time frame is annual, with data spans existing over two or three decades. The problem is thus constrained, but headway is being made. All the socialist countries of Eastern Europe, the USSR and China have had models estimated for their economies.[9] Many, but not all, developing countries have been modelled. There are sure to be more than 90 different developing countries for which models are available.[10]

These models have special features. The socialist systems must be built around the planning process. The LDC models must be sensitive to special export lines (often primary commodities), migrant workers, essential imports (capital and materials), servicing of external debts, and income distribution.

The econometric study of individual countries in the CPE or LDC categories has progressed far and will continue to improve with the study of single countries. Within Project LINK, the most recent research step has been to add some 30 or 40 LDC Models to those of the OECD and CPE regions already present on an individual country basis, and to integrate these models into the linkage mechanisms. In the spring of 1988, the matrices of trade in the worldwide LINK system consisted of 79 rows and columns, a formidable undertaking. There are many good years of research activity which remain to be taken up in polishing and augmenting models for developing countries; therefore this looks like an attractive direction for future work.

9   The reduction of exogeneity

Economic behaviour is a major part of societal behaviour; however it is obvious that the explanation of economic behaviour can fruitfully be expanded along research lines established in other disciplines. Promising work in neighbouring disciplines span demography, criminology, health, psychology, and engineering.

Demography already appears in macro-models and has been considered for a long time – since Malthus, in a sense, or since model-builders recognized at an early stage that per-capita formulations of economic relationships were advantageous. But, generally speaking, population size and composition were introduced as exogenous variables that had impacts on the economy without there being adequate analysis to explain population dynamics in their own right. Now there is much more concern with modelling population characteristics through birth rates, fertility rates, death rates, rates of immigration and emigration, and age–sex–race distributions of labour force, employment, income or wage earnings. The beginnings of an endogenous treatment of demography are in place, but much more needs to be done, and it can be expected that future models will go much further in this regard. Endogenous treatment of population should contribute to an overall improvement in accuracy and, for long-term models, this is a necessity. This is especially true in model-building for developing countries, where population characteristics are of predominant importance. But, most of all, the generation of population variables in econometric applications – projections, scenarios, policy simulations, multiplier analysis – will be another manifestation of the tendency to provide immediately useful information for users of model results. In specific industries, economic analysts need to know about the size of the infant, teenage, adult or aged population. Government policy – for social security retirement programmes, Medicare, unemployment compensation, disability pay – leans heavily on demographic projections, which ideally should go hand-in-hand with economic projections.

While demography may be the first externally related area to be incorporated endogenously into macroeconometric models, it is certainly not the only one. Criminal activity is already in the data base, implicitly, as crime in the form of shoplifting or theft from businesses shows up as a transfer payment (business to household sector) in the national income accounts, while the under-reporting of income from criminal operations may be partially embedded in the statistical discrepancy of the accounts. (Of course, conceptually the income from criminal activities does not form a part of national income, while the social costs of law enforcement are indeed a part of GNP, on both the expenditures and the income sides of the national accounts.) Crime is influenced by the state of the economy and has some feedback on the macro economy; therefore an explanation of its influence, together with related economic variables, should be integrated into models. The financial sums associated with crime are far from trivial. Since they play roles in day-to-day economic life, they must be explained, together with legitimate income sources, or, in other words, they must become conventional endogenous variables of macro-models.[11]

Health expenditures are closely associated with ageing, the raising of children, and other aspects of the life cycle; accordingly, a full endogenous treatment of demography would implicitly include health. There are, however, many aspects of health economics that arise, apart from the association with demography.

The health sector of the economy is an important producing sector. In a large-scale model with many inter-industry relationships (an input–output system), the health industry figures importantly because it is fast-growing; it is one of the high-technology sectors that figures importantly in future economic growth; it absorbs many people who gravitate towards the service industries; it is a sector where costs have been rising by unusually large amounts; and it is an important and growing sector of consumption. These and other aspects argue for its full explanation and integration into the equation systems of macroeconomics. When it is integrated, there should be careful attention paid to the professional medical side in order to capture technical progress.

Social psychology has played an important part in developing the use of sample surveys of human populations for the analysis of consumer and business behaviour. The writings of George Katona were replete with efforts to bring psychological methods and theory into economics. This has been done in large measure through the survey approach, which asks people about their plans, expectations and perceptions of the economy, as well as their own positions. The survey instrument provided some lead time from which to infer psychological influences on economic behaviour, but the 'shelf-life' of these pieces of information is only of a few months. In order to bring them effectively into models for longer time periods it is necessary to develop a theory or model of subjective attitudes, clearly a psychological problem, but also a problem with effect on, *and feedback from*, the economy.

An exposition of the way this problem has been handled in the past is provided by descriptions of the 'anticipations version' of the Wharton Model.[12] The new interest in the generation of expectations in economic models provides added incentive to turn to the problem of introducing psychology into economic models and developing endogenous explanation of many psychological magnitudes. Eventually this theoretical excursion should take up such problems as the spread of economic panic, imitative behaviour, fashion, fads and general bandwagon or contagion effects, as well as an investigation of whether expectations are 'rational'.

The entire input–output system, dealing with the laws of production, has strong engineering foundations. This extends to the concept of the production function – macro, micro or inter-industry. In medium- to long-term econometric applications, there is a strong engineering aspect to the study of technical progress.

In connection with the energy crisis, starting in 1973, the engineering foundations of energy analysis became important. Economists had to learn something about engineering aspects of energy before they could make a proper assessment of the impact of changing terms of trade for energy products. A proper technical or engineering treatment of energy supply and energy production became essential and finally emerged. Production functions of macroeconometric models shifted in great measure from:

$$X_{va} = f(L, K, t),$$

to

$$X_g = g(K, L, E, M; t), \text{ where}$$

$$
\begin{aligned}
X_{va} &= \text{real valued added;} \\
L &= \text{labour input;} \\
K &= \text{capital input;} \\
\\
X_g &= \text{real gross output;} \\
E &= \text{energy input;} \\
M &= \text{material input;}
\end{aligned}
$$

t = chronological time.

This latter type of production function (the so-called 'KLEM' production function) is an important, fundamental change in econometric specification and is engineering-based. The endogenous treatment of E and M is essentially an engineering problem, and we can look upon these two variables as a type of engineering variable because they are related to the structure of production.

In some models the analysis has been carried much further by introducing energy type and materials type. Types of labour and capital are also disaggregated. The engineering production function is capable of travelling far in the direction of disaggregation.

Finally, the explanation of technical progress, not just the statistical estimation of time trend effects, requires the introduction of engineering information. In moving forward over decades or more one needs the generation of technical progress, which is, to a large extent in one view, an exercise in engineering. In another view, technical progress is an endogenous phenomenon reflecting managerial considerations, particularly profitable opportunities for innovation.

10 Macroeconometric model-building under attack

In recent years, macroeconometric model-building has come under severe criticism from knowledgeable observers. Thus Hendry (1980) raises the question of whether applied econometrics is closer to 'alchemy' than to 'science', while Leamer (1983) suggests, 'Let's take the "con" out of econometrics'. In addition Sims (1980) suggested that current macroeconometric models are badly under-identified and that an alternative approach (based on employing unrestricted reduced forms which treat *all* variables as endogenous) be used.

Space does not permit a detailed comment on any of these three challenging papers. One can interpret Leamer's paper as reminding us that pure macroeconometric modelling can never replace judgement in the formulation of wise economic policies, or even in the tentative assessment of the state of the world.[13] Hendry, while he begins with an example of a regression that is quite spurious (but not much worse than many in the literature, he claims), argues that best-practice econometrics (characterized by heavy testing, particularly within the sample, of the fitted relationships) can go far to making applied econometrics (which presumably includes macroeconometric modelling) respectable.[14] Sims's critique is perhaps the most difficult of all, yet paradoxically perhaps the easiest with which to come to grips. Sims's arguments about under-identification really seem to be philosophical issues, about which reasonable scholars can indeed differ.[15] Moreover the constructive alternative that Sims proposes seems most unattractive for large systems, of the type that Sims appears to recognize are needed for policy purposes. The reluctance to impose some structure, in a large system, would appear to guarantee in advance that useful results could not be obtained. In terms of needed useful simplifications, we prefer our own (the orthodox variety) to those suggested by Sims.

The most formidable critique to the use of macroeconometric models as a guide to aggregative economic policy would appear, however, to originate with the 'rational expectations hypothesis' and the related 'Lucas critique' of macroeconometric model-building (Lucas, 1976). Briefly stated, the argument would appear to be the following: economic agents have preferred plans of action, and so they will take into account *any* systematic action of policy-makers. Accordingly, this will mean (Lucas gives several extended examples in the paper cited) that the parameters of the system are dependent on the policy regime in force when the relationships of the system were estimated. This would also imply that, were a new set of policies to be implemented (generally with the goal of improving economic welfare as the policy-makers see matters), the parameters of the system *will shift* systematically. Thus the system would break down and in particular would no longer permit a sound prediction (even a conditional prediction) of the likely consequences of a new policy action.[16] Obviously this would be quite a severe criticism of macroeconometric modelling in general – if the argument could be sustained.

However one can argue that the *empirical* significance of such a criticism is not terribly important. If this were the case, then (minor) regime changes from this source could easily be absorbed into the disturbance terms of the stochastic equations of the model, and previous techniques of using macroeconometric models could continue more or less as before. In his 1983 book, Otto Eckstein made an extensive study of past forecasting errors with the DRI Model of the US economy, to see whether he might detect a systematic tendency, on the part of the model, to produce greater forecasting errors when macroeconomic policy was undergoing obvious regime changes. His conclusion was negative: 'So far, the evidence suggests that changes in policy regimes are not among the principal causes of simulation error, that forecast error is largely created by other exogenous factors and the stochastic character of the economy' (Eckstein, 1983, p. 51). Instead, Eckstein points to other sources of regime change, such as wars, civil disturbances and OPEC oil price shocks. Indeed it is a somewhat contrived argument to claim that parameters in macroeconometric models are very particular functions of policy choices. In variable parameter systems that we attempt to deal with through non-linearities and equation shifts, other sources of parameter variation undoubtedly dominate policy changes.

Moreover one can criticize the Lucas critique and the associated rational expectations view of the macroeconomy on theoretical grounds also. One aspect of the Lucas critique asserts that the economic agents use all the information available, in order to produce expectations (or forecasts) of the endogenous variables that are unbiased. This is often interpreted to assert that, if one is using a macroeconomic model (econometric or other kind) for purposes of analysis, one should assume that the agents in general will have this information available to them. (In a complicated, non-linear model, it is not clear to us that this is equivalent to supposing that the agents have the ability to produce unbiased forecasts.) In criticizing this view, we may remark, following Klein (1982), that it is difficult to imagine a typical citizen, untrained in macroeconomics, coming to the same specific conclusions as a professional economist on an issue of macroeconomic policy, let alone following the same specific steps in the reasoning process.[17] The general statement that economic agents base their decisions on all the information available to them at the time that these choices are made is an excellent point that most model-builders have had in mind and have tried to implement for some time. There is nothing very special about rational expectations theory that proves that this way is the only way to interpret the behaviour of agents. Such an interpretation can be done in an infinite variety of ways, one of which has been extensively pursued by model-builders for more than 40 years, namely to generate sample survey response indicators as endogenous variables of models by relating them to many other endogenous variables that are available at the time decisions are made. In addition, two other considerations, pointed up by Eckstein, suggest limitations of the theoretical underpinning of the rational expectations hypothesis. Work with macroeconometric models in general (and the DRI model in particular) suggests that the hypothesis of continuous market-clearing is a quite inadequate description of the historical record. Second, more than first moments of subjective probability distributions may matter, if economic agents are risk-averse. Because both household and business decision-makers appear to be risk averters, the expected variances of outputs and prices may play a role, with agents reducing their planned spending on consumption and investment if the expected variance increases. (This is Eckstein's explanation of the apparently surprising result that the partial effect of increased inflation may be to *diminish* real consumption expenditure.) Accordingly, while the challenge raised by the rational expectations school has raised some important questions about the dynamics of the macroeconomy (in particular, with the nature and characteristics of expectations formation and also the kinds of lag distributions appropriate for macroeconomic variables), we doubt that this critique is applicable in its present form.

11   Structural change

A dilemma for econometricians in both micro and macro analysis has been that large samples of time-series data spanning periods of 50 to 100 years run the risk of encountering changes in the economic environment that induce structural changes in models; whereas confinement to small, short samples of time-series data, while preserving homogeneity of structure over the sample span, provides too few degrees of freedom for reliable statistical inference.

This is not an easy problem to resolve, but our tastes are for having as much information as possible in time-series that are as long as possible. If there is solid evidence of structural change, then this aspect of economic life should be incorporated into model structure. But we also take the view that there is more stability than volatility in economic behaviour. (In particular, we argued in the preceding section that changes in policy regimes are unlikely to produce *major* structural changes.) There is good evidence that fundamental economic behaviour survived the enormous upheaval of the Second World War. Interwar relationships from the much studied period of the 1920s and 1930s returned, after a transitional reconstruction period, to old patterns in the 1950s or at least by the 1960s. This was true in many countries – in North America, Europe and the Far East – where long time-series are available.

This issue is relevant in this forward-looking chapter, concluding our historical survey of macroeconometric model-building, because some people claim that we are now in a new era where the structure of the economy is different because we might have:

1. persistently large public deficits,
2. persistent trade imbalances,
3. unusual international currency alignments,
4. higher (than previous) levels of unemployment, and
5. stagflation.

Most of these new environmental conditions are manifestations of disequilibrium. It is not likely that they will persist indefinitely. But the most important thing to be pointed out is that individuals do not show evidence of changing fundamentally over long historical stretches. It is remarkable that some recent estimates of Engel curves from modern China (1982) (Hu *et al.*, 1984) show characteristics that are remarkably close to those reported by Houthakker (1957) for China of the 1920s in his article on the centenary of Engel's Law.

Politicians cannot repeal the laws of economics; they can distort them for relatively short periods of time. Short-run macroeconometric models should take account of these distortions and should also take account of new goods or new technical processes, but they should not be hasty in following fads that would try to negate the persistence of the patterns of fundamental human behaviour.

12 Conclusions

As this chapter suggests, we feel that there are a number of interesting, even fascinating, research problems that remain to be tackled. The current generation of young macroeconometricians have a number of challenges in front of them. There is no need for boredom or indifference in the face of the tasks which remain.

At the same time, we feel optimistic with regard to the solution of most, if not all, of the challenges outlined in this chapter. Models of the future will be better models, in part because most of the challenges outlined above will have been solved. New developments, as yet unforeseen, will also undoubtedly contribute to the improvement of future generations of macroeconometric models. We see these improvements as occurring not only in the realm of scientific discourse but also in the domain of practical applicability, for purposes of public policy and commercial applications. Thus it is our view that builders of macroeconometric models can face the future with hope and enthusiasm, both in terms of the contributions that will be made and also in terms of the demand for their services. As indicated in the initial section of this chapter, we see a continuation of growth, at least for the next decade or so, in the macroeconometric model-building industry.

Notes

1. See Klein, Pauly, and Voisin (1982). See also the discussion of Chapter 15.
2. See also the discussion of stochastic simulations and optimal control problems, in the context of large models, in the two preceding chapters.
3. A recent publication in this series of studies is McNees and Ries (1983).
4. We note with some satisfaction the adjustment in the exchange value of the US dollar between early 1985 and the time of writing (autumn 1989).
5. It may be noted that, in recent years even without explicit use of flow-of-funds accounts, many standard macroeconometric models have contained moderately detailed financial sectors.
6. An attempt has been made in this direction by Kanta Marwah and L. R. Klein (1983).
7. See Marwah (1985) and the references contained in this paper.
8. See Chapters 11 and 12 above, for a historical treatment of macroeconometric model-building in the case of two groups of LDCs. In the case of the CPEs, we were unsuccessful in an attempt to furnish a historical account of these developments.

9. See W. Welfe (1983).
10. Goetz Uebe *et al.* (1988) list approximately 90 LDCs (depending upon the classification) for which macroeconometric models are available.
11. Gary Becker's seminal article (1968) on the economics of crime has already inspired a number of econometric studies in this area.
12. See F. G. Adams and L. R. Klein (1972).
13. Of course, there is slightly more to Leamer's article than this. As a Bayesian, Leamer argues strongly for a Bayesian approach to the use of econometric tools to obtain new knowledge.
14. Hendry also comments that the then existing macroeconometric models 'broke down' in the face of the oil price shocks of 1973–4, which he implies would not have happened had the model-builders followed the 'best practice' that he recommends. We should only comment that this 'break-down' was a relative matter, as some models were able to function (make predictions and policy analyses) with suitable adjustment of the constant terms. But, wherever one stands in this evaluation, surely it is legitimate to allow model-builders to learn from past mistakes, particularly when the external environment shifts. One of our major themes in this book is the continuing (if not monotonic) progress in model-building, which of course implies that one will learn from the mistakes of the past.
15. As Sims recognizes, the argument is very similar to that put forward by T. C. Liu (1960) a generation ago. One of us (Klein) considered that point of view at that time and found it unattractive, from a philosophical point of view. Sims's repackaging of the argument has not led us to change our minds in this matter.
16. In the monetary area, this has come to be known as 'Goodhart's Law', after Charles Goodhart, a British monetary economist. As summarized by Goodhart himself (1986), this law asserts, 'Any statistical regularity, notably in the monetary area, will break down when pressure is placed upon it for control purposes.'
17. Of course, this assumes not only that the model in question is the true one, but also that the typical agent recognizes this and has no doubts on this score. (Mitigated conclusions follow if the typical agent considers the possibility that two or more models may be the 'correct' one; see Holden, Peel and Thompson (1982), Chapter 6.) But if professional economists cannot decide what is the true model, is it 'rational' (in the non-technical sense of this word) to expect the general public to be able to do so?

References

Adams, F. G. and L. R. Klein (1972) 'Anticipations Variables in Macro-Econometric Models', pp. 289–319 in B. Strumpel, J. N. Morgan and E. Zahn (eds), *Human Behavior in Economic Affairs* (Amsterdam: Elsevier).

Becker, G. S. (1968) 'Crime and Punishment: An Economic Approach', *Journal of Political Economy*, vol. 76, no. 2 (March/April) pp. 164–314.

Eckstein, Otto (1983) *The DRI Model of the U.S. Economy* (New York: McGraw-Hill).

Eckstein, O., E. W. Green and A. Sinai (1974) 'The Data Resources Model: Uses, Structure and Analysis of the U.S. Economy', *International Economic Review*, vol. 15, no. 2 (October) pp. 595–615.

Goldberger, A. S., A. L. Nagar and H. S. Odeh (1961) 'The Covariance Matrices of Reduced Form Coefficients and of Forecasts for a Structural Econometric Model', *Econometrica*, vol. 29, no. 4 (October) pp. 556–73.

Goodhart, C. A. E. (1986) 'Autobiographical Sketch' (pp. 322–3) in Mark Blaug (ed.), *Who's Who in Economics*, 2nd edn (Cambridge, Mass.: MIT Press).

Hendry, D. F. (1980) 'Econometrics – Alchemy or Science?', *Economica*, N. S., vol. 47, no. 188 (November) pp. 387–406.

Holden, K., D. A. Peel and J. L. Thompson (1982) *Modelling the UK Economy: An Introduction* (Oxford: Martin Robertson & Company).

Houthakker, H. S. (1957) 'An International Comparison of Household Expenditure Patterns, Commemorating the Centenary of Engel's law', *Econometrica*, vol. 25, no. 4 (October) pp. 532–50.

Hu, Teh-wei, Bai Jushan and Shi Shuzhong (1984) 'Household Expenditure Patterns in a Large Chinese City' (unpublished), Pennsylvania State University and Naokai University, Tianjian.

Klein, L. R. (1982) *The Present Debate about Macro Economics and Econometric Model Specification*, Chung-Hua Series of Lectures by Invited Eminent Economists, no. 5 (Taipei, Taiwan: Institute of Economics, Academia Sinica, July).

Klein, L. R., P. Pauly and P. Voisin (1982) 'The World Economy – A Global Model', *Perspectives in Computing*, vol. 2 (May) pp. 4–17.

Leamer, E. E., (1983) 'Let's Take the Con out of Econometrics', *American Economic Review*, vol. 73, no. 1 (March) pp. 31–43.

Liu, T. C. (1960) 'Underidentification, Structural Estimation and Forecasting', *Econometrica*, vol. 28, no. 4 (October) pp. 855–65.

Lucas, R. E. Jr (1976) 'Econometric Policy Evaluation: A Critique', pp. 19–46 in K. Brunner and A. H. Meltzer (eds), *The Phillips Curve and Labor Markets* (Amsterdam: North-Holland) Carnegie-Rochester Conference Series on Public Policy, vol. 1, *Supplement* to the *Journal of Monetary Economics*. Also reprinted in his (1981) *Studies in Business-Cycle Theory* (Cambridge, Mass: MIT Press), pp. 104–30.

Marwah, K. (1985) 'A Prototype Model of the Foreign Exchange Market of Canada: Forecasting Capital Flows and Exchange Rates', *Economic Modelling*, vol. 2, no. 2 (April) pp. 93–124.

Marwah, K. and L. R. Klein (1983) 'A Model of Foreign Exchange Markets: Endogenizing Capital Flows and Exchange Rates', pp. 61–95 in L. R. Klein and W. E. Krelle (eds), *Capital Flows and Exchange Rate Determination*, Supplementum 3, *Zeitschrift für Nationalokonomie/Journal of Economics*.

McNees, S. K. and J. Ries (1983) 'The Track Record of Macroeconomic Forecasts', *New England Economic Review*, Nov./Dec., pp. 5–18.

Schink, G. (1971) 'Small Sample Estimates of the Variance–Covariance Matrix of Forecast Errors for Large Econometric Models: The Stochastic Simulation Approach', unpublished PhD thesis, University of Pennsylvania, 1971.

Sims, C. A. (1980) 'Macroeconomics and Reality', *Econometrica*, vol. 48, no. 1 (January) pp. 1–48.

Tinbergen, J. (1952) *On the Theory of Economic Policy* (Amsterdam: North-Holland).

——— (1956) *Economic Policy: Principles and Design* (Amsterdam: North-Holland).

Uebe, Goetz, Georg Huber and Joachim Fischer (1988) *Macro-Econometric Models: An International Bibliography* (Aldershot: Gower).

Welfe, W. (1983) 'Models of the Socialist Economy', Appendix (pp. 197–227) to L. R. Klein, *Lectures in Econometrics* (Amsterdam, New York and Oxford: North-Holland).

Index